THE STATE

ELEMENTS OF HISTORICAL AND PRACTICAL POLITICS

BY

WOODROW WILSON

SPECIAL EDITION
REVISED TO DECEMBER, 1918
BY
EDWARD ELLIOTT, Ph.D.
PROFESSOR OF INTERNATIONAL LAW AND POLITICS
IN THE UNIVERSITY OF CALIFORNIA

D. C. HEATH & CO., PUBLISHERS

BOSTON   NEW YORK   CHICAGO

2E0

PREFACE

THE present edition of The State has been prepared to set forth the nature of the governments of the principal belligerent powers; the chapters dealing with ancient Greece, Rome, Norway, and Sweden have been omitted, and new chapters on Italy, Belgium, Serbia, Rumania, Bulgaria, modern Greece, Russia, Turkey, and Japan have been added, as has a chapter on After the War. The original chapters on England, France, the United States, Switzerland, Germany, and Austria have been revised. In view of the unsettled conditions in Germany and Austria, the governments of these countries have been described as they existed in 1914, and a brief statement made of their condition as it exists as this is written (December 1, 1918). The changes made in the revision have sought merely to bring the work up to date; they are relatively few, and the text of the original chapters remains for the most part that of the author, both in language and opinion. For the new chapters I must assume full responsibility.

It has seemed wise to include in this edition the chapters of a general character, dealing with the origin, nature, functions, and objects of government, and with the nature of law. Though they were written thirty years ago, it is believed that they represent substantially President Wilson's views to-day. In the new chapters I have not indicated specifically the sources upon which I have relied, nor can I do more here than make general acknowledgment of my indebtedness to those whose work has been most helpful.

I wish to express my appreciation of the aid given me by my colleague, Dr. Ludwik Ehrlich, who has freely placed at my service his wide knowledge of European governments and in particular of the governments of Germany and Austria.

EDWARD ELLIOTT.

BERKELEY, CALIFORNIA,
December 1, 1918.

iii

CONTENTS

v

I.

THE EARLIEST FORMS OF GOVERNMENT.

Nature of the Question. — The probable origin of government is a question of fact, to be settled, not by conjecture, but by history. Some traces we can still discern of the history of primitive societies. As fragments of primitive animals have been kept for us sealed up in the earth's rocks, so fragments of primitive institutions have been preserved, embedded in the rocks of surviving law or custom, mixed up with the rubbish of accumulated tradition, crystallized in the organization of still savage tribes, or kept curiously in the museum of fact and rumor swept together by some ancient historian. Limited and perplexing as such means of reconstructing history may be, they repay patient comparison and analysis as richly as do the materials of the archæologist and the philologian. The facts as to the origin and early history of government are at least as available as the facts concerning the growth and kinship of languages or the genesis and development of the arts and sciences. Such light as we can get from the knowledge of the infancy of society thus meagerly afforded us is, at any rate, better than that derived from *a priori* speculations founded upon our acquaintance with our modern selves, or from any fancies, how learnedly soever constructed, that we might weave as to the way in which history might plausibly be read backwards.

Races to be studied: the Aryans. — For purposes of widest comparison in tracing the development of government it would of course be desirable to include in a study of early society not only those Aryan and Semitic races which have played the chief parts in the history of the European world, but also every primitive tribe, whether Hottentot or Iroquois, Finn or Turk, of whose

1

institutions and development we know anything at all. Such a world-wide survey would be necessary to any induction which should claim to trace government in all its forms to a common archetype. But, practically, no such sweeping together of incongruous savage usage and tradition is needed to construct a safe text from which to study the governments that have grown and come to full flower in the political world to which we belong. In order to trace the lineage of the European and American governments which have constituted the order of social life for those stronger and nobler races which have made the most notable progress in civilization, it is essential to know the political history of the Greeks, the Latins, the Teutons, and the Celts principally, if not only, and the original political habits and ideas of the Aryan and Semitic races alone. The existing governments of Europe and America furnish the dominating types of to-day. To know other systems which are defeated or dead would aid only indirectly towards an understanding of those which are alive and triumphant.

Semitic and Turanian Instance. — Even Semitic institutions, indeed, must occupy only a secondary place in such inquiries. The main stocks of modern European forms of government are Aryan. The institutional history of Semitic or Turanian peoples is hardly part of the history of European governments : it is only analogous to it in many of the earlier stages of development. Aryan, Semitic, and Turanian races alike seem to have passed at one period or another through similar forms of social organization. Each, consequently, furnishes illustrations in its history, and in those social customs and combinations which have most successfully survived the wreck of change, of probable early forms and possible successive stages of political life among the others. Aryan practice may often be freed from doubt by Semitic or Turanian instance; but it is Aryan practice we principally wish to know.

Government rested First upon Kinship.[1] — What is known of the central nations of history clearly reveals the fact that social organization, and consequently government (which is the visible form of social organization), originated in *kinship*. The original

[1] The origin of government in kinship has been sharply questioned.

bond of union and the original sanction for magisterial authority were one and the same thing, namely, real or feigned blood-relationship. In other words, families were the original units of social organization; and were at first, no doubt, in a large degree separate. It was only by slow stages and under the influence of many changes of habit and environment that the family organization widened and families were drawn together into communities. A group of men who considered themselves in some sort kinsmen constituted the first State.

Early History of the Family; was it originally Patriarchal? — The origin of government is, therefore, intimately connected with the early history of the family. It is the more unfortunate that the conclusions to be drawn from what is known of the beginnings of the family should furnish matter for much modern difference of opinion. This difference of opinion may be definitely summed up in the two following contrasted views: —

(1) That the *patriarchal* family, to which the early history of the greater races runs back, and with which that history seems to begin, was the family in its original estate, — the original, the true archaic family.

> The patriarchal family is that in which descent is traced to a common male ancestor, through a direct male line, and in which the authority of rule vests in the eldest living male ascendant.

(2) That the patriarchal family, which is acknowledged to be found in one stage or another of the development of almost every race now civilized, was a developed and comparatively late form of the family, and not its first form, having been evolved through various stages and varieties of polyandry (plurality of husbands) and of polygyny (plurality of wives) out of a possibly original state of promiscuity and utter confusion in the relations of the sexes and of consequent confusion in blood-relationship and in the government of offspring.

In brief, it is held on the one hand that the patriarchal family was the original family; and on the other, that it was not the original but a derived form, others of a less distinct organization preceding it.

The Evidence. — It is of course impracticable to set forth here the miscellaneous evidence which has been swept together concerning so very obscure and complex a question. Suffice it to say that among many primitive races cases abound of the reckoning of kinship through mothers only, as if in matter-of-course doubt as to paternity; of consanguinity signified throughout the wide circle of a tribe, not by real or supposed common descent from a human ancestor, but by means of the fiction of common descent from some bird or beast, from which the tribe takes its name, as if for lack of any better means of determining common blood; of marriages of brothers with sisters, and of groups of men with groups of women, or of groups of men with some one woman. In the case of some tribes, moreover, among whom polygamy or even monogamy now exists, together with a patriarchal discipline, it is thought to be possible to trace clear indications of an evolution of these more civilized forms of family organization from earlier practices of loose multiple marriages or even still earlier promiscuity in the sexual relation.

The peoples, however, among whom such confusions of sexual relationships have been observed are not those who have emerged upon the European field. Among almost every European folk there is clear, unbroken tradition running back to a patriarchal power and organization. Roman law, that prolific mother of modern legal idea and practice, bears impressed upon every feature of it indubitable marks of its descent from a time when the father ruled as king and high priest in the family. Greek institutions speak hardly less unequivocally of a similar derivation. No belief is more deeply fixed in the traditions of the great peoples who have made modern history than the belief of direct common descent, through males, from a common male ancestor, human or divine; and nothing could well be more numerous or distinct than the traces inhering in the very heart of their polity of an original patriarchal organization of the family as the archetype of their political order.

The Warrantable Conclusion. — The evidence of more confused marriage relationships, moreover, is nowhere of such a character as to warrant the conclusion that promiscuity in sexual connections has among any people marked the first or any regular stage of social development. "All the evidence we possess tends to show that among our earliest human ancestors the family, not the tribe, formed the nucleus of every social group, and, in many cases, was itself perhaps the only social group." "It seems probable, moreover, that monogamy prevailed almost exclusively among our earliest human ancestors."[1] Promiscuity belongs, not to the most primitive times or to the regular order of social life, but rather to exceptional seasons of demoralization or confusion; to times of decadence rather than to the origins of the race. Polyandry has grown up only where the women were fewer than the men, and has almost necessarily broken down when the numerical balance between the sexes was restored. Polygyny "has been less prevalent at the lowest stages of civilization,— where wars do not seriously disturb the proportion of the sexes; where life is chiefly supported by hunting, and female labor is consequently of slight value; where there is no accumulation of wealth and no distinction of class, — than it is at somewhat higher stages."[2] Where it does exist, it is invariably confined to a small minority of wealthy and powerful men; the majority, from choice or necessity, are always monogamous. First and last, the strong monogamous instinct, has tended to exclude promiscuous or multiplied sexual connections, and to build up a distinct family order round about monogamous marriages.[3]

The efficient races who have dominated the European stage, at any rate, came into their place of leadership and advantage under the discipline of the patriarchal order of family life. Whether with several wives or with only one, the father was chief and master among them, and the family showed that clear authority and close organization which was to serve in fulness of time as the prototype and the model for the State.

From the Patriarchal Family to the State.— Among these Aryan peoples there was first the family ruled by the father as king and priest. There was no majority for the sons so long as their father lived. They might marry and have children, but they could have no entirely separate and independent authority during their father's life save such as he suffered them to exer-

[1] Westermarck, *History of Human Marriage*, pp. 538, 549.   [2] *Id.* 548.
[3] For a contrary view see Avebury, *The Origin of Civilization and the Primitive Condition of Man.* 6th ed., London, 1902.

cise. All that they possessed, their lives even and the lives of those dependent upon them, were at the disposal of this absolute father-sovereign. Such a group naturally broadens in time into the 'House,' or *gens*, and over this too a chief kinsman rules. There are common religious rites and observances which the *gens* regards as symbolic of its unity as a composite family; and heads of houses exercise many high representative and probably some imperative magisterial functions by virtue of their position. Then, as the social order widens, Houses are in their turn absorbed. The first distinctively political unit, no doubt, was the Tribe: broader than the *gens* and tending to subordinate it; a body in which kinship must still have been deemed the bond of union, but in which, nevertheless, it must have been a very obscure bond indeed, and in which family rights must steadily have tended to give way before the establishment of a common order within which the House served only as a unit of membership and a corporation for worship.

Tribes at length united to form a State. In days of nomadic habit the organization of the Tribe sufficed, and no more fixed, definite, or effective order was attempted. But when a people's travelling days were over, a settled life brought new needs of organization: a larger power must have sprung up almost of itself. Then a very significant thing happened. The State in effect ousted both the House and the Tribe from their functions as political units, and came itself to rest, not upon these for foundation, but upon the family, the original formation of the social substructure. Tribe and *gens* served henceforth only as religious corporations or as the convenient units of representation in the action of the State.

Prepossessions to be put away. — In looking back to the first stages of political development, it is necessary to put away from the mind certain prepossessions which are both proper and legitimate to modern conceptions of government, but which can have found no place in primitive thought on the subject. It is not possible nowadays to understand the early history of institutions without thus first divesting the mind of many conceptions most natural and apparently most necessary to it. The centuries which separate us from the infancy of society separate us also, by the whole length of the history of human thought, from the ideas into which the fathers of the race were born; and nothing but a most credulous movement of the imagination can enable the student of to-day to throw himself back into those conceptions of social connection and authority in which government took its rise.

The State and the Land. — How is it possible, for instance, for the modern mind to conceive distinctly a *travelling* political organization, a State without territorial boundaries or the need of them, composed of persons, but associated with no fixed or certain habitat? And yet such were the early tribal states, — nomadic groups, now and again hunting, fishing, or tending their herds by this or that particular river or upon this or that familiar mountain slope or inland seashore, but never regarding themselves or regarded by their neighbors as finally identified with any definite territory. Historians have pointed out the abundant evidences of these facts that are to be found in the history of Europe no further back than the fifth century of our own era. The Franks came pouring into the Roman empire just because they had had no idea theretofore of being confined to any particular Frank-*land*. They left no France behind them at the sources of the Rhine; and their kings quitted those earlier seats of their race, not as kings of France, but as kings of the Franks. There were kings of the Franks when the territory now called Germany, as well as that now known as France, was in the possession of that imperious race: and they became kings of France only when, some centuries later, they had settled down to the unaccustomed habit of confining themselves to a single land. Drawn by the processes of feudalization (pages 109, 115, 129), sovereignty then found at last a local habitation and a name.

The same was true of the other Germanic nations. They also had chiefs who were the chiefs of people, not the chiefs of lands. There were kings of the English for many a year, even for several centuries after A.D. 449, before there was such a thing as a king of England. John was the first officially to assume the latter title. From the first, it is true, social organization has everywhere tended to connect itself more and more intimately with the land from which each social group has drawn its sustenance. When the migratory life was over, especially, and the settled occupations of agriculture had brought men to a stand upon the land which they were learning to till, political life, like all the other communal activities, came to be associated more and more directly with the land on which each community lived. But such a connection between lordship and land was a slowly developed notion, not a notion twin-born with the notion of government.

Modern definitions of a State always limit sovereignty to some definite land. "A State" — runs the modern definition — "is a People organized for law within a definite territory." But the first builders of government would not have found such a definition intelligible. They could not have understood why they might not move their whole people, 'bag and baggage,' to other lands, or why, for the matter of that, they might not keep them moving their tents and possessions unrestingly from place to place in perpetual migration, without in the least disturbing the integrity or even the administration of their infant 'State.' Each organized group of men had other means of knowing their unity than mere neighborhood to one another; other means of distinguishing themselves from similar groups of men than distance or the intervention of mountain or stream. The original groups were knit together by bonds closer than those of geography, more real than the bonds of mere contiguity. They were bound together by real or assumed kinship. They had a corporate existence which they regarded as inhering in their blood and as expressed in all their daily relations with each other. They lived together because of these relations; they were not related because they lived together.

Contract versus Status. — Scarcely less necessary to modern thought than the idea of territoriality as connected with the existence of a State, is the idea of contract as determining the relations of individuals. And yet this idea, too, must be put away if we would understand primitive society. In that society men were *born* into the station and the part they were to have throughout life, as they still are among the peoples who preserve their earliest conceptions of social order. This is known as the law of *status*. It is not a matter of choice or of voluntary arrangement in what relations men shall stand towards each other as individuals. He who is born a slave, let him remain a slave; the artisan, an arti-san; the priest, a priest, — is the command of the law of *status*. Excellency cannot avail to raise any man above his parentage; aptitude is suffered to operate only within the sphere of each man's birthright. No man may lose 'caste' without losing respectability also and forfeiting the protection of the law. Or, to go back to a less developed society, no son, however gifted, may lawfully break away from the authority of his father, how-ever cruel or incapable that father may be; or make any alliance which will in the least degree draw him away from the family alliance and duty into which he was born. There is no thought of contract. Every man's career is determined for him before his birth. His blood makes his life. To break away from one's birth station, under such a system, is to make breach not only of social, but also of religious duty, and to bring upon oneself the curses of men and gods. Primitive society rested, not upon con-tract, but upon *status*. *Status* had to be broken through by some conscious or unconscious revolution before so much as the idea of contract could arise; and when that idea did arise, change and variety were assured. Change of the existing social order was the last thing of which the primitive community dreamed; and those races which allowed the rule of *status* to harden about their lives still stand where they stood a thousand years ago. "The leaving of men to have their careers determined by their efficien-cies," says Mr. Spencer, "we may call the principle of change in social organization."

Theories concerning the Origin of the State: the Contract Theory. — Such views of primitive society furnish us with destruc-tive dissolvents of certain theories once of almost universal vogue as to the origin of government. The most famous, and for our present purposes most important, of these theories is that which ascribes the origin of government to a 'social compact' among primitive men.

The most notable names connected with this theory as used to account for the existence of political society are the names of Hooker, Hobbes, Locke, and Rousseau. It is to be found developed in Hooker's *Ecclesias-tical Polity*, Hobbes' *Leviathan*, Locke's *Civil Government*, and Rousseau's *The Social Contract*.

This theory begins always with the assumption that there exists, outside of and above the laws of men, a Law of Nature.[1] Hobbes conceived this Law to include " justice," " equity," " modesty," " mercy " ; " in sum, ' doing to others as we would be done to.' " All its chief commentators considered it the abstract standard to which human law should conform. Into this Law primitive men were born. It was binding upon their individual consciences; but their consciences were overwhelmed by individual pride, ambition, desire, and passion, which were strong enough to abrogate Nature's Law. That Law, besides, did not bind men *together*. Its dictates, if obeyed, would indeed enable them to live tolerably with one another; but its dictates were not obeyed; and, even if they had been, would have furnished no permanent frame of civil government, inasmuch as they did not sanction magistracies, the setting of some men to be judges of the duty and conduct of other men, but left each conscience to command absolutely the conduct of the individual. In the language of the ' judicious Hooker,' the laws of Nature " do bind men absolutely, even as they are men, although they have never any settled fellowship, never any solemn agreement, amongst themselves what to do or not to do; but forasmuch as we are not by ourselves sufficient to furnish ourselves with competent store of things needful for such a life as our Nature doth desire, a life fit for the dignity of man, therefore to supply these defects and imperfections which are in us living single and solely by ourselves, we are naturally induced to seek communion and fellowship with others. This was the cause of men uniting themselves at first in politic societies." [2] In other words, the belligerent, non-social parts of man's character were originally too strong for this Law of Nature, and the ' state of nature,' in which that Law, and only that Law, offered restraint to the selfish passions, became practically a *state of war*, and consequently intolerable. It was brought to an end in the only way in which such a condition of affairs could be brought to an end without mutual extermination, namely, by common consent, by men's " agreeing together mutually to enter into one community

[1] For the natural history of this conception of a Law of Nature, see Maine, *Ancient Law*, Chap. III.

[2] *Ecclesiastical Polity*, Book I., sec. 10.

and make one body politic." (Locke.) This agreement meant sub-mission to some one common authority, which should judge between man and man; the surrender on the part of each man of all rights antagonistic to the rights of others; forbearance and coöperation. Locke confidently affirmed "that all men are naturally in that state [a state, *i.e.*, of nature], and remain so till, by their own consents, they make themselves members of some politic society." It was only as the result of deliberate choice, in the presence of the possible alternative of continuing in this state of nature, that commonwealths came into being.

Traditions of an Original Lawgiver. — Ancient tradition had another way of accounting for the origin of laws and institutions. The thought of almost every nation of antiquity went back to some single lawgiver at whose hands their government had taken its essential and characteristic form, if not its beginning. There was a Moses in the background of many a history besides that of the Jews. In the East there was Menu; Crete had her Minos; Athens her Solon; Sparta her Lycurgus; Rome her Numa; England her Alfred. These names do not indeed in every instance stand so far back as the beginning of government; but they do carry the mind back in almost every case to the birth of *national* systems, and suggest the overshadowing influence of individual statesmen as the creative power in framing the greater combinations of politics. They bring the conception of conscious choice into the history of institutions. They look upon systems as *made*, rather than as developed.

Theory of the Divine Origin of the State. — Not altogether unlike these ancient conceptions of lawgivers towering above other men in wisdom and authority, dominating political construction, and possibly inspired by divine suggestion, is that more modern idea which attributes human government to the immediate institution of God himself, — to the direct mandate of the Creator. This theory has taken either the definite form of regarding human rulers as the direct vicegerents of God, or the vague form of regarding government as in some way given to man as part of his original make-up

The Theories and the Facts. — Modern research into the early history of mankind has made it possible to reconstruct, in outline, much of the thought and practice of primitive society, and has thus revealed facts which render it impossible for us to accept any of these views as adequately explaining what they seek to explain. The defects of the social compact theory are too plain to need more than brief mention. That theory simply has no historical foundation. The family was the original, and *status* the fixed basis, of primitive society. The individual counted for nothing; society—the family, the tribe—counted for everything. Government came, so to say, before the individual and was coeval with his first human instincts. There was no place for contract; and yet this theory makes contract the first fact of social life. Such a contract as it imagines could not have stood unless supported by that reverence for 'law' which is an altogether modern principle of action. The times in which government originated knew absolutely nothing of law as we conceive it. The only bond was kinship,—the common blood of the community; the only individuality was the individuality of the community as a whole. Man was merged in society. Without kinship there was no duty and no union. It was not by compounding rights, but by assuming kinship, that groups widened into States,—not by contract, but by adoption. Not deliberate and reasoned respect for law, but habitual and instinctive respect for authority, held men together; and authority did not rest upon mutual agreement, but upon mutual subordination.

Of the theories of the origination of government in individual lawgiving or in divine dictate, it is sufficient to say that the one exaggerates the part played by human choice, and the other the part played by man's implanted instincts, in the formation and shaping of political society.

The Truth in the Theories. — Upon each of these theories, nevertheless, there evidently lies the shadow of a truth. Although government did not originate in a deliberate contract, and although no system of law or of social order was ever made 'out of hand' by any one man, government was not all a mere spontaneous growth. Deliberate choice has always played a part in its development. It was not, on the one hand, given to man ready-made by God, nor was it, on the other hand, a human contrivance. In its origin it was spontaneous, natural, twin-born with man and the family; Aristotle was simply stating a fact when he said, " Man is by nature a political animal." But, once having arisen, government was affected, and profoundly affected, by man's choice; only that choice entered, not to originate, but to modify government.

Conclusion. — Viewed in the light of "the observed and recorded experience of mankind," "the ground and origin of society is not a compact; that never existed in any known case, and never was a condition of obligation either in primitive or developed societies, either between subjects and sovereign, or between the equal members of a sovereign body. The true ground is the acceptance of conditions which came into existence by the sociability inherent in man, and were developed by man's spontaneous search after convenience. The statement that while the constitution of man is the work of nature, that of the state is the work of art, is as misleading as the opposite statement that governments are not made, but grow. The truth lies between them, in such propositions as that institutions owe their existence and development to deliberate human effort, working in accordance with circumstances naturally fixed both in human character and in the external field of its activity." [1]

The Beginnings of Government. — Government must have had substantially the same early history amongst all progressive races. It must have begun in clearly defined family discipline. Such discipline would scarcely be possible among races in which consanguinity was subject to profound confusion and in which family organization therefore had no clear basis of authority on which to rest. In every case, it would seem, the origination of what we should deem worthy of the name of government must have awaited the development of some such definite family as that in which the father was known, and known as ruler. Whether or not the patriarchal family was the first form of the family, it must have furnished the first adequate form of government.

The Family the Primal Unit. — The family was the primal unit of political society, and the seed-bed of all larger growths of government. The individuals that were drawn together to con·

[1] John Morley, *Rousseau*, Vol. II., pp. 183–4.

stitute the earliest communities were not individual men, as Locke and Locke's co-theorists would lead us to believe, but individual families; and the organization of these families, whether singly or in groups, furnished the ideas in which political society took its root. The members of each family were bound together by kinship. The father's authority bore the single sanction of his being the fountain-head of the common blood-relationship. No other bond was known, or was then conceivable, except this single bond of blood-relationship. A man out of this circle of kinship was outside the boundaries of possible friendship, was as of course an alien and an enemy.

Persistence of the Idea of Kinship. — When society grew, it grew without any change of this idea. Kinship was still, actually or theoretically, its only amalgam. The commonwealth was for long conceived of as being only a larger kindred. When by natural increase a family multiplied its branches and widened into a *gens*, and there was no grandfather, great-grandfather, or other patriarch living to keep it together in actual domestic oneness, it would still not separate. The extinct authority of the actual ancestor could be replaced by the less comprehensive but little less revered authority of some selected elder of the 'House,' the oldest living ascendant, or the most capable. Here would be the materials for a complete body politic held together by the old fibre of actual kinship.

Fictitious Kinship: Adoption. — Organization upon the basis of a fictitious kinship was hardly less naturally contrived in primitive society. There was the ready, and immemorial, fiction of *adoption*, which to the thought of that time seemed no fiction at all. The adopted man was no less real a member of the family than was he who was natural-born. His admittance to the sacred, the exclusive religious mysteries of the family, at which no stranger was ever suffered even to be present, and his acceptance of the family gods as his own gods, was not less efficacious in making him one with the household and the kin than if he had opened his veins to receive their blood. And so, too, Houses could grow by the adoption of families, through the engrafting of the alien branches into this same sacred stock of the esoteric religion of the kindred. Whether naturally, therefore, or artificially, Houses widened into tribes, and tribes into commonwealths, without loss of that kinship in the absence of which, to the thinking of primitive men, there could be no communion, and therefore no community, at all.

Kinship and Religion. — In this development kinship and religion operated as the two chief formative influences. Religion seems in most instances to have been at first only the expression of kinship. The central and most sacred worship of each group of men, whether family or tribe, was the worship of *ancestors*. At the family or communal altar the worshipper came into the presence of the shades of the great dead of his family or race. To them he did homage; from them he craved protection and guidance. The adopted man, therefore, when received into this hallowed communion with the gods of the family, accepted its fathers as his own, and took upon himself the most solemn duties and acquired the most sacred privileges of kinship. So, too, of the family adopted into the *gens*, or the *gens* received into the tribe. The new group accepted the ancestry by accepting the worship of the adopting House or community.

Religion was thus quite inseparably linked with kinship. It may be said to have been the thought of which kinship was the embodiment. It was the sign and seal of the common blood, the expression of its oneness, its sanctity, its obligations. He who had entered into the bonds of this religion had, therefore, entered into the heart of kinship and taken of its life-blood. His blood-relationship was thus rendered no fiction at all to the thought of that day, but a solemn verity, to which every religious ceremonial bore impressive witness.

The Bonds of Religion and Precedent. — The results of such a system of life and thought were most momentous. It is commonplace now to remark upon English regard for precedent, and upon the interesting development of 'common' and 'case' law. But not even an Englishman or an American can easily conceive of any such reverential regard for precedent as must have resulted from a canonization of ancestors. We have ourselves in a measure canonized our own forefathers of the revolutionary era, worshipping them around fourth of July altars, to the great benefit both of our patriotism and of our political morality. But the men of '76, we are all willing to acknowledge, were at their greatest only men. The ancestor of the primitive man became, on the contrary, a god, and a god of undying power. His spirit lived on to bless or to curse. His favor had to be propitiated, his anger appeased. And herein was a terribly effective sanction for precedent. It was no light matter to depart from the practices of these potent ancestors. To do so was to run in the face of the deities. It was to outrage all religious feeling, to break away from all the duties of spiritual kinship. Precedent was under such circumstances imperative. Precedent of course soon aggregated into custom, — such custom as it is now scarcely possible to conceive of, — a supreme, uniform, imperious, infrangible rule of life which brought within its inexorable commands every detail of daily conduct.

The Reign of Custom. — This reign of customary law was long and decisive. Its tendency was to stiffen social life into a formula. It left almost no room at all for the play of individuality. The family was a despotism, society a routine. There was for each man a rigorous drill of conformity to the custom of his tribe and house. Superstition strengthened every cord and knot of the network of observance which bound men to the practices of their fathers and their neighbors. That tyranny of social convention which men of independent or erratic impulse nowadays find so irksome, — that 'tyranny of one's next-door neighbor' against which there are now and again found men bold enough to rebel, — had its ideal archetype in this rigid uniformity of custom which held ancient society in hard crystallization.

Fixity of System the Rule, Change the Exception. — Such was the discipline that moulded the infancy of political society : within the family, the supreme will of the father; outside the family, the changeless standards of religious opinion. The tendency, of course, was for custom to become fixed in a crust too solid ever to be broken through. In the majority of cases, moreover, this tendency was fulfilled. Many races have never come out of this tutelage of inexorable custom. Many others have advanced only so far beyond it as those caste systems in which the law of *status* and the supremacy of immemorial custom have worked out their logical result in an unchanging balance of hereditary classes.

The majority of mankind have remained stationary in one or another of the earliest stages of political development, their laws now constituting as it were ancient records out of which the learned may rewrite the early history of those other races whom primitive custom did not stagnate, but whose systems both of government and of thought still retain many traces (illegible without illumination from the facts of modern savage life) of a similar infancy. Stagnation has been the rule, progress the exception. The greater part of the world illustrates in its laws and institutions what the rest of the world has escaped; the rest of the world illustrates what favorable change was capable of making out of the primitive practices with which the greater part of the world has remained *per force* content.

Changes of System outrun Changes of Idea. — The original likeness of the progressive races to those which have stood still is witnessed by that persistency of idea of which I have already spoken. Progress has brought nations out of the primitive practices vastly more rapidly than it has brought them out of the primitive ideas of political society. Practical reform has now and again attained a speed that has never been possible to thought. Instances of this so abound in the daily history of the most progressive nations of the world of to-day that it ought not to be difficult for us to realize its validity in the world of the first days of society. Our own guilds and unions and orders, merely voluntary and conventional organizations as they are, retain in their still vivid sense of the *brotherhood* of their members at least a reminiscence of the ideas of that early time when kinship was the only conceivable basis of association between man and man, when "each assemblage of men seems to have been conceived as a Family."[1] In England political change has made the great strides of the last two centuries without making the Crown any less the central object of the theoretical or lawyerly conception of the English constitution. Every day witnesses important extensions and even alterations of the law in our courts under the semblance of a simple application of old rules. Circumstances alter principles as well as cases, but it is only the cases which are supposed to be altered. The principles remain,

[1] Maine, *Early History of Institutions*, p. 232.

in form, the same. Men still carry their brides on wedding journeys, although the necessity for doing so ceased with the practice, once general, of stealing a bride. 'Good blood' still continues to work wonders, though achievement has come to be the only real patent of nobility in the modern world. In a thousand ways we are more advanced than we *think* we are.

How did Change enter? — The great question, then, is, How did change enter at all that great nursery of custom in which all nations once wore short clothes, and in which so many nations still occupy themselves with the superstitions and the small play of childhood? How did it come about that some men became progressive, while most did not? This is a question by no means easy to answer, but there are probabilities which may throw some light upon it.

Differences of Custom. — In the first place, it is not probable that all the groups of men in that early time had the same customs. Custom was doubtless as flexible and malleable in its infancy as it was inflexible and changeless in its old age. In proportion as group separated from group in the restless days of the nomadic life, custom would become differentiated from custom. Then, after first being the cause, isolation would become the natural result of differences of life and belief. A family or tribe which had taken itself apart and built up a practice and opinion all its own would thereby have made itself irrevocably a stranger to its one-time kinsmen of other tribes. When its life did touch their life, it would touch to clash, and not to harmonize or unite. Greeks, Romans, Celts, had probably once been a single people; but how unlike did they become!

Antagonism between Customs. — We need not specially spur our imaginations to realize how repugnant, how naturally antagonistic, to each other families or tribes or races would be rendered by differences of custom. "We all know that there is nothing that human beings (especially when in a low state of culture) are so little disposed to tolerate as divergencies of custom," says Mr. Hamerton, who is so sure of the fact that he does

not stop to illustrate it. How ' odd,' if not ' ridiculous,' the ways
of life and the forms of belief often seem to us in a foreign
country, — how instinctively we pronounce them inferior to our
own! The Chinaman manages his rice quite as skilfully with
his ' chop-sticks ' as we manage ours with our forks; and yet how
' queer,' how ' absurd ' chop-sticks are! And so also in the
weightier matters of social and religious practice.

Competition of Customs. — To the view of the primitive
man all customs, great or small, were matters of religion. His
whole life was an affair of religion. For every detail of conduct
he was accountable to his gods and to the religious sentiment
of his own people. To tolerate any practices different from those
which were sanctioned by the immemorial usage of the tribe was
to tolerate impiety. It was a matter of the deepest moment,
therefore, with each tribal group to keep itself uncontaminated
by alien custom, to stamp such custom out wherever and whenever it could be discovered. That was a time of war, and war
meant a competition of customs. The conqueror crushed out the
practices of the conquered and compelled them to conform to his
own.

The Better prevail. — Of course in such a competition the
better custom would prevail over the worse.[1] The patriarchal
family, with its strict discipline of the young men of the tribe,
would unquestionably be " the best campaigning family," —
would supply the best internal organization for war. Hence,
probably, the national aspect of the world to-day : peoples of
patriarchal tradition occupying in unquestioned ascendency the
choicest districts of the earth; all others thrust out into the heats
or colds of the less-favored continents, or crowded into the forgotten corners and valley-closets of the world. So, too, with the
more invigorating and sustaining religions. Those tribes which
were least intimidated by petty phantoms of superstition, least
hampered by the chains of empty but imperative religious ceremonial, by the engrossing observance of times and seasons, having
greater confidence in their gods, would have greater confidence in
themselves, would be freer to win fortune by their own hands,

[1] For the best development of the whole idea of this paragraph and others
in this connection, see Bagehot, *Physics and Politics*, Chap. II.

instead of passively seeking it in the signs of the heavens or in the aspects of nearer nature; and so would be the surer conquerors of the earth. Religion and the family organization were for these early groups of kindred men the two indexes of character. In them was contained inferiority or superiority. The most serviceable customs won the day.

Isolation, Stagnation. — Absolute isolation for any of these early groups would of course have meant stagnation; just as surely as contact with other groups meant war. The world, accordingly, abounds in stagnated nationalities; for it is full of instances of isolation. The great caste nations are examples. It is, of course, only by a figure of speech that we can speak of vast peoples like those of China and India as isolated, though it is scarcely a figure of speech to say that they are stagnated. Still in a very real sense even these populous nations were isolated. We may say, from what we discern of the movements of the nations from their original seats, that the races of China and India were the 'back-water' from the great streams of migration. Those great streams turned towards Europe and left these outlying waters to subside at their leisure. In subsiding there was no little commotion amongst them. There were doubtless as many intertribal wars in the early history of China before the amalgamation of the vast kingdom as there have been in the history of India. That same competition of custom with custom which took place elsewhere, also took place there. But the tribes which pressed into China were probably from the first much of a kind, with differing but not too widely contrasted customs, which made it possible for them to assume at a now very remote period a uniformity of religion and of social organization never known amongst the peoples that had gone to the West; so that, before the history that the rest of the world remembers had begun, China's wall had shut her in to a safe stagnation of monotonous uniformity. The great Indian castes were similarly set apart in their vast peninsula by the gigantic mountains which piled themselves between them and the rest of the continent. The later conquests which China and India suffered at the hands of Oriental invaders resulted in mere overlordships, which changed the destination of taxes, but did not touch the forms of local custom.

Movement and Change in the West. — It is easy to imagine a rapid death-rate, or at least an incessant transformation, amongst the customs of those races which migrated and competed in the West. There was not only the contact with each other which precipitated war and settled the question of predominance between custom and custom; there was also the slow but potent leaven of shifting scene and changing circumstance. The movement of the peoples was not the march of a host. It was only the slow progress of advancing races, its stages often centuries long, its delays fruitful of new habits and new aspirations. We have, doubtless, a type of what took place in those early days in the transformation of the Greeks after they had come down to the sea. We can dimly see them beginning a new life there. Slowly they acquired familiarity with their new neighbor, the sea. They learned its moods. They imagined new gods breathing in its mild or storming in its tempestuous winds. They at length trusted themselves to its mercy in boats. The handling of boats made them sailors; and, lured from island to island across that inviting sea, they reached those later homes of their race in Asia Minor. And they reached this new country changed men, their hearts strengthened for bolder adventure, their hands quick with a readier skill, their minds opened to greater enthusiasms and enriched with warmer imaginings, their whole nature profoundly affected by contact with Father Ægeus.

Migration and Conquest. — And so, to a greater or less extent, it must have been with other races in their movements toward their final seats. Not only the changes of circumstance and the exigencies of new conditions of life, but also the conquests necessarily incident to those days of migration, must have worked great, though slow, alterations in national character. We know the Latins to have been of the same stock with the Greeks; but by the time the Latins had reached Italy they were already radically different in habit, belief, and capacity from the Greeks, who had, by other routes, reached and settled Magna Græcia. Conquest changes not only the conquered, but also the conquerors. Insensibly, it may be, but deeply, they are affected by the character of the subdued or absorbed races. Norman does not merge with Saxon without getting Saxon blood into his own veins, and Saxon thoughts into his own head; neither had Saxon overcome Celt without being himself more or less taken captive by Celtic superstition. And these are but historical instances of what must have been more or less characteristic of similar events in 'prehistoric' times.

Intertribal Imitation. — There must, too, have been among the less successful or only partially successful races a powerful tendency towards *imitation* constantly at work, — imitation of the institutions of their more successful neighbors and rivals. Just as we see, in the histories of the Old Testament, frequent instances of peoples defeated by Jewish arms incontinently forsaking their own divinities and humbly commending themselves to the God of Israel, so must many another race, defeated or foiled in unrecorded wars, have forced themselves to learn the customs in order that they might equal the success of rival races.

Individual Initiative and Imitation. — And this impulse towards imitation, powerful as between group and group, would of course, in times of movement and conquest, be even more potent amongst individual men. Such times would be rich with opportunity for those who had energy and enterprise. Many a great career could be carved out of the events of days of steady achievement. Men would, as pioneers in a new country or as leaders in war, be more or less freed from the narrow restrictions of hard and fast custom. They could be unconventional. Their individual gifts could have play. Each success would not only establish their right to be themselves, but would also raise up after them hosts of imitators. New types would find acceptance in the national life; and so a new leaven would be introduced. Individual initiative would at last be permitted a voice, even as against immemorial custom.

Institutional Changes: Choice of Rulers. — It is easy to see how, under the bracing influences of race competition, such forces of change would operate to initiate and hasten a progress towards the perfecting of institutions and the final abolition of slavery to habit. And it is no less plain to see how such forces of change would affect the constitution of government. It is evident that, as has been said (p. 19), the patriarchal family did furnish the best campaigning materials, and that those races whose primitive organization was of this type did rapidly come to possess the "most-competed-for" parts of the earth. They did come to be the chief, the central races of history. But race aggregations, through conquest or adoption, must have worked considerable changes in the political bearings of the patriarchal principle. The direct line of male descent from the reputed common progenitor of the race could hardly continue indefinitely to be observed in filling the chieftainship of the race. A distinct element of choice — of election — must have crept in at a very early period. The individual initiative of which I have spoken, contributed very powerfully to effect this change. The oldest male of the hitherto reigning family was no longer chosen as of course, but the wisest or the bravest. It was even open to the national choice to go upon occasion altogether outside this succession and choose a leader of force and resource from some other family.

Hereditary replaced by Political Magistracy. — Of course mere growth had much to do with these transformations. As tribes grew into nations, by all the processes of natural and artificial increase, all distinctness of mutual blood-relationship faded away. Direct common lines of descent became hopelessly obscured. Cross-kinships fell into inextricable confusion. Family government and race government became necessarily divorced, — differentiated. The state continued to be conceived as a Family; but the headship of this huge and complex family ceased to be natural and became *political*. So soon as hereditary title was broken in upon, the family no longer dominated the state; the state at last dominated the family. It often fell out that a son, absolutely subject to his father in the family, was by election made master of his father outside the family, in the state. Political had at least begun to grow away from domestic authority.

Summary. — Enough has been said here to make plain the approaches to those systems of government with which we are familiar in the modern world. We can understand how custom crystallized about the primitive man; how in the case of the majority of mankind it preserved itself against all essential change; how with the favored minority of the race it was broken by war, altered by imperative circumstance, modified by imitation, and infringed by individual initiative; how change resulted in progress; and how, at last, kinsmen became fellow-citizens.

SOME REPRESENTATIVE AUTHORITIES.

Bachofen, Das Mutterrecht.

Bagehot, Walter, Physics and Politics, N. Y., 1884.

Coulanges, Fustel de, The Ancient City, Boston, 1882.

Darwin, Charles, The Origin of Species, 2 vols., London, 1888.

Draper, J. W., History of the Intellectual Development of Europe, 5th ed., N. Y., 1870.

Farnell, L. R., Cults of the Greek States, 5 vols., Oxford, 1896–1909.

Ford, H. J., The Natural History of the State, Princeton, 1915.

Freeman, E. A., Comparative Politics, London, 1873.

Hearn, W. E., The Aryan Household, London, 1879.

Howard, G. E., History of Matrimonial Institutions, Chicago, 1904.

Huxley, T. H., Evidence as to Man's Place in Nature, London, 1863.

Lang, Andrew, Custom and Myth, London, 1885; and article "Family," in the Encyclopædia Britannica.

Lecky, W. E. H., History of European Morals, 3d ed., N. Y., 1913.

Letourneau, Ch., The Evolution of Marriage, N. Y., 3d ed., London and N. Y., 1911.

Lord Avebury, The Origin of Civilization and the Primitive Condition of Man, 6th ed., London, 1902; and Prehistoric Times, 7th ed., London, 1913.

Lyall, Sir A. C., Asiatic Studies, Religious and Social, London, 1882.

McLennan, J. F., The Patriarchal Theory, London, 1885; and Studies in Ancient History, London, 1886; Studies in Ancient History, Second Series, London and N. Y., 1896.

Maine, Sir H. S., Ancient Law, with notes by Sir Frederick Pollock, 4th American from 10th London ed., N. Y., 1885; Early Law and Custom, N. Y., 1883, especially Chap. VII.; Early History of Institutions, N. Y., 1875; and Village Communities in the East and West, N. Y., 1880.

Mayne, J. D., Hindu Law and Custom, Madras, 1888.

Morgan, L. H., Ancient Society, London, 1877.

Peschel, O., The Races of Man, trans. London, 1876.

Smith, W. Robertson, Marriage and Kinship in Early Arabia, Cambridge 1885.

Spencer, H., Principles of Sociology, Vol. I., Part III.; "Ceremonial Institutions," and "Political Institutions."

Spencer and Gillen, The Native Tribes of Central Australia.

Starke, C. N., The Primitive Family, N. Y., 1889.

Tylor, E. B., Early History of Mankind, London, 1878; Primitive Culture, London, 1871, 3d ed., 1891.

Westermarck, Edward, History of Human Marriage, London, 1891.

The classical statements of the contract theory of the origin of government will be found in

Hooker, Ecclesiastical Polity.

Hobbes, Leviathan.

Locke, John, Essays on Civil Government.

Rousseau, J. J., The Social Contract.

II

NATURE AND FORMS OF GOVERNMENT

—————

Government rests upon Authority and Force. — The es‑sential characteristic of all government, whatever its form, is authority. There must in every instance be, on the one hand, governors, and, on the other, those who are governed. And the authority of governors, directly or indirectly, rests in all cases ultimately on *force*. Government, in its last analysis, is organized force. Not necessarily or invariably organized armed force, but the will of a few men, of many men, or of a community prepared by organization to realize its own purposes with reference to the common affairs of the community ; organized, that is, to rule, to dominate. The machinery of government necessary to such an organization consists of instrumentalities fitted to enforce in the conduct of the common affairs of a community the will of the ruling men: the ruling minority, or the ruling majority.

Not necessarily upon Obvious Force. — This is not, how‑ever, to be interpreted too literally, or too narrowly. The force behind authority must not be looked for as if it were always to be seen or were always being exercised. That there is authority lodged with ruler or magistrate is in every case evident enough; but that that authority rests upon force is not always a fact upon the surface, and is therefore in one sense not always practically significant. In the case of any particular government, the force upon which the authority of its officers rests may never once for generations together take the shape of armed force. Happily there are in our own day many governments, and those among the most prominent, which seldom coerce their subjects, seeming in their tranquil, noiseless operations to run of themselves. They in a sense operate without the exercise of force. But there is force behind them none the less because it never shows itself. The better governments of our day, — those which rest, not upon the armed strength of governors, but upon the free consent of the governed, — are founded upon constitutions and laws whose source and sanction are the habit of communities. The force which they embody is not the force of a dominant dynasty or of a prevalent minority, but the force of an agreeing majority. And the overwhelming nature of this force is evident in the fact that the minority very seldom challenge its exercise. It is latent just because it is understood to be omnipotent. There is force behind the authority of the elected magistrate, no less than behind that of the usurping despot, a much greater force behind the President of the United States than behind an autocratic monarch. The difference lies in the *display* of coercive power. Physical force is the prop of both, though in the one it is the last, while in the other it is the first, resort.

The Governing Force in Ancient and in Modern Society. — These elements of authority and force in government are quite plain to be seen in modern society, even when the constitution of that society is democratic ; but they are not so easily discoverable upon a first view in primitive society. It is common nowadays when referring to the affairs of the most progressive nations to speak of 'government by public opinion,' 'government by the popular voice '; and such phrases possibly describe sufficiently well the full-grown democratic systems. But no one intends such expressions to conceal the fact that the majority, which utters 'public opinion,' does not prevail because the minority are convinced, but because they are outnumbered and have against them not the 'popular voice ' only, but the 'popular power ' as well, — that it is the potential might rather than the wisdom of the majority which gives it its right to rule. When once majorities have learned to have opinions and to organize themselves for enforcing them, they rule by virtue of power no less than do despots with standing armies or concerting minorities dominating unorganized majorities. But, though it was clearly opinion which ruled in primitive societies, this conception of the might of majorities hardly seems to fit our ideas of primitive systems of

government.   What shall we say of them in connection with our
present analysis of government?   They were neither democracies
in which the will of majorities chose the ways of government,
nor despotisms, in which the will of an individual controlled, nor
oligarchies, in which the purposes of a minority prevailed.
Where shall we place the force which lay behind the authority
exercised under them?   Was the power of the father in the patriarchal family power of arm, mere domineering strength of will?
What was the force that sustained the authority of the tribal
chieftain or of that chief of chiefs, the king?   That authority
was not independent of the consent of those over whom it was
exercised; and yet it was not formulated by that consent.   That
consent may be said to have been involuntary, *inbred*.   It was
born of the habit of the race.   It was congenital.   It consisted
of a custom and tradition, moreover, which bound the chief no
less than it bound his subjects.   He might no more transgress the
unwritten law of the race than might the humblest of his fellow-
tribesmen.   He was governed scarcely less than they were.   All
were under bondage to strictly prescribed ways of life.   Where,
then, lay the force which sanctioned the authority of chief and
sub-chief and father in this society?   Not in the will of the
ruler: that was bound by the prescriptions of custom.   Not in
the popular choice: over that too the law of custom reigned.

The Force of the Common Will in Ancient Society. — The
real residence of force in such societies as these can be most easily
discovered if we look at them under other circumstances.   Nations
still under the dominion of customary law have within historical
times been conquered by alien conquerors; but in no such case
did the will of the conqueror have free scope in regulating the
affairs of the conquered.   Seldom did it have any scope at all.
The alien throne was maintained by force of arms, and taxes were
mercilessly wrung from the subject populations; but never did
the despot venture to change the customs of the conquered land.
Its native laws he no more dared to touch than would a prince of
the dynasty which he had displaced.   He dared not play with
the forces latent in the prejudices, the fanaticism of his subjects.
He knew that those forces were volcanic, and that no prop of
armed men could save his throne from overthrow and destruction

should they once break forth. He really had no authority to govern, but only a power to despoil, — for the idea of government is inseparable from the conception of *legal regulation*. If, therefore, in the light of such cases, we conceive the throne of such a society as occupied by some native prince whose authority rested upon the laws of his country, it is plain to see that the real force upon which authority rests under a government so constituted is after all the force of public opinion, in a sense hardly less vividly real than if we spoke of a modern democracy. The law inheres in the common will: and it is that law upon which the authority of the prince is founded. He rules according to the common will: for that will is, that immemorial custom be inviolably observed. The force latent in that common will both backs and limits his authority.

Public Opinion, Ancient and Modern. — The fact that the public opinion of such societies made no deliberate choice of laws or constitutions need not confuse the analogy between that public opinion and our own. Our own approval of the government under which we live, though doubtless conscious and in a way voluntary, is largely hereditary, — is largely an inbred and inculcated approbation. There is a large amount of mere *drift* in it. Conformity to what is established is much the easiest habit in opinion. Our constructive choice even in our own governments, under which there is no divine canon against change, is limited to *modifications*. The generation that saw our federal system established may have imagined themselves out-of-hand creators, originators of government; but we of this generation have taken what was given us, and are not controlled by laws altogether of our own making. Our constitutional life was made for us long ago. We are like primitive men in the public opinion which preserves; though unlike them in the public opinion which alters our institutions. Their stationary common thought contained the generic forces of government no less than does our own progressive public thought.

The True Nature of Government. — What, then, in the last analysis, is the nature of government? If it rests upon authority and force, but upon authority which depends upon the acquiescence of the general will and upon force suppressed, latent, withheld except under extraordinary circumstances, what principle lies behind these phenomena, at the heart of government? The answer is hidden in the nature of Society itself. Society is in no sense artificial; it is as truly natural as the individual man himself. As Aristotle said, man is by nature a social animal; his social function is as normal with him as is his individual function. Society, therefore, is compounded of the common habit and is an evolution of experience, an interlaced growth of tenacious relationships, a compact, living whole, structural, not mechanical.

Government an Organ of Society. — Government is merely the executive organ of society, the organ through which its habit acts, through which its will becomes operative, through which it adapts itself to its environment and works out for itself a more effective life. There is clear reason, therefore, why the disciplinary action of society upon the individual is exceptional; clear reason also why the power of the despot must recognize certain ultimate limits and bounds; and clear reason why sudden or violent changes of government lead to equally violent and often fatal reactions and revolutions. It is only the exceptional individual who is not held fast to the common habit of social duty and comity. The despot's power, like the potter's, is limited by the characteristics of the materials in which he works, of the society which he manipulates; and change which roughly breaks with the common thought will lack the sympathy of that thought, will provoke its opposition, and will inevitably be crushed by that opposition. Society can be changed only by evolution, and revolution is the antipode of evolution. The public order is preserved because order inheres in the character of society.

The Forms of Government: their Significance. — The forms of government do not affect the essence of government: the bayonets of the tyrant, the quick concert and superior force of an organized minority, the latent force of a self-governed majority, — all these depend upon the character and development of the community. "The obedience of the subject to the sovereign has its root not in contract but in force, — the force of the sovereign to punish disobedience ";[1] but that force must be backed by the general habit (pages 77, 80).   The forms of government are, nevertheless, in every way most important to be observed, for the very reason that they express the character of government, and indicate its history.   They exhibit the stages of political development, and make clear the necessary constituents and ordinary purposes of government, historically considered.   They illustrate, too, the sanctions upon which it rests.

Aristotle's Analysis of the Forms of Government. — It has been common for writers on politics in speaking of the several forms of government to rewrite Aristotle, and it is not easy to depart from the practice.   For, although Aristotle's enumeration was not quite exhaustive, and although his descriptions will not quite fit modern types of government, his enumeration still serves as a most excellent frame on which to hang an exposition of the forms of government, and his descriptions at least furnish points of contrast between ancient and modern governments by observing which we can the more clearly understand the latter.

Aristotle considered Monarchy, Aristocracy, and Democracy (Ochlocracy) the three standard forms of government. The first he defined as the rule of One, the second as the rule of the Few, the third as the rule of the Many.[2]   Off against these standard and, so to say, *healthful* forms he set their degenerate shapes.   Tyranny he conceived to be the degenerate shape of Monarchy, Oligarchy the degenerate shape of Aristocracy, and Anarchy (or mob-rule) the degenerate shape of Democracy.   His observation of the political world about him led him to believe that there was in every case a strong, an almost inevitable, tendency for the pure forms to sink into the degenerate.

The Cycle of Degeneracy and Revolution. — He outlined a cycle of degeneracies and revolutions through which, as he conceived, every State of long life was apt to pass.   His idea was this.   The natural first form of government for every state

[1] John Morley, *Rousseau*, Vol. II., p. 184.

[2] Not of the absolute majority, as we shall see presently when contrasting ancient and modern democracy (secs. 1403, 1406).

would be the rule of a monarch, of a single strong man with
supreme power. This monarch would usually hand on his kingdom to his children. They might confidently be expected to for-
get those pledges and those views of the public good which had
bound and guided him. Their rule would sink into tyranny.
At length their tyranny would meet its decisive check at
some Runnymede. There would be revolt; and the princely
leaders of revolt, taking government into their own hands, would
set up an Aristocracy. But aristocracies, though often public-
spirited and just in their youth, always decline, in their later
years, into a dotage of selfish oligarchy. Oligarchy is even more
hateful to civil liberty, is even a graver hindrance to healthful
civil life than tyranny. A class bent upon subserving only their
own interests can devise injustice in greater variety than can a
single despot: and their insolence is always quick to goad the
many to hot revolution. To this revolution succeeds Democracy.
But Democracy too has its old age of degeneracy, — an old age in
which it loses its early respect for law, its first amiability of
mutual concession. It breaks out into license and Anarchy, and
none but a Cæsar can bring it back to reason and order. The
cycle is completed. The throne is set up again, and a new series
of deteriorations and revolutions begins.

**Modern Contrasts to the Aristotelian Forms of Govern-
ment.** — The confirmations of this view furnished by the history
of Europe since the time of Aristotle have been striking and
numerous enough to render it still oftentimes convenient as a
scheme by which to observe the course of political history even
in our own days. But it is still more instructive to contrast the
later facts of political development with this ancient exposition
of the laws of politics. Observe, then, the differences between
modern and ancient types of government, and the likelihood that
the historian of the future, if not of the present and the immediate past, will have to record more divergencies from the cycle
of Aristotle than correspondences with it.

The Modern Absolute Monarchy. — In the vast absolute
Monarchies which have grown up in Europe since Aristotle, it
is evident that the modern monarch, if he be indeed monarch, has

a much deeper and wider reach of power than had the ancient monarch. The monarch of our day is a Legislator; the ancient monarch was not. Antique society may be said hardly to have known what legislation was. Custom was for it the law of public as well as of private life: and custom could not be enacted. At any rate ancient monarchies were not legislative. The despot issued edicts, — imperative commands covering particular cases or affecting particular individuals: the Roman emperors were among the first to promulgate 'constitutions,' — general rules of law to be applied universally. The modern despot can do more even than that. He can regulate by his command public affairs not only but private as well, — can even upset local custom and bring all his subjects under uniform legislative control. Nor is he in the least bound to observe his own laws. A word,— and that his own word,— will set them aside: a word will abolish, a word restore, them. He is absolute over his subjects not only, — ancient despots were that, — but over all laws also, — which no ancient despot was.

> Of course these statements are meant to be taken with certain important limitations. The modern despot as well as the ancient is bound by the habit of his people. He may change laws, but he may not change life as easily ; and the national traditions and national character, the rural and commercial habit of his kingdom, bind him very absolutely. The limitation is not often felt by the monarch, simply because he has himself been bred in the atmosphere of the national life and unconsciously conforms to it.

The Modern Monarchy usually 'Limited.' — But the absolute monarchy is abnormal in the Europe of to-day, as abnormal as that of the Turk, — a belated example of those crude forms of politics which the rest of Europe has outgrown. Turning to the other monarchies of to-day, it is at once plain that they present the strongest contrast possible to any absolute monarchy ancient or modern. In Europe, with the exception of Germany they are 'limited' by the resolutions of a popular parliament.[1] The people have a distinct and often an imperative voice in the conduct of public affairs.

Is Monarchy now succeeded by Aristocracy? — And what is to be said of Aristotle's cycle in connection with modern mon-

---

[1] The ' popular ' parliament, the Reichstag, in Germany, has no real power to ' limit ' the autocratic Kaiser.

archies? Does any one suppose it possible that when the despotism of the Czar falls it will be succeeded by an aristocracy; or that when the modified authority of the emperors of Austria and Germany or the king of Italy still further exchanges substance for shadow, a limited class will succeed to the reality of power? Is there any longer any place between Monarchy and Democracy for Aristocracy? Has it not been crowded out?

English and Ancient Aristocracy contrasted. — Indeed, since the extension of the franchise in England to the working classes, no example of a real Aristocracy is left in the modern world. At the beginning of the nineteenth century the government of England, called a 'limited monarchy,' was in reality an Aristocracy. Parliament and the entire administration of the kingdom were in the hands of the classes having wealth or nobility. The members of the House of Lords and the Crown together controlled a majority of the seats in the House of Commons. England was 'represented' by her upper classes almost exclusively. That Aristocracy has been set aside by the Reform Bills of 1832, 1867, 1885, and 1918; but it is worth while to look back to it, in order to contrast a modern type of Aristocracy with those ancient aristocracies which were present to the mind of Aristotle. An ancient Aristocracy *constituted* the State; the English aristocracy merely controlled the State. Under the widest citizenship known even to ancient democracy less than half the adult male subjects of the State shared the franchise. The ancient Democracy itself was a government by a minority. The ancient Aristocracy was a government by a still narrower minority; and this narrow minority monopolized office and power not only, but citizenship as well. There were no citizens but they. They were the State. Every one else existed for the State, only they were part of it. In England the case was very different. There the franchise was not confined to the aristocrats; it was only controlled by them. Nor did the aristocrats of England consider themselves the whole of the State. They were quite conscious,—and quite content,—that they had the State virtually in their possession; but they looked upon themselves as holding it in trust for the people of Great Britain. Their legislation was in fact class legislation, oftentimes of a very narrow sort; but they did not think that it was. They regarded their rule as eminently advantageous to the kingdom; and they unquestionably had, or tried to have, the real interests of the kingdom at heart. They led the State, but did not constitute it.

Present and Future Prevalence of Democracy. — If Aristocracy seems about to disappear, Democracy seems about universally to prevail. Ever since the rise of popular education in the last century has assured a thinking weight to the masses of the people everywhere, the advance of democratic opinion and the spread of democratic institutions have been most marked and most significant. They have destroyed almost all pure forms of Monarchy and Aristocracy by introducing into them imperative forces of popular thought and the concrete institutions of popular representation; and they promise to reduce politics to a single form by excluding all other governing forces and institutions but those of a wide suffrage and a democratic representation, — by reducing all forms of government to Democracy.

Differences of Form between Ancient and Modern Democracies. — The differences of form to be observed between ancient and modern Democracies are wide and important. Ancient Democracies were ' immediate,' while ours are ' mediate,' that is to say, *representative*. Every citizen of the Athenian State, — to take that as a type, — had a right to appear and vote in proper person in the popular assembly, and in those committees of that assembly which acted as criminal courts; the modern voter votes for a representative who is to sit for him in the popular chamber, — he himself has not even the right of entrance there. This idea of representation, — even the idea of a vote by proxy, — was hardly known to the ancients; but among us it is all-pervading.[1] Even the elected magistrate of an ancient Democracy was not looked upon as a representative of his fellow-citizens. *He was the State*, so far as his functions went, and so long as his term of office lasted. He could break through all law or custom, if he dared. It was only when his term had expired and he was again a private citizen that he could be called to account. There was no impeachment while in office. To our thought all elected to office, — whether Presidents,

---

[1] Where the initiative and referendum have been introduced, the electors vote directly upon laws, but the representative system has been continued.

ministers, or legislators, — are representatives. The limitations as to the size of the State involved in ancient practices and conceptions is obvious. A State in which all citizens are also legislators must of necessity be small. The modern representative State has no such limitation. It may cover a continent.

Nature of Democracy, Ancient and Modern. — The differences of nature to be observed between ancient and modern Democracies are no less wide and important. The ancient Democracy was a class government. As already pointed out, it was only a broader Aristocracy. Its franchise was at widest an exclusive privilege, extending only to a minority. There were slaves under its heel; there were even freedmen who could never hope to enter its citizenship. Class subordination was of the essence of its constitution. From the modern Democratic State, on the other hand, both slavery and class subordination are excluded as inconsistent with its theory, not only, but, more than that, as antagonistic to its very being. Its citizenship is as wide as its native population; its suffrage as wide as its qualified citizenship, — it knows no non-citizen class. And there is still another difference between the Democracy of Aristotle and the Democracy of Tocqueville and Bentham. The citizens of the former lived for the State; the citizen of the latter lives for himself, and the State is for him. The modern Democratic State exists for the sake of the individual; the individual, in Greek conception, lived for the State. The ancient State recognized no personal rights, — all rights were State rights; the modern State recognizes no State rights which are independent of personal rights.

Growth of the Democratic Idea. — In making the last statement embrace ' the ancient State ' irrespective of kind and ' the modern State,' of whatever form, I have pointed out what may be taken as the cardinal difference between all the ancient forms of government and all the modern. It is a difference which I have already stated in another way. The *democratic idea* has penetrated more or less deeply all the advanced systems of government, and has penetrated them in consequence of that change of thought which has given to the individual an importance quite independent of his membership of a State. I can here only indicate the historical steps of that change of thought; I cannot go at any length into its causes.

Subordination of the Individual in the Ancient State. — We have seen that, in the history of political society, if we have read that history aright, the rights of government, — the magistracies and subordinations of kinship, — antedate what we now call the rights of the individual. A man was at first nobody in himself; he was only the kinsman of somebody else. The father himself, or the chief, commanded only because of priority in kinship: to that all rights of all men were relative. Society was the unit; the individual the fraction. Man existed for society. He was all his life long in tutelage; only society was old enough to take charge of itself. The State was the only Individual.

Individualism of Christianity and Teutonic Institutions. — There was no essential change in this idea for centuries. Through all the developments of government down to the time of the rise of the Roman Empire the State continued, in the conception of the western nations at least, to eclipse the individual. Private rights had no standing as against the State. Subsequently many influences combined to break in upon this immemorial conception. Chief among these influences were Christianity and the institutions of the German conquerors of the fifth century. Christianity gave each man a magistracy over himself by insisting upon his personal, individual responsibility to God. For right living, at any rate, each man was to have only his own conscience as a guide. In these deepest matters there must be for the Christian an individuality which no claim of his State upon him could rightfully be suffered to infringe. The German nations brought into the Romanized and partially Christianized world of the fifth century an individuality of another sort, — the idea of allegiance to individuals (p. 101). Perhaps their idea that each man had a money-value which must be paid by any one who might slay him also contributed to the process of making men units instead of State fractions; but their idea of personal allegiance played the more prominent part in the transformation of society which resulted from their western conquests. The Roman knew no allegiance save allegiance to his State. He swore fealty to his *imperator* as to an embodiment of that State, not as to an individual. The Teuton, on the other hand, bound himself to his leader by a bond of personal service which the Roman either could not understand or understood only to despise. There were, therefore, individuals in the German State: great chiefs or warriors with a following (*comitatus*) of devoted volunteers ready to die for them in frays not directed by the State, but of their own provoking (pages 96–97). There was with all German tribes freedom of individual movement and combination within the ranks. When the German settled down as master amongst the Romanized populations of western and southern Europe, his thought was led captive by the conceptions of the Roman law, as all subsequent thought that has known it has been, and his habits were much modified by those of his new subjects ; but this strong element of individualism was not destroyed by the contact. It lived to constitute one of the chief features of the Feudal System.

The Transitional Feudal System. — The Feudal System was made up of elaborate gradations of personal allegiance. The only State possible under that system was a disintegrate state embracing, not a unified people, but a nation atomized into its individual elements. A king there might be, but he was lord, not of his people, but of his barons. He was himself a baron also, and as such had many a direct subject pledged to serve him ; but as king the barons were his only direct subjects ; and the barons were heedful of their allegiance to him only when he could make it to their interest to be so, or their peril not to be. They were the kings of the people, who owed direct allegiance to them alone, and to the king only through them. Kingdoms were only greater baronies, baronies lesser kingdoms. One small part of the people served one baron, another part served another baron. As a whole they served no one master. They were not a whole : they were jarring, disconnected segments of a nation. Every man had his own lord, and antagonized every one who had not the same lord as he (pages 103–109).

Rise of the Modern State. — Such a system was fatal to peace and good government, but it cleared the way for the rise of the modern State by utterly destroying the old conceptions. The State of the ancients had been an entity in itself, — an entity

to which the entity of the individual was altogether subordinate.
The Feudal State was merely an aggregation of individuals, —
a loose bundle of separated series of men knowing few common
aims or actions.   It not only had no actual unity : it had no
thought of unity.   National unity came at last, — in France, for
instance, by the subjugation of the barons by the king (page 115);
in England by the joint effort of people and barons against the
throne, — but when it came it was the ancient unity with a difference.   Men were no longer State fractions ; they had become
State integers.   The State *seemed* less like a natural, and more
like a deliberately organized association.   Personal allegiance to
kings had everywhere taken the place of native membership of
a body politic.   Men were now subjects, not citizens.

Renaissance and Reformation. — Presently came the
thirteenth century with its wonders of personal adventure and
individual enterprise in discovery, piracy, and trade.   Following hard upon these, the Renaissance woke men to a philosophical study of their surroundings, — and above all of their long-
time unquestioned systems of thought.   Then arose Luther to
reiterate the almost forgotten truths of the individuality of men's
consciences, the right of individual judgment.   Ere long the new
thoughts had penetrated to the masses of the people.   Reformers
had begun to cast aside their scholastic weapons and come down
to the common folk about them, talking their own vulgar tongue
and craving their acquiescence in the new doctrines of deliver-
ance from mental and spiritual bondage to Pope or Schoolman.
National literatures were born.   Thought had broken away from
its exclusion in cloisters and universities and had gone out to
challenge the people to a use of their own minds.   By using their
minds, the people gradually put away the childish things of their
days of ignorance, and began to claim a part in affairs.   Finally,
systematized popular education has completed the story.   Nations
are growing up into manhood.   Peoples are becoming old enough
to govern themselves.

The Modern Force of Majorities. — It is thus no acci-
dent, but the outcome of great permanent causes, that there is no
more to be found among the civilized races of Europe any sat·
isfactory example of Aristotle's Monarchies and Aristocracies.

The force of modern governments is not now often the force of minorities. It is getting to be more and more the force of majorities. The sanction of every rule not founded upon sheer military despotism is the consent of a thinking people. Military despotisms are now seen to be necessarily ephemeral. Only monarchs who are revered as seeking to serve their subjects are any longer safe upon their thrones. Monarchies exist only by democratic consent.

New Character of Society. — And, more than that, the result has been to give to society a new integration. The common habit is now operative again, not in acquiescence and submission merely, but in initiative and progress as well. Society is not the unity it once was, — its members are given freer play, fuller opportunity for origination; but its unified character is again prominent. It is the Whole which has emerged from the disintegration of feudalism and the specialization of absolute monarchy. The Whole, too, has become self-conscious, and by becoming self-directive has set out upon a new course of development.

SELECTED BIBLIOGRAPHY.

(For this and the two succeeding chapters.)

Amos, Sheldon, Science of Politics, London, 1890.
Aristotle, Politics.
Beaulieu, P. Leroy, The Modern State, London, 1891.
Burgess, John W., Political Science and Constitutional, Boston, 1891.
Garner, J. W., Introduction to Political Science, N. Y.
Graham, William, Socialism, 2d ed., London, 1901.
Jellinek, Georg, Das Recht des Modernen Staates, 2d ed., Berlin, 1905.
Lilly, W. S., First Principles in Politics, N. Y., 1899.
Mill, J. S., On Liberty, N. Y., 1877.
Plato, Republic.
Ral, John, Contemporary Socialism, 2d ed., 1891.
Ritchie, Principles of State Interference.
Sidgwick, Henry, Elements of Politics, London, 1891.
Spencer, Herbert, Man versus the State.
Willoughby, W. W., The Nature of the State, N. Y., 1896.

III.

THE FUNCTIONS OF GOVERNMENT.

———o⚬✺⚬o———

What are the Functions of Government? — The question
has its own difficulties and complexities: it cannot be answered
out of hand and by the list, as the physiologist might answer the
question, What are the functions of the heart? In its *nature*
government is one, but in its *life* it is many : there are governments *and* governments. When asked, therefore, What are the
functions of government? we must ask in return, Of what government? Different states have different conceptions of their
duty, and so undertake different things. They have had their
own peculiar origins, their own characteristic histories; circumstance has moulded them; necessity, interest, or caprice has
variously guided them. Some have lingered near those primitive
institutions which all once knew and upheld together; others
have quite forgotten that man ever had a political childhood and
are now old in complex practices of national self-government.

The Nature of the Question. — It is important to notice
at the outset that this is in one aspect obviously a simple *question
of fact;* and yet there is another phase of it, in which it becomes
as evidently a question of opinion. The distinction is important
because over and over again the question of fact has been con-
founded with that very widely different question, *What ought the
functions of government to be ?* The two questions should be kept
entirely separate in treatment. Under no circumstances may we
instructively or safely begin with the question of opinion : the
answer to the question of fact is the indispensable foundation of
all sound reasoning concerning government, which is at all points
based upon experience rather than upon theory. The facts of
government mirror the principles of government in operation.

41

What government does must arise from what government is: and what government is must determine what government ought to do.

Classification. — It will contribute to clearness of thought to observe the functions of government in two groups, I. *The Constituent* Functions, II. *The Ministrant.* Under the *Constituent* I would place that usual category of governmental function, the protection of life, liberty, and property, together with all other functions that are necessary to the civic organization of society, — functions which are *not optional* with governments, even in the eyes of strictest *laissez faire,* — which are indeed the very bonds of society. Under the *Ministrant* I would range those other functions (such as education, posts and telegraphs, and the care, say, of forests) which are undertaken, not by way of *governing,* but by way of advancing the general interests of society, — functions which *are* optional, being necessary only according to standards of convenience or expediency, and not according to standards of existence; functions which assist without constituting social organization.

Of course this classification is based primarily upon objective and practical distinctions and cannot claim philosophic completeness. There may be room for question, too, as to whether some of the functions which I class as Ministrant might not quite as properly have been considered Constituent; but I must here simply act upon my own conclusions without rearguing them, acknowledging by the way that the line of demarcation is not always perfectly clear.

"The admitted functions of government," said Mr. Mill, "embrace a much wider field than can easily be included within the ring-fence of any restrictive definition, and it is hardly possible to find any ground of justification common to them all, except the comprehensive one of general expediency."

I. The Constituent Functions.

(1) The keeping of order and providing for the protection of persons and property from violence and robbery.

(2) The fixing of the legal relations between man and wife and between parents and children.

(3) The regulation of the holding, transmission, and interchange of property, and the determination of its liabilities for debt or for crime.

(4) The determination of contract rights between individuals.

(5) The definition and punishment of crime.

(6) The administration of justice in civil causes.

(7) The determination of the political duties, privileges, and relations of citizens.

(8) Dealings of the state with foreign powers : the preservation of the state from external danger or encroachment and the advancement of its international interests.

These will all be recognized as functions which persist under every form of government.

II. The Ministrant Functions. — It is hardly possible to give a complete list of those functions which I have called Ministrant, so various are they under different systems of government. The following partial list will suffice, however, for the purposes of the present discussion :

(1) The regulation of trade and industry. Under this head I would include the coinage of money and the establishment of standard weights and measures, laws against forestalling and engrossing, the licensing of trades, etc., as well as the great matter of tariffs, navigation laws, and the like.

(2) The regulation of labor.

(3) The maintenance of thoroughfares, — including state management of railways and that great group of undertakings which we embrace within the comprehensive term 'Internal Improvements.'

(4) The maintenance of postal and telegraph systems, which is very similar in principle to (3).

(5) The manufacture and distribution of gas, the maintenance of water-works, etc.

(6) Sanitation, including the regulation of trades for sanitary purposes.

(7) Education.

(8) Care of the poor and incapable.

(9) Care and cultivation of forests and like matters, such as the stocking of rivers with fish.

(10) Sumptuary laws, such as 'prohibition' laws, for example.

These are all functions which, in one shape or another, all governments alike have undertaken. Changed conceptions of the nature and duty of the state have arisen, issuing from changed historical conditions and deeply altered historical circumstances; and part of the change which has thus affected the idea of the state has been a change in the method and extent of the exercise of governmental functions; but changed conceptions have left the functions of government *in kind* the same. Diversities of conception are very much more marked than diversities of practice.

History of Governmental Function: Province of the Ancient State. — Notable contrasts both of theory and of practice separate governments of the ancient omnipotent type from governments of the modern constitutional type. The ancient State, standing very near, as it did, in its thought, to that time, still more remote, when the State was the Kin, knew nothing of individual rights as contrasted with the rights of the state. "The nations of Italy," says Mommsen, "did not merge into that of Rome more completely than the single Roman burgess merged in the Roman community." And Greece was not a whit behind Rome in the absoluteness with which she held the subordination of the individual to the state.

This thought is strikingly visible in the writings of Plato and Aristotle, not only in what they say, but also, and even more, in what they do not say. The ideal Republic of which Plato dreams is to prescribe the whole life of its citizens; but there is no suggestion that it is to be set up under cover of any new conception as to what the state may legitimately do, — it is only to make novel experiments in legislation under the *old* conception. And Aristotle's objection to the utopian projects of his master is not that they would be socialistic (as we should say), but merely that they would be unwise. He does not fear that in such a republic the public power would prove to have been exalted too high; but.

speaking to the policy of the thing, he foresees that the citizens would be poor and unhappy. The state may do what it will, but let it be wise in what it does. There is no one among the Greeks to deny that it is the duty of the state to make its citizens happy and prosperous; nay, to *legislate* them happy, if legislation may create fair skies and a kind fortune; the only serious quarrel concerns the question, What laws are to be tried to this end?

Roman Conception of Private Rights. — Roman principles, though equally extreme, were in some respects differently cast. That superior capacity for the development of law, which made the Romans singular among the nations of antiquity, showed itself in respect of the functions of government in a more distinct division between public and private rights than obtained in the polity of the Greek cities. An examination of the conception of the state held in Rome reveals the singular framework of her society. The Roman family did not suffer that complete absorption into the City which so early overtook the Greek family. Private rights were not individual rights, but family rights: and family rights did not so much curtail as supplement the powers of the community. The family was an indestructible *organ of the state.* The father of a family, or the head of a *gens,* was in a sense a member of the official hierarchy of the City, — as the king, or his counterpart the consul, was a greater father. There was no distinction of principle between the power of king or consul and the power of a father; it was a mere difference of sphere, a division of functions.

> A son was, for instance, in some things exempt from the authority of the City only because he was in those things still subject, because his father still lived, to the dominion of that original state, the family. There was not in Rome that separation of the son from the family at majority which characterizes the Greek polity, as it now characterizes our own. The father continued to be a ruler, an hereditary state officer, within the original sphere of the family life, the large sphere of individual privilege and property.

This essential unity of state and family furnishes us with the theoretic measure of state functions in Rome. The Roman burgess was subordinated, not to the public authority exactly, but rather to the *public order,* to the conservative integrity of the community. He was subject to a law which embodied the steady, unbroken habit of the State-family. He was not dominated, but merged.

Powers of the Roman Senate. — The range of state power in ancient times, as a range broken only by limits of habit and convenience, is well illustrated in the elastic functions of the Roman Senate during the period of the Republic. With an unbroken life which kept it conscious of every tradition and familiar with every precedent ; with established standards of tested experience and cautious expediency, it was able to direct the movements of the compact society at whose summit it sat, as the brain and consciousness direct the movements of the human body ; and it is evident from the freedom of its discussions and the frequency of its action upon interests of every kind, whether of public or of private import, that the Roman state, as typified in its Senate, was in its several branches of family, tribe, and City, a single undivided whole, and that its prerogatives were limited by nothing save religious observance and fixed habit. Of that individual liberty which we cherish it knew nothing.

Government the Embodiment of Society. — As little was there in Greek politics any seed of the thought which would limit the sphere of governmental action by principles of inalienable individual rights. Both in Greek and in Roman conception government was as old as society, — was indeed nothing less than the express image and embodiment of society. In government society lived and moved and had its being. Society and government were one, in some such sense as the spirit and body of man are one : it was through government, as through mouth and eyes and limbs, that society realized and gave effect to its life. Society's prejudices, habits, superstitions, did indeed command the actions of government; but only because society and government were one and the same, not because they were distinct and the one subordinate to the other. In plain terms, the functions of government had no limits of principle, but only certain limits of wont and convenience, and the object of administration was nothing less than to help society on to all its ends : to speed and facilitate all social undertakings. So far as full citizens of the state were concerned, Greek and Roman alike was what we should call a socialist; though he was too much in the world of affairs and had too keen an appreciation of experience, too keen a sense of the sane and possible, to attempt the Utopias of which the modern socialist dreams, and with which the ancient citizen's own writers sometimes amused him. He bounded his politics by common sense, and so dispensed with 'the rights of man.'

Feudalism: Functions of Government Functions of Proprietorship. — Individual rights, after having been first heralded in the religious world by the great voice of Christianity, broke into the ancient political world in the person of the Teuton. But the new politics which the invader brought with him was not destined to establish at once democratic equality: that was a work reserved for the transformations of the modern world. During the Middle Ages, government, as we conceive it, may be said to have suffered eclipse. In the Feudal System the constituent elements of government fell away from each other. Society was drawn back to something like its original family groups. Conceptions of government narrowed themselves to small territorial connections. Men became sovereigns in their own right by virtue of owning land in their own right. There was no longer any conception of nations or societies as wholes. Union there was none, but only interdependence. Allegiance bowed, not to law or to fatherhood, but to ownership. The functions of government under such a system were simply the functions of proprietorship, of command and obedience: " I say unto one, Go, and he goeth; and to another, Come, and he cometh; and to my servant, Do this, and he doeth it." The public function of the baron was to keep peace among his liege-men, to see that their properties were enjoyed according to the custom of the manor (if the manor had been suffered to acquire custom on any point), and to exact fines of them for all privileges, whether of marrying, of coming of age, or of making a will. The baronial conscience, bred in cruel, hardening times, was the only standard of justice; the baronial power the only conclusive test of prerogative.

This was between baron and vassal. Between baron and baron the only bond was a nominal common allegiance to a distant king, who was himself only a greater baron. For the rest there was no government, but only diplomacy and warfare.

Government lived where it could and as it could, and was for the most part divided out piecemeal to a thousand petty holders. Armed feuds were the usual processes of justice.

The Feudal Monarchy. — The monarchy which grew out of the ruins of this disintegrate system concentrated authority without much changing its character. The old idea, born of family origins, that government was but the active authority of society, the magistrate but society's organ, bound by society's immemorial laws, had passed utterly away, and government had become the personal possession of one man. The ruler did not any longer belong to the state; the state belonged to him: he was himself the state, as the rich man may be said to be his possessions. The Greek or Roman official was wielded by the community. Not so the king who had swept together into his own lap the powers once broadcast in the feudal system: he wielded the community. Government breathed with his breath, and it was its function to serve him. The state had become, by the processes of the feudal development, his private estate.

Modern De-socialization of the State. — The reaction from such conceptions, slow and for the most part orderly in England, sudden and violent, because long forcibly delayed, on the Continent, was natural, and indeed inevitable. When it came it was radical; but it did not swing the political world back to its old-time ideas; it turned it aside rather to new. The ancient man had had no thought but to live loyally the life of society; but it became the object of the revolutionist and the democrat of the new order of things to live his own life. The antique citizen's virtues were not individual in their point of view, but social; whereas our virtues are almost entirely individual in their motive, social only in some of their results.

In brief, the modern State has been largely *de-socialized*. The modern idea is this: the state no longer absorbs the individual; it only serves him. The state, as it appears in its organ, the government, is the representative of the individual, and not his representative even except within the definite commission of constitutions; while for the rest each man makes his own social relations. 'The individual for the State' has been reversed and made to read, 'The State for the individual.'

More Changes of Conception than of Practice. — Such are the divergencies of *conception* separating modern from ancient politics, divergencies ·at once deep and far-reaching. How far have such changes of thought been accompanied by changes of function? By no means so far as might be expected. Apparently the new ideas which have been given prevalence in politics from time to time have not been able to translate themselves into altered functions, but only into somewhat *curtailed* functions, breeding rather a difference of degree than a difference of kind. Even under the most liberal of our modern constitutions we still meet government in almost every field of social endeavor. Our modern life is so infinitely wide and complex, it is true, that we may go great distances in any field of enterprise without receiving either direct aid or direct check from government; but that is only because every field of enterprise is vastly big nowadays, not because government is not somewhere in it: and we know that the tendency is for governments to make themselves everywhere more and more conspicuously present. We are conscious that we are by no means in the same case with the Greek or Roman: the state is ours, not we the state's. But we know at the same time that the tasks of the state have not been much diminished. Perhaps we may say that the matter stands thus: what is changed is not the activities of government but only the morals, the conscience of government. Government may still be doing substantially the same things as of old; but an altered conception of its responsibility deeply modifies *the way in which it does them*. Social convenience and advancement are still its ultimate standard of conduct, just as if it were still itself the omnipotent impersonation of society, the master of the individual; but it has adopted new ideas as to what constitutes social convenience and advancement. Its aim is to aid the individual to the fullest and best possible realization of his individuality, instead of merely to the full realization of his *sociality*. Its plan is to create the best and fairest opportunities for the individual; and it has discovered that the way to do this is by no means itself to undertake the administration of the individual by old-time futile methods of guardianship.

Functions of Government much the Same now as always. — This is indeed a great and profound change; but it is none the

less important to emphasize the fact that the functions of government are still, when catalogued, found to be much the same both
in number and magnitude that they always were. Government
does not stop with the protection of life, liberty, and property, as
some have supposed; it goes on to serve every convenience of
society. Its sphere is limited only by its own wisdom, alike where
republican and where absolutist principles prevail.

The State's Relation to Property. — A very brief examination of the facts suffices to confirm this view. Take, for example,
the state's relation to property, its performance of one of the
chief of those functions which I have called Constituent. It is
in connection with this function that one of the most decided contrasts exists between ancient and modern political practice; and
yet we shall not find ourselves embarrassed to recognize as natural
the practice of ancient states touching the right of private property. Their theory was extreme, but, outside of Sparta, their
practice was moderate.

In Sparta. — Consistent, logical Sparta may serve as the
point of departure for our observation. She is the standing classical type of exaggerated state functions and furnishes the most
extreme example of the antique conception of the relations of the
state to property. In the early periods of her history at least,
besides being censor, pedagogue, drill sergeant, and housekeeper to
her citizens, she was also universal landlord. There was a distinct
reminiscence in her practice of the time when the state was the
family, and as such the sole owner of property. She was regarded
as the original proprietor of all the land in Laconia, and individual tenure was looked upon as rather of the nature of a usufruct
held of the state and at the state's pleasure than as resting upon
any complete or indefeasible private title.

    Peculiar Situation of the Spartans. — There were in Sparta
special reasons for the persistence of such a system. The Spartans had
come into Laconia as conquerors, and the land had first of all been tribal
booty. It had been booty of which the Spartan host as a whole, as a
state, had had the dividing, and it had been the purpose of the early
arrangement to make the division of the land among the Spartan families
as equal as possible. Nor did the state resign the right of disposition in
making this first distribution. It remained its primary care to keep its
citizens, the favored *Spartiatæ*, upon an equal footing of fortune, to the

end that they might remain rich in leisure, and so be the better able to live entirely for the service of the state, which was honorable, to the avoidance of that pursuit of wealth which was dishonorable. The state, accordingly, undertook to administer the wealth of the country for the benefit of its citizens. When grave inequalities manifested themselves in the distribution of estates it did not hesitate to resume its proprietary rights and effect a reapportionment; no one dreaming, the while, of calling its action confiscation. It took various means for accomplishing its ends. It compelled rich heiresses to marry men without patrimony; and it grafted the poor citizen upon a good estate by means of prescribed adoption. No landed estate could be alienated either by sale or testament from the family to which the state had assigned it unless express legislative leave were given. In brief, in respect of his property the citizen was both ward and tenant of the state.

Decay of the System. — As the Spartan state decayed this whole system was sapped. Estates became grossly unequal, as did also political privileges even among the favored *Spartiatæ.* But these changes were due to the decadence of Spartan power and to the degeneration of her political fibre in days of waning fortune, not to any conscious or deliberate surrender by the state of its prerogatives as owner, guardian, and trustee. She had grown old and lax simply; she had not changed her mind.

In Athens. — When we turn to Athens we experience a marked change in the political atmosphere, though the Athenians hold much the same abstract conception of the state. Here men breathe more freely and enjoy the fruits of their labor, where labor is without reproach, with less restraint. Even in Athens there remain distinct traces, nevertheless, of the family duties of the state. She too, like Sparta, felt bound to dispose properly of eligible heiresses. She did not hesitate to punish with heavy forfeiture of right (*atimia*) those who squandered their property in dissolute living. There was as little limit in Athens as in Sparta to the theoretical prerogatives of the public authority. The freedom of the citizen was a freedom of indulgence rather than of right: he was free because the state refrained, — as a privileged child, not as a sovereign under Rousseau's Law of Nature.

In Rome. — When we shift our view to republican Rome we do not find a simple city omnipotence like that of Greece, in which all private rights are sunk. The primal constituents of the city yet abide in shapes something like their original. Roman society consists of a series of interdependent links: the family the *gens*, the city. The aggregate, not the fusion, of these makes up what we should call the state. But the state, so made up, was omnipotent, through one or other of its organs, over the individual. Property was not private in the sense of being individual; it vested in the family, which was, in this as in other respects, an organ of the state. Property was not conceived of as state property, because it had remained the undivided property of the family. The father, as a ruler in the immemorial hierarchy of the government, was all-powerful trustee of the family estates; individual ownership there was none.

Under Modern Governments. — We with some justice felicitate ourselves that to this omnipotence of the ancient state in its relations to property the practice of our own governments offers the most pronounced contrasts. But the point of greatest interest for us in the present connection is this, that these contrasts are contrasts of *policy, not of power.* To what lengths it will go in regulating property rights is for each government a question of principle, which it must put to its own conscience, and which, if it be wise, it will debate in the light of political history: but every government must regulate property in one way or another and may regulate it as much as it pleases. If the ancient state was regarded as the ultimate owner, the modern state is regarded as the ultimate heir of all estates. Failing other claimants, property *escheats* to the state. If the modern state does not assume, like the ancient, to administer their property upon occasion for competent adults, it does administer their property upon occasion for lunatics and minors. The ancient state controlled slaves and slavery. The modern state has been quite as absolute: it has abolished slaves and slavery. The modern state, no less than the ancient, sets rules and limitations to inheritance and bequest. Most of the more extreme and hurtful interferences with rights of private ownership government has abandoned, one may suspect, rather because of difficulties of administration than because of difficulties of conscience. It is of the nature of the state to regulate property rights; it is of the policy of the state to regulate them *more* or *less*. Administrators must regard this as one of the Constituent functions of political society.

The State and Political Rights. — Similar conclusions may be drawn from a consideration of the contrasts which exist in the field of that other Constituent function which concerns the determination of political rights, — the contrasts between the *status* of the citizen in the ancient state and the *status* of the citizen in the modern state. Here also the contrast, as between state and state, is not one of power, but one of principle and habit rather. Modern states have often limited as narrowly as did the ancient the enjoyment of those political privileges which we group under the word *Franchise.* They, too, as well as the ancient states, have admitted slavery into their systems; they too have commanded their subjects without moderation and fleeced them without compunction. But for all they have been so omnipotent, and when they chose so tyrannical, they have seldom insisted upon so complete and unreserved a service of the state by the citizen as was habitual to the political practice of both the Greek and the Roman worlds. The Greek and the Roman belonged each to his state in a quite absolute sense. He was his own in nothing as against the claims of his city upon him : he freely acknowledged all his privileges to be but concessions from his mother, the commonwealth. Those privileges accrued to him through law, as do ours; but law was to him simply the will of the organized community; never, as we know it in our constitutions, a restraint upon the will of the organized community. He knew no principles of liberty save only those which custom had built up : which inhered, not in the nature of things, not in abstract individuality, but in the history of affairs, in concrete practice. His principles were all precedents. Nevertheless, however radically different its doctrines, the ancient state was not a whit more completely master touching laws of citizenship than the state of to-day is.

As Regards the State's Ministrant Functions. — Of the Ministrant, no less than of the Constituent functions, the same statement may be made, that practically the state has been relieved of very little duty by alterations of political theory. It is natural enough that in the field of the Constituent functions the state should serve society now as always; in this field of the Ministrant functions one would expect the state to be less active now than formerly. But there is in fact no such difference: *government does now whatever experience permits or the times demand;* and though it does not do exactly the same things it still does substantially the same kind of things that the ancient state did. It will conduce to clearness if I set forth my illustrations of this in the order of the list of Ministrant functions which I have given (page 43).

(1) **The State in Relation to Trade.** — All nations have habitually regulated trade and commerce. In the most remote periods of which history has retained any recollection the regulation of trade and commerce was necessary to the existence of government. The only way in which communities. which were then seeking to build up a dominant power could preserve an independent existence and work out an individual development was to draw apart to an absolutely separate life. Commerce meant contact; contact meant contamination: the only way in which to develop character and achieve cohesion was to avoid intercourse. In the classical states this stage is passed and trade and commerce are regulated for much the same reasons that induce modern states to regulate them, in order, that is, to secure commercial advantage as against competitors or in order to serve the fiscal needs of the state. Athens and Sparta and Rome, too, regulated the corn trade for the purpose of securing for their citizens full store of food. In the Middle Ages the feuds and highway brigandage of petty lords loaded commerce with fetters of the most harassing sort, except where the free cities could by militant combination keep open to it an unhindered passage to and fro between the great marts of North and South. As the mediæval states emerge into modern times we find trade and commerce handled by statesmen as freely as ever, but according to the reasoned policy of the mercantilist thinkers; and in our own days according to still other conceptions of national advantage.

(2) **The State in Relation to Labor.** — Labor, too, has always been regulated by the state. By Greek and Roman the labor of the handicrafts and of agriculture, all manual toil

indeed, was for the most part given to slaves to do; and of course law regulated the slave. In the Middle Ages the labor which was not agricultural and held in bondage to feudal masters was in the cities, where it was rigidly ordered by the complex rules of the guild system, as were trade also and almost all other like forms of making a livelihood.   Where, as in England, labor in part escaped from the hard service of the feudal tenure the state stepped in with its persistent "statutes of laborers" and sought to tie the workman to one habitation and to one rate of wages. 'The rustic must stay where he is and must receive only so much pay,' was its command.   Apparently, however, all past regulation of labor was but elementary as compared with the labor legislation being tried by the governments of our own day.   The birth and development of the modern industrial system has changed every aspect of the matter; and this fact reveals the true character of the part which the state plays in the case.   The rule would seem to be that in proportion as the world's industries grow must the state advance in its efforts to assist the industrious to advantageous relations with each other.   The tendency to regulate labor rigorously and minutely is as strong in England, where the state is considered the agent of the citizen, as it was in Athens, where the citizen was deemed the child and tool of the state, and where the workman was a slave.

(3) **Regulation of Corporations.** — The regulation of corporations is but one side of the modern regulation of the industrial system, and is a function added to the antique list of governmental tasks.

(4) **The State and Public Works.** — The maintenance of thoroughfares may be said to have begun with permanent empire, that is to say, for Europe, with the Romans.   For the Romans, indeed, it was first a matter of moving armies, only secondarily a means of serving commerce; whereas with us the highway is above all things else an artery of trade, and armies use it only when commerce stands still at the sound of drum and trumpet. The building of roads may therefore be said to have begun by being a Constituent function and to have ended by becoming a Ministrant function of government.   But the same is not true of other public works, of the Roman aqueducts and theatres and

baths, and of modern internal improvements. They, as much as the Roman tax on old bachelors, are parts, not of a scheme of governing, but of plans for the advancement of other social aims, — for the administration of society. Because in her conception the community as a whole was the only individual, Rome thrust out as of course her magnificent roads to every quarter of her vast territory, considered no distances too great to be traversed by her towering aqueducts, deemed it her duty to clear river courses and facilitate by every means both her commerce and her arms. And the modern state, though holding a deeply modified conception of the relations of government to society, still follows a like practice. If in most instances our great iron highways are left to private management, it is oftener for reasons of convenience than for reasons of conscience. [1]

(5) **Administration of the Conveniences of Society.** — Similar considerations apply in the case of that modern instrumentality, the public letter-post, in the case of the still more modern manufacture of gas, and in the case of the most modern telegraph and telephone. The modern no less than the ancient government unhesitatingly takes a hand in administering the conveniences of society.

(6) **Sanitation.** — Modern governments, like the government of Rome, maintain sanitation by means of police inspection of baths, taverns, and houses of ill fame, as well as by drainage; and to these they add hospital relief, water supply, quarantine, and a score of other means.

(7) **Public Education.** — Our modern systems of public education are more thorough than the ancient, notwithstanding the fact that we regard the individual as something other than a mere servant of the state, and educate him first of all for himself.

(8) **Sumptuary Laws.** — In sumptuary laws ancient states of course far outran modern practice. Modern states have foregone most attempts to make citizens virtuous or frugal by law. But even we have our prohibition enactments; and we have had our fines for swearing.

---

[1] This is clearly shown in the taking over of the railroads by the government for the period of the war.

Summary. — Apparently it is safe to say with regard to the functions of government taken as a whole that, even as between ancient and modern states, uniformities of practice far outnumber diversities of practice. One may justly conclude, not indeed that the restraints which modern states put upon themselves are of little consequence, or that altered political conceptions are not of the greatest moment in determining important questions of government and even the whole advance of the race; but that it is rather by gaining practical wisdom, rather by long processes of historical experience, that states modify their practices. New theories are subsequent to new experiences.

THE OBJECTS OF GOVERNMENT.

———◦◦⚬⚬◦◦———

Character of the Subject. — Political interest and controversy have centred nowhere more acutely than in the question,
What are the proper objects of government? This is one of those
difficult questions upon which it is possible for many sharply
opposed views to be held apparently with almost equal weight
of reason. Its central difficulty is this, that it is a question
which can be answered, if answered at all, only by the aid of a
broad and careful wisdom whose conclusions are based upon the
widest possible inductions from the facts of political experience
in all its phases. Such wisdom is quite beyond the capacity of
most thinkers and actors in the field of politics; and the consequence has been that this question, perhaps more than any other
in the whole scope of political science, has provoked great wars
of doctrine.

The Extreme Views held. — What part shall government play in the affairs of society? — that is the question which
has been the gauge of controversial battle. *What ought the functions of government to be?* On the one hand there are extremists
who cry constantly to government, 'Hands off,' '*laissez faire,*'
'*laissez passer,*' who look upon every act of government which
is not merely an act of police with jealousy; who regard government as necessary, but as a necessary evil; and who would have
government hold back from everything which could by any possibility be accomplished by individual initiative and endeavor. On
the other hand, there are those who, with equal extremeness of
view in the opposite direction, would have society lean fondly
upon government for guidance and assistance in every affair of
life; who, captivated by some glimpse of public power and benefi-

cence caught in the pages of ancient or mediæval historian, or by some dream of coöperative endeavor cunningly imagined by the great fathers of Socialism, believe that the state can be made a wise foster mother to every member of the family politic. Between these two extremes, again, there are all grades, all shades and colors, all degrees of enmity or of partiality to state action.

Historical Foundation for Opposite Views. — Enmity to exaggerated state action, even a keen desire to keep that action down to its lowest possible terms, is easily furnished with impressive justification. It must unreservedly be admitted that history abounds with warnings of no uncertain sort against indulging the state with a too great liberty of interference with the life and work of its citizens. Much as there is that is attractive in the political life of the city states of Greece and Rome, in which the public power was suffered to be omnipotent, — their splendid public spirit, their incomparable organic wholeness, their fine play of rival talents, serving both the common thought and the common action, their variety, their conception of public virtue, — there is also much to blame, — their too wanton invasion of that privacy of the individual life in which alone family virtue can dwell secure, their callous tyranny over minorities in matters which might have been left to individual choice, their sacrifice of personal independence for the sake of public solidarity, their hasty average judgments, their too confident trust in the public voice. They, it is true, could not have had the individual liberty which we cherish without breaking violently with their own history, with the necessary order of their development; but neither can we, on the other hand, imitate them without an equally violent departure from our own normal development and a reversion to the now too primitive methods of their pocket republics.

Unquestionable as it is that mediæval history affords many seductive examples of an absence of grinding, heartless competition and a strength of mutual interdependence, confidence, and helpfulness between class and class such as the modern economist may be pardoned for wishing to see revived; and true though it be that the history of Prussia gives at least colorable justification to the opinion that state interference may under some circumstances be of benefit for the industrial upbuilding of a state, it must, on the other hand, be remembered that neither the feudal system, nor the mediæval guild system, nor the paternalism of Frederic the Great can be rehabilitated now that the revolutions in industry, in church, and in state have been wrought which have been witnessed since the beginning of the nineteenth century ; and that, even if these systems of the past could be revived, we should be sorely puzzled to reinstate their blessings without restoring at the same time their acknowledged evils. No student of history can wisely censure those who protest against state paternalism.

The State a Beneficent and Indispensable Organ of Society. — It by no means follows, nevertheless, that because the state may unwisely interfere in the life of the individual, it must be pronounced in itself and by nature a necessary evil. It is no more an evil than is society itself. It is the organic body of society : without it society would be hardly more than a mere abstraction. If the name had not been restricted to a single, narrow, extreme, and radically mistaken class of thinkers, we ought all to regard ourselves and to act as *socialists,* that is, believers in the wholesomeness and beneficence of the body politic.

If the history of society proves anything, it proves the absolute naturalness of government, its rootage in the nature of man, its origin in kinship, and its identification with all that makes man superior to the brute creation. Individually man is but poorly equipped to dominate other animals : his lordship comes by combination, his strength is concerted strength, his supremacy is the supremacy of union. Outside of society man's mind can avail him little as an instrument of supremacy ; and government is the visible form of society. If society itself be not an evil, neither surely is government an evil, for government is the indispensable organ of society.

Every means, therefore, by which society may be perfected through the instrumentality of government, every means by which individual rights can be fitly adjusted and harmonized with public duties, by which individual self-development may be made at once to serve and to supplement social development, ought certainly to be diligently sought, and, when found, sedulously fostered by every friend of society. Such is the view to which every true lover of his kind ought to adhere with the full grip of every noble affection that is in him.

Socialism and the Modern Industrial Organization. — It is possible, indeed, to understand and even in a measure to sympathize with, the enthusiasm of those special classes whom we have dubbed with the too great name of 'Socialists.' The schemes of social reform and regeneration which they support with so much ardor, however mistaken they may be, have the right end in view : they seek to bring the individual with his special interests, personal to himself, into complete harmony with society with its general interests, common to all. Their method is always some sort of coöperation, meant to perfect mutual helpfulness. They speak, too, a revolt from selfish, misguided individualism ; and certainly modern individualism has much about it that is hateful, too hateful to last.

The modern industrial organization has so distorted competition as sometimes to put it into the power of some to tyrannize over many, as to enable the rich and the strong to combine against the poor and the weak. It has given a woful material meaning to that spiritual law that "to him that hath shall be given, and from him that hath not shall be taken away even the little that he seemeth to have." It has magnified that self-interest which is grasping selfishness and has thrust out love and compassion not only, but free competition in part, as well. Surely it would be better, exclaims the Socialist, altogether to stamp out competition by making all men equally subject to the public order, to an imperative law of social coöperation! But the Socialist mistakes : it is not competition that kills, but unfair competition, the pretence and form of it where the substance and reality of it cannot exist.

A Middle Ground. — And there is a middle ground. The schemes which Socialists have proposed society cannot accept and live ; and no scheme which involves the complete control of the individual by government can be devised which differs from theirs very much for the better. A truer doctrine must be found, which gives wide freedom to the individual for his self-development and yet guards that freedom against the competition that kills, and reduces the antagonism between self-development and social development to a minimum. And such a doctrine can be formulated, surely, without too great vagueness.

The Objects of Society the Objects of Government. — Government is the organ of society, its only potent and universal instrument: its objects must be the objects of society. What, then, are the objects of society? What *is* society? It is an association of individuals organized for mutual aid. Mutual aid to what? To self-development. The hope of society lies in an infinite individual variety, in the freest possible play of individual forces: only in that can it find that wealth of resource which constitutes civilization, with all its appliances for satisfying human wants and mitigating human sufferings, all its incitements to thought and spurs to action. It should be the end of government *to assist in accomplishing the objects of organized society.* There must be constant adjustments of governmental assistance to the needs of a changing social and industrial organization. Not license of interference on the part of government, but only strength, and adaptation of regulation. The regulation that I mean is not interference: it is the equalization of conditions, so far as possible, in all branches of endeavor; and the equalization of conditions is the very opposite of interference.

Every rule of development is a rule of adaptation, a rule for meeting 'the circumstances of the case'; but the circumstances of the case, it must be remembered, are not, so far as government is concerned, the circumstances of any individual case, but the circumstances of society's case, the general conditions of social organization. The case for society stands thus: the individual must be assured the best means, the best and fullest opportunities, for complete self-development: in no other way can society itself gain variety and strength. But one of the most indispensable conditions of opportunity for self-development government alone, society's controlling organ, can supply. All combinations which necessarily create monopoly, which necessarily put and keep indispensable means of industrial or social development in the hands of a few, and those few, not the few selected by society itself, but the few selected by arbitrary fortune, must be under either the direct or the indirect control of society. To society alone can the power of dominating by combination belong. It cannot suffer any of its members to enjoy such a power for their own private gain independently of its own strict regulation or oversight.

Natural Monopolies. — It is quite possible to distinguish natural monopolies from other classes of undertakings; their distinctive marks are thus enumerated by Sir T. H. Farrer in his excellent little volume on *The State in its Relation to Trade* which forms one of the well-known English Citizen series: [1]

" 1. What they supply is a necessary," a necessary, that is, to life, like water, or a necessary to industrial action, like railroad transportation.

" 2. They occupy peculiarly favored spots or lines of land." Here again the best illustration is afforded by railroads or by telegraph lines, by water-works, etc.

" 3. The article or convenience they supply is used at the place and in connection with the plant or machinery by which it is supplied "; that is to say, at the favored spots or along the favored lines of land.

" 4. This article or convenience can in general be largely, if not indefinitely increased, without proportionate increase in plant and capital "; that is to say, the initial outlay having been made, the favored spot or line of land having been occupied, every subsequent increase of business will increase profits because it will not proportionately, or anything like proportionately, increase the outlay for services or machinery needed. Those who are outside of the established business, therefore, are upon an equality of competition neither as regards available spots or lines of land nor as regards opportunities to secure business in a competition of rates.

" 5. Certain and harmonious arrangement, which can only be attained by unity, are paramount considerations." Wide and systematic organization is necessary.

Such enterprises invariably give to a limited number of persons the opportunity to command certain necessaries of life, of comfort, or of industrial success against their fellow-countrymen and for their own

[1] P. 71. Sir Thomas Farrer was Permanent Secretary of the English Board of Trade.

advantage. Once established in any field, there can be no real competition between them and those who would afterwards enter that field. No
agency should be suffered to have such control except a public agency
which may be compelled by public opinion to act without selfish narrow-
ness, upon perfectly equal conditions as towards all, or some agency upon
which the government may keep a strong hold of regulation.

Control not necessarily Administration. — Society can by
no means afford to allow the use for private gain and without
regulation of undertakings necessary to its own healthful and
efficient operation and yet of a sort to exclude equality in competition. Experience has proved that the self-interest of those who
have controlled such undertakings for private gain is not coincident with the public interest: even enlightened self-interest may
often discover means of illicit pecuniary advantage in unjust discriminations between individuals in the use of such instrumentalities. But the proposition that the government should control
such dominating organizations of capital may by no means be
wrested to mean by any necessary implication that the government
should itself administer those instrumentalities of economic action
which cannot be used except as monopolies. In such cases, as Sir
T. H. Farrer says, " there are two great alternatives. (1) Ownership and management by private enterprise and capital under
regulation by the state. (2) Ownership and management by Government, central or local." Government regulation may in most
cases suffice. Indeed, such are the difficulties in the way of establishing and maintaining careful business management on the part
of government, that control ought to be preferred to direct administration in as many cases as possible, — in every case in which
control without administration can be made effectual.

Equalization of Competition. — There are some things
outside the field of natural monopolies in which individual action
cannot secure equalization of the conditions of competition; and
in these also, as in the regulation of monopolies, the practice of
governments, of our own as well as of others, has been decisively
on the side of governmental regulation. By forbidding child
labor, by supervising the sanitary conditions of factories, by limiting the employment of women in occupations hurtful to their
health, by instituting official tests of the purity or the quality of

goods sold, by limiting hours of labor in certain trades, by a hun·
dred and one limitations of the power of unscrupulous or heartless
men to out-do the scrupulous and merciful in trade or industry,
government has assisted equity.   Those who would act in moderation and good conscience in cases where moderation and good
conscience, if indulged, require an increased outlay of money, in
better ventilated buildings, in greater care as to the quality of
goods, etc., cannot be expected to act upon their principles so
long as more grinding conditions for labor or a more unscrupulous
use of the opportunities of trade secure to the unconscientious an
unquestionable and sometimes even a permanent advantage; they
have only the choice of denying their consciences or retiring from
business.   In scores of such cases government has intervened and
will intervene; but by way, not of interference, by way, rather,
of making competition equal between those who would rightfully
conduct enterprise and those who basely conduct it.   It is in this
way that society protects itself against permanent injury and
deterioration, and secures healthful equality of opportunity for
self-development.

Society greater than Government. — Society, it must always be remembered, is vastly bigger and more important than
its instrument, Government.   Government should serve Society,
by no means rule or dominate it.   Government should not be
made an end in itself; it is a means only, — a means to be freely
adapted to advance the best interests of Society.   The State
exists for the sake of Society, not Society for the sake of the
State.

Natural Limits to State Action. — And that there are
natural and imperative limits to state action no one who seriously
studies the structure of society can doubt.   The limit of state
functions is the limit of *necessary coöperation* on the part of Society as a whole, the limit beyond which such combination ceases
to be imperative for the public good and becomes merely convenient for industrial or social enterprise.   Coöperation is necessary in the sense here intended when it is indispensable to the
equalization of the conditions of endeavor, indispensable to the
maintenance of uniform rules of individual rights and relationships, indispensable because to omit it would inevitably be to

hamper or degrade some for the advancement of others in the scale of wealth and social standing.

There are relations in which men invariably have need of each other, in which universal coöperation is the indispensable condition of even tolerable existence. Only some universal authority can make opportunities equal as between man and man. The divisions of labor and the combinations of commerce may for the most part be left to contract, to free individual arrangement, but the equalization of the conditions which affect all alike may no more be left to individual initiative than may the organization of government itself. Churches, clubs, corporations, fraternities, guilds, partnerships, unions, have for their ends one or another special enterprise for the development of man's spiritual or material well-being: they are all more or less advisable. But the family and the state have as their end a general enterprise for the betterment and equalization of the conditions of individual development: they are indispensable.

The point at which public combination ceases to be imperative is not susceptible of clear indication in general terms; but it is not on that account indistinct. The bounds of family association are not indistinct because they are marked only by the immaturity of the young and by the parental and filial affections, — things not all of which are defined in the law. The rule that the state should do nothing which is equally possible under equitable conditions to optional associations is a sufficiently clear line of distinction between governments and corporations. Those who regard the state as an optional, conventional union simply, a mere partnership, open wide the doors to the worst forms of socialism. Unless the state has a nature which is quite clearly defined by that invariable, universal, immutable mutual interdependence which runs beyond the family relations and cannot be satisfied by family ties, we have absolutely no criterion by which we can limit, except arbitrarily, the activities of the state. The criterion supplied by the native necessity of state relations, on the other hand, banishes such license of state action.

The state, for instance, ought not to supervise private morals because they belong to the sphere of separate individual responsibility, not to the sphere of mutual dependence. Thought and conscience are private. Opinion is optional. The state may intervene only where common action, uniform law are indispensable. Whatever is merely convenient is optional, and therefore not an affair for the state. Churches are spiritually convenient; joint-stock companies are capitalistically convenient; but when the state constitutes itself a church or a mere business association it institutes a monopoly no better than others. It should do nothing which is not in any case both indispensable to social or industrial life and necessarily monopolistic.

The Family and the State. — It is the proper object of the family to mould the individual, to form him in the period of immaturity in the faiths of religion and in the practice of morality and obedience. This period of subordination over, he is called out into an independent, self-directive activity. The ties of family affection still bind him, but they bind him with silken, not with iron bonds. He has left his 'minority' and reached his 'majority.' It is the proper object of the state to give leave to his individuality, in order that that individuality may add its quota of variety to the sum of national activity Family discipline is variable, selective, formative: it must lead the individual. But the state must not lead. It must create conditions, but not mould individuals. Its discipline must be invariable, uniform, impersonal. Family methods rest upon individual inequality, state methods upon individual equality. Family order rests upon tutelage, state order upon franchise, upon privilege.

The State and Education. — In one field the state would seem at first sight to usurp the family function, the field, namely, of education. But such is not in reality the case. Education is the proper office of the state for two reasons, both of which come within the principles we have been discussing. Popular education is necessary for the preservation of those conditions of freedom, political and social, which are indispensable to free individual development. And, in the second place, no instrumentality less universal in its power and authority than government can secure popular education. In brief, in order to secure popular education the action of society as a whole is necessary; and popular education is indispensable to that equalization of the conditions of personal development which we have taken to be the proper object of society. Without popular education, moreover, no government which rests upon popular action can long endure: the people must be schooled in the knowledge, and if possible in the virtues, upon which the maintenance and success of free institutions depend. No free government can last in health if it lose hold of the traditions of its history, and in the public schools these traditions may be and should be sedulously preserved, carefully replanted in the thought and consciousness of each successive generation.

Historical Conditions of Governmental Action. — Whatever view be taken in each particular case of the rightfulness or advisability of state regulation and control, one rule there is which may not be departed from under any circumstances, and that is the rule of historical continuity. In politics nothing radically novel may safely be attempted. No result of value can ever be reached in politics except through slow and gradual development, the careful adaptations and nice modifications of growth. Nothing may be done by leaps. More than that, each people, each nation, must live upon the lines of its own experience. Nations are no more capable of borrowing experience than individuals are. The histories of other peoples may furnish us with light, but they cannot furnish us with conditions of action. Every nation must constantly keep in touch with its past; it cannot run towards its ends around sharp corners.

Summary. — This, then, is the sum of the whole matter: the end of government is the facilitation of the objects of society. The rule of governmental action is necessary coöperation. The method of political development is conservative adaptation, shaping old habits into new ones, modifying old means to accomplish new ends.

V.

LAW: ITS NATURE AND DEVELOPMENT.

————o·o:✺:o·o————

What is Law? — Law is the will of the State concerning
its own organization and conduct and the civic conduct of those
under its authority. This will may be more or less formally expressed: it may speak either in custom or in specific enactment.
Law may, moreover, be the will either of a primitive family-
community such as we see in the earliest periods of history, or of
a highly organized, fully self-conscious State such as those of our
own day. But for the existence of Law there is needed in all
cases alike (1) a community capable of having a will of its own,
and (2) some clearly recognized body of rules to which that community has, whether by custom or enactment, given life, character,
and effectiveness. Law is that portion of the established thought
and habit which has gained distinct and formal recognition in the
shape of uniform rules backed by the authority and power of
Government. The nature of each State, therefore, will be reflected
in its law; in its law, too, will appear the functions with which it
charges itself; and in its law will it be possible to read its history.

The Development of Law: its Sources. — Law thus follows
in its development, with slow, sometimes with uneven, but generally with quite certain steps, the evolution of the character, the
purposes, and the will of the organized community whose creation
it is. The sources whence it springs are as various as the means
by which a community can shape and express its will as a body
politic.

1. Custom.[1] — The earliest source of Law is Custom, and
custom is formed no one can say definitely how, except that it

---

[1] I adopt here the classification usual in English writings on Jurisprudence.
See, e.g., T. E. Holland, *Jurisprudence*, pp. 48 *et seq.*

is shaped by the coöperative action of the whole community, and not by any kingly or legislative command. It is not formed always in the same way; but it always rests upon the same foundation, upon the general acceptance of a certain course of action as best or most convenient. Whether custom originate in the well-nigh accidental formation of certain habits of action or in a conscious effort on the part of a community to adjust its practices more perfectly to its social and political objects, it becomes, when once it has been formed and accepted by the public authority, a central part of Law. It is difficult, if not impossible, to discover the exact point at which custom passes from the early inchoate state in which it is merely tending to become the express and determinate purpose of a community into the later stage in which it becomes Law; but we can say with assurance that it becomes Law only when it wins the support of a definite authority within the community. It is not Law if men feel free to depart from it.

> Under the reign of customary law that state of things actually did exist which modern law still finds it convenient to take for granted: everybody knew what the law was. The Teutonic hundred-moots, for example, the popular assemblies which regularly tried cases under the early polity of our own ancestors, declared the law by the public voice; the people themselves determined what it was and how it should be applied. Custom grew up in the habits of the people; they consciously or unconsciously originated it; to them it was known and by them it was declared.

2. Religion. — In the earliest times Custom and Religion were almost indistinguishable; a people's customs bore on every lineament the likeness of its religion. And in later stages of development Religion was still a prolific source of Custom. No primitive community contained any critic who could, even in his secret thought, separate Law from Religion. All rules of life bore for the antique mind the same sanction (page 15). There were not in its conception rules moral and rules political: politics, morals, and religion were indistinguishable parts of one great indivisible Law of Conduct. Religion and Politics very soon, it is true, came to have different ministers. In name often, if not always in fact, the priest was distinct from the magistrate.

But throughout a very long development, from the time of Greece and Rome, the magistrate either retained priestly functions or was dominated by rules which the priest declared and of which the priest was the custodian.

> Thus the early law of Rome was little more than a body of technical religious rules, a system of means for obtaining individual rights through the proper carrying out of certain religious formulæ ; and it marked the beginning of the movement of Roman law towards a broad and equitable system of justice when these rules of procedure were changed from sacerdotal secrets into published law by the publication of the Twelve Tables.

3. Adjudication. — One of the busiest and one of the most useful, because watchful, open-minded, and yet conservative, makers of Law under all systems has been the magistrate, the Judge. It is he who in his decisions recognizes and adopts Custom, and so gives it the decisive support of the public power; it is he who shapes written enactments into suitability to individual cases and thus gives them due flexibility and a free development. He is the authoritative voice of the community in giving specific application to its Law: and in doing this he necessarily becomes, because an interpreter, also a maker of Law. Whether deliberately or unconsciously, in expounding and applying he moulds and expands the Law. It is his legitimate function to read Law in the light of his own sober and conscientious judgment as to what is reasonable and just in custom, what practicable, rational, or equitable in legislation.

> It is this 'judge-made' law which is to be found, and is therefore so diligently sought for, in the innumerable law Reports cited in our courts. Except under extraordinary circumstances, our courts and those of England will always follow decisions rendered in similar cases by courts of equal jurisdiction in the same state. *A fortiori* do they follow the decisions of the highest courts: by these they are in a sense bound. In the courts of the continent of Europe, on the other hand, decisions are listened to as important expressions of opinion, but not as conclusive authority : are heard much as our own courts or those of England hear the decisions of courts of other states acting under like laws or similar circumstances.

4. Equity. — Equity too is judge-made Law; but it is made, not in interpretation of, but in addition to, the laws which already exist. The most conspicuous types of such Law are the decisions of the Roman Prætor and those of the English Chancellor. These decisions were meant to give relief where existing law afforded none. The Prætor declared, for instance, that he would allow certain less formal processes than had hitherto been permitted to secure rights of property or of contract, of marriage or of control, etc. The English Chancellor, in like manner, as keeper of the king's judicial conscience, supplied remedies in cases for which the Common Law had no adequate processes, and thus relieved suitors of hardships they might otherwise have suffered from the fixity or excessive formality of the Common Law, and enabled them in many things to obtain their substantial rights without technical difficulty.

> After the official decrees of the Prætors had been codified by the Prætor Salvius Iulianus, in the time of the Emperor Hadrian, and still more after they had been embodied in the Code of Justinian, the *Corpus Juris Civilis*, the Prætor's 'equity' became as rigid and determinate as the law which it had been its function to mend and ameliorate. In the same manner, our own state codes, many of which have fused law and equity in the same courts and under common forms of procedure, have given equity the sanction and consequently the fixity of written law. The English Judicature Act, also, of 1873, merging, as it does, the common-law and equity courts into a single homogeneous system, shows at least that a strong tendency in the same direction exists in England. The adjustments of Equity are less needed now that legislation is constantly active in mending old and creating new law and, when necessary, new procedure.
>
> In the same case with Equity must be classed the numerous so-called 'fictitious actions' which were the invention of the common-law courts and which, by means of imaginary suitors or imaginary transactions, duly recorded as if real, enabled things to be done and rights acquired which would have been impossible under any genuine process of the Common Law.

5. Scientific Discussion. — The carefully formed opinions of learned text-writers have often been accepted as decisive of the Law: more often under the Roman system, however, than under our own, though even we have our Cokes, our Blackstones, our Storys, and our Kents, whom our courts hear with the greatest possible respect. It is the proper function of legal science to interpret the law, not piecemeal, as the courts must, but in such way as to bring all its parts to their full development as doctrine and to their complete adjustment as members of a living system of thought and practice; to give the law system, study the conditions and forms of its genesis and development, and assist courts and legislatures alike in their functions of adaptation and creation.

6. Legislation. — That deliberate formulation of new Law to which the name Legislation is given is, for us of the modern time, the most familiar as well as the most prolific source of Law. For us Legislation is the work of representative bodies almost exclusively; but representation is no part of the essential character of the legislative act. Absolute magistrates or kings have in all stages of history been, under one system or another, makers of laws. Whether acting under the sanction of custom or under the more artificial arrangements of highly developed constitutions, father or prætor, king or archon has been a lawgiver. So, too, the assemblies of free men which, alike in Greece and in Rome, constituted the legislative authority were not representative, but primary bodies, like the *Lands gemeinden* of the smaller Swiss cantons.

Representation came in with the Germans; and with the critical development of institutions which the modern world has seen many new phases of Legislation have appeared. Modern law has brought forth those great private corporations whose bye-laws are produced by what may very fitly be called private legislative action. We have, too, on the same model, chartered governments, with legislatures acting under special grants of law-making power. Legislation has had and is having a notable development, and is now the almost exclusive means of the formulation of new Law. Custom of the older sort, which gave us the great Common Law, has been in large part superseded by acts of legislation; Religion stands apart, giving law only to the conscience; Adjudication is being more and more restricted by codification; Equity is being merged in the main body of the Law by enactment; Scientific Discussion now does hardly more than collate cases: all means of formulating Law tend to be swallowed up in the one great, deep, and broadening source, Legislation.

Custom again. — Custom at last enters again, with a new aspect and a new method. After judges have become the acknowledged and authoritative mouthpieces of Equity and of the interpretative adaptation of customary or enacted Law; after scientific writers have been admitted to power in the systematic elucidation and development of legal principles; even after the major part of all law-making has fallen to the deliberate action of legislatures, given liberal commission to act for the community, Custom still maintains a presiding and even an imperative part in legal history. It is Custom, the silent and unconcerted but none the less prevalent movement, that is, of the common thought and action of a community, which recognizes changes of circumstance which judges would not, without its sanction, feel, or be, at liberty to regard in the application of old enactments, and which legislators have failed to give effect to, by repeal or new enactment. Laws become obsolete because silent but observant and imperative Custom makes evident the deadness of their letter, the inapplicability of their provisions. Custom, too, never ceases to build up practices legal in their character and yet wholly outside formal Law, constructing even, in its action on Congresses and Parliaments, great parts of great constitutions. It constantly maintains the great forces of precedent and opinion which daily work their will, under every form of government, upon both the contents and the administration of Law. Custom is Habit under another name; and Habit in its growth, while it continually adjusts itself to the standard fixed in formal Law, also slowly compels formal Law to conform to its abiding influences. Habit may be said to be the great Law within which laws spring up. Laws can extend but a' very little way beyond its limits. They may help it to gradual extensions of its sphere and to slow modifications of its practices, but they cannot force it abruptly or disregard it at all with impunity.

The history of France since the Revolution affords a noteworthy example of these principles in the field of constitutional law. There we have witnessed this singular and instructive spectacle: a people made democratic in thought by the operation of a speculative political philosophy has adopted constitution after constitution created in the exact image of that thought. But they had, to begin with, absolutely no democratic habit, — no democratic custom. Gradually that habit has grown, fostered amidst the developments of local self-direction ; and the democratic thought has penetrated, wearing the body of practice, its only vehicle to such minds, to the rural populace. Constitutions and custom have thus advanced to meet one another, — constitutions compelled to adopt precedent rather than doctrine as their basis, thought, practical experience rather than the abstract conceptions of philosophy ; and habit constrained to receive the suggestions of written law. Now, therefore, in the language of one of her own writers, France has " a constitution the most summary in its text" (leaving most room, that is, for adjustments), " the *most customary in its application*, the most natural outcome of our manners and of the force of circumstances " that she has yet possessed.[1] Institutions too theoretical in their basis to live at first, have nevertheless furnished an *atmosphere* for the French mind and habit : that atmosphere has affected the life of France, — that life the atmosphere. The result that has been reached is normal liberty, political vitality and vigor, civil virility.

Typical Character of Roman and English Law. — Roman law and English law are peculiar among the legal systems of western Europe for the freedom and individuality of their development. Rome's *jus civile* was, indeed, deeply modified through the influence of the *jus gentium ;* it received its philosophy from Greece, and took some color from a hundred sources; and English law, despite the isolation of its island home, received its jury system and many another suggestion from the Continent, and has been much, even if unconsciously, affected in its development by the all-powerful law of Rome. But English and Roman law alike have been much less touched and colored than other systems by outside influences, and have presented to the world what may be taken as a picture of the natural, the normal, untrammelled evolution of law.

The Order of Legal Development. — As tested by the history of these systems, the order in which I have placed the Sources of Law is seen to be by no means a fixed order of historical sequence. Custom is, indeed, the earliest fountain of Law, but Religion is a contemporary, an equally prolific, and in some stages of national development an almost identical source; Adjudication comes almost as early as authority itself, and from a

[1] Albert Sorel, *Montesquieu* (Am. trans.), pp. 200, 201.

very antique time goes hand in hand with Equity. Only Legislation, the conscious and deliberate origination of Law, and Scientific Discussion, the reasoned development of its principles,
await an advanced stage of growth in the body politic to assert
their influence in law-making. In Rome, Custom was hardly
separable from Religion, and hid the knowledge of its principles
in the breasts of a privileged sacerdotal class; among the English,
on the contrary, Custom was declared in folk-moot by the voice
of the people, — as possibly it had been among the ancestors of
the Romans. In both Rome and England there was added to the
influence of the magistrate who adopted and expanded Custom
in his judgments the influence of the magistrate (Prætor or
Chancellor) who gave to Law the flexible principles and practices
of Equity. And in both, Legislation eventually became the only
source of Law.

But in Rome Legislation grew up under circumstances
entirely Roman, to which English history can afford no parallel.
Rome gave a prominence to scientific discussion such as never
gladdened the hearts of philosophical lawyers in England. The
opinions of distinguished lawyers were given high, almost conclusive, authority in the courts; and when the days of codification
came, great texts as well as great statutes and decrees were
embodied in the codes of the Empire. The legislation of the
popular assemblies, which Englishmen might very easily have
recognized, was superseded in the days of the Empire by imperial edicts and imperial codes such as the history of English legislation nowhere shows; and over the formulation of these codes
and edicts great jurists presided. The only thing in English
legal practice that affords a parallel to the influence of lawyers
in Rome is the cumulative authority of judicial opinions. That
extraordinary body of precedent, which has become as much a
part of the substance of English law as are the statutes of the
realm, may be considered the contribution of the legal profession
to the law of England.

The Forces Operative in the Development of Law. — The
forces that create and develop law are thus seen to be the same
as those which are operative in national and political development.

If that development bring forth monarchical forms of government, if the circumstances amidst which a people's life is cast
eradicate habits of local self-rule and establish habits of submission to a single central authority set over a compacted state, that
central authority alone will formulate and give voice to Law.
If, on the other hand, the national development be so favorably
cast that habits of self-reliance and self-rule are fostered and confirmed among the people, along with an active jealousy of any too
great concentration of only partially responsible power, Law will
more naturally proceed, through one instrumentality or another,
from out the nation : *vox legis, vox populi.* But in the one case
hardly less than in the other Law will express, not the arbitrary,
self-originative will of the man or body of men by whom it is formulated, but such rules as the body of the nation is prepared by
reason of its habits and fixed preferences to accept. The function of the framers of Law is a function of interpretation, of
formulation rather than of origination : no step that they can
take successfully can lie far apart from the lines along which
the national life has run. Law is the creation, not of individuals, but of the special needs, the special opportunities, the
special perils or misfortunes of communities. No 'law-maker'
may force upon a people Law which has not in some sense been
suggested to him by the circumstances or opinions of the nation
for whom he acts. Rulers, in all states alike, exercise the power
of the community, but cannot exercise any other. The community may supinely acquiesce in the power arrogated to himself by
the magistrate, but it can in no case really make him independent
of itself.

Here again France furnishes our best illustration. We have
a vivid confirmation of the truths stated in such an event as
the establishment of the Second Empire. The French people
were not duped by Louis Napoleon. The facts were simply these.
They were keenly conscious that they were making a failure of
the self-government which they were just then attempting ; they
wanted order and settled rule in place of fear of revolution and
the certainty of turbulent politics ; and they took the simplest,
most straightforward and evident means of getting what they

wanted. The laws of Napoleon were in a very real sense their own creation.

The Power of the Community must be behind Law. — The law of some particular state may seem to be the command of a minority only of those who compose the state: it may even in form utter only the will of a single despot; but in reality laws which issue from the arbitrary or despotic authority of the few who occupy the central seats of the state can never be given full effect unless in one form or another the power of the community be behind them. Whether it be an active power organized to move and make itself prevalent or a mere inert power lying passive as a vast immovable buttress to the great structure of absolute authority, the power of the community must support law or the law must be without effect. The bayonets of a minority cannot long successfully seek out the persistent disobediences of the majority. The majority must acquiesce or the law must be null.

There can be no reasonable doubt that the power of Russia's Czar, vast and arbitrary as it seemed, derived its strength from the Russian people. It was not the Czar's personal power; it was his power as head of the national church, as semi-sacred representative of the race and its historical development and organization. Its roots run deep into the tenacious, nourishing soil of immemorial habit. The Czar represented a history, not a caprice. Temporary, fleeting despots, like the first Napoleon, lead nations by the ears, playing to their love of glory, to their sense of dignity and honor, to their ardor for achievement and their desire for order.

Both a Mirror of Conceptions and an Active Force. — Looked at from an abstract point of view, Law is a body of principles, and as such constitutes a mirror of the prevalent conceptions as to ethical standards and social relationships in the communities in which it is accepted. But Law is also an active force, an expression of will. It is not merely a body of opinion; it is also a body of practical rules in operation. It is operative in two ways. It exercises both an ethical and a physical compulsion.

It involves (1), an *Ought*, in proportion as it is received as just or expedient. It is a source of conviction and motive in proportion as it is accepted as true. This ethical force is its principal force, its force for the majority. It is daily influential in moving men to do even what they conceive to be contrary to their individual interests. And this even when it is unjust in parts, provided it be deemed sound and just as a whole. (2) For the minority, who do not yield to its moral force or feel its moral compulsions, it involves a *Must*, and speaks harshly of the power of the state. That power is not great enough to venture to say ' You must' to a prevalent majority of any people. In cases of conquest, it is true, like that of the Normans in England, an actual physical compulsion may be operative for long periods together even against a numerical majority, and the law may seem to possess an ethical force only for the minority. But generally the compulsion is confined to the field of public law, in such cases; and there are majorities in affairs which are to be reckoned, not by number, but by capacity.

Roman Law an Example. — The law of Rome affords in this respect an admirable example of the normal character of law. It was the fundamental thought of Roman Law that it was the will of the Roman people. The political liberty of the Roman consisted in his membership of the state and his consequent participation, either direct or indirect, in the utterance of law. As an individual he was subordinated to the will of the state ; but his own will as a free burgess was a part of the state's will. He was an integral part of the community, his own power found its realization in the absolute *potestas et majestas populi*. This giant will of the people, speaking through the organs of the state, constituted a very absolute power, by which the individual was completely dominated ; but individual rights were recognized in the *equality* of the law, in its purpose to deal equally with high and low, with strong and weak ; and this was the Roman recognition of individual liberty.

The Power of Habit. — Legislators, those who exercise the authority of a community, build upon the habit of their so-called ' subjects.' If they be of the same race and sharers of the

same history as those whom they rule, their accommodation of
their acts to the national habit will be in large part unconscious :
for that habit runs in their own veins as well as in the veins of the
people. If they be invaders or usurpers, they avoid crossing the
prejudices or the long-abiding practices of the nation out of
caution or prudence. In any case their activity skims but the
surface, avoids the sullen depths of the popular life. They work
arbitrary decrees upon individuals, but they are balked of power
to turn about the life of the mass : that they can effect only by
slow and insidious measures which almost insensibly deflect the
habits of the people into channels which lead away from old into
new and different methods and purposes. The habit of the
nation is the material on which the legislator works ; and its
qualities constitute the limitations of his power. It is stubborn
material, and dangerous. If he venture to despise it, it forces
him to regard and humor it ; if he would put it to unaccustomed
uses, it balks him ; if he seek to force it, it will explode in his
hands and destroy him. The authority is not his, but only the
leadership.

Law's Utterance of National Character. — There is no
universal law, but for each nation a law of its own, which bears
evident marks of having been developed along with the national
character, which mirrors the special life of the particular people
whose political and social judgments it embodies (page 75).
The despot may be grossly arbitrary ; he may violate every principle of right in his application of the law to individuals ; he
may even suspend all justice in individual cases ; but the law,
the principles which he violates or follows at pleasure, he
takes from the people whom he governs, extracts from their
habit and history. What he changes is the application merely,
not the principles, of justice ; and he changes that application
only with reference to a comparatively small number of individuals whom he specially picks out for his enmity or displeasure.
He cannot violently turn about the normal processes of the
national law.

Germanic Law. — We have in Germanic law an example
of the influence of national character upon legal systems as conspicuous as that afforded by Roman law itself, and the example

is all the more instructive when put alongside of the Roman because of the sharpness of the contrasts between Roman and Germanic legal conceptions. Although so like the Romans in practical political sagacity and common-sense legal capacity, the Germans had very different conceptions as to the basis and nature of law. Their law spoke no such exaltation of the public power, and consequently no such intense realization of unity. The individual German was, so to say, given play outside the law ; his rights were not relative, but absolute, self-centred. It was the object of the public polity rather to give effect to individual worth and liberty than to build together a compact, dominant community. German law, therefore, took no thought for systematic equality, but did take careful thought to leave room for the fullest possible assertion of that individuality which must inevitably issue in inequality. It was a flexible framework for the play of individual forces. It lacked the energy, the united, triumphant strength of the Roman system ; but it contained untold treasures of variety and of individual achievement. It, no less than Roman law, rested broadly upon national character ; and it was to supply in general European history what the Roman system could not contribute.[1]

Sovereignty: who gives Law ? — If, then, law be a product of national character, if the power of the community must be behind it to give it efficacy, and the habit of the community in it to give it reality, where is the seat of sovereignty ? Whereabouts and in whom does sovereignty reside, and what is Sovereignty ? These, manifestly, are questions of great scope and complexity, and yet questions central to a right understanding of the nature and genesis of law. It will be best to approach our answers to them by way of an illustration.

In England, sovereignty is said to rest with the legislative power: with Parliament acting with the approval of the Crown, or, not to discard an honored legal fiction, with the Crown acting with the assent of Parliament. Whatever an Act of Parliament prescribes is law, even though it contravene every prin-

---

[1] What is here said of Germanic law and the Germans refers to the primitive, not to the modern Germans. The present German laws and Germans are all that those here spoken of were not.

ciple, constitutional or only of private right, recognized before the passage of the Act as inviolable. Such is the theory. The well-known fact is, that Parliament dare do nothing that will even seem to contravene principles held to be sacred in the sphere either of constitutional privilege or private right. Should Parliament violate such principles, their action would be repudiated by the nation, their will, failing to become indeed law, would pass immediately into the limbo of things repealed; Parliament itself would be purged of its offending members. Parliament is master, can utter valid commands, only so far as it interprets, or at least does not cross, the wishes of the people. Whether or not it be possible to say with the approval of those who insist upon maintaining the rules of a strict abstract logic that the sovereignty of Parliament is limited *de jure*, that is, in law, it is manifestly the main significant truth of the case that parliamentary sovereignty is most imperatively limited *de facto*, in fact. Its actual power is not a whit broader for having a free field *in law*, so long as the field in which it really moves is fenced high about by firm facts.

Sovereignty, therefore, as ideally conceived in legal theory, nowhere actually exists. The sovereignty which does exist is something much more vital, — though, like most living things, much less easily conceived. It is the will of an organized independent community, whether that will speak in acquiescence merely, or in active creation of the forces and conditions of politics. The kings or parliaments who serve as its vehicles utter it, but they do not possess it. Sovereignty resides in the community; but its organs, whether those organs be supreme magistrates, busy legislatures, or subtile privileged classes, are as various as the conditions of historical growth.

Certain Legal Conceptions Universal. — The correspondence of law with national character, its basis in national habit, does not deprive it of all universal characteristics. Many common features it does wear among all civilized peoples. As the Romans found it possible to put together, from the diversified systems of law existing among the subject peoples of the Mediterranean basin, a certain number of general maxims of justice out of which to construct the foundations of their *jus gentium*, so may jurists to-day discover in all systems of law alike certain common moral judgments, a certain evidence of unity of thought regarding the greater principles of equity. There is a common legal conscience in mankind.

Thus, for example, the sacredness of human life; among all Aryan nations at least, the sanctity of the nearer family relationships; in all systems at all developed, the plainer principles of 'mine' and 'thine'; the obligation of promises; many obvious duties of man to man suggested by the universal moral consciousness of the race, receive recognition under all systems alike. Sometimes resemblances between systems the most widely separated in time and space run even into ceremonial details, such as the emblematic transfer of property, and into many items of personal right and obligation.

Law and Ethics. — It by no means follows, however, that because law thus embodies the moral judgments of the race on many points of personal relation and individual conduct, it is to be considered a sort of positive, concrete Ethics, — Ethics crystallized into definite commands towards which the branch of culture which we call 'Ethics' stands related as theory to practice. Ethics concerns the whole walk and conversation of the individual; it touches the rectitude of each man's life, the truth of his dealings with his own conscience, the whole substance of character and conduct, righteousness both of act and of mental habit. Law, on the other hand, concerns only man's life in society. It not only confines itself to controlling the outward acts of men; it limits itself to those particular acts of man to man which can be regulated by the public authority, which it has proved practicable to regulate in accordance with uniform rules applicable to all alike and in an equal degree. It does not essay to punish untruthfulness as such, it only annuls contracts obtained by fraudulent misrepresentation and makes good such pecuniary damage as the deceit may have entailed. It does not censure ingratitude or any of the subtler forms of faithlessness, it only denounces its penalties against open and tangible acts of dishonesty. It does not assume to be the guardian of men's characters, it only stands with a whip for those who give overt proof of bad character in their dealings with their fellow-men. Its limitations are thus limitations both of kind and of degree. It addresses itself to the regulation of outward conduct only : that is its limitation of kind ; and it regulates outward conduct only so far as workable and uniform rules can be found for its regulation : that is its limitation of degree.

Mala Prohibita. — Law thus plays the rôle neither of conscience nor of Providence. More than this, it follows standards of policy only, not absolute standards of right and wrong. Many things that are wrong, even within the sphere of social conduct, it does not prohibit ; many things not wrong in themselves it does prohibit. It thus creates, as it were, a new class of wrongs, relative to itself alone : *mala prohibita,* things wrong because forbidden. In keeping the commands of the state regarding things fairly to be called morally indifferent in themselves men are guided by their *legal* conscience. Society rests upon obedience to the laws : laws determine the rules of social convenience as well as of social right and wrong ; and it is as necessary for the perfecting of social relationships that the rules of convenience be obeyed as it is that obedience be rendered to those which touch more vital matters of conduct.

Thus it cannot be said to be inherently wrong for a man to marry his deceased wife's sister ; but if the laws, seeking what may be esteemed to be a purer order of family relationships, forbid such a marriage, it becomes *malum prohibitum :* it is wrong because illegal.

It would certainly not be wrong for a trustee to buy the trust estate under his control if he did so in good faith and on terms manifestly advantageous to the persons in whose interest he held it ; but it is contrary to wise public policy that such purchases should be allowed, because a trustee would have too many opportunities for unfair dealing in such transactions. The law will under no circumstances hold the sale of a trust estate to the trustee valid. Such purchases, however good the faith in which they are made, are *mala prohibita.*

Or take, as another example, police regulations whose only

object is to serve the convenience of society in crowded cities. A street parade, with bands and banners and men in uniform is quite harmless and is immensely pleasing to those who love the glitter of epaulettes and brass buttons and the blare of trumpets ; but police regulations must see to it that city streets are kept clear for the ordinary daily movements of the busy city population, and to parade without license is *malum prohibitum.*

In all civilized states law has long since abandoned attempts to regulate conscience or opinion ; it would find it, too, both fruitless and unwise to essay any regulation of conduct, however reprehensible in itself, which did not issue in definite and tangible acts of injury to others. But it does seek to command the outward conduct of men in their palpable dealings with each other in society. Law is the mirror of active political life. It may be and is instructed by the ethical judgments of the community, but its own province is not distinctively ethical ; it may regard religious principle, but it is not a code of religion. Ethics has been called the science of the well-being of man, law the science of his right civil conduct. Ethics concerns the development of character ; religion, the development of man's relation with God ; law, the development of men's relations to each other in society. Ethics, says Mr. Sidgwick, "is connected with politics so far as the well-being of any individual man is bound up with the well-being of his society."

International Law. — International Law may be described as law in an incomplete state. It is law without a forceful sanction such as exists for the ordinary law of the land. There is no earthly power to which all nations are subject ; there is no power, therefore, above the nations to enforce obedience to rules of conduct as between them, yet International Law is not lacking in sanction altogether ; it rests upon those principles of right action, of justice, and of consideration which have so universal an acceptance in the moral judgment of men that they have been styled the Laws of Nature. Back of it in the first instance is the common public opinion of the world. When this public opinion is flouted, and the principles and practices of international Law are disregarded, then the physical force of individual states or groups of states may be brought to bear upon the law-breaker. International Law is the law of the international community of states; its principles are those upon which the successful life of that community depends. The society of states is not yet fully organized and International Law is incomplete just to the extent that this society lacks organization; its courts, its judges, its legislatures are rudimentary and are wanting as yet in that definiteness of constitution and authority which we find in individual states.

Early writers like Grotius and Vattel embodied it in distinct statements of what they conceived to be the almost self-evident principles of the Law of Nature. In process of time, the practice of nations has been recorded in state papers and in learned treatises by hosts of scholars; principles of international action have been agreed to in treaties by which states acting in pairs or in groups have agreed to be bound in their relations with each other, and both practice and agreements have found their way into the statutes or established judicial precedents of enlightened individual states. More and more international conventions have come to recognize certain elements of right, of equity and comity as settled, as always to be accepted in transactions between states. The practice of concerted action by the states of the world in formulating International Law is best exemplified in the First and Second Hague Conferences of 1899 and 1907, where much of the practice of International Law was formulated and definite rules accepted by the great body of states as binding upon them.

The formation of a " League of Nations " to bring pressure to bear upon a state unmindful of its international obligations will go far towards supplying the sanction of regulated force which International Law has hitherto lacked.

These rules concern the conduct of war, diplomatic intercourse, the rights of citizens of one country living under the dominion of another, jurisdiction at sea, the rights and duties of neutrals, etc. Extradition principles are settled almost always by specific agreement between country and country, as are also commercial arrangements, fishing rights, and all similar matters not of universal bearing. But even in such matters example added to example is turning nations in the direction of uniform principles ; such, for instance, as that political offences shall not be included among extraditable crimes, unless they involve ordinary crimes of a very heinous nature, such as murder.

Laws of Nature and Laws of the State. — The analogy between political laws, the laws which speak the will of the state, and natural laws, the laws which express the orderly succession of events in nature, has often been dwelt upon, and is not without instructive significance. In the one set of laws as in the other, there is, it would seem, a uniform prescription as to the operation of the forces that make for life. The analogy is most instructive, however, where it fails: it is more instructive, that is, to note the contrasts between the laws of nature and laws of the state than to note such likeness as exists between them. The contrasts rather than the resemblances serve to make evident the real nature of political regulation. " Whenever we have made out by careful and repeated observation," says Professor Huxley, "that something is always the cause of a certain effect, or that certain events always take place in the same order, we speak of the truth thus discovered as a law of nature. Thus it is a law of nature that anything heavy falls to the ground if it is unsupported. . . . But the laws of nature are not the causes of the order of nature, but only our way of stating as much as we have made out of that order. Stones do not fall to the ground in consequence of the law just stated, as people sometimes carelessly say ; but the law is a way of asserting that which invariably happens when heavy bodies at the surface of the earth, stones among the rest, are free to move."

Whatever analogies may exist between such generalized statements of physical fact and the rules in accordance with which men are constrained to act in organized civil society it may be profitable for the curious carefully to inquire into. What it is most profitable for the student of politics to observe is the wide difference between the two, which Professor Huxley very admirably states as follows: " Human law consists of commands addressed to voluntary agents, which they may obey or disobey; and the law is not rendered null and void by being broken. Natural laws, on the other hand, are not commands, but assertions respecting the invariable order of nature; and they remain law only so long as they can be shown to express that order. To speak of the violation or suspension of a law of nature is an absurdity. All that the phrase can really mean is that, under certain circumstances, the assertion contained in the law is not true; and the just conclusion is, not that the order of nature is interrupted, but that we have made a mistake in stating that order. A true natural law is a universal rule, and, as such, admits of no exception."[1] In brief, human choice enters into the law of the state, whereas from natural law that choice is altogether excluded: it is dominated by fixed necessity. Human choice, indeed, enters every part of political law to modify it. It is the element of change; and it has given to the growth of law a variety, a variability, and an irregularity which no other power could have imparted.

Limitations of Political Law. — We have thus laid bare to our view some of the most instructive characteristics of political law. The laws of nature formulate effects invariably produced by forces of course adequate to produce them; but behind political laws there is not always a force adequate to produce the effects which they are designed to produce. The force, the *sanction*, as jurists say, which lies behind the laws of the state is the organized armed power of the community: compulsion raises its arm against the man who refuses to obey (pages 26, 78). But the public power may sleep, may be inattentive to breaches of law, may suffer itself to be bribed, may be outwitted or thwarted: laws are not always 'enforced.' This element of weakness it is which opens up to us one aspect at least of the nature of Law. Law is no more efficient than the state whose will it utters. The law of Turkey shares all the imperfections of the Turkish power; the laws of England bespeak in their enforcement the efficacy of English government. Good laws are of no avail under a bad gov-

---

[1] These passages are taken from Professor Huxley's *Science Primer, Introductory.*

ernment; a weak, decadent state may speak the highest purposes in its statutes and yet do the worst things in its actual administration. Commonly, however, law embodies the real purposes of the state, and its enforcement is a matter of administrative capacity or of concerted power simply.

Public Law. — The two great divisions under which law may best be studied are these: (1) *Public Law*, (2) *Private Law*. Public law is that which immediately concerns the existence, the structure, the functions, and the methods of the state. Taken in its full scope, it includes not only what we familiarly know as constitutional law, but also what is known as administrative law, as well as all civil procedure in the courts and all criminal law. In brief, it is that portion of law which determines a state's own character and its relations to its citizens.

Private Law. — Private law, on the other hand, is that portion of positive law which secures to the citizen his rights as against the other citizens of the state. It seeks to effect justice between individual and individual; its sphere is the sphere of individual right and duty.

It is to the Romans that we are indebted for a first partial recognition of this important division in the province of Law, though later times have given a different basis to this distinction. I say 'indebted' because the distinction between public and private law has the most immediate connections with individual liberty. Without it, we have the state of affairs that existed in Greece, where there was no sphere which was not the state's; and where the sphere of the state's relations to the individual was as wide as the sphere of the law itself. Individual liberty can exist only where it is recognized that there are rights which the state does not create, but only secures.

Jurisprudence. — Jurisprudence is a term of much latitude, but when used strictly must be taken to mean the Science of Law. The science of law is complete only when it has laid bare both the nature and the genesis of law: the nature of law must be obscure until its genesis and the genesis of the conceptions upon which it is based have been explored; and that genesis is a matter, not of logical analysis, but of history. Many writers upon jurisprudence, therefore, have insisted upon the historical method of study as the only proper method. They have sought in the history of society and of institutions to discover the birth and trace the development of jural conceptions, the growths of practice which have expanded into the law of property or of torts, the influences which have contributed to the orderly regulation of man's conduct in society.

In the hands of another school of writers, however, jurisprudence has been narrowed to the dimensions of a science of law in its modern aspects only. They seek to discover, by an analysis of law in its present full development, the rights which habitually receive legal recognition and the methods by which states secure to their citizens their rights, and enforce upon them their duties, by positive rules backed by the abundant sanction of the public power. In their view, not only is the history of law not jurisprudence, but, except to a very limited extent, it is not even the material of jurisprudence. Its material is law as it at present exists. The history of that law is only a convenient light in which the real content and purpose of existing law may be made plainer to the analyst. The conclusions of these writers are subject to an evident limitation, therefore. Their analysis of law, being based upon existing legal systems alone and taking the fully developed law for granted, can be applied to law in the earlier stages of society only by careful modification, only by a more or less subtle and ingenious accommodation of the meaning of its terms.

Historical jurisprudence alone, — a science of law, that is, constructed by means of the historical analysis of law and always squaring its conclusions with the history of society, can serve the objects of the student of politics. The processes of analytical jurisprudence, however, having been conducted by minds of the greatest subtlety and acuteness, serve a very useful purpose in supplying a logical structure of thought touching full-grown systems of law.

The Analytical Account of Law. — In the thought of the analytical school every law is a command, "an order issued by a superior to an inferior." "Every positive law is 'set by a sovereign person, or sovereign body of persons, to a member or members of the independent political society wherein that person or body of persons is sovereign or superior.'" In its terms, manifestly, such an analysis applies only to times when the will of the state is always spoken by a definite authority; not with the voice of custom, which proceeds no one knows whence; not with the voice of religion, which speaks to the conscience as well as to the outward life, and whose sanctions are derived from the unseen power of a supernatural being; nor yet with the voice of scientific discussion, whose authors have no authority except that of clear reason; but with the distinct accents of command, with the voice of the judge and the legislator.

The Analytical Account of Sovereignty. — The analytical account of sovereignty is equally clear-cut and positive. Laws, "being commands, emanate from a determinate source," from a sovereign authority; and analytical jurisprudence is very strict and formal in its definition of sovereignty. A sovereign "is a determinate person, or body of persons, to whom the bulk of the members of an organized community are in the habit of rendering obedience and who are themselves not in the habit of rendering obedience to any human superior." It follows, of course, that no community which is not independent can have a law of its own. The law of the more fully developed English colonies, for example, though it is made by the enactment of their own parliaments, is not law by virtue of such enactment, because those parliaments are in the habit of being obedient to the authorities in London and are not themselves sovereign. The sovereignty which lies back of all law in the colonies is said to be the sovereignty of the parliament of England.

It would seem to follow that our own federal authorities are sovereign. They are a determinate body of persons to whom the bulk of the nation is habitually obedient and who are themselves obedient to no human superior. But then what of the authority of the states in that great sphere of action which is altogether and beyond dispute their own, which the federal authorities do not and cannot enter, within which their own people are habitually obedient to them, and in which they are not subject to any earthly superior?　It has been the habit of all our earlier writers and statesmen to say that with us sovereignty is divided.　But the abstract sovereignty of which the legal analyst speaks is held to be indivisible: it must be whole.　Analysis, therefore, is driven to say that with us sovereignty rests in its entirety with that not very determinate body of persons, the people of the United States, the *powers* of sovereignty resting with the state and federal authorities by delegation from the people.

The difficulty of applying the analytical account of sovereignty to our own law is in part avoided if law be defined as "the command of an authorized public organ, acting within the sphere of its competence.　What organs are authorized, and what is the sphere of their competence, is of course determined by the organic law of the state; and *this* law is the direct command of the sovereign."[1]　The only difficulty left by this solution is that of making room in our system for both a sovereign people of the single state and a sovereign people of the Union.

Summary. — Spoken first in the slow and general voice of custom, Law speaks at last in the clear, the multifarious, the active tongues of legislation.　It grows with the growth of the community.　It cannot outrun the conscience of the community and be real, it cannot outlast its judgments and retain its force. It mirrors social advance.　If it anticipate the development of the public thought, it must wait until the common judgment and conscience grow up to its standards before it can have life; if it lag behind the common judgment and conscience, it must become obsolete, and will come to be more honored in the breach than in the observance.

---

[1] This definition I have taken the liberty of extracting from some very valuable notes on this chapter kindly furnished me by Professor Monroe Smith, who upon this subject speaks authoritatively.

Several Representative Authorities.

Austin, John, Lectures on Jurisprudence, the Philosophy of Positive Law, 2 vols.

Gray, J. C., The Nature and Sources of the Law. N. Y., 1909.

Heron, D. C., Introduction to the History of Jurisprudence. London, 1880.

Holland, T. E., Elements of Jurisprudence. 11th ed. N. Y., 1910.

Ihering, v., Geist des Römischen Rechts. 3 vols., Leipzig.

Jellinek, Georg, Gesetz und Verordnung. Freiburg in B., 1887; Das Recht des Modernen Staates. 2d ed. Berlin, 1905.

Maine, Sir H. S., Ancient Law, and Early History of Institutions, Lectures XII., XIII.

Markby, Sir Wm., Elements of Law. Oxford (Clarendon Press), 1889·

Modern Legal Philosophy Series, Vols. 1–2, Boston.

Pollock, Sir Frederick, A First Book of Jurisprudence. London and N. Y., 1896.

Robertson, E., Article 'Law,' *Encyclopædia Britannica*, 9th ed.

Salmond, J. W., Jurisprudence. London, 1902.

Taylor, Hannis, The Science of Jurisprudence. N. Y., 1908.

Willoughby, W. W., The Nature of the State. N. Y., 1896.

VI

POLITY AND GOVERNMENT DURING
THE MIDDLE AGES.

———o‹o›o‹o›oo———

Contact of the Teutonic Tribes with Rome. — The Teutonic tribes which, in the fifth and following centuries, threw themselves into the Western Roman Empire to possess it were not all of them strangers to the polity which they overset. The Romans had often invaded Germany, and, although as often thrust out, had established a supremacy over the minds at least, if not over the liberties, of the Germans. Those tribes which had lived nearest the Rhine and the Danube, moreover, had long been in more or less constant contact with the masters of the Mediterranean and the western world, and had, of course, been deeply affected by the example of Roman civilization. Teutons had, besides, entered and, so to say, espoused the Roman world in great numbers, in search of individual adventure or advantage, long before the advent of the barbarians as armed and emigrant hosts. Rome had drawn some of her finest legions from these races which she could not subdue. Her armies were in the later days of the Empire full of stalwart, fair-haired Germans. Even her greater officers and officials were oftentimes of that blood.

Primitive Teutonic Institutions. — When Franks and Goths and Burgundians moved as militant races to the supplanting of Roman dominion, they, nevertheless, took with them into western Europe, torn as it was by Roman dissensions and sapped by Roman decay, an individuality of their own. They had their own contribution to make to the history of institutions. They had lived under a system of government combining, though in somewhat crude forms, tribal unity and individual independence. Amongst them, as amongst other Aryan peoples, kinship constituted the basis of association and the primal sanction of authority; and the family was the unit of government. Kinsmen, fellow-tribesmen, were grouped in villages, and each village maintained without question its privileges of self-government, legislating upon its common affairs and administering its common property in village meeting. Its lands were the property, not of individuals, but of the community; but they were allotted in separate parcels to the freemen of the community, upon would-be equitable principles, to be cultivated for private, not for communal, profit. Chiefs there were who exercised magisterial powers, but these chiefs were elected in village meeting. They did not determine the weightier questions of custom, in the administration of justice: that was the province of the village meeting itself; and such judicial authority as they did exercise was shared by 'assessors' chosen from the whole body of their free fellow-villagers.

Free, Unfree, and Noble. — Not all their fellow-villagers were free. There were some who were excluded from political privilege and who held their lands only as serfs of the freemen of the community; and there were others, lower still in rank, who were simple slaves. There were, again, on the other hand, some who were more than free, who, for one reason or another, had risen to a recognized nobility of station, to a position of esteem, and to an estate of wealth above those of the rest of the community. But nobility did not carry with it exceptional political privilege: it only assured a consideration which put its possessor in the way of winning the greater preferments of office in the gift of the village meeting. The power of the noble depended upon the franchises of his community rather than upon any virtue in his own blood.

Intercommunal Government. — It was not often that a village stood apart in entire dissociation from all similar tribal or family centres; but when it did, the powers of its *moot* (meeting) extended beyond the choice of magistrates, the management of the communal property, and the administration of communal justice. It also declared war and appointed leaders of the communal 'host.' Commonly, however, these greater matters of war and of 'foreign relations' were determined by assemblies representing more than one village. Communities sent out offshoots which remained connected with them by federal bonds; or independent communities drew together into leagues; and it was the grand folk-moot of the confederated communities which summoned the 'host' and elected leaders,— which sometimes even chose the chiefs who were to preside over the administration of the several villages.

Military Leadership : the Comitatus. — The leaders selected to head the 'host' were generally men of tried powers who could inspire confidence and kindle emulation in their followers; and such men, though in all cases chosen to official leadership only for a single campaign, never even in times of peace ceased to be, potentially at least, the heads of military enterprise and daring adventure. Not uncommonly they would break the monotony of peace and dull inactivity by gathering about them a band of volunteers and setting forth, spite of the peace enjoyed by their tribe, to make fighting or find plunder somewhere for their own sakes. About men of this stamp there gathered generally all the young blades of the tribe who thirsted for excitement or adventure, or who aspired to gain proficiency in arms. These became the military household, the *comitatus,* of their chosen chieftain, his permanent, inseparable retinue, bound to him by the closest ties of personal allegiance, sitting always at his table, and at once defending his person and emulating his prowess in battle; a band who looked to him for their sustenance, their military equipment, and their rewards for valor, but who rendered him in return a gallant service which added much to his social consideration and gave him rank among the most powerful of his fellow-tribesmen.

Contrasts between the Teutonic System and the Roman. — These features of tribal confederation and personal supremacy, though suggestive at many points of the primitive Roman state, were in strong contrast with the Roman polity as it existed at the time of the invasions. They were not only rude and primitive and characteristic every way of a very much less advanced stage of civilization, but they also contained certain principles which were in radical contradiction to conceptions obviously fundamental to Roman state life.

Roman Allegiance to the State. — The central contrast between the two systems may be roughly summed up in the statement that the Teutonic was essentially *personal*, the Roman essentially impersonal. Neither the Roman soldier nor the Roman citizen knew anything of the personal allegiance which was the chief amalgam of primitive German politics. His subordination was to the state, and that subordination was so complete that he was practically merged in the state, possessing no rights but those of a child of the body politic. His obligation to obey the magistrate in the city or his commander in the field lasted only so long as the magistrate's or commander's commission lasted. Allegiance had no connection with the magistrate or the commander as a person : magistrate and commander claimed allegiance only as representatives of the state, its temporary embodiment. To them *as the state*, the citizen or soldier owed the yielding of everything, even of life itself : for as against the state the Roman had no private rights. While he held office, therefore, and shared the *imperium*, magistrate or commander was omnipotent ; his official conduct could be called in question only after his term of office was at an end and he had ceased to be the state's self. Of course much decay had come into the heart of such principles ere the Empire was forced to break before the barbarian ; but they never ceased to be central to Roman political conception.

Teutonic Personal Allegiance. — With the Teutons, on the contrary, political association manifested an irresistible tendency towards just the opposite principles. When they came to their final triumph over the Empire they came ranked and associated upon grounds of personal allegiance. In their old life in Germany, as we have seen above, their relations to their commanders did not cease at the close of a war sanctioned by the community, though the commission of their leaders did expire then. Many, — and those the bravest and best, — remained members of their leaders' *comitatus*, bound to him by no public command or sanction at all, but only by his personal supremacy over them. They even made themselves members of his household,

depended upon the bounties of his favor, and constituted them·
selves a personal following of their chosen leader such as no
Roman but a fawning client would have deigned to belong to.
It was a polity of individualism which presented many striking
points of surprise to Roman observers. Individuals had under
such a system a freedom of origination and a separateness of
unofficial personal weight which to the Roman were altogether
singular and in large part repugnant.

Temporary Coexistence of the Two Systems. — For long
after the Teuton had established his dominion over the Romanized populations of Europe, Teutonic and Roman institutions
lived side by side, each set persistent for its own people. The
conquerors did not try to eradicate the old population or the
old laws of the Empire. They simply carried into the midst of
the Empire their own customs, which they kept for themselves,
without thrusting them upon their new subjects. They appro-
priated to their own uses large tracts of the conquered lands, and
established upon them such bodies of free landholders as they had
known and built their polity upon in their old seats, either casting out those who already occupied them or reducing the occupiers
to a servile condition; but much of the land they left untouched,
to be occupied as before. Of course Teutonic customs, being the
customs of the dominant race, more and more affected the older
Roman rights, even if only insensibly; and Roman principles of
right, belonging as they did to a much superior and much more
highly developed civilization, which the Teuton had already long
reverenced, must have had quite as great a modifying effect upon
the Teutonic customs, which now, so to say, lay alongside of
them. The Roman polity had entered into the whole habit of
the older provincials and still retained, despite the disorders
of the later days of the Empire, not a little of its old vigor and
potency. It had strongly affected the imaginations of the Germans when they had touched only its geographical borders, and
it did not fail in a certain measure to dominate them even now,
when it was at their feet. They made no attempt to stamp it
out. They, on the contrary, tolerated, respected, imitated it.

'**Personal**' **Law.** — What looked like tolerance on the
part of the Teutons was in reality for the most part only a natural

outcome of certain fixed conceptions of the race. The hosts which
had poured into the Roman territories were much greater and
more various in their make-up than any the Teutonic peoples
had gathered in their communal life in the forests of Germany.
They represented tribes united: kindred tribes, indeed, but still
tribes only very loosely confederated at home, if united there
under any common government at all.   These each had their own
law. Salian Frank had one law and custom, Ripuarian Frank
another; Frank had one right and practice, Burgundian another;
and it was a principle everywhere observed among Teutons that,
whether joined with others in a common enterprise or not, each
man must be judged and given his right by his own native law,
according to the custom of his own people.   Each had his 'personal' privilege of blood and custom, must be adjudged by his
own 'personal' law, the law of his own tribe or homeland.   So
at any rate we have now come to phrase it; and we know that in
giving leave to the people of the Roman territories to keep their
law also, the conquerors were but extending to them a habit of
their own, alike in thought and practice.

Relative Influence of Roman and Teutonic Systems. — So
far as any general description of this mixture of Roman and
Teutonic influences may be ventured, it may be said that the
Teutonic had their greatest weight on the side of political organization, the Roman on the side of the development of private
rights.   The Teutons, of course, tried to reproduce in their new
settlements the communal life peculiar to their own native institutions; they endeavored to organize their own power, according
to the immemorial fashion of their own politics, on the basis of
a freehold tenure of the land and local self-administration, — a
free division of the spoils on the principle of individual equality
among the freemen of the tribes.   They had stamped out the
Roman *state* in the invaded territory; Roman *public* law they had
of course displaced, destroyed.   It was Roman conceptions as to
private relations that gradually modified their Teutonic system.
That system rested, as regarded its political features hardly
less than at all other points, upon the relations of individual
to individual, and as the example of the Roman practices, still
preserved by the conquered populations about them, modified

these relations of individual to individual, great changes were by consequence inevitably wrought in political organization as well. Such changes were, however, not in the direction of a reproduction of Roman political method, but in the direction of the creation of that singular public polity which we designate as *mediæval*.

Roman Influence upon Private Law. — The Roman influence thus told most directly and most powerfully through the medium of Roman private law. That law had developed too complete and perfect a system, and was much too suitable to the new conditions in the midst of which they found themselves, to fail of influence amongst the new organizers. The Teutonic peoples, leaders and followers alike, were prepared to admire and heed Roman civil arrangements. The leaders had in many cases a fancy for seeming successors to the Roman Emperor. They were prompt, when their power was once established, to draw the law which was to be 'personal' to their Roman subjects into a crude but formal code, after the manner of Theodosius. King Gundobad, of the Burgundians, had such a code put together out of the older Roman codices, the writings of Paulus and Gaius, and the text-books and interpretations of the schools, so early as the year 500 A.D., five years after he had given his own people a similar statement of their own law. The new code was the "*Lex Romana Burgundionum*," the *Roman* law of the Burgundians, as contradistinguished from their own Burgundian law; and its provisions were chiefly for their conquered subjects, not for themselves. In the year 506 came the *Lex Romana Visigothorum*, the Roman code of the Visigoths, formulated at the command of Alaric II. and generally known now as the Breviary of Alaric, the best and most influential of the barbarian codes of Roman law. It was practically the only source of Roman law known in the south of France till the twelfth century. Germany and England drew their knowledge of that law from it until the eleventh century. In 511, or thereabouts, Theodoric the Great promulgated a like compilation of the Roman law for his Ostrogothic kingdom in Italy, a compilation which we know as the *Edictum Theodorici*. It was no small evidence of Roman influence that these rulers sought to give their subjects written law in both kinds; and the fact that only priests were literate enough to undertake the work of codification meant that Roman principles would creep unawares even into the statements of native law; for the polity and learning of the Church had its roots in the tradition and law of Rome. 'Personal' law, nevertheless, continued to prevail. Even the greatest statesmen, like Charles the Great, did not make use of their power to cut at the roots of local custom or personal right. Sometimes it was the plaintiff, sometimes the defendant, who established his right to his own personal law in a suit; but in every case custom reigned where it could.

Roman Towns. — It was in the towns that the law of Rome had its strongholds. There it had a centred and lively influence: and there it was long undisturbed by the conquerors. It took the Teuton a long time to learn how to live in a town, within limiting walls and amidst crowded houses. His native habit called him to a freer life: the pent-up town was too rigid, too conventional, too narrow a sphere for his restless energies. He at first contented himself, therefore, with the mere formal submission of the towns: it was long before he entered them to stay and to take part in their life. Meanwhile not only Roman private law, but also Roman municipal traditions, were preparing the cities for the power and independence which they were to claim and enjoy during the Middle Ages. They were to prove Rome's most vital fragments. They nursed her law and reproduced her politics. Not Italy only, but the Rhone and Rhine countries as well, were dotted over with these abiding places of the old influences which had once dominated the world: and from them those influences were eventually to issue forth again to fresh triumphs.

The Fusion of the Two Systems. — Gradually there was brought about that fusion of German customs with Roman law and conception which, after a long intermediate fermentation, and in conjunction with certain institutions developed apart from both was to produce the conditions of modern political life. During the Middle Ages government gradually worked its way out from the individualism inherent in the habits of the Germanic races back into an absolutism not unlike that of the Roman Empire. The intermediate stage was *Feudalism*.

Effects of Movements of Conquest upon Teutonic Institutions. — Feudalism was preceded, however, by modifications in the Teutonic system which were not the result of their contact with Romanized peoples so much as the direct effects of conquest.

The New Kingship. — The migratory conquests of the Teutons greatly emphasized for a time the principle of individualism, — the principle of personal allegiance. They advanced to their new seats not as separate marauding bands, but as emigrant nations. It was a movement of races, not of armies merely. All the freemen of the tribes came, bringing with them their families, their household goods, and their slaves, as having come to stay. But they could not preserve, when on such an errand, the organization of times of settlement and peace. They had not come, in fact, with nothing but their old and simple organization. They came with established discipline and subordination, it would seem, — with kingship already in some measure recognized amongst them, ready to be made permanent. They were forced to elevate the commander of the host to a new kingship. As confederated tribes in their old seats they had often chosen kings, who typified in their official dignity and sanctity the unity of tribal organization, who presided over the national councils, and who by reason of their preferred position enjoyed a somewhat greater state than their noble associates in the tribes. But these early kings, like the Greek kings of the Homeric songs, were scarcely more than patriarchal presidents, 'first among peers.' The later kings, in Gaul, in England, and in Spain, — the kings of the emigration, — on the other hand, ruled as well as reigned. They had first of all been the leaders who commanded the invading hosts, and who had met and routed the Roman forces which sought to withstand the stalwart immigrants; and so long as conquests remained incomplete they continued in command to complete them. Conquest being achieved, their authority was still necessary to keep their people together in dominant organization. It was only the logical and inevitable result that was reached, therefore, when they became possessed of sovereign powers of a sort such as German politics had never known before. Great as was the almost immediate transformation of commanders into kings, however, they were not yet kings such as later times were to see in France, after feudalism should have worked its perfect work.

The Modified Land Tenure. — The invading peoples doubt-less at first took possession of the conquered territory by a ten-ure not radically different from that by which they had held their older home fields, except as it was modified by the fact that the conquered lands were already occupied by a native population, whom it was not their policy altogether to dispossess, and whose presence even as serfs would necessarily affect the system of the new masters. Those who were suffered to retain their holdings only exchanged a Roman overlordship for a German; but they constituted a new class of citizens in the German polity, and inevitably touched with Roman influences Teutonic customs of tenure.

It was the circumstances of conquest, however, which were the chief causes of modification. The conquered territory was naturally disposed of, in large part at least, by the leaders of conquest in accordance with military and strategic require-ments. Such leaders, too, always get the lion's share of property won by arms, as these lands had been; and, by their gifts, their chief followers also are made specially rich in the new lands. Thus a new bond of personal connection is created, and conditions pregnant with profound social changes are established. It was by means of such gifts and their influence that the leaders of conquest raised up about them proprietors all but as powerful as themselves, and so both cheated themselves of full kingship, and robbed society of all chance of harmonious unity. Power fell apart into fragments, — into a vast number of petty lordships, and the Feudal System was born.

The Feudal System. — But the complex thing which we call the Feudal System was built up by no single or simple process. Feudalism was itself a process: the process by which armed and emigrant tribes, settled upon conquered territories, were compacted into states, and prepared for a new political order which should subdue the fierce individualism of the Teuton to a novel discipline of subordination and obedience. When the system had been thoroughly wrought out society resembled an army spread abroad and encamped, every freeman endowed with a portion of land indeed, for his own tillage, but holding it by 'military tenure,' upon the condition that he would serve him of whom he held it, his immediate overlord and commander, whenever his call came to the field: that he would in all things, with a soldier's fealty, prove himself his faithful follower. Before this migration and conquest and settlement in new lands the duty of each Teutonic freeman to come into the field when summoned had been only a personal duty, which fell upon him when the summons came from the free council of his people: it had had no connection with his title to his land. But under the new order of things it had become his duty as a tenant, and it was a duty which he owed, not to the host or to the leader with whom ne had voluntarily associated himself for some adventure of war, but to him of whom he held his land. And every freeman held his land thus of some one, save only the king himself. Military society had taken root in the soil. The land supported an army in which every man had a fixed place and function, failing which he was cut off from his land. A society that might have fallen to pieces, had not the unbridled independence of the Teuton been in some way checked and disciplined, was in this way held loosely together by a series of personal dependencies based upon the tenure of land. A connected series of greater and lesser landowners, the less dependent upon the greater, and all at least nominally dependent upon the king, the centre and titular head of the hierarchy: such was the pattern of feudal society.

Genesis of the System. — It is possible to distinguish in a general way the several stages by which this singular order of political life came into existence. It was many centuries in the making, and forces almost without number had their effect in creating it in its several parts; but the main outlines of what took place may be briefly stated. At first, no doubt, the Teutonic conquerors took possession of the land they had overrun like the rough freemen they were: every man, great or small, got his share of the conquered territory, and the land was covered, as in their original homes, with a yeomanry slow to call any man master or submit to any authority not of their own making. Inevitably, however, the shares of land that fell to the greater leaders of the invading hosts of freemen very greatly exceeded those which fell to the ordinary soldier, and the king's share was greatest of all. Those to whom the greater grants fell could not use them themselves, but they could perpetuate their personal power and importance by making gifts (*benefices*) out of them to their immediate followers, gifts revocable at will and given upon condition of continued allegiance and service. The new kings, moreover, bound their immediate servants and agents to themselves by a strict oath of *homage*, which rendered them their men and vassals, and made of them as it were a permanent *comitatus*. It was natural to reward such personal agents also with *benefices:* and such a process in time bred an inevitable association of ideas. It came to be expected that vassals should receive gifts of lands from their lords. It also came to be taken for granted that those who received such gifts should render homage to those of whom they accepted them. And so land and vassalage went at last together; and every man who had land enough gave *benefices* out of it in order that he might have bounden vassals.

The service rendered by a vassal was only such service as a freeman might render and not be degraded. It had never been degrading in the eyes of the Teutonic freeman to be of the *comitatus* or personal following of a great leader. It did seem to him degrading to pay money, to do any menial thing, to hold himself liable to any undefined or indefinable service : but military service degraded no man, nor anything that went naturally with it. Moreover, with the greater grants of land it became customary, as the new order of things developed, to grant also a certain wholesale right of jurisdiction and government, a long list of 'Immunities' or exemptions from higher authority in all matters not military, which in effect rendered a great estate a small kingdom. Those who received the greater holdings received also the right to be supreme lords within them: to make their own military levies, to coin their own money, if they chose, to lay taxes, and to hold their own independent courts of justice. Although at first such holdings were theoretically revocable at the will of the grantor, it naturally became more and more difficult to withdraw them. They inevitably became hereditary, and great families throve upon them. ·

The theory of the system was naturally opposed to the principle of inheritance. Each *fief* (as a feudal land gift was called) was held upon condition of military service, and no overlord or grantor could be sure that his vassal's son would be as faithful or as capable as his father. Though the heir took the estate, therefore, it became the practice for him to pay a price for the privilege of succession. The principle of inheritance, when once it crept in, was necessarily the principle of primogeniture: the fief and the responsibilities that went with it could not be divided. To grant any portion of it to another, merely for his use and service, moreover, was forbidden, except for a price paid. The fief must be kept a unit. Vassals, nevertheless, if they had land enough, made themselves masters in turn by granting portions of their land to others, upon a military tenure like their own, which rendered them more powerful without taking away from the obligations which they still owed to their own overlord and *seigneur*. The king was the nominal overlord of all; and upon some he had direct claims of authority. For to some he granted lands and immunities upon condition that they should act as his officers and representatives in the maintenance of his authority amongst the vassals about them. But the very offices became hereditary; grants and sub-grants filled the country with a long series of overlords and tenants; and the king's authority grew very remote indeed. A man's first duty was to his immediate overlord, and the king seemed very far away. The variety was completed by the granting of great territories to the Church; and then the Church feudalized its lands. "Monasteries and bishoprics parted with their land to fighting nobles on the tenure of military service [to be rendered at the call of the king], and received these persons as their vassals."

It was a long time before the small freeholders, come from the loins of the original conquerors, were drawn into the network of this hierarchy. Generation after generation they kept their independence and their separate ownership. But the process of feudalism was in the end too strong for them. The greater feudal lords grew to be too powerful to be safe neighbors; the feudal lawyers established it as a fundamental maxim of the law that there should be no land without its lord or *seigneur;*

and the poorer freemen, their ranks thinned by war, their properties too small to carry the burdens of independence, and their power to combine every year growing less, were fain to 'commend' themselves to the stronger owners near at hand: to give up their lands, that is, into their keeping, and receive them back again upon condition of vassalage.   For the feudal overlord owed protection and all that the word implied to his vassal.   Without an overlord, a man's only redress could be got in the distant courts of the king.   He had no protector at hand but himself. He was outside the fixed order of society, and might any day be compelled to yield to force.   And so, by the two processes of *benefice* and *commendation* the Feudal System was at last completed.

Local Differences in Feudal Development. — There was not, of course, exactly the same method of development everywhere.   In England, under the Saxons, and afterwards under their cousin Danes, the new polity seems to have been held together more than elsewhere by that old cement of personal allegiance, the relations of leader and *comitatus* (pages 96 and 97); in France, and elsewhere on the continent, it was generated more directly by *territorial* connections independent of leadership and following.   In the one case men were apt to own land and possess power because of their personal relations with the king; in the other, they were likely to stand in special personal relations to the king because they owned land of which circumstances had made him titular overlord.   Speaking generally, so as to include both France and England, it may be said that the *benefice* was of two kinds.   The English benefices were most often estates granted by the king to his personal following, to his *comites*, or to his local officers and agents, or to his less independent adherents, on condition that they should hold themselves ever ready to render him full aid and service, and ever continue to adhere to him with special fidelity.   The French benefices were more generally estates originally *allodial* (that is, held under no one, but by an independent title), which had been surrendered to the king, or to some other lord of the new hierarchy, to be received back again as his gift, for the sake of the mutual obligations of faith and support thus established.   Nevertheless, it is not to be understood that benefices were exclusively of the one kind in England, and exclusively of the other kind in France. In France such estates were very often direct gifts from the king or another superior; and in England they were as often surrendered freeholds as rewarding gifts. But each country had its predominant type of the benefice. Its common mark everywhere was that it was a landed estate: not an office or any other gift, but land held upon conditions of fealty to a superior.

Commendation, on the other hand, at first at any rate, had no necessary connection with land. Its predominant feature was a personal relationship which was rather that of master and man than that of landlord and tenant. It seems to have been made necessary by the creation of benefices. As great properties grew up about them, as they became encompassed by the great network of connected estates woven out of the principle of the benefice, small landholders found it necessary to avoid collision with the growing power of their princely neighbors by throwing themselves into the arms of that power, by hastening to conform and make of their own holdings fiefs held of the lord of the greatest contiguous manor; and as society fell thus into regular gradations of personal allegiance based upon property, the freeman who was without property and the native of the conquered territory who found himself suffered to have liberty but not to hold land by any such tenure as would enable him to become a '*beneficiary*,' were both left without a place in the new social order. Owing no definite service to the powerful persons about them, they could claim no protection from them. They could be oppressed without remedy. They were driven, therefore, to '*commend*' themselves to some lord who could afford them security — such security at least as the times permitted — in return for fealty. This was 'commendation.' It had, as I have said, no *necessary* connection with the land, though the small owner as well as the landless person probably became his lord's 'man' rather by commendation than by benefice. It became a universally recognized maxim of law that 'every man must have his lord.' Whether through benefice or through commendation, he must fall into a definite place in the minutely assorted and classified society of feudalism.

Political Disintegration. — The state was thus disintegrated. It no longer acted as a whole, but in semi-independent parts. There was no longer any central authority which acted directly upon all individuals alike throughout a common territory. The king controlled directly, as he had the power, only the greater lords, who were in feudal theory his immediate vassals; other men, lower down in the series, could be reached from above only through *their* immediate masters. Authority filtered down to the lower grades of society through the higher. It was a system, not of general obedience to a common law, but of personal obedience and subordination, founded upon land-ownership.

Such, then, was the Feudal System. The king had no immediate subjects except the greater barons and the vassals on his own baronial estates, and the greater barons were obedient subjects only when he had armed power sufficient to compel them to obey. Their vassals served the king only when they themselves did, and because they did, arming themselves for the king, as they would arm themselves against him, only as their lords commanded. In brief, every baron was himself practically sovereign of those holding under him. It was his decree that sent them into the field; it was his power that defended them against others who would have oppressed or plundered them; and it was in his courts that justice was administered between them. His strength and favor were their shield and title. Law indeed grew up in the shape of custom; but the customs of one barony differed from those of another. Except in so far as the priest and the lawyer revived, in their advice to the magnates who consulted them, the principles of the Roman law, still alive to the studies even of that time, no uniformity of practice prepared a unified system of law for the realm. It was an arrangement of governments within governments, a loosely confederated group of inharmonious petty kingdoms.

The Feudal Conception of Sovereignty. — The most notable feature of feudalism is that in its system sovereignty has become identified with *ownership*. The rights exercised by the barons were in many cases nothing less than sovereign. Not only did they decide property titles by the custom of their baronies and private rights by laws determined in their own courts, they often also coined money, they constantly levied tolls upon commerce, and they habitually made war when they pleased upon rival neighbors. They gathered about them, too, as the king gathered about himself, an immediate following of *knights*, whom they endowed with lands as, so to say, barons of these lesser kingdoms, the greater baronies. They commanded this retinue and exercised these sovereign powers, moreover, because of their relations as owners to the lands and tenantry of their domains. Sovereignty, in this petty parcelled kind, had become a private hereditary possession, an item in family assets. Whoever should be able to accumulate these territorial lordships into one really great kingship would be owner, and, as owner, sovereign of the realm (page 115).

Feudalism and the Towns. — The towns, meantime, stood out with not a little success against feudalization. Many a town was, indeed, dominated by the threatening pile of some baronial castle, built over against it on the strategic vantage ground of hill-summit or river peninsula; and all were constrained sooner or later to yield at least nominal overlordship to some feudal superior. They kept alive, if it were only in tradition, that true conception of political authority which made of it, not a piece of private property to be bartered or sold, but the organized, the uttered will of a community.

The Guilds. — Still, within the cities there early sprang up a semi-feudal organization of society altogether their own. The importance of a town rested, not upon the ownership of lands, though many towns owned not a little land, but upon wealth gained by trade and industry. The internal social organization of the towns, therefore, tended more and more to turn upon the relations of labor. The famous *guild* system sprang into existence. Every handicraftsman, every trader, — like every landowner and every freeman in the society outside the towns, — had to find his place in a sharply differentiated social classification. Each occupation was controlled by its guild; and that guild was a close corporation, admitting to membership only whom it chose. No one could enter save through the stringently guarded avenues of a limited and prescribed apprenticeship; and once in, the apprentice was bound by the rules of his order. City government became representative of the authority of associated guilds. No one was a citizen who was not within one of the privileged associations. It is a reminiscence of this old order of things that the building about which the city government of London, as of many other antique towns, still centres is known as the 'Guildhall.' Even the militia of the towns were train-bands from the several guilds. The town, also, had created its 'estates,' its orders, as the country had done. This was its feudal system.

The City Leagues. — The greater trading towns nearer the Baltic and along the Rhine in France and in Italy took advantage, during the thirteenth century, of the opportunities for independent action afforded by the piecemeal condition of feudal authority to draw together into leagues, the better to pursue their own objects; and for a long time these leagues exercised the powers of great states, making war and peace, levying custom, concluding treaties and alliances. Their primary object was to cure those disorders of the times which made the roads unsafe and interfered with their trade. The greatest of these leagues were the *Hansa*, more commonly known in English writings as the Hanseatic (*Hansa* means trade-guild), and the *Rhenish*. The former centred about the great cities of Lübeck and Hamburg, and at one time included ninety of the towns lying between the Baltic and the Elbe. The latter had Worms and Mainz as its leaders, and at one time or another had connections with seventy towns, some of which stood as far away from the Rhine as Bremen and Nuremberg, though the arteries of trade which it was meant to protect and keep open lay chiefly along the Rhine valley. Many great princes were constrained to connect themselves with these leagues in the heyday of their power. But trade alliances afforded too many occasions for jealous discords, and the growth of vast territorial monarchies too dangerous rivalries for the cities; and their leagues were eventually broken up.

Unifying Influences. — Two unifying influences operated more or less potently during the Middle Ages to counteract the disintegrating tendencies of the feudal system. These were the *Roman Catholic Church* and the *Holy Roman Empire*. Both the Church and the Empire may be said to have been shadows of imperial Rome. They were, by intention at least, the temporal and spiritual halves of the old empire of the Cæsars.

The Roman Catholic Church had, historically, a real connection with the veritable dominion of Rome. Before the Empire had been shattered by the onset of Teutons and Turks, Christianity had become its recognized official religion. The Pope in Rome represented one of the great primacies which had early grown up within the imperial Church: and this Church of the West, sundered from the Church of the East by irreconcilable differences of doctrine, showed an instinct for conquest which seemed a direct heritage from the great pagan Rome of the olden time. She mastered the new masters, the Teutons, and everywhere insinuated herself into the new political system which developed under their hand. Not only had every castle its chaplain, every city and country-side its priest, but the greater ecclesiastics themselves became feudal lords, masters of baronies, members alike of the civil and the religious hierarchies; and even monasteries owned vast estates which were parcelled out upon a feudal tenure.

But for all it was so interwoven with the feudal system, the Church retained its internal unity. The Pope's power did not fall apart as did the king's. The priest acknowledged in all things his allegiance to a universal kingdom, the spiritual kingdom of the Church of Rome. The Church recognized no boundaries, whether of baronies or of states, as limits to her own spiritual sovereignty. Her authority extended, she claimed, over all kings of whatsoever grade, over all men of whatsoever rank or estate. The silent, unarmed forces of her influence, therefore, stood always on the side of an ideal unity. And they certainly retarded disintegration. Her lesson was brotherhood and a common subjection; and that lesson, though often neglected, was never utterly lost sight of or forgotten. She kept alive, moreover, in her canon law, much of the civil law of Rome; *her* laws at any rate were not diverse, but always the same; they reached the people and the conceptions of the time through the administration not only of her ecclesiastical courts, but also, indirectly no doubt, through the judgments of the baronial courts of the baron-bishops : and whatever tended to unify law tended to unify politics. The ecclesiastical power was always on the side of any good Catholic who proved himself capable of creating larger wholes of political authority, larger areas of civil unity. By precept and by example the Church was imperial.

The Holy Roman Empire. — Under the direct descendants of Chlodwig, the once vast dominions of the Franks fell asunder in several pieces ; but Charles the Great (768–814) reunited and even extended them. He brought together under his sword much of the territory now included in Germany, Switzerland, Italy (all save the southernmost part), France, and Belgium. And neither any Teuton nor any successor of Teutons in western Europe ever gathered wide territories under his sway without dreaming of restoring the Roman Empire and himself ascending the throne of the Cæsars. From Charles the Great to the present German Kaiser the spell of the Roman example has bound the imagination of every European conqueror. Charles had this ambition clearly in his view, and circumstances peculiarly favored its realization. At the same time that he reached the height of his power, Rome reached the acme of her discontent with what she considered the heresies of the Eastern See, and the political disorders at Constantinople gave the Roman pontiff pretext for casting finally loose from all Eastern connections. The Empress Irene deposed her son and usurped his throne; the Italians declared that no woman could succeed to the titles of the Cæsars ; and the Pope, arrogating to himself the prerogatives of king-maker, crowned Charles the Great emperor of what later generations have known as the Holy Roman Empire, — ' Holy ' because created by the authority of mother Church.

Here was a real ' Western Empire '; the first had been only an administrative half of the once undivided dominions of the emperors. Charles gave to his empire real vitality while he lived ; he, moreover, did what he could to hasten civil unity by promulgating anew the Visigothic version of the Roman law (page 100) ; and, although his empire broke up upon his death, an almost uninterrupted line of emperors, of one great feudal house or another, carried the titles of Rome through the Middle Ages to modern times, now and again backing them with real power and always preserving for Germany a shadow at least of unity in a time of real disintegration. Believing themselves, besides, in the early times at any rate, the lineal and legitimate successors of the Cæsars, there was special reason why every emperor should continue to build, so far as he had the opportunity, as Charles the Great had begun to build, on the law of Rome as a foundation, never designedly, as Charles the Bald declared, enacting anything repugnant to it. All who from time to time drew to the side of the imperial power in the conflicts of disordered ages also naturally affected the language and principles of the same system. The Empire was, therefore, not only sometimes a silent witness and sometimes a great power for unification, but also always a steady influence on the side of a system of law more advanced and unifying than that of feudalism.

Centralizing Forces: the Carolingians. — The rise of the family of Charles the Great into power illustrates the character of the chief, indeed the only potent, centralizing forces of the feudal time. Those forces lay in the ambition of great barons. Under the descendants of Chlodwig (the Merowingians) the territory of the Franks tended more and more to become permanently divided into two distinct parts. There were often, it is true, more parts than two: for it was the Frankish custom to divide even a royal inheritance between all the sons of a deceased possessor. But, as it fell out in the long run, the most permanent division was that between Neustria (the western half) and Austrasia (the eastern). In both of these kingdoms the Merowingian rulers soon degenerated into mere shadows of their imperative, dominant ancestors; and they were presently displaced by a powerful family of Austrasia, the family of Charles Martel. Charles Martel was Mayor of the Palace under the Austrasian branch of the royal family. The office of Mayor of the Palace, though an office in the king's household, was, it would seem, filled rather by dictation of the powerful lords of the kingdom than by a free royal choice. It was filled, consequently, at any rate in the times of which I am now speaking, by the leader of the great territorial chiefs, by the leader, that is, of the king's rivals in power. It had indeed become an hereditary office held by the greatest of the baronial families. Charles Martel was a soldier of genius: he handed his office on to his son and his grandson: and they were men abler than he. His son, Pepin, with the sanction of the Pope, whom he had greatly served, became king of the Franks, in name as well as in reality, to the final ousting of the old line of 'do-nothing' monarchs; and Pepin's grandson was Charles the Great.

The Capets: Concentration of Feudal Power. — In the tenth century a similar change was wrought in France. The descendants of Charles Martel (Carolingians) had in their turn lost vigor and become unfit for power. They were displaced, therefore, in the western half of their dominions (in Neustria) by a family of warriors whom they had endowed first with the county of Paris, and afterwards with the duchy of France, as at once a reward for their services in withstanding the incursions of the Northmen and a stake in the threatened territory. The duchy of France was only a comparatively small district about Paris; but the vigor and capacity of the Capets, its dukes, speedily made it one of the most important feudal properties in the whole of the great territory to which it was eventually to give its name. They became the chiefs of the baronial party, and when discontent with the Carling kings culminated it was they who became first 'kings of the barons,' and finally kings of France. Refusing to degenerate, as the Merowingian and Carolingian princes had degenerated, they continued to develop, generation after generation, a kingdom destined one day to rank with the greatest of Europe; and that by a process planned as if meant to illustrate how best the feudal system might be used for its own destruction. By every means, — by war, by marriage, by contract, by stratagem, by fraud, — they drew all the greater feudal sovereignties into their own possession, until at length, their duchy of France and the kingdom of France were indeed identical; until, having absorbed all scattered authorities, they had made sovereignty, once possessed privately in sundered pieces, again a whole,— but a whole which, by the strict logic of feudalism, was their private estate; until they almost literally possessed the land, and Louis XIV. could say with little exaggeration, '*L'état c'est moi.*' They had gathered the fragments of the feudal system into a single hand, and had made the state itself a feudal possession, a family estate.

The Piecing together of Austria and Prussia. — Later still the same process was repeated in Prussia and in Austria. By conquest, inheritance, forfeiture, marriage, contract, fraud, powerful feudal families pieced together those great kingdoms, to become in after times the bases of national organization.   In neither Prussia nor Austria did the process go so far as in France, though Austria, under the house of Habsburg, became possessor of the imperial throne of the Holy Roman Empire, and Prussia, under the house of Hohenzollern, has become the central and dominant state of a new German Empire.

THE DIFFUSION OF ROMAN LAW IN EUROPE.

From the fifth to the twelfth centuries Roman law inhered in the confused civil methods of the times for the most part as a mere unsystematized miscellany of rules applicable to the descendants of the Roman provincials and observed largely within the towns.   As the old distinctions between Roman and Teuton faded away, however, in the gradual mixture of the populations, these rules entered more and more into the general mass of common custom.   This process was in great part unconscious; there was no scientific selection in the development.

The Barbaric Codes. — It was not from mere tradition, however,— not simply from Roman law transmuted into unrecorded provincial custom,— that the knowledge of these centuries concerning the civil law of the Empire was derived, but from fragments of the Theodosian legislation and of the writings of the jurists which had found embodiment in the Code of Alaric II. (page 100), which is known to quotation as the Breviary (*breviarium Alaricianum*).   The West Goths themselves had not long remained contented with that compend of the law.   In the seventh century there had been prepared in Spain a new *Lex Visigothorum* which contained a summary, not of Roman rules only, but of Gothic custom as well, and which, superseding the earlier compilation of Alaric, formed the basis for later codifications of Spanish law. But the south of France, which had once owned the dominion of the Visigoth, retained the Code of Alaric; it was transmitted thence to the north of France, to be handed on to Germany and England ; and for all of these countries it continued to be the chief, if not the only, source of Roman law until the eleventh or twelfth century. Charles the Great, as I have said, republished it, accepting it as the recognized manual of Roman legal principle. Even Italy had had the continuity of her legal tradition broken by barbarian invasion, — especially by the inroad of the raw Lombards, — and had had to keep the fragments together as best she might amidst just such a confusion of 'personal' laws as prevailed elsewhere in the once Roman world (page 98).

Custom and Written Law in France. — It was at this time that the north and south of France came to be distinguished as respectively the 'country of custom' (*pays de coutume*) and the 'country of written law' (*pays de droit écrit*). In the south, which had been thoroughly Romanized for centuries, there was the written law of Rome ; in the north, which had never been so thoroughly Romanized, and which was now in its northern part quite thoroughly Germanized, there reigned in unrestrained confusion the Teutonic customs of the barbarian masters.

The Study of the Roman Law. — But in the twelfth century the law of Rome fell upon the good fortune of being systematically studied once more by competent scholars, and once more cultivated by scientific lawyers. And not the Code of Alaric, but the vastly more perfect *Corpus Juris Civilis*, as the twelfth century called it, Justinian's (or, rather, Trebonian's) great compilation, was the basis of the revived study. The new cultivation of the law began, naturally enough, in the Italian cities. There the movements of trade were quick and various ; and there a various population was not only mixed of many elements but fused and united, by intermarriage no less than by close social, political, and commercial intercourse. For the quick, informal, multifarious operations of trade Teutonic law

had made no more suitable provision than had the *jus civile* in
the old days at Rome: a *jus gentium* was needed such as the
Roman jurisprudence stood ready to supply. 'Personal' law
could not obtain where elements were so fused and united by
common undertakings and interests as well as by an actual mixture of bloods. "In Justinian's Digest the Italian jurists of the
twelfth century found a system of law that was adequate to the
needs of the new commerce;" and great schools sprang promptly
into existence for its study and propagation. The first of these
was also to be the most famous, the University of Bologna, established late in the eleventh century, and destined to become the
chief seat of the study of the Roman code. Pisa and other Italian
cities then took up the new pursuit. Presently the interest
had spread to France and to Spain, going in France first to
Montpellier and Paris, afterwards to Bourges, Orléans, and Toulouse, the old capital of the West Goths; and in Spain creating
(A.D. 1254) the notable University of Salamanca. From Spain
and France, Holland caught the fashion, giving to Europe in the
seventeenth century the illustrious jurist Hugo Grotius, who
created out of the great principles of equity discoverable in
Roman Law the elevated and influential science of International
Law. In England, too, the same studies began to be affected
almost immediately after the rise of the school of Bologna, and
are said to have been regularly pursued there down to the sixteenth century.

This sudden spread and luxuriance of the study is impressive evidence of a common preparation and need for it. The
cultivation of the Roman law in the schools may in some instances indicate a clerical influence; but the study was too general
and too spontaneous to be attributable mainly to this or to any
other single cause.

Influence of the Schools. — The Italian schools of law
almost immediately drew to them students from all parts of
Europe, and, in time, "sent out masters and doctors by the hundreds." Priests and laymen alike got their training in them.
"Returning to their homes, the civil doctors crowded the hereditary expounders of local usage off the judicial bench. Under the
fostering care of kings and princes," interested to see a centralized

power built up by their courts, there grew up everywhere bodies of accomplished lawyers and a 'learned judiciary'; and "Europe obtained a common commercial law in the *Corpus Juris Civilis*, as it had obtained a common family law in the *Corpus Juris Canonici*," the developed jurisprudence of the Church.

> **The materials** upon which teachers and students alike worked in the schools were not the pure sources of the Roman law, but a mixture of Roman, canonical, and Lombard law which showed the influence of an earlier cultivation of jurisprudence by learned men among the Lombards in their school at Pavia.

Influence of the Church. — The Roman Church had early effected a conquest of the Teutonic invaders, and the new masters of Europe had left its organizations intact. "It cared for education and dispensed charity. It drew into its domain the entire control of the family relations. It undertook, partly in its own interest, to enforce testaments," or wills, after the Roman manner. The Teutonic peoples, held together by ties of consanguinity and accustomed to communal rather than to individual ownership in matters of property, had not admitted to their law conceptions of free contract, individual ownership, and succession by will such as the developed jurisprudence of Rome had given currency to. But the will, the contract, and the principle of separate ownership were indispensable to the Church if she was to build up her properties by the gifts and devises of pious persons to whom her priests were permitted to minister. "They were also characteristic and essential elements in the civilization amid which the Church had been reared to maturity." (Maine.) The whole weight of the Church's power was thrown, therefore, in favor of the adoption of these important doctrines and practices out of the law of Rome. And she was able to make her great influence tell in all the matters to which she gave her attention because she "had brought over from the Roman into the mediæval world a well-developed governmental organization. She added to this a complete set of courts, with appeal to Rome." (Smith.) And her priests possessed the learning of the time; were indispensable as counsellors and administrators, no less than as clerks; were the compilers of codes, whether of Roman or of Teutonic rules; had in all things the ascendency of training and knowledge.

The currency of the Latin language had also its influence
in spreading abroad the forces which were to bring in the Roman
law. It was everywhere in Europe the speech of commerce, of
learning, and of public business: the common repository and
vehicle of knowledge and of the forms of important transactions.

Entrance of Roman Law into the Legal Systems of Europe.
— Of course this widespread interest in the study of Roman law
was not all speculative. The study and the practice of the law
acted and reacted on one another. Its rules were more and more
consciously and skilfully fitted into the growing law of the kingdoms which were emerging from the feudal system because it was
being adequately mastered and systematized at the universities;
and it was being mastered and systematized at the universities
because it was being more and more called for in the actual administration of justice. Its use and its cultivation went hand in
hand.

In France. — Roman law came into use with much the
same pace with which the Capets advanced to complete power,
and triumphed with the perfecting of the centralization which
they effected. Louis IX. ordered the Roman law translated into
French; established the right of the crown to hear appeals from
the feudal courts in all cases; sent royal judges on circuit to
hear complaints of infringed rights; and erected at Paris the
famous *Parliament of Paris* as the supreme tribunal of the realm.
The feudal lords of France were the nominal members of this
court, but trained jurists (*legistes*), appointed as experts to assist
them, became in practice its real members. Schooled in the
Roman law, they admitted its principles into all their decisions;
and they gave to the king from the same source the maxim which
declared the will of the prince to be law. As the king's jurisdiction grew, the principles of Roman jurisprudence gained wider
and wider acceptance and supremacy.

The Method by which Roman law crept in was always the
same: it was introduced, not by legislation, but by adjudication,
by the decision of cases in the royal courts. It was here that the
learning of the trained lawyers told, and the desire of the king
to see the single power of the throne magnified. The royal

courts, as they were developed in the provinces, applied local custom in their decisions, for the most part, only upon very conclusive proof of its existence and its definiteness, and in the absence of definite and conclusive proof of a contrary custom resorted always to the Roman as to a 'common' law. The law grew thus, and was made consistent, by judgment, by written opinion, by royal ordinance; and a French jurisprudence began to make its appearance, working upon the various materials which were to enter into the final law of the land.

And presently the Roman law came, so to say, from out the nation to meet the royal system. Very early in Berri, Bourbonnais, and Auvergne, the central districts of France, the law of Rome had been consciously adopted as the common law of the land, to be appealed to in the absence of proof of any special custom or enactment. Subsequently it came to be considered as in some sort the supplementary common law of all France, for, though never established as such in the north of France, it was even there appealed to in doubtful cases as 'written reason.' The *Code Napoléon*, the last great codification of French law, has been described as in great part a republication of the laws of Justinian as those laws have been modified and fitted to new circumstances by the processes of French history.

Local Customs in France. — It is important to observe that the unifying, harmonizing influences exercised by the growing royal jurisdiction were, for a long time at any rate, influences which affected *procedure* much more than the internal, essential elements of legal principle. The differentiation between district and district which had taken place in the process of feudalization had been of the sharpest, most decided character. When the Capets first assumed the titles of kingship there were duchies as great as France. The work of extending and consolidating the kingdom consumed several centuries; and, meanwhile, each petty sovereignty was developing its own law apart. Much of the territory which afterwards became part of France was, during the same period, moreover, in foreign hands, held by England or Burgundy. The kingdom as finally consolidated, therefore, presented a very great variety of deeply rooted and persistent local laws and customs. Normandy had one set of customs, Berri a very different set, Anjou a third, Brittany a fourth; and so throughout the once piecemeal country.

Unifying Influence of the Royal Prerogative. — The influence of the royal jurisdiction upon this heterogeneous mass of differing laws was, as I have said, at first rather to unify and systematize the procedure of the local courts, which administered local law, than to effect changes in the local customs themselves. Since appeals to the king's justice were possible in all cases, the formal method of appeal tended to become the same everywhere; and the methods of the king's courts in dealing with appealed cases more and more tended to set the fashion of procedure throughout the loose system, though the royal judges continued to decide appealed cases according to the law of the district from which they were brought up.

By degrees, however, new ideas and principles, as well as new modes of procedure and appeal, were infused into local justice. The law and the legal practice of each district alike more and more distinctly and consciously approximated to the models of organization and to the standards of decision obtaining in the king's courts. The territorial tribunals accepted the services of lawyers trained in Roman principles and inclined towards regal precedents; and the local law officers of the crown were of course everywhere ready to effect whatever was within reach of their functions or example in the way of bringing local custom around to the rules of universal acceptance to be found in Roman law and regal decision. Independently, moreover, of the influence of the crown, the Roman law was entering the local courts, becoming common law in Auvergne and Bourbonnais, as we have seen, before it became the common law of France.

Through the *Parliament of Paris* the Roman law had, so to say, a double door of entrance. The jurisdiction of that court was both spiritual and temporal: so that both the Code of Justinian and the canons of the Church contributed their versions of Roman judicial practice and tradition to its findings.

In the Code Napoléon, the final codification of French law as it had emerged from the long processes of the Middle Ages, we find a statement of the law which was in fact made possible by the earlier labors of great French jurists, like the accomplished

Pothier. In matters of inheritance, in the rules which govern the family relations, and in the law of marriage the customs of France find their place, though as if they had been digested and formed anew under the influence of the Roman jurisprudence. In the law of contract, the law of property, the rules of judicial trial, and all questions of the legal burdens which may be placed upon land, Roman law has had a chief place of influence. Everywhere, however, there are traces and elements of fusion. It is a law written over with history and with the labors of trained students of the law.

In Germany there was no central power such as that which served to build together the legal systems of France and of England. The feudal system had done its work more thoroughly there than elsewhere : and Germany emerged from the Middle Ages, not a nation, but a congeries of petty states. There was a form of union among them, indeed, in the Holy Roman Empire, and throughout all the changes of German history the imperial influence had sought to shelter and to foster Roman law, the law of empire and of princely rule. The imperial courts, the imperial lawyers, the imperial party in Germany, were always administrators or advocates of its principles; and when the house of Habsburg came to the imperial throne, as when other powerful emperors had reigned, there was no small potency in these influences. But the final reception of the Roman law was postponed in Germany until the sixteenth century, and was due to other forces than those associated with the royal power.

Germany's Reception of Roman Law. — The reception of the Roman law into the law of Germany was due to various circumstances, but not entirely to the poverty or imperfections of German law. German law at some points may fairly be said to have been superior to Roman law in its suitability to the needs and conditions of the time. Neither was the law of Rome received as naturally supplementary to German law and of a sort to effect its further and more complete development; for there were not a few radical oppositions of principle between the two systems. For example, Roman law was based upon the recognition of the entire equality of persons, while German law ranked them in orders, with differing values and privileges ; Roman law allowed the free alienation of land and set up the principle of absolute individual ownership, while German law had at its root ideas of communal and family ownership and put many restrictions upon alienation.   Moreover, there could be no doubt that the law of feudal relationships had had as complete a development in Germany as anywhere else in the European world ; and yet, along with the Roman law, which she took from the schools and commentators of Italy, Germany took also the Italian Feudal Law, to which the Italian students had given a similar systematic formulation.

The Roman law was received in Germany largely because of the feebleness and disintegration of the judicial system there; because the old popular courts, which administered only an unchanging custom and tradition, inevitably decayed with the growth of society ; because single judges trained to the law were substituted, and the only law in which one could be trained was the Roman law of the Italian schools.   The introduction took place, not because princes controlled the courts, but because litigants insisted.   They were dissatisfied with the administration of justice in the unlearned courts.   They wanted a court, a judge, learned in the law.   " The single judge must be a learned judge, by the same necessity by which the old popular court was an unlearned court."

Throughout the Middle Ages the popular courts remained the only vital courts in Germany ; when they first began to give way their place was taken by courts that were no better, being made up of some unlearned agent of the feudal lord of the district, assisted by assessors as little trained for the function as he.   In France and in England a native jurisprudence grew up, because the royal power was able to set up a system of courts, to put trained officers into them, and to draw differing local customs to a common administration and development.   But there was no power capable of rendering the like service in Germany ; the decay of the popular courts did not mean the substitution of an indigenous learning.   The single judges finally set up there were learned, if trained at all to the law, in the Italian jurisprudence.   Germans had long studied in Italy ; and the Roman law of the Italian schools was taught from their foundation in the

German universities. All theological students were obliged to study the Roman and canonical law as part of their regular professional training; for it formed the basis of the administration of the spiritual courts, which had so long stood alongside the courts of ordinary law in every part of Europe.

The law that was received was not the *Corpus Juris* of Justinian, but the common law of Italy, founded upon the Roman, the canon, and the Lombard law. "The *Corpus Juris* was *terra incognita* to the German jurists of the period of the reception." They brought in, "not the Pandects, but the *Usus modernus Pandectarum* of the Italian lawyers." The new law was not, of course, accepted whole and in bulk. It entered, in Germany as elsewhere, as 'subsidiary' law, not as the native law of the land. It nevertheless received everywhere a decided preference in the courts. While accepting Roman legal rules as *prima facie* conclusive of the rights of a suitor, they imposed upon those who alleged established local usage in opposition to it the necessity of furnishing conclusive proof of the existence and acceptance of such usage as law. Roman law, in brief, they accepted on its own authority, Germanic custom only on the authority of indubitable circumstantial testimony.

The outcome was that, speaking most generally, the Roman law prevailed in the field of procedure, in the field of criminal law, in the field of contract, and in the field of the law of inheritance; while German law persisted in respect of the law of real property, in respect of family law, and wherever law was to be drawn on to the recognition of new relationships, like those of association and incorporation, in a changing society.

In England, a strong native jurisprudence kept the foreign law out. Always held off from the rest of Europe by the sea, a separate system of law was made possible for her, no less than an independent government. The royal power was able to make of the favored island a compact kingdom : and men of the masterful Plantagenet blood gave it a centralized administration of justice such as no other European state was able to obtain while yet it was in its early formative stage of growth. English judges put together a consistent English law, and there was no need for a foreign jurisprudence.

And yet the Roman law was not wholly excluded. The Romans had governed Britain four hundred years, bending the province to the purposes of their administration with their usual thoroughness. We know that Papinian, the greatest of Rome's jurists, himself administered the law in Britain, and we have every reason to believe that its promulgation there was thorough, its rootage full four hundred years deep. It can hardly be that the Saxons wholly eradicated it. We know that many Roman municipalities on the island survived all conquests: and we know that the priests of the Church of Rome early took back to Englished Britain conceptions steeped in Roman jurisprudence. Bede testifies that the Saxon laws were codified under the auspices of the clergy and that Roman codification was the model. We have seen that Roman law was studied in England almost as early as in mediæval Italy herself, the study being continued without serious break for more than three centuries (page 117); and the works of the earliest English legal text-writers, such as Glanvil, Bracton, and the author of the *Fleta*, abound in tokens of a close familiarity with the laws of the imperial codes, are full of their very phraseology indeed. The so-called laws of Henry I. are said by competent legal scholars to consist, to the extent of fully one-half their content, of precepts borrowed from Rome. Through the ecclesiastical courts, which down to the middle of the present century administered upon all estates in England, and upon all trusts; through the Court of Chancery, whence has issued the system of English equity, and which was presided over in its formative period by the great ecclesiastics who were the first chancellors, afterwards by great lawyers, such as Lord Hardwicke and Lord Thurlow, deeply versed in the civil law of Rome and apt to draw suggestion and even concrete rule from it; and through the Admiralty Courts, always controlled by the rules of the Civil Law, England has drawn directly or indirectly from Roman sources, in supplement of her own indigenous customs; and not many portions of her law have escaped being in some degree marked by the same influences that have moulded the law of the rest of Europe. Her borrowings, nevertheless, have been of form and method rather than of substance, and the great bulk of her law is her own.

REPRESENTATIVE AUTHORITIES.

Adams, George B., Civilization during the Middle Ages, New York, 1894.

Brunner, H., Deutsche Rechtsgeschichte. 2 vols., 1887–1892.

Bryce, The Holy Roman Empire. New York, 1911.

Church, R. W., The Beginning of the Middle Ages. (Series of *Epochs of Modern History.*) London, 1910.

Curteis, A. M., History of the Roman Empire from the Death of Theodosius the Great to the Coronation of Charles the Great, 395–800. 1875.

Duruy, Victor, Histoire du Moyen Âge, depuis la chute de l'Empire d'Occident jusqu'au milieu du XVe Siècle. 1 vol. Paris. 8th ed., 1875. Trans. by G. B. Adams, New York, 1891.

Emerton, E., Introduction to the Study of the Middle Ages, Boston, 1889, and Mediæval Europe, Boston, 1894.

Freeman, E. A., Historical Essays. Series I.

Gibbon, E., Decline and Fall of the Roman Empire. Smith's ed. New York, 1880.

Guizot, F., Lectures on the History of Civilization in France and in Europe.

Hallam, H., View of the State of Europe during the Middle Ages, especially Chapter II., which contains what is possibly the best brief account in English of the Feudal System.

Heeren, A. H. L., Manual of the History of the Political System of Europe and Its Colonies. Oxford, 1834.

Kingsley, Chas., The Roman and the Teuton.

Macaulay, T. B., Essay on Ranke's History of the Popes.

Milman, H. H., History of Latin Christianity. 8 vols. New York.

Oman, Ch., Europe, 476–918, New York and London, 1893.

Ranke, L. von, History of the Popes.

Schroeder, R., Lehrbuch der deutschen Rechtsgeschichte. 3d ed., 1898.

Sheppard, J. G., The Fall of Rome and the Rise of the New Nationalities. 1 vol. London and New York, 1861.

Concerning the introduction of Roman law into modern European legal systems, see, besides authorities mentioned at end of Chapter II. —

Jenks, Edward, Law and Politics in the Middle Ages, 2nd ed. London. 1913–1917.

Sohm, Rudolf, Die deutsche Rechtsentwickelung und die Codifications-frage, in Grünhut's *Zeitschrift für das Privat und Oeffentliche Recht der Gegenwart*, I., 245–280.

Stein, Lorenz, Das Wesen der Reception und die Reception des griech-ischen Rechts im römischen Recht, in Grünhut, I. 722 ff.

Stephen, Sir James, Lectures on the History of France, especially lectures I.–V., inclusive.

Tomkins, F. J., and *Jencken*, H. D., Modern Roman Law.

Vinogradoff, P., Roman Law in Mediæval Europe.   London and New York, 1909.

Waitz, Georg, Deutsche Verfassungsgeschichte, 8 vols.   The classical work on early Germanic institutions and the development of the German constitution.

VII.

THE GOVERNMENT OF FRANCE.

——oo⋮o⋮oo——

The Growth of the French Monarchy. — The full political significance of the history of France can be appreciated only by those who keep in mind the chief phenomena of the widening monarchy, the successive steps by which the Dukes of France, the capable Capets, extended their power and the name of their duchy over the whole of the great territory which was to be inherited by Louis XIV. The course of French history is from complex to simple. In the days of Hugh Capet 'France' was the name of only a single duchy centering in Paris, of but one of a great number of feudal lordships equally great, equally vigorous, equally wedded to independence. The duchy's advantage lay in the fact that her dukes had been chosen for leadership and that they were capable of leadership, rather than in the possession of preponderant strength or superior resources. To the west of her lay the solid mass of Normandy; to the north lay the territories of the Counts of Flanders and Vermandois, and to the east the territory of the Count of Champagne; southward lay the great duchies of Burgundy and Aquitaine, beyond them the lands of Toulouse; alongside of Normandy, Anjou and Brittany stretched their independent length to the west. And these were only the greater feudal sovereignties. Within and about them lay other districts not a few with masters ready to assert privileges without number in contradiction of all central rule. The early history of France is the history of a duchy striving to become a kingdom. 'France' holds a good strategic position, and fortune has made her dukes titular kings over their feudal neighbors, but still she is in reality only one among many duchies.

By slow and steady steps, nevertheless, a work of unification is wrought out by the Capets. In every direction they stretch out from their central duchy of France their hand of power and of intrigue and draw the pieces of feudalized Neustria together into a compact mass. The work is thoroughly done, moreover, at almost every stage. Out of populations as heterogeneous as any in Europe they construct a nation singularly homogeneous; out of feudal lordships as strong, as numerous, as heady, and as stiffly separate as any other equal territory could show, they construct a single kingdom more centralized and compacted than any other in Europe. The processes of these remarkable achievements give to the history of the French monarchy its distinctive political significance: the means which the Capets devised for solidifying, and, after its solidification, for enlarging and effectuating their power, furnish some of the most suggestive illustrative material anywhere to be found for the general history of government.

Perfection of the Feudal System in France. — The feudal system worked its most perfect work in France. The opportunities of feudalism there were great. Neustria, the western, Gallic half of the great Frankish kingdom, was early separated from Austrasia, the eastern, Germanic half (pages 114–115), and its separateness proved the cause of its disintegration. Burgundy, Brittany, and Aquitaine sprang to the possession of unchecked independent power round about it; the Normans thrust their huge wedge of territory into it; battle after battle between those who contended for the possession of the pieces of the great empire which Charles the Great had swept together first decimated and finally quite annihilated the sturdy class of Frankish freemen whose liberties had stood in the way of local feudal absolutism; privilege grew in the hands of feudal lords while prerogative declined in the hands of those who sought to be kings; those who possessed privilege built for themselves impregnable castles behind whose walls they could securely retain it: — and feudalism had its heyday in France.

It is reckoned that in Hugh Capet's day the "free and noble population" of the country out of which modern France was to be made numbered "about a million of souls, living on and taking their names from about seventy thousand separate fiefs or properties: of these fiefs about three thousand carried titles with them. Of these again, no less than a hundred, — some reckon as many as a hundred and fifty, — were sovereign states, greater or smaller, whose lords could coin money, levy taxes, make laws, administer their own justice." [1] Of these one hundred, however, only some eight or ten were really powerful states.

Materials of the Monarchy. — Such were the materials out of which the Capets had to build up their monarchy. It was their task to undo the work of feudalism. Nor were these the only materials that they had to handle in the difficult undertaking. There were other privileges besides those of the feudal barons which it was necessary to destroy or subordinate before they could see their power compact and undisputed.

Local Self-government. — Notwithstanding the fact that in most districts of the divided territory the power that ruled him was brought close to every man's door in the person of his feudal lord and master, there were many corners of the system which sheltered vigorous local self-government. The period of the greatest vitality of the feudal system was, indeed, the only period of effectual local self-government that France has ever yet known. The eventual supremacy of the Crown, which snatched their power from the barons, also destroyed local self-government, which the barons had in many cases suffered to grow; and neither the Revolution nor any of the governments which have succeeded the Revolution has yet restored it to complete life. Local liberties were taking form and acquiring vigor during the very period in which the monarchical power was making its way towards supremacy; and it was by these local liberties that the kings found themselves faced when their initial struggle with feudalism was over. It was their final task to destroy them by perfecting centralized administrative organization.

Rural Communes. — While feudalism was in its creative period, while the forces were at work, that is, which were shaping the relations of classes and of authorities to each other, it was not uncommon for feudal lords to grant charters to the rural communes lying within their demesnes. In and after the twelfth century these charters became very numerous. They permitted a separate organic structure to the communes, regulated the admission of persons to communal privileges, laid down rules for

[1] G. W. Kitchin, *History of France*, Vol. I., p. 186.

the administration of property in the commune, set forth feudal rights and duties, prescribed the corvées, etc. "Everywhere a general assembly of the inhabitants directly regulated affairs," delegating executive functions to communal officers, who acted separately, each in the function with which he was specially charged. These officers convoked the general assembly of the people for every new decision that it became necessary to take with reference to communal affairs. The principal affairs within the jurisdiction of the assembly were, "the administration of communal property, which in that period was very important, police, and the collection of the taxes both royal and local." [1]

In the administration of justice, also, the Middle Ages witnessed in France not a few features of popular privilege. The peasant as well as the nobleman had the right to be tried by his peers, — by persons of his own origin and station. In the courts of the feudal barons the vassals were present to act as judges, much as the freemen were present in the English county courts (secs. 836, 942).

Liberties of Towns: the Roman Municipalities. — The privileges of self-direction granted to the rural communes, however, were privileges granted, so to say, *inside vassalage:* the members of the communes were not freed from their constant feudal duties. Many towns, on the contrary, acquired and maintained a substantial independence. When the earliest Frankish kings failed in their efforts to establish a power in Gaul as strong and as whole as the Roman power had been, and the Frankish dominion fell apart into fragments whose only connection was a nominal subordination to a central throne, there were others besides the great landowners to avail themselves of the opportunity to set up independent sovereign powers of their own. The Franks, as we have seen, had found many Roman cities in Gaul, and, not at first taking kindly to town life, had simply conquered them and then let them be (page 101). In these, consequently, the old Roman organization had endured, freed from Roman dictation. The Franks who entered them later took character from them almost as much as they gave character to them. Germanic principles of moot-government and individual freedom entered,

---

[1] H. de Ferron, *Institutions Municipales et Provinciales Comparées*, p. 3.

to a certain extent, like a new life-blood into the Roman forms, and compact, spirited, aggressive, disciplined communities were formed which were quick to lay hold of large privileges of self-rule, and even to assume semi-baronial control of the lands lying about them, in the days when independent powers were to be had for the seizing. The organization which Roman influences had bequeathed to these towns was oligarchical, aristocratic: the governing power rested with close corporations, with councils (*curiæ*) which were coöptative, filling their own vacancies. But forces presently appeared in them which worked effectually for democracy. The Christian Church, as well as the barbarian Teuton, took possession of Gaul: the greater towns became the seats of bishops; and the bishops threw their weight on the side of the commons against both the counts outside the towns and the oligarchs inside. Only so could the magnates of the Church establish themselves in real power. In most cases the ecclesiastics and their restless allies, the commons, won in the contest for supremacy, and democracy was established.

The Italian towns, with their 'consuls' and their other imitations of the old Roman republican constitution, are perhaps the best examples of this renaissance of democracy.

The Non-Roman Municipalities. — These Roman towns, however, were to be found for the most part only in the south and along the Rhine. North of the Loire, as the Franks took gradually to city life, there sprang up other towns, of Germanic origin and character; and these were not slow to agitate for grants of special privileges from their baronial masters. In very large numbers they obtained charters, — charters, however, which were to give them a connection with the feudal system about them which the towns of the south, antedating feudalism, did not for some time possess. They were given substantial privileges of self-government, but they were not severed from baronial control. They conducted their affairs, on the contrary, under charters in which the relative (customary) rights of both seigneur and *burgher* were definitely ascertained, by which seigneurial authority as well as burgher privilege was fully recognized, and under which, moreover, the authority of the seigneur was actively exercised through the instrumentality of a *Prévot*, the lord's servant and representative in city affairs.

This, the more secure form of municipal self-government, because the form which was most naturally integrated with the political system about it, — a form, moreover, which very naturally connected itself, mediately, with the supreme seigneurial authority of the king, — became in course of time the prevalent, indeed the almost universal, type in France. The 'prévotal' town is the normal town down to the end of the fifteenth century.

Not all of this development was accomplished peacefully or by the complaisance of the barons. Many cities were driven to defend their privileges against the baronage by force of arms; some, unable to stand out unaided against feudal aggressions, were preserved from discomfiture only by succor from the king, whose interest it served to use the power of the townsmen to check the insolent might of the feudal lords; others, again, were repeatedly constrained to buy in hard cash from neighbor barons a grudging tolerance for their modest immunities. The kings profited very shrewdly by the liberties of the towns, drawing the townspeople very closely about themselves in the struggles of royal prerogative against baronial privilege. As supreme lords in France, they assumed to make special grants of municipal citizenship: they made frequent gifts of *bourgeoisie* to disaffected vassals of the barons, — gifts so frequently made, indeed, that there grew up a special class of royal townsmen, a special *bourgeoisie du roi*.

The Towns and the Crusades. — Not the least important element in the growth of separate town privileges was the influence of the crusades upon the power of the nobility. When the full fervor of crusading was upon France, her feudal nobility were ready to give up anything at home if by giving it up they might be enabled to go to the holy wars, to the prosecution of which Mother Church was so warmly urging them. Their great need was money; money the towns had; and for money they bought privileges from departing crusaders. Very often, too, their one-time lords never returned from Palestine — never came back to resume the powers so hastily and eagerly bartered away before their departure. When they did return they returned impoverished, and in no condition of fortune to compete with those who had husbanded their resources at home. On every hand opportunities were made for the perpetuation of town privileges.

Municipal Privileges. — The privileges extorted or bought by the sturdy townspeople were, to speak in general terms, the right to make all the laws which concerned only themselves, the right to administer their own justice, the right to raise all taxes (as well those demanded by king or baron as those which they imposed upon themselves for their own purposes) in their own way, and the right to discipline themselves with police of their own appointing. Such villages as contrived to obtain separate privileges could of course obtain none so extensive as these. They often had to seek justice before baronial rather than before their own tribunals; they could by no means always choose their own way of paying unjust charges; they had often to submit to rough discipline at the hands of prince's retainers; oftentimes the most they could secure for themselves was a right of self-direction in petty matters in which no one else was immediately interested.

> The administrative functions exercised by the towns have been thus summed up: the administration of communal property, the maintenance of streets and roads, the construction of public edifices, the support and direction of schools, and the assessment and collection of all taxes.[1]

Forms of Town Government. — The forms of self-government in the towns varied infinitely in detail, according to place and circumstance, but the general outline was almost everywhere the same. Often there were two assemblies which took part in the direction of municipal affairs, an Assembly of Notables and a General Assembly of citizens. These two bodies did not stand to each other in the relation of two houses of a single legislature; they were separate not only, but had also distinct functions. The popular body elected the magistrates; the select body advised the magistrates; the one was a legislative, the other an executive, council. More commonly, however, there was but one assembly, the general assembly of citizens, which elected the magistrates, exercised a critical supervision over them, and passed upon all important municipal affairs. The magistracy generally consisted of a mayor and aldermen who acted jointly as the executive of the city (its *corps de ville*), the mayor in most cases being only

---

[1] Ferron, p. 8.

the president, never the 'chief executive,' of the corporation, and mayor and aldermen alike being equal in rank and in responsibility in exercising their corporate functions.

Decay or Destruction of Municipal Self-government. — From this democratic model there were, of course, in almost all cases, frequent departures, quite after the manner formulated by Aristotle (page 31). Oligarchy and tyranny both crept in, time and again; nowhere did local liberties permanently preserve their first vigor; everywhere real self-government sooner or later succumbed to adverse circumstances, crushed in very many cases by the overwhelming weight of the royal power. Generally such changes were wrought rather by stress of disaster from without than because of degeneracy within: and in very few cases indeed did local liberty die before the community which had sought to maintain it had given proof of a capital capacity for self-government. The independence of the cities died hard and has left glorious memories behind it.

Pays d'États. — Early times saw self-government in the provinces also. Many a feudal province had had its own 'Estates,' its own triple assembly, that is, of nobles, clergy, and burghers, which met to discuss and in large part, no doubt, to direct provincial affairs. The provinces of old France, thirty-six in number, represented separate feudal entities, much as the English counties did (sec. 836). The towns, on the other hand, in the central and northern portions of France at least, represented nothing but grants of privilege, were nothing but communities which had been given a special and exceptional place in the feudal order. The assemblies of the provinces, accordingly, were not primary or democratic like those of the towns, but were made up *by 'estates,'* — models for the States-General which appeared in 1302 (page 139).

> The provincial Estates were probably in their origin nothing else than normal feudal councils, made up, as they were, of representatives of all who possessed corporate or individual privileges, whose judgments and advice feudal dukes and counts found it redound to their greater peace and welfare to hear and heed.

In several of the provinces, as, notably, in Languedoc and Brittany, these provincial Estates continued to meet and to exercise considerable functions down to the time of the Revolution. Such provinces came to be distinguished from the others as *pays d'états* (provinces having Estates), and it is largely from the privileges of their assemblies that we argue the general nature of the powers possessed by those which had passed out of existence before history could catch a glimpse of them. We see the Estates of the *pays d'états* clearly only after the royal power has bound together all the provinces alike in a stringent system of centralization; they sit only at the king's call; their resolutions must be taken in the presence of the king's provincial officers and must await the regal sanction; they live by the royal favor and must in all things yield to the royal will. Nevertheless their privileges were still so substantial as to make the *pays d'états* the envy of all the rest of France. They bought of the Crown the right to collect the taxes demanded by the central government; they retained to the last the right to tax themselves for the expenses of local administration and to undertake and carry through entirely without supervision the extensive improvements in roads and watercourses to which the local patriotism bred by local self-government inclined them. Restricted though their sphere was, they moved freely within it, and gave to their provinces a vitality and a prosperity such as the rest of France, administered, as it was, exclusively from Paris, speedily and utterly lost.

Territorial Development of the Monarchy. — The process of the organic development of the monarchy which centred in the duchy of France began with territorial expansion and consolidation. For eight centuries that expansion and consolidation went steadily on; but its successful completion was assured before the extinction of the first, the direct, line of Capets in 1328. Before that date Philip Augustus had wrung Normandy from England and had added Vermandois, Auvergne, Touraine, Anjou, Maine, and Poitou to the dominions of his Crown, and his successors had so well carried forward the work of expansion that before the Valois branch came into the succession only Flanders, Burgundy, and Brittany broke the solidity of the French power in the north, and only Aquitaine, still England's fief, cut France off from her wide territories in the southeast. It had been the mission of the direct line of the Capets to lay broadly and irremovably the foundations of French unity and nationality, and they had accomplished that mission. They gave to their monarchy the momentum which was afterwards to carry it into full supremacy over Brittany, Aquitaine, and Burgundy, over the Rhone valley, and over the lands which separated her from the Rhine.

The Crusades and the Monarchy. — The monarchy, even more than the towns (page 134), profited by the effects of the crusades on the feudal nobility. So great was the loss of life among the nobles, so great was their loss of fortune, that they fell an easy prey to the encroaching monarchy. During the first crusades the French kings stayed at home and reaped the advantages which the nobles lost; during the last crusades, the kings were strong enough themselves to leave home and indulge in the holy warfare in the East, without too great apprehension as to what might happen to the royal power in their absence.

Institutional Growth. — Of course along with territorial expansion there went institutional growth: and this growth involved in large part the destruction of local liberties. The amalgamation of France into a single, veritable kingdom was vastly more fatal to local self-government than the anarchy and confusion of feudal times had been. The cities could cope with neighbor lords; and during the period of contest between king and barons they could count oftentimes upon assistance from the king: his interests, like theirs, lay in the direction of checking baronial power. But when the feudal lords were no longer to be feared, the towns in their turn felt the jealousy of the king; and against his overwhelming power, when once it was established, they dared not raise their hands. The ancient provinces, too, had in the earlier days found ways of bringing local lords into their Estates, in which the right of the burghers to have a voice in the government was recognized (sec. 368). But they could no more resist the centralization determined upon by a king triumphant over all feudal rivals than the towns could. In the end the provincial assemblies, where they managed to exist at all in the face of the growing power of the Crown, were, like all other independent authorities of the later time, sadly curtailed in privilege, and at the last almost entirely lost heart and life.

The States-General. — At one time, indeed, it seemed as

if the nation, in being drawn close about the throne, was to be given a life of its own in a national parliament. Philip the Fair (1285–1314), bent upon making good his authority against the interference of the Pope in certain matters, bethought himself of calling representatives of the nation to his support. The kings of France had already often taken the advice upon public affairs of the baronage or of the clergy, each of which orders had a corporate existence and organization of its own, and therefore possessed means of influential advising: but Philip called in the burghers of the towns also and constituted (1302) that States-General (*États-Généraux*) in which for the first time in French history that 'third estate' of the Commons appears which in later times was to thrust both clergy and nobles out of power and itself rule supreme as 'the people.'

Character of the States-General. — The first States-General, summoned by Philip the Fair, reminds one not a little of the parliament called together in England in 1295 by Edward I. (secs. 848, 850). Apparently France was about to have a parliament such as England's became, a representative body, speaking, and at the end of every important contest bringing to pass, the will of the nation. But for France this first promise was not fulfilled. During three centuries, the fourteenth, fifteenth, and sixteenth (1302–1614), it was the pleasure of the French monarch to keep alive, at first by frequent, and later by occasional summons, this assemblage of the three Estates. This was the period during which feudal privileges were giving way before the royal prerogative, and it was often convenient to have the formal sanction of the Estates at the back of acts of sovereignty on the part of the Crown. But after the full establishment of the regal power the countenance of the Estates was no longer needed, and was no longer asked. The States-General never, moreover, even in the period of their greatest activity, became a legislative authority. For one thing, they had not the organization proper, not to say necessary, for the exercise of power. The three Estates, the Nobility, the Clergy, and the Commons (*Tiers État*), deliberated apart from each other as separate bodies; and each submitted its own list of grievances and suggestions to the king. They acted often in harmony, but never in union; their only common meeting was the first of each session, when they all three assembled in the same hall to hear a formal opening speech from the throne. They never acquired the right to be consulted with reference to that cardinal affair of politics, taxation; they never gained the right to sit independently of royal summons. They were encouraged to submit what suggestions they chose to the government concerning the administration of the kingdom; and, as a matter of fact, their counsels were often heeded by the king. But they never got beyond advising: never won the right to expect that their advice would be taken. Their sessions did, however, so long as they continued, contribute to keep alive a serviceable form of self-government which at least held the nation within sight of substantial liberties; and which, above all, secured national recognition for that 'third estate,' the people, whose sturdiest members, the burghers of the towns, were real representatives of local political life.

Administrative Development. — Of course along with the territorial expansion of the monarchy by annexation, absorption, and conquest there went also great administrative developments. As the monarchy grew, the instrumentalities of government grew along with it: possession and control advanced hand in hand.

Growth of the Central Administration. — In the earlier periods of the Capetian rule a Feudal Court and certain household officers constituted a sufficient machinery for the central administration. There was a *Chancellor*, who was the king's private secretary and keeper of both the public and the private records of the court; a *Chamberlain*, who was superintendent of the household; a *Seneschal*, who presided in the king's name and stead in the Feudal Court, and who represented the king in the direct administration of justice; a *Great Butler*, who was manager of the royal property and revenues; and a *Constable*, who was commander of the forces. The Feudal Court, composed of the chief feudatories of the Crown, exercised the functions of a tribunal of justice in suits between tenants *in capite*, besides the functions of a taxing body and of an administrative council.

The Council of State. — So long as 'France' was only a duchy and the real territory of the Crown no wider than the immediate domain of the Capetian dukes, the weight of administration fell upon the officers of the household, and the Feudal Court was of no continuous importance. But as France grew, the household officers declined and the Feudal Court advanced in power and importance. As the functions of the Court increased and the Court became a directing Council, the Council more and more tended to fall apart into committees, into distinct sections, having each its own particular part of the duties once common to the whole body to perform. The earlier Councils exercised without distinction functions political, judicial, and financial, and their differentiation, though hurried forward by monarchs like Louis IX., was not given definite completeness until 1302 (the year of the first States-General) when, by an ordinance of Philip the Fair, their political functions were assigned to the body which was to remain the Council, their judicial functions to a body which was to bear the ancient name of parliament (and which we know as the Parliament of Paris), their financial functions to a Chamber of Accounts. Alongside of the Chamber of Accounts there sprang up a Chamber of Subsidies which concerned itself with taxation. Into these bodies, whose activity increased from year to year, the old officials of the household were speedily absorbed, the Great Butler, for instance, becoming merely the president of the Chamber of Accounts.

The Parliament of Paris. — The judicial section of the Council of State consisted at first like the other sections, like the whole Council indeed, of feudatories of the Crown, as well as of administrative experts gradually introduced. More and more, however, this chief tribunal tended to become exclusively a body of technical officials, of trained jurists and experienced lawyers, the law officers and advisers of the Crown.

Growth of Centralized Local Administration: Louis IX.—

This expansion of the central organs of administration meant that the royal government was entering more and more extensively into the management of affairs in the provinces, that local administration was being centralized. This extension of centralized local administration may be said to have begun in earnest under Louis IX. Louis IX. did more than any of his predecessors to strengthen the grip of the monarchy upon its dominions by means of direct instrumentalities of government. He was a man able to see justice and to do it, to fear God and yet not fear the Church, to conquer men not less by uprightness of character than by force of will and of arms; and his character established the monarchy in its power. By combined strength and even-handedness he bore down all baronial opposition; the barons subjected to his will, he sent royal commissioners throughout the realm to discover where things were going amiss and where men needed that the king should interfere; he established the right of appeal to his own courts, even from the courts of the barons, thus making the Parliament of Paris the centre of the judicial system of the country; he forced limitations of power upon the feudal courts; he forbade and in part prevented judicial combats and private warfare. He drew the administration of the law in France together into a centralized system by means of royal *Baillis* and *Prévôts*, whom he subordinated to the Parliament of Paris.

Steps of Centralization. — It is not, of course, to be understood that Louis' work was to any considerable extent a work of creation : it was not, but rather a work of adaptation, expansion, systematization. The system which he perfected had been slowly growing under his predecessors. A *bailli* was, in the Middle Ages, a very common officer, representing king or seigneur, as the case might be, administering justice in his name, commanding his men-at-arms, managing the finances, caring, indeed, for every detail of administration. At first, it is said, "all of judicial, financial, and military administration was in his hands." It was an old system of royal *baillis*, set over districts known as *bailliages* (bailliwicks), that Philip Augustus instituted (1190) and Louis IX. extended and regulated, keeping an eye to it, the while, that the *baillis* should be made to feel their dependence upon the Crown so constantly that they should *per force* remain officials and not dream of following the example of dukes and counts and becoming independent feudal lords on their own. accounts.

Personal Government : Louis XIV. — Such measures naturally tended to subordinate all local magnates to the king. By the policy of Louis XIV. this tendency was completed : the whole of the nobility of France were, so to say, merged in the person and court of the king. Louis took care to have it understood that no man who remained upon his estate, who did not dance constant attendance upon his majesty, the king, at his court, to add to its brilliancy and servility, might expect anything but disfavor and loss. He made of the great landed nobility a court nobility, turning men from interest in their tenants and their estates to

interest in court intrigue alone. He drew all men of rank and ambition
to himself, merged them in himself, and left nothing between the monarchy and the masses whereby the terrible impact of the great revolution
which was to come might be broken.

The Completed Centralization: the Intendant. — Finally

came the completed centralization which followed the days of
Richelieu: the system whose central figure was the *Intendant*, a
direct appointee and agent of the king and absolute ruler within
the province; and whose lesser figures were the sub-delegates of
the Intendant, rulers in every district and commune. The rule of
these agents of the Crown almost totally extinguished the separate
privileges of the elected magistrates of the towns and of the other
units of local government.   In many places, it is true, the people
were suffered still to elect their magistrates as before; but the
usurping activities of the Intendant and his subordinates speedily
left elected magistrates with nothing to do.   In other cases elections ceased; the Crown sold the local offices as life estates to any
one who would buy them for cash.

> **The Province** was a military, not a civil, administrative district.
> The Provinces were grouped into *Generalities*, of which there were in all
> thirty-two, and it was over a *Generality* that each Intendant ruled. Ec-
> clesiastical administration was served by still another distinct division into
> *Dioceses*.

Judicial Centralization. — The local tribunals of justice in

like manner had their business gradually stolen from them.   The
principle of appeal established by Louis IX. at length worked its
perfect work.   Every case in which any interest cared for from
Paris (and what interest was not?) was either actually or by pretence involved was ' evoked ' to special courts set up by royal
commission.   No detail was too insignificant to come within the
usurpations of the king's government.

The Royal Council and the Comptroller-General. — The

Royal Council at Paris regulated, by 'orders in council,' every
interest, great or small, in the whole kingdom.   The Comptroller-
General, acting through the Intendants and their sub-delegates,
and through the royal tribunals, managed France.   Everybody's
affairs were submitted to him, and through him to the Royal
Council; and everybody received suggestions from Paris touching

his affairs. No labor of supervision was too overwhelming for the central government to undertake. Interference in local affairs, made progressively more and more systematic, more and more minute and inquisitive, resulted, of course, in the complete strangulation of local government. All vitality ran to the veins of the central organism, and, except for the lingering and treasured privileges of the *pays d'états,* and for here and there a persistent form of town life, France lay in the pigeon-holes of a bureau. *Tabula rasa* had been made of the historical elements of local government.

> **The Spirit of the Administration.** — This busy supervision of local and individual interests was always paternal in intent; and the intentions of the central power were never more benevolent than just when the Revolution was beginning to draw on apace. "The royal government was generally willing in the latter half of the eighteenth century to redress a given case of abuse, but it never felt itself strong enough, or had leisure enough, to deal with the general source from which the particular grievance sprang." [1]

The Revolution. — This whole fabric of government went for a moment to pieces in the storm of the Revolution. But the revolutionists, when their stupendous work of destruction had been accomplished, were under the same necessity to govern that had rested upon the monarch whom they had dethroned and executed; and they very soon proved themselves unable to improve much upon the old patterns of government. In denial of the indefeasible sovereignty of the king, they proclaimed, with huzzahs, the absolute sovereignty of the people; but Assembly and Convention could do no more than arrogate all power to themselves, as the people's representatives, and seek to reign in the king's stead through the king's old instrumentalities. They gave voice to a new conception, but they could not devise a new frame of administration. The result was confusion, Committees, the Terror, and — Napoleon.

The Reconstruction by Napoleon. — The Revolution removed all the foundations of French *politics,* but scarcely any of the foundations of French *administration.* The interests of the

[1] John Morley, *Miscellanies,* Vol. II. (last Macmillan edition), essay on " Turgot," p. 138.

royal administration had centred in the general government, rather than in its local parts, — in patronage, in the aggregate national power and prosperity, in finance. The true interests of republican government, on the other hand, centre in thorough local development: republican work, properly done, ought to tend to broaden and diversify administrative work by diversifying political life and quickening self-directive administrative agencies. But this the leaders of the Revolution neither saw nor could do; and Napoleon, whom they created, of course made no effort to serve republican development.

Napoleon simply reorganized despotism. In doing so, however, he did scarcely more than carry into effect the principal purposes of the Constituent Assembly. The legislation of that Assembly had sought, not to shatter centralization, but to simplify and systematize it; and it was this purpose that Napoleon carried out. For the Convention and Assembly, as representatives of the nation's sovereignty, he substituted himself; and then he proceeded to give to centralization a perfected machinery. The Convention and Assembly had endeavored to direct affairs through Committees, Commissions, Councils, Directories, — through executive *boards*, in a word. For such instrumentalities Napoleon substituted single officers as depositaries of the several distinct functions of administration; though he was content to associate with these officers advisory councils, whose advice they might ask, but should take only on their own individual responsibility. " 'To give advice is the province of several, to administer, that of individuals,' says the maxim which he engraved on the pediment of the administrative arrangements of France," to remain there to the present day. The Constituent Assembly, willing to obliterate the old Provinces of France, with their memories of feudal privilege, and the *Generalities*, with their ancient savor of absolutism, had redivided the country, as symmetrically as possible, into eighty-nine *Departments;* and it was upon this territorial framework that Napoleon superimposed a machinery of Prefects and sub-prefects, modelled, with simplifications and improvements of method, upon the system of Intendants and delegates of the old *régime*. This he accomplished in that celebrated "Constitution of the Year VIII." which still lies almost undisturbed at the foundation of French administration. The Revolution had resulted in imparting to centralization what it never had had before: namely, assured order and effective system. [1]

Advances towards Liberal Institutions. — Nevertheless, the Revolution had asserted a new *principle* of rule, and every change of government which has taken place in France since the Revolution has pushed her, however violently, towards genuine representative institutions and real republicanism. Louis XVIII., though he persisted in holding to the divine right of kings and in retaining for himself and his ministers an exclusive right of initiative in legislation, assented to the establishment of a parliament of two houses and conceded to it the responsibility of the ministers. Louis Philippe abandoned the delusion of the 'divine right,' acknowledged the sovereignty of the people, and shared with the chambers the right of initiative in legislation. With Napoleon III. came, reaction and a return to a system like that of the first Napoleon; but even Napoleon III. had consented to return to the practice of ministerial responsibility before the war with Germany swept him from his throne and gave birth to the present Republic.

The Third Republic. — Sedan having fallen (September 2), and the Emperor having been taken prisoner, the imperial government went to pieces, and on Sunday the fourth of September, 1870, the leaders of uneasy Paris proclaimed the Third Republic, Gambetta being their mouthpiece. A provisional government was at once set up by the republican leaders, under the name of the National Defence. The men who constituted it were fully aware that they legally represented nobody but themselves, that they had usurped power in the face of a national crisis and were acting by sufferance, and it was their purpose to call together a national assembly at once, an assembly chosen by universal suffrage, in order that the people's representatives might construct

---

[1] Since the war between France and Germany in 1870–'1, the Departments of France have numbered only eighty-six, the loss of Alsace and Lorraine having subtracted three Departments. There is also the territory of Belfort.

in more formal fashion a government of their own. Immediate preparations were accordingly made for an election. But the rapid and fatal progress of the war prevented. Germany pressed her victories to the utmost. It was not possible to hold an assembly at all until the end had come and it had become necessary to decide terms of submission and peace.

The National Assembly of 1871–1876. — On the 8th of February, 1871, a National Assembly was elected, and on the 13th of the same month it convened for the transaction of its business at Bordeaux. It turned out not to be a republican body. Of its seven hundred and sixty-eight members a majority were found to be in favor of a monarchical form of government. Had that majority been united, it could have undone the work of Gambetta and his colleagues and have set a prince once more upon the throne of France. But it could not unite. Some, the 'Legitimists,' wished to see the old house of Bourbon restored; others were partisans of the house of Orleans; a few were Imperialists and wanted the empire of the Bonapartes set up again. The first business of the Assembly was easily disposed of, humiliating though it was. Peace was concluded with Germany upon her own terms, only Belfort being saved by the diplomacy of Thiers. The matter of real difficulty was the establishment and maintenance of a government. For the time being, and until something better and more permanent could be agreed upon, the name and the forms of the Republic were kept. M. Grévy, a moderate Republican, was made President of the Assembly; M. Thiers, a moderate Orleanist, was chosen 'Chief of the Executive Power' of the Republic (a title presently changed to President); and the Assembly itself undertook to direct affairs, through the President as its responsible agent.

A Balance of Parties. — For five years the Assembly maintained its authority and hold upon affairs. It had been given no formal commission at the elections what it should do. It had been clearly enough understood, of course, that it was first of all to come to terms of peace with Germany; but no one knew what the voters had expected it would do after that. It had neither been commissioned to form a government nor to conduct one, and yet it certainly had not been forbidden to do either. The Republicans, finding themselves in a minority, urged that the Assembly had no authority to make a permanent constitution, and demanded that it should be dissolved and the people asked to choose a new assembly explicitly authorized to frame a government. The monarchical majority, however, feared that they should not have such another chance as the present to frame a government to their own liking, and claimed that as a National Assembly elected without instructions the existing body had practically received sovereign powers from the electors and might do as it pleased, watching, as prudent men should, the while, the temper of the country. The real difficulty was to hit upon a practicable programme, agreeable to all factions of the monarchists. The interests of the factions proved in fact irreconcilable and it soon became evident to conservative and observant men of every opinion that the Republic must be left standing. Thiers declared very frankly that he would have preferred a constitutional monarchy; but he believed a republic to be the real preference of the country, and he knew that to attempt the restoration of any one of the royal houses would be in the highest degree dangerous and revolutionary under the circumstances. "The Republic exists," he said; "it is the legal government of the country; to wish for anything else would be a revolution." The monarchists had at all events lost their opportunity by waiting; opinion ran steadily against them, and it was presently too late.

The Framing of the Constitution. — The more statesman-like and practical men amongst them saw at last very clearly that they must frame a republican government or none at all; but they determined to do as little as possible towards making the constitution they should frame definitive and difficult of alteration. They would make the forms of the new government such that it could at any rate be readily changed, and that without radical amendment, into a constitutional monarchy. They gave it, accordingly, as simple and rudimentary a frame as possible, leaving almost every detail, and even some of the main arrangements of its administration, to be settled by ordinary legislation; and they took care to make constitutional change as easy and informal a matter as might be without risking immediate instability. For four years they experimented with the government they had;

defining the powers of the President and their own relations to
him more than once, as if tentatively, and so as it were testing
and shaping the arrangements to which they should ultimately
give permanency. About a month after its convening the Assembly removed from Bordeaux to Versailles. While the Commune ruled Paris the leaders of the Assembly could of course
think of nothing but the measures necessary to establish order
and the authority of the government. When order had been restored, it was still necessary to handle the finances and arrange
many disordered matters of administration. What with the difficulties of governing the country and the even greater difficulty of
quieting its own factions, it proved impracticable for the Assembly to enter upon the work of constitution-making before 1873.
The work was not completed before the closing months of 1875.

Meanwhile (August 31, 1871), by the same act which conferred
upon him his new title of President of the Republic, the Assembly had
defined its relations to Thiers, constituting him its responsible minister,
with the right to appoint the other executive officers of the government and
to address the Assembly upon all matters of public business, and giving
him a term of office which should last until it should have finished its own
business. In March, 1873, thinking him too dominant in its counsels, it
had sought to exclude the President from its debates, except upon extraordinary occasions, and to put a responsible cabinet of ministers between
itself and the head of the government. Two months later it forced M.
Thiers to resign and elected Marshal MacMahon to exercise the office of
President in his stead, fixing his term at seven years and leaving the scope
of his authority and of his relations to the legislature to be determined by
the definitive constitutional laws it was about to frame. It had experimented long enough at governing and at the making and modifying of
Executives, and was ready, as it no doubt saw the country was, for its
final task.

Scope and Character of the Constitutional and Organic Laws of 1875.

— In framing the laws which were to give shape to
the new government the Assembly distinguished between those
which were to be 'constitutional' and subject to change only by
special processes of amendment, and those which, though 'organic,' were to be left subject to change by the ordinary processes
of statutory enactment by the two Houses of the Legislature.
The 'constitutional' laws, passed February 24th and 25th and July

16th, 1875, respectively, dealt in the simplest possible manner with the larger features of the new government's structure and operation: the election and general powers of the President; the division of the National Assembly into two houses, a Senate and Chamber of Deputies; the general powers and mutual relations of the two Houses, the President's relation to them, and the general rules which should control their assembling and adjournment. Two 'organic' statutes, bearing date August 2nd and November 30th, 1875, respectively, provided for the election of Senators and Deputies. The only radical amendment of the 'constitutional' laws since then effected was made in August, 1884, when almost the whole of the constitutional law regarding the composition and powers of the Senate was repealed, and replaced by an 'organic' law (that is, an ordinary statute) which introduced a number of important changes, and left the organization and authority of the Senate henceforth open to the freest legislative alteration, likely to be checked only by the circumstance that the Senate must itself assent to the changes made. The 'organic' laws of 1875 with regard to elections to the Chamber of Deputies have been several times amended.

The Sovereignty of the Chambers. — There can be no doubt that the National Assembly had invested Marshal MacMahon with the presidential power, upon the resignation of M. Thiers in May, 1873, with a distinct purpose. MacMahon was at once a popular and patriotic soldier and a partisan of monarchy. It was hoped that he might keep the chief executive place of the nation warm for some sovereign to be afterwards agreed upon and enthroned, — not necessarily by *coup d'état:* perhaps by a mere modification of the constitutional laws with regard to the person and powers of the head of the state. Sovereignty, nevertheless, passed under the new constitution to the new National Assembly, the Senate and Chamber of Deputies. The 'constitutional' laws of 1875 can be changed at will by the legislature which they called into existence: changed by the simple substitution of action in joint Assembly for the ordinary separate action in two houses. The Senators and Deputies have but to unite in National Assembly to become as sovereign as the Assembly which created them (see page 134). They are, besides, the sole judges of their own constitutional powers. No courts restrain them. France, like England, vests in her parliament a complete sovereignty of discretion as to its own acts.

> The principal difference between the two cases is, that the English Parliament may exercise all its powers in the same way, by the ordinary procedure of enactment, whether it changes by the act a mere detail of the common law or a chief arrangement of the constitution of the realm, while the French chambers are put under limitations of procedure in respect of every alteration of the fundamental law.

The constitutional arrangements thus effected have this admirable difference from all other previous constitutions France has had since the Revolution: they do not pretend to constitute the whole body of her fundamental public law. They exclude neither precedent nor growth. In practice even the precedents of previous constitutions have been suffered to have a part in supplementing them. So much of former constitutional usage as is not incompatible with the laws and character of the Republic is regarded as still in force. There has been no absolute break with the past, but only a new construction on old foundations.

The Chamber of Deputies. — It was the hope of the constitution-makers of 1875 that the Senate would have equal weight in affairs with the Chamber of Deputies; but that hope has been disappointed. Effective power has fallen from the first to the popular chamber, and the Senate has been thrust into a secondary rôle. Of the choice of members of the Chamber of Deputies, the constitutional laws say no more than that they shall be elected by universal suffrage. 'Organic' statute law has organized the Chamber on the basis of one deputy to every one hundred thousand inhabitants. Deputies must be at least twenty-five years of age, and their term, unless the Chamber be sooner dissolved, is four years. The eighty-six Departments into which the country is divided are the basis of representation in the Chamber, as in the Senate (page 153). To each Department is assigned a certain number of deputies, according to its population; every Department, however, whatever its population, being entitled to at least three representatives. The deputies are elected, not 'at large' for the whole Department, that is, on a general ticket, but by districts, as members of our federal House of Representatives are chosen in the States. The *Arrondissements* serve as ' congressional districts,' as we should call them,[1] — and this method of voting is accordingly known in France as *scrutin d'arrondissement* (ballot by arrondissement).

This was the original arrangement of 1875 ; but in 1885 the system of voting for deputies in each Department on a general ticket, as we vote for presidential electors in the States, was introduced, being called *scrutin de liste* (ballot by list). It was adopted at the suggestion of Gambetta, who thought that a system of general tickets would give his party a freer sweep of popular majorities. In 1889, however, *scrutin d'arrondissement* was reëstablished, because *scrutin de liste* had given too free a sweep to the popular majorities of General Boulanger.

The principal colonies, too, are entitled to representation in the Chamber. Algiers sends five deputies ; Cochin-China, Guadeloupe, Guyana, India, Martinique, Réunion, and Senegal each send one. In all, there are six hundred and two deputies. Elections to the Chamber do not take place at regular intervals and on fixed dates named by statute, but must be ordered by decree from the President of the Republic in each case. The law directs, however, that the President must order an election within sixty days, or, in case of a dissolution, within two months after the expiration of a term of the Chamber ; and that the new Chamber must come together within the ten days following the election. At least twenty days must separate decree and day of election.

Election by Majority. — The law governing the election of Deputies provides against choice by plurality on the first ballot ; and the result is unfortunate. If there are more than two candidates in an electoral district (an *arrondissement*), an election on the first ballot is possible only if one of the candidates receives an absolute majority of all the votes cast not only, but also at least one-fourth as many votes as there are registered voters in the district. If no one receives such a majority, another vote must be taken two weeks later, and at this a plurality is sufficient to elect. The result is, that the multiplication of parties, or rather the multiplication of groups and factions within the larger party lines, from which France naturally suffers overmuch, is directly encouraged. Rival groups are tempted to show their strength on the first ballot

[1] *Arrondissements* having a population of more than one hundred thousand people are divided into districts, called *circonscriptions* — one for each hundred thousand people or fraction thereof.

in an election, for the purpose of winning a place or exchanging favor for favor in the second. They lose nothing by failing in the first ; they may gain concessions or be more regarded another time by showing a little strength ; and rivalry is encouraged, instead of consolidation. France cannot afford to foster factions.

The Senate. — By an act of the National Assembly passed August 14th, 1884, almost the whole of the constitutional law of February 24th, 1875, relating to the organization of the Senate and to the qualifications and election of senators was stripped of its ' constitutional' character and became an ordinary statute. Four months later it was replaced by the act of December 9th, 1884. In all that respects its organization and in much that respects its powers the Senate has become a merely statutory body. So far as the ' constitutional ' laws are concerned, it might be constituted by executive appointment or by lot. By statute it has been made to consist of three hundred members chosen by ' electoral colleges ' specially constituted for the purpose in the several Departments and colonies, and the term of senatorship has been fixed at nine years.[1] Forty years has been declared the minimum age for senators. The electoral college for the choice of senators is composed in each Department of the deputies from the Department, the members of the ' General Council ' of the Department (page 169), and the members of the Councils of its several Arrondissements (page 171), together with delegates chosen in each Commune by the Communal Council, varying in number according to the numbers of the Communal Council. One-third of the membership of the Senate is renewed every three years. In legal powers the Senate is in all respects upon a footing of equality with the Chamber of Deputies, except that money bills must originate with the Chamber; and though it has in practice been conceded that the Senate may amend them, it has been doubted whether it can of strict legal right add to money bills. In political power, of course, the Chamber overshadows and dominates the Senate.

[1] Until 1884 the law provided that seventy-five of the senatorial seats were to be filled by the choice of the Senate itself, and held for life. By virtue of the constitutional change effected in 1884, all vacancies occurring in these life-memberships are now filled by election in the Departments, as other seats are, and for the usual term of nine years.

Legislation determines from time to time how many senators shall be elected by each Department. According to the present distribution ten are returned by the city of Paris, which itself constitutes most of the Department of the Seine. Other Departments vary in their representation from two to eight. "The following elect one senator each : the Territory of Belfort, the three Departments of Algeria, the four colonies, Martinique, Guadeloupe, Réunion, French Indies." (Law of Dec. 9, 1884.)

In Case of Usurpation. — In case the Chambers should be illegally dissolved or hindered from assembling, the General Councils of the Departments are to convene without delay in their respective places of meeting and take the necessary steps for preserving order and quiet. Each Council is to choose two delegates to join delegates from the other Councils in assembling at the place whither the members of the legal government and the regular representatives of the people who have escaped the tyranny have betaken themselves. The extraordinary assembly thus brought together is authorized to constitute itself for business when half the Departments shall be represented ; and it may take any steps that may be necessary to maintain order, administer affairs, and establish the independence of the regular Chambers. It is dissolved, *ipso facto*, so soon as the regular Chambers can come together. If that be not possible, it is to order a general election, within one month after its own assembling.

The National Assembly: its Functions. — The Senate and Chamber of Deputies meet together in joint session as a National Assembly for two purposes: the revision of the Constitution and the election of the President of the Republic. Since November, 1879, the Houses have met for the performance of their ordinary legislative functions in Paris; as a National Assembly they meet in Versailles, apart from the exciting influences of the great capital, which has led so many assemblies captive. Whether met for the election of the President or for the revision of the Constitution, the National Assembly must do the single thing which it has convened to do and then at once adjourn. For the election of the President there are clearly determined times and occasions: whenever the office of President falls vacant, whether by the death or resignation of the President or by the expiration of his term.

Revision of Constitution. — A revision of the Constitution may take place whenever the two Houses are agreed that revision is necessary. It has, thus far, been customary for the Houses to consider separately beforehand not only the propriety of *a* revision, — that standing constitutional rules require, — but also the particular points at which revision is necessary and the lines on which it should proceed; and to know each other's minds on these important heads before agreeing to a National Assembly. Alike for the election of a President and for the adoption of constitutional amendments an absolute majority vote of the united Chambers suffices.

It might easily happen that the majority in one of the Houses would be outvoted on joint ballot in National Assembly. If such were likely to be the case, that majority could hardly be expected to consent readily to a joint session. France has, not two, but many national parties, and it is not always possible to effect the same combination of factions in support of a measure in both the Houses. Cases must frequently arise in which a joint vote of the Houses upon a particular measure would carry with it defeat to the policy preferred in one of them. And yet there is no legal obstacle to prevent the majority in a joint session taking up and deciding questions not agreed upon beforehand. The only guarantee is good faith.

The National Assembly is the most completely sovereign body known to the Constitution, there being but one thing it cannot do under existing law : it cannot sit as long as it pleases. Its sessions must not exceed in length the duration of an ordinary legislative session (five months). It is, indeed, forbidden, besides, to consider the repeal of republican government; but it could repeal the law which forbids it.

The officers of the Senate act as officers of the National Assembly. They consist of a President, four Vice-Presidents, six Secretaries, and three Quæstors, elected for one year. The Chamber of Deputies has the same offices, with the addition of two more secretaryships.

The President of the Republic. — The president, elected by the joint ballot of the Chambers, is titular head of the Executive of France. His term of office is seven years. He has the power of appointing and removing all officers of the public service. He has no veto on legislation, but he is authorized to demand a reconsideration of any measure by the Houses. He can adjourn the Chambers at any time (though not more than twice during the same session) for any period not exceeding one month; he can close a regular session of the Houses at his discretion after it has continued five months, and an extra session when he pleases; and he can, with the consent of the Senate, dissolve the Chamber of Deputies, even before the expiration of the five months of its regular session. A dissolution of the Chamber of Deputies puts an end also to the sessions, though not to the life, of the Senate; for it cannot act, except as a court, without the Chamber. In the event of a dissolution, as has been said, the President must order a new election to be held within two months thereafter, and the Houses must convene within ten days after the election. "The President is responsible in case of high treason only," says the constitutional law of February 25th, 1875; and, in case of high treason the Chamber must impeach, the Senate try, him. As a matter of fact, however, four Presidents of the Republic have been forced or have chosen to resign.

The only limitation put by law upon the choice of the National Assembly in electing a President of the Republic is, that no one shall be chosen President who is a member of any family which has occupied the throne of France. Members of these families are also excluded from seats in either the Chamber or the Senate.

Influence of President and Senate. — The President and Senate, it will be seen, are given a really very great power of control over the Chamber of Deputies. It is within the choice of the President to moderate the excesses of the Chamber by returning bills to it for reconsideration,[1] or by adjourning it during a period of too great excitement; and it is within the choice of the President and Senate acting together to appeal from its decisions to the constituencies by a dissolution. The Senate, moreover, has once and again been given so many members of real weight of character and distinction of career that it would seem to have been in a position to act in restraint of the Chamber with firmness and success. But, though the National Assembly which elected Thiers and MacMahon and put together the framework of the constitution may have intended the new government to be in some real sense a government by the President, it has in fact never shown the President in any degree a master in affairs since the days of MacMahon himself. MacMahon exercised the power

---

[1] The President has no veto power and while the Chamber must reconsider bills thus returned to it, it may at once repass them without change.

of dissolution, with the approval of the Senate; but the change of Deputies only taught him the real character of the government, as a government subject to the will of the Chamber. Year by year the subordinate position of the Senate and the irregular but always irresistible power of the Chamber have become more and more obvious.

The Cabinet and the Council of Ministers. — *A Cabinet of ministers* constitutes a link between the President and the Chambers: and the political functions of this Cabinet are amongst the central features of government in France. Both the Cabinet and the Council consist of the same persons; but the Cabinet is a political body exclusively and is presided over by the Premier, while the Council has administrative functions and is presided over by the President. The distinction illustrates pointedly the double capacity of the ministers.

The Ministries. — There are now fourteen ministers: the Minister of *Justice*, filling the office filled before the Revolution by the Chancellor; the Minister of *Finance*, who has taken the place of the Comptroller-General of ante-revolutionary days (page 143); the Minister of *War*, who acts as head of the administrative department created in the time of Mazarin (1644); the Minister of *Marine;* the Minister of *Colonies;* the Minister of *Foreign Affairs* (1644); the Minister of the *Interior*, an office created by the Constituent Assembly in 1791, by a consolidation of the pre-revolutionary offices of Comptroller-General and Minister of the Royal Household, except so far as the functions of the Comptroller-General were financial and bestowed upon the Minister of Finance; the Minister of *Public Instruction* (1848) *and the Fine Arts;* the Minister of *Public Works and Transportation;* the Minister of *Agriculture* (an office created in 1812, but afterwards abolished, to be revived in 1828–30); the Minister of *Trade and Industry;* the Minister of *Labor;* the Minister of *Supplies*, and the Minister of *Munitions.*

The Cabinet. — As a Cabinet, the ministers represent the Chambers. They are commonly chosen from amongst the members of the Houses; but, whether members or not, they have, as ministers, the right to attend all sessions of the Chambers and to take a specially privileged part in debate.[1] The same right extends also to the Under-secretaries, who are, consequently, usually members of the Chambers.

The Council of Ministers. — As an administrative Council the ministers are, in official rank at least, subordinate to the President, who is the Chief Executive. The Council sits in his presence and under his presidency. Its duty is to exercise a general oversight of the administration of the laws, with a view to giving unity of direction to affairs of state. In case of the death, resignation, or incapacitation of the President of the Republic, the Council is to act in his stead until the National Assembly can meet and elect his successor. Its members are *ex officio* members of the Council of State, the highest judicial tribunal of the Republic for the determination of administrative cases (page 174).

Relation of the Ministers to the President. — The Council of Ministers is a body recognized by law, the Cabinet is not: it is only the ministers in consultation concerning matters affecting their political responsibility: it is, aside from such meetings for consultation, only a name representing their union in responsibility. But the two names, Council and Cabinet, furnish convenient means for making plain the various relations of the ministers to the President. As a Council they are, in a sense, his creation; as a Cabinet they are, in a sense, his masters. The Executive Departments or Ministries over which they preside are the creation, not of the Constitution or of statutes, but of the President's decree. No decree of the President is valid, however, unless countersigned by the minister whose department is affected. Any such decree must, too, almost necessarily affect the budget, and must in that way come within the control of the ministers and the Chambers. The ministers are the President's appointees; but he must appoint ministers who are in agreement with the majority in the Chambers, and they are responsible to the Chambers alone for their conduct in office. The President is the head of the administration; but his salary is dependent upon the

[1] A minister may speak at any time in the Chambers; not even the *clôture* (previous question) can exclude him. In 1888 the Minister of War was without a seat in the Chamber.

annual budget which the Minister of Finance presents to the Chambers : and the items of the budget are matter of agreement between the ministers and the Chambers.

All these ' buts ' are so many fingers pointing to the power of the Cabinet over the President. The Ministers are in fact not his representatives, but representatives of the Chambers. In this capacity they control not the policy only, but also the patronage of the government. Naturally the President's appointments, needing, as they do in every case, the countersignature of a minister, are in general the appointments of the ministers ; and their appointments are too often bestowed according to their interest in the Chambers, — are too often used, in short, to be cast as bait for votes.

The Patronage of Office, indeed, threatens to become even more of a menace to good government in France than it has been to good government in our own country under the federal system of appointment. The number of offices in the gift of the ministers in France is vastly greater than the number within the gift of the President of the United States ; and the ministers' need to please the Chambers by favors of any and all kinds is incomparably greater than our President's need to please Congress, since they are dependent upon the good-will of the Chambers for their tenure of office, while he is not dependent on Congress for his.

There have never yet been in France, however, any such wholesale removals from office upon the going out of one administration and the coming in of another as we have seen again and again in this country ; because there has really been no radical change of administration in France since the days of MacMahon. In this country, as in England, there are two great national parties, and the government is now in the hands of one and again in the hands of the other. But in France a change of cabinet means nothing more than a change from the leadership of one group to the leadership of another.

For some years after the establishment of the present form of government, the only real party opposed to the Republicans was made up of persons known or suspected to be hostile to the very form of government under which the country was living. The people never gave it a majority in the Chamber and were never willing to intrust it with office. With the general acceptance of the Republic this monarchical party has disappeared; support of the Republic has become unanimous. No well-defined issues have divided the people or their representatives into two great political parties; at present eight parties are represented in the Chamber of Deputies, ranging in number after the last election from 136 to 26, with 18 Independents. Since no party has a majority, a ministry must depend upon a *bloc*, or union of parties. There is thus no strong bond of support behind any ministry, and while ministries do not change with the disconcerting frequency of the earlier years of the Republic, their tenure is still far too insecure and short lived. Generally a new cabinet is composed in part of men who held office also in the cabinet just thrown out. It is a change only of chief figures. And so wholesale removals from office do not take place.

Ministerial Responsibility. — The responsibility of the ministers to the Chambers is of law, and not simply of custom as in England. Their tenure of office is dependent upon the favor of the Houses. It would doubtless be so without law, for no policy of theirs could succeed without legislative approval and support, and it is French precedent as well as English for ministers to resign when defeated. They resign because they will not carry out measures of which they disapprove. In theory their responsibility is to both Houses; but, as a matter of fact, it is almost wholly to the Chamber of Deputies. The votes of the Senate alone seldom make or unmake Cabinets[1]; that has come to be recognized as the prerogative of the popular Chamber, which is more directly representative of the nation.

Questions and Interpellations. — The ministers may be held closely to their responsibility at every turn of their policy by means of various simple and effective forms of inquiry on the part of the Chambers. First of all is the direct question. Any member of either House may, after due notice given to the minister concerned, ask any question as to affairs of state; and an answer is demanded, by custom at least, to every question which

[1] On March 18, 1913 Briand proposed a vote of confidence in the Senate on the question of proportional representation, and when it was not given, the ministry resigned.

can be answered publicly without detriment to the public interest. Next to the direct question, which is a matter between the individual questioner and the minister questioned, comes that broader form of challenging the policy of the Cabinet, known in France as the ' *Interpellation.*' The simple questioner must first get the consent of the minister to hear his question; an *interpellation*, on the contrary, can be brought on without awaiting the acquiescence of the minister. It is a special and formal challenge of the policy or action of the Cabinet on some matter of the day, and is commonly the occasion of a general debate. It usually results in a vote expressive of confidence or want of confidence in the ministers, as the case may be. It is the question exalted into a subject of formal discussion : it is the weightiest form of interrogating ministers : it makes them and all that they have done the objects of set attack and defence. A third and still more formal method of bringing administrative acts under the scrutiny of the Chambers consists in the appointment of a Committee of Investigation.

The power of interpellation has been so indiscriminately and unwisely used in France as seriously to discredit her system of cabinet government. Interpellation is unhesitatingly used to take the ministers by surprise. Deputies lie in wait to take them at a disadvantage. They are ' interpellated,' moreover, most often, not upon questions of first-rate importance or in any way representative of their policy, but upon trivial matters of the moment. A sudden impulse upon a minor question of administration often determines the vote, and a cabinet goes out, it may be, as if by a trick, — not because its policy has been rejected or discredited, but because a chance and temporary majority has been got together against it. Yet the French regard the interpellation, despite its abuses, as the essence of constitutional government and an indispensable element in securing ministerial responsibility. The Chambers have sought within recent years to lessen the evils of interpellation by restricting the opportunities for its use. Under the present rules of both the Senate and the Chamber interpellations can be made only on one day of the week. Demands for interpellations are so numerous that few can be made in the time allotted, and as each takes its turn in order, it has happened that interpellations have been reached as long as a year and a half after they were made. The Chamber is always mistress of its own order of the day and interpellations regarding important matters may be heard at once or may be specially set for an early day The number of interpellations is still so great as to impose a terrible tax upon the time of both ministers and Chambers.

Control during the War. — The Senate and the Chamber have exercised a wide degree of control over the government, not only with respect to questions of internal affairs but also with respect to its diplomatic policy and the general direction of military affairs. During 1915 and the early months of 1916, important groups in the Chamber demanded that interpellations upon diplomatic and military affairs should be discussed in secret session, but the government opposed this on the ground of the serious consequences that might result from a discussion of these matters, even in a secret session. The right of the Senate and Chamber to control was not questioned, but the government thought it could be done better by the great parliamentary committees on the army, finance, and foreign affairs. Finally the government was compelled to yield and on June 14–22, 1916, secret sessions were held for the first time in the history of the Third Republic. Though a vote of confidence in the Briand ministry was given, the Chamber resolved to appoint a special committee, which, with the concurrence of the government, should exercise effective control. But the Chamber was finally compelled to abandon the plan of a special committee of control and on July 26, 1916, it delegated to the great standing committees the powers necessary to exercise effective control.[1]

The Course of Legislation. — All propositions alike, whether made by ministers or by private members, have to go to a special committee for consideration before reaching a debate and vote by the whole House ; but the propositions of private members must, in the Senate, pass another test before they reach even a special committee. They must go first to the 'Monthly Committee on Parliamentary Initiative,' and it is only after hearing the report of that Committee upon bills submitted to it that the Senate determines whether particular measures shall be taken under further consideration and advanced to the special-committee stage. In the Chamber of Deputies every proposition of a private member goes to the president of the Chamber who refers it to the permanent committee within whose province it falls. A vote of emergency taken upon the introduction of a measure can, however, rescue a ministerial bill from all committee handling, and a private member's bill from the delays of the Initiative Committee.

The Committees.[2] — The committee organization of the House is worthy of special remark. Every month during the session, the members of the Senate are divided by lot into nine

[1] Duguit, *Manuel*, pp. 452 ff.   [2] *Ibid.*, pp. 431 ff.

bureaux. The business of these *bureaux* is not to consider bills but to elect the committees to which bills are referred.

In the Chamber of Deputies since 1915, at the opening of a new session eleven *bureaux* are chosen by lot and they proceed at once to examine the certificates of election·; other *bureaux* are chosen in the event the Chamber decides to establish a permanent or special committee, elected by the *bureaux*, in addition to the great standing committees.

Until 1902 the committees of both Senate and Chamber of Deputies were special and temporary : special in that they were appointed to consider one or more definite points and they could not consider anything else ; temporary, that is, they ceased to exist so soon as the matter with which they were intrusted was disposed of. Since 1902 the Chamber has adopted the system of permanent or standing committees, chosen for a year, among which all the business is distributed. In 1911 the Senate, though holding in principle to the theory of special committees, decided to establish a certain number of standing committees. The number of these committees in the Chamber is nineteen and in the Senate four. In the Senate they are chosen by the *bureaux*, but in the Chamber a method is used which gives proportional representation to the various political groups ; the *bureaux* of the different groups report to the president a complete list of their members and, after agreement among themselves, the list of candidates which they have determined in accordance with the rule of proportion. This list is regarded as having received the ratification of the Chamber unless fifty deputies have opposed it by a declaration in writing delivered to the president. In the event of opposition the Chamber proceeds to a vote by the *scrutin de liste.* Each committee consists of forty-four members and no deputy can serve on more than three committees at the same time.

The very existence of committees and of the matter-of-course reference of all measures to their consideration, means that the Chamber insists upon examining and sifting all proposals for itself, whether they have been introduced by the ministers or not. It means, consequently, that the leadership of the ministers is thus still further broken and embarrassed. The committees will always insist upon putting some touch at least of their own handiwork upon the bills submitted to them; and even the ministers may count upon seeing their proposals pulled about and altered.

The Budget Committee. — All financial matters are considered by special standing committees chosen for one year; in the Chamber of Deputies by a Budget Committee composed of forty-four members, and in the Senate by a Finance Committee composed of eighteen members; and these Committees, like other standing committees, arrogate to themselves something like absolute domination of the financial policy of the government, with the result of robbing financial legislation of order and consistency, and of sadly obscuring the responsibility of the ministers. Other committees simply consider and report; the Budget Committee undertakes often radically to revise, sometimes altogether to transform, ministerial proposals, originating when it was meant only to control.

Government by the Chambers. — Ministerial responsibility has rapidly degenerated in France into government by the Chamber of Deputies. Ministerial responsibility is compatible with ministerial leadership; and under a ministry really given leave to direct the course of public policy, the Chambers judging and controlling but not directing, that policy might have dignity, consistency, and strength. But in France the ministers have, more and more as the years of the Republic have multiplied, been made to substitute for originative leadership submissive obedience to the wishes, and even to the whims, of the Chamber of Deputies. The extraordinary functions which have been arbitrarily assumed by the Budget Committee simply mirror the whole political situation in France.

The Administrative and Judicial Powers of the Executive. — It must not be supposed, because the life of a ministry is short and its leadership in the houses uncertain, that it wholly lacks power while it lasts. It inherits the traditional prerogatives of the French Executive, and they are very great. The powers of the President are the powers of the ministers. His power to execute and administer the laws means, according to the immemorial practice in France, that he may freely interpret them to meet circumstances and cover cases which the legislature did not foresee or provide for. The laws are for the most part themselves without detailed provisions. They give the officers of state who are to execute them a principle by which to go rather than a body of minute instructions. He may not disregard the plain principles of the law, indeed, but he is not restrained by detail; and in shaping administrative arrangements, instructing officials, and developing plans to meet the requirements of public business the executive authority exercised by the ministers through the President's decrees is in most cases wholly free from the trammels of statute. The legality of administrative action, moreover, is tested, when challenged, not by the ordinary courts of law, in which private rights are determined and guarded, but by special administrative tribunals in which the utmost latitude of discretion on the part of officers of state is the principle chiefly respected and enforced. The Executive inherits a very absolute tradition of power.

The President's power to ' dispose of the armed force ' of the nation has been employed in such a way as almost to amount to a declaration of war, in some of the aggressive colonial schemes into which French ministries have allowed themselves to be drawn. There goes with the executive power of appointment, too, an absolute power of removal from office, and all the vast official machinery of a centralized state is under the hands of the ministers to use almost as they will.

Departmental Functions. — The main duties of most of the Departments are sufficiently indicated by their names and illustrate the range of function assumed by the government in France more conspicuously than they illustrate the form and spirit of her political institutions. A mirror of the political life of France is to be found in the organization of the Ministry of the Interior, which is more largely concerned than any other Department with the multifarious details of local government.

LOCAL GOVERNMENT.

France still preserves the administrative divisions created by the Constituent Assembly in December, 1789. Instead of the old system of ecclesiastical dioceses, military provinces, and administrative 'generalities' (page 143), with their complexities and varieties of political regulation and local privilege, there is a system, above all things simple and symmetrical, of *Departments* divided into Arrondissements, *Arrondissements* divided into Cantons, and *Cantons* divided into *Communes*. Much the most significant of these divisions is the Department: whether for military, judicial, educational, or political administration, it is the important, the persistent unit of organization ; arrondissement, canton, and commune are only divisions of the Department, — not fractions of France, but only fractions of her Departments. The canton, indeed, is little more than an election district; and the arrondissement is only a fifth wheel in the administration of the Department. The symmetry of local government is perfect throughout. Everywhere the central government superintends the local elective bodies ; and everywhere those bodies enjoy the same privileges and are hedged in by the same limitations of power.

The several parts of the system of local government in France will thus be seen to rest, not upon any historical groundwork, creating each a vital whole, with traditions of local self-government handed down from an older time of freedom, but upon a bureaucratic groundwork of system. France, therefore, in approaching confirmed democracy and complete self-government, is building, not upon a basis of old habit, fixed firmly in the stiff soil of want and prejudice, but upon a basis of new habit widely separated from old wont, depending upon the shifting soil of new developments of character, new aptitudes, new purposes. Her new ways run across, not with, the grain of her historical nature. Her self-government is a-making instead of resting upon something already made.

The Department: the Prefect. — The central figure of French administration is the Prefect, the legal successor of the Intendant (page 143). He is the agent of the central government in the Department. He is the recruiting officer of that district, its treasurer, its superintendent of schools,[1] its chief of police, its executive officer in all undertakings of importance, and the appointer of most of its subordinate officials. He fills a double capacity : he is the agent and appointee of the central government, and at the same time the agent of the local legislative authorities. He is at once member and overseer of the General

[1] He appoints and disciplines the teachers.

Council of his Department; and he is necessarily its agent, inasmuch as he commands, as representative of the authorities in Paris, all the instrumentalities through which its purposes must be effected.   A minister can veto any act of a Prefect, — for he is the representative of any minister who needs his executive aid in the Department, — but no minister can override him and act by his own direct authority.   Until he is dismissed the minister must act through him.

When acting as the agent of the central authorities in carrying out the provisions of general statutes or of general administrative regulations the Prefect has, of course, no choice but to obey the orders he receives from the ministers in Paris.   But when he acts in local matters, he may use his own discretion and can be brought to book only by judicial process and upon complaint. It is of great consequence, therefore, that his powers in the field of local government are so many and so important.   He prepares the budget of the Department not only but also all the other business upon which the General Council of the Department (pages 168, 169) is expected to act.   His initiative determines the greater part of what that Council does; and it can act only through him in getting its resolutions carried into effect.   His police power extends beyond the organization and government of the police of the Department to the, at any rate, indirect control of the police organization and the police regulations of the Communes, many of which are great cities, with elective officers of their own (page 171).   Every mayor's police appointments must be confirmed by him, and he alone can remove police officials from office in the Communes.   'Police' affairs, in France, moreover, cover not merely the preservation of order and the enforcement of the law, but also such important matters as those, for example, which concern the public health.   In respect of some matters of local management, too, the Prefect can act by direct orders of his own, addressed to the officials of the Communes, as if to his own immediate subordinates.   He can in his discretion suspend the mayor of a Commune from office for a month's time; he can suspend also the session of a communal council (page 173) for a like period.

The Prefect may take part in the proceedings of the General

Council of the Department at any time except when his accounts are being considered.

Such is the legal position of the Prefect. His actual position is somewhat different. The politics of the Republic, one of whose tendencies has been to contribute by degrees to local self-government, is making the Prefect more and more largely the executive agent of the General Council of his Department. He is appointed by the Minister of the Interior and is in law first of all and chiefly the representative of the Interior. But the other ministers also, as has been said, act through him in many things. He frequently owes his appointment to the favorable influence of the deputies and senators from his Department with the Minister of the Interior, and he is kept, by his personal relations with them, close to local influences. He is, consequently, not the autocrat he was under Napoleon.

The General Council of the Department. — The legislative body of the Department is the General Council, which is made up of representatives chosen, one from each canton, by universal suffrage. Except during a session of the Chambers, the President of the Republic may at any time dissolve the General Council of a Department for cause. The election of representatives to the General Council, like the election of deputies, does not take place upon days set by statute, but on days set by decree of the President. Councillors are elected for a term of six years, one-half of the membership of the Council being renewed every three years. In order that members of the General Council may be in fact representatives of at least a respectable number of the voters of the cantons, the law provides, as in the case of the election of Deputies (page 153), that no one shall be elected on a first ballot unless voted for on that ballot by an absolute majority in a poll of at least one-fourth of the registered voters. Attention having been called to the election by the failure of a first ballot, a plurality will suffice to elect on a second. In case of a tie, the *older* candidate is to be declared elected.

The membership of the Council varies in the several Departments, according to the number of cantons, from seventeen to sixty-seven.

The Council of State is judge of the validity of elections to its membership, and a seat may be contested on the initiative either of a member of the Council, the Prefect, or a constituent of the member whose rights are in question, or a defeated candidate.

There are two regular sessions of the General Council each year. The duration of both is limited by law: for the first to fifteen days, for the second to one month. Extra sessions of eight days may be called by the President of the Republic or by the Prefect at the written request of two-thirds of the members. If the Council in any case outsit its legal term, it may be dissolved by the Prefect; if it overstep its jurisdiction in any matter, its acts may be annulled by a decree of the President. Members are liable to penalties for non-attendance or neglect of duty. They are, however, on the other hand, paid nothing for their services.

At the first regular session of the year the Council considers general business; at the second and longer session it discusses the budget of the Department, presented by the Prefect, and audits the accounts of the year. At either session it may require from the Prefect or any other chief of the departmental service full oral or, if it choose, written replies to all questions it may have to ask with reference to the administration.

The supervisory and regulative powers of the General Council are of considerable importance; but its originating powers are of the most restricted kind. It has the right to appropriate certain moneys for the expenses of local government, but it has not the right to tax for any purpose. The amount and the source of the money it is to use are determined by the Chambers in Paris. Even such narrowed acts of appropriation as it can pass have to be confirmed by presidential decree. Its chief functions are directory, not originative. It sees to the renting and maintenance of the buildings needed for its own use, for the use of the Prefect and his subordinates, for the use of the public schools, and for the use of the local courts; it votes the pay of the police (*gendarmerie*) of the Department; provides for the cost of printing the election lists; supervises the administration of the roads, railroads, and public works of the Department; oversees the management of lunatic asylums and the relief of the poor. Most important of all, it apportions among the several arrondissements the direct taxes annually voted by the Chambers.

The Departmental Commission. — During the intervals between its sessions, the General Council is represented in local administration by a committee of its own members called the Departmental Commission, which it elects to counsel and oversee the Prefect. The powers of this Commission, however, are merely advisory.

Central Control. — The most noticeable feature of this system is the tutelage in which local bodies and the individual citizen himself are kept. Fines compel the members of the General Council to do their work, and then every step of that work is liable to be revised by the central administration. Irregularities in the election of a member may be brought to the attention of the General Council by the Prefect, as well as by its own members or by petition from the constituency affected. If the Council overstep the limits of its powers, it is checked by decree of the President, and not by such a challenging of its acts in the courts by the persons affected as, in English or American practice, strengthens liberty by making the individual alert to assert the law on his own behalf, instead of trusting inertly to the government to keep all things in order. Even expression of opinion on the part of the General Council is restricted. It may express its views on any matter affecting local or general interests, ' if only it never express a wish which has a political character.'

The Arrondissement is the electoral district for the Chamber of Deputies, the members of the Chamber of Deputies being elected, as we have seen, not 'at large,' for the whole Department, but by Arrondissements, — not by *scrutin de liste*, that is, but by *scrutin d'arrondissement* (page 152). It also serves as a judicial district and as the province of an arrondissemental Council. Its chief administrative officer is a Sub-Prefect. The Council of the Arrondissement (*conseil d'arrondissement*), elected from the Cantons, like the General Council of the Department, has no more important function than that of subdividing among the communes the quota of taxes charged to the Arrondissement by the General Council. For the rest, it merely gives advice to administrative officers appointed by the ministers in Paris. Its decisions are largely controlled by the Prefect, and may be annulled by the President of the Republic.

The Canton is the electoral district from which members are chosen to the General Council and the Council of the Arrondissement; it marks the jurisdiction of the Justice of the Peace; it is a muster district for the army, and serves as a territorial unit of organization for registration and for the departmental care of roads; but it has no administrative organization of its own. It is a mere region of convenient size for electoral and like purposes.

The Commune, unlike the Arrondissement and Canton, is as vital an organism as the Department. All towns are Communes; but there is, of course, a much larger number of rural than of town Communes.

There are 36,229 Communes, most of which have less than 1500 inhabitants and many of which have less than 500. One hundred and seventeen have more than 20,000. Every city of France, except Paris and Lyons, is organized as a Commune.

Paris has its special form of administration, which differs from that of all the other cities of France. It has no mayor, but its chief administrative officials are two Prefects — one, the Prefect of the Department of the Seine, which embraces Paris and the immediate environs, who exercises all the functions of a mayor except those relating to police; the other, the Prefect of police. The Municipal Council is composed of eighty members, four from each of the twenty Arrondissements into which the city is divided. Each Arrondissement has its own mayor, who is appointed by the central government.

The general rule of French administration is centralization, the direct representation of the central authority, through appointed officers, in every grade of local government, and the ultimate dependence of all bodies and officers upon the ministers in Paris. In one particular this rule is departed from in the Commune. The chief executive officer of the Commune, the mayor, is elected, not appointed. He is chosen by the Municipal Council from among its own members and is given one or more assistants elected in the same way.

Down to 1874 the mayors of the more populous Communes were appointed by the authorities in Paris, the mayors of the smaller Communes by the Prefects. Between 1831 and 1852 the choice of the appointing power was confined to the members of the Municipal Councils; between 1852 and 1874 the choice might be made outside those bodies. From 1874 to 1882 the smaller Communes elected their mayors, indirectly as now. Since 1882 all mayors have been elected.

The Communal Magistracy. — The mayor and his assistants do not constitute an executive *board:* the mayor's assistants are not his colleagues. He is head of the communal government: they have their duties assigned to them by him. The mayor is responsible to the central administration and its departmental representative, the Prefect. Once elected, he becomes the representative of the Minister of the Interior. If he will not do the things which the laws demand of him in this capacity, the Prefect may delegate some one else to do them, or even do them himself instead. For cause, both the mayor and his assistants may be suspended, by the Prefect for one month, by the Minister of the Interior for three months, and all their acts are liable to be set aside either by Prefect or Minister. They may even be removed by the Executive.

In case of a removal it is the duty of the Municipal Council to fill the vacancies, and to fill them with other men; for removal renders the mayor or his assistants ineligible for one year.

One of the duties of the mayor is to appoint the police force and other subordinate officers of the Commune; but in Communes of over forty thousand inhabitants the mayor's composition of the police force must be ratified by decree of the President, and in other Communes all his appointments must be confirmed by the Prefect.

The Municipal Council. — There is in every Commune a Municipal Council (of from ten to thirty-six members, according to the size of the Commune) which has, besides its privilege of electing the mayor and his assistants, pretty much the same place in the government of the Commune that the General Council has in the government of the Department; and, in the main, a like dependence upon the approval of the central administration. Unlike the General Council, the Municipal Council is liable to be suspended for one month by the Prefect; like the General

Council, it may be dissolved by decree of the President passed in the Council of Ministers. It holds four regular sessions each year, one of which it devotes to the consideration of the municipal budget, which is presented by the mayor. Its financial session may continue six weeks; none of its other sessions may last more than fourteen days. The mayor acts as its president, except when his own accounts are under consideration.

Neither the Municipal Council nor the Council of the Arrondissement is judge of the validity of the elections of its members. Contested election cases are heard by the Prefectural Council.

Until 1831 the Municipal Council was chosen by the Prefect from a list of qualified persons made up in the Commune. Between 1831 and 1848 its members were elected by a restricted suffrage. Since 1848 they have been elected by universal suffrage.

In case of a dissolution of the Municipal Council, its place may be taken, for the oversight of current necessary matters, by a delegation of from three to seven members appointed by the President of the Republic to act till another election can be had. This delegation cannot, however, take upon itself more than the merely directory powers of the Council.

Administrative Courts: the Council of State. — So thorough is the differentiation of functions in France that actions at law arising out of the conduct of administration are instituted, not in the regular law courts connected with the Ministry of Justice, but in special administrative courts connected with the Ministry of the Interior. French thought, inherited from days of unbounded royal prerogative, makes sharp separation between Public Law, which concerns the action of the government, and Private Law, which concerns the relations of individuals to one another. The ordinary courts will determine the rights of an individual when they concern the action of another individual; but the special courts of the administration must determine the questions involved in any challenge of official action, — in any challenge of the public power. (Comp. page 166.) The highest of these courts is the Council of State, which is composed of the ministers, and of various high administrative officers of the permanent service. It is the court of last resort on administrative questions. It is also charged with the duty of giving advice to the Chambers or to the government on all questions affecting administration that may be referred to it.

The Prefectural Council. — Below the Council of State are the Prefectural Council, a Court of Revision, a Superior Council of Public Instruction, and a Court of Audit. These are not subordinate to each other : each is directly subordinate to the Council of State. The Prefectural Council is directly associated with the Prefect and is the most important of them. It has, amongst other weighty functions, that of determining the validity of elections to the Council of the Arrondissement and to the Municipal Council. For the rest, it has jurisdiction over all administrative questions, and over all conflicts between administrative authority and private rights. Its processes of trial and adjudication are briefer and less expensive than those of the ordinary law courts. In almost all cases an appeal lies to the Council of State.

> The Prefect is the legal representative of the government in cases brought before the Prefectural Council ; but that court is not at all under his dominance. It is composed of permanent judges, one of whom, at least, is usually of long administrative experience. Its members are appointed, and, for cause, are removable, by the central administration.

The Administration of Justice.

Ordinary Courts of Justice. — The supreme court of France is the Cassation Court (the Court, that is, of reversals or appeals) which sits at Paris. Next below it in rank are twenty-six Courts of Appeal, the jurisdiction of each of which extends over several Departments. These hear cases brought up from the courts of first instance which sit in the capital towns of the arrondissements. These last consider cases from the Justices of the Peace, who hold court for the adjudication of small cases in the cantons. By decree of the President, passed in the Council of Ministers, the Senate may be constituted a special court for the consideration of questions seeming to involve the safety of the state ; and such questions may be removed by the same authority from the ordinary courts.

The appointment of all judges rests with the President, or, rather, with the Minister of Justice ; and the tenure of the judicial office, except in the case of Justices of the Peace, is during good behavior. In the case of Justices of the Peace, the President has power to remove.

Jury Courts. — In France, the ordinary civil courts are without juries; the judges decide all questions of fact as well as all questions of law. There are, however, special jury courts (*cours d'assises*) constituted four times a year in each Department for the trial of crimes, and of political and press offences; and in these the jury is sole judge of the guilt or innocence of the accused; the judges determine the punishment.

Tribunal of Conflicts. — Between the two sets of courts, the administrative and the ordinary, there stands a Tribunal of Conflicts, whose province it is to determine to which jurisdiction, the administrative or the ordinary, any case belongs whose proper destination, or forum, is in dispute. This Tribunal consists of the Minister of Justice as president, of three State Councillors chosen by their colleagues, and of three members of the Cassation Court selected, in like manner, by their fellow-judges, besides two members chosen by those already mentioned.

Some Representative Authorities.

Aucoc, Conférences sur l'administration et le droit administratif, 3d ed., Paris, 1885.

Bastard D'Estang, Les Parlements de France.

Beaulieu, Leroy, Administration locale en France et en Angleterre.

Berthélemy, H., Traité élémentaire de droit administratif, 8th ed., Paris, 1916.

Block, Dictionnaire de l'administration française, Paris, 1887, and subsequent annual supplements.

Bodley, J. E. C., France, 2 vols., London and N. Y., 1898.

Borgeaud, Charles, Adoption and Amendment of Constitutions in Europe and America. Trans. from the French by C. D. Hazen and J. M. Vincent, N. Y., 1895.

Boutmy, Émile, Studies in Constitutional Law: France — England — United States. Trans. from the French by E. M. Dicey, London, 1891.

Bozérian, Étude sur la revision de la constitution.

Bracq, J. C., France under the Republic, N. Y., 1910.

Brissaud, J., History of French Private Law, Boston, 1912.

Burgess, J. W., Political Science and Constitutional Law, 2 vols., Boston, 1891.

Chéruel, Dictionnaire historique des Institutions, Mœurs, et Coutumes de la France, 2 vols., 6th ed., Paris, 1884.

Cubertin, Pierre de, The Evolution of France, under the Third Republic, N. Y., 1897.

Currier, C. F. A., Constitutional and Organic Laws of France, 1875–'89, Philadelphia (Am. Acad. Pol. Sci.), 1893.

Demombynes, Les Constitutions Européennes, 2 vols., Paris, 1883. Vol. II., p. 1 *et seq.*

Dickinson, Reginald, Summary of the Constitution and Procedure of Foreign Parliaments, 2d ed.

Ducrocq, Cours de droit administratif, 2 vols., Paris, 1881.

Duguit, L., Manuel de droit constitutionnel, 3d ed., Paris, 1918, and Traité de droit constitutionnel. Paris, 1911.

Dupriez, L., Les Ministres dans les principaux Pays d'Europe et d'Amérique, 2 vols., Paris, 1892.

Edwards, M. Betham, France To-Day, 2 vols., London, 1892–'94.

Esmein, A., Éléments du droit constitutionnel, 6th ed., Paris, 1914.

Ferron, H. de, Institutions municipales et provinciales comparées, Paris, 1884.

Gazzi, L., L'Interpellation à l'assemblée nationale. Marseilles, 1909.

Goodnow, Frank J., Comparative Administrative Law, 2 vols., N. Y., 1893.

Haas, C. P. M., Administration de la France, 4 vols., 2d ed., Paris, 1861.

Hanotaux, Gabriel, Contemporary France, 4 vols., N. Y., 1903–'09.

Jezè, G., Les principes généraux du droit administratif, Paris, 1904.

Kitchin, G. W., History of France, 3 vols., Oxford, 1881–'85.

Laferrière, E., Traité de la Juridiction administrative et des recours contentieux, 2 vols., Paris, 1887.

Lebon, André, Französisches Verfassungsrecht, Tübingen, 1909 ; Modern France (*Story of the Nations* Series), London and N. Y., 1896 ; and (with P. *Pelet*) France As It Is, London, 1888.

Lowell, A. Lawrence, Governments and Parties in Continental Europe, 2 vols., Boston, 1896.

Munro, W. B., The Government of European Cities, N. Y., 1909.

Naquet, A., The French Electoral System, N. A. Rev., vol. 155.

Ogg, F. A., The Governments of Europe, N. Y., 1913.

Pierre, Eugène, Traité de droit politique, électoral et parlementaire, Paris.

Poincaré, Raymond, How France is Governed. Eng. Trans., London and N. Y., 1913.

Scherer, Edmond, La Democratie et la France.

Shaw, Albert, Municipal Government in Continental Europe, N. Y., 1895.

Stephen, Sir James, Lectures on the History of France, 2 vols., 3d ed., London, 1857.

Tocqueville, Alexis de, L'Ancien Régime et la Révolution, and Recollections (Trans. London, 1896).

Villeneuve, M. de la Bigne de, Éléments de Droit constitutionnel français, Paris, 1892.

VIII.

THE GOVERNMENT OF GREAT BRITAIN.

I. CENTRAL GOVERNMENT.

Origin of the English Constitution. — The history of government in England begins with the primitive politics of the Teutonic races. Those great race movements of the fifth century which put the Frank into the Roman's place in Gaul put the Angles and Saxons in the place of the Roman in Britain. The first Teutons who made a permanent settlement in Britain (A.D. 449) did not find the Roman there; the imperial legions had been withdrawn from the island almost forty years before (A.D. 410) to serve the Empire in her contest with invading hosts nearer home. But the new-comers from the lowlands about the Elbe and the Weser found there many splendid and impressive monuments of the civilization which everywhere kept company with Roman dominion. What effect these evidences of the displaced system of Rome may have had upon the rough seamen who made the new conquest, or how much of Roman influence may have remained with the people of Britain to be handed on, in faint reproduction, to future masters of the island, it is impossible to say. Certainly, however, there was nothing of Rome's handiwork in the forms of government which the Teutons established at the basis of English politics. Those forms were their own. They were reproductions, as nearly as the conditions of conquest would permit, of the institutions which the Romans had seen in use among their redoubtable foes beyond the Rhine before ever the Empire had suffered serious inroad.

Primitive Teutonic Institutions. — These institutions had none of the national character which they were in the course of

178

time to acquire. They illustrated the well-known historical sequence, in which local tribal government always precedes central national government. Men governed themselves as families and small communities before they were governed as nations. For the Germans of that early time the village was the centre of political life; national organization they at first scarcely knew except for purposes of war; kingship among them was honorary and typical rather than real. The freemen of each little community in times of peace directed their own affairs with quite absolute freedom in village meeting. Even in war each freeman had a vote in the distribution of booty and could set his own imperative individuality as a more or less effectual check upon the wilfulness of his commander (pages 94–98). A very fierce democratic temper seems to have ruled in the politics of that rough primitive time. And it is not at all likely that this temper was a whit abated among the hardy pirates, as tempestuous as the northern waters which they braved, who founded new tribal kingdoms in Britain in the fifth century.

Institutional Changes effected by Conquest. — Concerted, organized movements for conquest did the same thing for the Angles and Saxons that they did for the Franks (page 102): they made real kingship necessary as an abiding basis for national organization. The military leader was of necessity constituted permanent king, the same cohesion being needed to follow up and enjoy conquest that had been needed to effect it. But the new kingdoms were at first quite small, — small as the island was, it held many such, — and the internal organization of the tribes was probably not deeply affected by the fact that a throne had been set up. The people gathered, as was their long-time wont, into more or less compact but always small communities, round about the homesteads and villages the Romans had built; enjoying their lands according to some system of ownership which left the chief pastures and the principal water supply open to use by all and reserved only the arable land to separate use by individuals. Justice and government still proceeded, as of old, at first hand, from the meeting of village freemen.

The Hundred-moot and the Folk-moot. — But there was, besides, a wider organization, possessing features which possibly had not been quite so fully and symmetrically developed and integrated in earlier practice. Communities were combined into 'hundreds,' and it was a combination of 'hundreds,' doubtless, that constituted the little kingdoms of the first periods of Saxon dominion, — some of which at any rate became the 'shires' or counties of the later times when all England was united under one rule. The 'hundred,' like the smaller units of the system, the several villages or communities, had its 'moot' or meeting, composed of the priest, the reeve, and four men from each township within its limits. The principal functions of this hundred-moot were those of a court: for the hundred was distinctively a judicial rather than an administrative district. Above the hundred-moot, at the top of the primitive system, was the general folk-moot, a general assembly of the freemen, playing the same part as tribal or national council that Tacitus had seen similar assemblies play in Germany in the first century.

English Kingdom and English County. — When the English kingdoms were many, each, probably, had its general council, which sat under the presidency of the king, and which advised with him concerning the common interests with some at least of the old authoritativeness which its conclusions had possessed before the new kingship had been created. When England had been made a single kingdom, in the later days when the Norman conquest was drawing near, these divisions of the land, these kingdoms which had once had independent political life, sank to the rôle of counties, and their folk-moots, which had once been national assemblies, became mere shire-moots, mere county courts, presided over by the sheriff as representative of the king, the bishop as representative of mother Church, and the ealdorman as representative of the tribe, and composed of the landowners of the shire, the reeve, priest, and four men from each township, twelve representatives from each hundred, and all officials.

The Witenagemot. — National authority, meantime, had passed, so far as it had passed to any assembly, to an assembly of another kind, to a great council called the *Witenagemot*, or Assembly of the Wise. We have no certain knowledge of the exact character of this famous national body; but we are probably warranted in concluding that it was formed more or less closely upon the model of the assemblies which it had supplanted. The national councils of the smaller kingdoms of the earlier time, which had now shrunk into mere shire courts, handed on their functions of general counsel, and in theory also, it may be, their organization, to the *Witenagemot*. Possibly it was within the right of every freeman to attend and vote in this great meeting of the nation; but as a matter of fact, its membership was limited, apparently from the first, to the chief men of the shires and of the royal household. To it came the sheriffs, the ealdormen, the bishops, and the chief officers and thegns about the king's person. When the king wished a veritable national council he would sometimes summon the moots of all the shires to meet him in grand *Mycel-gemót* at some central point in the kingdom and declare their assent to his laws. This he did to spare himself the trouble of taking his laws to each shire moot in turn, as it had once been the king's custom to do.

Powers of the Witenagemot. — The powers of the *Witenagemot* were very great indeed, — in theory always, perhaps at first in practice also. To it belonged the old popular prerogative of electing, or upon occasion deposing, the king. It gave or withheld its consent to grants of the public land. It was the supreme court of the kingdom, for both civil and criminal cases. It shared with the king the lawmaking and appointing power, and joined him in the imposition of taxes. As the king grew in power and influence, the coöperation of the *Witenagemot* in judgment and legislation became more and more a matter of form only; but always there were two or three yearly meetings of the body, and its action, though in most things merely formal and perfunctory, was yet a necessary and, symbolically, a valuable form, preserving, as it did, the memory, if no more, of the nation's freedom.

The Norman Feudalization. — With the Norman conquest came profound changes in the government of England. The chief officers of the shire became royal officers merely, the ecclesiastical authority being set apart to itself, and the ealdorman being shut out from all administrative functions. The land William confiscated in vast quantities, in the ruthless thoroughness of his conquest, because of the stubborn resistance of its English own-

ers, and granted away in new estates to Normans or to submissive Englishmen, to be held in feudal subjection to himself.
The feudal system, so familiar to the historian of the Continent,
with its separated baronial jurisdictions and its personal dependencies of vassal upon lord and of lord upon overlord, was perfected in England also. Township courts in most places gave
way to baronial courts; hundred-moots lost their one-time importance; and all judicial power that did not pass into the hands of
feudal lords tended to pass to the court of the sheriff, the king's
lieutenant in the shire. Still William kept the barons under; he
did not suffer their power to become threatening to his own, but
kept them always dependent upon himself for the continued exercise of their privileges.

The Great Council of the Norman Kings. — More important still, he preserved, with modifications to suit his change of
system, the national assembly of the Saxon polity. He claimed
to come to the throne by natural right and legal succession, not
by conquest, and he sought to continue, so far as might be, the
constitution under which he claimed succession. He sought and
obtained formal election to the throne, as nearly as possible in
accordance with the ancient forms; and, his throne secure, he
endeavored to rule within the sanction of ancient custom. He
maintained the *Witenagemot*. But its character greatly changed
under his hands. Revolt hardened his rule, to the exclusion
of the old national element from the central assembly of the
realm. As the new organization of the country assumed a feudal character of the Norman type, that new character became
mirrored in the composition of the royal council. The *Mycel-
gemót* merged in the Great Council (*magnum* or *commune con-
cilium*) of the king's tenants-in-chief. To it came at first, besides
the earls, the barons, and the knights, who either in fact or in
feudal theory held their lands of the king, the archbishops also,
the bishops, and the abbots; subsequently, however, even these
ecclesiastical members were admitted only as barons, as holding
land of the king and so members of the feudal hierarchy. In
theory, it would seem, every landowner was entitled to claim a
seat in this Council; it was meant to hold the place of a national
assembly which could speak for the governing classes; but in

fact only the greater barons and churchmen as a rule attended, and 'tenure by barony ' became at length the only valid title to membership. The development of the Great Council of the Norman kings is the central subject of early English constitutional history ; for from it may be said to have sprung the whole effective organization of the present government of England. Out of it, directly or indirectly, by one process or another, have been evolved Parliament, the Cabinet, and the courts of law.

The Feudal System in England. — England was not feudalized by the Normans. Feudalization had grown there under Saxon and Dane as elsewhere under Frank and Goth. Society in England, as on the Continent, had divided into ranks of nobles, freemen, and slaves bound together by personal fealty and the principles of land ownership. What the Norman did was to give new directions to the indigenous growth of feudalism. The system had not gone to such lengths of disintegration in England as it afterwards went on the Continent, and William the Conqueror's first care when compacting his power in the island was to subordinate all feudal elements permanently to the Crown. He saw to it, by the unhesitating use of his great power, that no baron should be able to cope with the king without wide combination with other barons, such as watchful kings could probably always prevent ; and he dulled the edge of hostile feeling by giving to the greater barons of the kingdom a function of weight in the management of affairs by bringing them into peaceful and legitimate combination in the Great Council, which he called together three times every year, and whose advice he never refused at least to hear. The Council retained, formally at any rate, the right to choose the king, and all laws were declared to be enacted by and with its advice and consent.

Character of English Institutional Growth. — It has been

noted as a leading characteristic of the constitutional history of England that her political institutions have been incessantly in process of development, a singular continuity marking the whole of the transition from her most ancient to her present forms of government. It is not a history of breaks or of new establishments, or of successive new creations of instrumentalities of legislation and administration : all the way through it is a history of almost insensible change, of slow modification, and of unforced, almost of unconscious, development. Very great contrasts appear between the character of her government in one age and its character in another age distant one or more centuries from the first; but it is very difficult to perceive any alteration at all when comparison is made from generation to generation. Almost no changes can be given exact dates: each took place 'about' such and such a year, or in this or that long reign. The whole process, therefore, is one which may be outlined in brief epitome: its stages are long, its features large, its details unessential to clearness.

The Course of Development. — In briefest summary the facts are these: the Great (or National) Council itself became the Parliament of the realm; those of its members, as originally constituted, who were state officers and chief officials of the court became a Permanent royal Council, out of which, in course of time grew the more modern Privy Council and at length the Cabinet; and whose members of the Permanent Council whose duties were financial and judicial gradually drew apart from the rest for the exercise of their functions, their work being finally divided among them according to its nature, and the several bodies into which they thus fell apart becoming, in the end, the courts of Exchequer, of Chancery, and of common law.

The Permanent Council. — The body of state and court officers whom the king kept always about him as his 'Ordinary' or Permanent Council were originally all of them members of the Great Council and seem at first to have acted as a sort of "committee, or inner circle," of that greater body. The Great Council met but three times in the year; its organization was not permanent; its membership varied, both numerically and personally, from year to year. The officers of the permanent service, on the other hand, were always within easy reach of consultation; they were in a certain sense picked men out of the larger body of the national Council; it was natural that they should be consulted by the king and that their advice, given in their collective capacity as a smaller council, should carry with it the weight of their connection with the more authoritative Great Council. As a matter of fact at any rate, they acquired powers almost coincident with those of the national body itself. Their powers came, indeed, to possess an importance superior even to those of the more august assembly, being exercised as they were, not intermittently or occasionally, but continuously; not with a mere outside acquaintance with the posture of affairs, but with an inside intimacy of knowledge.

Composition of Permanent Council. — Under the Norman kings the membership of the Permanent Council consisted, usually, of the two archbishops (of Canterbury and of York), the Justiciar, the Treasurer, the Chancellor, the Steward, the Marshall, the Chamberlain, and the Butler, with the occasional addition of other officials, such as the king's Sergeant, and of such bishops and barons as the sovereign saw fit from time to time to summon. There was, however, no fixed rule as to its composition. Possibly every baron, as a member of the Great Council, could, if he had so chosen, have attended the sittings of this section of the Great Council also, which, while the Great Council was not in session, masqueraded as its deputy and proxy. Practically, it would seem always, as a rule, to have lain within the king's choice to constitute it how he would.

The Powers of the Permanent Council were enormous : were as large as those of the king himself, who constituted it his administrative, judicial, and legislative agent. Its " work was to counsel and assist the king in the execution of every power of the crown which was not exercised through the machinery of the common law " ;[1] and " the king could do nearly every act in his Permanent Council of great men which he could perform when surrounded by a larger number of his nobles ; except impose taxes on those nobles themselves." [2] But the Permanent Council very early ceased to act as a whole in the discharge of all its functions alike. Itself a committee, it presently, in its turn, began to split up into committees.

The Law Courts. — Men specially learned in the law were brought into its membership, the later kings not hesitating, when the needs of the service demanded, to introduce commoners, as the Council drifted away from even its nominal connection with the Great Council ; and to these the financial and judicial functions of the Crown were more and more exclusively entrusted. (Compare page 141.) It was not long before (a) a separate *Court of Exchequer*, which was at first charged principally with the

---

[1] Stubbs, *Constitutional History of England*, Vol. III., p. 252.
[2] A. V. Dicey, *The Privy Council*, p. ii.

audit of finance accounts, had been permanently assigned its
special ' barons ' as Justices, and had acquired jurisdiction over
all cases in which the king was directly concerned; (*b*) another
special bench of judges received, as a *Court of Common Pleas*,
jurisdiction over all civil cases between subject and subject; (*c*)
still another came to figure as a supreme court, or *Court of King's
Bench*, which always accompanied the sovereign wherever he
went, which was in theory presided over by the king himself, and
which was empowered to supervise local justice and itself control
all cases not specially set apart for the hearing of other courts; and
(*d*) the Chancellor, who had once been merely president, in the
king's absence, of the Permanent Council when it heard appeals
in its judicial capacity, absorbed to himself, in his *Court of
Chancery*, the whole of that so-called ' equitable ' function of the
Crown by virtue of which the king granted relief to suitors for
whose cases the common law provided no adequate process.   The
Chancellorship was thus put in the way of attaining to its later-
day partial ascendency over the ' courts of law.'   This process of
the differentiation and development of the courts began in the early
years of the twelfth century and may be said to have been completed by the middle of the fourteenth.

Parliament. — Meantime the national body, the Great
Council, from which the Permanent Council and courts had been
derived, had had its own expansions and changes of form and had
taken on a new character of the utmost significance.   Not greatly
altered in its composition during the century which followed the
Norman conquest, the Great Council was profoundly affected by
the outcome of Magna Charta (A.D. 1215) and the momentous
constitutional struggles which followed it.   It was then that the
principle of *representation* was first introduced into the constitution of Parliament and that commoners as well as nobles were
given seats in the national assembly.   The archbishops, bishops,
and abbots attended as of course, as always before, and the earls
and greater barons held themselves equally entitled to be summoned always by special personal summons; but the lesser barons,
who formerly had been called to the Council, not by personal
summons, but only by a general summons addressed to them,
along with all tenants-in-chief, through the sheriffs of the counties,

had given over attending because of the expense and inconvenience of the privilege, and were accordingly no longer called. Their place was filled by representation. Writs addressed to the sheriffs commanded the election of representatives of the lower clergy and, more important still, of representatives (knights) of the shires and (burgesses) of the towns. The Parliament which Edward I. summoned in 1295 contained all these elements and established the type for the composition of all future Parliaments.

In the fourteenth clause of Magna Charta John was made to promise that, besides summoning the archbishops, bishops, abbots, earls, and greater barons severally, by special personal letters, he would summon all lesser barons also by a general summons, through the sheriffs and bailiffs. But this general summons failed of the desired effect.

Representatives from the towns were summoned first in 1265 by Earl Simon of Montfort, who knew that he could count upon the support of the commons of England in his contest with the king, Henry III., and who called burgesses to the Parliament which he constituted during the brief period of his supremacy in order to give open proof of that support. Edward I. followed Montfort's example in 1295, not because he was deliberately minded to form a truly representative assembly as a wise step in constitutional development, but because he wanted money and knew that taxes would be most readily paid if voted by an assembly representing all classes.

Representatives from the shires (knights) had often been called to Parliament before 1265. Step by step, first one element of the nation and then another had been introduced into Parliament: first the lesser barons, by general summons, — only, however, to drop out again, — then the gentry of the shires by election in the counties, finally the burghers of the towns by similar election in county court.

Genesis of the Two Houses. — Such a body as the Parliament summoned by Edward was, however, too conglomerate, too little homogeneous to hold together. It did not long act as a single assembly; but presently fell apart into two 'houses.' Had the lower clergy continued to claim representation, there might and probably would have been three houses instead of two. But, instead of setting up a separate house in the civil Parliament, the clergy drew apart for the creation of an entirely distinct body, which, under the name of 'Convocation,' was to constitute a separate ecclesiastical parliament, devoting itself exclusively to the government of the Church. Their share in the management of temporal affairs they left altogether to the 'spiritual lords,' the few greater magnates of the Church who retained their places in the national council, and to such lay representatives as the clergy could assist in electing to the lower house.

There were left, therefore, in Parliament two main elements, lords and commoners. The lords, to whom the arch-bishops, bishops, and abbots adhered by immemorial wont, formed a house to themselves, the House of Lords. The commoners from the towns, who were soon joined by the middle order of gentry, the knights of the shires, who were neither great lords summoned by personal summons nor yet commoners, formed the other house, the House of Commons. These changes also were completed by the middle of the fourteenth century. Parliament was by that time, outwardly, just what it is now.

The Privy Council. — The Great Council and its direct heir, Parliament, were not a little jealous of the enormous powers wielded by the preferred counsellors of the king whom he main-tained in permanent relations of confidence with himself, and through whom he suffered to be exercised some of the greatest of the royal prerogatives. Especially did the arrangement seem obnoxious when the vitality of the Permanent Council passed to a still smaller 'Privy' Council. This body was to the Per-manent Council what the Permanent Council had been to the Great Council. It was still another "inner circle." It emerged during the reign of Henry VI. (1422–1461). The Permanent Council had become too large and unwieldy for the continuance of its intimate relations with the sovereign; it could no longer be used as a whole for purposes of *private* advice and resolution; and the king separated from the 'ordinary' councillors certain selected men whom he constituted his *Privy* Council, binding them to himself by special oaths of fidelity and secrecy. From that moment the Permanent Council was virtually superseded, and the Privy Council became the chief administrative and govern-ing body of the realm.

The Privy Council assumes Judicial Powers. — Many of the judicial prerogatives which really belonged to the king when sitting in his Great Council, or Parliament, had been claimed for the king's Permanent Council: hence the distinct law courts which were developed from its midst (sec. 847); and the same rights of exercising the powers of a court which had been assumed by the Permanent Council were in the later time arrogated to itself by the Permanent Council's proxy, the Privy Council. Out of it came, in course of time, the well-remembered Council of the North, the hated Star Chamber, and the odious High Commission Court, which were not abolished until 1641, when that great revolution had fairly set in, which was to crush arbitrary executive power forever in England, and to usher in the complete supremacy of Parliament.

Origin of the Cabinet. — Meanwhile, long before the parliamentary wars had come to a head, the same causes that had produced the Permanent and Privy Councils had again asserted their strength and produced the *Cabinet*, still a third "inner circle," this time of the Privy Council; a small body selected for special confidence by the king from the general body of his counsellors, and meeting him, not in the larger council chamber, but in a 'cabinet,' or smaller room, apart. The Privy Council had, in its turn, become "too large for despatch and secrecy. The rank of Privy Councillor was often bestowed as an honorary distinction on persons to whom nothing was confided, and whose opinion was never asked. The Sovereign, on the most important occasions, resorted for advice to a small knot of leading ministers. The advantages and disadvantages of this course were early pointed out by Bacon, with his usual judgment and sagacity; but it was not till after the Restoration that the interior Council began to attract general notice. During many years old-fashioned politicians continued to regard the Cabinet as an unconstitutional and dangerous board. Nevertheless, it constantly became more and more important. It at length drew to itself the chief executive power, and has now been regarded during several generations as an essential part of our polity. Yet, strange to say, it still continues to be altogether unknown to the law. The names of the noblemen and gentlemen who compose it are never officially announced to the public; no record is kept of its meetings and resolutions; nor has its existence ever been recognized by any Act of Parliament." [1]

[1] Macaulay, *History of England*, Vol. I., pp. 197, 198 (Harper's ed., 1849).

The Development of the Cabinet. — The Cabinet first comes distinctly into public view as a preferred candidate for the highest executive place in the reign of Charles II. It is now the central body of the English Constitution. The steps by which it approached its present position are thus summarized by a distinguished English writer: —

"(1) First we find the Cabinet appearing in the shape of a small, informal, irregular *Camarilla*, selected at the pleasure of the Sovereign from the larger body of the Privy Council, consulted by and privately advising the Crown, but with no power to take any resolutions of State, or perform any act of government without the assent of the Privy Council, and not as yet even commonly known by its present name. This was its condition anterior to the reign of Charles I.

"(2) Then succeeds a second period, during which this Council of advice obtains its distinctive title of Cabinet, but without acquiring any recognized status, or *permanently* displacing the Privy Council from its position of *de facto* as well as *de jure* the only authoritative body of advisers of the Crown. (Reign of Charles I. and Charles II., the latter of whom governed during a part of his reign by means of a Cabinet, and towards its close through a 'reconstructed' Privy Council.)

"(3) A third period, commencing with the formation by William III." of a ministry representing, not several parties, as often before, but the party predominant in the state, "the first ministry approaching the modern type. The Cabinet, though still remaining, as it remains to this day, unknown to the Constitution," had "now become *de facto*, though not *de jure*, the real and sole supreme consultative council and executive authority in the State." It was "still, however, regarded with jealousy, and the full realization of the modern theory of ministerial responsibility, by the admission of its members to a seat in Parliament," was "only by degrees effected.

"(4) Finally, towards the close of the eighteenth century, the political conception of the Cabinet as a body, — necessarily consisting (*a*) of members of the Legislature (*b*) of the same political views, and chosen from the party possessing a majority in the House of Commons; (*c*) prosecuting a concerted policy; (*d*)

under a common responsibility to be signified by collective resig
nation in the event of parliamentary censure; and (e) acknowledging a common subordination to one chief minister, — took
definitive shape in our modern theory of the Constitution, and
so remains to the present day." [1]

Parliament and the Ministers. — The principles concerning the composition of the modern Cabinets which are stated in
this last paragraph of Mr. Traill's summary may be said to have
been slowly developed out of the once changeful relations between
Parliament and the ministers of the Crown.   As I have said (page
188), the national council very early developed a profound jealousy of the power and influence of the small and private council
of state and court officials which the king associated with himself
in the exercise of his great prerogatives.   By every means it
sought to control the ministers.   Abandoning very soon, as revolutionary, all efforts to hold the king himself personally responsible for executive acts, Parliament early accepted the theory that
the king could do no wrong; that breaches of law and of right
committed by the government were committed always, — so the
theory ran, — by the vicious advice of the king's personal advisers;
they could do wrong (here the theory shaded off into fact), and
they should be held responsible for all the wrong done.   So early
as the close of the twelfth century the Great Council deposed William Longchamp, Justiciar and Chancellor of Richard I., for abuse
of power.   During the fourteenth century Parliament claimed and
once or twice exercised the right to appoint ministers and judges;
it beheaded Edward II.'s Treasurer and imprisoned his Chancellor for their part in Edward's illegal acts; and at the close of the
century (1386) it impeached Michael de la Pole, Richard II.'s
minister, notwithstanding the fact that he was able to plead the
king's direct commands in justification of what he had done.   In
the seventeenth century a new ground of impeachment was added.
From that time out, ministers were held responsible, by the severe processes of trial by Parliament for high crimes and misdemeanors, not only for illegal, but also for bad advice to the
Crown, for gross mistakes of policy as well as for overt breaches
of law and of constitutional rights.

[1] H. D. Traill, *Central Government* (English Citizen Series), pp. 23-25.

Disappearance of Impeachment. — The Act of Settlement and the policy of William and Mary inaugurated, however, the final period of Parliament's supremacy. Parliament's preferences began to be regarded habitually in the choice of ministers, and impeachment, consequently, began gradually to fall into disuse. Its place was taken by parliamentary votes, — finally by votes of the House of Commons alone. Ministers who cannot command a majority in the House of Commons for the measures which they propose resign, and Parliament has its own way concerning the conduct of the government.

The Executive. — The Executive, under the English system, so far as it may be described at once briefly and correctly, may be said to consist, therefore, of the Sovereign and a Cabinet of ministers appointed with the Sovereign's formal consent. All real authority is with the Cabinet; though the ministers are, in law, only the Sovereign's advisers, and the government is conducted in the Sovereign's name. The true place of the Sovereign in the system is that of an honored and influential hereditary councillor, to whose advice an exalted title and a constant familiarity with the greater affairs of state lend a peculiar weight. The king [1] is in fact, though of course not in legal theory, a permanent minister, differing from the other ministers chiefly in not being responsible to Parliament for his acts, and on that account less powerful than they.

The Sovereign is not a member of the Cabinet because George I. could not speak English. Until the accession of George I. the king always attended Cabinet councils; George did not do so because he could not either understand or be understood in the discussions of the ministers. Since his time, therefore, the Sovereign has not sat with the Cabinet. A similar example of the interesting ease with which men of our race establish and observe precedents is to be found in the practice on the part of Presidents of the United States of sending written messages to Congress. Washington and John Adams addressed Congress in person on public affairs; but Jefferson, the third President, was not an easy speaker, and preferred to send a written message. Subsequent Presidents followed his example as of course. Hence a sacred rule of constitutional action! [1]

[1] A rule which President Wilson, himself, was the first President to violate. He has never sent a written message to the Congress, but has always addressed it in person.

Position of the Cabinet. — The Cabinet consists of the principal ministers of state and has reached its present position of power in the government because of its responsibility to Parliament. The chief interest of English constitutional history centres in the struggle of Parliament to establish its supremacy over all other authorities in the conduct of the government; that struggle issued in the last century in the complete triumph of Parliament; it has reached its farthest logical consequence in **1911** in the concentration of parliamentary authority in the popular house of Parliament, the House of Commons. Parliament always claimed the right to direct in the name of the people, of the nation; that was the solid basis of all its pretensions; and so soon as reforms in the composition of the House of Commons had made it truly representative of the people, the House of Lords, which represents the hereditary, not the representative, principle, necessarily lost some part of its political authority. It is constantly recruited, by the creation of peerages, from all classes of successful men, scientists, manufacturers, lawyers, diplomatists, journalists, poets; but it is recruited by appointment, not by election; its votes are not controlled by the electorate; and precedence in affairs has fallen to the people's chamber.

Appointment of the Cabinet Ministers. — The responsibility of the ministers to Parliament constitutes their strength because it makes them the agents of Parliament: and the agents of a sovereign authority virtually share its sovereignty. The king appoints only such ministers as have the confidence of the House of Commons; and he does it in this way: he sends for the recognized leader of the political party which has the majority in the House of Commons and asks him to form a Cabinet. If this leader thinks that his party will approve of his assuming such a responsibility, he accepts the commission, and, usually after due consultation with other prominent members of his party, gives to the Sovereign a list of the men whom he recommends for appointment to the chief offices of state. These the Sovereign appoints and commissions as of course. They are always men chosen from among the members of both houses of Parliament, and generally because they have proved there their

ability to lead. They have, so to say, chosen themselves by a
career of steady success in the debates of the Houses : they have
come to the front by their own efforts, by force of their own ability, and usually represent tried parliamentary capacity. Such
capacity is necessary for their success as ministers ; for, after they
have entered the Cabinet, they constitute, in effect, a committee
of the majority of the House of Commons, commissioned to lead
Parliament in debate and legislation, to keep it, — and, through
it, the country at large, — informed concerning all important
affairs of state which can prudently be made public, and to carry
out in the conduct of the government the policy approved of by
the representatives of the people.

Composition of the Cabinet. — The Cabinet does not consist invariably of the same number of ministers. Until 1916
eleven officials always have had seats in it ; namely, the First
Lord of the Treasury, the Lord Chancellor, the Lord President of
the Council, the Lord Privy Seal, the Chancellor of the Exchequer,
the five Secretaries of State (for Home Affairs, for Foreign
Affairs, for the Colonies, for India, and for War), and the First
Lord of the Admiralty. To these were generally added from
three to six others, according to circumstances : often, for instance, the President of the Board of Trade, generally of late the
Chief Secretary for Ireland, frequently the President of the Local
Government Board. The general rule which governed these
additions was, that every interest which was likely to be prominent in the debates and proceedings of the House of Commons
ought to have a Cabinet minister to speak for it and to offer to
the House responsible advice. When Mr. Lloyd George became
Prime Minister in December, 1916, he formed a War Cabinet of
five members, expanded to six in 1917 with an occasional
seventh, but did not include any of the principal Secretaries
of State. Three members of the War Cabinet are ministers
'without Portfolio.' The word 'Ministry' is of wider meaning
than the word 'Cabinet.' The 'Ministry' consists of all those
executive officers who have seats in Parliament. These are the
'political' officers, who are expected to resign their offices when
the Cabinet is defeated in the Commons. But not all of them
are members of the Cabinet. The Coalition Cabinet of Mr.

Asquith in 1916 consisted of twenty-three persons; but besides these there are some forty-five non-Cabinet ministers in Parliament. (Compare p. 202.)

No member of the House of Commons may accept office without the approval of his constituents. Upon receiving an appointment as minister he must resign his seat in the House and seek reëlection, as representative *plus* minister.[1] The whole matter is merely formal, however, in most cases. The opposite party do not usually, under such circumstances, contest the seat a second time, and the minister is reëlected without opposition.

The custom of the Sovereign's selecting only the chief minister and intrusting him with the formation of a ministry also, as well as the Sovereign's absence from Cabinet meetings, originated with George I., who did not know enough of English public men to choose all the ministers, and so left the choice to Walpole.

This method of forming a ministry is the outcome of Parliament's efforts to hold the king's ministers to a strict responsibility to itself. None but members of their own party would suit the majority in Parliament as ministers; and since the ministers have to explain and excuse their policy to the Houses it is best that they should be members of the Houses with the full privileges of the floor. Only by such an arrangement could the full harmony desired between Parliament and the ministers be maintained: by face to face intercourse.

Ministerial Responsibility. — If the ministers are defeated on any important measure in the House of Commons, or if any vote of censure is passed upon them in that House, they must resign, — such is the command of precedent, — and another ministry must be formed which is in accord with the new majority. The ministers must resign together because the best form of responsibility for their conduct of the government can be secured only when their measures are taken in concert, and the House of Commons would be cheated of all real control of them if they could, upon each utterance of its condemnation of an executive act, or upon each rejection by it of a measure proposed or supported by them, 'throw overboard' only those of their number whose departments were most particularly affected by the vote,

[1] This requirement has been waived by acts of Parliament during the war.

and so keep substantially the same body of men in office. If a defeated or censured ministry think that the House of Commons in its adverse vote has not really spoken the opinion of the constituencies, they can advise the Sovereign to dissolve the House and order a new election; that advice must be taken by the Sovereign; and the ministers stand or fall according to the disposition of the new House towards them.

It should be added that exceptional cases do sometimes arise in which responsibility for an objectionable course of action can be so plainly and directly fixed upon a particular minister, who has acted, it may be, without the concurrence, possibly without the knowledge, of his colleagues, that his separate dismissal from office is recognized as the only proper remedy. A notable instance of this sort arose in England in 1851, when Lord Palmerston, then foreign secretary, was dismissed from office for adding to various other acts of too great independence an un-authorized expression of approval of the *coup d'état* of Louis Napoleon in France.

Legal Status of the Cabinet. — The peculiar historical origin of the Cabinet appears in a statement of its position before the law. As we have seen (page 189), it is not a body recognized by law: its existence, like the existence of not a few other political institutions in England, is only *customary*. The particular ministers who form the Cabinet have the legal right to be the exclusive advisers of the Crown, — that is, the sole executive power, — only by virtue of their membership of the Privy Council. They must all be sworn into the membership of that body before they can act as confidential servants of the Sovereign. The Privy Council itself, however (as a whole, that is), has not been asked for political advice for two centuries. It takes no part whatever in the function which certain ministers exercise by virtue of belonging to it; it is not responsible for the advice they give; and it cannot in any way control that advice. Membership of the Privy Council, moreover, is for life. The leaders of the minority in the Commons, having themselves once been ministers, are still members of the Council and have still the same *legal* right to advise the Crown.

Initiative of the Cabinet in Legislation. — Having inherited the right of initiative in legislation which once belonged to the Crown, the Cabinet shape and direct the business of the Houses. Most of the time of Parliament is occupied by the consideration of measures which they have prepared and introduced ; at every step in the procedure of the Houses it is the duty of the ministers to guide and facilitate business.

The Prime Minister. — ' Consistency in policy and vigor in administration' on the part of the Cabinet are obtained by its organization under the authority of one 'First' Minister. This Prime Minister generally holds the office of First Lord of the Treasury, though it is within his choice to hold another, if he will. It is not the office which gives him primacy in the Cabinet, but his recognized weight as leader of his party. The leader chosen by the Sovereign to form the ministry stands at its head when formed. He usually chooses to occupy the office of First Lord of the Treasury because the official duties of that place are nominal only and leave him free to exercise his important functions as leader of the party in power. The Prime Minister, though ' unknown to the constitution,' has been given indirect recognition by a Royal Proclamation of December 2, 1905, giving him ' place and precedence' above all his colleagues except the Lord Chancellor and next after the Archbishop of York. Recognition by statute fixing the order of precedence of public dignitaries followed in 1906.

The Departments of Administration. — So much for the relations of the Cabinet to the Sovereign and to Parliament. When we turn to view it in its administrative and governing capacity as the English Executive, we see the ministers as heads of departments, as in other governments. But the departments of the central government in England are by no means susceptible of brief and simple description as are those of other countries, which have been given their present forms by logical and self-consistent written constitutions, or by the systematizing initiative of absolute monarchs. They hide a thousand intricacies born of that composite development so characteristic of English institutions.

The Five Great ' Offices ' of State. — Not attempting detail, however, it is possible to give a tolerably clear outline of the central administration of the kingdom in comparatively few words. The Treasury I shall describe in a separate paragraph. The *Home Office* has a great variety of duties: it superintends the constabulary; oversees, to a limited extent, the local magistracy and the administration of prisons; advises the Sovereign with reference to the granting of pardons; and is the instrument of Parliament in carrying out numerous statutes regulating the hours and conditions of labor in mines and factories. The *Foreign Office* describes itself. So do also, sufficiently, the *Colonial Office*, the *War Office*, and the *India Office*.

These five great 'Offices' are all, historically considered, in a certain sense offshoots from a single office, that of the king's Principal Secretary of State. By one of the usual processes of English constitutional development, an officer bearing this title very early came into existence as one of the most trusted ministers of the Crown. At first only a specially confided-in servant of the Sovereign, employed in all sorts of confidential missions, he gradually assumed a more regular official place and began to absorb various important functions. At length it became necessary to double him and to have two Principal Secretaries of State, two men theoretically sharing one and the same office, and alternates of each other. At last he has, for the sake of convenience, been *quintupled*.

There are five Principal Secretaries of State, all, in theory, holding the same office, and each, in theory, legally authorized to perform the functions of any or all of the others; but in fact, of course, keeping each to a distinct department. There is a Principal Secretary of State for the Home Department, a Principal Secretary of State for Foreign Affairs, a Principal Secretary of State for the Colonies, a Principal Secretary of State for War, and a Principal Secretary of State for India. It is an interesting and characteristic case of evolution.

The Admiralty, the Board of Trade, and the Local Government Board. — The Admiralty is the naval office. It is presided over by a Commission of six, consisting of a chairman, entitled First Lord of the Admiralty, and five Junior Lords. *The Board* *of Trade* is, in form, a committee of the Privy Council. It is reconstituted at the opening of each reign by an order in Council. It consists, nominally, of "a President and certain *ex officio* members, including the First Lord of the Treasury, the Chancellor of the Exchequer, the Principal Secretaries of State, the Speaker of the House of Commons, and the Archbishop of Canterbury."[1] But it has long since lost all vital connection with the Privy Council and all the forms even of board action. Its President is now practically itself. Its duties and privileges are both extensive and important. It advises the other departments concerning all commercial matters, and is the statistical bureau of the kingdom; it exercises the state oversight of railways, inspects passenger steamers and merchant vessels, examines and commissions masters and mates for the merchant marine, administers the statutes concerning harbors, lighthouses, and pilotage, provides standard weights and measures, superintends the coinage, and supervises the Post Office. *The Local Government Board,* which is also in form a committee of the Privy Council, has also in reality none of the characteristics either of a committee or of a board. It is a separate and quite independent department, under the control of a President. Its other, nominal, members, the Lord President of the Council, the five Principal Secretaries of State, the Lord Privy Seal, and the Chancellor of the Exchequer, in reality take no part in its management. It is, in effect, the English department of the Interior. It is charged with supervising the administration, by the local authorities of the kingdom, "of the laws relating to the public health, the relief of the poor, and local government"; old age pensions; roads; — duties more important to the daily good government of the country than those of any other department. It also specially examines and reports upon every private bill affecting private interests.

The Board of Agriculture. — In 1889 still another department was set up which was to be in form a Board but in fact in charge of a single minister, its President. Since 1883 there had been a Committee of the Privy Council charged with the special

[1] Traill, pp. 126, 127.

superintendence of the agricultural interests of the kingdom; in 1889 it was given a more definite organization and larger powers, under the name of The Board of Agriculture, — a Board to consist nominally of the Lord President of the Council, the five Principal Secretaries of State, the First Commissioner of the Treasury, the Chancellor of the Exchequer, the Chancellor of the Duchy of Lancaster, and the Secretary for Scotland; but really to be under the direction of none of these gentlemen, but of its own independent President.

The duties of the Board embrace, besides the collection and publication of all information likely to be serviceable to the agricultural interest and the conduct and encouragement of inquiries and investigations touching agricultural processes and conditions and concerning the culture of forests, the inspection and subvention of schools in which instruction is given in such subjects, the duties hitherto attaching to the offices of the Land Commissioners and of the Commissioners of Works and Public Buildings, the enforcement of the acts concerning contagious diseases among animals, and a miscellany of duties of like kinds.

The Post Office is in England a subdivision of the Board of Trade. At its head is a Postmaster General. It controls, besides the usual business of a post-office department, the telegraph and telephone system of the country, which is owned by the government; and it has also under its direction a useful postal savings-bank system.

The war has made necessary the creation of a number of new ministerial posts, the most important of which are the Minister of Munitions of War, with Mr. Lloyd George as the first to hold the position, for the control and production of arms and ammunition of every sort; the Minister of Blockade; the Shipping Controller; the Food Controller; the President of the Air Board, and the Minister of Reconstruction.

The Treasury. — The history of this department, which may be reckoned the most important, may serve as another typical example of English departmental evolution. Originally the chief financial minister of the Crown was the Lord High Treasurer, with whom was associated at an early date a Chancellor of the Exchequer. But in the reign of George I. the great office of Lord High Treasurer was, in English phrase, put permanently 'into commission': its duties, that is, were intrusted to a board instead of to a single individual. This board was known as the "Lords Commissioners for executing the office of Lord High Treasurer," and consisted of a First Lord of the Treasury, the Chancellor of the Exchequer, and three others known as Junior Lords.

Evolution speedily set in, as in other similar English boards. That is, the board ceased to act as a board. Its functions became concentrated in the hands of the Chancellor of the Exchequer; the First Lordship, occupied almost invariably since 1762 by the Prime Minister, gradually lost all connection, except that of honorary chairmanship, with the Treasury Commission, its occupant giving all his energies to his political functions (page 197); and the Junior Lords were left none but parliamentary duties.

The Chancellor of the Exchequer, therefore, is the working head of the Treasury Department, and as such plays one of the most conspicuous and important rôles in the government of the country. He controls the revenue and expenditure of the state, submitting to Parliament, in the form of an annual 'budget,' careful comparisons of the sums needed for the public service and of the sums that may be expected to accrue from existing or possible sources of revenue, together with proposals to extend or curtail taxation, according as there is prospect of a deficit or of a surplus under existing arrangements.

The Estimates. — The various departments make up their own estimates; but those are subjected to a careful examination by the Chancellor of the Exchequer, and with him rests the prerogative of revising them where they may seem to admit of or to require revision. Thus changes in the clerical forces of the departments or redistributions of their work among sub-departments, etc., cannot, if they involve additional expense, be made without express approval by the Treasury.

Mr. Gladstone twice, with characteristic energy, held, when Prime Minister, both the office of the First Lord of the Treasury and the office of Chancellor of the Exchequer, thus in effect once more bringing the First Lord into vital connection with his nominal department.

Administrative Departments of the Privy Council. — Though superseded as advisory council to the Crown by the Cabinet and deprived of all actual executive control by the virtual erection of its several boards into independent departments, the Privy Council still has one or two vital parts. Chief among these is *The Education Department,* which consists of the Lord President of the Council, as nominal chief, a Vice-President as working chief, and certain *ex officio* members, among them the Chancellor of the Exchequer and the Secretary of State for Home Affairs, and which is charged with the administration of the public educational system of the country. This committee preserves in a rather more than formal way its collegiate character. The important judicial duties of the Privy Council I shall speak of in another connection (page 219).

The Lord Privy Seal exercises no important functions except those of keeping the great Seal of State and affixing it to such public documents as need its formal attestation; but the office is a 'Cabinet office.' The lightness of its duties leaves its incumbent the freer for his Cabinet functions of counsel. It is a berth for elderly men of intellectual and political weight who cannot or will not undertake onerous official duties.

The Chancellor of the Duchy of Lancaster holds an office whose duties (entirely legal and local) have all been delegated by longstanding custom to a Vice-Chancellor; but eminent politicians are brought into the Cabinet through this sinecure Chancellorship in order that they may give the ministry the benefit of their advice and countenance.

Political Under Secretaries. — There are often associated with the principal ministers of state certain 'political' Under Secretaries, whose function is one of very considerable importance. A political Under Secretary is one who goes in or out of office with his party, not having a place in the Cabinet but sharing its fortunes in the Commons. He is parliamentary spokesman for his chief. If the foreign minister, for instance, or any other member of the Cabinet, the affairs of whose department may be expected to call forth frequent comment or question in the lower House, be a member of the House of Lords, he is represented in the Commons by an Under Secretary, who there speaks as the minister's proxy. The representation of the ministers in both Houses is thus secured. (Compare page 194.)

Administration of Scotland and Ireland. — The affairs of Scotland are cared for through the agency of a Lord Advocate for Scotland, who is the legal adviser of the government concerning Scotch interests, and a Secretary for Scotland who is the intermediary between the Scotch members of Parliament and the ministry, and the official spokesman of the ministers regarding Scotch business in the House of Commons. Officially the Lord Advocate ranks as a subordinate of the Secretary of State for Home Affairs.

The Irish executive is, formally at least, separate from the English, being vested in a Lord Lieutenant and a Privy Council; but in fact it is completely controlled by the English Cabinet though the *Chief Secretary to the Lord Lieutenant,* who is always a member of the House of Commons and, when Irish affairs are specially prominent, a member of the Cabinet also; and who, though in titular rank a subordinate of the Lord Lieutenant, is, by virtue of his relations to the Cabinet and to Parliament, in effect his master.

For many years the agitation for Home Rule had been carried on but without success till the accession to power of the Liberals in 1906 and again in 1910.

A Home Rule Act for Ireland was passed by the House of Commons in the three consecutive sessions of 1912–13, 1913, and 1914, but was rejected by the House of Lords. Under the provisions of the Parliament Act it accordingly became a statute, but before it could be put into operation the war began and a Suspensory Act was passed postponing the time for putting it into operation for twelve months, or, if the war were not then ended, to such further time as should be fixed by the King in Council.

The Home Rule Act provided that the executive power, vested in the King, should be exercised by a Lord Lieutenant, acting for the King, through the Irish Ministers, heads of the Irish Departments.

The legislative authority is in an Irish Parliament, consisting of the King and two Houses — a Senate and a House of Commons. This Parliament has authority to " make laws for the peace, order, and good government of Ireland " subject to the plenary authority of the Parliament of the United Kingdom and to certain special limitations.

All money bills shall originate in the Commons and may not be rejected or amended by the Senate. The Senate is to be composed of forty members, — those of the first Parliament to be nominated by the Imperial Cabinet and thereafter to be elected by the four Irish provinces, by proportional representation for a period of five years and not to be affected by dissolution. The House of Commons will consist of 164 members, elected by the present Parliamentary electors. In constituencies returning three or more members the principle of proportional representation will be applied. The duration of a House of Commons is five years, but it may be sooner dissolved by the Lord Lieutenant under circumstances similar to those that would lead to a dissolution of the House of Commons at Westminster.

In case of conflict between the Senate and the Commons, a bill sent up to the Senate for a second time in the following session and again rejected, is to be submitted to a joint session of the two Houses and if adopted by a majority of those present and voting, it shall become a law.

Irish representation in the House of Commons at Westminster is fixed at 42. When the financial arrangements between Ireland and the United Kingdom has been reached, additional members may be summoned from the Irish House of Commons in such numbers as will make the representation of Ireland equivalent to that of Great Britain on the basis of population. These members so summoned shall be deemed members of the House of Commons at Westminster for the purposes of revision of the financial arrangements.

The Lord Chancellor, the only regular member of the Cabinet whose duties I have not yet indicated, is a judicial and legislative officer. His functions will be mentioned in another connection (page 219).

The Cabinet as Executive. — It would be a great mistake to suppose that, because the Cabinet is in reality a committee of the House of Commons, drawing all its authority from the confidence reposed in it by that chamber, it is a *mere* committee, possessing no separate importance as the executive body of the kingdom. In a sense the ministers have inherited the ancient prerogatives of the Crown; and Parliament is, in a very sensible degree, dependent upon them for the efficacy of the part it is to play in governing. Almost all important legislation waits for their initiative, and the whole business of the Houses to a great extent depends upon them for its progress. They can make treaties, of whatever importance, with foreign countries; they can shape the policy of the mother country towards her colonies; they can take what serious steps they please with reference to the government of India, can place troops and naval forces at pleasure, can make a score of momentous moves of policy towards the English dependencies and towards foreign countries, — in the field, that is, of many of the largest interests of the Empire, — which may commit the country to the gravest courses of action; — and all without any *previous* consultation with Parliament, whom they serve. The House of Commons, in brief, can punish but cannot prevent them.

Parliament: I. the House of Commons; its Original Character. — "The Parliament of the nineteenth century is, in ordinary speech, the House of Commons. When a minister consults Parliament he consults the House of Commons; when the Queen dissolves Parliament she dissolves the House of Commons. A new Parliament is merely a new House of Commons."[1] Such has been the evolution of English politics. But the processes which worked out this result were almost five centuries long. During a very long period, Parliament's first and formative period, the Commons held a position of distinct and natural subordination to the Lords, lay and spiritual; the great constitutional rôles were played by the king and baronage. The commoners in Parliament represented the towns, and spoke, for the most part, at first, only concerning the taxes they would give.

[1] Spencer Walpole, *The Electorate and the Legislature* (English Citizen Series), p. 48.

When the house of Parliament called the House of Commons first assumed a distinct separate existence, about the middle of the fourteenth century (page 187), it was by no means a homogeneous body. It held both the knights of the shires and the burgesses of the towns; and it was a very long time before the knights forgot the doubt which had at first been felt as to which house they should sit with, Lords or Commons. They were men of consideration in their counties; the only thing in common between them and the men from the towns was that election, and not hereditary possessions or rank, was the ground of their presence in Parliament. Long use, however, finally obscured such differences between the two groups of members in the lower House; their interests were soon felt to be common interests, because the chief questions they had a real voice in deciding were questions of taxation, which touched all alike.

Historical Contrasts between County and Borough Representatives. — The main object of the Crown in making the Commons as representative as possible would seem to have been to bring the whole nation, as nearly as might be, into coöperation in support of the king's government: and at first the lower House was a truly representative body. The knights of the shires were elected "in the county court, by the common assent of the whole country"; the burgesses of the towns were chosen by the borough freemen, a body numerous or limited according to the charter of each individual town, but generally sufficiently broad to include the better class of citizens. It was the decay of the towns and the narrowing of their franchises which made the Commons of the closing decades of the last century and the first decades of our own the scandalously subservient, unrepresentative Commons which drove the American colonies into revolt. So early as the reign of Henry VI., in the first half, that is, of the fifteenth century, the franchise was limited in the counties to freeholders whose landed property was of an annual value of forty shillings, and forty shilling freeholders were then men of means;[1] but this franchise remained unchanged until the parliamentary reforms of

---

[1] Forty shillings, it is estimated, were equivalent at that time in purchasing value to eighty pounds at present ($400). See *J. E. T. Rogers, Economic Interpretation of History*, p. 32.

the present century, and tended steadily, with the advancing wealth of the country and the relative decrease in the value of the shilling, to become more inclusive and more liberal. The borough franchise, on the contrary, went all the time steadily from bad to worse. It became more and more restricted, and the towns which sent representatives to Parliament became, partly by reason of their own decay, partly by reason of the growth and new distribution of population in the kingdom, less and less fitted or entitled to represent urban England. New boroughs had been given representatives from time to time; but all efforts to redistribute representation had virtually ceased before the dawn of the period of that great increase of population and that immense development of wealth and industry which has made modern England what it is. The towns which returned members to the House of Commons were mostly in the southern counties where the old centres of population had been. Gradually they had lost importance as the weight of the nation shifted to the central and western counties and Liverpool, Manchester, and Birmingham grew up, — and not their importance only, but their inhabitants as well. Some fell into ruins and merged in neighboring properties, whose owners pocketed both them and their parliamentary franchise; others, which did not so literally decay, became equally subject to the influence of neighbor magnates upon whom the voters felt more or less dependent; and at last the majority of seats in the Commons were virtually owned by the landed classes represented in the House of Lords.

The House of Commons consisted in 1801 of 658 members, and of these 425 are said to have been returned "on the nomination or on the recommendation of 252 patrons." It is said, also, that "309 out of the 513 members belonging to England and Wales owed their election to the nomination either of the Treasury or of 162 powerful individuals." [1]

Geographical Relations of Boroughs and Counties. — Borough populations had no part in the election of county members. The counties represented in Parliament were rural areas, exclusive of the towns. Thus the county of Derby was, for the purposes of parliamentary representation, the county of Derby *minus* its boroughs.

[1] Walpole, p. 55.

Parliamentary Reform. — It was to remedy this condition that the reforms since the beginning of the nineteenth century were undertaken. Those reforms have made the House of Commons truly representative and national : and in making it national have made it dominant. In 1832 a wholesale redistribution of seats was accomplished, and a complete reformation of the franchise. The decayed towns were deprived of their members, and the new centres of population were accorded adequate representation. The right to vote in the countries was extended from those who owned freeholds to those who held property on lease and those who held copyhold estates,[1] and to tenants whose holdings were of the clear annual value of fifty pounds. The borough franchise was put upon the uniform basis of householders whose houses were worth not less than ten pounds a year. This was putting representation into the hands of the middle, well-to-do classes ; and with them it remained until 1867. In 1867 another redistribution of seats was effected, which increased the number of Scotch members from fifty-four to sixty and made other important readjustments of representation. The franchise was at the same time very greatly widened. In the boroughs all householders and every lodger whose lodgings cost him ten pounds annually were given the right to vote ; and in the counties, besides every forty shilling freeholder, every copyholder and leaseholder whose holding was of the annual value of five pounds, and every householder whose rent was not less than twelve pounds a year. Thus representation stood for almost twenty years. Finally, in 1884, the qualifications for voters in the counties were made the same as the qualifications fixed for borough electors by the law of 1867, and over two millions and a half of voters were thus added to the active citizenship of the country.

In 1885 another great *Redistribution Act* was passed, which merged eighty-one English, two Scotch, and twenty-two Irish boroughs in the counties in which they lie, for purposes of representation ; gave additional members to fourteen English, three

---

[1] Copyhold estates are estates held by the custom of the manor in which they lie, a custom once evidenced by a ' copy ' of the rolls of the Manor Court.

Scotch, and two Irish boroughs ; and created thirty-three new urban constituencies. The greater towns which returned several members were cut up into single-member districts, and a like arrangement was effected in the counties, which were divided into electoral districts to each of which a single representative was assigned.[1] These changes were accompanied by an increase of twelve in the total number of members. Through the redistribution of seats in 1832 and 1867 the number had remained 658 ; in 1885 it was raised to 670.

Parliamentary Franchise. — The last and most far-reaching extension of the suffrage, through the Representation of the People Act of 1918, swept away all special qualifications existing at the time of its passage. Neither owners, lodgers, nor freemen are to be registered as such and the principle of woman suffrage has received wide recognition. Universal suffrage for men and women has been largely achieved.

By this Act the franchise was extended to all male subjects of full age, not subject to any legal incapacity, who have resided in a constituency for a period of six months terminable either on July 15th or January 15th in any year. This period is reduced to one month for discharged soldiers. Men who have the residential qualification and are also occupiers as owners or tenants of land on premises of the yearly value of not less than £10, are entitled to a second vote, provided the land or premises be used for the purposes of a business, trade, or profession and that the qualification is not in the same constituency as that in which they have their residence.

All men of full age and not under any legal incapacity who have received a degree (other than an honorary degree) from a University and all women thirty years of age who would be entitled to vote for a University if she were a man are entitled to vote for the University or group of Universities formed under the Act. This vote may be in addition to the residential vote, but no person may have more than two votes. Women of thirty years of age and not subject to any legal incapacity, who are

[1] This was establishing what the French, as we have seen (page 222), would call *scrutin d'arrondissement.*

entitled to be local government electors, in respect of the occupation, as owners or tenants, of land or premises of the value of £5 per annum or of a dwelling house, and women whose husbands are electors in a local government area for lands or premises of the value of £5 per annum or of a dwelling house, have received the franchise. It is estimated that the vote has thereby been extended to six million women and that the total number of electors under the new Act will be doubled.

A new redistribution of seats, based on one member for every 70,000 people, was also included, with a special act for Ireland, so that the new House of Commons will be composed of 707 members. In the new House of Commons England will have 492 members, Wales 36, Scotland 74, and Ireland 105, 372 sitting for counties, 320 for boroughs, and 15 for universities. All elections will be held on the same day; the cost of elections is cheapened and registration is simplified and put in charge of a responsible public official in every constituency.

Election and Term of the Commons. — Members of the House of Commons are elected, by secret ballot, for a term of five years.[1] Any male citizen is eligible for election except priests and deacons of the Church of England, ministers of the Church of Scotland, Roman Catholic priests, and sheriffs and other returning officers, — and except, also, English and Scotch peers. Irish peers not elected to the Lords are eligible and have often sat in the House.[2] The persons thus excepted, — all save the peers, at least, — can neither sit nor vote.

As a matter of fact no House of Commons previous to the present one has ever lived its full term. A dissolution, for the purpose of a fresh appeal to the constituencies, has always cut it off before its statutory time. The average duration of Parliaments has been less than four years. The longest Parliament of the nineteenth century (elected in 1820) lived six years, one month, and twelve days. The present Parliament has prolonged its own life to avoid a general election during the war and has been in existence since 1911.

---

[1] Until 1911 the term was seven years.

[2] Lord Palmerston, for example, was an Irish peer.

There is no property qualification for election to the House now, as there was formally; and the members receive £400 a year for their services.

Summons, Electoral Writ, Prorogation. — No standing statutes govern the time for electing Parliaments. Parliament assembles upon summons from the Crown (which, like all other acts of the Sovereign, now really emanates from the ministers); and the time for electing members is set by writs addressed to the sheriffs and the mayors. Parliament is also 'prorogued' (adjourned for the session) by the Sovereign (that is, the Cabinet); and assembles again, after recess, by special summons.

The summons for a new Parliament must be issued at least thirty-five days before the day set for its assembling; the summons to a prorogued Parliament at least fourteen days beforehand. It is now the invariable custom to assemble Parliament once every year about the middle of February, and to keep it in session from that time till about the middle of August.

If a seat fall vacant during a session, a writ is issued for an election to fill it upon motion of the House itself; if a vacancy occur during a recess, the writ is issued at the instance of the Speaker of the House.

Since 1867 the duration of Parliament has not been liable to be affected by a demise of the Crown; before 1695 Parliament died with the monarch. In that year it was enacted that Parliament should last for six months after the demise of the Crown, if not sooner dissolved by the new Sovereign. Parliament, it is now provided, must assemble immediately upon the death of the Sovereign. If the Sovereign's death take place after a dissolution and before the day fixed for the convening of the new Parliament, the old Parliament is to come together for six months, if necessary, but for no longer term.

Organization of the House. — The Commons elect their own Speaker (Spokesman); their clerk and sergeant-at-arms are appointed by the Crown. The business of the House is, as we have seen (page 197), quite absolutely under the direction of its great committee, the Cabinet. Certain days of the week are set apart by the rules for the consideration of measures introduced by private members, but most of the time of the House is devoted to 'government bills.'[1] The majority put themselves in the hands of their party leaders, the ministers, and the great contests of the session are between the minority on one side of the chamber and the ministerial party, or majority, on the other side.

Down the centre of the hall in which the House sits runs a very broad aisle. The Speaker's seat stands, upon an elevated place, at the farther end of this aisle, and below it are the seats and tables of the clerks and a great table stretching some distance down the aisle, for the reception of the Sergeant's mace and various books, petition boxes, and papers. The benches on either side of the aisle face each other. Those which rise, in tiers, to the Speaker's right are occupied by the majority, the Cabinet ministers, their leaders, sitting on the front bench by the great table. This front bench is accordingly called the 'Treasury Bench,' — the Treasury being the leading Cabinet office. On the benches which rise to the Speaker's left sit the minority, their leaders also (the 'leaders of the Opposition,' — the minority being expected, generally with reason, to be opposed to all ministerial proposals) on the front bench by the table, and so directly facing the ministers, only the table intervening.

The House of Lords: its Composition. — The House of Lords consisted on April 4th, 1918, of six hundred and fifteen English hereditary peers (Dukes, Marquises, Earls, Viscounts, Barons); the two archbishops and twenty-four bishops, holding their seats by virtue of their offices; sixteen Scottish representative peers, elected by the whole body of Scottish peers to sit for the term of Parliament; twenty-seven Irish peers, elected by the peers of Ireland to sit for life[2]; and seven judicial members known as Lords of Appeal in Ordinary (pages 216, 218, 219), sitting as life-peers only, by virtue of their office.

---

[1] Due to the war, the Government now possesses the whole time of the House except an hour allowed to members for general discussion on the motion for adjournment at each sitting.

[2] Earl Curzon of Kedleston, the 28th Irish Representative Peer, is also a Peer of the United Kingdom.

There is no necessary limitation to the number of hereditary English peers. Peers can be created at will by the Crown (that is, by the ministry), and their creation is in fact frequent. Two hundred and thirty-one peers have been created since 1900. The number of Scottish and Irish peers is limited by statute.

The House of Lords is summoned to its sessions when the House of Commons is, and the two must always be summoned together.

Function of the House of Lords in Legislation. — The House of Lords was until 1911, in legal theory, coequal in all respects with the House of Commons; but, in fact, its authority was politically very inferior. By the Parliament Act of 1911, this actual inferiority was given statutory recognition and the House of Lords became thereby a subordinate legislative chamber.

In the elections of 1906 the Liberals won an overwhelming victory and under the leadership of Lloyd George as Chancellor of the Exchequer radical changes in the system of taxation were proposed in the Finance Bill of 1909. When this Bill went to the Lords, it was rejected though the practice had been so long observed as to be regarded as one of the conventions of the constitution that the Lords must accept the financial legislation passed by the Commons. The House was dissolved and an appeal to the people was taken, with the result that the Liberals were returned to power but with a reduced majority. The Finance Bill was reintroduced and successfully passed. But the Liberals were determined that the powers of the Lords should be limited and a series of resolutions were introduced and passed in the Commons to the effect (1) that the House of Lords should by law be deprived of the power of rejecting or amending a money bill; (2) that the power of the Lords to veto other bills should be limited by law; and (3) that the duration of a parliament should be limited to a maximum period of five years. The House of Lords itself took up the question of its own reform and various proposals were introduced, looking, however, rather to a change in the method of constituting that body rather than to a change in its powers. These resolutions adopted by the Lords recognized the right of the Commons with respect to money bills of a purely financial character; provided a plan for determining whether or not a bill was of this character by a committee of the two Houses in which the Speaker of the House of Commons should have the deciding vote; that with respect to other bills about which the Houses might differ in two successive sessions with an interval of not less than a year, the matter should be settled at a joint sitting of the two Houses unless it referred to a matter of grave importance, in which case it should be submitted to the people by referendum; and that the hereditary principle should not be the sole basis of membership in the Lords.

A fresh appeal to the people was taken in December, 1910, and again the Liberals were returned to power and the Parliament Bill was reintroduced without change and passed with only minor amendment. The Commons claimed that the people had approved of the Bill at the general election, and when it went to the Lords and was there amended, the ministry let it be known that it would accept no compromise and that the Bill would be passed if enough new peers must be created to secure a majority. Faced with this threat the Lords yielded and the Bill was passed as approved by the House. Thus ended one of the most momentous struggles in English constitutional history, and as a result the House of Commons is practically supreme. The Lords have retained only a right of criticism and a suspensive veto.

The Parliament Act of 1911. — Both houses had accepted the principle of reforming the House of Lords by substituting a popular for the hereditary basis, and this principle was declared in the preamble to the Act, but as yet no steps have been taken to put such a reform into operation. The Lords remain an hereditary body but with greatly restricted powers.

In the first place the power of the Lords over Money Bills has been entirely taken away. If a Money Bill which has been passed by the House of Commons, and sent up to the House of Lords at least one month before the end of the session, is not passed by the House of Lords without amendment within one ·month after it has been so sent up, the Bill shall, unless the

House of Commons direct to the contrary, be presented to his Majesty and become an Act of Parliament on the royal assent being signified, notwithstanding that the House of Lords has not consented to the Bill. The decision as to what is a Money Bill under the terms of the Act rests with the Speaker of the House of Commons, who shall indorse thereon his certificate to that effect.

In the second place if any Public Bill other than a Money Bill, or a Bill containing any provisions to extend the maximum duration of Parliament beyond five years, is passed by the House of Commons in three successive sessions, whether of the same Parliament or not, and is rejected by the Lords in each of those sessions, the Bill shall, unless the House of Commons directs to the contrary, be presented to his Majesty and shall become an Act of Parliament on receiving the Royal Assent, notwithstanding that the House of Lords has not consented to the Bill. A period of two years must elapse between the date of the second reading of the Bill in the first of the three successive sessions of the House of Commons and its passage in the third session. The Speaker shall likewise put his certificate upon Bills of this character to the effect that all the provisions of the Parliament Act have been complied with.

The certificate of the Speaker shall in both cases be conclusive and shall not be questioned in any court of law. By this Act the time fixed for the maximum duration of Parliament was five years.

The House of Lords as a Supreme Court. — The House of Lords is still, however, in fact as well as in form, the supreme court of appeal in England, though it has long since ceased to exercise its judicial functions (inherited from the Great Council of Norman times) as a body. Those functions are now always exercised by the Lord Chancellor, who is *ex officio* president of the House of Lords, and four Lords of Appeal in Ordinary, who are learned judges appointed as life peers, specially to perform this duty. These special 'Law Lords' are assisted from time to time by other lords who have served as judges of the higher courts or who are specially learned in the law.

Legislation, therefore, is controlled by the House of Commons, the interpretation of the law by the judicial members of the House of Lords. The House of Lords has a limited share with the popular chamber in the right of law-making, but cannot assert that right further than to cause delay. The Sovereign has theoretically the right to negative legislation ; but the Sovereign is in the hands of the ministers, and the ministers are in the hands of the Commons ; and legislation is never negatived.

The Constitution of England consists of law and precedent. She has great documents like Magna Charta at the foundation of her institutions ; but Magna Charta was only a royal ordinance. She has great laws like the Bill of Rights at the centre of her political system; but the Bill of Rights was only an act of Parliament. She has no written constitution, and Parliament may, in theory, change the whole structure and principle of her institutions by mere Bill. But in fact Parliament dare not go faster than public opinion : and public opinion in England is steadily and powerfully conservative.

The Courts of Law. — The Administration of justice has always been greatly centralized in England. From a very early day judges of the king's court have 'gone on circuit,' holding their assizes (sittings) in various parts of the country, in order to save suitors the vexation and expense of haling their adversaries always before the courts in London. But these circuit judges travelled from place to place under special commissions from the central authorities of the state, and had no permanent connections with the counties in which their assizes were held : they came out from London, were controlled from London, and, their circuit work done, returned to London. It was, moreover, generally only the three courts of Common Law (the Court of King's Bench, the Court of Common Pleas, and the Court of Exchequer) that sent their judges on circuit; the great, overshadowing Court of Chancery, which arrogated so wide a jurisdiction to itself, drew all its suitors to its own chambers in Westminster.

The only thing lacking to perfect the centralization was a greater uniformity of organization and a less haphazard dis-

tribution of jurisdiction among the various courts. This lack
was supplied by a great Judicature Act passed in 1873. By that
Act (which went into force on the 1st November, 1875), and
subsequent additional legislation extending to 1879, the courts
of law, which had grown, as we have seen (page 185), out of that
once single body, the ancient Permanent Council of the Norman
and Plantagenet kings, were at last reintegrated, made up together into a coördinated whole.

Judicial Reform: the Reorganization of 1873-1879. — These
measures of reorganization and unification had been preceded, in
1846, by a certain degree of decentralization. Certain so-called
County Courts were than created, which are local, not peripatetic
Westminster, tribunals, and which have to a considerable extent
absorbed the assize business, though their function, theoretically,
is only to assist, not to supplant, the assizes. Now, therefore, the
general outlines of the judicial system are these. The general
courts of the kingdom are combined under the name, Supreme
Court of Judicature. This court is divided into two parts, which
are really two quite distinct courts : namely, the High Court of
Justice and the Court of Appeal; while over both, as the court of
last resort, still stands the House of Lords. The High Court
of Justice acts in three divisions, a Chancery Division, a King's
Bench Division, and a Probate, Divorce, and Admiralty Division ;
and these three divisions constitute the ordinary courts of law,
inheriting the jurisdictions suggested by their names. From
them an appeal lies to the Court of Appeal ; from the Court of
Appeal to the House of Lords. The County Courts stand related
to the system as the Assizes do.

"**The Chancery Division** has five judges besides its president, the Chancellor; the Queen's Bench Division has fifteen
judges, of whom one, the Lord Chief Justice, is its president;
the Probate, Divorce, and Admiralty Division has but two judges,
of whom one presides over the other." This arrangement into
divisions is a mere matter of convenience ; no very strict distinctions as to jurisdiction are preserved ; and any changes that
the judges think desirable may be made by an Order in Council.
Thus an Exchequer Division and a Common Pleas division, which

at first existed, in preservation of the old lines of organization, were abolished by such an Order in December, 1880. The judges assigned to the various Divisions do not necessarily or often sit together. Cases are generally heard before only one judge; so that the High Court may be said to have the effective capacity of twenty-three courts, its total number of judges being twenty-three. Only when hearing appeals from inferior tribunals, or discharging some other function different from the ordinary trial of cases, must two or more judges sit together.

The Court of Appeals may hear appeals on questions both of law and of fact. It consists of the Master of Rolls and five Lords Justices, who may be said to constitute a permanent and separate bench, and of the presidents of the three Divisions of the High Court, who may be called its occasional members. Since 1891 Ex-Chancellors are *ex officio* members, though they do not ordinarily sit. Three judges are necessary to exercise its powers, and, in practice, its six permanent members divide the work, holding the court in two independent sections.

The House of Lords may sit, when acting as a court, when Parliament is not in session, after a prorogation, that is, or even after a dissolution : for the House of Lords when sitting as a court is like its legislative self only in its modes of procedure. In all other respects it is totally unlike the body which obeys the House of Commons in law-making. It is constituted always, as a court, of the Lord Chancellor and at least two of the Lords of Appeal in Ordinary of whom I have spoken (page 212) ; only sometimes are there added to these a third Lord of Appeal in Ordinary, an ex-Lord Chancellor, or one or more of such judges or ex-judges of the higher courts as may have found their way to peerages. Other members of the House never attend; or, attending, never vote.

A Judicial Committee of the Privy Council, of which also the Lord Chancellor is a member, and which now consists mainly of the same Lords of Appeal in Ordinary who act in judicial matters as the House of Lords, constitutes a court of last resort for India, the Colonies, the Channel Islands, and the Isle of Man, as well as, within certain limits, as a court of appeal from the Probate, Divorce, and Admiralty Division of the High Court of Justice.

The Lord Chancellor is the most notable officer in the whole system. He is president of the House of Lords, of the Court of Appeal, of the High Court of Justice, and of the Chancery Division of the High Court, and he is a member of the Judicial Committee of the Privy Council; and he actually sits in all of these except the High Court, — in the House of Lords and the Privy Council always, in the Court of Appeal often. More singular still, he is the political officer of the law : he is a member always of the Cabinet, and, like the other members, belongs to a party, and goes in or out of office according to the favor of the House of Commons, exercising while in office, in some sense, the functions of a Minister of Civil Justice.[1]

Civil Cases are heard either by judges of the High Court in London, by judges of that court sitting on circuit in the various ' assize towns' of the county, of which there is always at least one for each county, or by the County Courts created in 1846, which differ from the old county courts, long since decayed and now deprived of all judicial functions, both in their organization and in their duties. They consist, not of the sheriff and all the freemen of the shire, but of single judges, holding their offices during good behavior, assisted by permanent ministerial officers, and exercising their jurisdiction not over counties but in districts much smaller than the counties. They are called county courts only by way of preserving an ancient and respected name.

The County Courts have jurisdiction in all cases of debt or damage where the sum claimed does not exceed £50, and in certain equity cases where not more than £500 is involved,— except that cases of slander, libel, seduction, and breach of promise to marry, as well as all matrimonial cases, are withheld from them. At least, such is their jurisdiction in rough outline. A full account would involve many details; for it has been the tendency of all recent judicial legislation in England to give more and more

[1] Maitland, p. 68.

business, even of the more important kind, to these Courts. Their normal importance may be judged from the fact, stated by Mr. Maitland, that " most of the contentious litigation in England is about smaller sums than " £50.

A judge of the High Court may send down to a county court, upon the application of either party, cases of contract in which the sum claimed does not exceed £100. Any case, however small the pecuniary claim involved, may be removed from the county to the High Court if the judge of the county court will certify that important principles of law are likely to arise in it, or if the High Court or any judge thereof deems it desirable that it should be removed. Appeals from a county court to the High Court are forbidden in most cases in which less than £20 is involved.

The county court system rests upon the basis of a division of the country into fifty-six circuits. All but one or two of these include several ' districts ' — the districts numbering about 500. Each district has its own separate court, with its own offices, registrar, etc.; but the judges are appointed for the circuits, — one for each circuit. They are appointed by the Lord Chancellor from barristers of seven years' standing.[1]

Juries are falling more and more into disuse in England in civil cases. In all the more important causes, outside the Chancery Division, whose rule of action, like that of the old Chancery Court, is ' no jury,' a jury may be impanelled at the desire of either party ; but many litigants now prefer to do without, — especially in the County Courts, where both the facts and the law are in a large majority of the cases passed upon by the judge alone, without the assistance of the jury of five which might in these courts be summoned in all cases of above £20 value.

Criminal Cases are tried either before the county Justices of the Peace, who are unpaid officers appointed by the Chancellor upon the recommendation of the Lords Lieutenant of the Counties; before borough Justices, who are paid judges much like all others ; or before judges of the High Court on circuit. The jurisdiction of the Justices may be said to include all but the gravest offences, all but those, namely, which are punishable by death or by penal servitude, and except, also, perjury, forgery, bribery, and libel. There are many Justices for each county, there being no legal limit to their number; and they exercise their more important functions at general Quarter Sessions, at general sessions, that is, held four times yearly. The criminal assizes of the High Court also are held four times a year. All

[1] The various Acts affecting the County Courts were amended and consolidated by the County Courts Act, 1888.

criminal cases, except those of the pettiest character, such as
police cases, are tried before juries.

" About one-half of the criminal trials," it is stated,[1] " take place
at county sessions, about one-fourth at borough sessions, the rest at Assizes
or the Central Criminal Court," the great criminal court of London.

Quarter and Petty Sessions. — For the exercise of all their
more important judicial functions the Justices meet quarterly, in Quarter
Sessions; but for minor duties in which it is not necessary for more than
two Justices to join, there are numerous Petty Sessions held at various
points in the counties. Each county is divided by its Quarter Sessions
into *petty sessional districts*, and every neighborhood is given thus its own
court of Petty Sessions, — from which in almost all cases an appeal lies to
Quarter Sessions. Thus the important function of licensing (page 233) is
exercised by Petty Sessions, subject to appeal to the whole bench of
Justices.

The Justices of the Peace were, as we shall see more particularly in another connection (pages 226–227), the general governmental
authorities of the counties until the reform of local government effected
in 1888, exercising functions of the most various, multifarious, and influential sort. They are generally country gentlemen of high standing in
their counties, and serve, as already stated, without pay. They are
appointed, practically, for life. The ' Commission of the Peace,' — the
commissioning, that is, of Justices of the Peace, — originated in the fourteenth century, and has had a long history of interesting development.
Considering the somewhat autocratic nature of the office of Justice, it
has been, on the whole, exercised with great wisdom and public spirit,
and during most periods with extraordinary moderation, industry, and
effectiveness.

The duties which Americans associate with the office of Justice of
the Peace are exercised in England, not by the bench of Justices sitting in
Quarter Sessions, — they then constitute, as we have seen, a criminal court
of very extensive jurisdiction, — but by the Justices singly, sitting either
formally or informally. A single Justice may conduct the preliminary
examination of a person charged with crime, and may commit for trial if
reasonable ground of suspicion be proved. A single Justice can also issue
search warrants to the constabulary for the detection of crime, etc.

Police. — The police force, or, in more English phrase,
the constabulary, of the kingdom is overseen from London by the
Home Office, which makes all general rules as to discipline, pay,
etc., appoints royal inspectors, and determines, under the Treasury, the amount of state aid to be given to the support of the

[1] Maitland, p. 86.

forces; but all the actual administration of the system is undertaken by the local authorities.   In the Counties a joint Committee of Quarter Sessions and the County Council appoint the
Chief Constable, who appoints and governs the force with powers
of summary dismissal and punishment, but who acts in all things
subject to the governing control of the Committee (page 235).   In
those towns which undertake to maintain a force distinct from
that of the County the Head Constable is chosen by the town
authorities and the direction of the force is superintended by a
'Watch Committee' of the Town Council.   London, which employs, it is stated, one-third of the entire police force of the
kingdom, has been given a special, exceptional system of its own.
The city police are governed by a Commissioner and two Assistant Commissioners who are appointed by the Home Secretary and
serve directly under his authority.

> The police throughout the country are given something like mili-
> tary drill and training, the organization being made as perfect, the training
> as thorough, and the discipline as effective as possible.   Ex-army officers
> are preferred for the office of Chief Constable.

II. Local Government.

Complex Character of Local Government in England. —
The subject of local government in England is one of extreme
complexity and, therefore, for my present purpose of brief description, one of extreme difficulty.   So perfectly unsystematic,
indeed, are the provisions of English law in this field that most
of the writers who have undertaken to expound them, — even to
English readers, — have seemed to derive a certain zest from the
despairful nature of their task, — a sort of forlorn-hope enthusiasm.   The institutions of local government in England have
grown piece by piece as other English institutions have, and not
according to any complete or logical plan of statutory construction.   They are patch-work, not symmetrical net-work, and the
patches are of all sizes, shapes, and materials.

> "For almost every new administrative function," complains one
> writer on the subject, "the Legislature has provided a new area contain-
> ing a new constituency, who by a new method of election choose candi-

dates who satisfy a new qualification, to sit upon a new board, during a new term, to levy a new rate [tax], and to spend a good deal of the new revenues in paying new officers and erecting new buildings." [1]

It has been the habit of English legislators, instead of perfecting, enlarging, or adapting old machinery, to create all sorts of new pieces of machinery with little or no regard to their fitness to be combined with the old or with each other. The Local Government Act of 1888 represents the first deliberate attempt at systematization; but even that Act did not effect system, and itself introduced additional elements of confusion by first adopting another Act (the Municipal Corporations Act of 1882) as its basis and then excepting particular provisions of that Act and itself substituting others in respect, not of all, but of some of the local administrative bodies meant to be governed by it. The supplementary legislation of 1894 introduced some further elements of consistent system; but did not after all very much simplify existing methods. It would seem as logical a plan of description as any, therefore, to discuss the older divisions and instrumentalities first and then treat afterwards of more recent legislative creations as of modifications, of however haphazard a kind, of these.

General Characterization. — In general terms, then, it may be said, that throughout almost the whole of English history, only the very earliest periods excepted, counties and towns have been the principal units of local government; that the parishes into which the counties have been time out of mind divided, though at one time of very great importance as administrative centres, were in course of time in great part swallowed up by feudal jurisdictions, and now retain only a certain minor part in the function, once exclusively their own, of caring for the poor; and that this ancient framework of counties, towns, and parishes has, of late years, been extensively overlaid and in large part obscured: (a) by the combination (1834) of parishes into 'Unions' made up quite irrespective of county boundaries and charged not only with the immemorial parish duty of maintaining the poor but often with sanitary regulation also and school superintendence,

---

[1] *Local Administration* (Imperial Parliament Series), by Wm. Rathbone, Albert Pell, and F. C. Montague, p. 14.

and generally with a miscellany of other functions; (b) by the creation of new districts for the care of highways; (c) by new varieties of town and semi-town government; and (d) by the sub-division of the counties (1889) into new administrative 'districts,' charged with general administrative functions. The only dis-tinction persistent enough to serve as a basis for any classifica-tion of the areas and functions of the local administration thus constructed is the distinction between Rural Administration and Urban Administration, — a distinction now in part destroyed by the Act of 1888; and of these two divisions of administration almost the only general remark which it seems safe to venture is, that Rural Administration has hitherto rested much more broadly than does Urban on old historical foundations.

The County: its Historical Rootage. — For the County, with its influential Justices of the Peace and its wide adminis-trative activities, is still the vital centre of rural government in England; and the Counties are in a sense older than the kingdom itself. Many of them, as we have seen (page 180), represent in their areas, though of course no longer in the nature of their government, separate Saxon kingdoms of the Heptarchy times. When they were united under a single throne they retained (it would appear) their one-time king and his descendants in the elder male line as their *eoldormen*. They retained also their old general council, in which *eoldorman* and bishop presided, though there was added presently to these presidents of the older order of things another official, of the new order, the king's officer, the Sheriff. To this council went up, as was of old the wont, the priest, the reeve, and four select men from every township, together with the customary delegates from the 'hundreds.'

Of course the Counties no longer retain these antique forms of government; scarcely a vestige of them now remains. But the old forms gave way to the forms of the present by no sudden or violent changes, and some of the organs of county gov-ernment now in existence could adduce plausible proof of their descent from the manly, vigorous, self-centred Saxon institutions of the ancient time.

Early Evolution of the County Organs. — In Norman times the *eoldorman's* office languished in the shadow of the Sheriff's great authority. The spiritual and temporal courts were separated, too, and the bishop withdrew in large measure from official participation in local political functions. The County Court became practically the Sheriff's Court; its suitors the free-holders. Its functions were, however, still considerable: it chose the officers who assessed the taxes; it was the medium of the Sheriff's military administration; and it was still the principal source of justice. But its duties were not slow to decay. As a Court it was speedily handed over to the king's itinerant justices, who held their assizes in it and heard all important cases, all 'pleas of the Crown.' Its financial functions became more and more exclusively the personal functions of the Sheriffs, who were commonly great barons, who managed in some instances for a little while to make their office hereditary, and who contrived oftentimes to line their own pockets with the proceeds of the taxes: for great barons who were sheriffs were sometimes also officials of the Exchequer, and as such audited their own accounts. The local courts at last became merely the instruments of the Sheriffs and of the royal judges.

Decline of the Sheriff's Powers. — It was the overbearing power of the Sheriffs, thus developed, that led to the great changes which were to produce the county government of our own day. The interests alike of the Court and of the people became enlisted against them. The first step towards displacing them was taken when the royal justices were sent on circuit. Next, in 1170, under Henry II.'s capable direction, the great baronial sheriffs were tried for malfeasance in office, and, though influential enough to escape formal conviction, were not influential enough to retain their offices. They were dismissed, and re-placed by Exchequer officials directly dependent upon the Crown. In 1194, in the next reign, it was arranged that certain 'custo-dians of pleas of the Crown' should be elected in the counties, to the further ousting of the Sheriffs from their old-time judicial prerogatives. Then came Magna Charta (1215) and forbade all participation by Sheriffs in the administration of the king's jus-tice. Finally the tenure of the office of Sheriff, which was by that time little more than the chief place in the militia of the county and the chief ministerial office in connection with the administration of justice, was limited to one year. The pulling down of the old system was complete; fresh construction had already become necessary.

Justices of the Peace. — The reconstruction was effected through the appointment of 'Justices of the Peace.' The expedient of 'custodians of pleas of the Crown' (*custodes placitorum coronæ*) elected in County Court, as substitutes for the Sheriff in the exercise of sundry important functions of local justice, had proved unsatisfactory. They, too, like the Sheriffs, were curtly forbidden by Magna Charta to hold any pleas of the Crown; and they speedily became only the *coroners* we know ('crowners' Shakspere's grave-digger in *Hamlet* very appropriately calls them), whose chief function it is to conduct the preliminary investigation concerning every case of sudden death from an unknown cause. Better success attended the experiment of Justices of the Peace. At first 'Conservators' of the peace merely, these officers became, by a statute passed in 1360, in the reign of Edward III., *justices* also, intrusted with a certain jurisdiction over criminal cases, to the supplanting of the Sheriff in the last of his judicial functions, his right, namely, to pass judgment in his *tourn* or petty court on police cases, — to apply the discipline of enforced order to small offences against the public peace.

Henceforth, as it turned out, the process of providing ways of local government was simple enough, as legislators chose to conduct it. It consisted simply in charging the Justices of the Peace with the doing of everything that was necessary to be done. Slowly, piece by piece, their duties and prerogatives were added to, till the Justices had become immeasurably the most important functionaries of local government, combining in their comprehensive official characters almost every judicial and administrative power not exercised from London. Not till the passage of the Local Government Act of 1888 were they relegated to their older and more characteristic judicial functions, and their administrative and financial powers transferred to another body, the newly created County Council.

Functions of Justices of the Peace prior to Recent Reforms. — The Justice of the Peace has been very happily described as having been under the old system "the state's man of all work." His multifarious duties brought him into the service (*a*) of the Privy Council, under whose Veterinary Department he participated in the administration of the Acts relating to contagious cattle diseases; (*b*) of the Home Office, under which he acted in governing the county constabulary, in conducting the administration of lunatic asylums, and in visiting prisons; (*c*) of the Board of Trade, under whose general supervision he provided and tested weights and measures, constructed and repaired bridges, and oversaw highway authorities; and (*d*) of the Local Government Board, under whose superintendence he appointed parish overseers of the poor, exercised, on appeal, a revisory power over the poor-rates, and took a certain part in sanitary regulation. The Justices, besides, formerly levied the county tax, or 'rate,' out of which the expenses of county business were defrayed; issued licenses for the sale of intoxicating drinks (as they still do), for the storage of gunpowder and petroleum, and for other undertakings required by law to be licensed; divided the counties into highway, polling, and coroner's districts; issued orders for the removal of paupers to their legal places of settlement; fulfilled a thousand and one administrative functions too various to classify, too subordinate to need enumeration, now that most of them have been transferred to the Councils. The trial of criminal cases, together with the performance of the various functions attendant upon such a jurisdiction, always constituted, of course, one of the weightiest duties of their office, and is now its chief and almost only duty.

"Long ago," laughs Mr. Maitland, speaking before the passage of the Act of 1888, "long ago lawyers abandoned all hope of describing the duties of a justice in any methodic fashion, and the alphabet has become the only possible connecting thread. A Justice must have something to do with 'Railroads, Rape, Rates, Recognizances, Records, and Recreation Grounds'; with 'Perjury, Petroleum, Piracy, and Playhouses'; with 'Disorderly Houses, Dissenters, Dogs, and Drainage.'"[1]

Character and Repute of the Office of Justice. — The office of Justice of the Peace is representative in the same sense, — not an unimportant sense, — in which the unreformed parliaments of the early part of the century were representative at any rate of the county populations. The Justices are appointed from among the more considerable gentry of the counties, and represent in a very substantial way the permanent interests of the predominantly rural communities over whose justice they preside. An interesting proof of their virtually representative character appears in the popularity of their office during the greater part of its history. Amidst all the extensions of the franchise, all the remaking of representative institutions which this century has witnessed in England, the Justiceship of the Peace remained all the while practically untouched, because on all hands greatly respected, until the evident need to introduce

[1] *Justice and Police*, p. 84.

system into local government, and the apparent desirability of systematizing it in accordance with the whole policy of recent reforms in England
by extending the principle of popular representation by election to county
government, as it had been already extended to administration in the
lesser areas, led to the substitution of County Councils for the Justices
as the county authority in financial and administrative affairs.

The Lord Lieutenant.— In the reign of Mary a '*Lord
Lieutenant*' took the place of the Sheriff in the County as head
of the militia, becoming the chief representative of the Crown in
the County, and subsequently the keeper of the county records
(*Custos Rotulorum*).   The Sheriff, since the completion of this
change, has been a merely administrative officer, executing the
judgments of the courts, and presiding over parliamentary elections.   The command of the militia remained with the Lords
Lieutenant until 1871, when it was vested in the Crown, —
that is assumed by the central administration.   (Compare pages
220–221.)

The Reform of 1888. — The reform of local administration
proposed by the ministry of Lord Salisbury, in the spring of 1888,
although not venturing so far as it would be necessary to go to
introduce order and symmetry into a patch-work system, suggested some decided steps in the direction of simplification and
coördination.   The confusions of the existing arrangements were
many and most serious.   England was divided into counties,
boroughs, urban sanitary districts, rural sanitary districts, poor-
law parishes, poor-law unions, highway parishes, and school districts; and these areas had been superimposed upon one another
with an astonishing disregard of consistent system, — without
either geographical or administrative coördination.   The confusions to be remedied, therefore, consisted (*a*) of the overlapping
of the various areas of local government, the smaller areas not
being in all cases subdivisions of the larger, but defined almost
wholly without regard to the boundaries of any other areas; (*b*)
of a consequent lack of coördination and subordination among
local authorities, fruitful of the waste of money and the loss of
efficiency always resulting from confusions and duplications of
organization; (*c*) of varieties of time, method, and franchise in
the choice of local officials; and (*d*) of an infinite complexity

in the arrangements regarding local taxation, the sums needed for the various purposes of local government (for the poor, for example, for the repair of highways, for county outlays, etc.) being separately assessed and separately collected, at great expense and at the cost of a great deal of vexation to the taxpayer.

The ministry at first proposed to remedy this confusion, at least in part, by largely centering administration, outside the greater towns, in two areas, the County and the District. The system of poor-relief, through parishes and unions, was to be left untouched, but a beginning was to be made in unification by making the Counties and Districts the controlling organs of local government; provision was to be made for extensive readjustments of boundaries so that the smaller rural areas might be brought into proper relation and subordination to the larger by making them in all cases at least subdivisions of counties; both County and District were to have representative councils presumably fitted ultimately to assume the whole taxing function; and the franchise by which these bodies were to be elected was to be assimilated to the simplest and broadest used in local and parliamentary elections.

Only a portion of this reform, however, it turned out, could be got through Parliament. The provisions relating to the formation of Districts were left out, and only the county was reorganized. The larger boroughs were given county privileges; the smaller were brought into new and closer relations with the reconstructed county governments. London, too, was given a county organization. The integration of the smaller areas of rural administration with the new county system was not accomplished till 1894.

Administrative Counties and County Boroughs. — The Act, as passed, coördinated Counties with what were thenceforth to be called 'county boroughs.' Every borough of not less than fifty thousand inhabitants at the time the Act was passed, or which was, before the passage of the Act, treated as a county (in all, sixty-one boroughs), was constituted a 'county borough,' and was formally put alongside the county in rank and privileges. This did not mean that these boroughs were to be given a county or·

ganization. Paradoxically enough, it meant just the opposite, that the counties were to be given an organization closely resembling that already possessed by the boroughs. The nomenclature of the Act would be more correct, though possibly less convenient, had it called the counties 'borough counties' instead of calling some of the boroughs 'county boroughs.' The measure has been very appropriately described as an Act to apply the Municipal Corporations Act of 1882, whose main provisions date back as far as 1835 (page 240), to county government, with certain relatively unimportant modifications.

> The counties designated by the Act are dubbed 'administrative counties,' because they are not in all cases the historical counties of the map. In several instances counties are separated into parts for the purposes of the reorganization. Thus the East Riding of Yorkshire constitutes one 'administrative county,' the North Riding another, and the West Riding a third ; Suffolk and Sussex also have each an East and West division ; Lincoln falls apart into three administrative counties, etc. All boroughs of less than 50,000 inhabitants not treated as counties are more or less incorporated with the counties in which they lie. (See page 242.)

The County Councils: their Constitution. — In pursuance of the purpose of assimilating county to borough organization, the counties are given representative governing assemblies composed of councillors and aldermen, presided over by a chairman whose position and functions reproduce those of the borough mayors, and possessing as their outfit of powers almost all the miscellany of administrative functions hitherto belonging to the Justices of the Peace. There is not, it should be observed, a Council *and* a Board of Aldermen, as in American cities, but a single body known as the Council and composed of two classes of members, the one class known as Aldermen, the other as Councillors. These two classes differ from each other, not in power or in function, but only in number, term, and mode of election. The Councillors are directly elected by the qualified voters of the County and hold office for a term of three years; the Aldermen are one-third as many as the Councillors in number, are elected by the Councillors, either from their own number or from the qualified voters outside, and hold office for six years, one-half of their number, however, retiring every three years, in rotation.

This single-chambered Council of Aldermen and Councillors elects its own chairman, to serve for one year, and pays him such compensation as it deems sufficient. During his year of service the chairman exercises the usual presidential, but no independent executive, powers, and is authorized to act as a Justice of the Peace, along with the rest of the ' Commission ' of the County.

Any one may be elected a councillor who is entitled to vote in parliamentary elections and is the owner of property held by freehold, copyhold, leasehold or other tenure within the area ; and in the counties, though not in the boroughs, peers owning property in the county and "clerks in holy orders and other ministers of religion " may be chosen to the Council. **The number of councillors** and the number of aldermen in each County Council (for the latter number is always one-third of the former) was fixed in the first instance by an order of the Local Government Board, and is in some cases very large. Thus Lancashire has a Council (aldermen, of course, included) of 140 members, the West Riding of Yorkshire a council of 120, Devon a council of 104. Rutland, whose Council is the smallest, has 28. The average is probably about 75. For the election of councillors the county, including such boroughs as are not ' county boroughs,' is divided into *electoral districts*, one councillor being chosen from each district. The number of these districts having been determined by the order of the Local Government Board, their area and disposition were fixed in the first instance by Quarter Sessions, or, within the non-county boroughs needing division, by the borough Council, due regard being had to relative population and to a fair division of representation between rural and urban populations. The number of councillors and the boundaries of electoral districts may be changed by order of the Local Government Board upon the recommendation of the Council of a borough or county.

Local Government Franchise. — In England, Wales, and Ireland the franchise for all local government areas has, by the Representation of the People Act of 1918, been extended to all men and women of full age not subject to any legal incapacity who are jointly or severally occupiers as owners or tenants of any land or premises in a local government area, if they have so occupied for six months ending either on the 15th of January or the 15th of July. Tenant includes lodgers in unfurnished quarters. In Scotland the local government franchise is enjoyed by men and women of full age who are owners or occupiers of lands and heritages of £10 yearly value ; or inhabitant occupiers of dwelling houses ; or occupiers of unfurnished lodgings of the yearly value of £10 ; or service occupiers.   Everywhere in the United Kingdom the wife of a qualified local government elector enjoys the franchise if she is thirty years old.

Powers of the County Councils. — The Council of each County is a body corporate and as such may have a common seal, hold property, make by-laws, etc.   Its by-laws, however, unless they concern nuisances, are subject to approval by the Secretary of State [the Home Secretary], and may be annulled by an order in Council.

(1) The Council holds and administers all county property, and may purchase or lease lands or buildings for county uses ;

(2) With it rests the duty of maintaining, managing, and, when necessary, enlarging, the pauper lunatic asylums of the county, and of establishing and maintaining, or contributing to, reformatory and industrial schools ; by the Education Act of 1902 it was given extensive authority over education.

(3) It is charged with maintaining county bridges, and all main roads in every part not specially reserved by urban authorities for their own management because lying within their own limits ; and it may declare any road a main road which seems to serve as such, and which has been put in thorough repair, before being accepted by the county, by the local highway authorities ;

(4) It administers the statutes affecting the contagious diseases of animals, destructive insects, fish preservation, weights and measures, etc. ;

(5) It appoints, pays, and may remove the county Treasurer, the county coroner, the public surveyor, the county analyst, and all other officers paid out of the county rates, — except the clerk of the Peace and the clerks of the Justices, — including the medical health officers, though these latter functionaries report, not to the Council (the Council receives only a copy of their report), but to the Local Government Board, and the only power of the Council in the premises is to address to the Board, independently and of their own motion, representations as to the enforcement of the Public Health Acts where such representations seem necessary ;

(6) It determines the fees of the coroner and controls the division of the county into coroners' districts ;

(7) It divides the county into polling districts also for parliamentary elections, appoints voting places, and supervises the registration of voters;

(8) It sees to the registering of places of worship, of the rules of scientific societies, of charitable gifts, etc.

> It is obviously impossible to classify or make any generalized statement of this miscellany of powers: they must be enumerated or not stated at all. They are for the most part, though not altogether, the administrative powers formerly intrusted to the Justices of the Peace.

The Licensing Function, being semi-judicial, is left in most cases with the Justices of the Peace; but the County Council is assigned the granting of licenses to music and dancing halls, to houses which are to be devoted to the public performance of stage plays, and for the keeping of explosives.

> Oddly enough, the County Council is, by another section of the Act of 1888, authorized to delegate its powers of licensing in the case of playhouses and in the case of explosives back to the Justices again, acting in petty sessions. The same section also permits a similar delegation to the Justices of the powers exercised by the Council under the Act touching contagious cattle diseases.

The Financial Powers of the Council are extensive and important. The Council takes the place of the Justices in determining, assessing, and levying the county, police, and hundred rates, in disbursing the funds so raised, and in preparing or revising the basis or standard for the county rates; though in this last matter it acts subject to appeal to Quarter Sessions. It may borrow money, "on the security of the county fund," for the purpose of consolidating the county debt, purchasing property for the county, or undertaking permanent public works, provided it first obtain the consent of the Local Government Board to the raising of the loan. That Board gives or withholds its consent only after a local inquiry, and, in case it assents, fixes the period within which the loan must be repaid, being itself limited in this last particular by a provision of law that the period must never exceed thirty years.

> If the debt of the county already exceed ten per cent. of the annual ratable value of the ratable property of the county, or if the proposed loan would raise it above that amount, a loan can be sanctioned

only by a *provisional* order of the Board, — an order, that is, which becomes valid only upon receiving the formal sanction of Parliament also, given by public Act. A county may issue stock, under certain limitations, if the consent of the Local Government Board be obtained.

Additional Powers. — The Act of 1888 provides that any othei powers which have been conferred upon the authorities of particular localities by special Act, and which are similar in character to those already vested in the County Councils, may be transferred to the proper County Councils by *provisional* order of the Local Government Board ; and also that a similar provisional order of that Board may confer upon a County Council any powers, *arising within the County*, which are now exercised by the Privy Council, a Secretary of State, the Board of Trade, the Local Government Board itself, or any other government department, provided they be powers conferred by statute and the consent of the department concerned be first secured.

The County Budget. — At the beginning of every local financial year (April 1st) an estimate of the receipts and expenditures of the year is submitted to the Council, and upon the basis of this, the Council makes estimate of the sums to be needed, and fixes the rates accordingly. The Council's estimate is made for two six-month periods, and is subject to revision for the second six-month period, provided the experience of the first prove it necessary either to increase or decrease the amounts to be raised.

Returns of the actual receipts and expenditures of each financial year are also made to the Local Government Board, in such form and with such particulars as the Board directs; and full abstracts of these returns are annually laid before both Houses of Parliament. The county accounts are, moreover, periodically audited by district auditors appointed by the Local Government Board. The accounts of the county Treasurer are audited by the Council.

Local rates are assessed exclusively upon real estate, and, until the passage of the Local Government Act of 1888, it was the habit of Parliament to make annual 'grants in aid of the rates' from the national purse, with the idea of paying out of moneys raised largely upon personal property some part of the expense of local administration. The Act of 1888 substitutes another arrangement. It provides that all moneys collected from certain licenses (a long list of them, from liquor licenses to licenses for male servants and guns), together with four-fifths of one-half of the proceeds of the probate duty, shall be distributed among the counties from the imperial treasury, under the direction of the Local Government Board, for the purpose of defraying certain specified county expenses, notably for the education of paupers and the support of pauper lunatics.

The Police Powers, long exercised by the Justices of the Peace, are now exercised by a joint committee of Quarter Sessions and the County Council. This committee is made up, in equal parts, of Justices and members of the Council; elects its own chairman, if necessary (because of a tie vote) by lot; and acts, when appointed, not as exercising delegated authority, but as an independent body. The term of the committeemen is, however, determined by the bodies which choose them.

The Parish. — Parishes there have been in England ever since the Christian church was established there; but the Parish which now figures in English local government inherits nothing but its name intact from those first years of the national history. The church, in its first work of organization, used the smallest units of the state for the smallest divisions of its own system : it made the township its parish; and presently the priest was always to be seen going up with the reeve and the four men of the township to the hundred and the county courts. Only where the population was most numerous did it prove necessary to make the parish smaller than the township; only where it was least numerous did it seem expedient to make the parish larger than the township. Generally the two were geographically coincident. During much the greater part of English history, too, citizenship and church membership were inseparable. The vestry, therefore, which was the assembly of church-members which elected the church-wardens and regulated the temporalities of the local church, was exactly the same body of persons that, when not acting upon church affairs, constituted the township meeting. It was the village moot 'in its ecclesiastical aspect.' And when the township privileges were, by feudalization, swallowed up in the manorial rights of the baronage, the vestry was all that remained of the old organization of self-government; for the court, or civil assembly, of the township was superseded by the baron's manorial court. But the church was not absorbed; the vestry remained, and whatever scraps of civil function escaped the too inclusive sweep of the grants of jurisdiction to the barons the people were fain to enjoy as vestrymen.

The Poor-law Parish. — It was in this way that it fell out that the township, when acting in matters strictly non-ecclesiastical, came to call itself the parish, and that it became necessary to distinguish the 'civil parish' from the 'ecclesiastical parish.' The vestry came at last to elect, not church-wardens only, but way-wardens also, and assessors; and in the sixteenth century (1535, reign of Henry VIII.) the church-wardens were charged with the relief of the poor. We are thus brought within easy sight of the parish of to-day. The legislation of the present century, which has been busy about so many things, has not failed to readjust the parish and in most cases, as altered by statute to suit the conveniences of political administration, "the modern civil parish coincides neither with the ancient civil parish, nor with the ecclesiastical parish"; but old parochial associations still survive, and many of the ancient parochial duties connected with the support of the poor. Until 1894 the parochial authority was still the ancient vestry, reduced almost to a minimum of powers, indeed, but not yet taken from its seat of control. In 1894 Parliament completed the reorganization of local government begun in 1888: vestries were relegated, at any rate in all rural districts, to the exercise of ecclesiastical functions alone; and the parishes, with a new democratic organization, became once more the vital units of local self-government.

The Reform of 1894. — All the legislation attempted in England during the present century with regard to local government, whether its object was first construction or reform, has carefully observed the difference between 'rural' and 'urban' areas; and the law of 1894 is no exception to the rule. The parishes which lie within the limits of boroughs or within the limits of those more thickly settled areas which, though without borough organization, are yet distinguished by the law as 'urban' in their means of local government (page 239), are not directly affected by the Act. But the organization and action of the rural parishes are revolutionized. They are made self-governing communes, with a very notable list of powers and privileges.

Every rural parish, great or small, has now its primary assembly, its *parish meeting*, of which every person of legal age in the parish, man or woman, is a member who is a qualified local government elector. In parishes which have less than three hundred inhabitants the *parish meeting* is the actual governing body, unless the County Council sees fit, with the consent of the parish electors, to set up a *parish council;* but in parishes which have a population of more than three hundred a *parish council* of from five to fifteen members, — the County Council determines the number in each case, — is given charge of affairs, and the *parish meeting* exercises only the functions of electing councillors, consenting to the larger sorts of loans, and voting upon the adoption and operation of certain statutes, known as the 'adoptive acts,' which Parliament has left it to them to adopt and act upon or not as they please. These are the statutes with regard to street lighting and watching, the establishment of baths and wash-houses, the undertaking of certain public improvements, the foundation of public libraries, and like matters. Women, whether married or single, are eligible for election to the *parish councils*, and even to the chairmanship of those bodies. The term of a *parish council* is three years.

Parishes which are governed by a *parish meeting* only, without a council, usually appoint one or more executive committees for the actual work of administration; and, if they accept the 'adoptive' acts mentioned in the last paragraph, they elect commissioners to carry them into execution; but in very many cases the County Councils have given these small parishes councils, and where there are councils they are the executive agents of the parish in practically every sort of business.

The chairman of a *parish council* is *ex officio* a Justice of the Peace for the county in which he resides; and this feature of the law has, in view of the very large number of parishes in every county, radically changed the character of the commission of the peace. Any one may be a parish councillor, and any one may be a chairman of a *parish council* who can be a member of a *parish meeting* (page 237), and a seat on the county bench of Justices is consequently no longer by any means the exclusive possession of country gentlemen.

The parish councillors are elected in *parish meeting*, by a mere show of hands, — unless a formal poll be demanded. No elector, whatever his property or interest, can cast more than one vote in any one parish; but those who have the requisite property qualification in more than one parish can be registered, and can vote in every parish in which they can prove the possession of the requisite amount of property. Married women cannot qualify, however, upon the same property upon which their husbands have qualified.

Parochial Powers. — The *parish councils* (or the *parish meetings*, as the case may be) exercise a miscellany of powers variously distributed, until 1894, amongst vestries, church-wardens, overseers of the poor, and commissioners of various sorts and functions. A *parish council* is a body corporate, and as such owns and manages the property of the parish. It may acquire property by gift or purchase, — not merely for the erection of parochial buildings and other directly parochial uses, but also for the establishment and maintenance of recreation grounds, and for the purpose of making allotments at a fixed rental to such residents of the parish as may wish to acquire holdings. It has control of the water supply of the parish, and is the local sanitary authority; it can acquire, maintain, or change public rights of way; it maintains the highways and the enclosed burial grounds of the parish; and it provides for the prevention and extinguishment of fires. It fixes the local assessment and tax rate, on appeal; prepares the parish register; and appoints the overseers and assistant overseers of the poor, who assess the poor rates and make out the jury lists and the lists of parliamentary and county voters. The right to appoint the overseers was taken over from the Justices of the Peace.

Supervision. — The County Councils are given supervisory charge of the new system of parish government. They group or divide the parishes for action under the law, in their discretion; they may create or dissolve *parish councils* in the smaller parishes; they determine the number of members in each *parish council;* supervise the action of the *parish councils* in the matter of loans and land allotments; regulate in some degree the custody and preservation of the parish books and documents; and in many other ways stand superintendent over their exercise of powers.

Urban parishes are for the most part unaffected by the Act of 1894, and still act in civil as well as in church matters through their vestries, as of old.

The Rural District. — Before 1894 the rural parishes were grouped in poor-law Unions, governed, in sundry other matters as well as in the care of the poor, by a Board of Guardians. Various Highway Boards, too, Burial Boards, Bath Commissioners, Library Commissioners, and Public Improvement Boards, acted for the parishes singly or in groups in the several special matters committed to their direction. The Act of 1894 substituted 'Rural Districts' for the Unions, gave to each District an administrative Council, and united in the hands of that Council the various local functions hitherto dispersed and separated. The *District Council* is elected for a term of three years (as the Board of Guardians was), and is charged with the general oversight and conduct of all business affecting the common interests of the parishes embraced within this District in matters of local government. It takes the place of the old Board of Guardians in the administration of the poor law, and is the general highway, sanitary, and administrative body of the District. Its members are elected by the parishes in *parish meeting*, and any one may be chosen who is a parochial elector in one of the parishes of the District, or who has resided in the District for a twelvemonth preceding the election. The chairman of a *District Council*, like the chairman of a *parish council*, is *ex officio* a Justice of the Peace for the county.

The Urban District. — The urban parishes, outside incorporated boroughs, are also grouped into Districts, each with its administrative Council, and to these Councils are assigned much the same powers as those which are exercised by the Councils of the rural Districts, except that they do not constitute the poor-law authority of the District. That is still, in the urban Districts, a distinct and separate Board of Guardians, selected for the purpose. The Local Government Board may, in its discretion, confer upon Urban District Councils, by order, any or all of the powers of rural *parish councils*, however, and so render them the most important administrative authorities for their area.

Women are eligible to serve upon District Councils as well as upon parish councils, and are eligible also to be chosen chairmen ; though a woman, if chairman, is not entitled to act as a Justice of the Peace.

The County Councils have a certain very considerable supervisory power over both Rural and Urban District Councils, fixing or altering the number of Councillors, hearing appeals from the parishes against their action or default, etc.

Municipal Corporations. — The constitution of those English towns which have fully developed municipal organizations rests upon the Municipal Corporations Act of 1835 and its various amendments, as codified in an Act of 1882 of the same name. This latter Act is, in its turn, in some degree altered by the Local Government Act of 1888. If the inhabitants of any place wish to have it incorporated as a municipality, they must address a petition to that effect to the Privy Council. Notice of such a petition must be sent to the Council of the county in which the place is situate and also to the Local Government Board. The Privy Council will appoint a committee to consider the petition, who will visit the place from which the petition comes and there see and hear for themselves the arguments *pro* and *con*. All representations made upon the subject by either the County Council or the Local Government Board must also be considered.

> Generally there is considerable local opposition either to such a petition being offered or to its being granted when offered ; for the government of the place is usually already in the hands of numerous local authorities of one kind or another who do not relish the idea of being extinguished; and there are always, besides, persons who do not care to take part in bearing the additional expenses of a more elaborate organization.

If the petition be granted, the Privy Council issues a charter of incorporation to the place, arranging for the extinction of competing local authorities, setting the limits of the new municipality, determining the number of its councillors, and often even marking out its division into wards.

Once incorporated, the town takes its constitution ready-made from the Act under whose sanction it petitioned for incorporation. That Act provides that the borough shall be governed by a mayor, aldermen, and councillors. The councillors hold office for a term of three years, one-third of their number going out, in rotation, every year. There are always added to the councillors one-third as many aldermen elected by the councillors for a term of six years, one-half of their number retiring from office every three years, by rotation. The mayor is elected by the Council, — by the aldermen and councillors, that is, who constitute but a single body, — holds office for one year only, and, unlike the councillors and aldermen, receives a salary.

Judicial Status of Boroughs. — Whatever powers are not specifically granted to a municipality remain with previously constituted authorities. The Municipal Corporations Act does not provide for the exercise of judicial powers by the authorities of a borough by virtue of their separate incorporation. Unless additional special provision is made to the contrary, a municipality remains, for the purposes of justice, a part of the county. By petition, however, it may obtain an additional ' commission of the peace' for itself, or even an independent Court of Quarter Sessions.

Either, then, (a) a borough contents itself in judicial matters with the jurisdiction of the county Justices; or (b) it obtains the appointment of additional Justices of its own, who are, however, strictly, members of the county commission and can hold no separate Court of Quarter Sessions; or (c) it acquires the privilege of having Quarter Sessions of its own.

In the latter case a professional lawyer is appointed by the Crown, under the title of Recorder, to whom is given the power of two Justices acting together and the exclusive right to hold Quarter Sessions, — who is made, as it were, a multiple Justice of the Peace.

Boroughs which have a separate commission of the peace are known as "counties of towns"; those which have independent Quarter Sessions as "quarter sessions boroughs." Every mayor is *ex officio* Justice of the Peace, and continues to enjoy that office for one year after the expiration of his term as mayor. This is true even when his borough has no separate commission of the peace.

County Boroughs. — In every borough the mayor, alder‧men, and councillors, who sit together as a single body, constitute the 'Council' of the corporation; and the powers of the Council, if the borough be a 'County Borough,' are very broad indeed. Since the passage of the Local Government Act of 1888, it is necessary to distinguish, in the matter of powers, several classes of boroughs. 'County Boroughs' stand apart from the counties in which they lie, for all purposes of local government, as com‧pletely as the several counties stand apart from each other. Ex‧cept in the single matter of the management of their police force, they may not even arrange with the county authorities for merg‧ing borough with county affairs. Their Councils may be said, in general terms, to have, within the limits of the borough, all the powers once belonging to the county Justices except those strictly judicial in their nature, all the sanitary powers of urban sanitary authorities, and powers of school administration, — all regulative and administrative functions except those of the poor-law Unions into which urban parishes are still grouped. In the case of these 'county boroughs,' all powers conferred upon counties are powers conferred upon them also.

If the Council of any borough or of a county make representation to the Local Government Board that it is desirable to constitute a borough which has come to have a population of not less than fifty thousand a 'county borough,' the Board shall, unless there be some special reason to the contrary, hold a local inquiry and provide for the gift of county *status* to the borough or not as they think best. If they order the borough con‧stituted a 'county borough,' the order is *provisional* merely, and must be confirmed by Parliament.

Other Boroughs. — Boroughs which have not been put in the same rank with counties and given full privileges of self-ad‧ministration as 'county boroughs,' fall into three classes in respect of their governmental relations to the counties in which they lie:

(1) Those which have their own Quarter Sessions and whose population is ten thousand or more. These constitute for several purposes of local government parts of the counties in which they are situate. The main roads which pass through them are cared for by the county authorities, unless within twelve months after the date at which the Act of 1888 went into operation (or after

the date at which any road was declared a 'main road') the urban authorities specially reserved the right to maintain them separately. They contribute to the county funds for the payment of the costs of the assizes and judicial sessions held in them. They send members, too, to the County Council. Their representatives, however, cannot vote in the County Council on ques·tions affecting expenditures to which the parishes of the borough do not contribute by assessment to the county rates. Beyond the few matters thus mentioned, they are as independent and as self-sufficient in their organization and powers as the 'county boroughs' themselves.

(2) Boroughs which have separate Quarter Sessions but whose population numbers less than ten thousand. These are made by the Act of 1888 to yield to the Councils of the counties in which they lie the powers once exercised by their own Councils or Justices in respect of the maintenance and management of pauper lunatic asylums, their control of coroners, their appointment of analysts, their part in the maintenance and management of reformatory and industrial schools, and in the administration of the Acts relating to fish conservation, explosives, and highways and locomotives.

(3) Boroughs which have not a separate court of Quarter Sessions and whose population is under ten thousand are for all police purposes parts of the counties in which they are situate, and have, since 1888, been, for all save a few of the more exclusively local matters of self-direction, merged in the counties, in whose Councils they are, of course, like all other parts of the counties, represented.

Every borough has its own paid Clerk and Treasurer, who are appointed by the Council and hold office during its pleasure, besides "such other officers as have usually been appointed in the borough, or as the Council think necessary." If a borough have its own Quarter Sessions, it has also, as incident to that Court, its own Clerk of the Peace and its own Coroner.

The Financial Powers of a municipal Council are in all cases strictly limited as regards the borrowing of money. "In each instance, when a loan is required by a municipal corporation, the controlling authority [the Local Government Board] is to be applied to for its consent. A local inquiry, after due notice, is then held, and if the loan is approved, a term of years over which the repayment is to extend is fixed by the central authority." [1] The same powers are exercised by the Local Government Board with regard to the larger loans of parish and district Councils also.

"The accounts of most local authorities are now audited by the Local Government Board, but boroughs are exempt from this jurisdiction. The audit is conducted by three borough auditors, two elected by the burgesses, called elective auditors, one appointed by the mayor, called the mayor's auditor." [2]

Boroughs and Urban Districts. —The difference between boroughs and urban districts is not at all a difference of size, — boroughs range from a few hundred to half a million inhabitants and urban districts from a few hundred to a hundred thousand ; [2] it has hitherto been a difference, apparently, of local preference, rather, and of legal convenience.   The boundaries of a borough, when once fixed by a charter of incorporation, could, until the passage of the Act of 1888, be altered only by a special Act of Parliament: it was much easier to apply to the Local Government Board, which could of its own authority create what was then known as an Urban *Sanitary* District.   As towns already incorporated grew, therefore, the added portions became independently incorporated as Urban Sanitary Districts, and thus the town was pieced out.   One writer was able to say, in 1882, "Nowhere, from one end of England to the other, do we find an instance (Nottingham alone excepted) of a large borough which is municipally self-contained, and consequently self-governing." [3]

In the Local Government Act of 1888 it was provided that the boundaries of a borough might be altered by provisional order of the Local Government Board, upon the address of the borough Council. This order, being provisional, must receive the sanction of Parliament, and is made only after local inquiry.   The proceedings, therefore, for changing the boundaries of a borough were still left much more elaborate and difficult than the free action of the Local Government Board with reference to urban districts.

Central Control of Urban Authorities. —Full municipal corporations look partly (in the matter of sanitary regulation, for example,)

[1] Bunce, *Cobden Club Essays*, 1882, p. 283; title, "Municipal Boroughs and Urban Districts."   [2] Chalmers, p. 87.   [3] Bunce, p. 298.

to the Local Government Board as a central authority exercising powers
of supervision, partly (in the management of the constabulary, for instance,) to the Home Office, and partly (if seaports) to the Board of
Trade.   Urban Districts, however, have but a single central authority set
over them, the Local Government Board.

London. — The metropolis was, until the passage of the
Act of 1888, the unsolved problem, the unregenerate monster,
of local government in England.   The vast aggregation of houses
and population known by the world as 'London,' spreading its
unwieldy bulk over parts of the three counties of Middlesex,
Surrey, and Kent, consisted of the *City* of London, a small corporation at its centre confined within almost forgotten boundaries,
still possessing and belligerently defending mediæval privileges
and following mediæval types of organization and procedure, and,
round about this ancient City as a nucleus, a congeries of hundreds
of old parishes and new urban districts made from time to time
to meet the needs of newly grown portions of the inorganic mass.
This heterogeneous body of mediæval trade guilds, vestries, and
sanitary authorities had been in some sort bound together since
1855 by a Metropolitan Board of Works which exercised certain
powers over the whole area outside the 'City.'
     The Local Government Act of 1888 made of the metrop-
olis, not a 'county borough,' but a county, — the 'Administrative County of London ' — with its own Lord Lieutenant, Sheriff,
and Commission of the Peace, as well as its own Council.   Its
numerous parishes were left to act, as formerly, under their several vestries ; and the Act of 1894 gave to those vestries the
same constitution and substantially the same powers that are
elsewhere in the kingdom possessed by the Urban District Councils (page 239).   The London Government Act of 1899 still further
consolidated and coördinated the administration by creating
twenty-eight metropolitan boroughs, each with its own mayor,
aldermen, and councillors, with specially defined powers, which,
in the matter of finance, are considerably limited.   The 'City '
is still left to occupy its separate place in the great metropolitan
county as a quarter sessions borough not enjoying separate county
privileges, — with some limitations special to its case.

The number of councillors in the London County Council is fixed at twice the number of members returned to Parliament at the time of the passage of the Act of 1888 by the various constituencies of the metropolitan area. The councillors, thus, number 118. The Council of the Metropolis is put upon an exceptional footing with regard to its quota of aldermen. The aldermen are to be one-sixth, instead of one-third, as many as the councillors. The total membership of the London Council is, therefore, 137.

Central Control. — The plan of central control in England is manifestly quite indigenous. The central government is not present in local administration in the person of any superintending official like the French Prefect (pages 167, 168, 170), or any dominant board like the 'Administration' of the Prussian Government District (pages 480–481). There has, indeed, been developing in England a marked tendency to bring local authorities more and more under the supervision in important matters of the government departments in London, — a tendency which has led to the concentration, since 1871, in the hands of the Local Government Board of various powers once scattered among such authorities as the Home Office, the Privy Council, etc. But this tendency, which is towards control, has not been towards centralization. It has, so far, not gone beyond making the advice of the central authority always accessible by local officers or bodies, and its consent necessary to certain classes of local undertakings. The central government has not itself often assumed powers of origination or initiative in local affairs. Even where the Local Government Board is given completest power the choice of the officers who are to put its regulations into force is generally left with the ratepayers in the districts concerned. Thus the authority of the Board over the Guardians of the Poor is complete ; but the Guardians are elected in the parishes. Its authority in sanitary matters makes its directions imperative as to the execution of the Public Health Acts ; but in many cases the local health officers are appointees of the local bodies. The by-laws enacted by the county authorities, unless they affect nuisances, may be annulled by an order in Council ; in the matter of borrowing money, too, local authorities are narrowly bound by the action of the Local Government Board ; and its assent to propositions to raise loans is seldom given without very thorough inquiry and without good reason shown.   But all these are *functions of system*, so to say, rather than of centralization.   Coördination in methods of poor-relief is sought, that relief being given under national statutes, and the coöperation of central with local judgment in financial matters, local debts constituting a very proper subdivision of national finance.   But the spirit in which the control is exercised, as well as the absence of permanent officials representing the central authority in local government, and even of permanent instrumentalities for the administration of financial advice, bespeak a system of coöperation and advice rather than of centralization.

Local Government in Scotland. — An Act of 1889 extended to Scotland a system of county government substantially the same as that created for England by the Act of 1888 ; and the Act of 1894 put *parish councils* like those of England into the place formerly held by parochial Boards, and erected a separate Local Government Board for Scotland, of which the Secretary for Scotland was made President.

The Government of the English Colonies.

English Colonial Expansion. — Doubtless the most significant and momentous fact of modern history is the wide diffusion of the English race, the sweep of its commerce, the dominance of its institutions, its imperial control of the destinies of half the globe.   When, by reason of the closing of the old doors of the East by the Turk and the consequent turning about of Europe to face the Atlantic instead of the Mediterranean, England was put at the front instead of at the back of the nations of the Continent, a profound revolution was prepared in the politics of the world.   England soon defeated Holland and Spain and Portugal, her rivals for the control of the Atlantic and its new continents ; and steadily, step by step, she has taken possession of almost every new land worth the having in whatever quarter of the globe.   With her conquests and her settlers have gone also her institutions, until now her people everywhere stand for types of free men, her institutions for models of free government.

English Colonial Policy. — It was only by slow degrees, however, that England learned the right policy towards her colonies. She began, as Rome did, by regarding her possessions as estates, to be farmed for her own selfish benefit. Nothing less than the loss of America sufficed to teach her how short-sighted such a policy was. But, unlike Rome, she was fortunate enough to lose the best part of her possessions without being herself overwhelmed; and even after the loss of America time and opportunity offered for the building up of another colonial empire scarcely less great.

Towards her present colonies her policy is most liberal; for the England of the present day is a very different England from that which drove America into rebellion. Even the notable lesson emphasized in the loss of America would not have sufficed to bring England to her senses touching her true interests in the colonies, had she not herself speedily thereafter been brought by other causes to a change of heart. The movements of opinion which stirred her to religious revival, to prison reform, to enlightened charity, to the reform of parliamentary representation, to a general social and political regeneration, stirred her also, no doubt, to vouchsafe to her colonists full rights as Englishmen.

Lord Durham in Canada. — The turning point was reached in 1837, when a rebellion broke out in Lower Canada. Lower Canada was French Canada. Its government, like the governments of the American states south of it in their own colonial times, consisted of an Executive, a Legislative Council nominated by the Crown, and a legislative chamber elected by the colonists. The colonists had been exasperated by just such arbitrariness and lack of sympathy on the part of the Governor and his Council, and just such efforts to make the salaries and the maintenance of the judicial officers of the colony independent of the appropriations voted by the popular assembly, as had hastened the separation of the United States from England; and at last rebellion had been made to speak the demands of the colonists for constitutional reform. The rebellion was put down, but the defeated colonists were not treated as they would have been in 1776. A royal commissioner was sent out to them from the mother country to redress their grievances by liberal measures of concession and reform. This commissioner was Lord Durham. He spoiled his mission by well-meant but arbitrary conduct which was misunderstood at home, and he was recalled ; but his report upon the condition of Canada and the measures necessary for her pacification may justly be called the fountain head of all that England has since done for the betterment of government in her colonies. Lord Durham recommended nothing less than complete self-government, with interference from England in nothing but questions immediately and evidently affecting imperial interests. 1847 saw independent responsible self-government completely established in Canada, and subsequent years have seen it extended to all the British colonies capable of self-direction.

The Self-governing Colonies. — The English colonies, as at present organized, may be roughly classified in two groups as (*a*) *Self-governing* and (*b*) *Crown* colonies. The self-governing colonies are five in number ; namely, Canada, Newfoundland, the Commonwealth of Australia, the Union of South Africa, and New Zealand. In all of these there is practically complete independence of legislation in all matters not directly touching imperial interests : and in all there is full responsible government, — government, that is, through ministers responsible to representatives of the people for their policy and for all executive acts, because chosen from and representing the majority in the popular chamber. In Tasmania, and the Commonwealth of Australia, both branches of the legislature are elected ; in the others the upper chamber is nominated by the Executive save in the Union of South Africa, where it is partly appointed and partly elected. But the origin of the upper chamber does not affect the full responsibility of the ministers or the practically complete self-direction of the colony.

The Government of Canada. — In 1840 Parliament provided by Act for the union of Upper and Lower Canada (now the provinces of Ontario and Quebec) upon a basis suggested by Lord Durham's report ; but the legislative union of these two provinces, the one English, the other almost wholly French, was ill-advised and proved provisional only. Although an Act of 1854 granted to the united colonies a government as nearly as might be modelled upon the government of England herself, no satisfactory basis of self-government was reached until, by the 'British North America Act' of 1867, the colonies were at once separated and re-integrated by means of a federal constitution. That Act is the present constitution of the 'Dominion of Canada.' Under that constitution the nine provinces now comprised within the Dominion, namely, Ontario, Quebec, Nova Scotia, New Brunswick, Manitoba, British Columbia, Prince Edward Island, Alberta, and Saskatchewan, have each a separate parliament and administration. In each a Lieutenant-Governor presides; in each, as in the Dominion itself, there is a ministry responsible for its policy and executive acts to a parliament fully equipped for self-direction in local affairs.

The provisions of the British North America Act were drafted in Canada and accepted by the Parliament in England without alteration. In the division of powers which they make between the government of the Dominion and the governments of the several provinces, they differ very radically in character from the provisions of our own federal constitution. Our constitution grants certain specified powers to the general government and reserves the rest to the states; the British North America Act, on the contrary, grants certain specified powers to the provinces and reserves all others to the government of the Dominion. Among the powers thus reserved to the federal government is that of enacting all criminal laws.

In all the provinces except Quebec and Nova Scotia the legislature consists of but a single house.

The government of the Dominion is for the most part a very faithful reproduction of the government of the mother country. The Crown is represented by the Governor-General, who acts in the administration of the colony as the Crown acts in the administration of the kingdom, through responsible ministers, and whose veto upon legislation is never used, though bills about whose bearing upon imperial policy there were serious doubts have been reserved for the approval of the king in Council (that is, of the ministry of the day in England).[1] The 'Cabinet' is a body unknown to the written constitution, but it comprises those

---

[1] Only one such bill has been refused the Royal assent.

members of the Privy Council who are also members of Parliament who for the time being represent the views and policies of the majority in the popular house of the legislature, leading that house in legislation, and in all its functions following the precedents of responsible cabinet government established in England. The legislature consists of two houses, the Senate and the House of Commons. The Senate consists of ninety-six members nominated for life by the Governor-General, — that is, in effect, appointed by the Dominion ministers; for in the composition of the Senate, as in the creation of peers at home, the advice of the ministers is decisive.[1] Each Senator must be at least thirty years of age, must reside in the province for which he is appointed, and must possess therein property, real or personal, to the value of four thousand dollars. The House of Commons consists of two hundred and twenty-one members elected from the several provinces, for a term of five years, upon the basis of one representative for every 22,688 inhabitants, it being understood, however, that Quebec shall never have less than sixty-five members.

The eighteen ministers composing the cabinet are, the Prime Minister and President of the Council, Secretary of State, Minister of Trade and Commerce, Ministers of Justice, Marine and Fisheries, Railways and Canals, Militia and Defence, Finance, Agriculture, Public Works, Interior, Labor, Customs, Inland Revenue, Solicitor-General, Postmaster-General, and two ministers without portfolios.

The distribution of representation in the Dominion House of Commons is at present as follows: Ontario has 92 members, Quebec 65, Nova Scotia 20, New Brunswick 14, Manitoba 7, British Columbia 6, Prince Edward Island 5, and the North West Territories 4. The representatives are elected by a franchise based upon a small property qualification.

The Parliament of the Dominion may be dissolved by the Governor-General upon the advice of the ministers, and a new Election

[1] The power is reserved to the sovereign, upon recommendation of the Governor-General, to direct that four or eight members be added to the Senate from the four divisions of Canada equally, but this power has never been exercised.

held, as in England, when an appeal to the constituencies is
deemed necessary or desirable.

THE COMMONWEALTH OF AUSTRALIA.

History of Federation. — The early settlements in Australia, treated as little more than convict stations, were ruled by the
Governor as he pleased, but as early as 1823 the need for a legislative body in New South Wales was met by vesting this function
in an appointed Council.   In 1842 the principle of representation
was introduced into the Council, though one-third of its number
remained appointive, and in 1850 two houses were substituted
for the single Council and responsible government was introduced
at the same time.   As the other colonies in Australia grew in population, representative institutions and responsible government
were introduced, the last colony to complete the process being
Western Australia in 1890.   The six colonies, New South Wales,
Victoria, South Australia, Tasmania, Queensland, and Western
Australia, were all in possession of substantially identical forms
of government, consisting of a Governor appointed by the Crown
and advised by a Council, composed in part by the ministers of
the day, and of a dual legislative body, the Parliament, to which
the ministers were responsible.   The constitutions of all the
colonies were originally framed in the colonies, and subsequently
enacted, with amendments, by the Parliament at Westminster.

Trade and the customs formed from the beginning a strong incentive toward federation, and in 1873 the Imperial Parliament
removed the legal bars which had made a Customs Union impossible, yet the divergent economic interests and tariff policies
of the colonies stood in the way.   The Federal Council of
Australasia Act, passed by Parliament in 1885, created a Council
with limited powers to deal with certain common interests in the
South Pacific.   There was no executive or judicial power created
by the Act, and the Council lacked the power to raise revenue or
expend money.   Membership in the Council was optional.   Yet
the Council legislated with respect to a number of matters, and
continued in existence till 1899.

The sentiment in favor of federation had been steadily gaining, and in 1887 the question of defence added its weight when, at the Imperial Conference at London, Australia as a whole agreed to furnish an annual subsidy of £ 226,000 towards the expense of a separate squadron on the Australian station. Conferences were held in 1890 and 1891, in which resolutions were passed laying down the basis on which federation should take place ; but it was not until 1897 that a convention assembled at Adelaide to frame a federal constitution. The proposed constitution was then submitted to the legislatures of the colonies, and after consideration by them, the convention reassembled at Sydney to consider the changes which had been suggested.

The larger colonies demanded that greater consideration should be given to population, and the smaller colonies sought to preserve their autonomy. The position and mode of election of the Senate was the source of the greatest difference of opinion, but finally a draft was agreed upon which, when submitted to the colonies, failed of ratification. Subsequently compromises were made to meet the objections, chiefly of New South Wales, and five colonies accepted the proposed constitution by popular vote. It was then forwarded to the Imperial Parliament for enactment. Western Australia, which had held aloof, asked for the right to join the federation, and in 1900 Parliament passed the Commonwealth of Australia Act. By proclamation the date of the establishment of the Commonwealth was fixed as January 1, 1901.

The Constitution. — The Constitution is an Act of the Imperial Parliament, and is in legal theory subject to change by that body whenever it chooses, though in practice it is not probable that any changes would be made which were contrary to the wishes of the Commonwealth. The Commonwealth differs from Canada in its fundamentals ; in the latter the provinces are far less independent of the Dominion government than are the states of the Commonwealth ; as provinces they have no participation or representation in the central government whereas in the former the separate character of the states finds representation in the Senate, as in the case of the United States. Moreover, the powers of the Commonwealth are delegated, while in Canada it is the government of the Dominion which possesses the reservoir of powers, and the provinces have only those powers which have been granted to them.   In Canada the lieutenant-governors of the provinces are appointed by the Governor-General, in Australia the governors of the states are appointed by the Crown. In short, Australia is far more of a federal state than is Canada.

The Executive. — The Executive of the Commonwealth is vested in a Governor-General, appointed by the King, and his power extends to the maintenance of the Constitution and the laws of the Commonwealth, but inasmuch as responsible government exists in the Commonwealth as it had existed and still exists in the individual states, the real executive power is vested in the ministry, which is responsible to Parliament. The ministry constitute the Governor-General's Executive Council, whose advice he must accept.   The following ministries have been established in the Commonwealth : External Affairs, Attorney-General, Home Affairs, Treasury, Trade and Customs, Defence, and the Postmaster-General.   There have also been ministers without portfolio.

Instability of Ministries. — Both in the Commonwealth and in the individual states changes of ministries have been frequent, due to the absence of questions on which parties could divide on party lines.   The Labor party is the only one which is effectively organized.   There is a conspicuous absence of loyalty to party leaders, and as a result ministries are weak and easily overthrown.   In the states the small size of the Parliament makes government more difficult, since the absence of a member or two in a small House may result in the overthrow of a government.

The Parliament. — The Parliament of the Commonwealth is composed of a Senate and a House of Representatives.   Until Parliament shall otherwise provide, the Senate is composed of six senators from each of the original states, directly chosen by the people of each state.   The number of senators may be increased or diminished, but the number of senators from each of the original states may not be less than six, and the equality of their representation must be maintained.   The term of senators is six years, and one-half retire every three years.   A senator must be twenty-one years of age, a native-born or naturalized citizen, and if the latter, he must have been a citizen at least five years; he must be entitled to vote at the election of members of the House of Representatives and have been for three years a resident of the Commonwealth; also he must not be under certain legal disabilities.

The membership of the House of Representatives is seventy-five, of whom 27 are from New South Wales, 22 from Victoria, 9 from Queensland, 7 from South Australia, and 5 each from Western Australia and Tasmania. The term of members is three years, unless sooner terminated by dissolution.

The powers of Parliament are fixed by the Constitution, and extend in general to all powers affecting the common interests of all the states. Except with respect to finance bills, the Senate and the House have equal power over legislation. All bills for raising revenue or appropriating money must originate in the House and cannot be amended by the Senate, but such bills may be returned to the House by message with the request for the omission or amendment of any items. The House may or may not accept the suggestions, as it sees fit. With respect to other legislation, if the Senate does not accept a bill which has passed the House, and if the House after an interval of three months, whether in the same session or the next, shall again pass the measure, the Governor-General may dissolve both the Senate and the House simultaneously; if after the dissolution the bill is again passed by the House and fails to pass the Senate, the Governor-General may convene a joint session of the two Houses, and if the bill is passed by a majority of the total membership of both Houses in joint session, it shall be taken as having been approved by Parliament and shall go to the Governor-General for the King's assent.

The Powers of the Colonial Courts. — The action of the courts in the colonies on certain questions furnishes an instructive counterpart to the constitutional functions of our own courts. The colonial governments are conducted under written constitutions as our own governments are, though their constitutions are imperial statutes, while ours are drafted by conventions and adopted by a vote of the people. And colonial courts exercise the same power of constitutional interpretation that belongs to our own courts and that has often been carelessly assumed to be a peculiar prerogative of theirs. They test acts of legislation by the grants of power under which they are enacted, an appeal lying from them to the Judicial Committee of the Privy Council in England, which serves as a general supreme court for the colonies.

The Union of South Africa. — Before the Boer War the two English colonies in South Africa, the Cape of Good Hope and Natal, both enjoyed responsible government, and the Cape Colony was one of the few English colonies in which both houses of the legislature were elected. The terms of surrender of the Boer forces in the field provided that representative institutions should be granted to the conquered colonies of the Transvaal and the Orange River, and that at the earliest possible moment they should be given self-government of the usual colonial type. Upon the accession to power, in 1906, of the Liberal ministry under Sir Henry Campbell-Bannerman, the time was thought ripe for carrying out these terms, and so full ministerial responsibility for the general government of these two colonies was established by letters patent, in the Transvaal in December, 1906, and the Orange River Colony in June, 1907.

These four English colonies in South Africa, so lately enemies, were faced with certain common interests and problems, which, despite race antagonisms and some conflicting interests, proved strong enough to draw them together into a union. Most pressing of all the problems — and one still awaiting a solution — is that of the native races, — the menace that South Africa might become a black man's country. Singly the colonies might have found their resources insufficient to meet a great native uprising, but united they are in large measure relieved from that fear. Railways and tariffs were other matters demanding common control and uniform action if the prosperity of all the colonies was to be fostered. Discrimination of one colony against the other created a strong incentive to union. A customs union of the four colonies and of Rhodesia, together with the territories under the administration of the High Commissioner for South Africa, had been formed in 1903 and was renewed in 1906. An

Intercolonial Council for the administration of the railways of the Transvaal and the Orange River Colony was inaugurated in 1902, so that the colonies were not without some experience of the habit and advantage of common action. The real stimulus to union came after the granting of self-government to the Transvaal and the Orange River Colony, at the conference of May, 1908, for the revision of customs and railway rates. Delegates from the several colonies were selected upon the authorization of the four colonial governments, who took up in convention the discussion of a basis of unification of South Africa. The work of this convention was done in secret, the members well knowing that a public discussion of the delicate questions with which it was confronted would prove fatal to any hope of union. The results of the convention's labors were submitted to the Parliaments of the colonies — and in Natal to a referendum — and after ratification delegates were appointed by the Parliaments to proceed to England and secure the enactment by Parliament of the proposed plan of union. This was done, and the Union of South Africa Act was passed in 1909, and the Union itself was inaugurated on May 31, 1910.

Plan of the Union. — The Union of South Africa differs fundamentally from the federal arrangements of Canada and Australia. In them are present the characteristic features of federalism — the supremacy of the constitution, the distribution of the powers of government among bodies of limited and coordinate authority, and the authority of the courts to interpret the constitution. Not one of these features is present in the Union of South Africa; the Parliament, not the constitution, is supreme; power is not divided among coördinate authorities with limited functions, but rests ultimately in the Parliament; the courts have not the right to interpret the constitution by declaring a law unconstitutional, but their function will be identical with that of the courts in England. In short, the supremacy of the Parliament within the Union has been secured in much the same way, though not to the same extent as the Parliament of the mother country — it is subject always to the ultimate authority of the latter, and with respect to certain provisions of the constitution of the Union its power is qualified.

As in Canada and Australia, the constitution of the Union is an Act of Parliament which legally may be changed by a Parliamentary Act, though in practice any change without the consent of the Union would be bitterly opposed as in the like case in Canada and Australia.

This supremacy of the Parliament of the Union has been generally approved in South Africa because of the belief in the need for a strong central government to meet the grave questions confronting it   An interesting feature accompanying the consummation of union in South Africa was the abolition of the previous governmental institutions of the colonies, and the institution by the Union of South Africa Act of a new framework of government within each colony.

The Executive. — The executive power is vested in the King and may be exercised by the King in person, or by a Governor-General as his representative, who shall be appointed by the King and hold office at his pleasure. Subject to the provisions of the Act, the Governor-General shall exercise such powers and functions as may be assigned him by the King. The salary of the Governor-General is fixed at ten thousand pounds, and shall not be altered during his continuance in office.

Executive Council. — The Governor-General is to be advised by an Executive Council, the members of which shall be appointed and summoned by him, and shall hold office during his pleasure. The real executive power is vested in the Governor-General in Council, which means the Governor-General acting with the advice of the Executive Council.

The Ministers. — The number of ministers is by the Act set at ten, who are appointed by the Governor-General, hold office at his pleasure, are members of the Executive Council, and who administer the departments of state. No minister shall hold office for a longer period than three months, unless he is or becomes a member of either House of Parliament. The ministries established are those of Agriculture, Interior, Mines and Defence, Native Affairs, Education, Finance, Lands, Public Works, Posts and Telegraphs, Railways and Harbors, Justice, and Commerce and Industries. A minister has the right to sit and speak in both Houses, but may vote only in the one of which he is a member.

All powers, authorities, and functions which had previously been exercised by the executive authorities of the separate colonies were conferred upon the Governor-General in Council, unless otherwise provided by the Act. The seat of the executive government was located at Pretoria.[1]

The Parliament. — The legislative power of the Union was vested in a Parliament, consisting of the King, a Senate, and a House of Assembly. The Governor-General may appoint such times as he sees fit for holding the sessions of Parliament, and he may prorogue Parliament and may dissolve both Houses simultaneously, or the House of Assembly alone. But the Senate may not be dissolved within a period of ten years after the establishment of the Union, and no dissolution of the Senate shall affect Senators nominated by the Governor-General in Council. Parliament shall meet at least once a year.

The Senate. — For ten years after the establishment of the Union the Senate shall be composed of eight Senators nominated by the Governor-General in Council, and for each province eight Senators shall be elected. Half of the Senators appointed by the Governor-General shall be selected on the ground of their thorough acquaintance with the reasonable wants and wishes of the colored races of South Africa. The elected Senators were chosen before the date of union by the two Houses of the Parliament of each colony, sitting together as one body on the principle of proportional representation with a single transferable vote, and presided over by the Speaker of the Legislative Assembly. The term of Senators is ten years, and vacancies among the appointed Senators shall be filled by the Governor-General in Council, and among the elected Senators by the Provincial Council of the Province from which such Senator had been chosen.

Parliament may provide for the manner in which the Senate

[1] The local rivalries of the colonies led to the unique arrangement of locating the three departments of government in three different places — the executive in Pretoria, the legislative in Cape Town and the judicial in Bloemfontein.

shall be constituted after the expiration of ten years, but until otherwise determined, the provisions respecting appointed Senators shall continue in force; the elected Senators shall be chosen by the Provincial Council and the House of Assembly in each Province, and shall hold office for ten years unless the Senate be sooner dissolved.

Qualifications of Senators. — A Senator must be not less than thirty years of age, must be qualified to be registered as a voter for the election of members of the House of Assembly of one of the provinces, must have resided for five years within the limits of the Union at the time when he is elected or appointed, must be a British subject of European descent, and in the case of an elected Senator must be the registered owner of immovable property within the Union of the value of not less than five hundred pounds over and above any special mortgages thereon.

House of Assembly. — Membership in the House of Assembly rests upon election by the voters of the Union, and members were allotted to the provinces as follows: Cape of Good Hope, 51; Natal, 17; Transvaal, 36; Orange Free State, 17. The number is subject to increase upon the basis of the census taken every five years beginning in 1911, until it reaches one hundred and fifty, but until that number is reached, or until a period of ten years has elapsed after the establishment of the Union, the number of representatives of any of the four original provinces may not be decreased. Thereafter, however, the representation shall be based upon the European male adults. Qualifications of electors shall be determined by Parliament, with the exception that no law shall disqualify any person in the province of the Cape of Good Hope, qualified by its laws, by reason of race or color only, unless the bill be passed by both Houses of Parliament sitting together and be agreed to by not less than two-thirds of the total number of members of both Houses, and no registered voter shall be removed from the register solely by reason of race or color. These exceptions were for the protection of the black voters of the Cape Colony.

The qualifications for members of the House of Assembly are the same as those for the Senate, except for the age and property requirements.

The House of Assembly shall, unless sooner dissolved by the Governor-General, continue for five years from the date of first meeting, but no longer.

Powers of Parliament. — Parliament has the supreme legislative authority for the Union, and it is its duty to make laws for the peace, order, and good government of the Union. The two Houses do not, however, stand upon an equal footing in the matter of legislation. All bills appropriating money or raising revenue must originate in the House of Assembly, and may not be amended so far as they are for the services of the government, and may not increase any proposed burden or charges upon the people. The House may not appropriate money unless such appropriation has been recommended by message from the Governor-General in the same session.

If the Senate fails to pass any bill passed by the House and if the bill is passed by the House in the next session, the Governor-General may during that session convene a joint session of the two Houses, and the bill, if passed by a majority of the Houses in joint session, shall become a law. In the case of money bills the Governor-General may convene the joint sitting during the same session.

Bills must be presented to the Governor-General, who may declare that he assents in the King's name, or that he withholds assent, or that he reserves the bill for the signification of the King's assent. Bills touching the House of Assembly, abolishing provincial councils, or abridging the powers conferred by the Act of Union upon provincial councils, must be reserved.

The King may within one year disallow any bill to which the Governor-General has given assent, and bills reserved for the King's pleasure shall have no force unless within a year the Governor-General shall make known to each of the Houses or by proclamation that the King's assent has been given.

The Provinces. — The executive power in each of the provinces is in the hands of an administrator, appointed by the Governor-General in council, who shall hold office for five years and who shall not be removed except by the Governor-General for cause assigned. The legislative power in the provinces is vested in an elective council which meets annually and shall continue for three years from the date of its first meeting. The administrator may prorogue but may not dissolve the council. Each provincial council chooses an executive committee of four members, from among its members or otherwise, who, together with the administrator, shall carry on the administration of provincial affairs. The powers of the provincial council are defined by the Act of Union, and may be said broadly to deal with the local affairs of the province, and any ordinance made by a provincial council shall have effect as long and as far only as it is not repugnant to any Act of Parliament.

The Crown Colonies. — All those colonies which have not responsible self-government are classed as Crown colonies, colonies more or less completely directed by the Colonial Office in London. They range in organization all the way from mere military administrations, such as have been established in St. Helena and Gibraltar, through those which, like Trinidad and the Straits Settlements, have both a nominated Executive and a nominated Legislative Council, and those like Jamaica, whose nominated Executive is associated with a Legislative Council in part elected, to those like the Bahamas and Bermuda, in which the Councils are altogether elected, but which have no responsible ministry.

Powers of Colonial Governors. — It is interesting to have the testimony of one of the most capable and eminent of English colonial administrators as to the relative desirability of the post of governor in a colony in which he is governor indeed, with no ministers empowered to force their advice upon him, and in a colony where he must play the unobtrusive part of constitutional monarch. Lord Elgin says with great confidence, in his *Letters*, that his position as governor of Canada was a position of greater official power than his position, previously held, as governor of Jamaica. He declares his unhesitating belief that there is " more room for the exercise of influence on the part of the governor" in such a colony as Canada, where he must keep in the background, and scrupulously heed his ministers, than under any other arrangement that ever was before devised, although his influence there is of course " wholly moral — an influence of suasion, sympathy, and moderation, which softens the temper while it elevates the aims of local politics."[1] This is but another way of stating the unquestionable truth that it is easier, as well as wiser, to govern with the consent and coöperation of the governed than without it, — easier to rule as a friend than as a master.

India. — India stands in matters of government, as in so many other respects, entirely apart from the rest of the British Empire.[2] It is governed, through the instrumentality of its Governor-General and his Council, directly from London by a member of the Cabinet, the Secretary of State for India. The Secretary of State is assisted by a Council of ten or more members appointed by the Crown from among persons who have resided or served in India. Acting under the Secretary of State and his Council in London, there is the Governor-General of India, who is also assisted by a Council of from five to six members, appointed by the Crown, — a Council which is first of all administrative, but which, when reënforced by additional members nominated by the Governor-General or elected under the Indian Councils Act of 1909, has also the functions of a legislative council.

The work of the Governor-General's Council is divided among ten departments, one of which, that of foreign affairs, is generally kept in the hands of the Governor-General himself. These departments do not constitute a ministry ; they are regarded simply as committees of the Council.

The sessions of the legislative council are held always in public. The number of members is 68, of whom 36 are official and 32 are non-official, which secures to the government the control of the action of the council. Special provision is made for representation of the Mohammedan part of the population. The legislative council makes laws, subject to some restrictions, for all persons in British India, for all British subjects in native states, and for all native Indian subjects in any part of the world.

Not all of India is directly administered by the English government. There are numerous native states which act with

[1] *Letters and Journals of Lord Elgin*, ed. by Theodore Walrond, London, 1872, p. 126.

[2] The Government of India Act, 1915, as amended by a like Act in 1916.

substantial independence in local affairs, though under English overlordship and control. Such part of the vast territory as is administered directly by English officials is divided into fifteen provinces, of which the chief in importance are under governors who are appointed by the Crown and are assisted, as the Governor-General is, by two councils, administrative and legislative. Lieutenant-Governors, appointed by the Governor-General, and assisted by similar councils, preside over the provinces next in importance. The Commissioners or agents of the other provinces, who are also appointed by the Governor-General, also have their councils. In all provincial legislative councils the majority is elected.

There has been a growing demand in India for a larger participation on the part of Indians in the government of India, and, among a few, a feeling of nationality.

In 1885 there was held the first Indian national Congress, and in the succeeding Congresses there has been a considerable agitation in favor of throwing off British rule and of establishing a national Indian state. The nationalists are Hindus, and the interests of the Moslem part of the population were not cared for by their program. In 1906 the All-India Moslem League was founded on the basis of complete loyalty to the Crown.

The war has produced profound changes in the situation. The princes have contributed largely of men and money to aid in its prosecution, and thousands of Indians have been organized into labor units for work in various parts of the world.

The Government of India Act of 1915 confers a larger participation in affairs of the government upon native Indians, and Indians may now become officers in the British army. India also is represented in the Imperial War Conference.

The policy of the present British government toward India was stated by the Secretary of State for India in the House of Commons on August 20, 1917, as follows: "The policy of His Majesty's government . . . is that of the increasing association of Indians in every branch of the administration, and the gradual development of self-governing institutions, with a view to the progressive realization of responsible government in India as an integral part of the British Empire."

Greater Britain. — Greater Britain, the world of English colonies, differs very materially from Greater Greece, the wide-spread Hellas of the ancient world.   Hellas was disintegrate: the Greeks carried with them, as of course, Greek institutions, but only to allow those institutions wide differentiation.   In no way did Greek settlement signify race integration or a national nexus of rule.   Englishmen, on the contrary, in English colonies, maintain a homogeneity and integration both of race and of in-stitutions which have drawn the four parts of the world together under common influences, if they have not compacted them for a common destiny.   Throughout Europe reformers have copied English political arrangements; the colonists have not copied them, they have extended and are perpetuating and perfecting them.

Imperial Unity or Federation. — For the past fifteen years there has been much discussion of the future relations of the Dominions to the mother country and the means by which they might be drawn closer together.   The Dominions felt a grow-ing desire to participate actively in the decision of questions affecting imperial interests, particularly in view of the contribu-tions they were making to the Imperial defence, but nothing beyond Colonial and Imperial Conferences had been achieved. At the outbreak of the war the Dominions responded instantly to the need of the mother country, and their efforts in the war have been worthy of the best traditions of Englishmen.   The war has shown them their need of defence by the United Kingdom, and the latter has received with gratitude the assistance so loyally given.

On the part of the United Kingdom there has been practical acknowledgment of the need to draw the mother country and the Dominions into closer relations and a participation by the latter in the decisions affecting Imperial questions.   A War Conference was summoned in 1917 to which the Premiers of the Dominions were invited, and all sent representatives with the exception of Australia.   In 1916 the visiting Premiers had been asked to sit at special meetings of the general Cabinet Council, but in 1917 Lloyd George went further and took the Premiers into the inner War Cabinet of five members which he had constituted upon assuming the position of Prime Minister. It was decided to hold meetings annually, or oftener if need be, " to discuss foreign affairs and other subjects of Imperial policy." The Imperial Cabinet for the future should consist of the Prime Minister of the United Kingdom and such of his colleagues as dealt specially with Imperial affairs, the Prime Minister of each of the Dominions or a special representative clothed with equal authority, and a representative of the Indian people appointed by the government of India.

What shape the closer relation between the United Kingdom and the Dominions should take was left for determination after the War.

REPRESENTATIVE AUTHORITIES.

Anson, Wm. R., The Law and Custom of the Constitution, 3 vols., 4th ed., Oxford, 1907–1909.

Bagehot, Walter, The English Constitution, London, 1867; N.Y., 1882.

Bourinot, John G., Federal Government in Canada (Johns Hopkins Univ. Studies in Historical and Political Science), Baltimore, 1889; and Parliamentary Procedure and Practice in the Dominion of Canada, 4th ed., Toronto, 1916.

Boutmy, Émile, The English Constitution, trans. out of the French by Isabel M. *Eaden;* and Studies in Constitutional Law, trans. by E. M. *Dicey.* Both, London, 1891.

Brand, R. H., The Union of South Africa, Oxford, 1909.

Burgess, J. W., Political Science and Constitutional Law, 2 vols., Boston, 1890.

Cameron, E. R., The Canadian Constitution, Winnipeg, 1915.

Clark, W. Inglis, Australian Constitutional Law, Melbourne, 1901.

Clement, The Law of the Canadian Constitution, 3d ed., Toronto, 1916.

Cobden Club Essays, 1882: Local Government and Taxation in the United Kingdom. London.

Dicey, A. V., The Privy Council, London, 1887; and The Law of the Constitution, 8th ed., London, 1915.

Dilke, Sir C. W., Problems of Greater Britain, London, 1890.

Dupriez, L., Les Ministres dans les principaux Pays d'Europe et d'Amérique, 2 vols., Paris, 1892.

Egerton and *Grant*, Canadian Constitutional Development, London, 1907.

Egerton, Confederations and Unions.

English Citizen Series: H. D. *Traill*, Central Government.

M. D. *Chalmers*, Local Government.

F. W. *Maitland*, Justice and Police.

S. *Walpole*, The Electorate and the Legislature.

T. W. *Fowle*, The Poor Law.

Gneist, R., History of the English Constitution, 2 vols., N.Y., 1886; Student's History of the English Parliament, N.Y., 1887; Self-government, Communalverfassung und Verwaltungsgerichte, 3d ed., Berlin, 1871; Das Englische Verwaltungsrecht der Gegenwart in Vergleichung mit dem deutschen Verwaltungswesen, 3d ed., 2 vols., 1883–1884.

Goodnow, F. J., Comparative Administrative Law, 2 vols., New York, 1893.

Hallam, H., Constitutional History of England, 2 vols., N.Y., 1880.

Hearn, W. E., The Government of England, 2d ed., London, 1887.

Ilbert, Courtenay, Parliament, N.Y., 1911.

Imperial Parliament Series: Local Administration, by W. *Rathbone*, A. *Pell* and F. C. *Montague*, London, 1885.

Keith, A. B., Responsible Government in the Dominions, 3 vols., Oxford, 1912; and Imperial Unity and the Dominions, Oxford, 1916.

Lefroy, A. H. F., Canada's Federal System, Toronto, 1913.

Low, Sydney, The Government of England, Rev. ed., London, 1914.

Lowell, A. L., The Government of England.

Macy, Jesse, The English Constitution, London and N.Y., 1907.

May, Sir T. E., Constitutional History of England, 3 vols., N.Y., 1912.

McIlwain, C. H., The High Court of Parliament, Yale University Press, 1910.

Moore, W. H., The Constitution of the Commonwealth of Australia, London, 1902.

Munro, J. E. C., The Constitution of Canada, Cambridge University Press, 1889.

Munro, W. B., The Government of European Cities, N.Y., 1909.

Ogg, F. A., The Governments of Europe, N.Y., 1913.

Quick and *Garran*, Constitution of the Commonwealth of Australia.

Redlick and *Hirst*, Local Government in England, 3 vols., London, 1903.

Riddell, W. R., The Constitution of Canada in its History and Practical Working, Yale University Press, 1917.

Shaw, Albert, Municipal Government in Great Britain, N.Y., 1895.

Stubbs, William, Constitutional History of England, 3 vols., Oxford, 1883.

Taswell-Langmead, L., English Constitutional History, London and Boston, 3d ed., 1886.

Taylor, Hannis, The Origin and Growth of the English Constitution, 2 vols., Boston, 1889 and 1898.

Todd, Alpheus, Parliamentary Government in England, new ed., London and N.Y., 1888–1889; and Parliamentary Government in the British Colonies, 2d ed., London, 1894.

   Local Government Reforms:

Baker, Charles E., The Local Government Act, 1888, with Notes and Index, London, 1888.

Jenks, Edward, An Outline of English Local Government, London, 1894.

Ryde, Walter C., The Local Government Act, 1894, London, 1894.

IX

THE GOVERNMENT OF THE UNITED STATES.

—⚬⚬⁘⚬⚬—

The English Occupation of America. — The political in-stitutions of the United States are in the main the political insti-tutions of England, transplanted by English colonists to a new soil and worked out through a fresh development to new and characteristic forms. Though they now show so large an ad-mixture of foreign blood, the main stock of the people of the United States is still of British extraction. For several genera-tions the settlements of New England and the South contained scarcely any other element. In the North, in what is now Canada, and at the mouth of the Mississippi, there were French settlements; in Florida there were colonists from Spain; the Dutch had settled upon the Hudson and held the great port at its mouth; and the Swedes had established themselves on the Delaware: all along the coast there was rivalry between the western nations of Europe for the possession of the new conti-nent. But by steady and for the most part easy steps of aggres-sion the English extended their domain and won the best regions of the great coast. New England, Virginia, and the Carolinas were never seriously disputed against them; and, these once securely taken possession of, the intervening foreigner was soon thrust out: so that the English power had presently a compact and centered mass which could not be dislodged, and whose ultimate expansion over the whole continent it proved im-possible to stay. England was not long in widening her colo-nial borders. The French power was crushed out in the North, the Spanish power was limited in the South, and the colonies had only to become free to develop energy more than sufficient to make all the most competed-for portions of the continent thoroughly English, — thoroughly Anglo-American.

Adaptation of English Institutions. — This growth of the English power in America involved a corresponding expansion of English institutions. As America became English, English institutions in the colonies became American. They adapted themselves to the new conditions and the new conveniences of political life in separate colonies, — colonies struggling at first, then expanding, at last triumphing; and without losing their English character gained an American form and flavor. Some institutions set up in New England the men who formed Plymouth had doubtless learned to know and to like while they were exiles in Holland; but they brought nothing with them that was not suitable to English habit.

It would be misleading to say that the English planted states in America. They planted small isolated settlements, and these settlements grew in their own way to be states. The slow process was from local, through state, to national organization. And not everywhere among the English on the new continent was the form of local government at first adopted the same : there was no invariable pattern, but everywhere, on the contrary, a spontaneous adjustment of political means to place and circumstance. By all the settlements alike English precedent was followed, but not the same English precedent. Each colony, with the true English sagacity of practical habit, borrowed what was best suited to its own situation, and originated what it could not borrow. New England had one system, Virginia another, New Jersey and Pennsylvania still a third, compounded after a sort of the other two.

The New England Colonies. — In New England the centre of government was always the town, with its church and schoolhouse and its neighborly cluster of houses gathered about these. The soil on the coast where the first settlers established themselves was shallow and slow to yield returns even to hard and assiduous toil; the climate was rigorous, with its long winters and bleak coast winds; every circumstance invited to close settlement and trade, to the intimate relationships of commerce and the adventures of sea-faring rather than to the wide-spreading settlements characteristic of an agricultural population.

The first New Englanders, moreover, were most of them religious refugees. They had left the Old World to escape the Old World's persecutions and in order to find independence of worship; they were establishing a church as well as a community; they acted as organized congregations; their life was both spiritually and temporally organic. Close geographical association, therefore, such as was virtually forced upon them by the conditions of livelihood by which they found themselves constrained, accorded well with their higher social purposes. The church could be made, by such association, the vital nerve-centre of their union: the minister was the ruling head of the community, and church membership was in several of the settlements recognized as identical with citizenship.

The Separate Towns. — The several parts of the New England coast were settled by independent groups of settlers. There was the Plymouth colony at Plymouth, and altogether distinct from it, the Massachusetts Bay colony at Salem and Charlestown and Boston. To the south of these, founded by men dissatisfied with the Massachusetts government, were Portsmouth, Newport, and Providence, in what is now Rhode Island. On the Connecticut river other wanderers from Massachusetts built Hartford and Windsor and Wethersfield. Saybrook, at the mouth of the Connecticut river, was settled direct from England; so also was the colony of New Haven, on the coast of Long Island Sound west of the Connecticut. From year to year the planting of towns went diligently on: almost every town became the prolific mother of towns, which either sprang up close about it and retained a sort of dependence upon it, or, planted at a distance, ventured upon an entirely separate life in the wilderness.

Union of the Towns. — Gradually the towns of each of the general regions mentioned drew together into the colonies known to later times, the colonies which were to form the Union. Plymouth merged in Massachusetts; Portsmouth, Newport, and Providence became but parts of Rhode Island; New Haven was joined to Connecticut. But at first these larger colonies were scarcely more than town leagues. It sometimes happened that each town retained unaltered its separate organization and its virtual independence in the regulation of its own local affairs.   In Rhode Island, particularly, their jealousy of each other and their reluctance to expose themselves to anything like a loss of perfect autonomy long kept the common government which they most of the time maintained at a balance between union and dissolution. In the other New England colonies the same influences manifested themselves, though in a less degree.   The town system which everywhere prevailed was by its nature an extremely decentralized form of government : government, so to say, came to a separate head in each locality : and the chief vitality was in the self-governing units of each group rather than in the bonds which connected them with each other.

Forms of Town Government. — The form of town government was everywhere such as it was quite natural that Englishmen should have set up.   The names of the town officers were borrowed from the borough governments at home, and their duties were, as nearly as circumstances permitted, the same as the duties of the officers whose names they bore.   The New England town was, at the same time, in many of its most important and characteristic features, rather a reversion to older types of government than a transplanted cutting of the towns which the settlers had left behind them in the England of the seventeenth century.   There was in it none of the elaborated class privilege that narrowed the town governments of the England of that time.   All the townsmen met in town-meeting and there elected their officers : those officers were responsible to them and always rendered careful account of their actions to the body which elected them.   Generally the most important of these officers were called Selectmen, — men selected by the town-meeting to carry on the necessary public business of the community, — and these Selectmen stood in the closest relations of counsel and responsibility to the town-meeting.   In the earliest times the franchise was restricted, in Massachusetts and New Haven at least, to those who were church members, and many were excluded by this rule from participation in the government; but even under such circumstances there was real and effective self-government.   The towns lacked neither vitality nor energy, for they did not lack liberty.   In the late days when great cities grew up, the simple township system had to be abandoned in part; as the colonies expanded, too, they gained in energy and vitality as wholes, and their component parts, the towns, fell by degrees to a place of less exclusive importance in colonial affairs; but this basis of the township was never lost and has remained to the present day the foundation of local government in New England.

Colonial Organization. — As the towns came together into the groupings which constituted the later colonies other areas of government naturally came into use. Townships were, for judicial purposes, combined into counties, and by various other means of organization a new nexus was given to the several parts of the now extended state. From the first the colonists had their 'general courts,' their central legislative assemblies representative of the freemen. To these assemblies went delegates from the several towns comprised in the colony. As the colonies grew, their growth but strengthened their assemblies: it was in the common ruling function of these that the union of the several parts of each colony was made real and lasting.

The sheriffs of the counties of colonial Massachusetts were appointed by the Governor. The development of the county organization brought into existence, too, Justices of the Peace who met in Quarter Sessions, afterwards called 'General Sessions,' and who were the general county authority quite after the fashion of the mother country.[1]

The Southern Colonies. — To this picture of the political institutions of colonial New England political and social organization in the Southern colonies offered many broad contrasts. The settlers in Virginia were not religious refugees: they had come out for a separate adventure in political, or rather in social, organization, but not for a separate venture in religion; and the coast they happened upon, instead of being rugged and bleak, was low and fertile, with a kindly climate, deep rivers, broad stretches of inviting country, and a generous readiness to yield its fruits in their season. They had been sent out by a Company (the 'Virginia Company' it was called) in England, to which the Virginia territory had been granted by the Crown, and they had no thought

---

[1] See *Town and County Government in the English Colonies of North America*, by Edward Channing, Johns Hopkins University Studies in Historical and Political Science, 2d Series, pp. 40–42.

but to live under the governors whom the Company had placed over them.   They founded Jamestown some hundred miles above the mouth of the James river; but Jamestown was in no way like the New England towns, and it soon became evident that town life was not to be the characteristic habit of the colony. The rich soil invited to agriculture, the numerous rivers, full and deep, stood ready to serve as natural highways, and as the population of the colony increased it spread far and wide along the courses of the rivers.

Contrasts of Character. — There was much more, besides soil and climate and the differing conditions of settlement, that made the Southern colonies unlike the colonies of New England. The New Englanders came for the most part out of the town and village population of the mother country: out of a very distinctly marked middle class with common motives and ideals: the more distinctly marked because most of them had had the same experiences and were of the same way of thinking in matters of religion.   They naturally drew together for the sort of life they had left behind them over sea.   The settlers of the Southern colonies, on the contrary, came from no single class and had no common habit, — except the general habit of the English race. They had been taken by fortune, as if at haphazard, out of the general mass of Englishmen at home, some gentle, some common, some bred to comfort, some not, all bent upon an independent life and carrying in their purpose the general ideals of their race. Prominent among these ideals, no doubt, was this, that a gentleman must live with space of good acres about him, a lord of the soil.   The life of the Southern colonists was not more English than that of the New Englanders; but it was much more of the general pattern of English life, and more likely to keep near the models set up by English gentlemen outside the towns.   There came a time, too, when Virginia received a strong infusion of Cavalier blood, and men came to her quiet lands who had the air and habit of courts, the ambitions of men of caste and estate; not a little of the color of English country life went out of them into all the ways of the broad tide-water properties; and the genial air told kindly upon the new fashions.   Virginia grew more than ever like rural England; and followed the new ways until the Scots-Irish came into the valley, to add another quality and the spice of variety.   Alike in the North and in the South, climate, soil, and every natural quality of the region chosen fitted the instinct of the settlers.   Both lived after their kind.

Expansion without Separation. — There would appear to have been no idea of organic separation in this southern process of expansion, as there was so often in the spreadings of the New England colonists.   Great plantations indeed grew up with an almost entirely separate life of their own, with their own wharves on the river fronts and their own direct trade with the outer world by vessels which came and went between them and England, or between them and the trading colonies to the north; but all this took place without any idea of organic political separateness. This diffused agricultural population, thus living its own life on the great rural properties which steadily multiplied in all directions, still consciously formed a single colony, living at first under the general government of the Company which had sent out the first settlers, and afterwards, when the Company had been deprived of its charter and possessions, under the authority of royal governors.   Its parts hung loosely together, it is true, but they did not threaten to fall apart: the plan was expansion, not segregation.

Southern Colonial Society. — The characteristics of the society formed under such circumstances were of course very marked.   Slaves were early introduced into the colony, and served well to aid and quicken the development of the plantation system.   A great gap speedily showed itself between the owners of estates and the laboring classes.   Where slavery exists manual toil must be considered slavish and all the ideas on which aristocracy are founded must find easy and spontaneous rootage.   Great contrasts of condition soon appeared, such as the more democratic trading communities of New England were not to know until the rise of the modern industrial organization; and the governing power rested with the powerful, propertied classes.

Government of Colonial Virginia. — The government of colonial Virginia bore, in all its broader features, much the same character as the rural government of England.   Organization was effected through a machinery of wide counties, instead of by means of compacted townships. There was at the head of each county, under this first order of things, a Lieutenant whose duties corresponded roughly with those of the Lords Lieutenant in England. The other important executive officer of the county, too, in Virginia as in England, was the Sheriff. The Lieutenant was appointed by the Governor, was chief of the military (militia) organization of the county, and, by virtue of his membership in the Governor's Council, exercised certain judicial functions in the county. The Sheriff also was appointed by the Governor, upon the nomination of the Justices of the county. His duties an English sheriff would have regarded as quite normal. And added to these officers there was, as in England, a 'commission of the peace,' a body of justices or commissioners authorized to hold county court for the hearing of all ordinary cases not of grave import; authorized to levy the county taxes, to appoint surveyors of highways, to divide the county into precincts; empowered to act as the general administrative authority of the county in the management of all matters not otherwise assigned. The Episcopal church had the same official recognition in Virginia as in England and contributed the same machinery, — the machinery of the vestry, — to local government. Even the division of the 'hundred' was recognized, so close was the outline likeness between the institutions of the mother country and those of her crude child in the west. The system was undemocratic, of course, as was its model: "the dominant idea," as Mr. Ingle says, "was gradation of power from the Governor *downward*, not upward from the people."[1] The Justices, like the other officers of the county, were appointed by the Governor, and held only during his pleasure: the whole system rested upon a frank centralization. But still there was liberty. There was strong local feeling and individual pride to counteract the subserviency of the officers: those officers showed a more or less self-respecting independence in their administration; and at least the spirit of English self-government was kept alive.

[1] *Local Institutions in Virginia*, by Edward Ingle, Johns Hopkins University Studies in Historical and Political Science, 3d Series, p. 97 (continuous, p. 199).

Virginia's Colonial Assembly. — The vital centre of the political life of the colony was her representative assembly. So early as 1619, only twelve years after the foundation of the colony (1607), the Virginia Company, then still in control, had called together in the colony, through its governor, an assembly repre-senting the several plantations then existing, which were in this way treated as independent corporations entitled to a represent-ative voice in colonial affairs. Later years saw the Assembly developed upon the basis of a representation by towns, hundreds, and plantations : and even after the governors sent out by the Company had been supplanted by royal governors this represent-ative body, this House of Burgesses, as it came to be styled, continued to exist, and to wax strong in control. It was some time before the area of the colony justified that broader division into counties which was so characteristic of later days, and which changed very radically the system of representation. The 'towns' and 'plantations' of the early days seem to have been known, at any rate for purposes of representation, as 'boroughs,' and the representative house got its name, 'House of Burgesses,' before county representation grew up. The first Assembly, that of 1619, sat in joint session with the Governor and his Council, but the more fully developed assembly of later times sat apart as a distinct and independent body. It was this elective repre-sentation in the government of the colony which made and kept Virginia a vital political unit, with a real organic life and feeling.

The Constitutions of the other Southern Colonies corre-sponded in the main with the constitution of Virginia. They, too, had the county system and the general representation in a central assembly, combined with governors and councils ap-pointed by the Crown. All save Maryland. Her constitution differed from the others mainly in this, that in place of the king stood a 'proprietor,' to whom the fullest prerogatives of govern-ment had been granted.

The Middle Colonies had a mixed population. New York had been New Netherland, and the Delaware had been first settled by the Swedes and then conquered by the Dutch. When the territory which was to comprise New York, New Jersey, Delaware, and Pennsylvania fell into the hands of the

English the foreign element was not displaced but merely dominated; and to a large extent it kept its local peculiarities of
institution. For the rest, the English settlers of the region
followed no uniform or characteristic method of organization.
The middle colonies, though possessed of a rich soil, had also
fine seaports which invited to commerce; their climate was
neither so harsh as that of New England, nor so mild and be-
guiling as that of the southern colonies. Their people were of
all sorts and origins. They built towns and traded, like the
people of New England ; they also spread abroad over the fertile
country and farmed, like the people of Virginia. They did these
things, moreover, without developing either the town system of
New England or the plantation system of Virginia. Townships
they had, but counties also; they were simple and democratic,
like the New Englanders, and yet they were agricultural also,
like the Virginians: in occupation and political organization, as
well as in geographical situation, they were midway between
their neighbors to the north and south.

The Charters: Massachusetts. — The political relations
of the colonies to the mother country during the various developments of which I have spoken were as various as their separate
histories. The three New England colonies, Massachusetts,
Rhode Island, and Connecticut, possessed charters from the
king which virtually authorized them to conduct their own
governments without direct interference on the part of the
Administration at home. During the first years of English
settlement on the American coast it had been the practice of
the government in England to grant territory on the new
continent to companies like the Virginia Company of which I
have spoken, — grants which carried with them the right of
governing the new settlements subject only to a general supervision on the part of the home authorities. The colony of
Massachusetts Bay was established under such an arrangement:
a Company, to which special privileges of settlement and government had been granted, sent out colonists who founded Salem
and Boston ; but the history of this Company was very different
from the history of the Virginia Company. The Virginia Company tried to manage their colony from London, where the

members of the Company, who were active liberals and therefore not very active courtiers, presently got into trouble with the government and had both their charter and their colony taken away from them. The Massachusetts Company, on the other hand, itself came to America, and, almost unobserved by the powers in London, erected something very like a separate state on the new continent. Its charter was received in 1629; in 1630 it emigrated, governor, directors, charter, and all, to America, bringing a numerous body of settlers, founded Salem, Boston, and Cambridge, and put quietly into operation the complete machinery of government which it had brought with it. It created not a little stir in official circles in England when it was discovered that the Company which had been given rights of settlement on the New England coast had left the country and was building a flourishing set of independent towns on its territories; but small colonies at a great distance could not long retain the attention of busy politicians in London, and nothing was done then to destroy the bold arrangement. Fatal collision with the home government could not, however, it turned out, be permanently, or even long avoided by the aggressive, self-willed rulers of the Massachusetts Company. Many of the laws which they passed did not please the Crown, — particularly those which set up an exclusive religion and tolerated no other; they would not change their laws at the Crown's bidding; and, though the evil day was postponed, it came at last. In 1684 the contest between Crown and colony came to a head, and the charter of the Massachusetts Company was annulled. Before a change could be effected in the government, indeed, the king, Charles II., died, and at the end of the troublous reign of James II. the colonists quietly resumed their charter privileges; but in 1692 the government of William and Mary was ready to deal with them, and a new form of colonial organization was forced upon them. They were compelled to take a governor from the king; the royal governor appointed the judicial officers of the colony and controlled its military forces; and, although the colonists retained their assembly and through that assembly chose the governor's council, the old charter privileges were permanently lost.

The Connecticut Charter. — Rhode Island and Connecticut were smaller and more fortunate. The town of Saybrook, at the mouth of the Connecticut river, had been founded under a charter granted to two English noblemen, and consisted, therefore, of immigrants direct from England; but Saybrook did not grow rapidly and proved a comparative failure. The successful and dominant settlement on the Connecticut was that which was founded higher up the river at Hartford, by men from Massachusetts who had neither charter nor any other legal rights, but who had simply come, settled, and made a written constitution for themselves. New Haven, westward of the river on the shore of the sound, had been established by a band of English immigrants equally without charter rights, but equally ready and able to construct a frame of government for themselves. Some thirty years after their settlement, the leaders of the 'Connecticut colony,' up the river, which meantime had become an extended cluster of towns, decided that it was time to obtain a charter. Accordingly they sent their governor, Winthrop, to England to procure one. He was entirely successful, much more successful than was pleasant to the settlers of the New Haven district; for he had obtained a grant which included their lands and colony and which thus forced them to become a part of 'Connecticut.' Saybrook had already been absorbed. The charter gave the colonists substantially the same rights of self-government that they had had under their own written constitution, adopted upon their first settlement; it was, in other words, just such a charter as Massachusetts then enjoyed. And, unlike Massachusetts, Connecticut kept her charter, kept it not only through colonial times to the Revolution, but made it at the Revolution her state constitution, and was content to live under it until 1818. Her shrewdness, her acts of timely concession, and her inoffensive size enabled her to turn away from herself each successive danger of forfeiture.

Rhode Island's Charter. — Rhode Island was similarly protected by fortune and sagacious management. Roger Williams, the energetic leader of settlement in that region, obtained a charter from Parliament in 1644, which was confirmed in 1654, and replaced by a new charter, from Charles II., in 1663, the year after Connecticut obtained its legal privileges through the instrumentality of Winthrop. As New Haven and Connecticut were joined by Winthrop's charter, so were the towns of the Rhode Island country united by the charters obtained by Williams, under the style ' Rhode Island and Providence Plantations,' — a title which is still the full official name of the state. The charter of 1663 was retained by the people of Rhode Island even longer than the people of Connecticut retained theirs. It was not radically changed until 1842.

Proprietary Governments. — The governments of almost all the other colonies were at first 'proprietary'; those of Maryland, Pennsylvania, and Delaware remained proprietary until the Revolution. Maryland was granted to the Calverts, Lords Baltimore; Pennsylvania and Delaware were both included in the grant to William Penn; New York was bestowed upon James, Duke of York, upon whose ascension of the throne, as James II., it became an immediate province of the Crown; New Jersey, originally a part of New York, was first bestowed by the Duke of York on Lord John Berkeley and Sir John Carteret, was afterwards divided, then sold in part, and finally surrendered to the Crown (1702); the Carolinas and Georgia in the same way, given at first to proprietors, passed very soon into the hands of the royal government. New Hampshire, after several attempts to unite with Massachusetts, fell quietly into the status of a royal colony, without having had either a charter or even any regularly ordered proprietary stage of existence.

Government under proprietors meant simply government by governors and councils appointed by the proprietors, with in all cases a right on the part of the people to exercise a substantial control over the government through representative assemblies. The private proprietors, like the great public proprietor, the Crown, granted charters to their colonies. The charter which Penn bestowed upon Pennsylvania is distinguished as one of the best-conceived and most liberal charters of the time; and under it his colony certainly enjoyed as good government as most of the colonies could secure.

Direct Government by the Crown, which came in turn to every colony except Rhode Island, Connecticut, Pennsylvania, and

Delaware, involved the appointment of governors by the Crown, and also, everywhere except in Massachusetts, the appointment of the governor's council.   It generally involved also the dependence of the colonial judiciary, and in general of the whole administrative machinery of government, upon the royal will; but it, nevertheless, did not exclude the colonists from substantial powers of self-government.   Everywhere legislators disciplined governors with the effective whip of the money power, and everywhere the people grew accustomed to esteem the management of their own affairs, especially the control of their own taxes, matter-of-course privilege, just as much the inalienable right of Englishmen in America as of Englishmen in England.

Development of the Assemblies. — It was, indeed, as a matter of course rather than as a matter of definite legal right that the powers of the colonial assemblies waxed greater and greater from year to year.   Parliament would have been wise to continue the policy of neglect which had been the opportunity of the colonies in the development of their constitutional liberties. Left to themselves, they quickly showed what race they were of.

As Burke said, in their justification, they "had formed within themselves, either by royal instruction or royal charter, assemblies so exceedingly resembling a parliament, in all their forms, functions, and powers, that it was impossible they should not imbibe some opinion of a similar authority.   At the first designation of these assemblies, they were probably not intended for anything more (nor perhaps did they think themselves much higher) than the municipal corporations within this island, to which some at present love to compare them.   But nothing in progression can rest on its original plan. . . .   Therefore, as the colonies prospered and increased to a numerous and mighty people, spreading over a very great tract of the globe, it was natural that they should attribute to assemblies so respectable in their formal constitution some part of the dignity of the great nations which they represented.   No longer tied to by-laws, these assemblies made acts of all sorts and in all cases whatsoever.   They levied money, not for parochial purposes, but upon regular grants to the Crown, following all the rules and principles of a parliament, to which they approached every day more and more nearly. . . .   Things could not be otherwise ; and English colonies must be had on these terms, or not had at all.   In the meantime neither party felt any inconvenience from this double legislature [the parliament of England, that is, and a colonial legislature], to which they had been formed by imperceptible habits, and old custom, the great support of all the gov-

ernments in the world. Though these two legislatures were sometimes
found perhaps performing the very same functions, they did not very
grossly or systematically clash. . . . A regular revenue, by the authority
of Parliament, for the support of civil and military establishments, seems
not to have been thought of until the colonies were too proud to submit,
too strong to be forced, too enlightened not to see all the consequences
which must arise from such a system." [1]

In such assertions of a right of parliamentary self-government it might be expected that the charter colonies would be
most forward; but, as a matter of fact, such was not the case.
Massachusetts was ever, indeed, very stubbornly and heroically
attached to her liberties, but the royal colony of Virginia was not
a whit behind her. The assemblies of the royal colonies, no less
than those of the charter governments, early, and as if by an
instinct and habit common to the race, developed a consciousness
and practice of local sovereignty, which comported well enough,
indeed, with a perfect loyalty, — long-suffering in respect of Navigation Acts and all like attempts of the mother country to regulate their place in the politics and commerce of the outside world,
— but which was from the first prompt to resent and resist all
dictation as to the strictly interior affairs of the settlements.
And the same was true of the proprietary colonies, also. Maryland assumed the same privileges that Virginia insisted upon, and
even Pennsylvania, with its population compounded of English,
Dutch, and Swedes, manifested not a little of the same spirit of
independent self-direction.

Development of Constitutional Liberty in the Colonies. —
There was, therefore, a comparatively uniform development of
constitutional liberty throughout the colonies. Everywhere the
same general causes were operative. The settlement and development of a new country gave to the elective governing bodies of
the colonies a wide and various duty of legislative regulation;
the newness of the country created everywhere substantially the
same new conditions of social relationship; everywhere, and
more and more as the years went on, there was a very general
participation in communal and colonial affairs by the mass of

[1] "Letter to the Sheriffs of Bristol," *Works* (ed. Boston, 1880), Vol. II.,
pp. 232, 233.

the people most interested: and democratic institutions brought in their train equality of law and a widespread consciousness of community of interest. Each colony grew, the while, more and more vividly conscious of its separate political personality in its relations with the other colonies and with the ruling powers in England.

Political Sympathy of the Colonies. — The substantial identity of institutional development in the several colonies appears in nothing more clearly or conclusively than in their close and spontaneous alliance against England at the Revolution. Despite very considerable outward differences of social condition and many apparent divergencies of interest as between colony and colony, they one and all *wanted the same revolution.* Almost without hesitation they ran together to coöperate by the same means for the same ends. They did not so much *make* a common cause as *have* a common cause from the first. The real concrete case of revolution, it happened, was made up between England and Massachusetts. To the politicians in the mother country it seemed possible to divide the colonies on grounds of self-interest. Apparently colonies so utterly different in every outward aspect, so strongly contrasted in actual economic condition as Massachusetts and Virginia, could easily be played off against one another. But we now know how little foundation of fact such a view had. Boston's trade was offered to Salem, her commercial rival, as a bait to catch Salem's acquiescence in the stringent Boston Port Bill which shut Boston off from all trade; but Salem would not have it. What was to prevent similar treatment of herself in the future? More striking still, distant Virginia sounded the call to revolution in behalf of Massachusetts. The contest was *political,* she clearly perceived, not economical, — a contest of principle, not a contest for any temporary interest or momentary advantage. From the point of view of politics Massachusetts' quarrel was Virginia's also. Virginia spoke at once, therefore, and as a leader, for combination, for a joint resistance to the aggressions of the home government, and at length for independence and a perpetual union between the colonies. For the shortest possible time did the struggle remain local; almost immediately it became 'continental.'

American as compared with English Constitutional Development. — There was in this development of self-government in America a certain very close resemblance to the development of self-government in England; but there were also other points of very strong and obvious contrast between the institutional histories of the two countries. Both in England and in America the process of institutional growth was in the same direction. It began with small, hardy, deep-rooted local institutions, with small self-directing communities, and widened from these to national institutions which bound the constituent communities together in a strong and lasting central union. England began with her village communities and her judicial 'hundreds,' with the primitive communal institutions of the Teutonic folk; these were first gathered to a head in the petty kingdoms of the days of the Saxon Heptarchy; another step, and these one-time petty kingdoms were merely the counties of a wider union, and England was ready for the amalgamation of the Norman rule, — for the growth of her parliaments and her nationality. In like manner, the United States began with isolated settlements upon a long coast, settlements separate, self-contained, self-regulative; these in time merged in numerous petty colonial states; and finally these colonial states fitted themselves together into a national union.

Process of Growth in America Federation, in England Consolidation. — But the means of integration were in the two cases quite diverse. American integration has been federal; English, absorptive, incorporative. The earlier stages of federation did not appear in the Southern colonies; because there the unity of the first settlement was generally not broken; the Virginia of the Revolution was but an expansion of the Jamestown settlement; growth by agricultural development was not disintegration like growth by town establishment. But in New England the process was federative from the first, finding its most perfect type, probably, in Rhode Island, whose town atoms drew so slowly and reluctantly together and so long stoutly resisted the idea that they had in any sense been absorbed or subordinated under the operation of the charters of 'Rhode Island and Providence Plantations.' What was at first mere confederation

between these smallest units, however, by degrees became virtual
coalescence, and the absorbed towns finally formed but subordinate parts in the new and larger colonial units which drew
together in the Continental Congresses. Between these larger
units, these full-grown colonial states, union was from the first
distinctly federative, matter of concession and contract. They
were united in entirely voluntary association, as the Saxon
kingdoms were not.

Conscious Development of Institutions in America. —
Throughout their development the colonies presented a marked
contrast to English development in this, that the formulation
of their institutions was conscious and deliberate. The royal
colonies, like the proprietary and the charter colonies, exercised
their rights of self-government under written grants of privilege
from the Crown : their institutions grew within the area of
written constituent law ; from the first they had definite written
' constitutions' wherein the general fabric of their governments
was outlined. Constitution by written law, therefore, became
very early one of the matter-of-course habits of colonial thought
and action. When they cast off their allegiance to Great Britain
their self-constitution as independent political bodies took the
shape of a recasting of their colonial constitutions simply. Rhode
Island and Connecticut, as we have seen, did not even find it
necessary to change their charters in any important particular :
they already chose their own governors and officials as well as
made their own laws. The other colonies, with little more
trouble, found adequate means of self-government in changes
which involved hardly more than substituting the authority of
the people for the authority of the English Crown. But the
charter, the written constituent law, was retained : the new governments had their charters which emanated from the people, as
the old governments had had theirs given by the king. Popular
conventions took the place of the Privy Council. The colonists
were not inventing written constitutions ; they were simply continuing their former habitual constitutional life.

English Law and Precedent. — Whatever the form of
colonial institutions, however, their substance and content were
thoroughly English. In a sense, indeed, even the forms of colo-

nial constituent law may be said to have been English, since it was English practice which originated the idea and habit of giv- ing written grants of privilege to distant colonies. The colonial law of Canada and Australia stands to-day in much the same relation to the law of the mother country that the law of the American colonies bore to the law which created them (page 255). Within the constitutions of the colonial and revolutionary time, at any rate, English law and precedent were closely followed. The English common law has gone with Englishmen to the ends of the world. The English communities in America were but pro- jected parts of the greater English community at home; the laws of private and personal relationship which obtained in England were recognized and administered also in the colonies; and when, at the time of the Revolution, the colonists developed out of their charters the constitutions under which they were to live as inde- pendent commonwealths their first care was to adopt this common law under which they had always acted. Important modifications were made, it is true, in the law thus adopted. It was purged of all class privilege, of all church prerogative, of all things in- compatible with the simple democratic society of the new world ; but no real break was made with the principles of English legal precedent and practice.

Quite as naturally and quite as completely was English practice adhered to in the public law of the colonies and of the independent commonwealths into which they grew. The re- lations of the colonial legislatures with the colonial governors were substantially the relations of King and Parliament repro- duced on a small scale, but with scarcely less earnestness and spirit. In all respects, except that of the erection of a responsible ministry representing and shielding the executive, the relations of the people to their governments suggest English precedent. The powers of the executive were, in small, the powers of the Crown. The courts were constituted as the English courts were, and followed the same rules of procedure. The English in America, being men of the same practical political race as Eng- lishmen in England, struck out not a few lines of development of their own in suiting their institutions to the daily needs of a new civilization and to novel conditions of social organization; Ameri-

can politics were not long in acquiring in many respects a character peculiarly their own. But the manner of development was
English throughout: there was nowhere any turning of sharp
corners: there was nowhere any break of continuity. To the
present day our institutions rest upon foundations as old as the
Teutonic peoples.

Union: Preliminary Steps. — How much of political
precedent that was their own the colonists had developed appeared most distinctly when they came to put the timbers of
their Union together in the days succeeding the Revolution. The
colonies cannot be said to have framed any federative constituent
law until 1777, when the Articles of Confederation were drawn
up. Before that time they had coöperated without any determinate law of coöperation, acting rather upon the suggestions of
international procedure than upon any clear recognition of corporate combination. Preparations for union there had been, and
signs of its coming; but no more. For a period of forty years
following the year 1643 the New England colonies had held
together in a loose confederation against the Indians; in 1754
colonial delegates who had met at Albany for conference with
representatives of the Six Nations discussed a premature plan of
union; in 1765 delegates from nine of the colonies met at New
York and uttered in behalf of all English Americans that protest
against taxation by Parliament which gave the key-note to the
revolutionary movement that followed; and in 1774 sat the first
of the series of 'Continental Congresses' with which began
American union. But in none of these steps was there any
creation of organic union: that was to be the result of slow
processes, and was to be effected only by the formulation of an
entirely new body of law.

Separateness of the Colonial Governments. — It is very
important, if a just view is to be formed of the processes by which the
Union was constructed, to realize the complete separateness of the governments of the colonies. They all held substantially the same general
relation to the English authorities; they had a common duty as towards
the distant country from which they had all come out; but they were not
connected with each other by any bonds of government on this side the
sea. Each of the colonies had its separate executive officials, legislature,

and courts, which had no connection whatever with the officers, legisla-tures, and courts of any other colony. Their coöperation from time to time in meeting dangers which threatened them all alike was natural and spontaneous, but it was intermittent; it rested upon mere temporary necessity and had no basis of interior organic law. The colonists had many grounds of sympathy. Besides possessing the same blood and the same language, they entertained the same ideas about political justice ; their dangers, whether proceeding from aggressions on the part of the French and Indians which threatened their lives, or from aggressions by Parliament which threatened their liberties, were common dangers : they were one and all equally interested in the successful development and liberal government of the new country with which they had identified themselves. But the motive of their endeavors was always the preserva-tion of their internal and separate self-government; their liberties were historically coincident with their separate organization and rights as dis-tinct governments. It was only by a slow and hard experience of the fatal consequences of any other course that the colonies were brought to subordinate themselves to a central authority which could go further than mere conference and command them. They saw from the first the neces-sity for coöperation, but they did not see from the first the absolute necessity for union. Very slowly, considering the swift influences of revolution amidst which they worked, and very reluctantly, considering the evident dangers of separation which daily looked them in the face, did they construct the union which was to deprive them of the fulness of their loved independence.

The Confederation. — It was not until 1781 that a founda-tion of distinct written law was put beneath the practice of union; it was not till 1789 that the law of the union was made organic. In 1781 the Articles of Confederation were finally adopted which had been proposed by the Continental Congress of 1777. But those Articles gave no real integration to the confederated states: they were from the first a rope of sand which could bind no one. They did little more than legitimate the Continental Congress. Under them the powers of the Confederation were to be exercised by its Congress; its only executive or judicial organs were to be mere committees or agencies of the Congress; and it was in fact to have no real use for executive parts, for it was to have no executive rights. Its function was to be advice, not command. It hung upon the will of the states, being permitted no effective will of its own. The Articles were in effect scarcely more than an international convention.

The Articles of Confederation formally vested the exercise of federal functions in a Congress just such as the Continental Congresses had been, — a Congress, that is, consisting of delegates from the several states, and in whose decisions the states were to have an absolutely equal voice. No state, it was arranged, should have her vote in the Congress unless represented by at least two delegates, and no state, on the other hand, was to be entitled to send more than seven delegates; whether she sent two or seven, however, her vote was to be a single vote, upon which her delegates were to agree. The government thus constituted was officially known as "The United States in Congress assembled." For the exercise of representative functions it was very liberally and completely equipped. To it the independence of the several states in dealing with foreign powers was entirely subordinated. It alone was to conduct international correspondence and sanction international agreements; it was to control the army and navy of the Confederation; it was to preside over federal finances, doing all the borrowing and all the spending that might be necessary for the purposes of the common government; it was to determine the value of current coin and the standards of weights and measures; it was to be arbitrator in disputes between the states; in brief, it was to be the single and dominant authority for all the graver common interests of the constituent states: its representative position was eminent and complete.

Weakness of the Confederation. — But it was given absolutely no executive power, and was therefore helpless and contemptible. It could take no important resolution without the difficult concurrence of nine states, — a concurrence made all the more difficult by the fact that the removal of the pressure of the war with England very greatly abated the interest of the states in the functions of the central Congress, and led some of them to fail again and again to send any delegates to its sessions. Its chief executive agency was a committee of its members representing all the states (hence called the "Committee of States") and bound by the same hard rule of obtaining the concurrence of nine of its thirteen members to every important executive step. Above all, its only power to govern was a power to advise. It could ask the states for money, but it could not compel them to give it; it could ask them for troops, but could not force them to heed the requisition; it could make treaties, but must trust the states to fulfil them; it could contract debts, but must rely upon the states to pay them. It was a body richly enough endowed with prerogatives, but not at all endowed with powers. "The United States in Congress assembled" formed a mere consultative and advisory board.

Need of a Better Union. — It was the fatal executive impotency of the Confederation which led to the formation of the present stronger and more complete government. The old Continental Congresses had sufficed, after a fashion, to keep the colonies together so long as the pressure of the war continued. Throughout that war there had been, despite much indifference now and again on the part of some of the colonies to their duty, and of not a little positive dereliction of plain obligations, a remarkable degree of energy and unity of action among the confederated colonists. But when the pressure of the war was removed there was an ominous access of indifference, an ill-boding decrease of respect for plighted faith between the states. Signs fast multiplied both of the individual weakness of the states and of the growth of threatening jealousies between them. A war of tariffs began between neighbor states on the seaboard, notably between New York and New Jersey and between Virginia and Maryland. In Massachusetts there flared out, by reason of the poverty engendered by the war, a rebellion of debtors under Daniel Shays which it was for a moment feared the state authorities might find it impossible to cope with. It speedily became evident that, both for the sake of internal order and of interstate peace and goodwill, a real central government was needed. Central consultation would not suffice; there must be central government. The Confederation, therefore, was no real advance upon the old Continental Congresses. Before a single decade had passed over the new government with its fair-spoken Articles a new union had been erected and the real history of the United States begun.

The Constitution : Colonial Precedents. — The present Constitution erects a very different government. It is the charter of a federal state, which has a commanding law and an independent power of its own, whose Constitution and law are the supreme law of the land. The Convention which framed the new Constitution met in Philadelphia in May, 1787, and fused together over the slow fires of prolonged debate the elements of English and colonial precedent which were to constitute the government of the United States. In the debates of that Convention during that memorable summer are to be read the particulars of the translation of English precedent into American practice made during the formative colonial period. Through the instrumen-

tality of the able men who composed that extraordinary assembly, the government of the United States was fitted out
with the full experience of the colonies and of the revolutionary states.[1] It was arranged that the legislature of the new
federal government should consist of two houses, not in direct
imitation of the English system, whose House of Lords we
did not have the materials for reproducing, but in conformity
with an almost universal example set by the states. A single
state furnished the precedent in accordance with which a real
difference of character was given to the two houses. The lower
house of the Connecticut legislature was constituted by an equal
representation of the towns of the state, while her upper house,
composed of the governor, lieutenant-governor, and twelve ' assistants,' represented her people at large: and Connecticut's
example showed the Convention a convenient way of compromise by which they could reconcile the two parties within it
which were contending, the one for an equal representation of
the states in Congress after the absolute manner of the Confederation, the other for a proportional representation of the people.
The Senate, it was agreed, should represent the states equally,
the House of Representatives the people proportionally. The
names Senate and House of Representatives were to be found
already in use by several of the states. The single Executive,
the President, was an obvious copy of the state governors, many
of whom at that time bore the name of president; his veto power
was to be found formulated ready to hand in the constitution of
New York; a method of impeachment was already prepared in
the constitutions of half a dozen states. Several states had also
the office of Vice-President. With a fine insight into the real
character of the government which they were constructing, the
Convention provided that its judiciary should be placed, not
under the President or the houses, but alongside of them, upon

[1] In describing the work of the Convention I follow here Professor Alexander Johnston's admirable exposition given in the *New Princeton Review*
for September, 1887, under the title "The First Century of the Constitution." A convenient brief survey of the chief features of the state constitutions at the time of the formation of the present government of the Union
may be found in Hildreth, Vol. III., Chap. XLIV.

a footing of perfect equality with them.   A similar arrangement obtained under the state constitutions.   The function of constitutional interpretation was nowhere explicitly conferred, but existed in the nature of the case.   It, necessarily as old as written charters and constitutions, was an inevitable corollary to their fundamental proposition of a gift of limited powers.   Written constituent law is by its very nature a law higher than any statute the legislature acting under it can enact, and by that law, as by an invariable standard, must the courts test all acts of legislation.[1] The colonial courts had once and again upon this principle questioned the validity of colonial legislation, and the Supreme Court of the United States had long had a prototype in the Judicial Committee of the Privy Council, whose function it was to hear appeals from the colonies, and whose practice it had been to pronounce against all laws incompatible with the royal charters (pages 219, 255).[2]

When they came to equip Congress with powers, the Convention adopted the plan of careful enumeration.   They set out the acts of government which were to be permitted to the legislature of the new government in a distinctly cast list of eighteen items.   Even in doing this, however, they may be said to have been simply recording the experience of the Confederation.   They were giving Congress the powers for lack of which the Congress of the Confederation had proved helpless and ridiculous.   It was only when they came to construct the machinery for the election of the President that they left the field of American experience and English example and devised an arrangement which was so original that it was destined to break down almost as soon as it was put in operation.

It is an instructive fact that the work of the Convention was a work of selection, not a work of creation, and that the success of their work was not a success of invention, always most dangerous in government, but a success of judgment, of selective wisdom, of practical sagacity, — the only sort of success in politics which can ever be made permanent.

[1] See A. V. Dicey, *The Law of the Constitution*, Chap. III ; and J. Bryce, *The American Commonwealth*, Chap. XXIII.

[2] See Brinton Coxe, *Judicial Power and Unconstitutional Legislation*.

Character of the New Government. — It is one of the dis-tinguishing characteristics of the English race whose political habit has been transmitted to us through the sagacious generation by whom this government was erected that they have never felt themselves bound by the logic of laws, but only by a practical understanding of them based upon slow precedent. For this race the law under which they live is at any particular time *what it is then understood to be;* and this understanding of it is compounded of the circumstances of the time. Absolute theories of legal consequence they have never cared to follow out to their con-clusions. Their laws have always been used as parts of the practical running machinery of their politics, — parts to be fitted from time to time, by interpretation, to existing opinion and social condition.

Character of the Government Changes with Opinion. — It requires a steady, clear-viewed, thoroughly informed historical sense, therefore, to determine what was at any given time the real character of our political institutions. To us of the present day it seems that the Constitution framed in 1787 gave birth in 1789 to a national government such as that which now constitutes an indestructible bond of union for the states; but the men of that time would certainly have laughed at any such idea, — and for the English race, as I have said, every law is what those who admin-ister it think that it is. The men of 1789 meant to form "a more perfect union" than that which had existed under the Confedera-tion: they saw that for the colonies there must be union or disin-tegration; they thought union needful and they meant to have it in any necessary degree. But they had no special love for the union which they set about consummating, and they meant to have as little of it as possible, — as little as might be compatible with wise providence in respect of the welfare of the new-fledged states. They were even more afraid of having too strong a cen-tral government than of having one which was too weak, and they accepted the new constitution offered them by the Convention of 1787 because convinced of the truth of the arguments urged by its friends to the effect that the union would be federal merely and would involve no real sacrifice of individuality or autonomy on the part of the states.

Early Sentiment towards the Union. — It is astonishing to us of this generation to learn how much both of hostility and of indifference was felt for the new government, which we see to have been the salvation of the country. Even those who helped to make it and who worked most sincerely for its adoption enter-tained grave doubts as to its durability; some of them even, in despondent moments, questioned its usefulness. Philosophic statesmen like Alexander Hamilton supported it with ardent pur-pose and sustained hope; but for the average citizen, who was not in the least degree philosophic, it was at first an object of quite unexciting contemplation. It was for his state, each man felt, that his blood and treasure had been poured out: it was that Massachusetts and Virginia might be free that the war had been fought, not that the colonies might have a new central government set up over them. Patriotism was state patriotism. The states were living, organic persons: the union was an arrangement, — possibly it would prove to be only a temporary arrangement; entirely new adjustments might have to be made.

Early Tolerance of Threats of Secession. — It is by this frame of mind on the part of the first generation that knew the present Constitution that we must explain the undoubted early tolerance for threats of secession. The Union was too young to be sacred; the self-love of the states was too pronounced to be averse from the idea that complete state independence might at any time be resumed. Discontent in any quarter was the signal for significant hints at possible withdrawal. As the new system lived on from year to year and from year to year approved itself strong and effective it became respected; as it gathered dignity and force regard was added to respect, until at last the federal government became a rallying centre for great parties moved by genuine national sentiment. But at first neither love nor respect shielded the federal authorities from the jealousies and menaces of the states. The new government was to *grow* national with the growth of a national history and a national sentiment.

Growth of the National Idea. — The career and fate of the Federalist party very well illustrate the first state of opinion concerning the Union. The Federalist party was the party of the Constitution, — the party which had been chiefly instrumental in bringing about the adoption of the new frame of government. Immediately upon the inauguration of the present Union this party of its friends was put in charge of the new central body politic. It presided over the critical period of its organization, and framed the first measures which gave it financial credit, international consideration, security, and energy. But it soon became evident that the Federalists held views as to the nature of the new government which not all of those who had voted for the adoption of the Constitution were willing to sanction. They assumed for the federal authorities prerogatives of too great absoluteness, and seemed to many to be acting upon the idea that the purpose of the Constitution was to subordinate, and if need be sacrifice, state interests to the interests of the general government. Very speedily, therefore, they brought a reaction upon themselves, and were displaced by a party which felt that the limitations put by the Constitution upon federal authority ought to be very strictly observed. This new party, calling itself 'Democratic-Republican,' may be said to have been created by the injudicious excesses of the Federalists; and from this point of view the Federalist party may be said to have effected its own destruction. After its first national defeat it never again came into power. Rapidly in some places, slowly in others, it went utterly to pieces.

But, although the Federalist party was destroyed, time worked in favor of its political conceptions. The Democratic-Republicans soon found that success in conducting the affairs of the federal government was, even for them, conditioned upon a very liberal reading of the authority conferred by the Constitution; and by slow degrees they drifted into practices of 'broad construction' quite as abhorrent to their own first principles as the much berated measures of the Federalists had been. But the Democratic-Republicans, — or the Democrats as they were before long more briefly called, — had the advantage of a corresponding change in public opinion. That, too, was steadily becoming nationalist in its tendencies.

Railroads, Expansion, and War aid the National Idea. — So long as the people of one section of the country saw little or nothing of the people of the other sections, separateness of feeling and localness of view continued to exist and to exercise a controlling force; the majority of the people continued to put the states before the nation in their thoughts and to demand more or less punctilious regard for state prerogatives. But when railroads began to be built and to multiply; when people from all parts of the Union began to go out and settle the West together; when seeing each other and trading with each other began to make the people of all the states very much alike in most of the greater things of habit and institution, and even in most of the smaller things of opinion and conduct; when new states which had grown up in the West without any of the old conservative colonial traditions began to be admitted to the Union in increasing numbers, regarding themselves as born in and of the Union; when a second war with England and a hot struggle with Mexico had tested the government and strengthened a sentiment of national patriotism, — then at length it began to be very generally thought that the Federalists had been right after all; that the federal government ought to come first in consideration, even at the cost of some state pride.

Slavery stands in the Way of Nationality. — What stood most in the way of the universal growth of this sort of national feeling was the great difference between the northern and southern portions of the Union caused by the existence of slavery in the South. So long as the laborers in the South were slaves and those of the North free men, these two sections could not become like one another either socially or politically, and could not have the same national feeling. The North and Northwest meant one thing when they spoke of the nation; while the South meant quite another thing. Each meant a nation socially and politically like itself. The two sections, therefore, rapidly became dissatisfied with living together under the same political system, and the secession so much talked about in various quarters in the earlier days of the Union at last became a reality. Inevitably came the war of secession, by means of whose fiery processes the differences of institution between North and South were to be swept utterly away

Civil War completes the Union. — The war wrought changes of the most profound character. Secession was prevented, the Union was preserved, and slavery was forever abolished; these were the immediate effects of the struggle. But the remoter results were even more important. They penetrated to the changing of the very nature of the Union, though the form of the federal government remained in all essential features unaltered. <u>The great effect of the war was, that the nation was made, in social institutions, at last homogeneous.</u> There was no longer any permanent reason why the South should not become like the rest of the country in character and sentiment. Both sections were brought to the same modes of life and thought; there was no longer any legal obstacle to their being in reality one great nation. The effort made in the war, moreover, to preserve the Union, and the result of the war in making the country at last socially homogeneous throughout, has made the federal government, as the representative of the nation, seem greater in our eyes than ever before, and has permanently modified in the profoundest manner the way in which all the old questions concerning constitutionality and state rights are regarded.

Present Character of the Union. — It by no means follows that because we have become in the fullest organic sense a nation, ours has become a unitary government, its federal features merged in a new national organization. The government of the Union has indeed become permanent, the cherished representative, the vital organ of our life as a nation; but the states have not been swallowed up. Their prerogatives are as essential to our system as ever, — are indeed becoming more and more essential to it from year to year as the already vastly complex organism of the nation expands. But, instead of regarding the government of the United States and the government of a state as two governments, as our fathers did, we now regard them, — if we may make a matter-of-fact analysis of our working views in politics, — as two parts of one and the same government, two complementary parts of a single system. The value of the plan of government which our statesmen adopted at the first, the plan of functions divided between national and state authorities, has **depreciated** not a whit: we are only a little less anxious about the clearness of the lines of division. The national government still has its charter, somewhat enlarged since the war, but substantially the same document as of old; and the national authorities must still confine themselves to measures within the sanction of that charter. The state governments, too, still have their charters, and still have valid claim to all powers not specifically delegated to the government of the Union. Liberal construction of the federal charter the nation wants, but not a false construction of it. The nation properly comes before the states in honor and importance, not because it is *more* important than they are but because it is all important to them and to the maintenance of every principle of government which we have established and still cherish. The national government is the organic frame of the states: it has enabled, and still enables, them to exist.

Present Character of the Government of the Union. — It is perhaps most in accordance with the accomplished results of our national development to describe the government of the United States, not as a dual government, but as a *double* government, so complete is the present integration of its state and federal parts. Government with us has ceased to be plural and has become singular, the *government* of the United States. Distinct as are its parts, they are not separate. The state and federal systems are so adjusted under our public law that they may not only operate smoothly and effectively each in the sphere which is exclusively its own, but also fit into each other with perfect harmony of coöperation wherever their jurisdictions cross or are parallel, acting as parts of one and the same frame of government, with an uncontested subordination of functions and an undoubted common aim.

Although these two parts of our government are thus vitally united, however, thus integrated into what is in reality a single scheme of government, state law by no means depends upon federal law for its sanction. The Constitution of the United States and the laws and treaties passed in pursuance thereof are indeed the supreme law of the land, but their supremacy does not trench upon or displace the self-originated authority of the states in the immensely important sphere reserved to them. Although it is true, taking our system as a whole, that the governments of the states are subordinate in our political order to the government of the Union, they are not subordinate in the sense of being subject to be commanded by it, but only in being less than national in their jurisdiction.

The States not Administrative Divisions but Constituent Members of the Union. —The common and convenient distinction between central and local government furnishes here no appropriate ground of discrimination. A central government, as contradistinguished from a local government within the meaning of that distinction, is a government which prescribes both the constitution and the mode of action of the lesser organs of the system to which it belongs. This the governments of the states do with reference to the townships, the counties, the cities within their territories: these local bodies are merely administrative divisions of the states, agencies delegated to do the daily work of local government. But there is no such relationship between the federal government and the states. They are not administrative divisions but constituent members of the Union, coördinate with the Union in their powers, in no sense subject to it in their appropriate spheres. They are excluded, indeed, by the federal Constitution from the exercise of certain functions, but the great and all-important functions which they do exercise are not given them by that Constitution: they are exercised, on the contrary, upon the completest principles of self-direction. We may properly distinguish the government of a county and the government of a state by the distinction between local and central government, but not the government of a state and the government of the Union.

CHARACTER, ORGANS, AND FUNCTIONS OF THE STATES.

The States properly come first in a description of the government of this country, not only because it was in conformity with state models and precedents that the federal government was constructed, but also and more particularly because the great bulk of the business of government still rests with the state authorities. The states still carry by far the greater part of the weight of the governing function, still constitute the ordinary fountains of justice and of legal right, still stand nearest the people in the regulation of all their social and legal relationships. : Like the Swiss Cantons, our states have given to the government which binds them together their own forms of constitution. Even more than the Cantons, our states have retained their right to rule their citizens in all ordinary matters without federal interference. They are the chief creators of law among us. They are the chief constituent units of our political system not only, but are also self-directive units. They make up the mass, the body, the constituent tissue, the organic stuff of the government of the country. " The federal government," as Tocqueville said, " is the exception; the government of the states is the rule." To them is intrusted our daily welfare, to the federal government only certain collective interests. Upon the character of the state governments depends the character of the nation in its several constituent members; upon the character of the federal government depends the character of the nation as a whole. If we are to begin our study of our institutions at the centre, at the heart of self-government, we must begin with the states.

The Law of the States: its Character. — The law of each state consists of two great parts, (1) the Constitution, statutes, and treaties of the United States and (2) the constitution and statutes of the state. The Constitution, statutes, and treaties of the United States are the supreme law of the land not so much in the sense of being set above the constitutions and laws of the states as in the sense of being, by virtue of the principles of our public law, integral parts of the law of the states. The constitutions of several of the states explicitly declare the Constitution of the United States to be a part of their fundamental law: but such declarations are only formal recognitions of a principle now in all cases indubitable. On their legal as well as on their political side the two parts of our system have been completely integrated. Upon the state courts as well as upon the courts of the United States rests the duty of administering federal law. The federal Constitution is a negative portion of state law in respect of the limitations which it sets to the sphere of state activity; but the laws passed by Congress under the authority of that Constitution are also positive portions of state law, whose mandates all officers of government, whether state or federal, are bound to obey.

The constituted authorities of the states do not stand in the same relation, however, to the Constitution and laws of the Union that they bear to state law. Of state law they are the final interpreters, but of federal law they are only provisional interpreters. In acting upon federal law state officers always act subject to the supervision of the federal tribunals.

The functions of the state courts with regard to the interpretation of federal law very forcibly illustrate the adjustments of our system. If in any case brought in a state court the question arise whether a certain state law involved in the case is or is not in violation of the Constitution of the United States, the court may freely give its judgment upon the question, and if its judgment be that the state law is *not* constitutional that judgment is conclusive. If, however, it should declare the law to be in agreement with the federal Constitution, its opinion may be cited to a federal tribunal for revision. The federal law is, thus, not regarded as a thing apart from the law of a state, too sacred to be handled by any but the federal courts, its specially constituted guardians: it is a part of state law and the state courts may declare and apply its principles. But in the last resort the federal courts must themselves shield it from a too liberal or too prejudiced judgment by state judges, who may very conceivably be interested to vindicate the statutes of their state as against any objections drawn from the law of the Union. Both for the sake of making it uniform and for the sake of keeping it supreme federal law must receive its final adjudication in its own courts.

Scope of State Law. — A moment's thought suffices to reveal how very great a field of activity, how preponderant a part remains under our system to the states. The powers of the federal government seem great by enumeration. Besides being intrinsically powers of the greatest importance, they are made the more imposing in the Constitution by the fact of their being set forth in an exhaustive list. The *residuum* of powers that remains to the states, consisting as it does of unenumerated items, is vague, and because vague seems unimportant by comparison. A moment's examination of this *residuum* however, a moment's consideration of its contents, puts a very different face on the matter. It is worth while for the sake of an adequate understanding of the real division of powers under our government to give to the powers remaining with the states something like the same setting forth that is given to those granted to the Union.

Legislative Powers of the Union. — The Constitution of the United States grants to Congress first of all the power to lay and collect taxes, duties, imposts, and excises for the support of the government of the Union, the payment of its debts, and the promotion of the common defence and welfare, and also the power to borrow money on the credit of the United States; but these powers of taxation and borrowing belong also to the states, except that they must raise their revenues without resort to duties, imposts, and excises, the privilege of imposing these being reserved to the Union exclusively. The powers which distinguish the general government from the governments of the states are not these powers of raising money but these others: To control the monetary system of the country, to maintain post-offices and post-roads, to grant patents and copyrights, to deal with crimes committed on the high seas or against the law of nations, to shape the foreign relations of the country, to declare war and control the military forces of the nation, and to regulate commerce both with foreign countries and among the states. It is empowered also to establish uniform rules of naturalization and uniform laws concerning bankruptcy; but these powers do not belong to it exclusively. In case Congress does not act in these matters, the states may adopt laws for themselves concerning them. All the powers of the general government are plainly such as affect interests which it would be impossible to regulate harmoniously by any scheme of separate state action, and only such; all other powers whatever remain with the states.

Powers withheld from the States. — Some powers, it is true, the Constitution of the United States expressly withholds from the states, besides those granted exclusively to the general government. No state may pass any bill of attainder, *ex post facto* law, or law impairing the obligation of contracts, or grant any title of nobility; no state may, without the consent of Congress, lay any imposts or duties, keep troops or ships of war in time of peace, enter into any agreement with another state or with a foreign power, or engage in war unless actually invaded or in such immediate danger as will not admit of delay. But these prohibitions obviously curtail scarcely at all the sphere which the states would in any case normally occupy within the scheme of federal union.

Powers left with the States. — Compared with the vast prerogatives of the state legislatures, these limitations seem small enough. All the civil and religious rights of our citizens depend upon state legislation; the education of the people is in the care of the states; with them rests the regulation of the suffrage; they prescribe the rules of marriage, and the legal relations of husband and wife, of parent and child; they determine the powers of masters over servants and the whole law of principal and agent, which is so vital a matter in all business transactions; they regulate partnership, debt and credit, and insurance; they constitute all corporations, both private and municipal, except such as specially fulfil the financial or other specific functions of the federal government; they control the possession, distribution, and use of property, the exercise of trades, and all contract relations; and they formulate and administer all criminal law, except only that which concerns crimes committed against the United States, on the high seas, or against the law of nations. Space would fail in which to enumerate the particular items of this vast range of power; to detail its parts would be to catalogue all social and business relationships, to set forth all the foundations of law and order.

A striking illustration of the preponderant part played by state law under our system is supplied in the surprising fact that only one out of the dozen greatest subjects of legislation which engaged the public mind in England during the nineteenth century would have come within the powers of the federal government under the Constitution as it stood before the war, only two under the Constitution as it stands since the addition of the war amendments. I suppose that I am justified in singling out as these twelve greatest subjects of legislation the following: Catholic emancipation, parliamentary reform, the abolition of slavery, the amendment of the poor-laws, the reform of municipal corporations, the repeal of the corn laws, the admission of the Jews to Parliament, the disestablishment of the Irish church, the alteration of the Irish land laws, the establishment of national education, the introduction of the ballot, and the reform of the criminal law. Of these every one except the corn laws and the abolition of slavery would have been under our system, so far as they could be dealt with at all, subjects for state regulation entirely; and it was only by constitutional amendment made in recognition of the accomplished facts of the war that slavery, which was formerly a question reserved for state action, and for state action alone, was brought within the field of the federal authority.[1]

Non-constitutional Provisions in State Constitutions. —

One of the most characteristic circumstances connected with our state law is the threatened loss of all real distinction between constitutional and ordinary law. Constitutions are in their proper nature bodies of law by which government is *constituted*, by which, that is, government is given its organization and functions. Private law, the regulation of the relations of citizens to each other in their private capacities, does not fall within their legitimate province. This principle is fully recognized in the construction of our federal Constitution, which is strong and flexible chiefly because of its great, its admirable simplicity and its strictly *constitutional* scope. But constitution-making in the states, especially in the newer states, has proceeded upon no such idea. Not only do the constitutions of the states go very much more into detail in their prescriptions touching the organization of the government; they go far beyond organic provisions and undertake the ordinary, but very different, work of legislative enactment. They commonly embody regulations, for example, with reference to the management of state property, such as canals and roads, and for the detailed administration of the state debt; they determine the amounts and sorts of property which are to be exempt from seizure for private debt; they formulate sumptuary laws, such as those forbidding the sale of intoxicating liquors; at a score of points they enter without hesitation or restraint the field usually reserved for the action of legislative bodies.

Distrust of Legislation. —

The motive is dissatisfaction with legislation, distrust of legislators, a wish to secure for certain classes of law a greater permanency and stability than is vouchsafed to statutes, which stand in constant peril of altera-

[1] Compare J. F. Jameson, *Introduction to the Constitutional and Political History of the Individual States,* Johns Hopkins University Studies in Historical and Political Science, 4th Series, p. 9 (continuous p. 189).

tion or repeal. A further motive is the desire to give to such laws the sanction of a popular vote. It is the almost universal practice throughout the Union to submit constitutional provisions to a vote of the people; and the non-constitutional provisions which are becoming so common in our constitutions are virtually only ordinary laws submitted to popular sanction and so placed, along with the rest of the instrument of which they form incongruous parts, beyond the liability of being changed otherwise than through the acquiescence of the same ultimate authority. The practice perhaps discovers a tendency towards devising means for making all very important legal provisions dependent upon direct popular participation in the process of enactment.

The objections to the practice are as obvious as they are weighty. General outlines of organization, such as the Constitution of the United States contains, may be made to stand without essential alteration for long periods together; but, in proportion as constitutions make provision for interests whose aspects must change from time to time with changing circumstance, they enter the domain of such law as must be subject to constant modification and adaptation. Not only must the distinctions between constitutional and ordinary law hitherto recognized and valued tend to be fatally obscured, but the much to be desired stability of constitutional provisions must in great part be sacrificed. Those constitutions which contain the largest amount of extraneous matter, which does not concern at all the structure or functions of government, but only private or particular interests, must of course, however carefully drawn, prove subject to most frequent change. In some of our states, accordingly, constitutions have been as often changed as important statutes. The danger is that constitution-making will become with us only a cumbrous mode of legislation.

Distrust of the legislatures is further indicated by the introduction in several states of the initiative and the referendum for ordinary laws. By the former a certain percentage of the electorate may initiate legislation by a petition which, when properly signed and forwarded to the Secretary of State, compels the submission to popular vote of the measure set out in the petition. By the referendum a certain percentage of the electorate, generally smaller than in the case of the initiative, may compel the submission to popular vote of a measure already passed by the legislature.

The objections to the initiative and the referendum are that they assume a discriminating judgment and a fullness of information on the part of the people touching questions of public policy which they do not often possess, and that it lowers the sense of responsibility on the part of legislators. In their behalf it may be urged that they enable the people to pass good measures and to kill bad ones and that their educational value is large.

Constitutional Amendments. — The amendment of state constitutions, like the amendment of the federal Constitution, can be effected only by elaborate, formal, and unusual processes which are meant to hedge the fundamental law about with a greater dignity and sanctity than attaches to any other body of legal precepts. The theory of our whole constitutional arrangement is, that the people have not only, in establishing their constitutions, bound their agents, the governing bodies and officials of the states, but have also bound themselves, — have bound themselves to change the fundamental rules which they have made only by certain formal and deliberate processes which must mark the act of change as at once solemn and fully advised.

The distinction between constitutional provisions and ordinary laws is further lessened in those states which have adopted the initiative and the referendum both for constitution making and amending and for the passage of ordinary laws. By their introduction the formal difference between the constitution and a statute, adopted through their use, has been very largely removed.

In England, constitutional amendment is not distinguishable from simple legislation (page 216). Parliament may, by simple Act, change any, even the most fundamental, principle of government that the deliberate opinion of the nation wishes to see changed. Where the constitution consists for the most part of mere precedent, and for the rest of Acts of Parliament or royal ordinances simply, it may be altered as easily as precedent may be departed from. In England that is not easily. The great conservative force there is the difficulty with which Englishmen abandon established courses.

In France constitutional amendment differs from ordinary legislation only in this, that the two chambers must sit together at Versailles, as a single National Assembly, when passing laws which affect the constitution (page 156).

In Germany constitutional amendment differs from ordinary legislation only in the number of votes required for the passage of an amendment through the *Bundesrath*, in which fourteen negative votes will defeat it. In the United States, on the contrary, constitutional amendment differs from ordinary legislation both in formal procedure and in the political powers called into action to effect it.

Preliminary Steps of Amendment. — Legislatures, with us, cannot of themselves undertake any general revision of the fundamental law. In case a general revision of a state constitution is sought to be effected, the legislature is empowered to propose the calling of a popular convention to be chosen specially for the purpose; the question whether or not such a convention shall be called must be submitted to the people; if they vote for its being summoned, it is elected by the usual suffrage; it meets and undertakes the revision, and then usually submits the results of its labors to the popular vote, which may either accept those results, or reject them and fall back upon the old constitutional arrangements.

In many of the states a proposition for the calling of such a convention may be submitted to the people only if adopted by a two-thirds vote of both houses of the legislature. The new state constitution, adopted in South Carolina (1895) and in Delaware (1897) were not submitted to the popular vote, but were promulgated as law by the conventions which framed them. This method of adoption was once not uncommon; but it is now very unusual.

Proposal of Amendments. — Legislatures may, however, themselves propose particular amendments to constitutional provisions. In some of the states a mere majority vote suffices for the preliminary adoption of amendments by the legislature, though in most states larger majorities, ranging from three-fifths of a quorum to two-thirds of all the elected members of each house, must be obtained. But in almost all cases popular sanction must follow: a vote of the people being made an indispensable condition precedent to the incorporation of an amendment in the fundamental law. In many states, indeed, amendments proposed thus by the legislature must be adopted by two *successive* legislatures, besides receiving the people's sanction, before they can become part of the constitution. In some a popular vote intervenes between the two legislative adoptions which must be had before the desired amendment is effected. In Delaware amendments may be made without a popular vote, if adopted by a two-thirds vote in two successive legislatures, a renewal of the representative house by election intervening.

In some of the states amendments to the constitution can also be proposed by the initiative of the people and when so proposed must be submitted to popular vote and, if adopted, become part of the constitution without the participation of the legislature.

The details of these processes differ widely in different states. In Vermont only the senate can propose amendments, and it only at intervals of ten years. In Connecticut amendments can be originated only by the house of representatives. Various restrictions, too, are in many of the states put upon the number of clauses of the constitution to which amendments can be proposed at any single legislative session, the number of times amendments may be submitted to the people within a specified term of years, and the method to be followed in the popular vote when more than one amendment is submitted. In most states, too, special popular majorities are required for the adoption of all constitutional changes.

These processes of amendment have been found by no means so difficult as they seem. The habit of inserting in state constitutions enactments not properly belonging with constitutional provisions, and which must be subject to frequent alteration, has led to frequent appeals to the people for purposes of amendment, and has served to show how easy amendment may be made. So easy and normal, indeed, have appeals to the people in state affairs become that the constitution of New Hampshire goes the length of providing for the submission to the vote of the people every seven years of the question whether or not the state constitution shall be revised by a convention called for the purpose, while that of Iowa commands the submission of the same question to the people every ten years, that of Michigan every sixteen years; and the constitutions of New York, Ohio, Oklahoma, and Maryland direct its submission every twenty years.

Conflict of Laws. — The plan of leaving to the states the regulation of all that portion of the law which most nearly touches our daily interests, and which in effect determines the whole structure of society, the whole organic action of industry and business, has some very serious disadvantages : disadvantages which make themselves more and more emphatically felt as modern tendencies of social and political development more and more prevail over the old conservative forces. When the Constitution of the Union was framed the states were practically very far distant from one another. Difficulties of travel very greatly restricted intercourse between them : being, so to say, physically separate, it was no inconvenience that they were also legally separate. But now that the railroad and the telegraph have made the country small both to the traveller and to the sender of messages the states have been geographically and socially compacted. Above all, they have been commercially and industrially knit together. State divisions, it turns out, are not natural economic divisions; they practically constitute no boundaries at all to any distinctly marked industrial regions. Variety and conflict of laws, consequently, have brought not a little friction and confusion into our social and business arrangements.

Detrimental Effects. — At some points this diversity and multiformity of law almost fatally affect the deepest and most abiding interests of the national life. Above all things else, it has touched the marriage relation, that tap-root of all social growth, with a deadly corruption. Not only has the marriage tie been very greatly relaxed in some of the states, while in others it retains its old-time tightness, so that the conservative rules which jealously guarded the family, as the heart of the state, promise amid the confusion to be almost forgotten; but diversities between state and state have made possible the most scandalous processes of collusive divorce and fraudulent marriage.

In the Matter of Taxation so great a variety of law obtains among the states as to preclude in part a normal and

healthy economic development. Special taxes drive out certain
employments from some states, special exemptions artificially
foster them in others ; and in many quarters ill-judged or ill-
adjusted systems of taxation tend to hamper industry and
exclude capital. So, too, in the matter of corporations diversity
of state law works great confusion and partial disaster to the
interests of commerce and industry, not only because some
states are less careful in their creation and control of corporations than others, and so work harm to their own citizens, but
also because loosely or unwisely incorporated companies created
by the laws of one state may do business and escape proper
responsibility in another state.

In the Criminal Law, again, variety works social damage,
tending to concentrate crime where laws are lax, and to under-
mine by diffused percolation the very principles which social
experience has established for the control of the vicious classes.
So, too, in laws concerning **debt**, special exemptions or special
embarrassments of procedure here, there, and everywhere impair
that delicate instrument, credit, upon whose perfect operation the
prosperity of a commercial nation depends.

Proposals of Reform. — It is in view of such a state of
affairs, such a multiformity and complexity of law touching matters which ought, for the good of the country, to be uniformly
and simply regulated throughout the Union, that various extensions of the sphere of the federal government have been proposed
by sanguine reformers, who would have all interests which need
for their advancement uniform rules of law given over to the care
of Congress by constitutional amendment.

Evils of the Case Easily Exaggerated. — The extent of
the legal friction and confusion complained of may, however,
easily be exaggerated. It is in most cases a confusion of detail
and of procedure rather than of principle or substance, and has
more exasperations for the lawyer than for the layman. Unquestionably there is vastly more uniformity than diversity. Nearly
all the states have built up their law upon the ancient and common foundation of the Common Law of England, the new states
borrowing their legislation in great part from the old. Nothing
could afford clearer evidence of this than the freedom with which,

in the courts of nearly every state in the Union, the decisions of the courts of the other states, and even the decisions of the English courts, are cited as suggestive or illustrative, some-times also as authoritative, precedent. Everywhere, for instance, the laws of property rest upon substantially the same bases of legal principle, and everywhere those laws have been similarly freed from the burdens and inequalities of the older system from which they were derived. Everywhere there is the same facility of transfer, the same virtual abolition of all feudal character-istics of tenure, the same separation between the property in-terests of man and wife, the same general rules as to liens and other claims on property, the same principles of tenancy, of disposition by will, and of intestate inheritance. Every-where, too, contracts, common carriage, sales, negotiable paper, and partnership rest upon similar principles of practically uni-versal acceptance. We feel the conflicts, because we suffer under their vexations; while we fail to realize and appreciate the uni-formities, because they are normal and have come to seem matters of course. It must be acknowledged, moreover, that even within the area of irritation there are strong corrective forces at work, a growing moral sentiment and a fashion of imitation, promising the initiation and propagation of reform. As the country grows socially and politically, its tendency is to compact, to get a com-mon thought and establish common practices. As it compacts, likenesses will be emphasized, diversities pared and worn away.

Louisiana and New Mexico stand apart with a peculiar law of their own, unlike the law of the rest of the states, because based upon the civil law of France and Spain, which is Roman law filtered through the histories of the Romance nations. Inevitably, however, the laws of these exceptional com-munities have approximated in some degree to the legal systems of the rest of the Union ; and they will draw still closer to them in the future.

Interstate Law: Commerce. — In a country being thus compacted, thus made broader than its states in its feelings and interests, thus turned away from the merely local enterprise of its early industrial history to the national commerce and produc-tion of the present generation, state lines must coincide with the lines of very few affairs which are not political: there must be many calls for the adjusting weight of an authority larger than that of any single state. Most such interests, happily, are commercial in their nature, and with the regulation of interstate commerce Congress has always been charged. It was to give Congress this power, indeed, that the great constitutional convention was called: interstate commerce was one of the chief sources of the alarming friction between the states which marked that time of crisis. It is by the operation of this power that the great railroad systems of this country, and the endless telegraph and telephone lines, have come under the guardianship, and, so far as Congress has chosen, under the regulation of the federal government. Federal law cannot touch agencies of commerce which lie wholly within a single state; but there are nowadays very few such agencies, and the jurisdiction of Congress over commerce, where it does exist, is exclusive of all interference by the states. Federal law controls all navigable waters which constitute natural highways of interstate traffic or intercourse, whether directly or only through their connections; it extends to such waters, not only, but also to the control of the means by which commerce may cross them in its land passage, to the construction, that is, of bridges over navigable waters for the facilitation of land traffic. It excludes every state tax or license law, every state regulation whatever, that in any way affects by way of restriction or control any movement of commerce or intercourse between the states.

Posts and Telegraphs. — Directly supplementary to the power of Congress over interstate commerce is its power to establish post-offices and post-roads. This has been interpreted to bestow upon Congress the right to facilitate telegraphic intercourse between the states by taking measures to break down exclusive privileges granted by a state; and it must undoubtedly be taken as rounding out to a perfect wholeness the control of the general government over the means of communication between state and state.

Of course, too, this is a jurisdiction which must necessarily advance with lengthening strides as the movements of our already vast commerce become yearly even wider still and more rapid. It has been made, indeed, to carry also a promise even of federal ownership of the telegraph systems of the country, and of a very much more extensive regulation of railway management than has yet been ventured upon.[1] The most significant step yet taken was the creation, in 1887, of an Interstate Commerce Commission charged with the prevention of unjust discriminations in railroad rates either for freight or passage. This Commission has already become one of the most important judicial bodies of the nation, and illustrates a very important experiment in federal control.

Citizenship. — Citizenship in the United States illustrates the double character of the government. Whoever possesses citizenship at all is a citizen both of the United States and of the state in which he lives. He cannot be a citizen of the United States alone, or only of a state ; he must be a citizen of both or of neither : the two parts of his citizenship cannot be separated. The responsibilities of citizenship, too, are both double and direct. Under our federal system punishment for the violation of federal law falls directly upon individuals, as does punishment for the violation of state law ; the obligation of obedience is in both cases direct : every citizen must obey both federal law and the law of his own state. His citizenship involves direct relations with the authorities of both parts of the government of the country, and connects him as immediately with the power of the marshals of the United States as with the power of the sheriff of his own county, or the constable of his own town.

The population of the United States is probably less stationary in its residence than the population of any other country in the world, and frequent changes of residence have led to a great facilitation of the transfer of citizenship from one state to another. A very brief term of residence in a new home in another state secures the privileges of citizenship there : but in transferring his state citizenship a citizen does not affect his

---

[1] The control of both the railroads and the telegraph systems has been taken over by the federal government for the period of the war.

citizenship of the United States at all. The term of residence required for the acquirement of the privilege of suffrage varies from three months to two years and a half, but is in most cases one year.

Elements of Confusion. — A very considerable amount of obscurity, it must be admitted, surrounds the question of citizenship in the United States. The laws of our states have so freely extended to aliens the right to hold property, and even the right to vote after a mere declaration of intention to become naturalized citizens (see page 320), — have, in brief, so freely endowed aliens with all the most substantial and distinguishing *privileges* of citizenship, — that it has become extremely difficult to draw any clear line, any distinction not merely formal, between citizens and aliens. Of course if a person who is not formally naturalized exchanges residence in a state in which he was allowed the privileges of citizenship for residence in a state in which those privileges are denied him, he can complain of no injustice or inequality. The Constitution of the United States commands that " the citizens of each state shall be entitled to all the privileges and immunities of citizens in the several states "; but only federal law admits aliens to formal citizenship, and only formal citizenship can give to any one, wherever he may go, a right to the privileges and immunities of citizenship. The suffrage in particular is a privilege which each state may grant upon terms of its own choosing, provided only that those terms be not inconsistent with a republican form of government, and with the Constitution of the United States.

Naturalization. — Naturalization is the name given to the acquirement of citizenship by an alien. The power to prescribe uniform rules of naturalization rests with Congress alone, by grant of the Constitution. The states cannot make rules of their own in the matter, though they may, singularly and inconsistently enough, admit to the privileges of citizenship on what terms they please (page 220). The national naturalization law requires that the person who wishes to become a citizen must apply to a court of law in the state or territory in which he desires to exercise the rights of citizenship for formal papers declaring him a legal citizen; that before receiving such papers he must take oath to be an orderly and loyal citizen and must renounce any title of nobility he may have held; and that in order to obtain such papers he must have lived in the United States at least five years, and in the state or territory in which he makes application at least one year; and at least two years before his application he must have declared in court under oath his intention to become a naturalized citizen.

It is not necessary for a person who became a resident of the United States three years before coming of age to make such a sworn declaration of his intention to become a citizen. If a man who has made such sworn declaration dies before taking out his papers of naturalization, his widow and minor children may become citizens by merely taking the necessary oath of citizenship at the proper time. The children of persons who become naturalized, if they live in the United States, and are under twenty-one years of age when their parents take the oath of citizenship, become citizens by virtue of the naturalization of their parents.

In Germany, the terms and conditions upon which foreigners are to be admitted to citizenship are also regulated by federal law; while in Switzerland citizenship in its fulness can be conferred only by cantonal law, though naturalization is regulated by federal provision. The European states have, however, very few of the problems of naturalization which confront and confound us in the United States. The whole world is not coming to them as it is coming to us.

Citizenship under a Confederation. — The possession of a national naturalization law is one of the practical political features which distinguish our general government from the government of a mere confederation. The states which compose it are the only 'citizens' of a confederation: for the individual there is no federal citizenship; and the transfer by an individual of his citizenship from one state to another within the confederation is as much a mere matter of international comity as if the states were not bound together by any common law.

Central Governments of the States. — The governments of the states depend for their structure and powers entirely upon written fundamental law, — upon documents which we may call popular charters. It was, as I have said, upon the models and precedents furnished by the governments of the thirteen original states that the federal government was constructed, and this was one of the features copied: the state governments, no less dis tinctly than the federal government, rest upon fundamental law based upon the explicit assent of the people or their representatives.

A very great uniformity of structure is observable among the central governments of the states in all general features. One of the most obvious points of resemblance between them is the complete separation and perfect coördination of the three great departments of governmental action, — the legislative, the executive, and the judicial; and these are set apart and organized under the state constitutions with a very much greater particularity than characterizes the provisions of the federal constitution.

The State Legislatures: their Powers. — The state constitutions supplement the Constitution of the Union, providing for the exercise of all powers not bestowed by the federal charter; and the legislatures of the states may be said, in general terms, to possess all law-making powers not given to Congress. But this is by no means a complete statement of the case. State constitutions contain strict limitations of power no less than does the Constitution of the United States. Some powers there are which are altogether withheld: which cannot under our system be exercised by any existing authority: which have been granted neither to Congress nor to the legislatures of the states. Such, for example, are the power to grant to any person or class of persons exclusive political privileges or immunities, the power to bestow hereditary privileges or honors, and the power to abridge in any way the equal rights to life, liberty, and property. These may safely be said, however, to be powers which no state legislature would in any case dream of exercising, inasmuch as they would have to be exercised, if exercised at all, in the face of a public opinion which would certainly refuse reëlection to any legislator who should violate the principles of republican government so strenuously worked out in our history, from Magna Charta down, and now so warmly cherished by all classes of our people that no denial of them could stand upon our statute books a single twelve-month. These are at most limitations put upon reaction.

Limitations of Length of Session, etc. — There are other limitations, however, of a very different character contained in our state constitutions: limitations meant especially to control the action of legislatures within the sphere of their proper and undoubted powers, and unquestionably based upon a general distrust of the wisdom, if not of the honesty, of legislators. Thus our constitutions very commonly forbid all private or special legislation, confining legislatures to the passage of general laws applying uniform rules to all persons and all cases alike. They limit, moreover, in very many cases, the length and frequency of legislative sessions,[1] providing that the legislature shall convene, for instance, only once in every period of two years, and shall continue its biennial session for not more than a certain number of days, except under special or exceptional conditions, when extra sessions may be called by the governor or regular sessions extended by a special two-thirds or three-fifths vote. Many constitutions contain, also, minute provisions concerning the conduct of legislation, forbidding the introduction of bills later than such and such a day of a limited session, prescribing the general form of bills, limiting their subject-matter to a single object each, and even commanding the manner of their consideration.

Other Limitations. — More than this, as we have seen, there are certain classes of legislative provisions which have been removed beyond the cognizance of legislatures by being put into the constitutions themselves : such as exemptions of certain classes of property from seizure for private debt (generally called "homestead exemptions"), 'prohibition' provisions, etc. The embodiment of such measures in constitutions is intended to put them beyond legislative interference, — is a limitation of the same indirect sort as a Bill of Rights. It is usual, also, for our state constitutions to limit the power of legislatures to create corporations, by provisions which direct the passage of general laws of incorporation to be applied in a formal administrative manner by the courts, to which applications for incorporation are to be made.

State Legislatures not Sovereign Bodies. — It will thus be seen that our state legislatures are not in any sense 'sovereign'

---

[1] The period to which the duration of legislative sessions is restricted varies, when imposed, from forty days (Wyoming) to ninety days (Colorado and Minnesota), the most common period being sixty days.

bodies. There is a certain serviceable clearness of view to be had by regarding the state governments as, in their legal aspect, like corporations. Their legislatures are *law-making bodies* acting within the gifts of charters, and are by these charters in most cases very strictly circumscribed in their action. It is this fact which gives so unique a place of power under our system to the courts, the authoritative interpreters of the fundamental law to which all legislation and all executive action must conform.

Legislative Organization. — In every state the legislature consists of two houses, a senate and house of representatives, and in most of the states the term of senators is four years, that of representatives two years, one-half of the senate being renewed every two years at the general elections. There is no such difference in character, however, between the two houses of the state legislatures as exists between the Senate and the House of Representatives of the United States. Connecticut, as we have seen (page 289), furnished the suggestion upon which the framers of the federal Constitution acted in deciding upon the basis and character of representation in the two federal houses; for in the Connecticut legislature of that time one house represented the towns, as the confederate units of the state, while the other represented the people directly. Even Connecticut has now abandoned this arrangement, however, and in almost all the states representation in both houses is based directly upon population, the only difference between the senate and house being that the senate consists of fewer members representing larger districts. Often, for instance, each county of a state is entitled to send several representatives to the lower house of the legislature, while several counties are combined to form a single senatorial district.

Reasons for Two Houses in State Legislatures. — There is, consequently, no such historical reason for having two houses in the states as exists in the case of the federal government. The object of the federal arrangement is the representation of the two elements upon which the national government rests, namely, the popular will and a federal union of states. The state legislatures have two houses simply for purposes of deliberateness in legislation, in order, that is, that legislation may be filtered through the debates of two coördinate bodies, representing slightly differing constituencies, though coming both directly from the people, and may thus escape the taint of precipitation too apt to attach to the conclusions of a single all-powerful popular chamber. The double organization represents no principle, but only an effort at prudence.

The reason for our having double legislatures cannot, however, be so simply explained. It is compounded of both deliberate and historical elements. Its historical grounds are sufficiently clear: the senates of our states are lineal descendants of the councils associated with the colonial governors, though they now represent a very different principle. The colonial councils emanated from the executive, and may be said to have been parts of the executive, while our senates emanate from the people. Then, too, there was the element of deliberate imitation of English institutions. One hundred years ago England possessed the only great free government in the world ; she was, moreover, our mother land, and the statesmen who formed our constitutions at the revolution naturally adopted that English fashion of legislative organization which has since become the prevailing fashion among all liberalized governments. Possibly, too, they were influenced by more ancient example. The two greatest nations of antiquity had had double legislatures, and, because such legislatures existed in ancient as well as in modern times, it was believed that they were the only natural kind.

Historical Precedents. — Greeks, Romans, and English alike had at first, it is true, only a single law-making body, a senate representing the elders or nobles of the community, associated with the king, and, because of the power or rank of its members, a guiding authority in the state. In all three nations special historical processes produced at length legislatures representing the people also ; popular assemblies were, on one plan or another, coördinated with the aristocratic assembly, and presently the plan of an aristocratic chamber and a popular chamber in close association appeared in full development. We copied the English chambers when they were in this stage of real coördination ; before her legislature had sustained that great change, which Greece and Rome also had witnessed, whereby all real power virtually came to rest again with a single body, the popular assembly.

Terms of Senators and Representatives. — Among the older states of the union there is a more noticeable variety of law as to the *terms* of senators and representatives than is to be found in most of the constitutions of the newer states. In Massachusetts, for instance, the term of both senators and representatives is a single year only.

In New Jersey senators are elected for three years, one-third of the senate being renewed every year at the election for representatives, whose term in New Jersey is but one year. A few of the states, however, both new and old, limit the term of senators to two years, the usual term of representatives; while in Louisiana representatives are given the term usually assigned to senators, namely, four years.

Names of the Houses. — There is some variety among the states as regards the name by which the lower house of the legislature is known. In New York the popular house is called "the Assembly"; in Virginia, the "House of Delegates"; in New Jersey, the "General Assembly," — a name usually given in most of the states to the two houses taken together.

The Qualifications required of senators and representatives vary widely in the different states, but not in any essential point of principle. It is universally required, for example, that members of the legislature shall be citizens; it is very generally required that they shall be residents of the states, sometimes that they shall be residents of the districts for which they are elected; and it is in almost all cases required that a member of the legislature shall have reached a certain age. Variety appears in these provisions only in respect of details, as to the length of time citizenship or residence shall have been acquired before election, the particular age necessary, etc. The age required varies in the case of senators from twenty-one to thirty years, in the case of representatives from twenty-one to twenty-five.

Legislative Procedure. — The same general rules of organization and procedure are observed in the constitution and business both of Congress and of the state legislatures. The more numerous branch is in all cases presided over by an officer of its own election who is called the 'Speaker'; and the senate sits under the presidency, generally, of a *Lieutenant-Governor*, who occupies much the same place in the government of the state that the Vice-President of the United States occupies in the national government. He is contingent substitute for the governor. In twenty-seven of the states it is required that the votes of a majority, not of a *quorum* merely, but of the full number of members elected to each house, shall be necessary for the passage of a bill.

Standing Committees. — The houses of the state legis-latures, too, being separated from the executive in such a way as to be entirely deprived of its guidance, depend upon stand-ing committees for the preliminary examination, digestion, and preparation of their business, and allow to these committees an almost unquestioned command of the time and the conclu-sions of the legislature. The state legislatures of the early time served as models for Congress. They and the legislatures of the later states, made like them, have retained substantially their first plan of organization, following the rules of parlia-mentary practice universally observed among English-speaking peoples; and they and Congress alike have had in the main the same development. As they have grown larger they have grown more dependent upon their advisory parts, their com-mittees.

In several states the constitutions themselves command the refer-ence of all bills to committees and forbid the passage of any measure which has not been referred and reported upon.

The Suffrage. — The suffrage is in all the states given by constitutional provision to male citizens twenty-one years of age; but it does not in all the states stop there. Several of the states extend the privilege of voting also to every male resi-dent of foreign birth who is twenty-one years of age and has declared his intention to become a naturalized citizen; and several of the states grant it to every male citizen or '*inhabi-tant*' of voting age. The laws of almost all the states require residence in the state for a certain length of time previous to the election in which the privilege is sought to be exercised (the period varies all the way from three months to two years and a half), as a condition precedent to voting; most require a certain length of residence in the county also where the privilege is to be exercised; some a certain length of residence in the voting precinct. Many states require all voters to have paid certain taxes; in Delaware they are required to have paid a fixed registration fee; but no state except Rhode Island and South Carolina has a property qualification properly so-called. In South Carolina it is required that each voter shall be able to read and write, *or*, if illiterate, shall own property valued at three hundred dollars.

In several of the states the suffrage is confined to those who can read the constitution or the laws of the state. It is common, of course, throughout the country to exclude criminals, insane persons, and idiots ; and in several states the privilege is withheld from those who bet on elections. In Florida betting on an election not only excludes from the election in connection with which the offence is committed, but is punished, upon conviction, by entire and permanent disfranchisement.

Women are accorded the privilege of voting in school elections in a number of states, and in a still larger number they are made eligible to be elected to school boards. Several states have extended the franchise to them in municipal elections ; and, although the constitutions of most of the states declare the suffrage to be restricted to males, fifteen have conferred it upon women in all elections.[1]

The ballot, or voting paper, is throughout all the states the instrument of voting, and they have adopted the so-called Australian ballot system, by which voters are secured a complete privacy in the preparation of the voting papers and in the casting of their votes when prepared.

The State Courts. — A very great variety exists among the laws of the several states regarding the constitution, functions, and relative subordination of the courts. A general sketch of the state courts must, therefore, be made in very broad outline. Perhaps in this department of state law, as in others, there may be said to be, despite a bewildering variety of detail, sufficient unity of general feature to warrant a generalized description, and to render unnecessary the unsatisfactory expedient of choosing the institutions of a single state as in some broad sense typical, and describing them alone.

The courts of our states are in no sense organs of federal justice, as the courts of the German states are. They have an entirely independent standing and organization and an entirely independent jurisdiction. Their constitution and procedure are in no way affected by federal law, — except of course by way of limitation ; — their sphere is a sphere apart. The series of courts

[1] These are Arizona, California, Colorado, Idaho, Kansas, Michigan, Montana, Nevada, New York, Oklahoma, Oregon, South Dakota, Utah, Washington and Wyoming. Illinois has conferred upon women the suffrage in certain elections.

in each state, therefore, is complete.   Every state has its supreme court, as well as its inferior tribunals, and appeals lie from the state courts to the courts of the United States only in cases involving federal law or in cases where the character of the parties to the suit does not give any state court complete jurisdiction.

One of the most characteristic features of our state courts is what I may call their *local attachment*.   In most cases the judges are not appointed by any central authority but are elected by the voters of the district or circuit in which they hold court; they, like members of legislatures, may be said to have 'constituents.'   Their responsibility is thus chiefly a responsibility to the electors, a popular rather than an official responsibility.   The courts are held together in a common system and to a common duty only *by law*, therefore, and not by discipline or official subordination to superior judicial authorities.   The courts may be said to be local rather than central organs; they are integrated only *in opinion*, — only by the course of appeal, the appellate authority of the higher over the lower courts in points of law.

This *localization* of the organs of government, in their origin as well as in their functions, is a general characteristic of American political organization, — a characteristic which appears most conspicuously in the arrangements of local government, which is not so much organized as left to organize itself under general statutes, for whose enforcement no central administrative machinery is provided.

Common Law Courts. — There are, usually, four grades of jurisdiction in the judicial systems of the states, with four grades of courts corresponding.   There are generally (1) *Justices of the Peace*, who have jurisdiction over all petty police offences and over civil suits for trifling sums; who conduct preliminary hearings in cases of grave criminal offence, committing the accused, when there is *prima facie* proof of guilt, for trial by a higher court; and who are, in general terms, conservators of the peace.   They act separately and have quite lost the high judicial estate which still belongs to the English Justices, from whom they take their name.   Their decisions are in almost all cases subject to appeals to higher courts.

Mayor's courts in the towns are generally the same in rank and jurisdiction, so far as criminal cases are concerned, as the courts of Justices of the Peace.

(2) **County or Municipal Courts,** which hear appeals from Justices of the Peace and from Mayor's courts, and whose own original jurisdiction is one step higher than that of the Justices, including civil cases involving considerable sums, and criminal cases generally not of the gravest character.

Often, however, courts of this grade, especially the municipal courts of the larger towns, are given a much higher jurisdiction and are coördinated in some respects with courts of the next higher grade, the Superior Courts. In New York, New Jersey, and Kentucky the county courts retain the English name of Quarter Sessions.

(3) **Superior Courts,** which hear appeals from the county and municipal courts, and generally from all inferior courts, and which are themselves courts of high original jurisdiction of the most general character in both civil and criminal cases. They may be said to be the general courts which give to the courts of lower grade their name of 'inferior.' County and municipal courts, as their names imply, sit only for certain small districts; but the districts over which superior courts have jurisdiction usually cover a wide area, necessitating the sitting of each such court in several places in succession. In other words, superior courts are generally circuit courts, and in many states bear that name.

'Circuit courts' is, indeed, the most generally used name for courts of this grade, that is, for the principal courts of the state; though in almost as many states they are called 'district courts.' In most of the states these courts have special judges of their own; but in Maine and New Hampshire they are held by the judges of the supreme court on circuit.

In some states civil is separated from criminal jurisdiction in this grade, and distinct courts are created for each. Thus in Texas there are District courts for civil causes, District Criminal courts for criminal cases. In Pennsylvania courts of Quarter Sessions are the courts of general criminal jurisdiction, as in England, civil causes going to the courts of Common Pleas. Delaware has criminal courts called courts of Gaol Delivery.

(4) **Supreme Courts,** which in most of the states have no original jurisdiction at all, but only appellate jurisdiction, hearing

appeals in all classes of cases (except such as involve only trifling offences or small sums of money) from the superior courts and from various inferior courts.

(5) In several states there are *supremest* courts above the 'supreme.' Thus in New York there is a Supreme Court, which has its Appellate Division ; the Appellate Division has four several parts or sections which sit and hear appeals in the four judicial districts into which the state is divided ; and over all there is a Court of Appeals, a court of general revision. In New Jersey there is a supreme court above the circuit, which is itself of high appellate jurisdiction, and a Court of Errors and Appeals above the supreme ; in Louisiana the order is reversed and there is a supreme court above a court of appeals ; in Illinois a supreme court above certain district " appellate courts " ; and in Kentucky a somewhat similar arrangement prevailed until the Constitutional revision of 1891. In Texas there are two coördinate supreme courts : one, called the supreme, for the hearing of civil cases only, the other, called the court of appeals, for the hearing of criminal cases and of civil cases brought up from the county courts.

The name 'court of appeals' is found also in California, Maryland, Virginia, and West Virginia.

In five of the original states (New Hampshire, Massachusetts, Rhode Island, New York, New Jersey), and in Maine, the supreme courts have, anomalously enough, *original* as well as appellate jurisdiction in all cases ; but in the newer states such an arrangement is never found. In the case of New York, however, it is hardly accurate to say that the Supreme Court has original jurisdiction, but rather that its judges have, acting separately, and subject to the oversight of the several sections of the 'Appellate Division.'

In several of the larger cities of the country there are complete sets of courts, reproducing the state judiciary in small. Thus in Baltimore, for example, there are city courts from the lowest grade up to a ' Supreme Bench of Baltimore City.'

Courts of Equity. — ' Equity ' is defined, under the legal systems of England and the United States, as "that portion of remedial justice which is exclusively administered by a court of equity, as contradistinguished from that portion of remedial justice which is exclusively administered by a court of common law " (Story). In other words, it is that portion of remedial justice which was administered in England by the Chancellors, who were 'the keepers of the king's conscience,' and from whose court, as if from the king's sense of justice, there issued writs from time to time for the remedy of wrongs for which the common law made no adequate provision (page 185). The early Chancellors were ecclesiastics imbued with Roman law as it had come down through the medium of the canon law, and both in their hands and in those of their lay successors of later times, who were the heirs of their principles and prerogatives, equity law and procedure became a very different thing from the law and procedure of the common law courts.

Fusion of Law and Equity. — As time has gone on equity and law have been largely fused, even in England, just as the *jus gentium* and the *jus civile* became merged in the development of the Roman law; and in most of the states of the Union the same courts exercise both equitable and common law jurisdiction. In several states the whole procedure even, in both jurisdictions has been made practically identical, and law is hardly distinguishable from equity. Generally, however, the distinctive procedure at least has been preserved, and only courts of the superior and supreme grades have been given equitable jurisdiction, — jurisdiction, that is, over cases in which the remedy is equitable. In Alabama, Delaware, Michigan, Mississippi, New Jersey, Tennessee, and Vermont there are still special chancery courts.

Equity processes of trial differ from common law processes, outwardly, chiefly in the fact that the testimony is written instead of oral, and that decisions of fact as well as of law rest with the judge instead of with a jury. For its special subject-matter equity jurisdiction generally embraces such matters as trusts, mistakes, frauds, etc., — matters hardly tangible by ordinary remedies.

Probate Courts. — In most of the states there are special probate courts, — special courts, that is, charged with jurisdiction over the proof of wills, the administration of estates, the appointment of guardians, administrators, etc., the care of the estates of wards, and, in general, of the proper disposition of the property of persons deceased. In some of the states, however, these functions are left to the ordinary courts of law.

In England this probate jurisdiction was, from the first until a very recent date, a prerogative of the ecclesiastical courts, and in two of our states the probate courts retain the names of the officers who exercised this function in the place of the bishop ; in Georgia the court is called the court of the ' Ordinary,' in New York the ' Surrogate's ' court. In New Jersey, with a reminiscence of the same origin, it is called the ' Prerogative ' court. In several states, on the other hand, it is known, by virtue of one side of its function, as the ' Orphan's ' court.

Judges. — The judges of most of the state courts are elected, generally by the people, in a few cases by the legislature; but in several states they are nominated by the governor and appointed by and with the advice and consent of the Senate. In New Hampshire they are appointed by the governor by and with the advice and consent of the Council.

> Supreme court judges are usually elected by the people of the state at large ; circuit, district, county, municipal, and other judges by the electors of the areas in which they serve.
>
> The terms of judges range all the way from two years to a tenure during good behavior. The constitutions of more than three-fourths of the states permit the removal of judges by the legislature, or by the governor at the request of the legislature. In Florida, Massachusetts, and Rhode Island all judges of the higher courts hold during good behavior ; in New Hampshire until seventy years of age. The length of the term varies with the grade of the court, the tendency being to give longer terms to the judges of the higher courts.

The qualifications required of judges by state law are not stringent. Only fourteen of the states require by law any identification of their judges with the legal profession ; and only ten require ' learning in the law ' ; though custom and public opinion invariably confine the choice of judges to professional lawyers. Generally a certain age is required of judges (varying, where there is such a requirement, from twenty-five to thirty-eight years), besides, in most cases citizenship and residence in the state or circuit. As a rule single judges hold all the courts except the highest. Supreme courts have a more or less numerous ' bench.'

The ministerial officers of the state courts, the sheriffs, are generally not appointed by the judges or responsible to them, but elected by the people and answerable to ' constituents,' just as the judges themselves are. Even the clerks of the courts are often elected.

> The position of sheriff thus differs very materially from the position of a United States marshal (sec. 1317), the sheriff's counterpart

in the federal judicial system. The marshal is appointed by the President of the United States, and is responsible to a central authority, is part of a centralized organization of justice. The sheriff, on the contrary, is the organ of an extremely decentralized, an almost disintegrated, organization of justice. The bailiffs, the sheriff's deputies, are usually the appointees of the sheriff.

The State Executives. — The Executives of the states are the least distinct parts of state organization, the least susceptible of being adequately pictured in outline, or indeed in any broad and general way. Under our system of state law the executive officers of a state government are neither the servants of the legislature, as in Switzerland, nor the responsible guides of the legislature, as in England, nor the real controlling authority in the execution of the laws, as under our own federal system. The Executive of a state has an important representative place, as a type of the state's legal unity; it has a weighty function of superintendence, is the fountain of information, the centre and source of advice, the highest organ of administration to the general eye; but it cannot be said to have any place or function of guiding power. Executive power is diffused by our law throughout the local organs of government; only a certain formal superintendence remains with the authorities at the state capitals.

Of course this does not apply to the governor's *veto* power, — that contains real energy, — but only to executive functions proper; these are localized, not centralized, after the extremest pattern.

Not all of the states have the same central executive officers. All have governors; a majority of them have lieutenant-governors; all have secretaries of state; all have treasurers; almost all have attorneys-general; and a majority, superintendents of education. Many have also auditors: eleven have comptrollers, and fifteen boards of education; four (Massachusetts, New Hampshire, Maine, and North Carolina) associate councils with their governors.

For the rest, there are a great many minor officers of various functions in the different states; superintendents of prisons, for instance, registrars of land offices, superintendents of labor, bureaux of agriculture, commissioners of mines, commissioners of immigration, etc. There is no uniformity between the administrations of the states as regards these special offices; different states undertake different functions, new or old, and create new, or revive old, offices accordingly.

The governor's term of office is in almost all of the states either two or four years, although Massachusetts gives her governor a term of but a single year, while New Jersey elects hers for three. The lieutenant-governor, where such an officer is elected, has the same term as the governor, and is generally required to have the same qualifications.

These *qualifications* consist, almost always, of citizenship of from two to twenty years' standing, residence within the state of from one to ten years, and age of from twenty-five to thirty-five years. In Maine it is required that the governor shall be a *native-born* citizen.

The terms of the other principal state officers are usually the same as the term of the governor, though it is not uncommon to give to treasurers, secretaries of state, attorneys-general, and auditors a longer tenure. The qualifications required of the different officers are of the most various nature.

> The constitutions of many of the states still exhibit the jealousy of long terms of office which was so characteristic of the extreme democratic feeling generated in the colonies by the constant friction between the representatives of the people and officials who owed their offices, not to election, but to royal appointment. Seven states limit official tenure to a maximum period of seven years; Texas makes two years the maximum; and Massachusetts, Virginia, and Maryland give express constitutional sanction to *rotation in office*.

> Many states effect such a limitation with reference to the tenure of the governor's office by provisions setting bounds to the reëligibility of the governor. Thus some exclude their governors from successive terms; others allow only a single term to any one man within a specific period of, say, eight years; while still others withhold reëligibility altogether.

Contrast between State and Federal Executives. — The federal executive was, as we have seen (page 289), constituted in quite close accordance with the models of previous state organization; but the imitation can scarcely be said to have gone further than the adoption of the suggestion that the United States should have a single governmental head, a president, because the states had tried and approved a single presidency. For the rest, the president was given the character, as regards his relations with the other officials of the federal system, rather of an English sovereign than of a state governor. Certainly the contrast between the official place and power of the president and the place and power of the state governors of the present day is a very sharp and far-reaching contrast indeed. The president of the United States is the only executive officer of the federal government who is elected; all other federal officials are appointed by him, and are responsible to him. Even the chief of them bear to him, in theory at least, only the relation of advisers; though in fact, it must be acknowledged, they are in effect his colleagues. Of state officials associated with the governor it may, on the other hand, be said that both in law and in fact they are colleagues of the governor, in no sense his agents, or even his subordinates, except in formal rank and precedence. They, like himself, are elected by the people; he is in no way concerned in their choice. Nor do they serve him after election. They are not given him as advisers; they are, on the contrary, coördinated with him. North Carolina, indeed, calls her chief officers of state a 'cabinet'; but they are not dependent upon each other even in counsel, and they are quite as independent of the governor as Congress is of the president. The only means of removal to which the principal officers of the states are subject is, ordinarily, *impeachment*, to which the governor also is equally exposed. Both they and he may be charged with official crimes and misdemeanors by the house of representatives, and tried, convicted, and removed by the senate of the state. Their only other responsibility is to the courts of law, to which, like other citizens, they are answerable, for actual breaches of law. Governor, treasurer, secretary of state, attorney-general, — all state officers alike, serve, not other officers, but the people, who elected them; upon the people they are dependent, not upon each other; they constitute no hierarchy, but stand upon a perfect equality.

In the states of Delaware, Maryland, New Jersey, Pennsylvania, and Texas the secretaries of state are appointed by the governor, subject to confirmation by the senate ; in several states the attorney-general also is appointed ; nor is it uncommon for the state superintendent of education

to be an appointee of the governor ; and these facts offer apparent contradiction to the statement that the several constituent parts of the state executives stand always apart in complete independence and coördination,
— especially when it is added that in one or two states officers so important as the secretary of state and the attorney-general *hold during the
pleasure of the governor.* Several of the states empower their governors
to suspend or remove subordinate officers against whom charges are preferred, and to institute criminal proceedings against them in the courts.
Maryland authorizes the summary removal of sundry minor officials by
the governor, and Michigan and New York even the suspension of the secretary of state or the treasurer, in case of corruption or gross misconduct,
until the legislature can act ; and in Delaware the governor can remove
any public officer " convicted of misbehaving while in office, or of any in-
famous crime." But these cases constitute in fact no real exceptions :
for the duties of such officers, after their appointment, are prescribed by
constitutional provision or by statute, not by the governor ; and the
governor may remove them, not at his whim, or for mere administrative reasons, but for just cause only, and as if he acted as an officer of
justice. In brief, even when appointed by him, they do not depend upon
him.

Real Character of a State 'Executive.' — The governor
therefore, is not the 'Executive'; he is but a single piece of the
executive. There are other pieces coördinated with him over
which he has no direct official control, and which are of less
dignity than he only because they have no power to control
legislation, as he may do by the exercise of his veto, and because
his position is more representative, perhaps, of the state government as a whole, of the people of the state as a unit. Indeed it
may be doubted whether the governor and other principal officers
of a state government can even when taken together be correctly
described as 'the executive,' since the actual execution of the
great majority of the laws does not rest with them but with the
local officers chosen by the towns and counties and bound to
the central authorities of the state by no real bonds of responsibility whatever. Throughout all the states there is a significant
distinction, a real separation, between 'state' and 'local' officials;
local officials are not regarded, that is, as state officers, but as
officers of their districts only, responsible to constituents, not to
central authorities. Throughout the country the sheriffs and
other county officers, the county treasurers, clerks, surveyors.

commissioners, etc., and the town and city officials also, as well as the judges of the courts and the solicitors or district attorneys who represent the public authority before the courts, are, almost without exception, chosen by the voters of limited areas, and are regarded, for the most part, as serving, not the state, but *their part of the state.* Minor 'state' officers there are, — minor officers, that is, who ministerially serve the central offices, — and these are often appointed by the governor; but it is exceptional for the governor to control the local authorities by whom the laws are in fact put into actual operation. The president of the United States is the veritable chief and master of the official forces of the federal government; he appoints and in most cases can remove all federal marshals, district attorneys, revenue officers, post-office officials. But the governor of a state occupies no such position; nor does any high 'state' official; the central offices of a state constitute a system of supervision and report often, but seldom a system of control.

In Michigan, it is true, all officials not legislative or judicial may be removed by the governor for just legal cause ; in New York, too, sheriffs, coroners, district attorneys, and county clerks are removable by the same authority, and in Wisconsin sheriffs, coroners, district attorneys, and registrars of deeds ; but such provisions are exceptional, and are not accompanied by a system of continuous central control. Government remains disjointed, — still lies in separated parts.

Relations of the Local to the Central Organs of Government in the States. — It is characteristic of our state organization, therefore, that the counties, townships, and cities into which the states are divided for purposes of local government do not serve as organs of the states exactly, but rather as independent organisms, constituted what they are by state law, indeed, but, after being set up, left to themselves almost as entirely as if they were self-constituted. They elect their own officers, and, except for the occasional mandates of the courts, go their own paces in enforcing the general laws of the state.

Our local areas are not *governed*, in brief ; they act for themselves. Self-government implies, when used in its strict historical meaning, that the officers of local administration are officers of the *state*, of the central authority, whatever may be the machinery of their appointment, and that their responsibility is central, instead of to their neighbors merely. The only sense in which the local units of our state organizations are *governed* at all is this, that they act under general laws which are made, not by themselves, but by the central legislatures of the states. These laws are not executed by the central executive authorities, or under their control, but only by local authorities acting in semi-independence. They are, so to say, left to run themselves.

The Governor. — The usual duties of a state governor may be conveniently summed up under four general heads: (1) As towards the legislature, it is his duty to transmit to the houses at each regular session, and at such other times as may be required, full information concerning the state of the commonwealth, and to recommend to them such measures as seem to him necessary for the public good. It is also his duty in case of necessity for such a step, or upon the requisition of a sufficient number of legislators, to summon the houses to extra session. (2) He is commander-in-chief of the state militia, and as such is bound to see, not only that foreign invasion is repelled, but also that internal order is preserved. (3) He exercises the clemency of the state towards condemned persons, having the right to grant pardons to persons convicted of crime, to remit fines and penalties, under certain conditions, and to remove political disabilities incurred in consequence of conviction of crime; though he exercises these high prerogatives subject always to a definite responsibility to public opinion and to the laws.

In some states, as notably in Pennsylvania, the power of granting pardons is given to the governor, however, only in form, the sanction of a Board of Pardons being made necessary, whose action is semi-judicial. In New Jersey there is a *judicial committee* on pardons; and in Connecticut the legislature alone can pardon: the governor can only reprieve until the end of the next session of the legislature.

(4) In all the states with the single exception of North Carolina the governor's assent is made necessary to the validity of all laws not passed over his dissent by a special legislative vote upon a second consideration made in full view of his reasons for withholding his signature. And in Rhode Island, Ohio, and North Carolina, though the governor has no

veto properly so-called, he can compel the reconsideration of any measure by the legislature.

All bills which the governor signs, or upon which he does not take any action within a certain length of time, become law ; those which he will not sign he must return to the legislature with a statement of his objections. Generally he must return bills which he thus rejects to the house in which they originated, though in Kansas he must return them always to the house of representatives.

The vote by which a bill may be passed over the governor's veto varies very widely among the states. In Connecticut a mere majority suffices for its second passage ; in other states a three-fifths vote is required, in some a two-thirds vote ; sometimes a majority of elected members (instead of a special number within a mere *quorum*) must concur in a second passage ; and sometimes two-thirds of the elected members. In Missouri it is provided that the votes of two-thirds of the elected members shall be necessary in the house in which the measure originated, while a mere majority of the other house will suffice.

In many of the states the governor is given the power to veto particular items in appropriation bills ; as regards all other bills his approval or disapproval must cover all of the measure or none of it.

The Secretary of State. — The title 'Secretary of State,' borne by a conspicuous officer in each of the states, is very apt to mislead those who have studied the English executive or the functions of our own federal minister of foreign affairs. The federal Secretary of State is first of all an executive minister, only secondarily a secretary ; and the five principal Secretaries of State in England are equally without prominent secretarial functions. They are one and all executive heads of department.

The federal Secretary of State is entitled to his official name chiefly by virtue of certain minor duties seldom thought of by the public in connection with the Department of State. He has charge, for example, of the seal of the United States ; he preserves the originals of all laws and of all orders, resolutions, or votes of the houses which have received the force of law ; he furnishes to Congress, besides consular and diplomatic reports, lists of passengers arrived in the United States from foreign countries, etc.

The chief clerical features of the office which the five Principal Secretaries of State in England theoretically share (page 198) would seem to be represented by the necessity of the countersignature of some one of them to the validity of the sign-manual.

The Secretaries of State in the commonwealths of our Union, on the contrary, can show substantial cause for holding their title; the making and keeping of records is the central duty of their office. It is usually their duty to register the official acts of the governor, to enroll and publish the Acts of the Legislature, to draw up all commissions issued to public officers, to keep all official bonds, to record all state titles to property, to keep and affix, where authorized, the seal of the commonwealth, to preserve accurate maps and careful records of the boundaries of the various civil districts of the state, (the counties, townships, etc.) and to give to all who legally apply duly attested copies of the public documents in their keeping. In brief, the Secretary's office is the public record office.

Often other duties are assigned to the Secretary of State. In one state, for instance, he is constituted Internal Improvement Commissioner; in another Surveyor-general. But such additional functions are not necessarily characteristic of his office.

1200. It is to the Secretary of State in each commonwealth that the votes of the state's electors for President and Vice-President are returned; and it is he who transmits them to the president of the Senate to be opened in the joint session of the two houses.

Votes in state elections also are generally returnable to the Secretary of State's office, and the Secretary of State is very commonly one of the state canvassers of election returns. Such duties manifestly flow very naturally from the general duties of his office.

The Comptroller, or that equivalent officer, the state *Auditor*, is public accountant. It is his function to examine and pass upon all claims presented against the state under existing provisions of law; to audit the accounts of all officers charged with the collection of the revenue of the state, filing their vouchers, requiring of them the necessary bonds, and crediting them with all sums for which they present the state Treasurer's receipt; to ensure uniformity in the assessment and collection of the public revenue by preparing and furnishing to the local fiscal officers the proper forms and instructions; to issue warrants for all legal disbursements of money from the treasury of the state, keeping a careful account with the state treasurer; to submit his books and accounts at any time to examination by the legislature, — in a word, to regulate the assessment, collection, and disbursement of the public moneys.

The State Treasurer may be said simply to keep the public moneys subject to the warrants of the Comptroller. Without such warrant he can pay out nothing.

These, manifestly, are not offices of control. The Comptroller, for example, can generally proceed against local fiscal officers through the local law-representatives of the state, the local states-attorneys, in the ordinary courts, for the purpose of securing the necessary bonds when these are not promptly or properly given, or of enforcing the payment of moneys withheld or uncollected ; and he may make test of the validity or sufficiency of official bonds by any means within his reach ; but he has none but this indirect control, exercised through the courts over officers who refuse bond or who neglect the forms and instructions issued to them regarding the assessment and collection of taxes. The whole machinery of control is local, not central, — through courts and states-attorneys who are themselves elected by the same persons, in town or county, by whom the collecting officers themselves are chosen. The local fiscal officers are not officers of the state treasury, but officers of the towns and counties whom the state employs as its agents.

The State Superintendent of Education often occupies a somewhat different position. It is frequently his prerogative to prescribe the qualifications of teachers and the methods by which they are to be selected ; he is required to make a thorough inspection of the schools throughout the state ; often he is given power to secure proper reports of school work through special inspectors appointed to act instead of local superintendents whose reports are irregular or unsatisfactory. School administration is recognized to require a certain degree of centralization of administrative authority, and so to constitute a legitimate exception to the general rules as to the constitution of executive power in the states. Still, even the power of a state Superintendent of Education does not often go very much beyond supervision. The powers of district or township school directors remain in most cases very absolute as regards the management of the schools. They are governed by statute, not by the state Superintendent.

Constitutional Diffusion of the Executive Power. — The constitutions of at least seven of the states make very frank confession of the diffusion of executive authority upon which I have dwelt as character-istic of our state system. Thus the constitution of Alabama provides that the executive power "shall consist of the governor, secretary of state, state treasurer, state auditor, attorney-general, and superintendent of education, *and the sheriff for each county*." The constitutions of Arkansas, Colorado, Illinois, Minnesota, Pennsylvania, and Texas make similar enumerations, with the exception of the sheriffs of the counties. The Florida constitution of 1868 provided that the governor should be "assisted by a cabinet of administrative officers" appointed by himself, subject to the confirmation of the senate ; but clothed these officers with functions which made them in fact not assistants but colleagues.

The constitutions of most of the other states declare the executive power to be vested in the governor, but are hardly through with outlining his functions before they provide for the erection of executive departments among which the greater part of executive power shall be parcelled out; so that the arrangement is everywhere practically that of those states which in effect declare the executive office to be 'in commission' by enumerating the officers who are to divide its duties.

Full Legal, but no Hierarchical, Control. — This, then, is the sum of the whole matter : the control of law, exercised through the courts, is thorough and complete : statutes leave to no officer, either central or local, any considerable play of discretionary power : so far as possible they command every officer in every act of his administration. But no hierarchy stands between an officer and the law. The several functions of executive power are segregated, — each official, so to say, serves his own statute. So thorough is the control attempted by legislation, — and so potent among us is the legal habit and conscience, the law-abiding sense, — that no official control, no hierarchical organization has been deemed necessary.

LOCAL GOVERNMENT.

General Characteristics. — The large freedom of action and broad scope of function given to local authorities is the distinguishing characteristic of the American system of government. Law is central, in the sense of being uniform and the command of the central legislature in each state; and its prescriptions are minute; but function and executive power are local. There is a single comprehensive statutory plan, but a host of unassociated deputies to carry it into effect, an infinite variety in the local application of its principles. General laws are given to the localities by state legislation, and these laws are generally characterized by a very great degree of particularity and detail of provision; but no central authority has executive charge of their application: each locality must see to it for itself that they are carried out.

Duties of Local Government. — The duties of local government include Police, Sanitation, the Care of the Poor, the Support and Administration of Schools, the Construction and Maintenance of Roads and Bridges, the Licensing of Trades, the Assessment and Collection of Taxes, besides the Administration of Justice in the lower grades, the maintenance of Court Houses and Jails, and every other affair that makes for the peace, convenience, comfort, and local good government of the various and differing communities of each commonwealth. In many places libraries are included among the institutions given into the charge of the officers of local government. Local officers look to state laws for their authority; but practically state administration represents only the unifying scheme of local government. Local administration is *the* administration of the state.

Local Varieties of Organization. — Almost without exception the states which have been added to the original thirteen by which the Union was formed have derived their local institutions, whether by inheritance or by imitation, from the mother states of the Atlantic seaboard. Wherever New England settlers have predominated the *township* has taken quick rootage and had a strong growth; wherever Southern men have gone the *county* has found favor above other forms of local organization; wherever the people from the two sections have met and mixed, as in the early days they met and mixed in New York, New Jersey, and Pennsylvania, the same combination or mixture of institutions that is characteristic of the middle Atlantic states is found in full prominence. But in all cases the new foundations in the West have this common feature: they have all been in a greater or less degree artificially contrived. Towns have not grown up in the Northwest for the same reasons that led to their growth in New England, in the days when isolation was necessary and when isolation involved compact and complete self-government: they have, on the contrary, been deliberately constructed in imitation of New England models. Neither have Western counties been developed by processes of pioneer agricultural expansion like those which made the irregular, and in a sense geographically natural, counties of Virginia (pages 271–273); they have, on the contrary, been geometrically laid off in the exact squares of the government survey and deliberately organized after the Southern fashion because the settlers wanted to reproduce by statute the institutions which in their old homes had been evolved by slow, unpremeditated growth.   The institutions of the admitted states, in a word, were transplanted by enactment, whereas the institutions of the original states were sown by habit.   It by no means follows that these newer institutions lack naturalness or vigor: in most cases they lack neither, — a self-reliant race has simply readapted institutions common to its political habit; but they do lack the individuality and the native flavor often to be found in the institutions in whose likeness they were made.

The differences of institution, then, which show themselves in the East between local government in New England, local government in the South, and local government in the central belt of Atlantic states extend also into the West.   There, too, we find the three types, the township type, the county type, and the compound type which stands between the two; but the compound type is in the West naturally the most common.   The Westerner has had the sagacity to try to combine the advantages of all the experiments tried in the older states, rejoicing in being fettered by no hindering traditions, and profiting by being restrained by no embarrassing incapacity for politics.

Keeping these facts in mind, it will be possible to consider without confusion, the Township, the County, the School District, the Town, and the City as elements of local government in the United States.   The different place and importance given to each of these organs in different sections may be noted as we proceed.

The Township: its Historical Origin. — The township is entitled to be first considered in every description of local government in the United States not only because it is a primary unit of administration, but also by reason of its importance and because of its ancient and distinguished lineage.   It is a direct

lineal descendant from the primitive communal institutions which
Cæsar and Tacitus found existing in the vigor of youth among
the peoples living in the ancient seats of our race. The New
England town was not an American invention; and the settlers
upon the northern coasts did not adopt the town system simply
because they were obliged to establish themselves in isolated
settlements in a harsh climate and among hostile native tribes.
We have seen (pages 268, 269) that they kept together in close
settlements for religious purposes, for mutual defence, and for
purposes of trade, and that their settlements were often completely isolated by stretches of wild primeval forest; but their
form of government, or at least the talent and disposition for
it, they brought with them, an inheritance of untold antiquity.
Their political organization was like a spontaneous reproduction of the ancient Germanic mark. In most cases they regarded the land upon which they settled as the property of
the community, just as their remote barbarian ancestors had
done; like those ancestors, they divided the land among families
and individuals or worked it in common as might be decided by
public vote in general assembly, in open ' folk-moot ' we may call
it. This same ' town-meeting,' as they styled it, voted the common discipline, elected the officers, and made the rules of common
government. Each group of colonists constituted themselves a
state with a governing primary assembly. They reëstablished,
too, the old principles of folk-land. Whether they tilled their
lands in common or divided them in severalty, they had always
a communal domain, part of which was kept as open common
for the general pasturage, and the rest of which was given over
in parcels, from time to time, for settlement. They were inventing nothing; they were simply letting their race habits and instincts have natural play. Their methods showed signs at almost
every point of having been filtered through intervening English
practices; but they rested, none the less, upon original Teutonic
principles.

The exceptions to the principle of folk-land occurred where, as
in the Hartford, Windsor, and Wethersfield settlements on the Connecticut, the land was held, not in common by the civil community, but in
common by a sort of corporation of joint owners under whose supervision

the new colonies were established.   These joint owners were quite distinct from the communal authorities.[1]

Absorption of the Town in Larger Units of Government.

— It was towns of this primitive pattern that were drawn together ultimately into the New England colonies of the later time, by the processes I have already described (page 269); and in becoming parts of larger organizations they lost to some extent their independence of movement, as well as in some slight degree their individuality also.   In some cases, as for instance in the coalescence of 'Connecticut' and New Haven (page 278), the establishment of central state legislative control over the towns took the shape of a mere confirmation to them of their old functions and privileges, and in this way fully recognized their elder and once sovereign place in the historical development of the commonwealth; but it in all cases necessarily resulted in their virtual subordination.   It led also to the creation of new areas of local government.   Towns were grouped, at first for judicial purposes only, into counties, and the counties came in time to furnish a very convenient basis for certain administrative functions once vested exclusively in the smaller areas. Great cities, too, presently grew up to demand more complex, less simply and directly democratic, methods than those of the towns.   But no change has seriously threatened town organization with destruction.   The 'town' is still the most characteristic and most vital element of local government in New England; and it still has substantially the same officers, substantially the same functions, that it possessed at its foundation in America.

> An influx of foreigners has in many places disturbed and impaired the town system, and the cities, which draw to themselves so rapidly the rural population, but which are too big for the primitive methods of town government, are powerful disintegrating elements in the midst of the old organization; but the new adaptation and development of the township in the West, and the tendency to introduce it in some parts of the South, seem still to promise it honor and length of days.

[1] See Andrews, *The River Towns of Connecticut* (Johns Hopkins Studies, 'th Series).

Town-meeting. — The sovereign authority, the motive power, of town government is the Town-meeting, the general assembly of all the qualified voters of the town, which has reminded so many admiring observers of the ancient Grecian and Roman popular assemblies and of the *Landsgemeinde* of Switzerland. The regular session of this assembly is held once a year, usually in the spring,[1] but extra sessions are held from time to time throughout the year as occasion arises, due notice being given both of the time of meeting and of the exact business to be considered. Town-meeting elects all officers, — its regular annual session being the session for elections, — and decides every affair of local interest.[2] It is presided over by a 'Moderator' and attended by the town officers, who must give a full account of their administration, and who must set before the Meeting a detailed statement of the sums of money needed for local government. These sums, if approved, are voted by the Meeting and their collection ordered, on a prescribed basis of assessment. Everything that the officials and committees of the town have done is subject to be criticised, everything that they are to do is subject to be regulated by the Meeting.

The Town Officers. — The officers of the town are certain 'Selectmen,' from three to nine in number, according to the size and needs of the town, who constitute the general executive authority for all matters not otherwise assigned; a Town Clerk, who is the keeper of the town records and registers; a Treasurer; Assessors, whose duty it is to make valuation of all property for tax assessment; a Collector of the taxes voted by the Meeting or required by the county and state authorities; a School Committee; and a variety of lesser officers of minor function, such as Constables, together with certain committees, such as library trustees, etc. Generally there are also overseers of the poor and surveyors of highways.

To this corps of officers all the functions of local government belong. The county authorities cannot enter their

[1] In Connecticut in the autumn.

[2] In some of the coast towns (townships), as notably in Connecticut, the regulation of the use of the oyster beds is a very prominent question in town-meeting.

domain, but must confine themselves to the judicial duties proper to them and to such administrative matters as the laying out of inter-town roads, the issuing of certain county licenses, the maintenance of county buildings, etc., for the due oversight of which larger areas than the town seem necessary. County expenses are defrayed by taxes raised by the towns: the county authorities apportion such taxes, but do not lay them.

> In Rhode Island the only county officials are those connected with the administration of justice.

The Township of the Northwest. — The town may, therefore, be said to exist in New England in its full historical character and simplicity, though much overshadowed by great cities, and everywhere modified and partially subordinated by the later developments of state and county. In the *Northwest*, whither New England emigrants have gone, it has entered another phase and taken on another character, — a character which may perhaps foreshadow its ultimate organization, should the country have at any future time the uniform practices of local government now dimly promised by certain incipient forces of institutional interchange and imitation.

In the first place, the Northwestern township is more thoroughly integrated with the county than is the New England township. County and township fit together as pieces of the same organism. In New England the township is older than the county, and the county is a grouping of townships for certain purposes; in the Northwest, on the contrary, the county has in all cases preceded the township, and townships are divisions of the county.

The county preceded the township because the county furnishes, for our people, the natural basis of organization for a scattered agricultural population; the township came afterwards, in obedience to the habit of the New England settlers, as the natural organization for a population which had become more numerous and which had drawn together into closer association.

Its Origin. — It was *school organization* that supplied the beginnings of the township system in all the more newly settled portions of the country. The Western township has sprung out

of the school as the New England township of the earliest days
sprang out of the church. The government surveyor, who has
everywhere preceded final settlement in the West, has in all cases
mapped out the land in regular plots of thirty-six square miles
each, which, for convenience, he called 'townships'; and in every
township Congress has reserved at least a square mile of land
(one 'section') for the endowment of schools. This endowment
had to be administered by the settlers; school organization had
to be effected; the name *township* had already been given to
the district so endowed; and there was, therefore, naturally
school organization on the basis of the township. From this
there eventually issued an equally natural growth of local political institutions.[1]

Spread of Township Organization. — In the newer portions of the country the development of the township has progressed almost in direct ratio with the development of local
government : in many sections, even where population is comparatively dense, county organization has been made to suffice
for such districts as have not assumed the structure and privileges of village or city incorporation ; but wherever any special
effort has been made to perfect local rural organization for administrative purposes, the township has been accepted as the best
model of political association.

> It has received its widest acceptance in such middle states as
> New York and Pennsylvania, and in the great Northwestern states of
> Michigan, Wisconsin, Illinois, and Minnesota. Elsewhere, in the middle
> West, in Ohio, Indiana, and Kansas, for example, and in such states of
> the far West as California, it is less fully developed, and occupies a much
> more subordinate place as compared with the county. The county,
> indeed, may be said to be the prevalent unit of local government in Cali-
> fornia, as well as in Colorado, Oregon, Nebraska, and Nevada.

Township Organization. — The *organization* of the township outside of New England varies with its development.
Where it is most vigorous there is the town-meeting, exercising powers strictly defined and circumscribed by statute and
somewhat less extensive than the powers of the town-meeting in

[1] See p. 10 of *Local Government in Illinois*, by Dr. Albert Shaw (Johns
Hopkins Studies in Historical and Political Science, First Series).

New England, but still covering a multitude of local interests and representing a very real control. Where it is less developed there is no town-meeting, but instead only the processes of popular election to local office. In all cases the 'selectmen' have disappeared : at least we find no officers bearing their name, and no officers possessing exactly their functions. Where the township is most completely organized we find one or more 'supervisors' standing at the front of township administration, who are clothed with the duties of overseers of the poor, exercise oftentimes a certain control over the finances of the township, and are in general function the presiding and directing authorities of the administration.

Where there are several supervisors or trustees in the township, it is common to associate them together as a Board, and under such an arrangement they very closely resemble the New England board of selectmen in their administrative functions. Township boards also exist under the laws of some states in which there is but a single supervisor for each township, being composed, usually, besides the supervisor, of such officers as the town clerk and the Justices of the Peace. In Michigan such a board has rather extensive supervisory powers ; in Illinois it is a committee of audit simply.

The number of township officers varies with the degree of development to which the township system has attained. In Ohio, where the system is still more or less in germ, there are, besides the three trustees, no township officers save a clerk and a treasurer.

In Michigan, even, where the township system is fully accepted, there is neither an assessor nor a collector of taxes, the supervisor acting as assessor and the treasurer as collector. In Illinois, on the other hand, there is always a full corps of officers : supervisor, collector, assessor, clerk, commissioners of highways, justices of the peace, constables, etc., — and for the school township a body of school trustees.

The term of all officers except justices of the peace, road and school commissioners, and constables is generally but a single year, as in New England ; the terms of the other officers named are often three or four years. Where there is a town-meeting the officers are elected by it; where there is no town-meeting they are chosen at the polls.

The Township in the Middle Atlantic States. — It is reversing the historical order to speak of the townships of the middle Atlantic states after discussing the townships of the newer West; but it is not reversing the order of convenient exposition. The processes of formation are plainly visible in the West; in the East they are more complex and obscure, being the formations of history rather than of legislation.

The New York township is like the townships of Michigan and Illinois in its structure and functions; but like because it is an original, not because it is a copy. Over it presides a single supervisor who is the treasurer and general financial officer of the area. It has its clerk, its assessor, its collector, its commissioners of highways, its constables, its justices of the peace. It has also special overseers of the poor. An annual town-meeting, under the presidency of the justices of the peace, or of the town clerk, elects all officers, passes sundry by-laws, votes taxes for schools and poor relief, and constitutes the general governing authority.

In counties containing 300,000 or more inhabitants there is a provision for the election of township officers at the polls.

The Pennsylvania Township. — The New York township system suggested the system of the states about the lakes, and stands nearest in the order of development to the township of New England. The township of Pennsylvania, on the other hand, suggests the township system of the next lower belt of middle Western states. In it there is no town-meeting, but only an executive machinery. A board of two or three supervisors, holding for a term of three years, presides over the township, and has as its most prominent function the care of highways. For the rest, there are the usual officers, with the somewhat uncommon addition of the auditors. Where the township is charged with the care of the poor, two special overseers are elected.

Origins of Local Government in the Middle States. — Local government in New York, Pennsylvania, Delaware, and most of New Jersey runs back, as to a common source, to the system established in colonial times by the Duke of York as proprietor. Under that system the township was the principal organ of local government. Its officers were certain constables and overseers; and above the township was only an artificial ' Riding,' presided over by a sheriff. Certain General Courts levied highway and poor rates, appointed overseers of highways, etc. After the period of the Duke's proprietorship, the development of local government in the several parts of his domain exhibited a considerable variety. The township retained its importance in New York, but further south, particularly in Pennsylvania, the county gained the superior place.

The Township in the South. — Wherever, in the South, the principle of local taxation for local schools has been fully recognized, there the township has begun to show itself, at least in bud. Virginia, the oldest of the southern states, and in most respects the type of all the rest in institutional development, for six years (1868–1874) tried the township system in its full form. But the experiment proved unsatisfactory. The system, instead of being gradually introduced and allowed to take a normal way of growth, was adopted whole, proved too artificial, and was very soon abolished by constitutional amendment. North Carolina and West Virginia have adopted a township system of a very much more rudimentary sort, and with better results in practical administration.

The County. — The division of power between township and county can be most intelligibly discussed in connection with the following outline of county organization. The natural history of the county is best studied in the South, where, despite the partial adoption of township organization here and there, the county remains the chief and almost the only organ of local order and government. We have seen (pages 271–273) how natural a basis of government it was for a widespread agricultural population. The county was imported into the West by Southern settlers, and also found there at first its natural reason for existence in a similarly diffused population. New England immigration and new conditions of industrial and social combination have created the township within the county in the West, as similarly altered conditions have begun to create it in the South also.

In all cases, it would seem, the county was originated primarily for judicial purposes, as an area in and for which courts were to be held, though in such confederate colonies as Connecticut it was also in part the outgrowth of the union of different groups of once independent towns. In the South the county became also the single area for the administrative organization of local government, being given the functions elsewhere divided between the county and smaller areas like the township. In New England certain general functions of a limited character have been conferred upon it by subtraction from the townships. In the Northwest, county and township have been created almost simultaneously and side by side, and are carefully integrated.

The American county was of course in the first instance a frontier copy of the English shire; but its growth affords no analogy to the growth of its English prototype. The English shire in a great many instances traces its history back to the time when it was a separate Saxon kingdom, and may be said to have as natural boundaries as France; American counties, on the other hand, have all been deliberately 'laid out,' as judicial and administrative subdivisions, and have no such independent historical standing.

The Southern county, which undertakes all of local administration, has a complete set of officers. At its head is a small board of *county commissioners.* Acting under the general superintendence of the commissioners, there are generally a county treasurer, auditor, superintendent of roads, superintendent of education, and superintendent of the poor. On its judicial side, the county has its sheriff, its clerk, its ordinary or surrogate, its coroner, and its state-attorney, the latter generally acting for a judicial district inclusive of several counties. The functions of the county embrace the oversight of education, the maintenance of jails and poorhouses, the construction and repair of highways, and all local matters. County officers are in almost all instances elected by popular vote. Under the Southern county system the sheriff is commonly also tax-collector.

Where the township exists there is great variety of county organization, almost the only point of common likeness being the organization of justice. The county always has its sheriff, and generally its separate courts, with the usual coroner and clerk. The variety shows itself in the field of administrative structure. Sometimes, as in New York, Michigan, and Illinois, the county administrative authority is a board composed of the supervisors of all the townships; sometimes, as in Pennsylvania and Minnesota, the county authority is a board of three commissioners. In Wisconsin the county board consists of members each of whom is chosen by two or more townships. Where the county is given least power, as in New England, its administrative functions hardly extend beyond the maintenance of county buildings such as the jail and courthouse, the granting of certain licenses, and the partial supervision of the highway system. In New York and the Northwest the county authorities often undertake the relief of the poor, sometimes exercise an extensive control over the debt-contracting privileges of the smaller areas, often audit the accounts of local officers, and supervise taxation for purposes of equalization.

Where townships exist, then, the division of functions may be said to be as follows: the township is the area for the administration of schools, for the relief of the poor (unless by special popular vote this function be given to the county), police, the construction and maintenance of highways, and sanitation ; while the county is the area for the administration of justice, for the maintenance of jails, courthouses, and sometimes poorhouses, for tax equalization, and often for the exercise of certain other general supervisory powers.

Villages, Boroughs, Cities. — Counties and townships are areas of rural organization only. With the compacting of population in great towns and cities other and more elaborate means of organization became necessary, and a great body of constitutional and statutory law has grown up in the states concerning the incorporation of urban areas. There is no complete and general municipal corporations act in any of our states such as that under which, in England, cities of all sizes may acquire the privileges and adopt the organization of full borough government (page 240): the largest towns are left to depend for their incor-

poration upon special acts of legislation. The large cities of the country consequently exhibit a great variety of political structure, and even cities in the same state often differ widely in many material points of organization and function.

. The electors or freeholders of less populous urban dis-tricts are in most of the states empowered to obtain a simple sort of urban organization and considerable urban powers, by certain uniform routine processes, from the courts of law; *villages* (as they are called in New York), *boroughs* (as they are styled in Pennsylvania), *towns* (as they are sometimes designated in the South),[1] *cities of the lesser grades* (in states where towns are classi-fied according to population), may usually get from the courts as of course, upon proof of the necessary population and of the con-sent of the freeholders or electors, the privilege of erecting them-selves into municipal corporations under general acts passed for the purpose; very much as private joint-stock companies may get leave to incorporate upon showing to the court evidence of the possession of the necessary membership, stock, or paid-up capital.

> The town or borough is, however, a public, not a private, corpo-ration, receiving by delegation certain powers of government; and many states have left with their legislatures the power to create all public cor-porations by special act. The incorporation of towns is not, therefore, universally governed by general statute.

The Authorities of urban districts thus erected into separate corporations succeed, generally, to all the powers of township officers within their area and constitute a local body apart; but usually the area thus incorporated does not cease to be a part of the county in which it lies. It continues to pay county taxes and its electors continue to take their part in the choice of county officials. In some cases, however, cities have been definitely separated from the counties in which they lie. This has been the virtually uniform policy of Virginia. In other cases cities have by growth absorbed the counties in which they were situated, as has happened, for example, by the expansion of New York, Philadelphia, New Orleans, and San Francisco. Balti-more and St. Louis have been made independent of county gov-

---

[1] The name *town* when used in New England always means, not an urban district, but a town*ship*.

ernment and county obligations by special legal arrangement. The organization of incorporated towns is unlike that of either county or township principally in this, that they have at the front of their government a representative council which within its sphere is a law-making authority.

A common model of organization for the smaller urban areas is : a mayor, president, or chief burgess ; a small town council given extensive power of making by-laws, considerable power of taxation for local improvements as well as for local administration, and other powers of local direction which quite sharply differentiate it from the merely executive boards often found in the townships and always found in the counties ; a treasurer ; a clerk ; a collector; a street commissioner ; sometimes overseers of the poor ; and generally such other minor officers as the council sees fit to appoint.

Organization of Government in Cities. — The difference between the organization of these smaller urban areas and the organization of great cities is a difference of complexity not only but often also a difference of kind. Cities, we have seen (page 324), are often given a separate judicial organization, being made in effect separate judicial circuits or counties, with their own courts, sheriffs, coroners, and state-attorneys ; and are sometimes also made quite independent of the counties in which they lie (page 349). They are given also larger councils, with larger powers ; a larger corps of officers ; and greater energy of self-direction than other local areas possess.

The Council of a great city usually consists of two sections or ' houses,' — a board of *aldermen* and a board of *common councilmen*, differing very much as the two houses of a state legislature differ, in the number and size of the districts which their members represent. In most of the cities of New York state, however, there is but a single legislative chamber, called sometimes the Board of Aldermen, sometimes the Common Council.

These boards always constitute the law-making (or rather *ordinance*-making) and taxing power of the city ; and always until recent years they have been constituted overseers of administration also, by being given the power to control it not only by withholding moneys, but also through direct participation in the power of appointment to the minor city offices, — all those, that is to say, not filled by popular election. The chief officers of every city have usually been elected, but all others have, as a rule, been appointed by the mayor subject to confirmation by the city council. The tendency of all very recent legislation with reference to the constitution of city governments has been to concentrate executive power, and consequently executive responsibility, in the hands of the mayor, leaving to the council only its ordinance-making power and its function of financial control. Some of the most recent charters have even extended the appointing power of the mayor so as to include the most important executive offices of the city administration. Local bills are submitted to the mayors of the cities which they affect, for their approval. But, if they do not approve, the repassage of the act by a mere majority in the legislature suffices to make it law, notwithstanding.

Commission Form of Government. — The most recent development in municipal government is the commission form, where the old form of organization, consisting of a mayor and an elected council, has been replaced by a single elective commission, small in number, which combines in itself both executive and legislative functions. The commission form has been widely adopted in smaller towns and cities, in a few cities of size, but not in any of the very largest cities. Its merit lies in the concentration of powers in the hands of a few men whom it is easier to hold responsible than was formerly the case when authority was divided and parceled out among many. In some cities the plan has been introduced of selecting a city manager, who under the control of the commission, by whom he is appointed and removed, is the actual administrative head of the city government.

School Administration. — Wherever the public school exists there we find the school district the usual administrative area for educational purposes. Where the county system prevails the county is divided into school districts; where the township system prevails the township is divided into school districts. In every case there are district directors or trustees who control school administration, and usually control it so entirely as to prevent in great part the existence of any uniform system of education for the whole state; but where the township system prevails there is generally more participation on the part of the people, gathered in district-meeting, in school administration, and generally a fuller power of local taxation.

In New England recent years have been witnessing the disappearance of the separate school district in some states, and its absorption by the township. Thus in Maine, in New Hampshire, and in Connecticut school administration is being transferred from district to township officers, and the township is being made the school area. In Massachusetts the school district system was entirely abolished in 1882, and township school administration substituted. And outside New England the same substitution has here and there been made, — as, for example, in Pennsylvania.

In the Northwest schools usually receive support from three distinct sources: from the land granted to each township by the federal government; from a general state tax for education, whose proceeds are distributed among the townships, to be further distributed by the township authorities among the districts; and from district taxes levied by the district directors. In New England there is generally state and township taxation for the support of the schools. In the South, under the county system, there is state taxation only, for the most part, save in certain exceptional localities, and in the greater towns. In many cases in the Northwest the school district is coincident in area with the civil township, though distinct and separate in organization.

Nowhere is there sufficient centralization of control. State superintendents or other central educational authorities are without real administrative powers (compare page 335); county superintendents seldom have much authority; township trustees or committees, as a rule, have little more than a general supervision and power of advice; usually the directors of the smallest area have the greater part of the total of administrative authority, applying their *quota* of even the state taxes according to their own discretion. The result is, variety in the qualifications of teachers, variety in the method of their choice, variety in courses of study, variety in general efficiency.

Taxation. — The most striking feature regarding local taxation in the United States is the strict limitations put upon it by constitution or statute. Commonly no local authorities can tax beyond a certain fixed percentage of the appraised value of the property of their district. Under the county system, requisition is made upon the officers of the counties for the taxes voted by the legislature for state purposes, and the county boards raise them, together with the county taxes, upon the basis of the county assessment. Where the township exists, the process goes one step further: requistion is made upon the townships for both the state and county taxes, and the townships raise these, together with their own taxes, upon the basis of the assessment made by their own assessors.

An effort is made in most of the states, however, to equalize assessments. Some county authority acts as *a board of equalization* with reference to the assessments returned by the assessors of the several townships, and above the equalization boards of the counties there is generally a state board of equalization, whose duty it is to harmonize and equalize, upon appeal, taxation in the several counties. Appeals always lie from the local assessors to these boards of equalization. The system is, however, only partially successful. It has proved practically impossible, under the present system of localized authority, to avoid great varieties and inequalities of assessment: local officials try to cut down the shares of their districts in the general taxes as much as possible.

General Remarks on Local Government. — Several features observable in our systems of local government taken as a whole are worthy of remark. (1) In the first place, outside of the towns and cities, the separately incorporated urban districts, there is a marked absence of representative, law-making bodies. Almost everywhere local officers and boards have merely executive powers and move within narrow limits set by elaborate statute law.

(2) In the second place, where there are local law-making bodies, they act under strict constitutional law: under charters, that is, possessing thus a strong resemblance, of *kind*, to state legislatures themselves.

(3) In the third place, central control of local authorities exists only in the enforcement, in the regular law courts, of charters and general laws: there is nowhere any central Local Government Board with discretionary powers of restriction or permission (page 246).

(4) In the fourth place, relatively to the central organs of the state, local government is, administratively, the most vital part of our system: as compared either with the federal government or with local authorities, the central governments of the states lack vitality not only, but do not seem to be holding their own in point of importance. They count for much in legislation, but, so far, for very little in administration.

THE FEDERAL GOVERNMENT.

The Constitution of the United States does not contain all the rules upon which the organization of the federal government rests. It says that there shall be a Congress which shall exercise the law-making power granted to the general government; a President who shall be charged with the execution of the laws passed by Congress; and a Supreme Court which shall be the highest court of the land for the determination of what is lawful to be done, either by individuals, by the state governments, or by the federal authorities, under the Constitution and laws. It prescribes also in part the organization of Congress. But it does not command how Congress shall do its work of legislation, how the President shall be enabled to perform his great function, or by what machinery of officers and subordinate courts the Supreme Court shall be assisted in the exercise of its powers. It leaves all detail of operation to be arranged by statute: and statute accordingly plays an all-important part in the organization of the government.

The Constitution furnishes only the great foundations of the system. Those foundations rest upon the same firm ground of popular assent that supports the several constitutions of the states. Framed by a federal convention and adopted by representative conventions in the states, it stands altogether apart from ordinary law both in character and sanction.

Amendment of the Constitution. — The Constitution cannot be amended without the consent of two-thirds of Congress and three-fourths of the states. Amendments may be *proposed* in one of two ways: either (*a*) two-thirds of the members of each house of Congress may agree that certain amendments are necessary; or (*b*) the legislatures of two-thirds of the states may petition Congress to have a general convention called for the consideration of amendments, and such a convention, being called, may propose changes. In both cases the mode of *adoption* is the same. Every change proposed must be submitted to the states, to be voted upon either by their legislatures or by state conventions called for the purpose, as Congress may determine. Any amendment which is agreed to by three-fourths of the states becomes a part of the Constitution.

The seventeen amendments so far made to the Constitution were all proposed by Congress. No general constitutional convention has been called since the adjournment of the great body by which the Constitution was framed in 1787.

None of the written constitutions of Europe is so difficult of alteration as our own. In Germany a provision changing the imperial constitution passes just as an ordinary law would pass, the only limitation upon its passage being that fourteen negative votes in the *Bundesrat* will defeat it (14 out of 58). In France (pages 154, 155) constitutional amendments pass as ordinary laws do, except that they must be adopted by the two houses of the legislature acting, not separately in Paris, but jointly at Versailles, as a National Assembly. In Switzerland such amendments must pass both houses of the federal legislature and must also be approved, in a popular vote, by a majority of the voters, *and* by a majority of the Cantons. In England the distinction between constitutional law and statute law can hardly be said to exist.

The Federal Territory. — The territory of the United States is of three different sorts : there is (*a*) the District of Columbia, over which the nation exercises exclusive jurisdiction as the seat of its government, and the arsenals and dock-yards, which it has acquired by purchase, and over which the states have given it jurisdiction for military purposes; and (*b*) the great national property, the territories, which the federal authorities hold in trust for the nation as a seed-bed for the development of new states, and (*c*) the dependencies.

The District of Columbia. — It would have been inconvenient for the federal government to have no territory of its own on which to build its public offices and legislative halls, and where it could be independent of local or other state regulations. The Constitution itself therefore provided that Congress should have exclusive authority within any district not more than ten miles square which any state might grant to the federal government for its own uses. Acting upon this hint, Maryland and Virginia promptly granted the necessary territorial jurisdiction, it having been decided to establish the seat of government upon the Potomac. A part of the home-land of the federal government, thus ceded, was laid out under the name of the *District of Columbia :* there the public buildings were erected, and there, after the removal of the government offices thither in 1800, the city of Washington grew up.

The first Congress of the United States met in New York City ; there the first President was inaugurated, and the organization of the new government effected. In 1790 it was determined that the federal officers should live and Congress meet in Philadelphia (as the Continental Congress had generally done) for ten years ; after that, in the district specially set apart for the use of the federal government.

The creation of this federal home-plot is a feature peculiar to our own federal arrangements. Berlin is the capital of Prussia, not the exclusive seat, or in any sense the property, of the imperial government. Berne, too, is cantonal, not federal, ground. Our government would have been in the same case as those of Germany and Switzerland had our federal authorities remained the guests of New York or Pennsylvania.

The several *arsenals, dock-yards, forts, and light-houses* established by the federal government in different parts of the Union are built upon land purchased by the federal government, generally of individuals. It is the practice for the several states in which such pieces of property lie to grant to the federal government exclusive jurisdiction over them, — usually with the proviso that the jurisdiction shall lapse when the property ceases to be used for the federal purposes specified.

The Territories. — As the different parts of our vast national domain have been settled it has been divided, under the direction of Congress, into portions of various sizes, generally about the area of the larger states, though sometimes larger than any state save Texas. These portions have been called, for want of a better name, *Territories,* and have been given governments constituted by federal statute. First they have been given governors and judges appointed by the President; then, as their population has become numerous and sufficiently settled in its ways of living, they have been given legislatures chosen by their own people and clothed with the power to make laws subject to the approval of Congress; finally, upon becoming still more developed, they have been granted as full law-making powers as the states. The territorial stage of their development passed, they have one by one been brought into the Union as states. The only territories remaining are Alaska and Hawaii.

Until 1803 the only territory of the United States consisted of the lands east of the Mississippi which had belonged to the thirteen original states individually, and had by them been granted to the general government. In 1803 the vast tract known as Louisiana was bought; in 1848, by conquest, and in 1852, by negotiation, the Pacific coast lands were acquired from Mexico; in 1846 the right of the United States to a portion of the Oregon country was finally established, by treaty.

The Dependencies. — With the acquisition of Porto Rico and the Philippines as a result of the war with Spain, the United States acquired non-contiguous lands, already inhabited by peoples differing from ourselves in language, customs and institutions. Unlike the territory previously acquired, — with the exception of Alaska and Hawaii, — the insular possessions are not adapted for the progressive development from territories to states. They are dependencies, and will remain as such until they reach the stage when they may become independent or self-governing.

The post-offices, federal court chambers, custom-houses, and other like buildings erected and owned by the general government in various parts of the country, are held by the government upon the ordinary principles of ownership, just as they might be held by a private corporation. Their sites are not separate federal territory.

Congress. — As in the states, so in the federal government, the law-making power is vested in a double legislature, a Congress consisting of a Senate and a House of Representatives. Unlike the two houses of a state legislature, however, the two houses of Congress have distinct characters: the Senate differs from the House not only in the number of its members, but also in the principle of its composition. It represents the federal principle upon which the government rests, for its members represent the states. The House of Representatives, on the other hand, represents the national principle, upon which also the government has now been finally established, without threat of change. Its members represent the people.

The Senate. — The Senate consists of two representatives from each of the states of the Union. It has, therefore, the states being forty-eight in number, ninety-six members. Each senator is elected, for a term of six years, by the people of the state which he represents; and a state is legally free to choose any one as senator who has been a citizen of the United States nine years, who has reached the age of thirty, and who is at the time of the election a resident of the state which he is chosen to represent.

The Constitution directed that, immediately after coming together for its first session, the Senate should divide its members, by lot, as nearly as it could into three equal groups; that the members assigned to one of these groups should vacate their seats after the expiration of two years, the members assigned to another after the expiration of four years, and the members of the third after the expiration of six years; after which arrangement had been accomplished, the term of every senator was to be six years as provided. It was thus brought about that one-third of the membership of the Senate is renewed by election every two years. The result is, that the Senate has a sort of continuous life, — no one election year affects the seats of more than one-third of its members.

The Senate is the *federal* house of Congress. Its members represent the states as the constituent members of the Union. They are not, however, in any sense delegates of the governments of the states. They are not subject to be instructed as to their votes, as members of the German *Bundesrat* are, by any state authority. Each senator is entitled and expected to vote according to his own individual opinion. Senators, therefore, may be said to represent, not the governments of the states, but the people of the states organized as corporate bodies politic.

There is no rule which obliges senators from the same state to vote together after the fashion once imperative in the Congress of our own Confederation, and still imperative in the German *Bundesrat* (p. 288). Each senator represents his state, not in partnership, but singly.

The *equal* representation of the states in the Senate more strictly conforms to the federal principle than does the unequal representation characteristic of the German *Bundesrat* ; but the rule observed in Germany, that the representatives of each state must vote together, must, in turn, be admitted to be more strictly consistent with the idea of state representation than is the rule of individual voting followed in our Senate.

The Vice-President of the United States is president of the Senate. Unless the President die, this is the only function of the Vice-President. He is not a member of the Senate ; he simply presides over its sessions. He has a vote only when the votes of the senators are equally divided upon some question and his vote becomes necessary for a decision. If the President die or resign, or be removed from office, or be rendered unable " to discharge the duties and powers " of his office, the presidency devolves on the Vice-President.

Organization of the Senate. — The Senate makes its own rules of procedure, the Vice-President being of course bound to administer whatever rule it adopts. Naturally the internal organization of the body is the matter with which its rules principally concern themselves, and the most important feature of that organization is the division of the members of the Senate into standing committees ; into small groups, that is, to each of which is entrusted the preparation of a certain part of the Senate's business. The Senate itself would not have time to look into the antecedents and particulars, the merits and bearings, of every matter brought before it ; these committees are, therefore, constituted to act in its stead in the preliminary examination and shaping of the measures to be voted on. Whenever any proposal is made concerning any important question, that proposal is referred to the standing committee which has been commissioned to consider questions of the class to which the proposed action belongs. The committee takes the proposal under consideration, in connection with all other pending proposals relating to the same subject, and reports to the Senate what it thinks ought to be done with reference to it, — whether it is advisable to take any action or not, and, if it is advisable to act, what action had best be taken.

> Thus there is a Committee on Finance, to which all questions affecting the revenue are referred; a Committee on Appropriations, which advises the Senate concerning all votes for the spending of moneys; a Committee on Railroads, which considers all railroad questions; a Committee on Foreign Affairs, which prepares for consideration all questions touching our relations with foreign governments, etc.

Influence of the Standing Committees. — Its standing committees have a very great influence upon the action of the Senate. The Senate is naturally always inclined to listen to their advice, for each committee necessarily knows much more about the subjects assigned to it for consideration than the rest of the senators can know. Its committee organization may be said to be of the essence of the legislative action of the Senate: for the leadership to which a legislative body consigns itself is of the essence of its method and must affect, not the outward form merely, but the whole character also of its action. Under every great system of government except our own, leadership in legislation belongs for the most part to the ministers, to the Executive, which stands nearest to the business of governing; it is a central, and, as evidenced by its results, extremely important characteristic of our system that our legislatures *lead themselves*, or, rather, that they suffer themselves to be led along the several lines of legislation by separate and disconnected groups of their members.

> **The Senate and the Executive.** — One of the chief uses of the committees is to obtain information for the Senate concerning the affairs of the government. But, inasmuch as the executive branch of the government is quite separate from Congress, it is often very difficult for the Senate to find out through its committees all that it wishes to know about the condition of affairs in the executive departments. The action of the two houses upon some questions must of course be greatly influenced, and

should be greatly influenced, by what they can learn of administrative experience in the departments, and the Senate, as well as the House, has the right to ask what questions it pleases of executive officers, either through its committees or by requiring a written report to be made directly to itself by some head of a department. Upon financial questions, for example, the Senate or its Finance Committee must constantly wish to know the experience of the Treasury. But it is not always easy to get legislative questions fully and correctly answered ; for the officers of the government are in no way responsible to either house for their official conduct. They belong to an entirely separate and independent branch of the government : only such high crimes and misdemeanors as lay them open to impeachment expose them to the power of the houses. The committees are, therefore, frequently prevented from doing their work of inquiry well, and the Senate has to act in the dark. Under other systems of government, the ministers are always present in the legislative bodies to be questioned and dealt with, directly, face to face.

The President Pro Tempore. — It is the practice of the Senate to make itself independent of all chances of the Vice-President's absence by electing statedly from its own membership a president *pro tempore*, to act in case of the absence or disability of the Vice-President.

The House of Representatives. — The House of Representatives represents, not the states, but the people of the United States. It represents them, however, not in the mass, but by states. Representation is apportioned among the states severally according to population, and no electoral district crosses any state boundary.

Apportionment of Representatives. — Congress itself decides by law how many representatives there shall be; it then divides the number decided upon among the states according to population ; after which each state is divided by its own legislature into as many districts as it is to have representatives, and the people of each of these districts are entitled to elect one member to the House. The only limitation put by the Constitution itself upon the number of representatives is, that there shall never be more than one for every thirty thousand inhabitants. The first House of Representatives had, by direction of the Constitution itself, sixty-five members, upon the proportion of one to every thirty-three thousand inhabitants. The number has, of course, grown, and the proportion decreased, with the growth of population. A census is taken every ten years, and the rule is to effect readjustments and a redistribution of representation after every census.

In states which send but one representative (there are now — 1918 — five of these), the representative is chosen by the voters of the whole state. In some of the other states also it sometimes happens that one or more representatives are chosen thus 'at large,' pending a redistribution among districts, — or for some other reason.

At present there are four hundred and thirty-five members in the House, and the states are given one member for every 211,877 of their inhabitants. In cases where a state has many thousands more than an even number of times that many inhabitants, it is given an additional member to represent the balance. Thus, if it have four times 211,877 inhabitants and a very large fraction over, it is given five members instead of four only. If any state have less than 211,877, it is given one member, notwithstanding, being entitled to at least one by constitutional provision. The reason for allowing a state an extra representative when there is a large fraction remaining over after a division of its population by the standard number is that the apportionment of representatives is made according to states, and not by an even allotment among the people of the country taken as a whole, and that under such a system a perfectly equal division of representation is practically impossible. Congress makes the most equitable arrangement practicable each time it reapportions the membership of the House upon the basis of the decennial census which Congress directs to be taken for this purpose in pursuance of a special constitutional command.

Elections to the House. — Any one may be chosen a representative who has reached the age of twenty-five years, has been a citizen of the United States for seven years, and is at the time of his election an inhabitant of the state from which he is chosen. The term of a representative is two years : and two years is also the term of the whole House; for its members are not chosen a section at a time, as the senators are ; the whole membership of the House is renewed every second year. Each biennial election creates ' a new House.'

Although the Senate has a continuous life, we speak habitually of different ' Congresses,' as if a new *Congress*, instead of a new House of Representatives merely, were chosen biennially. Thus the Congress of

1917–1919 is known as the sixty-fifth Congress, because the House of Representatives of that period is the sixty-fifth that has been elected since the government was established.

Federal law does not determine who shall vote for members of the House of Representatives. The Constitution provides, simply, that all those persons in each state who are qualified under the constitution and laws of the state to vote for members of the larger of the two houses of the state legislature may vote also for members of the House of Representatives of the United States. The franchise is regulated, therefore, entirely by state law.

In the fourteenth amendment to the Constitution (passed 1866–1868) a very great pressure is, by intention at least, brought to bear upon the states to induce them to make their franchise as wide as their adult male population. For that amendment provides that, should any state deny to any of its male citizens who are twenty-one years of age the privilege of voting for members of the more numerous branch of its own legislature (and thus, by consequence, the privilege of voting for representatives in Congress), for any reason except that they have committed crime, its representation in Congress shall be curtailed in the same proportion that the number of persons thus excluded from the franchise bears to the whole number of male citizens twenty-one years of age in the state. This provision has in practice, however, proved of little value. It is practically impossible for the federal authorities to carry it satisfactorily into effect.

Organization of the House. — The House, like the Senate, has its own rules, regulative of the number and duties of its officers and of its methods of doing business; and these rules, like those of the Senate, are chiefly concerned with the creation and the privileges of a great number of standing committees. The committees of the House were until **1910** appointed by the presiding officer of the House, the 'Speaker'[1];

[1] The House of Representatives is not given a president by the Constitution, as the Senate is. It elects its own presiding officer, whose name, of 'Speaker,' is taken from the usage of the English House of Commons, whose president was so called because whenever, in the old days, the Commons went into the presence of the king for the purpose of laying some matter before him, or of answering a summons from him, their president

and this power of the Speaker to appoint the committees of the House made him one of the most powerful officers in the whole government. For the committees of the House are even more influential than those of the Senate in determining what shall be done with reference to matters referred to them. They as a matter of fact have it in their power to control almost all the acts of the House. The Senate, being a comparatively small body, has time to consider very fully the reports of its committees, and generally manages to shape its own conclusions. But the House is too large to do much debating : it must be guided by its committees or it must do nothing. It is this fact which made the Speaker's power of appointment so vastly important. He determined who should be on the committees, and the committees determined what the House should do. He nominated those who shaped legislation. More than that, he shaped the rules and determined the course of business. For he was chairman of the Committee on Rules, which had but four other members, whom be regarded as his 'assistants,' and that committee guided the House quite absolutely in the use of its time. The Speaker will not 'recognize' (that is, will not give the floor to) any member who seeks to upset the programme it has fixed.

The extraordinary power of the Speaker often made his election a very exciting part of the business of each new House : for he was always selected with reference to what he would do in constituting the principal committees, and in shaping and administering the rules.

So great had become the power of the Speaker, not only to control legislation but also to discipline recalcitrant members, and so arbitrarily did Speaker Cannon exercise his power, that at length opposition developed within his own party, the 'insurgents,' who finally in 1910 combined with the Democrats to change the Committee on Rules. It was enlarged from five to ten members, six of the majority and four of the minority party, elected by the House, and the Speaker was deprived of his membership.

was their spokesman or Speaker. This name is used also in the legislative bodies of all the English colonies, — wherever, indeed, English legislative practices have been directly inherited.

In the next session the Democratic party had a majority in the House and it carried through a complete change in the method of constituting committees. The House now elects its own committees, and in practice the following method is used. Each party holds a caucus which elects a party committee on committees. These party committees select the party members for committees; the names thus selected are nominated to the House by the respective party committees and the House elects the members thus nominated. These changes have taken away much of the Speaker's power and have placed it in the hands of the party leaders, for the party committees on committees are naturally composed of the party leaders. The autocratic character of the Speaker's power has been replaced by a more democratic control by the party. Yet the influence of the Speaker is still great, and more than any one individual he can aid or hinder legislation.

The House has so many standing committees that every representative is a member of one or another of them, — but many of the committees have little or nothing to do. Some of them, though still regularly appointed, have no duties assigned them by the rules. One of the most important committees is that on Appropriations, which has charge of the general money-spending bills introduced every year to meet the expenses of the government, and which, by virtue of its power under the rules to bring its reports to the consideration of the House at any time, to the thrusting aside of whatever matter, virtually dominates the House by controlling its use of its time. Special appropriation bills, which propose to provide moneys for the expenses of single departments, — as, for example, the Navy Department or the War Department, — are, by a rule of the House, taken out of the hands of the Committee on Appropriations and given to the committees on the special departments concerned. Scarcely less important than the Committee on Appropriations, though scarcely so busy as it, is the Committee on Ways and Means, which has charge of questions of taxation.

The House has to depend, just as the Senate does, upon its standing committees for information concerning the affairs of the government and the policy of the executive departments, and is just as often and as much embarrassed because of its entire exclusion from easy, informal, and regular intercourse with the departments. They cannot advise the House unless they are asked for their advice; and the House cannot ask for their advice except indirectly through its committees, or formally by requiring written reports.

Acts of Congress. — In order to become a law or Act of Congress a bill must pass both houses and receive the signature of the President. Such is the ordinary process of legislation. But the President may withhold his signature, and in that case the measure which he has refused to sanction must receive the votes of two-thirds of the members of each house, given upon a reconsideration, before it can go upon the statute book. The President is given ten days for the consideration of each measure. If he take no action upon it within the ten days, or if within that period he sign it, its provisions become law; if within the ten days he inform Congress by special message that he will not sign the bill, returning it to the house in which it originated with a statement of his reasons for not signing it, another passage of the measure by a majority of two-thirds in each house is required to make it a law.

There are, therefore, three ways in which a bill may become law: either (a) by receiving the approval of a majority in each house, and the signature of the President, appended within ten days after its passage by the houses; or (b) by receiving the approval of a majority in each house, and not being acted upon by the President within ten days after its passage; or (c) by receiving the approval of two-thirds of each house after having been refused signature by the President within ten days after its passage by a majority in each house. If Congress adjourn before the expiration of the ten days allowed the President to consider bills sent him, such bills lapse unless he has signed them before the adjournment.

Neither house can do any business (except send for absent members or adjourn) unless a majority of its members are present, — a majority being in the case of all our legislatures, both state and federal, the necessary *quorum*.

In the practice of some foreign legislatures the *quorum* is much less than a majority of the members. In the English House of Commons, for instance, it is only forty members, although the total number of members of the House of Commons is seven hundred and seven.

When it is said that under certain circumstances a bill must be passed by a vote of two-thirds in order to become a law, it is understood to mean that it must be voted for by two-thirds of the members *present*, not necessarily by that proportion of the whole membership of the body. In the case of bills which the President refuses to sign, however, the Constitution expressly says that it cannot be made law unless a second time passed by *two-thirds of each house*.

A bill may ' originate ' in either house, unless it be a bill relating to the raising of revenue. In that case it must originate in the House of Representatives, though the Senate may propose what amendments it pleases to a revenue bill, as to any other which comes to it from the House.

If one of the houses pass a bill, and the other house amend it, the changes so proposed must be adopted by the house in which the bill originated before it can be sent to the President and be made a law. When the two houses disagree about amendments they appoint conference committees; that is to say, each house appoints a committee to consult with a similar committee appointed by the other house, to see what can be done towards bringing about an agreement between the two houses upon the points in dispute.

The Federal Judiciary : its Jurisdiction. — The Judiciary of the United States consists of a Supreme Court, nine Circuit Courts of Appeals, nine Circuit Courts, eighty-three District Courts, and a Court of Claims. Its organization and functions rest more than do those of either of the other branches of the general government upon statute merely, instead of upon constitutional provision. The Constitution declares that " the judicial power of the United States shall be vested in one supreme court, and in such inferior courts as the Congress may, from time to time, ordain and establish," and that " the judges, both of the supreme and inferior courts, shall hold their offices during good behavior, and shall, at stated times, receive for their services a compensation which shall not be diminished during their continuance in office." It provides also that the judicial power of the federal government shall extend to all cases in law or equity which may arise under the Constitution, laws, or treaties of the United States; to all cases affecting ambassadors, other public ministers, and consuls; to all admiralty and maritime cases; to controversies in which the United States is a party, controversies between two or more states, between a state and citizens of another state (the state being the suitor), between citizens of different states, between citizens of the same state claiming lands under grants from different states, and between a state or its citizens and foreign states, citizens, or subjects. And it directs that in cases affecting ambassadors, other public ministers and consuls, and in cases in which a state is a party the Supreme Court shall have original jurisdiction; while in all other cases it is to have appellate jurisdiction only, "with such exceptions, and under such regulations, as the Congress shall make."

The judicial power of the federal government is thus made to embrace two distinct classes of cases: (a) those in which it is manifestly proper that its authority, rather than the authority of a state, should control, *because of the nature of the questions involved:* for instance, admiralty and maritime cases, navigable waters being within the exclusive jurisdiction of the federal authorities; and cases arising out of the Constitution, laws, or treaties of the United States or out of conflicting grants made by different states. (b) Those in which, *because of the nature of the parties to the suit,* the state courts could not properly be allowed jurisdiction; cases affecting, for instance, foreign ambassadors, who are accredited to the government of the United States and with whom our only relations are national relations, whose privileges rest upon the sovereignty of the states they represent; or cases in which the state courts could not have complete jurisdiction because of the residence of the parties; for instance, suits arising between citizens of different states. It is always open to the choice of a citizen of one state to sue a citizen of another state in the courts of the latter's own domicile, but the courts of the United States are the special forum provided for such cases.

Power of Congress over the Judiciary. — But these provisions of the Constitution leave Congress quite free to distribute the powers thus set forth among the courts for whose organization it is to provide, and even, if it so chooses, to leave some of them entirely in abeyance. In other words, the Constitution defines the sphere which the judicial power of the United States *may* fill, while Congress determines how much of that sphere shall actually be occupied, by what courts and in what manner, subject to what rules and limitations.

With regard to the organization of the judiciary Congress determines not only what courts shall be created inferior to the Supreme Court, but also of what number of judges the Supreme Court itself shall consist, what their compensation and procedure shall be, and what their specific duties in the administration of justice. It might also determine, should it see fit, what qualifications should be required of occupants of the supreme bench.

The Existing Federal Courts. — In pursuance of these powers, Congress has passed the Judiciary Act of September, 1789, and the Acts amendatory thereto upon which the national judiciary system now rests. In 1911 all previous legislation was codified and the organization and jurisdiction of the lower courts were greatly modified. The Supreme Court consists of a chief justice and eight associate justices ; it is required to hold annual sessions in the city of Washington — sessions which begin on the second Monday of each October — any six of the justices constituting a quorum. Next below the Supreme Court are nine Circuit Courts of Appeal. The territory of the United States, including Alaska, Porto Rico, and Hawaii, is divided into nine circuits, in each of which there is a Circuit Court of Appeals, consisting of two judges in the fourth circuit, three judges in the first, third, fifth, sixth, and ninth circuits and of four judges in the second, seventh, and eighth circuits.

The chief justice and associate justices of the Supreme Court are allotted among the circuits by order of the court ; the chief justice and the associate justices assigned to each circuit are competent to sit as judges of the Circuit Court of Appeals within their respective circuits and when so sitting shall preside. In case the full court is not made up, one or more district judges shall sit in the court.

The Circuit Courts of Appeal exercise appellate jurisdiction to

370   THE GOVERNMENT OF THE UNITED STATES.

review by appeal or writ of error final decisions in the District Courts which may not be appealed direct to the Supreme Court, and for the most part the decisions of the Circuit Courts of Appeal are final; they may, however, certify to the Supreme Court such questions of law as they may deem best.

The nine circuits are divided into eighty-three districts, which, like Congressional districts, never cross state lines; and for each of these districts there has been established a district court. Some of the less populous states constitute each a single district; others are divided into two, while still others furnish sufficient business to warrant their being divided into four. The District courts are the lowest courts of the federal series, and have their own separate judges.

The Court of Claims was established in 1855, to relieve Congress of the necessity of determining the validity of claims against the United States, for the settlement or adjudication of which no provision had been made. It consists of a chief justice and four associates, and sits always in Washington. Pension claims, war claims, and claims already rejected were excluded from its jurisdiction; but all other claims against the United States, which are of such a kind that they could not be settled by an ordinary suit at law, in equity, or in admiralty (if the United States were suable like an individual) are referred to it. In some instances it is authorized to enter judgment; in others it can only find the facts; but in either case the claimant must wait for an appropriation by Congress for the satisfaction of his claim.

The Court of Customs Appeals is composed of a presiding judge and four associates. It has exclusive jurisdiction over appeals from the Board of General Appraisers of the Treasury Department as to the classification of imported goods and the rate of duty imposed thereon under such classifications. The court is always open for business and sessions may be held in any circuit at the discretion of the Court.

The division of jurisdiction between the Circuit Courts of Appeal and the District courts is effected by act of Congress; and, inasmuch as Congress has not seen fit to vest in the courts complete jurisdiction over *all* cases arising under the Constitution, laws, and treaties of the United States, but has given to each court power in certain specified cases, and left the rest in abeyance, it would be impossible to give in brief compass a detailed account of the jurisdiction of the several courts. It must suffice for present purposes to say, that the District courts are given cognizance of all ordinary civil cases falling within the federal jurisdiction, of all common law suits brought by the United States, all torts under international law or the treaties of the United States, suits against consuls or vice consuls, land condemnations, and all cases brought under the civil rights laws; and that they have exclusive original jurisdiction in postal law cases, prize cases, admiralty and maritime cases, and suits against the United States for money claims not exceeding $10,000. The Circuit Courts are given appellate jurisdiction only.

All judges of the United States are appointed by the President, with and by the consent and advice of the Senate, to serve during good behavior. There are in all eighty-three federal judicial districts, and for each of these, as a rule, a special district judge is appointed, though in thickly populated sections of the country it is customary to have more than one judge hold court in a district. Thus at present there are one hundred and four district judges.

Federal judges of the inferior courts are, so to say, interchangeable. When necessary, a district judge can go into another district than his own and either aid or replace the district judge there. A district judge may also, when it is necessary for the despatch of business, sit as circuit judge; and a circuit judge may, in his turn, upon occasion hold District court. This seems the less anomalous when it is remembered that the earliest arrangement was for the district judges to hold Circuit court always in the absence of the justices of the Supreme Court from circuit, or in conjunction with them, and that special circuit judges were appointed only because of the necessity for more judges consequent upon a rapid increase of federal judicial business.

The District Attorney and the Marshal. — Every district has its own federal *district attorney* and its own United States *marshal*, both of whom are appointed by the President. It is the duty of the federal district attorney to prosecute all offenders against the criminal laws of the United States, to conduct all civil cases instituted in his district in behalf of the United States, and to appear for the defence in all cases instituted against the United States; to appear in defence of revenue officers of the United States where they are sued for illegal action, etc. The marshal is the ministerial officer of the federal Circuit and District courts. He executes all their orders and processes, arrests and keeps all prisoners charged with criminal violation of federal law, etc., and has within each state the same powers, within the scope of United States law, that the sheriff of that state has under the laws of the state. He is the federal sheriff.

The orders and processes of a state court are binding and operative only within the state to which the court belongs; the orders and processes of United States courts, on the contrary, are binding and operative over the entire Union.

The Courts of the District of Columbia and of the territories are courts of the United States, but they are not federal courts; they bear, so far as their jurisdiction is concerned, the character of state and federal courts united. The only laws of the territories and of the District of Columbia are laws of the United States, inasmuch as the legislatures of the territories act under statutory grant from Congress.[1] The territorial legislatures are, so to say, commissioned by Congress; and the laws which they pass are administered by judges appointed by the President.

The territorial courts and the courts of the District of Columbia do not come within the view of the Constitution at all. With reference to them Congress acts under no limitations of power whatever. The rule of tenure during good behavior, for example, which applies to all judges of the United States appointed under the Constitution, does not apply to judges of the territories or of the District of Columbia. The term of office of territorial judges is fixed at four years. The federal courts sitting in the states, and the United States courts established in the territories, ought not to be thought of as parts of the same system, although the Supreme Court is the highest tribunal of appeal for both.

The procedure of a federal court follows, as a rule, the procedure of the courts of the state in which it is sitting; and

[1] Congress early enacted that the people of the District of Columbia should continue to live under the laws which had previously had force in the District before its cession to the federal government.

state law is applied by the courts of the United States in all matters not touched by federal enactment. Juries are constituted, testimony taken, argument heard, etc., for the most part, according to the practice of the state courts ; so that, so far as possible, both as regards the outward forms observed and the principles applied, a federal court is domestic, not foreign, to the state in which it acts.

It is not within the privilege of Congress to delegate to the courts of the states the functions of courts of the United States ; for the Constitution distinctly provides that, besides the Supreme Court, there shall be no court authorized to exercise the judicial powers of the United States except such as Congress " may, from time to time, ordain and *establish.*" The adoption of state courts by Congress is excluded by plain implication. A very interesting contrast is thus established between the federal judicial system of the United States and the federal judicial systems of Germany and Switzerland.

The Federal Executive. — " The executive power," says the Constitution, " shall be vested in a President of the United States of America," who " shall hold his office during a term of four years." Of course it is impossible for one man actually to exercise the whole executive power. The President is assisted by numerous heads of departments to whom falls so large a part of the actual duties of administration that it has become substantially correct to describe the President as simply presiding over and controlling by a general oversight the execution of the law ; which is doubtless all that the sagacious framers of the Constitution expected. The Vice-President has no part in the executive function. He is the President's substitute, and is chosen at the same time and in the same manner that the President is chosen.

Election of a President. — The choice is not direct by the people, but indirect, through electors chosen by the people. In each state there are elected as many electors as the state has representatives and senators in Congress, the " electoral vote " of each state being thus equal to its total representation in Congress.

The electors are voted for on the Tuesday following the first Monday of November in the year which immediately precedes the expiration of a presidential term. They assemble in the several state capitals to cast their votes on the second Monday of the January following. Their votes are counted in the house of Congress sitting in joint session on the second Wednesday of the following February. The President is inaugurated on the fourth of March.

Practical Operation of the Plan : the Party Conventions. — The original theory of this arrangement was that each elector was really to exercise an independent choice in the votes which he cast, voting for the men whom his own judgment had selected for the posts of President and Vice-President. In fact, however, the electors only register party decisions made during the previous summer in national conventions. Each party holds during that summer a great convention composed of party delegates from all parts of the Union, and nominates the candidates of its choice for the presidency and vice-presidency. The electors, again, are, in their turn, chosen according to the nominations of party conventions in the several states ; and the party which gains the most electors in the November elections puts its candidates into office through their votes, which are cast in obedience to the will of the party conventions as a matter of course. The party conventions, of which the Constitution knows nothing, are in fact by far the most important part of the machinery of election.

Qualifications for the Office of President. — "No person, except a natural-born citizen, or a citizen of the United States at the time of the adoption of this constitution shall be eligible to the office of president; neither shall any person be eligible to that office who shall not have attained to the age of thirty-five years, and been fourteen years a resident within the United States."[1] In respect of age there is here only a slight advance upon the qualifications required of a senator ; in respect of citizenship it is very much more rigorous than in the case of members of Congress.

It is provided by the Constitution that the compensation received by judges of the United States shall not be diminished during their terms of office ; concerning the President, whose tenure of office is much briefer,

[1] Constitution, Art. II., sec. i., par. 5.

it is provided that his compensation shall neither be diminished *nor in-creased* during his term.

Duties and Powers of the President. — It is the duty of the President to see that the laws of the United States are faithfully executed; he is made commander-in-chief of the army and navy of the United States, and of the militia of the several states when called into the actual service of the United States; he is to regulate the foreign relations of the country, receiving all foreign ministers and being authorized to make treaties with the assent of two-thirds of the Senate; he is to appoint and com-mission all officers of the federal government; and he may grant reprieves and pardons. The Constitution makes all his appoint-ments subject to confirmation by the Senate; but it also gives Congress the power to remove from the superintending view of the Senate the filling of all inferior official positions, by vesting the appointment of such subordinate officers as it thinks proper in the President alone, in the courts of law, or in the heads of departments. As a matter of fact, legislation has relieved the Senate of the supervision of the vast majority of executive appointments. The confirmation of the Senate is still neces-sary to the appointment of ambassadors, other public ministers, and consuls, of judges of the courts of the United States, of the chief military, naval, and departmental officials, of the principal post-office and customs officers, — of all the more important servants of the general government: but these con-stitute only a minority of all the persons receiving executive appointment. The majority are appointed without legislative oversight.

The unfortunate, the demoralizing influences which have been allowed to determine executive appointments since President Jackson's time have affected appointments made subject to the Senate's confirmation hardly less than those made without its coöperation; senatorial scrutiny has not proved effectual for securing the proper constitution of the public service. Indeed, the "courtesy of the Senate," — the so-called "courtesy" by which senators allow appointments in the several states to be regulated by the preference of the senators of the predominant party from the states concerned, has frequently threatened to add to the improper motives of the Executive the equally improper motives of the Senate.

Reform of Methods of Appointment to Federal Offices. — The attempts which have been made at various times to reform by law the system of appointments have not been directed towards the higher offices filled with the consent of the Senate, but only towards those inferior offices which are filled by the single authority of the President or of the heads of the executive departments; have touched in their results, indeed, only the less important even among those offices. The Act which became law in June, 1883, and which is known as the "Pendleton Act," may be said to cover only 'employees': it does not affect any person really *in authority*, though it does affect a large body of federal servants. It provides, in brief, for the appointment by the President, by and with the advice and consent of the Senate, of a *Civil Service Commission* consisting of three persons, not more than two of whom shall be adherents of the same political party, under whose recommendation, as representatives of the President, selections shall be made for the lower grades of the federal service upon the basis of competitive examination. It forbids the solicitation of money from employees of the government for political uses, and all active party service on the part of members of the civil administration. It endeavors, in short, to "take the civil service out of politics."

The carrying out of those portions of the Act which relate to the method of choosing public officers is, however, almost entirely subject to the pleasure of the President. The Constitution vests in him the power of appointment, subject to no limitation except the possible advice and consent of the Senate. Any Act which assumes to prescribe the manner in which the President shall make his choice of public servants must, therefore, be merely advisory. The President may accept its directions or not as he pleases. The only force that can hold him to the observance of its principle is the force of public opinion.

The Presidential Succession. — In case of the removal, death, resignation, or disability of both the President and Vice-President, the office of President is to be filled *ad interim* by the Secretary of State, or, if he cannot act, by the Secretary of the Treasury, or, in case he cannot act, by the Secretary of War; and so on, in succession, by the Attorney-General, the Postmaster-General, the Secretary of the Navy, or the Secretary of the Interior, the Secretary of Agriculture, the Secretary of Commerce, and the Secretary of Labor. None of these officers can act, however, unless he have the qualifications as to age, citizenship, and residence required by the Constitution of occupants of the presidential chair. Until 1886, the 'succession' passed first to the president *pro tempore* of the Senate, and, failing him, to the Speaker of the House of Representatives. This was found inconvenient, because there are intervals now and again when there is neither a president *pro tempore* of the Senate nor a Speaker of the House. These officers, moreover, are by no means always of the same political party as the President and Vice-President. Some doubt was felt, too, as to whether they were 'officers' within the meaning of the Constitution, in the clause in which Congress is authorized to designate the 'officers' upon whom in such cases the presidential office was to devolve.

Relations of the Executive to Congress. — The only provisions contained in the Constitution concerning the relation of the President to Congress are these : that, " he shall, from time to time, give to the congress information of the state of the union, and recommend to their consideration such measures as he shall judge necessary and expedient"; and that " he may, on extraordinary occasions, convene both houses, or either of them," in extra session, "and, in case of disagreement between them, with respect to the time of adjournment, he may adjourn them to such time as he shall think proper " (Art. II., sec. iii.). His power to inform Congress concerning the state of the Union and to recommend to it the passage of measures is exercised only in annual and special ' messages.'

Washington and John Adams interpreted this clause to mean that they might address Congress, in person, as the sovereign in England may do : and their annual communications to Congress were spoken addresses. But Jefferson, the third President, being an ineffective speaker, this habit was discontinued, and the fashion of written messages was inaugurated and firmly established.[1] (Compare page 193.) Possibly, had the President not so closed the matter against new adjustments, this clause of the Constitution might legitimately have been made the foundation for a much more habitual and informal, and yet at the same time much more public and responsible, interchange of opinion between the Executive and Congress. Having been interpreted, however, to exclude the President from

[1] President Wilson reverted to the original practice, and has read his messages to Congress.

any but the most formal and ineffectual utterance of advice, our federal executive and legislature have been shut off from coöperation and mutual confidence to an extent to which no other modern system furnishes a parallel. In all other modern governments the heads of the administrative departments are given the right to sit in the legislative body and to take part in its proceedings. The legislature and executive are thus associated in such a way that the ministers of state can lead the houses without dictating to them, and the ministers themselves be controlled without being misunderstood, — in such a way that the two parts of the government which should be most closely coördinated, the part, namely, by which the laws are made and the part by which the laws are executed, may be kept in close harmony and intimate coöperation, giving coherence to the action of the one and energy to the action of the other.

The Executive Departments. — The Constitution does not explicitly provide for the creation of executive departments, but it takes it for granted that such departments will be created. Thus it says (Art. II., sec. ii., par. 1, 2) that the President " may require the opinion, in writing, of the principal officer in each of the executive departments, upon any subject relating to the duties of their respective offices," and that Congress may vest the appointment of such inferior officers as it may see fit " in the heads of departments." The executive departments consequently owe their creation and organization to statute only.

The first Congress erected three such departments, namely, the departments of State, of the Treasury, and of War ; providing, besides, for the creation and exercise of the office of Attorney-General, but not erecting a Department of Justice.   In 1798 the management of the navy, which had at first been included in the duties of the War Department, was intrusted to a special Department of the Navy ; in 1829 the post-office, which had been a sub-division of the Treasury, was created an independent Department ; and in 1849 a Department of the Interior was organized to receive a miscellany of functions not easy to classify, except in the feature of not belonging properly within any department previously created.[1]   In 1870 the Attorney-General was put at the head of a

[1] A character like that of the Department of the Interior, it is interesting to remark, may be attributed to some corresponding department, bearing either this name or a name of like significance, in almost every other modern government.   There is everywhere some department of state to receive functions not otherwise specially disposed of.

regularly constituted Department of Justice; and in 1889 the Department of Agriculture, which had existed as a subordinate executive bureau since 1862, was given full standing under a Secretary of 'cabinet' rank; in 1903 the Department of Commerce and of Labor was established, and in 1913 the Department of Labor.

We have, thus, at present, ten executive departments, viz. : (1) **A Department of State**, which is what would be called in most other governments our 'foreign office,' having charge of all the relations of the United States with foreign countries.

(2) **A Department of the Treasury**, which is the financial agency of the government, and whose functions cover the collection of the public revenues accruing through the customs duties and the internal revenue taxes, their safe keeping and their disbursement in accordance with the appropriations from time to time made by Congress; the auditing of the accounts of all departments; the supervision and regulation of the national banks and of the currency of the United States; the coinage of money; and the collection of certain industrial and other statistics. This Department, therefore, contains within it the treasury and comptrolling functions which in the states are separated.

To this Department is attached also the *Bureau of Printing and Engraving*, by which all the printing of the paper currency, bonds, and revenue stamps of the government is done.

(3) **A Department of War**, which has charge of the military forces and defences of the Union. It has charge of the Military Academy at West Point, and supervision of the various military schools to which Congress gives aid.

(4) **A Department of the Navy**, which has charge of the naval forces of the general government; and which has charge of the Naval Academy at Annapolis and the Naval War College at Newport.

(5) **A Department of Justice**, from which emanates all the legal advice of which the federal authorities stand in need at any time, and to which is intrusted the supervision of the conduct of all litigation in which the United States may be concerned. To it are subordinate all the marshals and district attorneys of the United States, — all ministerial, non-judicial law officers, that is,

in the service of the government.   It may be compendiously described as the lawyer force of the government.   It is presided over by an Attorney-General, all the other departments, except the Post-Office, being under 'Secretaries.'

(6) **A Post-office Department**, under a Postmaster-General, which is charged with the carrying and delivery of letters and parcels, with the transmission of money by means of certain 'money orders' issued by the Department, or under cover of a careful system of registration, and with making the proper postal arrangements with foreign countries.

These arrangements with foreign countries may be made without the full formalities of treaty, the consent of the President alone being necessary for the ratification of international agreements made by the Postmaster-General for the facilitation of the functions of the Department.   The United States is a member of the Universal Postal Union, to which most of the civilized countries of the world belong.   The central office of this Union is under the management of the Swiss administration. Its administrative expenses are defrayed by contribution of the various governments belonging to the Union.

(7) **A Department of the Interior**, which has charge: (I) Of the management of the public lands (*General Land Office*); (II) Of the government's dealings with the Indians, a function which is exercised through a special Commissioner of Indian Affairs in Washington and various agencies established in different parts of the Indian country.

It is through this *Indian Bureau*, for example, that all laws concerning the settlement, assistance, or supervision of the tribes are administered, as well as all laws concerning the payment of claims made upon the federal government for compensation for depredations committed by the Indians, and laws touching the distribution and tenure of land among the Indians.

(III) Of the paying of pensions and the distribution of bounty lands, a function which it exercises through a special *Commissioner of Pensions;* (IV) Of the issuing and recording of patents and the preservation of the models of all machines patented. For the performance of these duties there is a *Patent Office*. (V) Of the keeping and distribution of all public documents

(*Superintendent of Public Documents*); (VI) Of the collection of statistical and other information concerning education, and the diffusion of the information so collected for the purpose of aiding the advance and systematization of education throughout the country (*The Office of Education*); (VII) Of the superintendence of the government hospital for the insane and the Columbia Asylum for the Deaf and Dumb; (VIII) Of the Geological Survey ; (IX) Of the Freedmen's Hospital and the Howard University.

Many of these subdivisions of the Interior, through in strictness subject to the oversight and control of the Secretary of the Interior, have in reality a very considerable play of independent movement.

(**8**) **A Department of Agriculture**, which is charged with furthering in every possible way, by the collection of information not only, but also by the prosecution of scientific investigation with reference to the diseases of plants, etc., the agricultural interests of the country, and under which there are maintained a special *Forestry Division*, and the national Weather Bureau.

(**9**) **A Department of Commerce.** — By an Act of 1903 a Department of Commerce and Labor was established which in 1913 was divided, the Department of Labor becoming a separate Department. It is the province and duty of the Department of Commerce to foster, promote and develop the foreign and domestic commerce, the mining, manufacturing, shipping and fishing industries of the United States. From the Treasury Department there have been transferred to the Department of Commerce the Light-House Board and Establishment, the Steamboat-Inspection Service, the Bureau of Navigation, the United States Shipping Commissioners, the National Bureau of Standards, the Coast and Geodetic Survey; from the Department of the Interior, the Census Office; from the Department of State, the Bureau of Foreign Commerce; and under it were placed also the Fish Commission, and the office of Commissioner of Fish and Fisheries.

(**10**) **A Department of Labor.** — In 1913 the Department of Commerce and Labor was divided and a separate Department of Labor was created, charged with the duty to foster, promote and develop the welfare of the wage earners, to improve their working conditions, and to advance their opportunities for profitable employment. Under its direction were placed the Bureaux of Labor Statistics, Immigration, Naturalization, and the Children's Bureau.

Set apart to themselves, and therefore without representation in the Cabinet, there are (1) the *Interstate Commerce Commission*, a semi-judicial body by which the federal statutes forbidding unjust discrimination in railway rates in interstate freight or passenger traffic, prohibiting certain sorts of combinations in railroad management, etc., are interpreted and enforced. (2) The *Civil Service Commission*, by which the Act mentioned on page 376 is administered. (3) The Government Printing Office, which prints all public documents. (4) The Smithsonian Institution, the National Museum, and the Bureau of Ethnology.

SOME REPRESENTATIVE AUTHORITIES.

Histories:

Adams, Henry, The History of the United States under the Administrations of Jefferson and Madison, 9 vols., N.Y., 1889–1891; Documents relating to New England Federalism, Boston, 1877.

Adams, Herbert B., Maryland's Influence upon Land Cessions to the United States, in the *Johns Hopkins Studies in Historical and Political Science*, 3d Series, No. 1.

American Nation Series.

American Statesman Series, a series of Biographies. 26 vols., 12mo, Boston, 1882–1891.

Bancroft, George, History of the United States, from the discovery of America to the adoption of the federal constitution. Revised ed., 6 vols., 8vo, N.Y.

Benton, Thomas H., Thirty Years' View; or, A History of the Working of the American Government for Thirty Years, 1820–1850. 2 vols., 8vo, N.Y., 1854–1856.

Bishop, Cortlandt F., History of Elections in the American Colonies (in Columbia University Studies in History, Economics, and Public Law), N.Y., 1896.

Curtis, George T., History of the Origin, Formation, and Adoption of the Constitution of the United States. 3 vols., N.Y., 1854, 1858, 1896.

Doyle, J. A., The English Colonies in America. 5 vols., N.Y., London and N.Y., 1882–1907.

Fisher, George P., The Colonial Era, N.Y., 1892.

Fiske, John, The Critical Period of American History, Boston, 1888, 1897.

Frothingham, Richard, Rise of the Republic of the United States, 3d ed., Boston, 1881.

Hart, Albert B., Formation of the Union, 23d ed., London and N.Y.

Hildreth, R., History of the United States from the Discovery of America to the End of the Sixteenth Congress (1821). Two Series, 6 vols., New ed., N.Y., 1879.

Holst, H. von, The Constitutional and Political History of the United States. Trans. from the German. 7 vols., Chicago, 1877–1892.

Jameson, J. F. (editor), Essays in the Constitutional History of the United States in the Formative Period, 1775–1789, Boston, 1889.

Johnston, Alexander, History of American Politics, 3d ed., revised, N.Y., 1890; The First Century of the Constitution, in the *New Princeton Review*, September, 1887.

Landon, Judson S., The Constitutional History and Government of the United States. A Series of Lectures. Boston, 1889.

Lodge, Henry C., A Short History of the English Colonies in America, N.Y., 1881.

MacMaster, John B., History of the People of the United States, 8 vols., N.Y., 1913.

Pitkin, Timothy, Political and Civil History of the United States of America from their Commencement to the Close of the Administration of Washington, 2 vols., 8vo, New Haven, 1828.

Rhodes, James F., History of the United States from the Compromise of 1850, 8 vols., N.Y., 1893–1906.

Roosevelt, Theodore, The Winning of the West, 4 vols., London and N.Y., 1889–1896.

Schouler, James, History of the United States of America under the Constitution, 7 vols., N.Y., 1889–1913.

Scott, Eben G., Development of Constitutional Liberty in the English Colonies of America, N.Y., 1882.

Sloane, William M., The French War and the Revolution, N.Y., 1893.

Stanwood, Edward, A History of the Presidency, 2 vols., Boston and N.Y., 1916.

Sumner, William G., Politics in America, 1776–1876. *North American Review*, January, 1876, p. 47.

Taylor, Hannis, The Origin and Growth of the English Constitution, 2 vols., Boston, 1889–1898.

Thwaites, Reuben G., The Colonies, 1492–1750, 22d ed., London and N.Y., 1910.

Tucker, George, The History of the United States from their Coloniza-
    tion to the End of the Twenty-sixth Congress in 1841, 4 vols.,
    Phila., 1856–1857.
Walker, Francis A., The Making of the Nation, N.Y., 1895.
Wilson, Woodrow, Division and Reunion, 1829–1889, 13th ed., London and
    N.Y., 1898; and History of the American People, 5 vols., N.Y., 1908.
Winsor, Justin (editor), Narrative and Critical History of America,
    Vol. VII., Boston, 1888.   Contains full bibliographical notes.

The controversial literature accompanying and preceding the War of
Secession may be seen, representatively, in :

Adams, John, Works.
Bledsoe, Albert T., Is Davis a Traitor?   Balto., 1866.
Brownson, O. A., The American Republic: its Constitution, Tendencies,
    and Destiny, N.Y., 1866 and 1886.
Calhoun, John Caldwell, Works.
Centz, P. C. (B. J. *Sage*), The Republic of Republics, 4th ed., Boston,
    1881.
Hurd, J. C., The Theory of Our National Existence, Boston, 1881.
Jefferson, Thomas, Works.
Stephens, Alexander H., A Constitutional View of the War between the
    States, 2 vols., 8vo, Phila., 1868.
Webster, Daniel, Speeches.

Commentaries and Treatises:

Atkinson, C. T., The Committee on Rules and the Overthrow of Speaker
    Cannon, N.Y., 1911.
Beard, C. A., American Government and Politics.
Borgeaud, Charles, The Adoption and Amendment of Constitutions in
    Europe and America, N.Y., 1895.
Boutmy, Émile, Studies in Constitutional Law, London and N.Y.,
    1891.
Bryce, James, The American Commonwealth, 2 vols., Revised ed.,
    N.Y., 1915.
Burgess, John W., Political Science and Constitutional Law, 2 vols.,
    Boston, 1891.
Carter, C.H., Connecticut Boroughs, in *New Haven Historical Society's
    Papers*, Vol. IV.
Cooley, Thomas M., Treatise on the Constitutional Limitations which
    rest upon the Legislative Power of the States of the American
    Union, 2d ed., Boston, 1871; The General Principles of Con-
    stitutional Law in the United States of America, Boston, 1880,
    and several later editions.   And (with others) Constitutional

History of the United States as seen in the Development of American Law, a survey of the successive constitutional decisions of the Supreme Court of the United States, N.Y., 1889.

Convin, E. S., The Doctrine of Judicial Review, Princeton, 1914.

Coxe, Brinton, Judicial Power and Unconstitutional Legislation, Phila., 1893.

Dicey, Albert V., Lectures Introductory to the Study of the Law of the Constitution, 8th ed., London, 1915.   This book, though a commentary on the English constitution, contains much excellent comment also on our own.

Digest of State Constitutions.   Prepared for the use of the New York State Constitutional Convention.   Albany, 1915.

Dupriez, L., Les Ministres dans les principaux Pays d'Europe et d'Amérique, 2 vols., Paris, 1892.   Vol. II., pp. 3 *et seq.*

Ely, Richard T., Taxation in American States and Cities, N.Y., 1888.

The Federalist, by Alexander *Hamilton*, James *Madison*, and John *Jay*.

Fiske, John, Civil Government in the United States considered with Some Reference to its Origins, Boston, 1890.

Follett, M. P., The Speaker of the House of Representatives, London and N.Y., 1896.

Ford, H. J., The Rise and Growth of American Politics.

Ford, W. C., The American Citizen's Manual.   Part I.   N.Y., 1882.

Goodnow, Frank J., Comparative Administrative Law, 2 vols., London and N.Y., 1893; Municipal Home Rule, London and N.Y., 1895.

Haines, C. G., The American Doctrine of Judicial Supremacy, N.Y.

Harrison, Benjamin, This Country of Ours, N.Y., 1897.

Hart, A. B., Actual Government, 3d ed., 1910.

Hart and McLaughlin, Cyclopedia of American Government, N.Y. and London, 1914.

Howard, George E., Local Constitutional History of the United States, Vol. I , 8vo, Balto., 1885.

Jameson, J. F., Introduction to the Constitutional and Political History of the Individual States, in the *Johns Hopkins University Studies in Historical and Political Science*, 4th Series, No. V.

Johns Hopkins Studies in Historical and Political Science, 14 vols., Balto., 1883–1896.

Maine, Sir H. S., Popular Government, N.Y., 1886.   Especially Chap. VI.

McConachie, L. C., Congressional Committees.

McCall, S. W., The Business of Congress, N.Y., 1911.

Oberholzer, E. P., The Referendum in America, New ed., N.Y., 1911.

Parker, Joel, Jaffrey Address, 1873.   Origin, Organization, and Influence of the Towns of New England. *Proceedings* Mass. Hist. Soc'y, June, 1886.

Poore, Ben: P., Federal and State Constitutions, Colonial Charters, and other Organic Laws of the United States, 2 vols., Washington, 1877.

Schouler, James, Constitutional Studies, N.Y., 1897.

Shires and Shire Towns in the South. *Lippincott's Magazine*, Aug., 1882.

Sloane, W. M., Party Government in the U.S., N.Y. and London, 1914.

Stevens, C. E., Sources of the Constitution of the United States, London and N.Y., 1894.

Story, Joseph, Commentaries on the Constitution.   Ed. by T. M. Cooley.

Thorpe, Francis N., Compiled Federal and State Constitution, 7 vols., Govt. Printing Office, 1909.

Tocqueville, Alexis de, Democracy in America.   Translated by Henry Reeve.   New ed., London, 1875.

Wilson, Woodrow, Congressional Government, A Study in American Politics, Boston, 1885; and Constitutional Government in the United States, N.Y., 1908.

Young, J. T., The New American Government and its Work, N.Y., 1916.

X.

THE GOVERNMENTS OF SWITZERLAND.

Feudalism in Switzerland. — Until the beginning of the fourteenth century the towns and communes of the country now called Switzerland were all held fast in the meshes of the feudal system. Real vassalage, indeed, such as the low countries of France and Germany knew, had never penetrated to all the valleys of the Alps; many a remote commune had never known anything but a free peasantry; and hardly anywhere near the heart of the great mountains had feudal fealty meant what it meant elsewhere. Still great neighbor lords and monasteries had swept even these mountain lands at least nominally within their overlordships, and most of the Swiss Cantons of to-day represent pieces of old feudal domains.

First Movements towards Cantonal Independence. — In 1309, however, began the process which was to create the Switzerland of our time. In that year the Cantons of Schwyz, Uri, and Unterwalden, lying close about the lake of Lucerne, won from the Emperor Henry VII. the recognition of their freedom from all supremacy save that of the Empire itself. They had already, about the middle of the thirteenth century, drawn together into a league which was to prove the seed of the modern Confederacy. That Confederacy has two distinguishing characteristics. It has brought down to us, through an almost unbroken tradition, the republican institutions of the Middle Ages; and it has by slow processes of cautious federation drawn together into a real union communities the most diverse alike in point of race, of language, and of institutions without destroying their individuality.

The Processes of Confederate Growth. — In its briefest terms the story is this. The Cantons broke from the toils of the feudal system while still in possession of those local liberties which the disintegrateness of that system gave leave to grow wherever courageous men could muster numbers enough to assert their independence; having a common cause against the feudal powers about them, they slowly drew together to each other's support; and, having allied themselves, they went on to show the world how Germans, Frenchmen, and Italians, if only they respect each the other's liberties as they would have their own respected, may by mutual helpfulness and forbearance build up a union at once stable and free. Several centuries elapsed before the development was complete, for the Confederation, as finally made up, consisted of two very different elements: of strong and for the most part aristocratic free cities and of quiet rural peasant democracies. It was necessarily a long time before even common dangers and common interests brought proud Cantons like Bern and aristocratic cities like Geneva into cordial relations with Schwyz, Uri, and Unterwalden, the humble originators of the Confederacy. But circumstances constrained and wisdom prevailed: so that union was at last achieved.

French Interference. — The year 1513 may be taken as marking the close of the period during which the Confederacy won the place it was always to keep among the powers of Europe. In that year the League was joined by the last of those thirteen German Cantons which were to constitute its central membership down to the French Revolution. It was not till 1848, however, that its constitution was put upon its present foundations; and not till 1874 that that constitution received at all points its present shape. In the meantime events of the greatest magnitude gave direction to Swiss affairs. The great powers had recognized the independence of Switzerland in the Treaty of Westphalia, 1648. The thirteen original Cantons had received great French cities, like Geneva, to the west, and various Italian lands, to the south, either into close alliance or into fixed subjection. The French Revolution had sent French troops into Switzerland, in support of a fruitless attempt to manufacture out of the always stiffly independent Cantons, hitherto only confederates, a compact and centralized 'Helvetic Republic,' after the new model just set up in unhappy France (1798–1802). Napoleon had intervened (1803–1814) for the purpose of both loosing these artificial bonds and creating a new cement for the League in the shape of a common allegiance to himself. And, in 1815, the pressure of the French power being removed, reaction had come. The irritated Cantons, exasperated by the forms of a government not of their own choosing, had flung apart, to the practice of principles of cantonal sovereignty broader, extremer even than those upon which they had based their Union before 1798. And then reaction, in its turn, brought its own penalties. Troubles ensued which read very much like those, so familiar to Americans, which forced a strong federal government upon the United States.

The Sonderbund War. — It was, however, differences of religious, not of political, opinion which were in Switzerland the occasion of the strife which was to bring union out of disunion. After the power of Napoleon had been broken, the Congress of Vienna had sought to readjust all the arrangements that he had disturbed, and Swiss affairs had not been overlooked. The Cantons were induced to receive Geneva, Valais, Neuchâtel, and the territories hitherto held as dependencies, into full confederate membership, and to agree to a Pact (known as the Pact of 1815) which gave to the League, with its increased membership of twenty-two Cantons, a new basis of union. One of the clauses of that Pact contained a solemn guarantee of the rights and privileges of the monasteries still maintained in the Roman Catholic Cantons: and upon that guarantee were based the hopes of all parties for peace among the members of the League. But the guarantee was broken down. The wave of democratic reform swept steadily and resistlessly through Switzerland during the revolutionary period of 1830–1848, and where the Protestant and Roman Catholic parties were nearly equal in popular force threatened not a few of the oldest foundations of the mediæval church. The crisis was first felt in Zürich, where the excesses of a radical party temporarily in control brought about, in 1839, a violent reaction. The next year saw the disturbance transferred to Aargau. There the anti-Catholic party, commanding, during a period of constitutional revision, a narrow popular majority, and exasperated by the violent opposition tactics of the clerical party, forced a vote in favor of the abolition of the eight monasteries of the Canton. The Diet of the Confederation was thereupon asked by the aggrieved party whether it would permit so flagrant a breach of the Pact of 1815. It was forced by a conflict of interests to a compromise, agreeing to the abolition of four of Aargau's eight monasteries. This was in August, 1843. The next month saw the formation of a separate League (*Sonderbund*) by the seven Roman Catholic Cantons, Schwyz, Uri, Unterwalden, Luzern, Freiburg, Valais, and Zug. The deputies of these Cantons were, however, slow in withdrawing from the Diet, and the Diet was reluctant to come to open strife with its recalcitrant members. Four years this league within a league was permitted to continue its obstructive agitation. But at last, in November, 1847, war came,—a sharp, decisive contest of only eighteen days' duration, in which the seceded Cantons were overwhelmed and forced back to their allegiance.

The New Constitution. — Constitutional revision followed immediately. The Pact of 1815 was worn out: a strong and progressive constitution had become a necessity which not even the party of reaction could resist or gainsay. By the Constitution of 1848 there was created, out of the old discordant Confederation of States (*Staatenbund*) the present federal State (*Bundesstaat*). That Constitution, as modified and extended by the important revision of 1874, is the present Constitution of Switzerland.

Character of the Constitution. — The federal government thus established has many features which are like, as well as many which are very unlike, the familiar features of our own national system. It has had, since 1874, a federal Supreme Court, which is in many important fields of jurisdiction the highest tribunal of the land; and it has had since 1848 a Legislature consisting of two branches, or Houses, the one representative of the people, the other representative of the states of the Confederation. The popular chamber is called the 'National Council' (*der Nationalrat*), the federal senate, the 'Council of States' (*der Ständerat*). The former represents the people as a whole; the latter, the States as constituent members of the Confederation.

Much of the resemblance of these arrangements to our own is due to conscious imitation. The object of the reformers of 1848 and 1874 was not, however, to Americanize their government, and in most respects it remains distinctively Swiss.

Nationality and State Sovereignty. — Much as such institutions resemble our own federal forms, the Constitution of Switzerland rests upon federal foundations such as our own government had during the first half century of its existence rather than upon national conceptions such as have dominated us since the war between the States. The Swiss Constitution does indeed expressly speak of the Swiss nation, declaring that "the Swiss Confederacy has adopted the following Constitution with a view to establishing the union (*Bund*) of the Confederates and to maintaining and furthering the unity, the power, and the honor of the Swiss nation": and not even the war between the States put the word *nation* into our Constitution. But the Constitution of Switzerland also contains a distinct and emphatic assertion of that principle of divided sovereignty which is so much less familiar to us now than it was before 1861. It speaks of the Confederation as formed by "the people of the twenty-two sovereign Cantons," and it explicitly declares that "the Cantons are sovereign, so far as their sovereignty is not limited by the federal Constitution, and exercise as such all rights which are not conferred upon the federal power"; and its most competent interpreters are constrained to say that such a constitution does not erect a single and compacted state of which the Cantons are only administrative divisions, but a federal state, the units of whose membership are themselves states, possessed, within certain limits, of independent and supreme power. The drift both of Switzerland's past history and present purpose is unquestionably towards complete nationality; but her present Constitution was a compromise between the advocates and the opponents of nationalization; and it does not yet embody a truly national organization or power.

Large Constitutional Grants. — At the same time, the grants of power under the Swiss Constitution have from the first been both larger and less definite than those contained in the Constitution of the United States. It contains such indefinite grants as these: that the federal legislature shall have power to pass "laws and resolutions concerning those subjects which the Confederacy is commissioned by the federal Constitution to act upon"; to control the foreign relations of the Cantons; to guarantee the constitutions and territories of the Cantons; to provide for the internal safety, order, and peace of the country; to adopt any measures "which have the administration of the federal Constitution, the guaranteeing of the cantonal constitutions, or the fulfilment of federal duties for their object"; and to effect revisions of the federal Constitution.

It adds to such federal powers as we are familiar with the authority to regulate religious bodies and monastic orders, to control the manufacture and sale of alcoholic liquors, to establish general sanitary regulations in the case of certain diseases, to control the construction and operation of all railroads, to regulate labor in factories, to provide for the compulsory insurance of workmen, and to legislate throughout the whole field of commercial law. The federal government is given, besides, a large power of superintendence. It has supervision of streams and forests, and of the more important roads and bridges; it has the right to disapprove of and annul the press laws of the several cantons, and their regulations with regard to the acquisition of residence and the franchise in the communes; and it exercises in many another matter a general oversight and guardianship.

Guarantee of the Cantonal Constitutions. — The Swiss federal Constitution is more definite in guaranteeing to the Cantons their constitutions than our federal Constitution is in guaranteeing to the States "a republican form of government." The guarantee is made to include the freedom of the people and their legal and constitutional rights; the exercise of those rights under representative or democratic forms; and the revision of any cantonal constitution whenever an absolute majority of the citizens of the Canton desire a revision.

This ' guarantee ' is not used or understood in Switzerland as it is in the United States. Here the sanction and support of the federal government is taken for granted, unless the constitutional arrangements of a State are challenged as unrepublican. In Switzerland it is expected that each Canton shall seek the explicit sanction or guarantee of the federal government for its constitution, and even for each amendment as added.

The Cantonal Governments.

The Cantonal Constitutions and the Federal Constitution.
— So deeply is Swiss federal organization rooted in cantonal precedents, that an understanding of the government of the Confederation is best gained by studying first the political institutions of the Cantons. At almost all points the federal government exhibits likeness to the governments of the Cantons, out of whose union it has grown. As our own federal Constitution may be said to generalize and apply colonial habit and experience, so the Swiss Constitution may be said to generalize and apply cantonal habit and experience: though both our own Constitution and that of Switzerland have profited largely by foreign example also.

In some respects the Swiss Constitution is more conservative — or, if you will, less advanced — than the Constitution of the United States. Those who have fought for union in Switzerland have had even greater obstacles to overcome than have stood in the way of the advocates of a strong central government in this country. Differences of race, of language, and of religion, as well as stiffly opposing political purposes, have offered a persistent resistance to the strengthening and even the logical development of the prerogatives of the federal power. The Constitution of the Confederation, therefore, bears many marks of compromise. It gives evidence at certain points of incomplete nationalization not only, but even of imperfect federalization. Cantonal institutions are, consequently, upon a double ground entitled to be first considered in a study of the governments of Switzerland. Both their self-assertive vitality and their direct influence upon federal organization make them the central subject of Swiss politics.

Position of the Legislative Power. — The development of
political institutions has proceeded in the Swiss Cantons rather according to the logic of practical democracy than according to the logic of the schools. The Swiss have not, for one thing, hesitated to ignore in practice all dogmas concerning the separation of legislative, executive, and judicial functions. I say 'in practice'; for in theory such distinctions are observed. The

constitutions of fully half the Cantons say explicitly that legislative, executive, and judicial functions shall be kept fundamentally distinct; but in the practical arrangements actually made the line of demarcation is by no means sharply drawn. The leading principle according to which they proceed in all political arrangements is, that in every department of affairs the people must, either immediately or through representatives, exercise a direct, positive, effective control. They do not hesitate, therefore, to give to their legislative bodies a share both in the administration and in the interpretation of laws; and these bodies are unquestionably the axes of cantonal politics.

A Single House. — A very great variety of practice marks the organization of government in the Cantons. Each Canton has had its own separate history and has, to a certain extent, worked out its own individual political methods. But there is one point of perfect uniformity, — the Legislature of each Canton consists of but a single House. The two Houses of the federal legislature have been made after foreign, not after Swiss, models. In Uri, Upper and Lower Unterwalden, Glarus, and Appenzell Interior and Exterior this single lawmaking body is the *Landsgemeinde*, the free assembly of all the qualified voters, the *folkmoot ;* but in the other Cantons the legislative assembly is representative. Representatives are elected by popular vote in all the Cantons, and in ten by the method of proportional representation.

Elections are for a term which varies from two years to five in the different Cantons, the rule being a term of from three to four years. The number of representatives bears a proportion to the number of inhabitants which also varies as between Canton and Canton. In Zug there is one member of the legislature for every 350 inhabitants ; in Bern one to every 3000. As a result of the low ratios, the cantonal legislators have a relatively large membership.[1]

In most of the Cantons the legislative body is called the Great Council (*Grossrat*)— the executive body being the Lesser Council — in some it is called the Cantonal Council (*Kantonsrat*).

Functions of the Cantonal Legislatures. — The functions of these councils have the inclusiveness characteristic of Swiss

---

[1] Brooks, *Government and Politics of Switzerland*, p. 313.

political organization. Not only are they entrusted with such legislative power as the people are willing to grant ; they also, as a rule, select many of the administrative officers of the Canton, and exercise, after such election, a scrutiny of administrative affairs which penetrates to details and keeps executive action largely within their control. It is a recognized principle of cantonal government, indeed, that the executive body — executive power, as we shall see, being vested in a board or commission, not in an individual — is a committee of the representatives of the people, — a committee of the legislative council.[1] To that council they are responsible, as the selectmen of a New-England town are responsible to the town-meeting (page 341).[1]

The Executive Power is collegiate in all the Cantons, is exercised, that is, not by a single individual or by several individuals acting independently of each other, but by a commission. This commission is variously called in the different Cantons. In some it is known as the "*Landammann* and Council," in others as the "Estates-Commission" (*Standeskommission*), in some as the "Smaller Council"; but in most as the "Administrative Council" (*Regierungsrat*). Its term of office varies in the different Cantons with the term of the legislative body, with which it is always coincident; but the custom is reëlection, so that the brief tenure does not in practice result in too frequent changes in executive *personnel*. The members of the executive have always in the mountain Cantons been chosen by the people themselves ; in the others they were formerly elected always by the legislative council — whence the name, "smaller council," which they bear in some Cantons. Now, however, direct election by the people has been substituted in all but two of the Cantons. Whether elected by the people or by the Great Council, however, the Administrative Council remains, in function, a committee of the legislative body. Its members freely take part in the business of legislation and in the debates of the Great Council. It in fact originates most of the measures of each session, and is looked to for guidance in every matter of consequence. It does not resign if outvoted upon its proposals. It is, on the contrary, regarded in most of the Cantons rather as a business head than as a body of

[1] Orelli, p. 99.

party leaders, and its membership is usually made up, not from one, but from the several political parties of the Canton.

The Administrative Council usually consists of from five to seven members, though in the Cantons of Bern and Appenzell Interior it contains nine, and in Lower Unterwalden, eleven. It has proved necessary of late years to give over the attempt to act in all matters as a Board, and it has become usual to divide the work of the Council among departments. But these departments are under the general direction of the Council as a whole, and the administration of a canton has usually a very real coherence and an intimate coördination.

The People's Control over Legislative Action. — Although the people have delegated their legislative powers to representative chambers in all the Cantons except those which still retain their primitive *Landsgemeinden*, they have nevertheless kept in their own hands more than the mere right to elect representatives. The largest of the Cantons (Bern) has but a little more than half a million inhabitants; the majority of the Cantons have less than one hundred thousand apiece; and the average population, taking big and little Cantons together, is only about one hundred and twenty thousand. Their average area scarcely reaches six hundred and forty square miles. The people of such communities stand, as it were, in the midst of affairs. They are in a sense always at hand to judge of the conduct of the public business. Their feelings and their interests are homogeneous, and there is the less necessity to part with their powers to representatives. In seven of the German Cantons a certain number of citizens (the number varies from one to twelve thousand) can demand a popular vote upon the question whether the Great Council shall be dissolved or not; and if the vote goes in the affirmative the chamber's term is ended and a new election takes place at once. If this method of control is no longer used, it is because more effective methods have been substituted. In all the Cantons the question of constitutional revision can be brought to popular vote upon petition, and the revision, if undertaken, may go any length in changing or reversing the processes of legislation.

The Initiative: Imperative Petition. — So far has the apparent logic of democracy been carried in Switzerland that the people exercise in several ways a direct part in lawmaking. The right of petition, which is recognized in every country where popular rights exist at all, has become in Switzerland a right of initiative in legislation. In every Canton the people have been granted the right to initiate constitutional reforms by petition; and in all except Freiburg the same right has been established with regard to the revision or enactment of ordinary laws. In the Confederation petitions signed by fifty thousand voters have, since 1891, been imperative in respect of the introduction of constitutional amendments. In the case of ordinary legislation, specific laws may be proposed by petition, in all the Cantons except the one I have named; the legislature must submit the law proposed to the popular vote; and its adoption at the polls puts it upon the statute book.

In the case of constitutional amendments, it is generally provided that either general or specific changes may be proposed: that is, that the changes may be proposed either in general terms or in definitive and final form, ready for adoption. If the proposal is couched only in general terms, the legislature may either formulate the desired amendment at once and submit it to the people, or, if it disapprove of the change proposed, it may first submit the general question to the vote of the electors. If, in the latter event, the vote be in the affirmative, the legislature must proceed to formulate the necessary article or articles, and these must be submitted in their definitive shape once more to the popular verdict. If the petition itself embody a specific change already drawn and formulated, the amendment must go in that shape to the vote, and its adoption makes it part of the fundamental law. The number of signatures required for these imperative petitions varies with the size of the Cantons. Petitions demanding a change in the fundamental law of the Confederation must be signed, as we have seen, by not less than fifty thousand voters.

In the earlier years of its use, the constitutional initiative in the Confederation gave rise to severe criticism through the adoption of a constitutional amendment which aimed a blow at the Jews, under the disguise of forbidding the slaughtering of animals by bleeding; but since 1900 the use of the initiative has justified itself. "The measures submitted during the later period were moderate and progressive. Those which failed laid an educational foundation for reforms which are likely to be made in the not distant future, while the two successful amendments represent substantial achievement."[1] In the Cantons the experience has been similar.

The Referendum. — In every Canton of the Confederation, except Freiburg only, the right of the people to have all important legislation referred to them for confirmation or rejection has now been, in one form or another, established by law. In the smaller Cantons, which have had, time out of mind, the directest forms of democracy, this legislation by the people is no new thing; they have always had their *Landsgemeinden*, their assemblies of the whole people, and the legislative function of their Councils has long been only the duty of preparing laws for the consideration of the people. Among the Cantons which have representative institutions, on the other hand, the *Referendum* assumes a different form. In some of them laws must be submitted to the vote of the electors only when their submission is demanded by petition, with the requisite number of signatures. This is called the 'optional' or 'facultative' *Referendum*. In the rest of the Cantons (always excepting Catholic and conservative Freiburg) substantially all substantive changes in the laws must be submitted to the electors, and the action of their legislatures is periodically voted upon. This is known as the 'obligatory' *Referendum*.[2] The Federation itself has had the optional *Referendum* since 1874. The *Referendum* is, moreover, everywhere obligatory, whether in the Confederation or in the several Cantons, in the case of every constitutional change. Administration and the ordinary budget are usually excepted from its operation, and it is made to apply, within the field of ordinary legislation, only to laws of a general character; but in most of the Cantons it is made to cover also all appropriations of an unusual character or above a certain sum; and in Valais it applies only to certain financial measures.

[1] Brooks, *Government and Politics of Switzerland*, p. 152.

[2] Eleven Cantons have adopted the obligatory referendum for ordinary legislation.

Origin of the Referendum. — The term *Referendum* is as old as the sixteenth century, and contains a reminiscence of the strictly federal beginnings of government in two of the present Cantons of the Confederation, Graubünden, namely, and Valais. These Cantons were not at that time members of the Confederation, but merely districts allied with it (*zugewandte Orte*). Within themselves they constituted very loose confederacies of Communes (in Graubünden three, in Valais twelve). The delegates whom the Communes sent to the federal assembly of the district had to report every question of importance to their constituents and crave instruction as to how they should vote upon it. This was the original *Referendum*. It had a partial counterpart in the Constitution of the Confederation down to the formation of the present forms of government in 1848. Before that date the members of the central council of the Confederation acted always under instructions from their respective Cantons, and upon questions not covered by their instructions, as well as upon all matters of unusual importance, it was their duty to seek special direction from their home governments. They were said to be commissioned *ad audiendum et referendum.* The *Referendum* as now adopted by almost all the Cantons bears the radically changed character of legislation by the people. Only its name now gives testimony as to its origin.[1]

Its Operation. — In respect of constitutional changes the use of the *Referendum* is not peculiar to Switzerland. In that field its use in this country is older than its use in Switzerland. And in its application to ordinary laws it is modern even in Switzerland. Its earliest adoption was in 1831, and it was not until the decade 1864–1874 that it won its way into the constitutional practice of the greater Cantons. It led in the earlier years to the rejection of radical legislation, even to the rejection of radical labor legislation, such as the ordinary voter might be expected to accept with avidity. The Swiss populations, being both homogeneous and deeply conservative, long resisted the infection of modern radical opinion, but in recent years progress toward social legislation has been marked. They have shown themselves apt to reject, also, complicated measures which they do not fully com-

[1] Orelli, p. 104.

prehend, and measures involving expense which seems to them unnecessary. And they have shown themselves not a little indifferent, too. The vote upon most measures submitted to the ballot is usually very light; there is not much popular discussion; and the *Referendum* by no means creates that quick interest in affairs which its originators had hoped to see it excite.

Local Government : The Districts. — Local government in the Cantons exhibits a twofold division, into Districts and Communes. The District is an area of state administration, the Commune an area of local self-government. The executive functions of the District, the superintendency of police, namely, and the carrying into effect of the cantonal laws, are entrusted, as a rule, not to a board, but to a single officer, — a *Bezirksamman* or *Regierungs-Statthalter,* — who is either elected by popular vote in the District or appointed by one of the central cantonal councils, the legislative or the administrative. Associated with this officer, there is in some Cantons a District or county Council chosen by vote of the people.

The *Gemeinde,* or Commune, enjoys in Switzerland a degree of freedom in self-direction which is possessed by similar local organs of government hardly anywhere else in Europe. It owns land as a separate corporation, has charge of the police of its area, of the relief of its poor, and of the administration of its schools, and acts in the direction of communal affairs through a primary assembly of all its freemen which strongly reminds one of the New-England town-meeting (page 241). Besides its activities as an organ of self-government in the direction of strictly local affairs, the Commune serves also as an organ of cantonal administration, as a subdivision of the District. Thus it is an electoral district, and a voting district in the case of a *Referendum;* and in so far as it is used as a district of the Canton it is subject to the supervision of the local authorities of the state.

There is by no means a fixed and uniform organization in the local government of the Cantons. In most of the smaller Communes the people themselves act directly in affairs, in township meeting, while in the large cities a city council (Stadtrat) is elected by popular vote. In all the Communes, as in the Cantons, the executive power is vested in a board of officials, presided over by a *Hauptmann*, a *Gemeindeamman*, a *Syndic*, or a *Maire*. This communal or municipal council is chosen by the freemen in assembly or by direct popular election. The *Hauptmann* has often separate powers of his own, apart from and independent of his colleagues; but in most matters he is merely the presiding officer of the administrative council, and executive action is collegiate.

Citizenship in Switzerland is associated very closely with the Commune, — the immediate home-government of the citizen, — the primary and most vital organ of his self-direction in public affairs. The Commune is, so to say, the central political family in Switzerland; it is to it that the primary duties of the citizen are owed. Every citizen of a Canton is by the Federal Constitution a Swiss citizen. Naturalization is regulated by cantonal law subject only to approval by the Federal Council, upon the advice of its Political Department. The result has been the greatest diversity of practices in regard to a matter of vital consequence to the whole state, and the full rights of citizenship can be conferred only by cantonal and communal law.

THE FEDERAL GOVERNMENT.

The Federal Executive. — In no feature of the federal organization is the influence of cantonal example more evident than in the collegiate character of the Executive. The executive power of the Confederation, like the executive power of each Canton, is vested not in a single person, as under monarchical or presidential government, but in a board of persons. Nor does Swiss jealousy of a too concentrated executive authority satisfy itself with thus putting that authority 'into commission': it also limits it by giving to the legislative branch of the government, both in the Cantons and in the federal system, an authority of correction as regards executive acts such as no other country has known. The share of the legislative branch in administrative affairs is smaller, indeed, under the Federal Constitution than under the laws of the Cantons; but it is large even in the federal system, and it seems inherent in Swiss political thought.

The executive commission of the Confederation is known as the Federal Council (*Bundesrat*). It consists of seven mem-

bers elected for a term of three years by the two houses of the
federal legislature acting together in joint session as a Federal
Assembly (*Bundesversammlung*). The Constitution forbids the
choice of two of its seven members from one and the same Canton: they must represent seven of the twenty-two Cantons. The
Council is organized under a President and Vice-President chosen
by the Federal Assembly, from among the seven councillors, to
serve for a term of one year, the Constitution insisting upon the
extreme democratic doctrine of rotation. Neither President nor
Vice-President can fill the same office for two consecutive terms;
nor can the President be immediately nominated to the office of
Vice-President again upon the expiration of his term. There is
nothing to prevent the Vice-President succeeding the President,
however; and it has hitherto been the uniform practice to follow
this natural and proper line of promotion.

The Federal Assembly may elect to the Council any Swiss citizen
who is eligible to either Chamber of the Legislature. As a matter of fact,
however, they almost invariably make their choice from amongst the
members of the Chambers, though an election to a place in the executive
body necessitates a resignation of the legislative function. Bern and
Zürich have always been represented in the *Bundesrat*, and are considered to have acquired a sort of prescriptive right to places on it. Vaud
has almost always had a member, too ; and Aargau was represented continuously till 1891.

The choice of the Federal Assembly in constituting the executive has
hitherto been admirably conservative. Some of the more prominent
members of the Council have been retained upon it by repeated reëlection
for fifteen or sixteen years ; one has served for thirty years ; and those
who have left its membership have generally done so of their own accord,
Only twice, indeed, since 1848, have members who wished reëlection been
refused it.

The Federal Assembly fills all vacancies in the membership of the
Council, electing, however, only for the unexpired term.

The three-years term of the Council is coincident with the three-years
term of the National Council, the popular branch of the Legislature. At
the beginning of each triennial term of this lower House, the two Houses
come together as a Federal Assembly and elect (in practice reëlect) the
Federal Council. If the National Council be dissolved before the close of
its three-years term, the election of the *Bundesrat* must be renewed by the
two Houses upon the assembling of the new National Council. The *Bundesrat* is thus not, strictly speaking, elected for three years, but for the
term of the National Council, whatever that may turn out to be.

The precedence of the President of the Council is a merely formal precedence: he is in no sense the Chief Executive. He represents the Council in receiving the representatives of foreign powers; he enjoys a somewhat enhanced dignity, being addressed in diplomatic intercourse as 'His Excellency'; and he receives a little larger salary than his colleagues receive; but he is in all practical matters merely the Council's chairman.

The Executive and the Legislature. — The members of the Federal Council, though they may not be at the same time members of either ·House of the Legislature, may attend the sessions of either House, may freely take part in debate, and may introduce proposals concerning subjects under consideration: may exercise most of the privileges of membership, except the right to vote. They are expected, indeed, to prepare and guide the business of the Houses, and every bill is submitted to them for an opinion before its passage. They thus to a certain extent occupy a position resembling that which a French or English ministry occupy; but there is this all-important difference: the English or French ministers are subject to 'parliamentary responsibility,' — must resign, that is, whenever any important measure which they favor is defeated; whereas the Swiss ministers are subject to no such responsibility. Defeat in the Legislature does not at all affect their tenure. They hold office for a term of years, not for a term of legislative success; and they are the servants of the Houses, not their leaders. They have habitually been chosen from both the chief parties in the Confederation, and since 1891 a third political group has been represented among them. They are not expected to speak the same opinions even on the floor of the Houses. But they are expected to act in harmony in all business, and to mediate between extreme views in matters of deliberation.

At the outbreak of the war in 1914 the Federal Assembly conferred by resolution unlimited power upon the Council "to take all measures necessary to the security, integrity, and neutrality of Switzerland, and to protect the credit and economic interests of the country, especially including the assurance of its food supply. For this purpose the Federal Council shall possess unlimited credit to meet expenses. It is especially authorized to conclude all necessary loans. The Federal Council shall account to the Federal Assembly at its next session with regard to its employment of the unlimited powers hereby conferred upon it." [1] It is doubtful if any permanent change in the relations between the executive and the legislature will be produced by this emergency measure. The jealousy with which the two Houses have regarded the exercise of the powers thereby conferred would indicate a return to former conditions with the return of peace.

The Executive Departments. — The Council acts as a body of Ministers. It was the purpose of the Constitution that all executive business should be handled by the Council as a whole, but of course such collegiate action has proved practically impossible: it has been necessary to divide the work among seven Departments. Each member of the Council presides over a Department, conducting it much as an ordinary minister would under a Cabinet system, though there is a somewhat closer union of the several Departments than characterizes other systems, and a greater degree of control by the several ministers over such details of administration as the 'permanent' subordinates of Cabinet ministers generally manage, by virtue of possession, to keep in their own hands, to the restraint and government of transient political chiefs. All important decisions emanate from the Council as a whole; and, so far as is practicable, the collegiate action contemplated by the Constitution is adopted.

The seven Departments are (1) Political, including Foreign Affairs, (2) Justice and Police, (3) Interior, (4) War, (5) Finance and Imposts, (6) National Economy, and (7) Posts and Railways. The department of Foreign Affairs is associated with the presidency. The arrangement of administrative business in Departments is effected in Switzerland, as in France and Germany, by executive decree, and not by legislative enactment, as in the United States.

It is considered the capital defect of this collegiate organization of the Swiss executive, combined as it is with the somewhat antagonistic arrangement of a division of executive business among Departments, that it compels the members of the Council to exercise at one and the same

---

[1] *Bundessbeschluss* of August 3, 1914, A. S. XXX, 347, quoted in Brooks, p. 114.

time two largely inconsistent functions. They are real, not simply nominal, heads of Departments, and are obliged as such to give their time and attention to the routine, the detail, and the technical niceties of administration ; and yet as a body they are expected to impart to the administration as a whole that uniformity, breadth, and flexibility of policy that can be imparted only by those who stand aloof from detail and routine and command the wider views of general expediency. They are called to be both technical officials and political guides. It has been suggested by thoughtful Swiss publicists that it would be vastly better to give the Departments permanent heads and leave to a board of ministers such as the present Council only a general oversight. Political and administrative functions require different aptitudes, must be approached from very different points of view, and ought seldom to be united in the same persons.

Mixed Functions of the Executive. — Swiss law, as I have said, makes no very careful distinction between executive, legislative, and judicial functions. Popular jealousy of executive power has resulted, alike in the cantonal systems and in the system of the Confederation, in the vesting of many executive functions either wholly or in part in the lawmaking bodies, and a very singular confusion between executive and judicial functions has resulted in the possession by both the executive and the legislative bodies of prerogatives which should, on any strict classification, belong only to regularly constituted courts of law. It is, consequently, somewhat difficult to get a clear summary view of the rôle played in Swiss federal affairs by the central executive Council. Its duties give it a touch both of legislative and of judicial quality.

(1) It stands closely connected with the Legislature because of its part in shaping legislation. The Council both originates proposals in the Houses and gives its opinion upon proposals referred to it, either by the Houses or by the Cantons. It renders annual reports to the Houses concerning its conduct of administration and the condition of the Confederation, which give it opportunity to urge upon them necessary measures of reform or amelioration; and which, being freely debated, give the members of the Houses, also, an opportunity to press their own criticisms and suggestions with reference to the conduct of the administration. It presents the budget of the Confederation also to the Houses and leads in its debates of financial legislation. It is, in

brief, the intimate servant and in part the authoritative guide of the Legislature, both taking and giving advice. The Houses may reverse whatever action of the Executive they please, even though it be merely administrative in character ; but they usually suggest, they do not often condemn action already taken.

(2) In the exercise of several of its most important duties the action of the Council is essentially judicial. It is empowered to examine the agreements made by Cantons among themselves or with foreign governments and to judge of their conformity with federal constitutional law, withholding its approval at its discretion. In like manner there are other cantonal laws and ordinances whose validity is made dependent upon its approval; and until 1893 to a very limited extent, a jurisdiction like that entrusted to the Federal Court in hearing complaints concerning breaches of federal law was given it. It has also authoritative oversight of the administration of federal law by the cantonal officials. There are not many federal officials ; federal law is for the most part executed by local officers, the Federal Council supervising.

> Here are some of the topics touching which the authoritative opinion of the Council may be taken : cantonal school affairs ; freedom of trade and commerce, and the interpretation of contracts with foreign states which concern trade and customs-levies, patent rights, rights of settlement, freedom from military service, free passage, etc.; rights of settlement within the Cantons ; freedom of belief ; validity of cantonal elections, votes, etc.; gratuitous equipment of the militia.[1]

(3) Its strictly executive functions are, however, its most prominent and important functions. It appoints all officers whose selection is not otherwise specially provided for by law; it of course directs the whole executive action of the government, controlling federal finance, and caring for all federal interests; equally of course, it manages the foreign affairs of the Confederation. Besides these usual executive and administrative functions, it exercises, however, others less common. It is the instrument of the Constitution in making good to the Cantons the federal guarantee of their constitutions. It executes the judgments of the Federal Court, and also all agreements or decisions

of arbitrators concerning matters in dispute between Cantons. In cases of necessity it may call out and itself direct the movements of such cantonal troops as are needed to meet any sudden danger, provided the Legislature is not in session to command such measures, and provided the call is for not more than two thousand men for a service of more than three weeks. If more men or longer service seem necessary, the Legislature must be called at once and its sanction obtained. This power of the Council to call out troops to meet a pressing peril of war or riotous disorder is a logical part of the duty imposed upon it of guarding the external and internal safety and order of the Confederation, a duty which embraces the general police function of keeping the peace.

The Army. — Compulsory military service is required by the constitution of 1848 which at the same time forbade the federation to maintain a standing army. The consequence was that the Cantons were left in charge of military administration. The constitution of 1874 gave the federation a much enlarged control over the army, though the prohibition against the maintenance of a standing army was retained. The law of 1907, passed upon referendum by a large popular vote, is the basis of the army organization. Liability to military service extends from the twentieth to the forty-eighth year, but the periods of service are short.

Detail of Federal Supervision. — The federal government is directed by the Constitution to see to it that the Cantons provide free, compulsory, non-sectarian education for their people, and that the political rights and liberties of individuals are respected by cantonal law. It is likewise authorized, in case of internal disturbances, to intervene to preserve the public order upon its own initiative, whenever the cantonal authorities are unable to call upon it for assistance. It has been held, moreover, that it may exercise many of these extensive powers of oversight and direction upon the initiative of individuals whose rights are affected, as well as upon the initiative of the cantonal governments ; and its powers of superintendence and intervention have shown a marked tendency to grow. The people have come to feel the Cantons in many things too small to do without the aid and countenance of the federal power.

Execution of Federal Law. — Although the supervisory powers of the federal government are very great, however, its active administrative duties are not many. The federal laws are for the most part executed by cantonal officials, under the superintendence of the Federal Council. In all that concerns foreign affairs the federal government acts for itself and through its own officials ; it directly administers the custom house, too, and the postal and telegraph systems of the country. It has charge of its own arsenals ; and it is entrusted with the management of the government

alcohol monopoly and of the national polytechnic school. But in almost
all other matters it is served by cantonal officials. Even the Federal
Court has no executive officers of its own.

Appeal in Judicial Cases. — Following the example of the
cantonal constitutions, which provide for a very absolute dependence of the executive upon the representatives of the people and
freely neglect, in practice, the careful differentiation of legislative
from administrative functions, the Federal Constitution of 1848
allowed an appeal in all cases from the Federal Council to the
Federal Assembly (*Bundesversammlung*). The constitutional revision of 1874, which had as one of its chief objects the development and strengthening of the judiciary of the Confederation,
transferred many appeals to a Federal Court, but it left the
action of the Federal Council no less subject to the Assembly
than before, and it did not exclude the Legislature from judicial
functions. It was, indeed, provided that the Federal Court,
rather than the Assembly, should in most cases hear appeals
from the Federal Council; but it was also arranged that certain
'administrative' cases might be reserved to the Assembly by
special legislative action. Religious and 'confessional' questions
have, accordingly, been retained by the Legislature — questions
which would seem to be as far as possible removed from the
character of administrative matters.

It seems to have been the conscious purpose of the more advanced
reformers in 1874 to bring the Federal Court as near as possible in character and functions to the Supreme Court of the United States; but they
were able to realize their purpose only in part. The most important prerogative of our own Court, its powers, namely, of constitutional interpretation, was denied the Federal Court in Switzerland. Most constitutional
questions are decided by the Legislature, except when specially delegated
to the Court by legislation. The chief questions of this nature now taken
cognizance of by the Court are disputes as to constitutional rights between
cantonal and federal authorities.

The Federal Chancellor. — The office of Federal Chancellor is
worth noting as an inheritance of the present from the older Confederation, in whose days of incomplete federalization the Chancellor typified
the unity of the Cantons. The Chancellor is elected by the Federal
Assembly at the same time and for the same term (three years) as the
Federal Council. He is chief clerk of both Houses of the Federal Assembly, is keeper of all the federal records, and exercises a semi-executive

function as preserver of diplomatic forms and usages. A Vice-Chancellor acts under the Chancellor as Secretary of the Council of States (*Stände-rat*), the Chancellor acting chiefly for the popular chamber.

The Federal Legislature. — Properly speaking, the legislative powers of the Confederation are vested in the Federal Assembly (*Bundesversammlung*); but that Assembly consists of two distinct Houses, the National Council (*Nationalrat*) and the Council of States (*Ständerat*); and the Houses act separately in all strictly legislative matters, coming together as a single Assembly only for the exercise of certain electoral and judicial functions. The two Houses stand in all respects upon an equal footing: there is no difference of function between them. The originative work of each session — that is, the first handling of measures — is divided between them by a conference of their Presidents at the beginning of the session. The Constitution requires that at least one session be held annually: as a matter of practice there are usually two sessions of about four weeks each every year, one beginning in June, the other in December, and a shorter extra session in March. Special sessions may be called either by resolution of the Federal Council or upon the demand of five Cantons or of one-fourth of the members of the National Council. An absolute majority of its members constitutes a *quorum* in each House.

Composition of the Houses: I. The National Council. — The popular chamber of the Assembly consists of one hundred and eighty-nine members chosen from forty-nine federal electoral districts (*Wahl-Kreise*) in the proportion of one representative for every 20,000 inhabitants. The federal electoral districts cannot, however, cross cantonal boundary lines and include territory in more than one Canton. If, therefore, in the apportionment of representatives among the Cantons, the division of the number of inhabitants of any Canton by the number 20,000 shows a balance of 10,000, or more, that balance counts as 20,000, and entitles to an additional representative. Reapportionments are made from time to time to meet changes in the number of inhabitants as shown by decennial censuses. If any Canton have less than 20,000 inhabitants, it is, nevertheless, entitled to a representative.

There are now six single-member Cantons. Bern has thirty-two representatives, and Zürich, twenty-five, and Vaud has sixteen.

In those electoral districts which send more than one representative, candidates are voted for upon a general ticket, each voter being entitled to vote for as many representatives as the district returns. It requires an absolute majority to elect, and if no one secures a majority at the first election, a second is held in which a plurality suffices.

Every Swiss twenty years of age who is not a clergyman and who is qualified to vote by the law of his Canton may vote for members of the National Council. The term of the National Council is three years. Elections take place always in October, on the same day throughout the country, — and that day is always a Sunday.

It is upon the assembling of each new National Council that the election of the Federal Council takes place (pages 402, 403). The three-years term of the executive Council is thus made to extend from the beginning of the first session of one National Council to the beginning of the first session of the next.

The National Council elects its own officers ; but in selecting its President and Vice-President it is bound by a rule similar to that which limits the yearly choice of a President of the Confederation. The President or Vice-President of one session cannot be reëlected for the session next following. For the officers of the National Assembly, like the officers of most European law-making bodies, are elected every session instead of for the whole term of the body, as in our House of Representatives and the English House of Commons.

II. **The Council of States** (*Ständerat*) is composed of forty-four members : two from each of the twenty-two Cantons. It would thus seem to resemble very closely in its composition our own federal Senate and to represent distinctively the federal feature of the union between the Cantons. In fact, however, it has no such clearly defined character : for the mode in which its members shall be elected, the qualifications which they shall possess, the length of time which they shall serve, the salary which they shall receive, and the relations they shall bear to those whom they represent, in brief, every element of their character as representatives, is left to the determination of the Cantons themselves, and the greatest variety of provisions consequently prevails. From some Cantons the members are sent for one year only ; by some for three ; by others for four ; by still others for two. In most of the Cantons they are elected by popular vote, as the members of the National Council are; in seven Cantons they are elected by the legislative body of the Canton.[1] Differing, thus, from the National Council, as regards at least very many of its members, only in the fact that every Canton sends the same number as each of the others and chooses the term for which they shall be elected, the Council of States can hardly be called the federal chamber : neither is it merely a second chamber. Its position is anomalous and obviously transitional.

694. The Council of States elects its own President and Vice-President, but subject to the restriction that neither President nor Vice-President can be chosen at any session from the Canton from which the President for the immediately preceding session was taken, and that the office of Vice-President cannot be filled during two successive regular sessions by a member from the same Canton.

695. The Cantons, upon enumeration, number, not twenty-two, but twenty-five, because three of them have been divided into ' half-cantons,' namely, Unterwalden, Basel, and Appenzell. The half-cantons send each one member to the Council of States. The following is a list of the Cantons : Zürich, Berne, Luzern, Uri, Schwyz, Obwalden, Nidwalden, Glarus, Zug, Freiburg, Solothurn, Baselstadt, Baselland, Schauffhausen, Outer Appenzell, Inner Appenzell, St. Gallen, Graubünden, Aargau, Thurgau, Ticino, Vaud, Valais, Neuchâtel, Geneva.

696. **Functions of the Houses.** — It may be said, in general terms, that its Legislature is the supreme, the directing organ of the Confederation. It is difficult, therefore, to classify the functions which the Houses exercise, because they extend into every field of government; but the following may serve as a distinct arrangement of them: 1. They exercise the sovereignty of the Confederation in its dealings with foreign states, controlling all alliances or treaties with foreign powers, determining questions of peace and war, passing all enactments concerning the federal army, and taking the necessary measures for maintaining the neutrality and external safety of Switzerland. 2. They maintain the authority of the Confederation as against the Cantons, taking care to pass all the measures necessary for preserving internal safety and order and for fulfilling the federal guarantee of the cantonal constitutions, and deciding, upon appeal from the Fed-

[1] They are Bern, Freiburg, St. Gallen, Aargau, Vaud, Valais, and Neuchâtel.

eral Council, the validity of agreements between the Cantons or between a Canton and a foreign power. 3. They exercise the general legislative powers of the Confederation, providing for the carrying out of the Federal Constitution and for the fulfilment of all federal obligations. 4. They pass upon the federal budget and control the federal finances. 5. They organize the federal service, providing for the creation of all necessary departments or offices and for the appointment and pay of all federal officers. 6. They oversee federal administrative and judicial action, hearing and acting upon complaints against the decisions of the Federal Council in contested administrative cases. 7. With the concurrence of the people, they revise the Federal Constitution.

Legislative Procedure.— Each House is served in the conduct of its business by a President, a Vice-President, and four Tellers. These six officers constitute a ' Bureau,' whose duty it is not only to count the votes upon a division, but also to look after absentees, and to appoint such committees as the chambers do not themselves choose to elect. Much of the business introduced is referred to committees for detailed consideration ; but the Federal Council is the grand committee. All important legislation either comes from it or goes to it for final formulation, and its part is generally a guiding part in debate.

Revision of the Constitution. — When the two Houses can agree concerning a revision of the Constitution, it is effected by the ordinary processes and under the ordinary rules of legislation, though it is followed by an obligatory *Referendum* to the people. But a revision may also be otherwise accomplished. If one House demands particular changes and the other House refuses to assent, or if 50,000 qualified voters call for a revision by petition, the question whether or not a revision shall be undertaken must be submitted to popular vote; and if there be a majority of the whole of such popular vote in the affirmative, new Houses must be elected and the revision proceeded with. In every case the amendments adopted by the Houses must be voted upon by the people and must be accepted by a majority of the people and by a majority of the Cantons also in order to go into force. In reckoning up the votes by Cantons, on such occasions, the vote of a half-canton counts as half a vote.

The Federal Referendum. — "Federal laws, as well as generally binding federal resolutions, which are not of a pressing nature, shall be laid before the people for their acceptance or rejection upon the demand of 30,000 qualified Swiss citizens or of eight cantons." Such is the command of Article 89 of the Federal Constitution which establishes for the Confederation the 'facultative' or 'optional' *Referendum* (page 398).

The whole detail of the exercise of the *Referendum* is regulated by federal legislation. A period of ninety days, running from the date of the publication of the law, is set within which the demand for a popular vote must be made. Copies of all federal laws which are subject to *Referendum* are sent to the authorities of each Canton, and by them published in the Communes. For the Communes are constituted the districts in which the popular demand is to be made up. That demand must be made by written petition addressed to the Federal Council; all signatures must be autographic; and the chief officer of the Commune must attest the right of each signer to vote. Demands from Cantons for the *Referendum* are made through the cantonal councils, subject to the right of the people, under the provisions of the cantonal *Referendum*, to reverse the action. In case it appears that 30,000 voters or eight Cantons demand *Referendum*, the Federal Council must set a day for the popular vote; a day which must be at least four weeks later than the resolution which appoints it.

Functions of the Federal Assembly. — The functions which the Houses exercise in joint session, as the Federal Assembly, are not legislative but electoral and judicial. 1. The Assembly elects the Federal Council, the federal judges, the Chancellor, and the generals of the federal army. 2. It exercises the right of pardon. 3. It determines conflicts of jurisdiction between federal authorities.

The President of the National Council presides over the sessions of the Federal Assembly, and the rules of the National Council for the most part govern its proceedings.

Administration of Justice: I. The Cantonal Courts. — The Cantons are left quite free by the Federal Constitution to organize their courts as they please. Not even a general uniformity of system is prescribed; nor are the cantonal courts subordinated to the Federal Court except in certain special cases provided for by statute. It may be said, in general terms, that justice is administered by the Cantons, with recourse in selected cases to the tribunal of the Confederation.

There is, however, a certain amount of uniformity in judicial organization throughout Switzerland. There are usually two ranks of courts in each Canton : District Courts (*Bezirksgerichte* or *Amtsgerichte*) which are courts of first instance, and a supreme Cantonal Court (*Kantonsgericht*) which is the court of final instance. There are also everywhere Justices of the Peace whose duty it is, in many places, first to act as mediators in legal disputes, — and as magistrates only when they fail as mediators. Petty police cases are heard by the District Courts ; but for the hearing of criminal cases there is trial by jury under the presidency of a section of the supreme court justices, or by a special criminal court acting without a jury.

In some of the larger Cantons, there are special Cassation Courts formed by a division of the Cantonal Court. Special Commercial Courts (*Handelsgerichte*), and industrial courts (*Gewerbegerichte*) have been established in industrial districts.

In many of the Cantons the Supreme Court exercises certain semi-executive functions, taking the place of a Ministry of Justice, in overseeing the action of the lower courts and of all judicial officers, such as the states-attorneys.

In most of the Cantons, too, the Supreme Court makes annual reports to the legislative Council, containing a full review of the judicial business of each year, discussing the state of justice, with criticisms upon the system in vogue and suggestions of reform. These reports are important sources of judicial statistics.

The terms of cantonal judges vary. The usual terms are three, four, and six years. The judges of the inferior courts are as a rule elected directly by the people : those of the supreme courts commonly by the legislative Council.

No qualifications for election to the bench are required by Swiss law except only the right to vote. But here, as well as in regard to the very brief terms of the judges, practice is more conservative than the law. To the higher courts, at least, competent lawyers are generally elected ; and reëlection is in most cases the rule.

In Geneva the States-attorney, instead of the Supreme Court, is given the general duties of superintendence which, outside of Switzerland, are vested in a Minister of Justice ; and in other Cantons similar officers are given prerogatives much more extensive than are usually associated with such offices elsewhere.

II. The Federal Court. — The Federal Court was created by the Constitution of 1848. Before that time arbitration had been the only form of adjudication between the Cantons. Even in creating it, however, the Constitution of 1848 withheld from the Federal Court all real efficiency : its jurisdiction was of the most restricted kind and was condemned to be exercised under the active superintendence of the omnipotent Federal Assembly. It was one of the chief services of the constitutional reform of 1874 that it elevated the Federal Court to a place of substantial influence and real dignity. It still rests with the Houses to determine by statute many of the particular questions which shall be submitted to the Court; but its general province, as well as its organization, is prescribed in considerable detail by the Constitution.

The Federal Court consists of twenty-four judges chosen by the Federal Assembly (with due regard to the representation of the three official languages of Switzerland, — German, French, and Italian) for a term of six years. Every two years, also, the Federal Assembly selects two of these twenty-four to act, the one as President, the other as Vice-President, of the Court. The Court sits, not at Berne, the legislative capital of the Confederation, but at Lausanne.

The Federal Assembly elects, at the same time that it chooses the judges, nine substitutes also, who sit, as occasion demands, in place of any judge who cannot act, and who receive for their occasional services a *per diem* compensation.

The members of the Court may not hold any other office or follow any other business during their term as judges; nor can they be members of any business corporation.

Criminal Jurisdiction of the Federal Court. — In the exercise of its criminal jurisdiction the Federal Court goes on circuit.

The country is divided into three assize districts (*Assisenbezirke*), one of which embraces French- and Italian-speaking Switzerland ; the other two, German-speaking Switzerland.

The Court annually divides itself, for criminal business, into four bodies: A Criminal Chamber, the Federal Penal Court, a Chamber of Complaints, and a Chamber of Appeals. The Criminal Chamber decides at what places in the several Districts assizes shall be held. The places selected furnish, at their own cost, a place of meeting. The cantonal police and court officers serve as officers of this Court. A States-attorney appears for the Federal Council in all cases.

Cases in Public Law. — The jurisdiction of the Federal Court covers a great variety of causes. There are (1) Cases in Public Law. These include disputes between Cantons concerning such matters as the fulfilment of inter-cantonal agreements, the settlement of boundary lines, conflicts of jurisdiction between the authorities of different Cantons, and extradition; also the enforcement of agreements between Cantons and foreign governments; and, most fertile of all, cases involving the constitutional rights of citizens, whether those rights rest upon the federal or upon a cantonal constitution. Its jurisdiction does not, however, cover questions as to the constitutionality of federal legislation. The federal Houses are the sole judges, under public opinion, of their own powers.

It is considered "the proper and natural province of the Federal Court" in Switzerland "to defend the people and the citizens against abuses of power, whether they proceed from federal or cantonal authorities." Such a province is, however, in the very nature of the case, insusceptible of definite limitations; and the powers of the Federal Court have gradually spread far abroad by reason of the temptations of this vague prerogative. The most usual and proper cases arising under it are infringements of the federal guarantee to citizens of equality before the law, of freedom of settlement, of security against double taxation, of liberty of the press, etc., but the Court has gone much beyond these. Its jurisdiction has been extended to the hearing of complaints against cantonal authorities for ordinary alleged failures of justice, such as the Constitution can hardly have contemplated giving into the hands of the Federal Court. The Court has even "brought within the circle of its judgments cases where the appellant asserts a denial of his claims by a cantonal judge grounded upon merely obstructive motives or an arbitrary application of the law."[1]

[1] Orelli, p. 42.

The Federal Court has also cognizance of contested citizenship cases between Communes of different Cantons. For citizenship in Switzerland is first of all of the Commune. The Commune is, so to say, the unit of citizenship, and it is through communal citizenship that cantonal citizenship is held (p. 401).

(2) **Civil Cases in Private Law.** — The administration of justice between individuals under federal laws is left for the most part to the cantonal courts, which thus serve in a sense as federal tribunals ; but if, in any case falling under federal law, a sum of 3000 francs be involved, or if the matter involved be not susceptible of money valuation, an appeal may be taken to the Federal Court from the court of last resort in the Canton. Certain other private law cases, even when they do not involve federal law, may be brought, — not by appeal, but in the first instance, — before the Federal Court upon another principle, because, *i.e.*, of the nature of the parties to the suit, *viz.:* Cases between Cantons and private individuals or corporations ; cases in which the Confederation is defendant; cases between Cantons ; and cases between the Confederation and one or more Cantons.

Cases of the first two of these four classes can be brought in the Federal Court only if they involve a sum of 3000 francs. Otherwise they must be instituted and adjudged in the cantonal Courts.

By agreement of both parties, the jurisdiction of the Federal Court may be invoked in any case in which the subject of litigation is rendered important by virtue of federal legislation.

A special railroad jurisdiction, too, has been given by statute to the Federal Court, covering cases concerning right of way and the right of eminent domain, and cases in private law between railroads and the Confederation.

(3) **Criminal Cases.** — The criminal jurisdiction of the Federal Court covers cases of high treason and of outbreak or violence against the federal authorities, breaches of international law, and political offences which were the cause or the result of disorders which have necessitated the intervention of the Confederation. It may, however, in the discretion of certain authorities, include a variety of other matters in addition to these. Federal officers, whose breaches of duty are ordinarily punished

upon judgment of the cantonal tribunals, may, by resolution of the Federal Council or of the Federal Assembly, be handed over to the Federal Court to be judged. Cases may even, also, be assigned to the federal tribunal by cantonal constitutions or laws, if the Federal Assembly assent to the arrangement.

The Chamber of Appeals of the Federal Court takes cognizance, besides, of complaints concerning judgments of the cantonal courts given under certain fiscal, police, and banking laws of the Confederation.

By amendments to the constitution adopted in 1898, the federation was expressly authorized to deal with all matters of civil and criminal law. To carry out this power and bring about uniformity a civil code was drafted and put into operation by the Federal Assembly on January 1, 1912. A similar codification of the criminal law is in process.

The Federal Council: (4) **Administrative Cases.** — The administrative jurisdiction of the Confederation, which is exercised, not by the Federal Court, but by the Federal Council, includes a great number of important cases. It covers questions touching the calling out of the cantonal militia, the administration of the public-school system of the Cantons, freedom of trade, occupation and settlement, consumption taxes and import duties, freedom of belief and worship, the validity of cantonal elections and votes, and rights arising out of contracts with foreign powers regarding trade relations, the credit to be given to patents, exemption from military service, freedom of passage, etc. In all these cases an appeal lies from the Federal Council either to the Houses or to the Federal Court.

In 1914 an amendment to the Constitution was adopted, providing for the establishment of an administrative court to exercise such jurisdiction in administrative cases as the Federal Assembly may confer upon it.

Inter-Cantonal Judicial Comity. — The Swiss Constitution, in close imitation of the provision on the same subject in the Constitution of the United States, requires that full force and credit be given the judgments of the courts of each Canton throughout the Confederation.

Some Representative Authorities.

Adams, Sir F. O., and *Cunningham*, C. D., The Swiss Confederation. 8vo, London and N.Y., 1889.

Blumer, J. J., Handbuch des schweizerischen Bundesstaatsrechts, 2 vols., 1863–1865; New ed. completed by J. *Morel*, 1887.

Bluntschli, J. C., Geschichte des schweizerischen Bundesrechts von den ersten ewigen Bünden bis auf die Gegenwart, 2 vols., 1849–1852; 2d ed., Vol. I., 1875.

Borgeaud, Chas., Adoption and Amendment of Constitutions in Europe and America. Trans. by C. D. *Hazen* and J. M. *Vincent*. New York and London, 1895. Pp. 250 ff.

Brooks, R. C., Government and Politics of Switzerland, N.Y., 1918. Excellent and has critical bibliography.

Burakhardt, W., Kommentar der Schweizerischen Bundesverfassung, Bern, 2 ed., 1914.

Coolidge, Early History of the Referendum, in the *English Historical Review*, 1891, p. 674.

Curti, Th., Le Referendum; histoire de la legislation populaire en Suisse, Paris, 1915.

Demombynes, G., Les Constitutions Europénnes, Ed. 1883, Vol. II., pp 304 ff.

Deploige, S., Le Referendum en Suisse, Brussels, 1893.

Dodd, W. E., Modern Constitutions, 2 vols., Chicago, 1909.

Droz, Numa, Études et portraits politiques.

Dubs, J., Das öffentliche Recht der schweizerischen Eidgenossenschaft, 2d ed., Zürich, 1878.

Dupriez, L., Les Ministres dans les principaux pays d'Europe et d'Amérique, 2 vols., Paris, 1892. Vol. II., pp. 167 ff.

Hilty, C., Die Bundesverfassung der schweizerischen Eidgenossenschaft, Bern, 1891.

Lowell, A. L., Governments and Parties in Continental Europe, 2 vols., Boston, 1896. Chaps. XI.–XIII.

Macy, Jesse and Gannaway, Comparative Free Government, N.Y., 1915.

Moses, Bernard, The Federal Government of Switzerland, An Essay on the Constitution. A comparative study. San Francisco, 1889.

Ogg, F. A., The Government of Europe, N.Y., 1913.

Orelli, Alois von, Das Staatsrecht der schweizerischen Eidgenossenschaft (in *Marquardsen's* Handbuch des öffentlichen Rechts), Freiburg im B., 1885.

Rambert, Eugène, Études historiques et nationales, — Les Alpes Suisses, 1889.

Richman, Irving B., Appenzell, Pure Democracy and Pastoral Life in Inner Rhoden.   A Swiss Study.   London and N.Y., 1895.

Snell, Ludwig, Handbuch des schweizerischen Staatsrechts, 2 vols., Zürich, 1837–1845.   Contains a great deal of original material for the period preceding the formation of the present federal government.

Stüssi, Referendum und Initiative in den Sweizerkantonen, Zürich, 1893.

Vincent, J. M., Government in Switzerland.   N.Y., 1900.

Winchester, Boyd, The Swiss Republic, Philadelphia and London, 1891.

XI

THE GOVERNMENT OF ITALY.

—∘∘⟩⟨∘∘—

The Empire. — The overthrow of the Roman Empire by the barbarian tribes in the fifth century did not destroy the tradition of supremacy associated with the name of Rome, any more than it destroyed Roman law and civilization. As the latter survived and profoundly modified the civilization imposed upon it, so Rome survived as the traditional mistress of the world and became again under the Frankish kings, in name at least, the head of a new Empire, that of Charlemagne and his successors. The imperial tradition thus revived and centered in Rome had a profound influence upon subsequent Italian history and had much to do with the late realization of Italian unity. While other nations, as France, England, and Spain, were developing into the modern national states, unified under their own national kings, Italy was ruled for the most part by foreigners; in the first instance by the Emperors of the Holy Roman Empire, who were German, and at a later date by these German Emperors and by the French and Spanish who established claims to various parts of the peninsula.

The Church. — Throughout all this period the Church was a temporal power, at times rivalling in influence the Emperor and always supreme in the States of the Church, a territory stretching across central Italy from northeast to southwest and for centuries forming a competing temporal power.

The City Republics. — In the later Middle Ages there grew up, particularly in northern Italy, great free city Republics, such as Genoa, Florence, Pisa, Milan, and Venice — and for a brief moment, Rome itself. These city Republics felt the full force of the Renaissance and its awakening spirit, and for a space played a great part in the history of the world. In time they lost their republican character for the most part and sank into subjection or obscurity, but left behind them a strong republican tradition.

Napoleon. — At the end of the eighteenth century Italy remained but a geographical designation for a great number of petty kingdoms and principalities, most of them under the control of foreign princes. Napoleon, with the conqueror's ruthlessness, swept them all away and established the Kingdom of Italy. Brief as was the existence of this artificial union, it nevertheless left its impression of a united Italy — an impression which added strength to the growing sentiment in favor of national unity.

But Napoleon's Kingdom of Italy had been preceded by the establishment of a number of Republics in northern Italy when he was still the leader of nominally republican France. They were Republics created out of hand by the conqueror and were as readily dissolved by the same hand, yet they revived the medieval tradition of the city Republics and gave expression to the awakening spirit of the people. Thus Napoleon contributed to the development of the aspiration both for national union and for a republican form of government.

Congress of Vienna. — At the Congress of Vienna, the former condition of Italy was in large measure reëstablished — everywhere were small kingdoms and principalities under rulers whose powers were nowhere limited by constitutional restraints and many of whom were tyrannical. Foreign influence was again reëstablished. But the democratic spirit engendered by the French Revolution was very much alive and led to the organization of secret societies whose object was the establishment of a united Italy under a republican form of government.

House of Savoy. — In the northwestern part of the peninsula, stretching from the mountains to the sea, was the Kingdom of Sardinia, under the rule of the House of Savoy, which was destined to become the leader in the unification of Italy, but as a kingdom and not as a republic. In response to the Revolutionary movement of 1848, Charles Albert, its king, granted to his people a constitution, called the *Statuto*, and in 1848–49 he sought to free Italy from the oppression of Austria. Though defeated and compelled to abdicate in favor of his son, Victor Emmanuel, he had centered the thought of the Italians upon the House of Savoy as the possible liberators of Italy. Despite the threats of Austria, Victor Emmanuel refused to repeal the *Statuto*.

The four principal figures in the struggle for Italian unity were Mazzini, the revolutionary enthusiast; the King, Victor Emmanuel; Cavour, his great minister; and Garibaldi, the dashing soldier of fortune. Mazzini's part was played in the earlier years in filling the place of high minded advocate of liberty, in stirring the spirit of freedom throughout Italy, and in conspiring to secure its realization. The king formed the rallying point about which the sentiment in favor of unification could gather, and the high place which he held in the respect and admiration of the people contributed much to the willingness of the republicans to yield their preference and accept a monarchy. Cavour was a truly great statesman who realized that the Austrian power must be driven out before Italy could be united. Accordingly he induced Napoleon III. to declare war on Austria in 1859, in conjunction with Sardinia. The full success of the war was lost by the sudden withdrawal of Napoleon, leaving Venice still in the hands of Austria. Garibaldi fired the imagination of the people, and his successful operations in overrunning Sicily and in driving out the rulers of Naples occurred at a most opportune time.

Cavour's original plan had been for a federation of the Italian states under the nominal headship of the Pope, but with the real leadership in the King of Sardinia. With the conclusion of the war against Austria, leaving Venice in her hands, he concluded that the only solution lay in unification under the House of Savoy. The northern states had risen in 1860 and driven out their rulers; they now voted for union with Sardinia. Sicily and Naples, freed by Garibaldi, likewise decided by popular vote to join the new kingdom. With the exception of Venice, held by Austria, and Rome, held by French troops, the rest of Italy soon followed.

Venice was not added to the new Kingdom of Italy till 1866, when Italy joined Prussia in the war against Austria; but Italy failed then to acquire two districts, preponderantly Italian in population and sympathy — the Trentino, a mountain district, and Italia Irredenta, that part of the Adriatic sea coast adjoining

Venice, of which Trieste is the most important city. Both of these districts will have been added to Italy as a result of the Great War, 1914–1918. Rome was acquired in 1870 at the time of the Franco-Prussian war, when Italian soldiers took possession of the city and Rome became the capital of a united Kingdom of Italy. Thereby the last remnant of the temporal power of the Pope was destroyed.

The Statuto. — The *Statuto* granted by Charles Albert in 1848 remains to-day the constitution of Italy — not the whole constitution, for both custom and enactment have greatly modified the original instrument, but it is still the principal source of governmental arrangements. As the Kingdom of Sardinia expanded into the Kingdom of Italy the *Statuto* was extended to the new territories. The *Statuto* contained no provision for its amendment, and the custom that the constitution may be amended by an ordinary act of Parliament has become so firmly established as to be regarded as a part of the constitution.

The eighty-four articles of the constitution deal with the rights and duties of citizens, the Crown, the Ministers, the Senate, the Chamber of Deputies, and the Judiciary. All inhabitants are guaranteed equality before the law; liberty of person; freedom of the press and of assembly, though the latter is subject to qualifications; inviolability of property and of domicile; and exemption from taxation not authorized by Parliament.

The King. — According to the *Statuto* the form of government is a "representative monarchical government," with an hereditary king who succeeds under the Salic law, that is, only by and through the male line. The executive power is vested in the King, who approves and promulgates the laws, concludes treaties, declares war, appoints all officers of state, makes decrees and ordinances, creates Senators, and commands the military and naval forces. These powers, though vested in the King, are not exercised by him but by ministers responsible to the Chamber of Deputies. No act of the king is valid unless countersigned by one of his ministers, and this fact is the legal foundation for the responsibility of the ministers to the Chamber of Deputies.

The actual powers exercised by the King are slight, and no attempt has been made by any one of the three kings to be other than a constitutional monarch, but each has recognized whole-heartedly that the actual government is carried on by the ministers under responsibility to the popular house of Parliament. The "representative" function of the King is not without importance ; his opinions in matters of foreign relations have much weight and at times of cabinet crises, when the ministry resigns the King may exercise a certain amount of choice with respect to the man who shall be selected to form a new cabinet and in doing so may exert some influence upon the course of government.

The Ministry. — As in other countries with responsible cabinet government, the ministers are both political leaders and heads of the administrative department. Of the latter there are at present thirteen, which are as follows : Foreign Affairs ; War ; Marine ; the Interior ; Finance ; the Treasury ; Public Instruction ; Public Works ; Justice and Ecclesiastical Affairs ; Commerce, Industry, and Agriculture ; Posts and Telegraphs ; Colonies ; and Railways and Merchant Marine.

In the exercise of their functions as political leaders, the ministers, who are members either of the Senate or of the Chamber of Deputies, have a right to appear upon the floor and to speak in both houses, though their right to vote is confined to the house of which they are members. The king may appoint to the post of minister one who is not a member of Parliament, but such a minister must be appointed a member of the Senate or stand for election to the Chamber at the first vacancy. Also there have been ministers without portfolio. The premier has generally held the post of Minister of the Interior.

As the head of the government, responsible to the Chamber, the cabinet takes the initiative in legislation, though private members may introduce bills ; but by reason of the multiplicity of parties, cabinets have usually been lacking in internal unity and in the power of controlling the Chamber, with the result that it is difficult for a cabinet to inaugurate and put through an extended programme and that ministries change with frequency.

The Senate. — The Italian Senate is unlike any other second chamber in its composition. Its membership is unlimited in number (395 in 1916), and aside from the royal princes, of whom there are six, its members are appointed by the king for life from certain classes of the people as defined in the *Statuto*. Generally these classes may be said to comprise high state officials, — church officials also are eligible but since the break with the Vatican in 1870 none have been appointed, — persons of fame in science or literature or who have performed a distinguished service for the state, and persons who pay over 3000 lire ($600) in taxes. Appointment by the king means of course appointment by the ministry in power, but the Senate has a right to decide whether or not the proposed appointee comes from one of the recognized classes and in a number of instances it has decided that the requirements had not been met and in consequence the appointment failed. Members must not be less than forty years of age. The president and vice-president are designated by the crown. The power of appointment has been exercised on several occasions for the purely political purpose of changing the opinion of the body, as many as seventy-five senators being appointed at one time in 1890, and through this power the equality of the Senate with the chamber has been destroyed.

Legally the Senate has an equal voice with the Chamber in law-making, and no bill can become a law without its consent, but its consent can be forced by the method of appointment. The Senate lacks popular character and cannot stand against the Chamber. Ministers are responsible to the Chamber and not to the Senate and those cases in which opposition in the Senate has led to the resignation of a ministry may be regarded as accidental.

The Senate may act as a High Court for the trial of ministers impeached by the Chamber and to try cases of high treason and attempts upon the safety of the state.

The Chamber of Deputies. — The popular house of the Italian Parliament is elected on the basis of universal manhood suffrage, except that those under thirty years of age who have neither performed military service nor learned to read and write are excluded. In the earlier years of the Kingdom the electorate was narrowly limited, due to the backward condition of the country and to the large proportion of illiterates. With the establishment of better school facilities, and with the economic and commercial development of the country, the suffrage has been extended until by the Electoral Law of 1912 universal manhood suffrage was all but reached. There is still a large ignorant and illiterate population but no bad effects therefrom have as yet made themselves felt in serious fashion; and universal manhood suffrage is in keeping with the democratic spirit of the people.

The Chamber is composed of 508 members, or one to each 71,000 inhabitants, elected each from a district. Originally the deputies were elected from separate districts but in 1882 the *scrutina di lista,* or the election of a number of deputies from a single district, was introduced. It was hoped that the new system would lead to the choice of deputies having more of a national and less of a local point of view, but the experiment did not prove a success and was abandoned in 1891 and the former system was reëstablished. A candidate in order to be elected must receive the votes of more than one-tenth of the inscribed electors and more than one-half of the votes cast. If no candidate secures the necessary number of votes, a second election is held a week later.

Qualifications of Members. — Members of the Chamber must be citizens, at least thirty years of age, and in possession of full civil and political rights. It is not necessary that a member should reside in the district which he represents. Priests, salaried government officials, except the officers of the army and navy, ministers and under-secretaries, and a few other high officials and all persons receiving stipends from the state are ineligible. Of those government officials who are eligible there can never be more than forty who are members at the same time, but ministers and under-secretaries are not counted in the forty. Deputies are elected for a period of five years, which is the maximum period for the duration of Parliament, but they seldom fill out the term because of the earlier dissolution of Parliament.

The members receive 2000 lire ($400) to cover the cost of correspondence and 4000 lire a year if not in receipt of an income from a public source. Those who are in receipt of a public income receive the difference to make up this income to four thousand lire. All travel free on government railroads. Since the budget and the contingent of recruits is determined by annual laws, the houses must meet at least once a year unless, as frequently happens, the sessions are prolonged for more than a year.

Procedure. — The president and vice-president of the

Senate are appointed by the Crown, but the Chamber chooses
its own president, who is continued in office without regard to
party affiliations.   The business of the houses is transacted by
committees.   The president of the Chamber appoints the committees on rules and contested elections; in each house the
budget committee is elected directly by the houses.   For the
rest, the Senate is divided into five and the Chamber into nine
sections by lot every two months and these sections choose the
committees not otherwise provided for.

The ministers appear regularly upon the floor of the houses to
defend their measures and to answer questions.   The interpellation, or challenge of the policy of the ministry, exists, but the
vote must follow after an interval of several days, and the ministry is protected from the rashness of a snap vote taken immediately which has proved so destructive to ministries in France.

The Judiciary. — The judicial system of Italy is the
result of a compromise between the existing order in the individual states at the establishment of the Kingdom and the needs
of the new Kingdom.   As a result there is lacking that centralization and coördination of courts which makes for unity.   Instead
of a single supreme court there are five courts of Cassation, located
in Turin, Florence, Rome, Naples, and Palermo, — each supreme
within its own territory, and each interpreting the law in accordance with its own views, — so that it is possible to have five different interpretations of the same law, each affecting a different
district.   The Court of Cassation at Rome has had conferred
upon it exclusive jurisdiction to decide in cases of conflict of
jurisdiction between different courts, conflicts between the courts
and the administrative authorities, the transfer of cases from
one court to another, writs of error in criminal cases, and some
other special matters, but in all other cases involving the ordinary
civil law the five courts of Cassation are all equal.   The lower
courts are more symmetrically organized, for they are new creations and do not differ materially from the French plan.

Administrative Courts. — In Italy, as in the rest of continental Europe, there are administrative courts to try cases affecting administrative officers.   In England no distinction is made
between public and private law and all offences are subject to trial

by the ordinary courts. Administrative law and administrative courts are sharply differentiated in France from the ordinary law and courts. In Italy the distinction is made but it has not been so clearly carried out as in France. A special section of the Council of State, composed of a president and eight councillors appointed by the king, serves as the highest administrative court, while inferior jurisdiction has been conferred upon the prefects and certain assistants in the provinces. It has in general the right to decide whether the acts of the local or central officers are authorized by law, unless some special provision to the contrary has been made by law.

Local Government. — The local government in Italy is modeled on that of France and is even more centralized than that of the latter. Familiarity with the French system and the need for a strongly centralized government to meet the unsettled conditions in parts of the newly formed kingdom combined to sweep away all preëxisting territorial divisions and forms of local government. In its place was substituted an artificial division of the country into provinces, circondari, mandamenti, and communes, lacking in real local life.

Prefect. — At the head of each province — they are sixty-nine in number — is a prefect appointed by the king and directly responsible to the minister of the Interior. His functions correspond very closely to those of the French prefect, for he is both a political and an administrative official. He publishes and executes the laws, supervises the administration of the provinces, opens and closes the sessions of the provincial council, sanctions or vetoes the acts of that body, and protects the interests of the central government in the province.

Council. — With the prefect there is associated a council of from twenty to sixty members, elected for a period of six years, with one-half of the members renewed every three years. The Council meets regularly once a year and its most important business is the voting of the provincial budget. A commission, elected by the Council from its members, carries on the business of the Council in the interval between its meetings. The prefect has large powers of control over the proceedings of the Council and he is not responsible to it but only to the central government.

The *circondari* are primarily electoral districts and the *mandamenti*, or cantons, are mere administrative subdivisions of the provinces.

The Commune. — The commune is the most vital of Italian local government units. It has the duty of maintaining streets, roads and markets; to provide elementary education; to provide poor relief; to see to the registration of electors; to keep a register of births and deaths; and to provide police protection. In addition to its duties, it may provide for every sort of local enter-. prise. The government of the commune is composed of a syndic, or mayor, and a council. The syndic is elected by the council from among its members for a term of three years. Though chosen by the council the syndic is a representative of the central government and may be removed, save in exceptional circumstances, only with the consent of the prefect and is responsible not to the council but to his superiors. The council is composed of from fifteen to eighty members and its members are elected for a period of six years, one-half being renewed every three years. The council meets regularly twice a year and its work is carried on between meetings by a committee chosen from its members.

The Pope. — The relation of the Kingdom of Italy to the Papacy has been extremely difficult of a satisfactory solution. The temporal power of the Popes had existed for centuries and was regarded as necessary for full religious freedom on the part of the church. But the continued existence of the Papal states stretching across the central portion of the peninsula was a bar to Italian unity. Accordingly the Papal states, with the exception of Rome, were added to the Kingdom in 1860. But there was a feeling that without Rome, united Italy was incomplete.

Advantage was taken of the Franco-Prussian war, when Napoleon III. was in no position to aid the Pope, and on September 20, 1870, Italian troops entered Rome and took possession of the city. Before moving the seat of government to Rome it was thought best to settle the position of the Pope, so the Law of the Papal Guarantees of May 13, 1871, was passed. According to this law the Pope enjoys the personal rights and privileges of a sovereign. His person is declared sacred and inviolable; public officials are not permitted to enter his palace or grounds in the ex ercise of their duties; and persons accredited to him enjoy all the immunities of diplomats. He is guaranteed freedom of intercourse and protection for papers and messages; he is granted annually the sum of six hundred and forty-five thousand dollars, but this he has never consented to receive; and he is left in undisturbed possession of the palaces of the Vatican, the Lateran, and Castel Gandolfo, with their gardens free from taxation.

The Popes have never been willing to recognize the loss of their temporal power or to acquiesce in the present arrangements. For a time there was a hope that foreign powers might intervene to reëstablish their claims, but when this hope vanished, Pope Pius IX. in 1883 promulgated a decree, the *non expedit*, by which it was declared "inexpedient" for Catholics to participate in Parliamentary elections, and in 1895 what had been declared "inexpedient" was forbidden. This prohibition did not apply to municipal elections and was not widely observed by Catholics, many of whom strongly opposed it. Ten years later it was found necessary to relax the prohibition; the socialist party had been so rapidly growing in strength that Pope Leo XIII yielded to the argument that it was the duty of the Church to oppose socialism, and in 1905 he issued an encyclical which made it the duty of Catholics to support the social order and enjoined that they take part in political contests in its defense wherever it was threatened. The participation in political struggles must, however, be under the direction and control of the Church. The result has been to found a strictly Catholic and conservative party and to unite more closely the radical-republican-socialist groups through a common anti-clerical sentiment.

SOME REPRESENTATIVE AUTHORITIES.

Cesaresco, M., The Liberation of Italy, London, 1895, London, 1898.

Dodd, W. E., Modern Constitutions, 2 vols., Chicago, 1909.

Dupriez, L., Les Ministres dans les principaux pays d'Europe et L'Amerique, 2 vols., Paris, 1892.

Godkin, G., Life of Victor Emmanuel II., London, 1880.

King, B., A History of Italian Unity, 2 vols., London, 1899. Mozzini, London, 1902.

King and *Okey*, Italy To-day.

Lowell, A. L., Governments and Parties in Continental Europe, 2 vols., Boston, 1896.

Ogg, F. A., The Governments of Europe, New York, 1913.

XII.

THE GOVERNMENT OF BELGIUM.

———o○⦂⊗⦂○o———

THE history of Belgium justifies the statement that it has been the battle ground of Europe. It has formed a part of three great Empires: those of Charlemagne, of Charles the Fifth, and of Napoleon. It had been successively Spanish, Austrian, French, and Dutch, before finally attaining independence. From the days of Charles the Fifth it has had a separate existence. In the eighteenth century the Austrian Netherlands appear as a territory distinct from the hereditary possessions of the Habsburgs, and under French dominion, administration and legal uniformity were gained. Thus through all the centuries and under so many different powers, the Belgians retained their identity and prepared the way for political independence. By the terms of the Congress of Vienna, there was established the United Kingdom of the Netherlands with William of Orange as sovereign. The Kingdom was composed of Holland, the bishopric of Liege, and the Austrian Netherlands, but the union was from the first an unhappy one. The constitution, drawn up in Holland, was rejected by the Belgians, but was nevertheless put into operation. Dutch was made the official language though French was spoken in a large part of the Kingdom. The Protestant Dutch antagonized the Catholic Belgians and the administration was more favorable to the Dutch than to the Belgian provinces.

The French revolution of 1830 inspired the Belgians to follow a like course, and a national congress proclaimed the independence of Belgium. A constitution was adopted February 7, 1831 and Leopold of Saxe-Coburg was chosen king. In spite of Dutch opposition, the conference of The Powers in London in 1831 recognized the independence of Belgium, and Holland was forced to acquiesce.

Plan of the Constitution. — The Belgian constitution consists of 139 articles divided into eight titles as follows : the territory and its divisions; citizens and their rights; concerning powers; finances; the army; general provisions; revision of the constitution; and temporary and supplementary provisions. The constitution extends a rather long list of individual rights guaranteed by the constitution and safeguarded by law. Among the constitutional rights of Belgians may be mentioned equality before the law; no distinction of classes; individual liberty; no arrest for longer than twenty-four hours without a warrant; inviolability of domicile and of property; religious liberty, freedom of the press, of speech, and of assembly, and the right of petition.

Powers of Government. — All power emanates from the people and can only be exercised in the manner provided by the constitution. The legislation is exercised collectively by the King, the House of Representatives, and the Senate, each of which has the right of initiative; but money bills and laws relating to the army contingent must be voted first by the House of Representatives.

The executive power is vested in the King, subject to the provisions that his ministers are responsible and that no decree of the King shall take effect unless it is countersigned by a minister who thereby renders himself responsible for it.

The judicial power is exercised by the courts and the tribunals, but the authoritative interpretation of the laws is vested in the legislative power. Belgian courts cannot declare laws unconstitutional and the legislative power is the supreme power in the government.

Made under the impulse of revolution, the Belgian constitution was remarkable for its liberality and democracy; at a time when the reactionary forces were in control in Europe, it represents complete popular supremacy and legislative omnipotence under the form of a constitutional monarchy.

The Legislative Power; the Senate. — The country is divided into nine provinces, and from each province senators are chosen in two ways, some directly by the people and some by the provincial councils, to the number of two for each province having less than 500,000 inhabitants, of three for each province having from 500,000 to 1,000,000 inhabitants, and of four for each province having more than 1,000,000 inhabitants. The number of senators to be elected directly by the voters shall be equal to one half the number of members of the House of Representatives.

Senators are elected for a term of eight years, one half being elected every four years. In case of dissolution the whole Senate is renewed. The Senate is then divided, one half serving for four years and the other for eight. The qualifications for senator are Belgian citizenship and residence, civil and political rights, the payment of at least 1200 francs direct taxes or the proprietor or usufructuary of real estate in Belgium, the assessed income of which amounts to at least 12,000 francs. In the provinces in which those eligible do not reach the proportion of one for every 5000 inhabitants, there are added a sufficient number of the highest taxpayers to make this proportion. In the case of senators elected by the provincial council, there is no property qualification. Senators must be at least forty years of age; they receive no salary or emoluments. Sons of the King, or if there be none, the Belgian princes of the branch of the royal family designated to succeed to the throne, are senators at the age of eighteen but have no vote until the age of twenty-five.

House of Representatives. — The members of the House are chosen by direct election for a term of four years, one half being elected every two years. In the event of a dissolution, the whole House is renewed and the members are divided into two groups, one of which serves for two years and the other for four.

Plural voting exists for members both of the House and of the Senate. All male citizens twenty-five years of age and resident for one year in the same commune and not otherwise disqualified by law have the suffrage. An additional vote is given all married men, and widowers with children, who have reached the age of thirty-five and pay a tax of not less than five francs as householders, unless exempt on account of a profession, and likewise to all those who have reached the age of twenty-five, who own real estate of the value of at least 2000 francs or possess an income from land corresponding to such value, or are inscribed in the great book of the public debt or possess obligations of the Belgian savings bank bearing at least 100 francs interest.

Two additional votes are given to citizens who have reached the age of twenty-five years and who hold a diploma from an institution of higher instruction or a certificate showing the completion of a course of secondary education of the higher degree or who hold or have held a public office or position or who practice or have practiced a private profession which presupposes at least the knowledge imported in the secondary instruction of higher degree. But no one shall have more than three votes, and voting is obligatory under penalties ranging from a reprimand and a fine of twenty-five francs to a temporary deprivation of the right to vote and hold office. The system of proportional representation is employed. The number of representatives is fixed by law according to the population, but must not exceed one for every 40,000 inhabitants.

Qualifications. — Members of the House must be Belgian citizens, resident in Belgium, and in the enjoyment of civil and political rights and at least twenty-five years old. The compensation of members is 4000 francs a year and free transportation on government railroads from the place of residence to the city where the session is held.

The King and the Ministers. — The succession to the throne, or rather to the constitutional powers of the King, is hereditary in the House of Saxe-Coburg according to the Salic law. The powers of the King are limited to those conferred by the constitution and the laws; these he can exercise only through a responsible minister who must countersign all his decrees.

The parliamentary system of government through responsible ministers is established by the constitution, and powers conferred upon the King are in reality the powers of the ministers who are responsible to the House of Representatives. The King appoints and dismisses the ministers, but he must appoint those who can secure support for their policies from a majority in the House of Representatives, and he cannot in practice dismiss ministers so long as they enjoy that support. The King approves and promulgates the laws and must issue all regulations and decrees necessary for the execution of the laws, but he cannot suspend or dispense with the laws. The King commands the military and naval forces, declares war, makes treaties of peace, alliance, and commerce, but treaties which may burden the state or bind Belgians individually take effect only after having received the approval of the two Houses.

The Houses meet annually the second Tuesday in November, but the King may summon them earlier; he may dissolve one or both of the Houses and he may adjourn them, but not for longer than a month and not oftener than once in a session without the consent of the Houses.

The ministers are the leaders of the majority in the House of Representatives and also the administrative heads of the departments, of which there are ten: Foreign Affairs; Interior; Science and Arts; Agriculture; Industry and Labor; Justice; Finance; Public Works; War; and Railroads. Ministers have the right to appear and be heard in both Houses but can vote only in the House of which they are members. The Houses have the right to demand the presence of ministers.

As under other systems of parliamentary government, the question and the interpellation are the normal means by which the Houses exercise control over the government. The question demands an answer from the minister but not a vote; if a vote is demanded, it becomes an interpellation and there is a debate, followed by a vote.

Committees. — The House is divided into six sections, renewed every month by lot. Bills are referred to the sections for examination unless a special committee is appointed for a particular bill. Each section appoints a reporter, and the six reporters, together with the president of the Chamber, form the central section, which in turn appoints its reporter. There are two permanent committees of the House, elected by secret ballot at each session — a committee of finance and accounts and a committee of agriculture, industry, and commerce. The House also elects special committees whenever it sees fit, and this is the normal procedure in the Senate.

The Judiciary. — The judicial system consists of a Court of Cassation for the whole of Belgium, which sits at Brussels. Its members are appointed by the King from two lists, one presented by the Court itself and the other by the Senate. Below the Court of Cassation are three courts of appeal, whose members are appointed by the King from two lists, one presented by these courts and the other by the provincial councils. Next in sequence come the courts of first instance who are appointed by the King, but the presidents and vice-presidents of these courts are appointed from two lists, one presented by the courts and the other by the provincial council. In addition there are courts of assizes to hear criminal cases, military courts, courts of commerce and justices of the peace. All judges are appointed for life and no judge shall be deprived of his office or suspended till after trial and judgment. Nor can they be transferred except by a new appointment and with their consent. Belgium differs from other continental countries in that it has no administrative courts but in this particular has followed the English system.

XIII

THE GOVERNMENTS OF GERMANY.

———o◦;◦;◦o———

The Feudalization of Germany was in some points strongly contrasted with the feudalization of France. There was in Germany no Romanized subject population such as existed in Gaul, with habits which should enter like a leaven into the polity of their conquerors. Beyond the Rhine all were of one general kin, all bred to the same general customs. What was new there was the great Frankish kingship of Merowingian and Carolingian, — the new size and potency of the regal power bred amidst the readjustments of conquering migration by the dominant Franks. For the rest, there was at first the old grouping about elective or hereditary princes, the old tribal individualities of custom, the old organization into separate, semi-independent, self-governing communities. Feudalism came, not so much through fresh gifts of land and novel growths of privilege based upon such fresh gifts, not so much through 'benefice' and 'commendation' (pages 104–106, 108), as through the official organization of the Frankish monarchy.

Official System of the Frankish Monarchy : the Counts. — In order to exercise their kingly powers the more effectually, the Frankish monarchs adopted the natural plan, for which there was Roman precedent, of delegating their functions to officers commissioned to act as their representatives in various districts of their extensive domains. There does not seem to have been any symmetrical division of the territory into districts to fit the official system. Here and there there were counts (*Grafen*), the king's vicegerents in the exercise of the financial, judicial, and military prerogatives of overlordship; but the limits of their jurisdiction were not always sharply defined. There were, for one thing,

438

many exemptions from their authority within the general districts allotted them. There were the dignity and pretensions of provincial princes to be respected, more important still, there were the claims of the great landowners to a special jurisdiction and independent lordship of their own to be regarded. As a matter of policy such claims were generally allowed. The demesnes of the greater landowners were cut out from the administrative territory of the count and given separate political functions. Barons, such as we have seen in France, — local autocrats with law courts and a petty sovereignty of their own, — were freely created. The king apparently could not deny them the 'immunities' they demanded.

The Magistracy of Office and the Magistracy of Proprietorship. — There thus grew up, side by side, a double magistracy — a magistracy of office and a magistracy of proprietorship. The count ruled by virtue of his office; the baron by virtue of his landed possessions: there were lords by privilege, and lords by commission. As time went on the two sets of magnates drew nearer and nearer to the possession of a common character through an interchange of qualities. The office of count tended more and more to become hereditary and to connect itself with the ownership of large estates. Heredity of title and prerogative was the almost irresistible fashion of the age: the men of greatest individual consequence, besides, — the men who were fit because of their individual weight to be delegated to exercise the royal authority, — were commonly the men of large properties. Either there went, therefore, along with the grafship, gifts of land, or else men already sufficiently endowed with lands were given the grafship: and as the office connected itself with proprietorship it took from proprietorship its invariable quality of heredity. This was the double process: counts became hereditary territorial lords; and hereditary territorial lords acquired either the grafship itself or powers quite as great.

Hereditary Chiefs. — Add to this hierarchy the more ancient dukes of the tribes, and the tale of greater lords is complete. These dukes were, by traditional title at least, rulers of the once self-governing communities which Frankish ascendency had in the days of conquest united under a common authority. In many cases, no doubt, they retained a vital local sway. They were intermediate, in the new political order, between the king and the barons.

Full Development of Territorial Sovereignty. — By the thirteenth century German feudalization was complete. Dukes, counts, and barons had all alike become lords within their own territories (*Landesherren*). Bishops and abbots, too, as in France, had entered the competition for power and become themselves counts and barons. That territorial sovereignty, that private ownership of political authority which is the distinguishing mark of feudalism, and which we have seen so fully developed in France, is present in as full development here in Germany also. But the elements of the development are very different in the two countries. In France we have seen the appointment of royal delegates come after the perfecting of feudalism and lead, through the gradual concentration of judicial and other authority in the king's hands, to the undermining and final overthrow of baronial sovereignty (pp. 195, 197). In Germany, on the contrary, the royal representatives, appointed while feudalism was taking shape, themselves entered and strengthened the baronage, quitting their dependent functions as officials for the independent privileges of territorial lords.

The Markgraf. — One office especially fostered feudal independence in Germany. Outside the hierarchy I have described, and standing in special relations with the king, was the *Markgraf*, — the count of the march or border, set to defend the kingdom against inroads by hostile peoples. He was of course chosen chiefly because of his capacity in war, and was of the most imperative, masterful soldier breed of the times. To him, too, were necessarily vouchsafed from the first extraordinary powers. He was made virtual dictator in the unsettled, ill-ordered border district which he was appointed to hold against foreign attack ; and he was freely given all the territory he could conquer and bring under the nominal authority of the king. It was thus that the Mark Brandenburg spread itself out to the northeast, to become at last a great kingdom, and that the *Ostmark*, established by Charles the Great as a barrier against the Hungarians, increased till it became the great state of Austria. The *Markgraf* was not

long in becoming virtually a ruler in his own right, little disturbed by the nominal suzerainty of a distant monarch, and possessed by fast hereditary right of the titles and powers which
would one day make of him a veritable king.

The Empire. — Charles the Great set for his successors
the example of a wide rule and a Roman title. But for many
a long age it seemed as if he had left behind him nothing but a
tradition and a scheme of power which no man was able to take
up. His great empire fell to pieces, never to be put together
again, except as it seemed to rise once more for a little space in
the days of Charles V. Even the greater fragments of it fell
apart beyond the Rhine, shattered by the disintegrating forces
of feudalism. But the name and shadow of the imperial power
persisted from age to age with a strange vitality. First a line
of Saxon princes, then men of the Franconian house, after them
the masterful Hohenstaufen essayed the office Charles had made
great, wielding such authority as they could as power came and
went amidst the shifting scene of German politics. Finally the
succession fell to the house of Habsburg, who were building a
veritable kingdom together upon the southern skirts of Germany,
where the *Ostmark* had grown to be Austria. As their strength
increased, their presidency amidst the German states became an
unmistakable power of command, and Germany had at last a
leader, if not a master.

The Imperial Cities. — While the imperial power languished a notable thing happened. Germany gave birth to great
free cities, set like independent states in the midst of their weak
neighbors. The cities of the Empire had, as feudalism developed, fallen into its order in two classes. Some of them held
their privileges of the Emperor himself, were his immediate vassals; others were subordinated to some feudal lord and were subjects of the Empire only through him. The position of those
immediately dependent upon the Emperor was much more advantageous than the position of those who had lesser and nearer
masters. The imperial supervision was apt to be much less
exacting than the overlordship of princes who, having less wide
interests to care for than those which busied the Emperor, could
render their power greater by concentration. They were always

near at hand and jealous of any movement of independence on the part of the towns within their domain; the Emperor, on the other hand, was often far away and never by possibility so watchful. He was represented always by some deputy; but the presence of this officer did not greatly curtail municipal self-government. In the thirteenth century even this degree of control was got rid of at the suit of some of the cities. They were allowed to become 'free' imperial cities, bound to the Emperor only by sworn allegiance, not by any bonds of actual government. The next step in the acknowledgment of their independence and importance was their admission to representation in the Diet of the Empire, — and such recognition was not long delayed. The rôle of these great free cities in imperial affairs became one of the most important of the many independent rôles played on the confused stage of that troubled time. Lübeck, Hamburg, and Bremen retain to this day a certain privilege of position as free cities in the German Empire.

484. **The Swiss Confederation.** — Almost at the very time that the Habsburgs first won the imperial crown and acquired the duchy of Austria, some of their Swiss dependencies broke away from them, and established an independence never since permanently broken. Schwyz, Uri, and Unterwalden, the sturdy little mountain communities grouped about the southern end of quiet Lucerne, with whose struggle for freedom the glorious story of the Swiss Confederation begins, contained some part of the estates of the Counts of Habsburg, whose hereditary domains touched the other end of Lucerne, and stretched wide to the north about the further shore of Lake Geneva, and southward again on the West. The region of the Alps contained the notable imperial cities of Zürich, Berne, Basle, and Schaffhausen ; and Schwyz, Uri, and Unterwalden claimed to be immediate vassals of the Emperor, as these cities were. The Counts of Habsburg, in despite of this claim, sought to reduce them to submission to themselves. The result was a long struggle in which the three little cantons, at first joined only by their neighbor canton, Lucerne, but afterwards by Zürich, Glarus, Zug, and Berne, were eventually completely victorious. By the formation of this famous league of free cantons and cities, at first known as the " Old League of High Germany," but ultimately as Switzerland (the land of Schwyz), there emerged from the German Empire one of the most interesting states known to history. It may be said to have been the offspring of the disintegrating forces of the Empire, — a living proof of its incoherence.

Austria's Rival, Prussia. — While Austria's power was on the make a formidable rival had grown up in the north, out of the North Mark established in the tenth century as the Empire's barrier against the Wends. Men of energy and daring had steadily pushed forward the eastern boundaries of the Mark until it had become a great territory, the Mark Brandenburg. In the fifteenth century the markgrafship fell into the hands of a race more capable than the Habsburgs, the Hohenzollerns of Nuremberg. Under them it waxed greater yet alike in territory and in organized power: took in Prussia, the district from which it was to get its later name, and got ready for the rôle it was to play in the seventeenth, eighteenth, and nineteenth centuries. In 1640 Frederic William, the Great Elector (1640–1688), came upon the stage, to make his power a determining element in the politics of Europe. His son was Frederic, the first ' king in Prussia.'

Frederic the Great. — Frederic, the first king of Prussia, governed from 1688 to 1713. His son, Frederic William I. (1713–1740), rounded out Brandenburg's possessions and hoarded the money and prepared the army with which his son, Frederic the Great (1740–1786), was to complete the greatness of Prussia. Frederic took Silesia from Austria, and then, joining in the heartless and scandalous partition of Poland in 1772, filled up the gap between Brandenburg and East Prussia with West Prussia and the Netze district. The second and third partitions of friendless Poland in 1793 and 1795 added to Prussia the district now known as Posen and a part of East Prussia.

Prussia was at last ready for her final rivalry with Austria for the leadership of Germany. But first there was to be the great storm of the Napoleonic wars, which was to sweep away so much that was old in German political arrangements, and create the proper atmospheric conditions for German nationality.

Napoleon: the Confederacy of the Rhine. — One of the earliest acts of Napoleon in his contest with Austria and Prussia was to isolate these two great German states by thrusting between them a barrier of smaller German states attached to the French interest. So little coherent was Germany, so little had the Empire made of the Germans a single nation, that Napoleon was able to detach from all alliance with either Austria or Prussia every one of the German states except Brunswick and the electorate of Hesse. Of these the chief were the kingdoms of Bavaria and Württemberg and the grand-duchy of Baden. Napoleon organized out of these allies the so-called 'Confederacy of the Rhine,' of which he constituted himself 'Protector,' and which lasted from 1806 till 1813.

The year 1806 had marked also the formal end of the 'Holy Roman Empire' over which the Habsburgs had so long presided. The eighteenth century had witnessed a notable decline in their power; the sweeping conquests of Napoleon put them at his mercy; and in 1806 Francis of Austria was forced to abdicate and forever renounce the imperial office. There was no more to be a German Empire till Prussia should draw one about her, and Austria be once for all ousted from her place of leadership in Germany.

The German Confederation (1815-1866). — Despite the ease with which he at first divided Germany in order to conquer it, Napoleon discovered at last that he had himself aroused there a national feeling which was to cast him out and ruin him. In 1813 Germany rose, the Confederacy of the Rhine went to pieces, and all Napoleon's plans were undone. He had done Germany the inestimable service of making her patriotic. The Congress of Vienna, which met at the close of the Napoleonic wars to recompose Europe, could not revivify the German Empire: that had been dead for some time before Napoleon forced a winding up of its affairs. But Germany was not to remain disintegrate. The year 1815 witnessed the formation of a new union of the German states, the German Confederation, which, loose as it seemed, held them more closely together than they had been held for many generations. Austria was the president of the Confederation. The organ of government was a Diet of ambassadors from the thirty-nine component states (kingdoms, duchies, cities, principalities) authorized to mediate between the states in all matters of common concern; and the Confederation maintained an army of thirty thousand men. The arrangement was little enough like national union: the large states had a preponderant representation in the Diet, Austria dominating all; and each state, whether great or small, was suffered to go its own way, make its own alliances, and fight its own wars, if only it refrained from injuring any one of the Confederates or the interests of the Confederation. But there was sufficient cohesion to keep the states together while German national feeling grew, and while the political revolutions of the century (1830 and 1848) liberalized political institutions.

Period of Constitutional Reform. — By 1848 most of the German states, except Prussia, granted constitutions to their people. In the same year a 'German National Parliament' met at Frankfort (the seat of the Diet of the Confederation) and attempted to formulate a plan for more perfect union under the leadership of Prussia; but its leaders proposed much more than was possible, the time was not yet ripe, and the attempt failed. Still earlier, in 1833, Prussia had led in the formation of a 'Customs Union' (*Zollverein*) between herself and all[1] the states of the Confederation except Austria, which laid a free-trade basis for those subsequent political arrangements from which also Austria was to be excluded. In 1850 Prussia received from the hands of her king the forms, at least, of a liberal government, with parliamentary institutions.

The North German Confederation (1867–1871). — Finally, in 1866, came the open breach between Prussia and Austria. The result was a six weeks' war in which Austria was completely defeated and humiliated. The Confederation of 1815 fell to pieces; Prussia drew about her the Protestant states of Northern Germany in a 'North German Confederation'; the middle states, Bavaria, Württemberg, Baden, etc., held off for a while to themselves; and Austria found herself finally excluded from German political arrangements.

Austria out of Germany. — Thereafter Austria, originally predominantly German, devoted herself to the fruitless task of amalgamating the various nationalities of Southeast Europe under her hegemony, and so became in large part a non-German state. Prussia became the head and front of Germany, in her stead. Meantime Prussia has grown more than one-fifth in territory. The rearrangement at Vienna in 1815 gave her Swedish Pommerania and the northern half of Saxony; the war of 1866 gained

[1] The Union did not at first include this 'all,' but it did eventually.

for her the possession of Schleswig-Holstein, Hannover, Hesse-Cassel, Hesse-Nassau, and Frankfort.

The German Empire. — The finishing impulse was given to the new processes of union by the Franco-Prussian war of 1870–1871. Prussia's successes in that contest, won, as it seemed, in the interest of German patriotism, broke the coldness of the middle states towards their great northern neighbor; they joined the rest of Germany; and the German Empire was formed (Palace of Versailles, January 18, 1871).

GOVERNMENT OF THE EMPIRE.

Austria and Germany: Character of the German Empire. — When he ceased to be Emperor of the Holy Roman Empire (1806), Francis I. still remained Emperor of Austria. He had assumed that title in 1804; and there became in full form, — what there had long been in reality, — an Austrian Empire. In 1871 there arose by its side a new German Empire, but the two empires were thoroughly unlike one another. The Austrian Empire, though wearing the form of a dual monarchy as Austria-Hungary, was composed of the hereditary possessions of the House of Habsburg; the German Empire, on the other hand, was a federal state composed of four kingdoms, six grand-duchies, five duchies, seven principalities, three free cities, and the imperial domain of Alsace-Lorraine, these lands being united in a great 'corporation of public law' under the hereditary presidency of the king of Prussia as German Emperor.

The four kingdoms were Prussia, Bavaria, Saxony, and Württemberg; the grand-duchies, Baden, Hesse, Mecklenburg-Schwerin, Saxe-Weimar, Oldenburg, and Mecklenburg-Strelitz; the duchies, Brunswick, Saxe-Meiningen, Anhalt, Saxe-Coburg, and Saxe-Altenburg; the principalities, Waldeck, Lippe, Schwarzburg-Rudolstadt, Schwarzburg-Sondershausen, Reuss-elder line, Schaumberg-Lippe, and Reuss-younger line; the free cities, Hamburg, Lübeck, and Bremen.

The Central German States and the Empire. — The first step towards the new union was taken in 1870, when Baden, Bavaria, and Wurttemberg, fearing that the object of Napoleon

III. was to conquer the central German states or renew the Confederation of the Rhine, decisively espoused the side of Prussia and the North German Confederation. While the siege of Paris was in progress these three states sent delegates to King William at Versailles and formally united themselves with their northern compatriots: the North German Confederation became the German Confederation, with King William as president. Almost immediately, thereafter, the influences of the time carried the Confederates a step farther: the president-king was crowned Emperor, and the German Confederation became the German Empire.[1]

The Character of the Empire. — These changes of membership and of title did not, however, change the character or, at first, the constitution of the union. It remained a federal state, and the king of Prussia was still its president only; he was not its monarch. Its make-up and powers were not radically altered. Prussia, indeed, was very great: in territory nearly three times as large as all the other states of the union put together, her population three-fifths that of all Germany; and the king of Prussia had other means of mastery than those afforded by the law. But as Emperor he occupied not an hereditary throne, but only an hereditary office. Sovereignty did not reside in him, but "in the union of German federal princes and the free cities." He was the chief officer of a great political corporation, whose object it was to "form an eternal union for the protection of the realm and the care of the welfare of the German people."

The Emperor. — Still his constitutional prerogatives were of the most eminent kind. He was irresponsible: he could not be removed, his office belonging inalienably to the throne of Prussia. He summoned, opened, adjourned, and closed the two Houses of the federal legislature, the *Bundesrat* and the *Reichstag*, the latter of which he could also, with the consent of the *Bundesrat*, dissolve. He appointed, and might at his pleasure remove, the Imperial Chancellor, who was both the vital centre of all imperial administration and the chairman of the *Bundesrat;* and he appointed also, under the countersignature of the Chancellor, all minor officers of the imperial service, whom, with a like coöperation of the Chancellor, he might also dismiss. He controlled the

[1] The constitution of the Empire bears date April 16, 1871,

foreign affairs of the Empire and commanded its vast military forces; and in this latter capacity, of commander-in-chief of the imperial army, it rested with him, acting at the suggestion of the *Bundesrat,* to coerce into obedience such states of the Empire as might at any time wilfully and pertinaciously neglect to fulfil their federal duties. He had, in brief, to the fullest extent, both the executive and the representative functions now characteristic of the head of a powerful constitutional state. There were distinct limits to his power as Emperor, limits which marked and emphasized the federal character of the Empire; but those limits nevertheless lay abundantly wide apart. Adding, as he did, to his powers as hereditary president of the Empire his commanding privileges as king of Prussia and, as king of Prussia, the dominant member of the Union, he possessed no slight claim to be regarded as the most powerful ruler of our time.

Sovereignty of the Empire in Legislation. — So complete, so unlike that of a mere confederation, was the union of German states that the sovereign legislative power of the Empire was almost unlimited. The constitution could be amended by the federal legislature; amendment might change all the existing allotments of power as between the federal and the state governments; powers reserved to the states could, except in one or two instances in which they were explicitly guaranteed, be withdrawn from them without their consent. The individual states virtually retained their general rights " only by sufferance of the Empire." [1] Amendments of the constitution were not submitted either to the people or to the governments of the states : nor were they passed by any special or peculiar procedure, as in France (p. 401). They were originated and acted upon as ordinary laws would be. The only limitations put upon their passage were, first, that fourteen negative votes in the *Bundesrat* would defeat a proposed amendment, and, second, that no state could be deprived of any right guaranteed to it by the constitution, without its own consent. From the first the legislative power of the Empire covered the entire field of the law of contracts, of commercial law, and of criminal law; and by an amendment of December 20, 1873, it was

[1] Laband, *Das Staatsrecht des deutschen Reiches* (Marquardsen's *Handbuch*), p. 22.

extended to the whole field of civil law as well. For some time it did not exercise its power over the whole domain of these great subjects, but it later enacted, besides full codes of commercial and criminal law, an exhaustive civil code which brought practically all of private law under the statutes of the imperial government.

The Bundesrat: its Composition and Character. — The central and characteristic organ of the Empire was the *Bundesrat*, the Federal Council, which was alike in make-up and function, the lineal successor of the Diet of the older Confederation. In form, in theory, and indeed in fact, the *Bundesrat* was a body of ambassadors. Its members represented the governments of the states from which they came, and were accredited to the Emperor as diplomatic agents, plenipotentiary *chargés d'affaires*, to whom he must extend the same protection that was extended to the like representatives of foreign states. It was a fundamental conception of the German constitution that " the body of German sovereigns together with the senates of the three free cities, considered as a unit, — *tanquam unum corpus*, — is the repository of imperial sovereignty "; [1] and the *Bundesrat* was the organ of this body. It was therefore the organ through which the sovereignty of the Empire was expressed. The Emperor did not exercise sovereignty : he only shared it as king of Prussia, so far as the Empire was concerned, and took part in its exercise only through the Prussian members of the *Bundesrat.* It followed, of course, from this principle that the members of the *Bundesrat* were only the agents of their governments, and acted under instructions from them, making regular reports of the proceedings of the *Bundesrat* to their home administrations. The votes of a state were valid, whether cast by its representatives in accordance with their instructions or not; but the delegates were responsible for every breach of instructions to their home authorities. In practice they were generally themselves members of the governments they represented, entrusted also with high administrative functions at home, and representing their governments in the local legislative bodies of their own states, as well as in the *Bundesrat.* The *Bundesrat* was thus used, as it was intended to be, and as it was used under the somewhat looser forms of the earlier Confederation, as a body of con

[1] Laband, p. 40.

sultation and guidance, a larger sort of imperial cabinet, in which the responsible ministers of the several states drew together to determine all questions of general interest, whether they affected the making or the administration of the laws.

Representation of the States in the Bundesrat. — The states of the Empire were unequally represented, according to their size. Prussia had seventeen votes; Bavaria six; Saxony and Württemberg four each; Baden, Hesse and Alsace-Lorraine,[1] each three; Mecklenburg-Schwerin and Brunswick each two; the other seventeen states one apiece. The votes of each state which was entitled to more than one vote were cast together as a unit, and each such state could cast her full vote whether or not it had its full number of representatives present.

Members were sent and withdrawn at the pleasure of their respective governments, like the responsible agents they were; and their constant responsibility made formal instruction as to their votes upon particular measures for the most part unnecessary. The smaller states found the duty of maintaining representatives at times very onerous; and, inasmuch as it was not required by law that their delegates should be chosen from among their own citizens, it became a common practice for them to serve economy and their own convenience by combining to maintain joint representatives. Groups of them combined, and each group delegated its powers to a single person, who was authorized to represent them severally.

The significance of the constitutional provision that amendments to the constitution could not pass even if there be fourteen negative votes cast in the *Bundesrat* is quite evident. A combination of the small states could in theory defeat any organic change of law proposed by the large states; and Prussia alone could bar any amendment to which she was opposed. The seventeen votes of Prussia on the one side and the seventeen votes of the small states on the other might be said, were there any real offset to the power of Prussia, to have constituted the central balance of the system, but the control by Prussia of the four additional votes destroyed even the semblance of a balance.

[1] The one vote of Waldeck was permanently in the hands of the King of Prussia and the three votes of Alsace-Lorraine were controlled by Prussia.

Functions of the Bundesrat. — The *Bundesrat* occupied a position in the German system in some respects not unlike that which the Roman Senate held in the government of Rome. It was, so to say, the residuary legatee of the constitution. All functions not specifically entrusted to any other constitutional authority remained with it, and no power was in principle foreign to its jurisdiction. It had a composite character, and was the presiding organ of the Empire. It was at one and the same time an administrative, a legislative, and a judicial body.

In its *legislative* capacity, it presided over the whole course of lawmaking. The *Reichstag* had the right to originate measures, but, as a matter of practice, originated very few. Most bills first passed the *Bundesrat* and went with its sanction to the *Reichstag*. If passed by the people's house, they were returned to the *Bundesrat*, and there once more adopted. All the more important legislation, moreover, was framed by the imperial officials and presented to the *Bundesrat* by the Chancellor, who was not only president of the federal chamber but also chief of the Prussian delegation. Prussia, therefore, in reality presided over the process of legislation. Hers was the chief initiative; and the federal chamber, in which she controlled twenty-one votes, was the usual source of every great measure. The *Reichstag* had, of course, the right of amendment, and sometimes exercised it; but nothing that it suggested could become law without the assent of the guiding and overseeing *Bundesrat*. The consent of the *Bundesrat*, as well as of the *Reichstag*, was necessary to every treaty which affected any matter that fell within the legislative powers of the Empire.

The measures sent down from the *Bundesrat* to the *Reichstag* were generally advocated there, if not by the chancellor himself, by members of the federal chamber specially delegated for that purpose; and the *Reichstag* was usually kept advised of the amendments which the *Bundesrat* would accept. All members of the *Bundesrat* had, however, the right to be present in the *Reichstag*, and to express the views of their governments upon its floor concerning pending legislation, even when the views were not those which had been accepted by the majority in the *Bundesrat*.

The *administrative* function of the federal chamber may be summed up in the word *oversight*. It considered all defects or needs which discovered themselves in the administrative arrangements of the Empire in the course of the execution of the laws, and might, in all cases where that duty had not been otherwise bestowed, formulate the necessary regulation to cure such defects and meet such needs. It had, moreover, a voice in the choice of some of the most important officers of the imperial service. It nominated or elected the members of the Court of Accounts, of the Supreme Court of the Empire (*Reichsgericht*), and of the ' Chamber of Discipline,' as well as the officials who administered the imperial pension funds, and those who constituted the directory of the Imperial Bank. It confirmed the nomination, also, either directly or through one of its committees, of consuls and of the officers who exercise the imperial control over the duties and taxes laid by the states under laws of the Empire. The consent of the *Bundesrat* was also necessary to a declaration of war [1] (except in case of invasion, when the Emperor could act alone), to a dissolution of the *Reichstag* during a legislative period, and to coercive action against a state of the Empire.

The *judicial* functions of the *Bundesrat* sprang in part out of its character as the chief administrative council of the Empire. When acting as such a council, many of its conclusions partook of the nature of decisions of a supreme administrative court of appeal. But its jurisdiction as a court was much wider than questions of administration. It could declare a state of the Empire delinquent, and order execution to issue against it. It was the court of highest instance in every case of the denial of justice to an individual in a state court arising out of a defect or deficiency in the law of the state ; it being within its competence in such a case to compel the state to cure the deficiency and afford the suitor the proper remedy. It was the court of appeal in all cases of dispute between the imperial government and a state, and in all cases arising between two or more states of the Empire which involved not mere private law questions (such cases go to the ordinary civil courts), but points of public law.

---

[1] That this power was illusory is shown by the declaration of war in 1914 when the *Bundesrat* was not in session.

In case it could not agree upon a conclusion in such disputes, the whole legislative power was brought into play and a law was passed covering the matter in controversy. If in any case it considered itself unfitted by its organization, or for any other reason, to act as a court in controversies brought before it, it might delegate its judicial powers to a court or to experts. This it did in 1877 with reference to the dispute between Prussia and Saxony concerning the Berlin-Dresden railway.[1]

Organization of the Bundesrat. — The Imperial Chancellor was chairman of the *Bundesrat.* He was appointed by the king of Prussia, and he must also be one of Prussia's seventeen representatives, — for it is the better opinion among German constitutional lawyers that the Chancellor's membership in the federal chamber was necessary to his presidency of the body. In case of a tie vote, the Chancellor's vote was decisive: that is to say, *the side on which Prussia's votes were cast prevailed,* for her vote must be undivided: — the Chancellor's vote was not his own, but was one-seventeenth part of Prussia's whole vote.

Inasmuch as it was not merely the legislative but also the administrative organ of the Empire, the *Bundesrat* might be convened without the *Reichstag.* It must be called together if one-third of its members demanded a session. Its business, moreover, was continuous from session to session, being taken up at each session where it was left off at the last: an arrangement by which it gained both efficiency and expedition in action. Its sessions were secret: for it preserved the reserve of a guiding cabinet. Its compromises and quarrels did not go abroad.

Imperial law made no provision with regard to a *quorum* in the *Bundesrat.* It is believed by German jurists, however, that its business could go forward, after proper notice, if only the Chancellor, its president, were present. No state could cast its vote upon any question in which it was not interested.

Committees. — The *Bundesrat* followed the practice of other deliberative bodies in referring various matters to special committees of its members. It had, too, like other bodies, certain standing committees. These were four: one on Alsace-Lorraine, one on the Constitution, one on the Order of Business, and one on Railroad Freight Rates

[1] Laband, p. 43, *n.*

Much more important than these, however, were eight delegations of its members which, though called committees, may be more properly described as *Commissions*, for, like the executive committee of our own Congress under the old Confederation (p. 288), they continued to sit during the recesses of the chamber which they in a sense represented. Of these Commissions two were appointed by the Emperor, namely a Commission "for the Land Forces and Fortifications" and a Commission "for Naval Affairs": five were chosen yearly by the *Bundesrat*, namely, those "on Tariffs and Taxation," "for Trade and Commerce," "for Railways, Posts, and Telegraphs," "on Justice," and "on Accounts" (*Rechnungswesen*); the eighth and most important, the "Commission on Foreign Affairs," consisted of the representatives of Bavaria, Saxony, and Württemberg, and of two other members chosen by the *Bundesrat*. At least five states must be represented on each of these Commissions, and Prussia must always be one of the five, except in the case of the Commission on Foreign Affairs. On this last Prussia needed no representation; she had committed to her, through her king who is also Emperor, the whole conduct of the foreign affairs of the Empire; the Commission was appointed simply to watch the course of international relations, and to inform the several states of the posture of foreign affairs from time to time. "It has to prepare no conclusion for the *Bundesrat* and to make no reports to it: it serves to receive communications concerning the foreign affairs of the Empire and to exchange opinions with the imperial administration concerning" those affairs.[1] Its action was thus independent of its connection with the *Bundesrat;* and this is the chief point of contrast between it and the other Commissions. Their duties were principally to the *Bundesrat:* they for the most part only made reports to it.

Besides their right to representation on the Commission on Foreign Affairs, of which Bavaria had the presidency, Württemberg, Bavaria, and Saxony had also the right to appointments on the Commissions for Land Forces and Fortifications and for Naval Affairs which it was the privilege of the Emperor to name. Prussia was entitled to the presidency of all the Commissions except that on Foreign Affairs. Each state represented had one

[1] Laband, p. 46.

vote in the action of a Commission, and a simple majority controlled.

The Reichstag : its Character and Competence. — It would lead to very serious misconceptions to regard the *Bundesrat* and the *Reichstag* as simply the two houses of the imperial legislature, unlike each other only in some such way as our Senate and House of Representatives are unlike, only, *i. e.*, because the upper house was differently constituted and was entrusted with a certain share in functions not legislative. Properly conceived, the *Bundesrat* and *Reichstag* stood upon a very different footing with reference to each other. The *Bundesrat* was the sovereign organ of the Empire, the authoritative representative of the " body of German sovereigns and the senates of the free cities." Though it initiated most of the legislation of the Empire, legislation was no more peculiarly its business than was the superintendence of administration or the exercise of judicial functions. It, as part of the administration, governed ; the *Reichstag*, as representing the German people, was supposed to control. The control of the *Reichstag* was exercised, not only through its participation in legislation, but also through the giving or withholding of its sanction to certain ordinances to whose validity the constitution made its concurrence necessary ; through its power of refusing to pass the necessary laws for the execution of treaties of which it does not approve ; through its right to inquire into the conduct of affairs ; and through its right of remonstrance. Its powers were not enumerated ; they were, exercised in one form or another, in theory as wide as the activities of the Empire. The legislative competence of the Empire was, after 1873, legally unlimited as to private law : it covered the whole field of civil and criminal enactment.

Composition of the Reichstag.— The *Reichstag* represented, not the states, or the people of the several states regarded separately, but the whole German people. Representation was distributed on the basis of about one representative to every one hundred and thirty-one thousand inhabitants. Representatives were, however, elected by districts, one for each district, and no district could cross a state line and include territory lying in more than one state. If, therefore, any state of the Empire had less than one hundred and thirty-one thousand inhabitants, it must, nevertheless, be constituted a district and send a representative to the *Reichstag*.

The *Reichstag* consisted (1917) of three hundred and ninety-seven members; and of this number Prussia returned two hundred and thirty-five, about three-fifths of the whole number. The electoral districts were fixed so long ago that Berlin, though it had grown to possess more than two million inhabitants, had only six members in the *Reichstag*.

The members of the *Reichstag* were elected for a term of five years by universal suffrage and secret ballot. The voting age in Germany was twenty-five years; and that was also the earliest age of eligibility to the *Reichstag*.

> The election districts were determined in the northern states according to laws passed under the North German Confederation; in Bavaria, by the Bavarian legislature; in the other southern states, by the *Bundesrat*. The subdivisions of the districts, the voting precincts, were determined by the administrations of the states.
>
> An absolute majority was required for election, as in France (p. 152). In case no candidate received such a majority, the commissioner of election — an officer appointed by the state administration for each district — ordered a new election to take place within fourteen days after the official publication of the result of the first, the voting to be for the two candidates who received the highest number of votes. Should this second election result in a tie, the lot decided.

Election to the *Reichstag* took place, not on days set by statute, but on days appointed by executive decree. For the *Reichstag* could be dissolved by the Emperor, with the consent of the *Bundesrat* (by a vote in which Prussia concurred) before the completion of its regular term of five years.

In case of a dissolution, it was required that a new election must be ordered within sixty days, and the *Reichstag* must reassemble within ninety days. The Emperor could also adjourn the *Reichstag* without its own consent (or, in English phrase, prorogue it) once during any session, for not more than thirty days.

Sessions of the *Reichstag*. — The *Reichstag* met at the call of the Emperor, who must call it together at least once each year; and who might convene it oftener. He must summon at the same time the *Bundesrat*. The sessions of the *Reichstag* were public; it was not within its choice to make them private. A private session was regarded as, legally, only a private conference of the members of the *Reichstag*, and could have no public authority whatever.

Members of the *Reichstag* who accepted a salaried office under the Empire or one of the states, or an imperial or state office of higher rank or power than any they may have held when elected, were compelled to resign and offer themselves for reëlection.

Organization of the Reichstag. — The *Reichstag* elected its own president, vice-presidents (2), and secretaries. For the facilitation of its business, it divided itself by lot, for the session, into seven 'Sections' (*Abteilungen*), each Section being made to contain, as nearly as might be, the same number of members as each of the others. These Sections divided among them the work of verifying the election of members and the choice of special committees. The *Reichstag* had no standing committees; but from time to time, as convenience suggested, temporary committees were named, whose duty it was to prepare information for the body, which they presented in reports of a general nature. These committees it was which the Sections selected. Each Section contributed its quota of members to each committee. The party leaders, however, always determined beforehand the division of places on the Committees and the Sections merely did their will in the matter. Government bills, moreover, were not referred to the committees. They played no such part in revision as is played by the committees of the French Chamber of Deputies. One-half of the members constituted a *quorum;* and an absolute majority was requisite to a valid vote.

Election of Officers. — The initial constitution of a newly elected *Reichstag* was interesting. It came to order under the presidency of the oldest member; it then elected its president, two vice-presidents, and secretaries; the president and vice-presidents for a term of only four weeks. At the end of these four weeks a president and vice-presidents were elected for the rest of the session. There was no election of officers for the whole legislative term, as in England and the United States: at the opening of each annual session a new election took place. It was only at the first, however, that there was a, so to say, experimental election for a trial term of four weeks.

Powers of the Reichstag : the Budget. — The *Bundesrat,*
as I have said, governed ; the *Reichstag* in a measure controlled.
But only in a measure.   Its assent was necessary to the validity
of all legislation.   Though the *Bundesrat* originated, it could not
rule in the field of law without the coöperation of the popular
chamber.   Like other popular assemblies, too, the *Reichstag*
voted the taxes and subjected the government to criticism
when it asked for money.   But the annual budget came to it like
other subjects of legislation, from the *Bundesrat,* and with the
sanction of that great chamber already behind it; many of the
principal revenue laws were not annual but permanent; the army,
for whose maintenance the larger votes were asked, was organized
for periods of several years together and must be paid ; and there
was really very little latitude of choice with regard to any but
new or subordinate expenditures.   No minister was responsible to
the *Reichstag* for what he did or proposed.   The Emperor might
dissolve the *Reichstag* at any time, if the *Bundesrat* consented,
and he frequently exercised the power with the result of obtaining in the new elections the majority he desired.   The *Reichstag*
might influence affairs, might win slow victories by persistent and
well-directed criticism, might force modifications of policy ; but it
was constantly made to realize the fact that it could not govern,
and that its chief function was not origination but control.[1]

Classes and Parties. — The majority of its members, moreover, were Prussians, and Prussia was above all things else a military state, trained to the compact order and instinctive obedience
of a strong monarchy.   Classes, too, were sharply marked in Prussia.   An active and influential landed aristocracy furnished the
army with its best officers, the court with its most devoted servants,
the public assemblies with their most conservative leaders.   The
parties that desired democratic privilege worked against ancient
prestige, against the habit of the community, against the organization and the prejudices of long-established classes.   National
parties, moreover, were broken athwart by the divergent feelings
and variant interests of the different states of the unequal Empire.   Prussia supported the monarchy whose power galled the

---

[1] On at least two occasions unfavorable votes upon the resolution after interpellation had no effect upon the government.

lesser states; her statesmen withstood the process of liberalization which men of some of the smaller states would fain have seen pressed forward. Neither responsible party government nor any kind of clear-cut constitutional rule was possible.

Imperial Administration. — While the distinction between the executive and legislative functions of government was sharply enough preserved in Germany, no equally clear discrimination was made in practice between executive and judicial functions. The judiciary was a branch of the administration. The caption 'Imperial Administration' covered, therefore, all activities of the government of the Empire which were not legislative.

Although it was a fundamental principle of the imperial constitution that 'the Empire has sovereign legislative power, the states only autonomy,' the Empire occupied only a part of the great field thus opened to it, and confined itself as a rule to mere oversight, leaving to the states even the execution of imperial laws. The judges of all but the supreme imperial court, for instance, the tariff officials and gaugers, the coast officers, and the district military authorities, were state officers.

The Imperial Chancellor. — The Empire had, nevertheless, its own distinct administrative organs, through which it took, whether through oversight simply or as a direct executive, a most important and quite controlling part in affairs; and the head and centre of its administration was the Imperial Chancellor, an officer who has no counterpart in any other constitutional government.

(1) Looked at from one point of view, the Chancellor may be said to have been the Emperor's responsible self. If one could clearly grasp the idea of a responsible constitutional monarch standing beside an irresponsible constitutional monarch from whom his authority was derived, he would have conceived the real, though not the theoretical, character of the Imperial Chancellor of Germany. He was the Emperor's responsible proxy. Appointed by the Emperor and removable at his pleasure, he was still, while he retained his office, virtually supreme head of the state, standing between the Emperor and the *Reichstag*, as the butt of all criticism and the object of all punishment. He was not a responsible minister in the English or French sense (pages 160 and 196); there

was, strictly speaking, no 'parliamentary responsibility' in Germany. In many respects, it is true, the Chancellor occupied with regard to the *Reichstag* much the same position that a French or English ministry holds towards the representatives of the people; he must give an account of the administration to them, when a debate was forced upon him. But an adverse vote did not unseat him. His 'responsibility' did not consist in a liability to be forced to resign, but consisted simply in amenability to the laws. He did not represent the majority in the *Reichstag*, but he must obey the law.

This 'responsibility' of the Chancellor's, so far as it went, shielded, not the Emperor only, but also all other ministers. "The constitution of the Empire knows only a single administrative chief, the Imperial Chancellor." [1] So all-inclusive was the representative character of the chancellorship that all powers not specifically delegated to others rested with the Chancellor. Thus, except when a special envoy was appointed for the purpose, he conducted all negotiations with foreign powers. He was also charged with facilitating the necessary intercourse between the *Bundesrat* and the *Reichstag*.

The Chancellor's relation to the *Reichstag* was typified in his duty of submitting to it the annual budget of the Empire.

(2) Still further examined, the chancellorship is found to have been the centre, not only, but also the source of all departments of the administration. Theoretically at least the chancellorship *was* the administration: the various departments were offshoots from it, differentiations within its all-embracing sphere. In the official classification adopted in German commentaries on the public law of the Empire, the Chancellor constituted a class by himself.[2] There were (1) The Imperial Chancellor, (2) Administrative officials, (3) Independent (*i.e.*, separate) financial officials, and (4) Judicial officials. The Chancellor dominated the entire imperial service.

(3) A third aspect of the Chancellor's abounding authority was his superintendency of the administration of the laws of the Empire by the states. With regard to the large number of imperial laws which were given into the hands of the several

[1] Laband, p. 57.   [2] Laband, p. 56.

states to be administered, the Empire could not only command what was to be done, but might also prescribe the way in which it should be done: and it was the duty of the Chancellor to superintend the states in their performance of such behests. In doing this he did not, however, deal directly with the administrative officials of the states, but with the state governments to whom those officials were responsible. In case of conflict between the Chancellor and the government of a state, the *Bundesrat* decided.

The expenses of this administration of federal laws by the states fel[1] upon the treasuries of the states themselves, not upon the treasury of the Empire. Such outlays on the part of the states constituted a part of their contribution to the support of the imperial government. The states were required to make regular reports to the imperial government concerning their conduct of imperial administration.

(4) When acting in the capacity of chairman of the *Bundesrat*, the Chancellor was simply a Prussian, not an imperial, official. He represented there, not the Emperor, for the Emperor as Emperor had no place in the *Bundesrat*, but the king of Prussia. During most of the time since the institution of the Empire the Chancellor was also chief minister of Prussia as president of the Council. Theories aside, the Prussian government guided imperial affairs through the Chancellor.

The Vice-Chancellorship. — The laws of the Empire made a double provision for the appointment of substitutes for the Chancellor. As already said, in connection with his presidency of the *Bundesrat* he could himself appoint a substitute, for whose acts he was, however, responsible. In addition to this a law of March 17, 1878, empowered the Emperor to appoint a *responsible* Vice-Chancellor. This appointment was made, upon the motion of the Chancellor himself, for the administration of all or any part of his duties, when he was himself hindered, even by an overweight of business, from acting; the Chancellor himself judging of the necessity for the appointment. The Chancellor might, at any time, too, resume any duties that might have been entrusted to the Vice-Chancellor, and himself act as usual. He was thus, in effect, ultimately responsible in every case, — even for the non-exercise of his office. The vice-chancellorship was only a convenience.

Foreign Affairs. — The full jurisdiction over the foreign affairs of the Empire conferred upon the imperial government by the constitution of the Empire did not exclude the several states from having their own independent dealings with foreign courts : it only confined them in such dealings to matters which concerned them without immediately affecting imperial interests. The subject of extradition, for instance, of the furtherance of science and art, of the personal relations and private affairs of dynasties, and all matters which affect the interests of private citizens individually, were left to be arranged, if the states desired, independently of the imperial Foreign Office. The states, therefore, had as full a right to send ambassadors for their own constitutional purposes as the Empire had to send ambassadors for its greater objects affecting the peace and good government of Europe. It might thus often happen that the Empire and several of the states of the Empire were at the same time separately represented at one and the same court. In the absence of special representatives from the states, their separate interests were usually cared for by the representative of the Empire. The department of the imperial administration which had charge of the international relations of the Empire was known as the Foreign Office simply (*das Auswärtige Amt*).

Internal Affairs. — The general rule of government in Germany was that administration was left for the most part to the states, only a general superintendence being exercised by the imperial authorities. But the legislative sphere of the Empire was very much wider than is the legislative sphere of the central government in any other federal state. Imperial statutes prescribed in very great variety the laws which the states administered, and constantly extended farther and farther their lines of prescription. From the Empire emanated not only laws which it was of the utmost moment to have uniform, — such as laws of marriage and divorce, — but also laws of settlement, poor laws, laws with reference to insurance, and even veterinary regulations. Its superintendence of the local state administration of imperial laws, moreover, was of a very active and systematic sort.

Weights and Measures. — Imperial methods of supervision are well illustrated in the matter of weights and measures. The laws with reference to the standard weights and measures to be used in commerce were passed by the imperial legislature and administered by state officials acting under the direction and in the pay of the state authorities; but thorough control of these state officials was exercised from Berlin. There was at the capital a thoroughly organized Weights and Measures Bureau (*Normal-Eichungskommission*), which supplied standard weights and measures, superintended all the technical business connected with the department, aud was in constant and direct association with the state officials concerned, to whom it issued from time to time specific instructions.

Money. — With regard to money the control of the Empire was, as might be expected, more direct. The states were forbidden to issue paper money, and imperial legislation alone determined money-issue and coinage. But even here the states were the agents of the Empire in administration. Coining was entrusted to state mints, the metal to be coined being distributed equally among them. This, however, was not really state coinage. The state mints were the mere agents of the imperial government: they coined only so much as they were commanded to coin; they operated under the immediate supervision of imperial commissioners; and the costs of their work were paid out of the imperial treasury. They were state mints only in this, that their officers and employees were upon the rolls, not of the imperial, but of the state civil service. The Empire would doubtless have had mints of its own had these not already existed ready to its hand.

Railways. — The Empire made comparatively little use of the extensive powers granted it in this field by its constitution. It could virtually control; but it in practice only oversaw and advised. The Imperial Railway Office (*Reichs-Eisenbahnamt*) had advisory rather than authoritative functions; its principal supervisory purpose was to keep the various roads safe and adequately equipped. Some railways the Empire itself owned, but most of the lines were owned by the several states; and the states were bound by the constitution to administer them, not independently or antagonistically, but as parts of a general German system. Here again the Empire refrained from passing any laws compelling obedience to the constitution on this point; possibly because the states assiduously complied of their own accord.

Using the *Bundesrat* for informal conference on the matter (though the *Bundesrat* has no constitutional authority in railway administration) they effected satisfactory coöperative arrangements.

The railways of Bavaria stood upon a special footing: for Bavaria came into the federation on special terms, reserving an independence much greater than the other states retained in the management of her army, her railways, and her posts and telegraphs.

For military purposes, the Empire could command the services of the railways very absolutely. It was as aids to military administration primarily that their proper construction and efficient equipment were insisted on through the Imperial Railway Office. Even the Bavarian railroads could be absolutely controlled when declared by formal imperial legislative action to be of military importance to the Empire. With reference to any but the Bavarian roads a simple resolution of the *Bundesrat* alone sufficed for this declaration.

The duty of the states to administer their roads as parts of a single system was held to involve the running of a sufficient number of trains to meet all the necessities of passenger and freight traffic, the running of through coaches, the maintenance of proper connections, the affording of full accommodations, etc.

At times of scarcity or crisis, the Emperor could, with the advice of the *Bundesrat*, prescribe low tariffs, within certain limits, for the transportation of certain kinds of provisions.

Posts and Telegraphs. — Here the administrative arrangements of the Empire were somewhat complicated. Bavaria and Württemberg retained their own systems and a semi-independence in their administration, just as Bavaria did with regard to her railways also; being subject to only so much of imperial regulation as brought their postal and telegraphic services into a necessary uniformity with those of the Empire at large. In most of the states the imperial authorities directly administered these services ; in a few — Saxony, Saxe-Altenburg, the two Mecklenburgs, Brunswick, and Baden — there was a sort of partnership between the states and the Empire. The principle throughout was, however, that the Empire controlled.

Patents, etc. — Besides the administrative activities with reference to internal affairs which have been mentioned, the Empire issued patents, granted warrants to sea-captains, naval engineers, steersmen, and pilots ; and examined sea-going vessels with a view to testing their seaworthiness.

Military and Naval Affairs. — The Empire as such had a navy, but no troops. Prussia was the only state of the Empire that ever maintained a naval force, and she freely resigned to the Empire, which she virtually controls, the exclusive direction of naval affairs. But the case was different, in form at least, with the army. That was composed of contingents raised, equipped, drilled, and, in all but the highest commands, officered by the states. This at least was the constitutional arrangement : the actual arrangement was different. Only Bavaria, Saxony, and Württemberg really maintained separate military administrations. The other states handed over their military prerogatives to the king of Prussia. Bavaria's privileges extended even to the appointment of the commander of her contingent. The Emperor was commander-in-chief, however, appointing all the higher field officers ; and the imperial rules as to the recruitment, equipment, discipline, and training of troops and as to the qualifications and relative grading of officers were of the most minute kind and were imperative with regard to all states alike.

Finance. — The expenses of the Empire were met partly from imperial revenues, and partly from contributions by the states. The Empire levied no direct taxes ; its revenues came principally from customs duties and excises, certain stamp taxes, the profits of the postal and telegraph system, of imperial railways, of the imperial bank, and like sources. So far as these did not suffice, the states assisted, being assessed according to population. And here, again, the states undertook much of the actual work of administration : the customs officials, for example, being state officers acting under imperial supervision. The financial bureaux, like all other branches of the imperial government, were immediately subordinated to the Imperial Chancellor.

Justice. — In the administration of justice, as in so many other undertakings of government, the Empire superintended, merely, and systematized. The state courts were also courts of the Empire : imperial law prescribed for them a uniform organization and uniform modes of procedure : and at the head of the system stood the Imperial Court (*Reichsgericht*) at Leipzig, created in 1877 as the supreme court of appeal. The state governments appointed the judges of the state courts and determined the judicial districts ; but imperial laws fixed the qualifications to be required of the judges, as well as the organization that the courts should have. The decisions of the court at Leipzig gave uniformity to the system of law.

Citizenship. — Every citizen of a state of the Empire was a citizen of the Empire also and enjoyed the rights and immunities of a citizen in every part of the Empire ; but citizenship, though rooted in the states by way of *locus*, was conferred only upon terms fixed by federal law. The Empire determined in nearly all respects this fundamental question of civil *status;* and every citizen was thereby made the more directly and immediately a citizen of the Empire. It remained, nevertheless, the theory of the relationship that citizenship was primarily state citizenship and that citizenship of the Empire flowed out of citizenship of the state. A law of the Empire of 1913 provided that a German, becoming naturalized in another country, might nevertheless retain his German citizenship. The oath of allegiance to his adopted country was not to hinder him from being still a loyal subject of the Fatherland.

THE GOVERNMENT OF PRUSSIA.

The organization of government in Prussia had, for the student of German political institutions, a double interest and importance. In the first place, Prussia's king was Germany's Emperor ; Prussia was the presiding and controlling state of the Empire; and many of her executive bureaux were used as administrative agencies of the Empire. Her government was in a very real sense an organ and representative of the imperial government. In the second place, Prussia's administrative system served as a type of the highest development of local government in Germany.

Stages of Administrative Development. — Until the time when she emerged from the long period of her development as the Mark Brandenburg and took her place among the great military states of Europe, Prussia's administrative organization was of a very crude sort, not much advanced beyond the mediæval pattern.   Later, under the Great Elector and his immediate successors, though well out of her early habits, she was still little more than a mere military state, and her administration, though more highly developed, had almost no thought for anything but the army.   Only since the close of the Napoleonic wars has her system of government become a type of centralized civil order

Process of Centralization. — The Great Elector reduced the feudal Estates of the Mark to complete subjection to his will.   He it was, also, who began the policy by which local affairs as well were to be centralized.   In the towns the process was simple enough.   In them there was little effective obstruction: the channels were already open.   There the military authorities, directly representative of the Elector, had all along dictated in police and kindred matters; direct ordinances of the Elector, moreover, regulated taxation and the finances, and even modified municipal privileges at pleasure.   It did not take long, such being the system already established, to make burgomasters creatures of the royal will, or to put effective restrictions upon municipal functions.

In the provinces, however, it was quite another matter to crush out local privilege.   The Prussia of the Great Elector and his successors was no longer the Mark Brandenburg, but the extended Prussia of conquest.   There were many Estates to deal with in the several principalities of the kingdom; and these Estates, exercising long-established prerogatives, very stubbornly contested every step with the central power.   *They* were the channels through which the sovereign's will had at first to operate upon provincial government, and they were by no means open channels.   They insisted, for a long time with considerable success, that the chief officers of the provinces should be nominated by themselves; and they nominated natives, men of their own number.   Only by slow and insidious processes did the Elector, or his successors the kings of Prussia, make out of these representative provincial officials subservient royal servants.

First Results of Centralization. — The system pursued in the process of centralization, so far as there was any system, was a system by which central control was grafted upon the old growths of local government derived from the Middle Ages. The result was of course full of complexities and compromises. In the vast royal domains *bailiffs* administered justice and police, as did *Schulzen* in the manorial villages. In the larger rural areas a *Landrath*, or sheriff, "nominated by the county nobility, usually from among their own number, and appointed by the king," saw to the preservation of order, to the raising of the levies, to tax collection, and to purveyance. In the towns there was a double administration. Magistrates of the towns' own choosing retained certain narrow local powers, constantly subject to be interfered with by the central authority; but royal tax-commissioners, charged with excise and police, were the real rulers. Above this local organization, as an organ of superintendence, there was in each province a 'Chamber for War and Domains,' which supervised alike the *Landrath* and the city tax-commissioners.

> A War and Domains Chamber consisted of a president, a "director or vice-president, and a number of councillors proportioned to the size, populousness, or wealth of the province." The president of a chamber was "expected to make periodical tours of inspection throughout the province, as the *Landraths* did throughout their counties." In the despatch of business by a Chamber, the councillors were assigned special districts, special kinds of revenue, or particular public improvements for their superintendence or administration, the whole board supervising, auditing, etc.[1]

Justice and Finance. — Much progress towards centralization was also made by the organization of justice and finance. "The administration of justice was in the hands of boards, the *Regierungen*, or governments, on the one hand [the whole organization of administration in Prussia being characteristically collegiate], and the courts on the other."

In finance also there was promise of systematization. During the period preceding the Napoleonic wars, when Prussia figured as a purely military state, the chief concern of the central government was the maintenance and development of the army. The chief source of revenue was the royal domains: the chief

---

[1] Tuttle, *History of Prussia*, Vol. III., pp. 107–109.

need for revenue arose out of the undertakings of war.[1] There were, therefore, at the seat of government two specially prominent departments of administration, the one known as the 'General War Commissariat,' and having charge of the army, the other known as the 'General Finance Directory,' commissioned to get the best possible returns from the domains; and here and there throughout the provinces there were 'War Commissariats' and 'Domains Chambers' which were the local branches of the two great central departments.[2] These two departments and their provincial ramifications were, however, instead of being coördinated, kept quite distinct from each other, clashing and interfering in their activities rather than coöperating.

Fusion of Departments of War and Domains. — Such at least was the system under the Great Elector and his immediate successor, Frederic I., if system that can be called which was without either unity or coherence. Frederic William I. united War and Domains under a single central board, to be known as the 'General Supreme Financial Directory for War and Domains,' and brought the local war and domains boards together in the provinces as Chambers for War and Domains. Under this arrangement the various 'war councillors' who served the provincial Chambers were charged with a miscellany of functions. Besides the duties which they exercised in immediate connection with military administration, they were excise and police commissioners, and exercised in the cities many of the civil functions which had formerly belonged to other direct representatives of the Crown. In the rural districts the Chambers were served in civil matters by the several *Landräthe.*

Differentiation of Central Bureaux. — This arrangement speedily proved as cumbrous as the name of its central organ, and an internal differentiation set in. The General Directory separated into Committees; and, as time went on, these committees began to assume the character of distinct Ministries, — though upon a very haphazard system. Frederic the Great further confused the system by creating special departments immediately

---

[1] The army consumed about five-sevenths of the entire revenue.

[2] Seeley, *Life and Times of Stein*, Vol. I., Chap. II. Also Tuttle, Vol. I., pp. 421, 422.

dependent upon himself and a special cabinet of advisers having no connection with the General Directory. He was himself the only cohesive element in the administration: it held together because clasped entire within his hand.

Reforms of Stein and Hardenberg. — Order was at last introduced into the system through the influence of Baron vom Stein and the executive capacity of Count Hardenberg, the two most eminent ministers of Frederic William III., who together may be said to have created the present central administration of Prussia. Prussia owes to the genius of Stein, indeed, the main features of both her central and her local organization. Her central organization is largely the direct work of his hands; and her local organization derives its principles from his thought not only, but also from the provisions of the Ordinance by which he reconstructed the administration of the towns.

Reform of Local Government before 1872. — The county law (*Kreisordnung*) of the 13 December, 1872, has been called the *Magna Charta* of Prussian local government. Upon it all later changes and modifications rest. Between the period of Stein's reforms and the legislation of 1872 the organization of local government was substantially as follows:[1] The provinces were divided into 'Government Districts,' as afterwards, the Government Districts into 'Circles' or Counties. An administrative Board established in the Government District was then, as afterwards, the vital organ of local administration. In the province there was also a board, exercising general supervisory powers, the eye of the central bureaux in the larger affairs of administration, the affairs, that is, which extended beyond the area of a single Government District; and, as the chief officer of the province, a 'Superior President' of influential position and function. But alongside of this quite modern machinery stood the old provincial Estates (revived in 1853), representing, not the people, but the social orders of a bygone age, and possessing certain shadowy powers of giving advice. In the 'Circle' or County, there was still the *Landrath*, as formerly, appointed from a list of local

---

[1] See R. B. D. Morier's essay on *Local Government in Germany*, in the volume of *Cobden Club Essays* for 1875.

landed proprietors, and associated with the 'Estates of the Circle,' a body composed of the county squires and a few elected representatives from the towns and the rural townships, — a body of antiquated pattern recalled to life, like the Estates of the province, in 1853. In the towns, which had directly received the imprint of Stein's reforming energy and sagacity, administration was conducted by boards of magistrates chosen by popular councils and associated with those councils in all executive business by means of a joint-committee organization, the burgomasters being presidents rather than chief magistrates.

Landgemeinde and Manors. — Besides these areas of administration there were rural communes (*Landgemeinde*) still connected, quite after the feudal fashion, with adjacent or circumjacent manors, their government vested in a *Schulze* and two or more *Schöffen* (sheriffs or justices), the former being appointed either by the lord of the manor, or, if the village was a free village, as sometimes happened, by the owner of some ancient freehold within the commune with which manorial rights had somehow passed. The commune had, besides, either a primary or an elective assembly. The communes were often allowed, under the supervision of the official board of the Government District, to draw up charters for themselves, embodying their particular local laws and privileges. Within the manors police powers, poor-relief, the maintenance of roads, etc., rested with the proprietor. Local government was within their borders private government.

Reform of 1872. — The legislation of 1872 took the final steps towards getting rid of such pieces as remained of the antiquated system. It abolished the hereditary jurisdiction of the manor and the dependent office of *Schulze*, and established in place of the feudal *status* an equal citizenship of residence. In place of the Estates of the province and county it put real representative bodies. It retained the *Landrath*, but somewhat curtailed his powers in the smaller areas within the Circle, and associated with him an effective administrative board, of which he became little more than president. It carried out more thoroughly than before in the various areas the principle of board direction, integrating the lesser with the greater boards, and thus giving to the smaller areas organic connection with the larger. It reformed also the system of local taxation.

It is upon this legislation that the system of local government later obtaining in Prussia was erected.[1]

The Central Executive Departments. — Stein's scheme for the development of the central organs of administration brought into existence five distinct ministries, which no longer masqueraded as committees of a cumbrous General Directory, and whose functions were distributed entirely upon a basis of logical distinction, not at all upon any additional idea of territorial distribution. These were a Ministry of Foreign Affairs, a Ministry of the Interior, a Ministry of Justice, a Ministry of Finance, and a Ministry of War. This, however, proved to be by no means a final differentiation. The Ministry of the Interior was at first given a too miscellaneous collection of functions, and there split off from it in 1817 a Ministry of Ecclesiastical, Educational, and Sanitary Affairs, and in 1848 a Ministry of Trade, Commerce, and Public Works and a Ministry of Agriculture. In 1878 a still further differentiation took place. The Ministry of Finance, retaining distinct reminiscence of its origin in the administration of the royal domains, had hitherto maintained a Department of Domains and Forests. That department was in 1878 transferred to the Ministry of Agriculture. At the same time the Ministry of Trade, Commerce, and Public Works was divided into two, a Ministry of Trade and Commerce and a Ministry of Public Works.

There were, then, nine ministries : (1) a Ministry of Foreign Affairs (Stein, 1808) ; (2) a Ministry of the Interior (1808); (3) a Ministry of Ecclesiastical, Educational, and Sanitary Affairs (1817) ; (4) a Ministry of Trade and Commerce (1848) ; (5) a Ministry of Agriculture (1848), Domains, and Forests (1878) ; (6) a Ministry of Public Works (1878) ; (7) a Ministry of Justice (1808) ; (8) a Ministry of Finance (1808) ; and (9) a Ministry of War (1808).

The Council of State. — Most of these ministries were created before Prussia had any parliamentary system, and when, consequently, there was no instrumentality in existence through which there could be exercised any legislative control over the executive. Stein would have revived for the exercise of some

[1] Morier, p. 434.

such function the ancient Council of State (*Staatsrath*) founded by Joachim Friedrich in 1604, which had at first presided over all administration but whose prerogatives of oversight and control had gradually decayed and disappeared. This council, which bore a general family resemblance to the English Privy Council, had a mixed membership made up in part of princes of the blood royal, in part of certain civil, military, and judicial officials serving *ex officio*, and in part of state officials specially and occasionally summoned. It was Stein's purpose to rehabilitate this body, which was in a sense representative of the classes standing nearest to government and therefore presumably best qualified to test methods, and to set it to oversee the work of the ministers : to serve as a frame of unity in the administration without withdrawing from the ministers their separate responsibility and freedom of movement. This part of his plan was not, however, carried out, and the Council of State, though still existing, a shadow of its former self, never regained its one-time prominence in administration.

Staatsministerium. — Instead of adopting Stein's plan, Count Hardenberg integrated the several ministries by establishing the *Ministry of State,* or College of Ministers (*Staatsministerium*), which stood in much the same relation to Prussian administration that the French Council of Ministers (page 157) occupies towards administration in France, though it in some respects resembled also the French Council of State (page 173). It was composed of the heads of the several ministries and met, once a week or oftener, for the consideration of all matters which concerned all the executive departments alike, to discuss proposed general laws or constitutional amendments, to adjust conflicts between departments, to hear reports from the ministers as to their policy in the prosecution of their separate work, to exercise a certain oversight over local administration, to concert measures to meet any civil exigency that might arise, etc. It served to give unity and coherence to administration.

The Supreme Chamber of Accounts. — The same purpose was served by the Supreme Chamber of Accounts (*Oberrechnungskammer*) and by the Economic Council (*Volkswirthschaftsrath*). The Supreme Chamber of Accounts was founded in 1714 by

Frederic William I.   Its members had the tenure and responsibility of judges.   Its president was appointed by the Crown on the nomination of the Ministry of State; its other members were appointed by the Crown upon the nomination of its president, countersigned by the president of the Ministry of State.   It constituted a distinct branch of the government, being subordinate, not to the Ministry of State, but directly responsible to the Crown. Its duty was the careful oversight and revision of the accounts of income and expenditure from all departments; and the oversight of the state debt and of the acquisition and disposition of property by the state.   It watched, in brief, the detailed administration of the finances, and was the judicial guardian of the laws concerning revenue and disbursement.

The Economic Council. — The Economic Council considered proposals for laws or ordinances affecting weighty economic interests which fell within the domains of the three ministries of Trade and Commerce, of Public Works, and of Agriculture.   Such proposals, as well as the proposals for the repeal of such laws and ordinances, might be submitted to its debate before going to the king for his approval.   It was also privileged to consider the question how Prussia's votes should be cast upon such matters in the *Bundesrat*.   Of course, however, its part in affairs was merely consultative.   It was composed of seventy-five members appointed by the king for a term of five years, forty-five of this number being appointed upon the nomination of various chambers of commerce, mercantile corporations, and agricultural unions.

The Ministers in the Legislature. — The king — or, more properly, the Administration — was represented in the legislative houses by the ministers, who need not be members in order to attend and speak on the public business.

The Landtag: the House of Lords. — The Prussian *Landtag*, or Legislature, consisted of two houses, a House of Lords (*Herrenhaus*) and a House of Representatives (*Abgeordnetenhaus*). The House of Lords might better be described as a house of classes. It contained not only hereditary members who represented rights of blood, but also life members who represented landed properties and great institutions, and officials who represented the civil hierarchy.   There sat in it princes of the blood royal nominated to membership by the king; the heads of families once royal whose domains had been swallowed up by Prussia; certain greater noblemen appointed by the Crown, together with eight others elected by the resident landowners of the provinces; the four chief officials of the province of Prussia (the Supreme Burggraf, the High Marshal, the Grand Master of the Teutonic Order, and the Chancellor); and a great number of life members appointed by the king upon the presentation of various bodies: certain evangelical foundations, namely, certain colleges of counts, and of landholders of great and ancient possession, the nine universities, and forty-three cities which received the right of nomination. The king could, besides, issue special summons to sit in the House of Lords to such persons as he thought worthy. There was no limit placed upon the number of members, — the only restriction concerned age: members must be at least thirty years old. The number of members was about 300. Of these quite one-third were of the landed nobility, and almost as many more were the nominees of the landed classes; so that the House stood for the loyalty to the Crown and opposition to liberal change.

The House of Representatives. — Though in a sense representing every Prussian twenty-five years of age who was not specially disqualified to vote, it was not constituted by a direct popular franchise, or even by an equal suffrage. The vote was indirect and was proportioned to taxable property. The country was divided into districts; the qualified voters of each district were divided into three classes in such a way that each class should represent one-third of the taxable property of the district; each of these classes selected by vote a third of the number of electors to which the district was entitled; and the electors so chosen elected the members of the House of Representatives.

The Electoral System. — One elector was chosen for every two hundred and fifty inhabitants; the voting was not by the ballot, but was public, and an absolute majority of the electors was required to elect. The total number of members of the House was 443. The term was five years. Any Prussian who was thirty years of age and in full possession of civil rights might be chosen. In case a vacancy occurred in the House, no choice of electors was necessary. Once chosen, the electors were competent to act throughout the legislative term.

It need hardly to be remarked that the division of the primary voters into classes according to the amount of taxes they pay gave a preponderance to wealth. The three classes were of course very unequal in numbers. It required a comparatively small number of rich men to represent one-third of the taxable property in a district; it took a considerably larger number of the well-to-do to represent another third; and the last third was represented by the great majority of the inhabitants of the district. For the classes were not constituted with a view to distributing the small taxpayers and equalizing the classes numerically. Those who paid most taxes constituted the first class; those who paid less, the second; those who paid least or none, the third; and it might thus very well happen that a very small number of persons elected a third of the electors.

Equality and Competence of the House. — The consent of both Houses was necessary to the passage of a law, and they stood upon a perfect equality as regards also the right of initiative in legislation, — except that all financial measures must originate in the lower house, and that the upper house could pass upon the budget, which must be presented first to the House of Represent- atives, only as a whole. The Lords could not amend the budget in part: they must accept or reject it entire.

The King's Power of Adjournment and Dissolution. — The king could adjourn the House of Representatives for a period not exceeding thirty days, once during any one session without its consent. He could also dissolve it. When a dissolution was resorted to he must order a new election within sixty days, and the newly elected House must assemble within ninety days. (Compare p. 155.)

Local Government. — The organization of local govern- ment in Prussia is rendered complex by a mixture of historical and systematic elements: it is compounded of old and new, — of the creations of history and the creations of Stein and Gneist. Stein's hand is even more visible in local organization in Prussia than in the organization of the central ministries. More conserva- tive than the Constituent Assembly and Napoleon in France, he did not sweep away the old provinces of Prussia, whose boundaries, like those of the French provinces of the old *régime*, were set deep in historical associations. The twelve provinces were given a place, — a function of superintendence, — in the new system established. The country was, indeed, divided into Districts (*Bezirke*) corresponding in general character and purpose with the French Departments; but these Districts were grouped under a superintendent provincial organization. There were, therefore, in Prussian local organization (1) the Province, (2) the Government District, (3) the Circle (*Kreis*) or County, and (4) the township and the town. The township and the town were coördinate, standing in the same rank of the series.

The usual organs of local government throughout all the series of the Prussian system were "first, a representative body with an exclusive control over the economic portion of the communal business; secondly, an executive board with an exclusive control over the public portion of the communal business; thirdly, mixed committees, composed of members of both bodies, for the ordinary management of the affairs of the community; fourthly, the division of the communal area into administrative districts under overseers responsible to the executive board."[1]

The Province. — There were in the Province two sets of governmental organs: one of which represented the state and its oversight, the other the Province and its self-government. (1) The state is represented by a Superior President and a *Provinzialrat* associated with him. The original purpose in retaining the provincial organization was to secure broad views of administration through officials charged with the oversight of extended areas and so elevated above the near-sightedness of local routine and detail. Nearer to the particulars of local administration than the minister at Berlin, but not so near as the officials of the Government Districts, the provincial representatives of the state were charged with the care "of all such affairs as concern the entire province or stretch beyond the jurisdiction of a single [district] administration."[2] These were such matters as affect

[1] R. B. D. Morier, *Cobden Club Essays* (1875) on *Local Government and Taxation*, p. 433.

[2] Schulze, *Das Staatsrecht des Königreichs Preussen* (in Marquardsen's *Handbuch*), p. 63.

imperial interests or the whole Prussian state; the concerns of public institutions whose functions extend beyond a District; insurance companies; extensive plans of improvement; road and school management, etc. In exercising most of these functions the provincial authorities acted, however, not through officers of their own, but through the District Administrations. There lay with the Superior President, also, the duty of overseeing district administration, the provincial tax directors, and the general Commission for the regulation of the relations between landlords and tenants. He represented the central government, too, in all special, occasional duties, and under all extraordinary circumstances. He had, besides, initial jurisdiction in cases of conflict between District Administrations, or between such Administrations and specially commissioned officials not subject to their orders.

> The extraordinary powers of the 'Superior President' are illustrated by the fact that, in case of serious civil disturbance, of war or the danger of war, he was authorized to assume the whole authority of administration, local as well as general, within the Province. In overseeing the District Administration, however, he had no executive, but only advisory, powers. He was merely the eye of the Ministries at Berlin, advising them of all matters needing their action. Like the French Prefect, he was the servant of all Ministries alike, though most directly and intimately associated with the Ministry of the Interior. The defect of the provincial organization in Prussia was said to be lack of vitality. Critics like Professor Gneist thought that it rendered the system of local government cumbrous without adding to its efficacy. It was too much restricted to gratuitous advice, and too little authorized to take authoritative action.

The *Provinzialrat*, the administrative Council associated with the Superior President, consisted, besides the President or his representative as presiding officer, of one professional civil official of high rank, appointed by the Minister of the Interior, practically for life, and of five lay members chosen by the Provincial Committee for a term of six years. The assent of the *Provinzialrat* was necessary to every ordinance issued by the Superior President.

(2) The organs representing the Province and its self-government were the Provincial *Landtag*, the Provincial Committee, and the *Landeshauptmann* or *Landesdirektor*. In a Prussian law concerning local government the province is described as "a communal union established with the rights of a corporation for

self-government of its own affairs."[1] The provincial legislative body, the *Landtag*, was composed of representatives elected from the Circles or Counties by the Diets of the Circles : for, when looked at from the point of view of self-government, the Province was a union of Circles, not of Districts : the Districts were organs of the central government only. The functions of the *Landtag* lay within the narrow field of such matters as the apportionment of taxes among the Circles (which in their turn apportioned them among individuals), the examination of the local budget, the care of provincial property, and the election of certain officials, — though it was at liberty to take cognizance of anything that was of local concern.

It might also, on occasion, give its opinion on bills concerning the Province and on other matters referred to it, for an expression of opinion, by the authorities at Berlin. The Superior President could be present at its sessions and could annul all acts in which it overstepped its jurisdiction. Its by-laws were subject to the Crown's approval, as were also many of its votes of appropriation ; and the king might dissolve it.

The *Landtag* elected the Provincial Committee and the *Landeshauptmann*, who were the executive organs of provincial self-government. The *Landeshauptmann* and the Committee stood related to each other very much as do the Superior President and *Provinzialrat*, or the French Prefect and the Prefectural Council : the *Landeshauptmann* was the executive, the Committee the advisory organ of local self-administration, though it in effect directed the action of the *Landeshauptmann* in most matters.

The spheres of the representatives of the state and of the representatives of local self-government were quite sharply distinguished in Prussia. The Provincial Committee and the *Landeshauptmann* had nothing to do with the general administration : that was altogether in the hands of the Superior President and the *Provinzialrat*, who on their part had nothing to do with local self-government. The sphere of local self-government, though narrow, was somewhat more guarded against the constant interference of the central authorities in Prussia than in France. (Compare page 170.)

[1] Schulze, *Das Staatsrecht des Königreichs Preussen* (in Marquardsen's *Handbuch*), p. 85.

The Government District (*Regierungsbezirk*). — Unlike the Province, the Government District had no organs of self-government: it was exclusively a division of *state* administration. Its functionaries were the principal, — it may even be said the universal, — agents of the central government in the detailed conduct of administration : they were charged with the local management of all affairs that fall within the sphere of the Ministries of the Interior, of Finance, of Trade and Commerce, of Public Works, of Agriculture, of Ecclesiastical and Educational Affairs, and of War, exclusive, of course, of such matters as were exceptionally entrusted to officers specially commissioned for the purpose. In brief, they served every ministry except the Ministry of Justice.

Collectively the functionaries of the District were called the 'Administration' (*Regierung*), and their action is for the most part collegiate, *i.e.*, through Boards. The exception to this rule concerned matters falling within the province of the Ministry of the Interior. That Ministry acted in the District, not through a board of officials, but through a single official, the President of the Administration (*Regierungspräsident*). In dealing with all other matters the action was collegiate ; but the Boards were not independent bodies : they were divisions (*Abteilungen*) of the 'Administration' taken as a whole, and in certain affairs of general superintendence the 'Administration' acted as a single council (*im Plenum*). Each Board was presided over by a 'Superior Administrative Councillor' (*Oberregierungsrat*), and that on Domains and Forests had associated with it a special functionary known as the Forest-master. The members of the 'Administration' were all appointed by the central government, which placed upon the Boards whose functions require for their proper discharge a special training, certain so-called " technical members " : for instance, school experts, medical experts, road-engineers, and technically instructed forest commissioners.

These 'Administrations' took the place of the old-time War and Domains Chambers, and which, like the Administrations, acted through Boards as a sort of universal agency for all departments of government. In 1883 the affairs of the Interior were given into the sole charge of the President of the Administration. Before that date they also were in the hands of a Board.

"Every head of a department, as well as every *Rat* and assessor, is bound each year to make a tour through a portion of the
district, to keep an official journal of all he sees, to be afterwards
preserved amongst the records of the Board, and thus to make
himself practically acquainted with the daily life and the daily
wants of the governed in the smallest details."[1] (Compare page
468.)

The President of the Administration (*Regierungspräsident*) was
the most important official in the Prussian local service. Not
only did he preside over the 'Administration,' the general and
most important agency of local government; he was also equipped
for complete dominance. He might, upon occasion, annul the
decisions of the 'Administration' or of any of its Boards with
which he did not agree, and, in case delay seemed disadvantageous,
could himself command necessary measures. He could also, if he
would, set aside the rule of collegiate action and arrange for the
personal responsibility of the members of the 'Administration,'
whenever he considered any matter too pressing to await the meeting and conclusions of a Board, or, if when he was himself present
where action was needed, he regarded such an arrangement as
necesary.[2] In brief, he was the real governing head of local administration. The jurisdiction of the 'Administration' covered such
matters as the state taxes, the churches, the schools, and the
public domain.

The District Committee. — Although the Government
District was not an area of self-government, a certain part in the
oversight of governmental action in the District was given to lay
representatives chosen by the provincial agents of the people.
A District Committee (*Bezirksausschuss*), composed of two professional members (one of whom must be qualified for judicial
office, the other for the higher grades of the administrative
service) appointed by the king for life, and of four members
chosen by the Provincial Committee (page 479) for a term of
six years, was allowed an oversight of such matters as it were
thought best to put under lay supervision. The President of the
Administration was *ex officio* a member of the Committee and usu-

[1] Morier (*Cobden Club Essays*), p. 422.
[2] Schulze (in Marquardsen), p. 64.

ally presided over its sessions.   All orders or arrangements which
he wished to make with regard to local police were subject to its
confirmation, and all questions regarding the control of subordinate local authorities fell to it.   More important than its administrative functions were the judicial functions with which it was
invested.   Since 1883 the District Committee was the Administrative Court of the District (page 488).   When acting in
this capacity the Committee was presided over by its judicial
member, and the President of the Administration did not sit with
it.   The Government Districts numbered thirty-five, and were
grouped within the twelve Provinces.

The Circle (*Kreis*). — In the Circle, as in the Province,
there emerged a double set of functions : there was the state administration and, alongside of it, the narrower function of self-government.   This double set of functions was performed, however,
by a single set of functionaries : by a professional officer known as
the *Landrat*, associated with a Circle Committee (*Kreisausschuss*),
which acted by delegation for the Diet of the Circle (*Kreistag*),
the consultative and supervisory authority.   There were not, as
in the Province, one council and one executive for the state,
another council and another executive for the locality.

The Landrat and the Circle Committee. — The *Landrat*
stood upon a peculiar footing : his office was ancient and retained
some of its historical features.   Originally the *Landrat* represented the landed gentry of various districts of Brandenburg ; he
was appointed upon their nomination and in a sense represented
their interests.   In some parts of Prussia traces of this right of
presentation to the office by the landowners remained ; and in
almost all parts of the kingdom the privilege of nomination
was transferred to the Circle Diet, as heir of the control once
exercised by the local lords of the soil.   The *Landrat* was, therefore, formally, the representative of the locality in which he
officiated.   In reality, however, he was predominately the agent of
the state, serving both the District Administration and the departments at Berlin.   He was appointed by the Superior President
of the Province in which the Circle lay, and was always a professional officer who had passed, by examination, into the higher
grades of the civil service.   He was chief of police within the

Circle, and superintendent of all public affairs. The Circle Committee was associated with him in the administration of his office and organized under his presidency. It consisted, besides himself, of six members chosen by the Circle Diet. It constituted the Administrative Court of the Circle (page 488), hearing appeals from the acts of subordinate officials as well as supervising administrative action.

The Diet of the Circle represented, not the people, but groups of interests, — was based upon the economical and social relations of the people. Each Circle included all towns lying within it which had less than 25,000 inhabitants, and representation in the Diet was divided between town and country. The country representation, in its turn, was divided between the rural Communes and the greater landowners.

The cities elected representatives either singly or in groups ; if singly, through their magistrates and councils acting together ; if in groups, through electors who assembled under the Presidency of the *Landrat*. As 'greater landowners' were classed all those who paid, in their own right, 75 thalers annual land or building tax ; and these were organized for electoral purposes in Unions (*Verbände*). The rural Communes elected in groups through electors. The term of members of the Circle Diet was six years. Cities having more than 25,000 inhabitants constituted separate Circles, and combined in their town governments both Circle and Commune under the forms of city government.

The Circle the Basis of Local Government. — A moment's review of the electoral arrangements which underlay Prussian local government as outlined will show how literally the whole structure, so far as it was a system of self-government, rested upon the electoral organization of the Circle. The Diet of the Circle was the only representative body I have yet named which was chosen by the qualified voters of the locality : and it was not chosen directly. The larger towns elected their quota of members through their councils, while the smaller towns united and chose through electors. The rural communes elected in groups, through electors. The greater landowners sent their separate quota. And then from the Circle Diet, when once it was chosen, proceeded, indirectly, all the other lay bodies of administration in the larger areas. It nominated the *Landrat,* elected the Circle Committee, and united with the Diets of the other Circles of the Province in choosing the provincial *Landtag.* The provincial *Landtag,* in turn, elected the *Landeshauptmann* and the Provincial Committee. The Provincial Committee elected five out of the seven members of the *Provinzialrat* and four out of the six members of the District Committee. Each Provincial Committee chose, on an average, two District Committees. It was in only a very restricted sense a system of popular control in local affairs. It was a long way from the people to the District Committee.

The Magisterial District (*Amtsbezirk*). — The rural Communes were grouped in Magisterial Districts containing each about fifteen hundred inhabitants ; and each District was presided over by a Reeve or Justice (*Amtsvorsteher* or *Amtsmann*) who was appointed by the king upon the nomination of the Circle Diet, usually from among the landowners of the locality. The Reeve's term was six years. He was given charge of the police of the District, and was entrusted with the administration of the laws for the relief of the poor and the preservation of health. As police commissioner he was put over the mayors of the several Communes within his district. He acted under the supervision of the Committee of the Circle.

The Rural Commune (*Landgemeinde*). — The larger rural Communes acted through small representative assemblies or councils, while the less populous regulated their affairs by mass meeting. In some Communes the executive officer was known as ' mayor,' in others as ' village judge,' in still others as ' president.' In most localities he was assisted by one or more aids or assessors. The electoral privilege was based upon the three-class system of voting already described, except that those who paid no taxes at all were usually excluded from the franchise. The powers of the Communes covered all matters of strictly local interest.

The City Communes (*Stadtgemeinde*). — Among the City Communes there was great variety of organization. In some cities there was a single executive, — a single Burgomaster, — perhaps assisted by certain Boards ; in others the Burgomaster had colleagues ; in still others the magistracy was collegiate, — was itself a Board. In all there were councils more or less directly representative of the people. In the cities, as in every other unit of local administration, the subjects of finance, police, and the military were largely controlled from Berlin; and in these branches of administration the city governments were agencies of the central government. They thus had a double character; they were at one and the same time representatives of the authorities at the capital and of the citizens at home. When acting as agencies of state administration they were, of course, responsible to the central Departments at Berlin.

General Principles of Prussian Town Government. — Although without uniformity of structure, town government in Prussia had certain uniformities of principle at its basis. The mayor of a Prussian city was a trained official, taken from the professional service; but he was not the Executive; he was simply president of the executive. There was associated with him a board of Aldermen most of whose members were elected from the general body of citizens, to serve without salary, but an important minority of whose members were salaried officials who, like the mayor, had received a thorough technical training in their various branches of administration, and whose tenure of office was in effect permanent: and this board of Aldermen was the centre of energy and rule in city government. But it acted under check. A town council represented the citizens in the exercise of a control over the city budget, and citizens not of the Council as well as Councilmen acted with the Aldermen in the direction of executive business. The Aldermen did their administrative work in Committees, and acted always in association with certain delegations of town-councilmen and certain 'select citizens' named by the council. In the wards of the larger towns the Aldermen commanded also the assistance of local committees of citizens, by whom the conditions and needs of the various districts of the town were familiarly known. Thus in the work of poor relief, in the guardianship of destitute orphans, in education, and in tax assessment 'select citizens' commonly reinforced the more regular, the official, corps of city officers. This literal self-government, which breaks down the wall of distinction between the official and the non-official guardian of city interests and presses all into the service of the community, was not optional; it was one of the principles of the

system that service as a ' select citizen' was to be enforced by penalties, — by increasing the taxes of those who refused to serve.

The citizens chosen for ward work or for consultation with the
central committees of Aldermen and town-councillors included
merchants, physicians, solicitors, manufacturers, head-masters of
public schools, and like representative persons.

The three-class system of voting obtained also in all municipal
elections in Prussia, so that weight in the electoral control of city
affairs was proportioned to tax-assessment. One-third of the
elected Aldermen and town-councillors represented the wealthy
class, one-third the middle class, one-third the ' proletariat.' It
was said that in Berlin the first class contained " less than two
per cent of the voters, the second class less than thirteen per cent,
and the third eighty-six per cent." The arrangement bred discontent in the lowest class and they largely refrained from voting.

The Administration of Justice. — The Prussian courts of
justice, like those of the other states of the Empire, had the
general features of their organization and jurisdiction prescribed
by imperial law (p. 465). They were Prussia's courts; but they
also served as courts of the Empire; Prussian law commanded only
their *personnel* and their territorial competence. At the head of
the system sat the supreme court of the Empire (*Reichsgericht*),
to which the courts of all the other states stood subordinated.[1]
In each Province there was a Superior District Court (*Oberlandes-
gericht*), and, next below it, a District Court (*Landgericht*). In
each magisterial District there was an *Amtsgericht*.

The *Amtsgericht*, which was the court of first instance in
minor civil cases, consisted of one or of several judges, according
to the amount of business there was for the court to despatch : for
when there was more than one judge the work was not handled by
them together, but separately ; it was divided, either logically or
territorially.

The higher courts, the District Court, and the Superior District
Court consisted each of a number of judges. At the beginning of
each year, the full bench of judges in each court determined a
division of the business of the court among themselves, constituting

---

[1] Prussia is vouchsafed by imperial law the privilege of retaining her own
supreme court ; but she has not availed herself of the permission.

themselves in separate 'chambers' for separate classes of cases. There was always a 'civil chamber' and a 'criminal chamber,' and often a chamber for commercial cases (*Kammer für Handelssachen*). Each chamber had its own president and its own independent organization.

Minor criminal cases were tried in sheriffs' courts (*Schöffengerichte*) sitting in the Magisterial Districts; more serious offences by the criminal chamber of the District Court; all grave crimes by special jury-courts (*Schwurgerichte*) which sat under the presidency of three judges of the District Court.

An appeal from a sheriff's court on the merits of the case could go no further than the District Court. Appeals on the merits of the case from the criminal chamber of the District Court were not allowed; but a case could be taken from that court to the Superior District Court on the ground of neglect of a rule of law, and on other legal grounds to the Imperial Court, for revision.

The nomination of all judges rested with the king : but the appointment was for life and the judges stood in a position of substantial independence. The Minister of Justice, however, completely controlled all criminal prosecutions : for no criminal prosecution could be instituted except by the states-attorneys who represented the government in the several courts, and these held their offices by no permanent tenure, but only at the pleasure of the Minister.

Purity in the administration of justice was sought to be secured by public oral proceedings. Until a very recent period all proceedings in the Prussian courts were written : the plea and the answer constituted the suit. Later public oral proceedings were made imperative.

The organization of justice in Prussia provided for the assumption by the state of a certain 'voluntary' jurisdiction, some of which, such as the exercise of guardianship and the probate of wills (which latter was made a function of the *Amtsgericht*) are quite familiar to the practice of other countries; but others of which, such as an oversight over certain feudal interests, are somewhat novel in their character. The system knew also certain officially commissioned Arbitrators (*Schiedsmänner*) and certain trade judges, which were in some respects peculiar to itself.

Administrative Courts (*Verwaltungsgerichte*). — The same distinction between administrative and ordinary courts of justice that we have observed in France obtained also in Prussia (page 173). Here again appeared the organizing hand of Stein. He established for Prussia the principle that cases arising out of the exercise of the state's sovereignty should be separated in adjudication from cases between private individuals and should be allotted to special courts. Such were cases of damage done to an individual through the act of an administrative officer, or cases of alleged illegal action on the part of a public official, — in brief, all cases of conflict between the public power and private rights, as well as all questions between administrative authorities.

The courts charged with this jurisdiction were, (1) in the Circle, the *Circle Committee* (page 482), presided over, as in dealing with other matters, by the *Landrat*, and in the cities which themselves constitute Circles, the *City Committee* (*Stadtausschuss*), consisting of the Burgomaster as president and four members, all of whom must be qualified for judicial service or for the higher grades of administrative office, elected by the magistracy of the city, acting collegiately, for a term of six years. (2) In the Government District, the *District Committee* (page 481), to whose presidency when sitting in this capacity, the king could appoint, as representative of the President of the Administration, one of the members of the 'Administration' under the title of Director of the Administrative Court (*Verwaltungsgerichtsdirektor*). (3) The *Superior Administrative Court* in Berlin (*Oberverwaltungsgericht*), whose members were appointed by the king, with the consent of the Council of Ministers, for life. This court stood upon the same footing of rank with the supreme federal tribunal, the *Reichsgericht*. Its members were qualified, half of them for high judicial, half for high administrative office. It acted, like the other courts, in divisions or "senates," each of which had its separate organization ; and these sections came together only for the settlement of certain general questions.

The Court of Conflicts (*Gerichtshof für Kompetenz-konflikte*). — Between the two jurisdictions, the ordinary or private and the administrative, stood, as in France, a Court of Conflicts. It consisted of eleven judges appointed for life (or for the term of their chief office, in case they acted *ex officio*) ; and of these eleven six were members of the Superior District Court of Berlin, — must belong, that is, to a court of the ordinary jurisdiction. The other five were persons eligible to the higher judicial or administrative offices. (Compare p. 174.)

The Prussian Courts and Constitutional Questions. — The Prussian courts had no such power of passing upon the constitutionality of laws as is possessed by the courts of the United States. They could not go beyond the simple question whether a law had been passed, or, in administrative cases, an official order issued, in due legal form.

Revolution in Germany. — At the time this is written (December 1, 1918) all Germany is in a state of revolution. The Emperor has abdicated and taken refuge in Holland and a provisional government has been established with the Socialists in control. Soldiers' and Workmen's Councils have been established in numerous places and have assumed control of local affairs. In all the monarchical states of the Empire, the rulers have abdicated or have been deposed, and it appears that a democratic form of government will be established both in the Empire and in the individual states.

A general election in the Empire has been called for January, 1919 and upon the body then chosen will devolve the task of formulating the new governmental arrangements.

This much may safely be predicted — that the Empire will lose Alsace-Lorraine and Prussia will lose that part of Poland which it acquired through the partitions of the unhappy country.

SOME REPRESENTATIVE AUTHORITIES.

Ashley, Local and Central Government, London, 1906.

Barker, J. E., Modern Germany, new ed., London, 1912.

Binding, K., Die Rechtliche Stellung des Kaisers, Dresden, 1898.

Borgeaud, Ch., Adoption and Amendment of Constitutions, trans. by C. D. Hazen and J. M. Vincent, N.Y., 1895.

Burgess, J. W., Political Science and Constitutional Law, 2 vols., N.Y., 1891.

Dawson, W. H., Germany and the Germans, 2 vols., 8vo, London, 1894, and The Evolution of Modern Germany, London, 1908.

Demombynes, G., Constitutions Européennes, 2 vols., 8vo., Paris, 1883. See Vol. II., pp. 487 and 733.

Dodd, W. F., Modern Constitutions, 2 vols., Chicago, 1909.

Dupriez, L., Les Ministres dans les principaux pays d'Europe et d'Amérique, 2 vols., Paris, 1892.

Fleiner, F., Institutionen des deutschen Verwaltungsrecht, Tübingen, 1911.

Goodnow, F. J., Comparative Administrative Law, 2 vols., 8vo, N.Y., 1893.

Grais, Graf Hué de, Handbuch der Verfassung und Verwaltung in Preussen und im deutschen Reiche, 8th ed., Berlin, 1907.

Howard, B. E., The German Empire, N.Y., 1906.

James, E. J., The Federal Constitution of Germany (Translation), Am. Acad. Social and Political Science, Phila., 1890.

Laband, Paul, Das Staatsrecht des deutschen Reiches, 4 vols., 4th ed., Tübingen, 1901. *Also*, under same title, a briefer commentary in *Marquardsen's* Handbuch des Oeffentlichen Rechts der Gegenwart, Freiburg in B., 1883.

Lowell, A. L., Governments and Parties in Continental Europe, 2 vols., Boston, 1896.

Mayer, O., Deutsches Verwaltungsrecht, Leipzig, 1895–1896.

Morier, R. B. D., in Cobden Club Essays on Local Government and Taxation, 1875.

Munro, W. B., The Government of European Cities, N.Y., 1909.

Ogg, F. A., The Governments of Europe, N.Y., 1913.

Rönne, L. v., Das Staatsrecht des deutschen Reiches, 2d ed., Leipzig, 1876. Das Staatsrecht der preussischen Monarchie, 5 vols., 4th ed., 1881–1883.

Sarwey, O. von, Allgemeines Verwaltungsrecht, in *Marquardsen's* Handbuch des Oeffentlichen Rechts der Gegenwart, Freiburg in B., 1884, pp. 112–117.

Seeley, J. R., Life and Times of Stein. Part I., Chap. V.; Part III., Chap. I.; Part V., Chaps. II., III.

Schulz, Hermann, Das preussische Staatsrecht, auf Grundlage des deutschen Staatsrechtes, 2 vols., Leipzig, 1872–1877. Das Staatsrecht des Königreichs Preussen, in *Marquardsen's* Handbuch, Freiburg in B., 1884.

Stengel, K. von, Wörterbuch des deutschen Verwaltungsrechts, 2 vols., Freiburg in B., 1889–1890.

Turner, Sam'l Epes, A Sketch of the Germanic Constitution, N.Y., 1889.

Zorn, P., Das Staatsrecht des deutschen Reiches, 2d ed., Berlin, 1895–1897.

XIV

THE GOVERNMENTS OF AUSTRIA–HUNGARY.

Austria's Historical Position. — Until the middle of the last century Austria stood at the front of German political union; not until 1866 was she deposed from leadership in Germany and set apart to attempt alone the difficult task of amalgamating the polyglot dual monarchy of Austria-Hungary (page 445).

Acquisition of Hungary and Bohemia. — It was unquestionably Austria's headship in the Empire which enabled the Habsburg princes at once to broaden and to consolidate their domain in the southeastern border-land between Slav and Teuton. Their power and influence within the Empire gave them their opportunity to control the destiny of border states like Bohemia and Hungary, lying at Austria's doors. Both Hungary and Bohemia fell to Habsburg in the same year, the year 1526, when Ferdinand I. mounted their throne.

Bohemia. — Bohemia was a Slavonic wedge thrust into the side of Germany. Compassed about by hostile powers, it was a prize to be fought for. Alternately conquered by several neighboring kingdoms, it finally fell into German hands and became an apanage of the Empire. It was as such that the Habsburgers seized it when its throne became vacant in consequence of the extinction of a Luxemburg line of princes. In 1526 their hold upon it became complete, and they were thenceforth able to keep it secure as an hereditary possession within their family.

Moravia. — Moravia also was and is Slavonic. Slavs early drove out its Teutonic possessors, and were prevented from joining the Slavs of the southeast in the formation of a vast Slavonic kingdom only by the intervention of the Magyars, the conquerors of Hungary. This dominant race in the tenth century thrust themselves in between the Slavs of the northwest and those of the southeast, and, driving back the Slavs of Moravia, reduced the once 'Great Moravia' to the dimensions of the present province. Striven for by Hungary, by Poland, and by Bohemia, Moravia finally met her natural fate in incorporation with Slavonic Bohemia (1029), and passed, along with thàt kingdom, into Austrian hands, in 1526.

Hungary. — Hungary is the land of the Magyars, a Turanian race which retains even to the present day its distinctive Oriental features, habits, and bearing among the native European races about it. After having suffered the common fortune of being overrun by numerous barbaric hordes at the breaking up of the Roman Empire, the territory of Hungary became, in 889, the realm of the Magyar duke Árpád, the Conqueror. In the year 1000 the duke Vaik, who had succeeded to the duchy in 997, received at the hands of Pope Sylvester II. the title of 'apostolic king' of Hungary, and, under the name of Stephen, became the first of a line of native monarchs which kept the throne until 1301. From 1301 till 1526 kings of various families and origins won places upon the throne. During this period, too, Hungary felt the full power of the Turk, since 1453 master of Constantinople. The battle of Mohács (29 August, 1526) brought terrible overthrow upon the Hungarian forces at the hands of Soliman the Magnificent, and death to Louis, the Hungarian king. Louis was childless; his widow, Maria, was sister to Ferdinand I. of Austria; and it was her influence which led the more powerful party of nobles within the kingdom to elect the Habsburger to the throne and so put Austria permanently in the Hungarian saddle. Not, however, until 1665–1671, a period of insurrection in Hungary, did the Habsburgers convert their elective into an hereditary right to the throne.

Transylvania, Slavonia, Croatia. — Transylvania, Slavonia, and Croatia, annexed at various times to Hungary, passed with Hungary to the house of Habsburg. Except during the period 1848 to 1867, the period during which Hungary was being disciplined for her revolt of 1848–1849, these provinces remained apanages of Hungary, though Croatia occupied a distinctive position, and was always accorded a representative of her own in the Hungarian ministry.   From 1848 to 1867 Transylvania, Slavonia, and Croatia were treated as Austrian crown lands.

Galicia, Dalmatia. — Galicia, a district much fought for and often divided, formerly a part of Poland, came to Austria upon the first partition of Poland, in 1772.   Dalmatia, once part of ancient Illyria, afterwards a possession of Venice, much coveted and sometimes held by Croatia and by Hungary, came to Austria through the treaty of Campo Formio, in 1797.

Bosnia and Herzegovina. — The Congress of Berlin, 1878, which met to fix upon a basis for the new settlements resulting from the victories of Russia over Turkey, added to Austria's multifarious duties as ruler of many races the protectorate of Bosnia and Herzegovina, districts inhabited by a Servian race and long subject to Turkish dominion.   They were annexed by Austria in 1908.

Austria-Hungary: Nature of the Union. — The constitution of the Austro-Hungarian monarchy practically recognized but two parties to the union, Austria and Hungary.   Bohemia, for all she had so much individuality and boasted so fine a history of independence, was swallowed up in Austria : only the Magyars of Hungary, among all the races of the heterogeneous realm of the Habsburgers, obtained for the kingdom of their making a standing of equality alongside of dominant Austria.

Variety of Race. — The commanding difficulty of government throughout the whole course of Austro-Hungarian politics has been the variety of races embraced within the domain of the monarchy.   First and most prominent was the three-sided contrast between German, Slav, and Magyar.   Within this general classification, again, Slav differed from Slav by reason of many sharp divergencies of history, of speech, and of religion ; and outside this classification, there was added a miscellany of Italians, Croats. Serbs, Rumanians, Jews, — men of almost every race and people of eastern Europe.   This variety was emphasized by the fact that only the Czechs (Bohemians), among all these peoples, had a separate home land in which they were in the majority.   In Bohemia and Moravia the Czechs constituted considerably more than half the population ; whilst in Hungary the Magyars, though greatly outnumbering any other one element of the population, were less than half the whole number of inhabitants; and in Austria, though men of German blood were very greatly in the majority in the central provinces which may be called Austria proper, they constituted in Austria taken as a whole very little more than one-third of the population.

Home Rule: Bohemia, Hungary. — At least two among these many races, moreover, were strenuously, restlessly, persistently devoted to independence. No lapse of time, no defeat of hopes, seemed sufficient to reconcile the Czechs of Bohemia to incorporation with Austria. Pride of race and the memories of a notable and distinguished history kept them always at odds with the Germans within their gates and with the government set over their heads. They desired at least the same degree of autonomy that had been granted to Hungary.

Not 'granted' either. No doubt it would be more correct to say the degree of autonomy *won* by Hungary. Dominant in a larger country than Bohemia, perhaps politically more capable than any Slavonic people, and certainly more enduring and definite in their purposes, the Magyars, though crushed by superior force in the field of battle, were able to win a specially recognized and highly favored place in the dual monarchy. Although for a long time a land in which the noble was the only citizen, Hungary has been a land of political liberties almost as long as England herself has been. The nobles of Hungary won from their king, Andreas II., in 1222, a "Golden Bull" which was a veritable Magna Charta. It limited military service in the king's army, it regulated taxation, it secured for every noble trial by his peers, it gave order and propriety to judicial administration, it even enacted the right of armed resistance to tyranny. The nobles, too, established their right to be personally summoned to the national *Reichstag*. Standing upon these privileges, they were long able to defeat the absolutism of the Austrian monarchs. Ferdinand I. acquired the throne of Hungary only after recognizing her constitution; not for more than a hundred years did the crown become hereditary in the Austrian house; and not till 1687 did the ancient right of armed resistance lose its legal support.

The period of reaction which followed the Napoleonic wars

and the Congress of Vienna found kings everywhere tightening where they could the bonds of absolutism: and nowhere were those bonds more successfully strengthened than in Austria-Hungary under the reigning influence of the sinister Metternich. 1848, however, saw the flames of insurrection break forth more fiercely in Hungary than anywhere else in terror-stricken Europe: only by the aid of Russia was Austria able once more to get control of her great dependency. So completely was Hungary prostrated after this her supreme effort that she had for a little no choice but to suffer herself to be degraded into a mere province of Austria.

The Constitution of 1867. — Wars and disasters presently burst upon the absolutist Austria, however, in an overwhelming storm. Thrust out from Germany (page 445) she was made at length to feel the necessity, if she would give her realm strength, to give her subjects some rights. Her eyes were at last opened to the supreme folly of keeping the peoples under her rule weak and spiritless, poor and motionless, in order that her monarchs might not suffer contradiction. She assented, accordingly, 18 February, 1867, to a constitutional arrangement which recognized the kingdom, not as Austria's, but as the joint kingdom of Austria-Hungary, and which gave to the Empire its political organization.

Dual Character of the Monarchy. — The Austro-Hungarian monarchy, although compacted by the persistent forces of a long historical development, was not a unitary state, a territorial and legal unit, but simply a " real union of two constitutionally and administratively independent states." This union was, indeed, more substantial than that formerly existing between Sweden and Norway: the latter began only in 1815, and was only an arrangement by which two kingdoms might subsist under a single king, as partners in international undertakings but as something less than partners in affairs of nearer interest; while Austria-Hungary, on the contrary, held as a dual possession by a single royal house for more than three hundred and fifty years, subjected by that house to the same military and financial services, and left the while in possession of only such liberties as could be retained by dint of turbulent insistence, consisted of two countries at many points interlaced and amalgamated in history and in institutional life.

The Fundamental Laws. — The constitutional law of the dual kingdom rested upon grants of privilege from the Crown. It is divisible into three parts : the laws of the union, the laws of Austria, and the laws of Hungary. (a) The laws of the union embraced, beside various other rules concerning succession to the throne, the Pragmatic Sanction of 1713, which was formally adopted by the representatives of the Hungarian group of states ; and the identical Austrian and Hungarian laws, passed in December, 1867, which fixed the relations of the two kingdoms to one another and arranged for the administration of their common affairs. (b) The fundamental law of Austria consisted of various royal decrees, 'diplomas,' and patents, determining the membership, privileges, etc., of the national *Reichsrath* and of the provincial *Landtags*. Of these the chief are five fundamental laws of December, 1867, by which a general reconstruction of the government was effected, in agreement with the new constitution given to the union in that year. (c) The constitutional arrangements of Hungary rested upon the Golden Bull of Andreas II., 1222, touching the privileges of the Estates (page 494) ; upon certain laws of 1790–1791 concerning the political independence of Hungary, and her exercise of legislative and executive powers ; upon laws of 1847–1848 granting ministerial responsibility, annual sessions of the *Reichstag*, etc. ; and upon a law of 1868 (amended in 1873) whereby Croatia-Slavonia was given certain distinct privileges to be enjoyed independently of Hungary. These were most of them older laws than the Austrian. Although able for long periods together to keep Austria at their feet, the Hapsburgers were never able to keep Hungary for long in a similar attitude of submission. Her constitutional separateness and independence, though often temporarily denied in practice, were never destroyed. The coöperative rights of the Estates in government, communal self-administration, and the privileges of the free cities triumphantly persisted spite of all efforts made to suppress them.

The Common Government : the Emperor-King. — The Emperor of Austria bore also the titles King of Bohemia and 'Apostolic' King of Hungary (page 492). He stood at the head, not of one of the branches of the government, but of the whole government in all its branches. In theory, indeed, he alone governed : he made, while legislatures and provincial assemblies only assented to, the laws. Law limited his powers : the sphere of his authority was fixed in each kingdom by definite constitutional provisions ; but, whatever practical concessions modern movements of thought and of revolution may have compelled, it yet remained the theory, and to a certain extent the fact, of constitutional development in Austria-Hungary that the monarch had himself of his own free will created such limitations upon his prerogative as existed. There was, therefore, significantly enough, nothing to be said by constitutional commentators in Austria-Hungary either concerning the king's veto or concerning any special arrangements for constitutional change. It was thought to go without the saying that the monarch's negative would absolutely kill, his 'let it be' abundantly vitalize, all laws, whether constitutional or other.

Succession, Regency, etc. — The laws touching the succession to the Austro-Hungarian throne provided so minutely for the widest possible collateral inheritances that provision for a vacancy was apparently not necessary. Permanent laws vested the regency in specific representatives of the royal house. The royal age of majority was sixteen years.

The Common Ministries. — The Emperor-King was assisted in his direction of the common affairs of his two kingdoms by three Ministries and an Imperial Court of Audit. There was (1) a *Ministry of Foreign Affairs* and of the Imperial Household, which, besides the international functions indicated by its name, was charged with oversight of the foreign trade and shipping interests of the dual kingdom. (2) *The Ministry of War*, by which the common standing army of the two kingdoms was administered. The legislation upon which the maintenance of this common standing army was based originated with the legislatures of the two kingdoms acting separately. It was, that is, matter of agreement between the two countries. It covered such points as the size of the army, liability to military service, rules and methods of recruiting, etc., and was embodied in identical laws adopted by the two legislatures, each acting for itself and without constitutional compulsion.

As commander-in-chief of the army, the Emperor-King had the full right of discipline, full power to appoint, remove, or transfer officers of the line, and the determination of both the war and peace organizations of the army, quite independently of any action whatever on the part of the minister of war. In most other concerns of the military administration, however, his acts require the countersignature of the minister. The militia, or reserve, services of the two kingdoms were separate, and separately maintained ; but in war the militia of both countries became supplementary to the regular army.

(3) *The Ministry of Finance:* acting under the Emperor, the minister of finance prepared the joint budget, apportioned the costs of the common administration between Austria and Hungary, saw to the raising of the relative quotas, applied the common income in accordance with the provisions of the budget, and administered the common floating debt.

The chief sources of the common revenue in Austria-Hungary were customs duties and direct contributions from the treasuries of the two states. Certain parts of the customs duties were assigned to the common treasury ; and such expenses as these were not sufficient to meet were defrayed by the contributions, Austria paying sixty-three and six tenths (63.6), and Hungary thirty-six and four tenths (36.4) per cent of the sums needed.

The Economic Relations of Austria and Hungary were regulated in the important matters of commerce, the money system, the management of those railroads and telegraph lines whose operation affected the interests of both kingdoms, the customs system, and the indirect taxation of industries by formal agreements of a semi-international character entered into every ten years, and brought into force by separate but of course identical laws passed in the national legislatures of both countries. Each state controlled for itself the collection of customs duties within its own territory ; but Austria-Hungary was regarded as forming only a single customs and trade territory, and the laws touching administration in these fields were identical in the two countries.

There was a joint stock Austro-Hungarian bank at Vienna ; the two kingdoms had by treaty the same system of weights and measures ; and there was separate coining but the same coinage.

Patents, Posts, and Telegraphs. — A common system of patents and copyrights was maintained ; and both countries had the same postal and telegraph service.

The Delegations. — The most singular, interesting, and characteristic feature of the common government of Austria-Hungary was the Delegations, which constituted, in germ at least, a common legislature.   There were two Delegations, an Austrian and a Hungarian.   They were respectively committees of the Austrian and Hungarian legislatures.   Each Delegation consisted of sixty members, twenty of whom were chosen by the upper, forty by the lower chamber of the legislature which they represented. But, although thus in form a committee of the legislature which sent it forth, each Delegation may be said to have represented the kingdom from which it came rather than the legislature of that kingdom.   It was not subject to be instructed, but acted upon its own judgment as an independent body.   The two Delegations sat and acted separately, though they exercised identical functions. Each passed judgment upon the budget of the common administration, each was at liberty to take action upon the management of the common debt, each superintended the common administration, and could freely question and ' interpellate' the ministers, from whom each heard periodical reports ; and each had the privilege of initiative as regards all measures coming within their competence.   These functions were concurrent, not joint. They were, nevertheless, obviously functions which must under such a system be exercised in full agreement : the common administration could not serve two masters.   If, therefore, after a triple exchange of resolutions no agreement was reached between the two bodies, a joint session was held, in which, without debate, and by a mere absolute majority vote, the question at issue was decided.

As a matter of fact the legislative powers of the Delegations were very narrow indeed.   Their independent action was confined for the most part to the granting of supplies and the superintendence of the administrative action of the three common ministries.   The very supplies they granted came out of taxes voted separately by the parliaments of the two kingdoms ; and almost every agency they used rested upon treaties and identical laws independently passed. The term for which the Delegations were elected was one year. They were called together by the monarch annually, one year at Vienna, the next at Buda-Pest. In the selection of members of the Delegation the Austrian crown lands (the provinces once separate or independent) were entitled to representation, as was also Croatia-Slavonia on the Hungarian side. When the two Delegations met in joint session, the number of members present from each must be equal to the number of those present from the other, any numerical inequality being corrected by lot.

Citizenship. — There was no common citizenship for the two kingdoms; but in all business relationships the citizens of each state were regarded as citizens of the other.

The Government of Austria: the Executive. — The governing power rested in Austria with the Emperor. The recent Emperors by no means ventured upon the centralization of authority attempted and in part effected by Maria Theresa and Joseph II; but Austrian constitutional law did not assign duties to the head of the state: it assigned functions to the ministers and granted privileges to the representative bodies. All powers not explicitly so conferred remained with the Emperor. He directed all the administrative activities of the state; he appointed the life members of the upper house of the *Reichsrat;* and, through his ministers, he in large measure controlled legislation. But he must act in administration through the ministers and in legislation through the parliament. The countersignatures of the ministers were, by statute, made necessary for the validity of his decrees; and the consent of the *Reichsrat* was indispensable to the determination of the policy and content of all legislation. The only judicial prerogative that remained with him was the power of pardon. On all sides his power was circumscribed by the legally necessary coöperation of other regularly constituted authorities.

The Ministry, which consisted of a Minister-President and seven heads of departments, acted as the Emperor's council, but it did not constitute a board whose majority vote decided administrative questions. Action was taken, rather, in each department upon the individual responsibility of the minister at its head. The ministers had a threefold office: they were the Emperor's councillors, they executed his commands, and they were the responsible administrators of special branches of the public service. They acted for the Emperor also in introducing measures in the *Reichsrat.* They must attend both Houses to defend the policy of the executive and to answer 'interpellations.' There were eight executive departments : Interior, National Defence, Religion and Education, Trade, Agriculture, Finance, Justice, and Railways. The Minister-President often held no portfolio, and constituted a ninth minister.

Legislation : the National and Provincial Legislatures. —

In all legislation of whatever kind the coöperation of the representatives of the people was necessary ; but not all of this coöperative privilege belonged to the *Reichsrat*, the national legislative body. Coöperation in the greater matters of legislation was expressly given by law to the *Reichsrat*, but all legislative powers not expressly granted to it belonged to the sphere of the *Landtags* of the seventeen provinces (kingdoms, grand-duchies, archduchies, duchies, and counties), of which the conglomerate realm was made up.

The Reichsrat. —

The *Reichsrat* consisted of a House of Lords (*Herrenhaus*) and a House of Representatives (*Abgeordnetenhaus*). To the House of Lords came princes of the blood royal who had reached their majority, the archbishops and certain bishops, nobles of high rank who had acquired hereditary seats in the chamber, and such life members as the Emperor chose to appoint in recognition of special services to the state, to the church, to science, or to art. To the other House came representatives chosen by general, equal, and direct manhood suffrage.[1] The term of the lower house was six years. The number of members in the House of Representatives by the law of 1907 was 516. Representation was apportioned among the several lands which form the Austrian domain.

The assent of the chambers was required not only in legislation but also for the validity of treaties which affected the trade of the country, which laid economic burdens upon the state, which affected its legal constitution, or which concerned an alienation or extension of territory. The powers of the two Houses were the

[1] Law of 1907.

same, except that financial measures and bills which affected recruitment for the army must originate in the House of Representatives. It was the general rule that the assent of both Houses was necessary to every resolution or action of the *Reichsrat;* but an interesting exception is to be noted. If a disagreement arose between the chambers upon a question of finance or of military recruitment, the lowest figures or numbers were to be considered adopted.

The Emperor named not only the life members but also the president and vice-president of the House of Lords. He called and opened the sessions of the *Reichsrat,* and might close, adjourn, or dissolve it. It was within the prerogative of the Emperor, acting with the advice of his ministers, to enact any laws which seemed to be immediately necessary during a recess of the *Reichsrat,* provided they were not financial laws, or laws which in any way permanently encumbered the state. But such laws must be submitted to the *Reichsrat* within four weeks after its next assembling (going first to the House of Representatives), and altogether lapsed unless submitted to the *Reichsrat* within that time, and sanctioned by it.

Ministerial Responsibility. — In theory, the ministers were responsible to the Houses, and resigned if defeated; but the theory found no realization in practice. Race lines determined party lines in the Houses, and even members of the same race did not keep steadily together in purpose or policy; so that there were no governing parties, and no majorities that could be reckoned beforehand. The Emperor might placate now this group, and again the other, and so keep his own ministers and pursue his own policy.

The Landtags. — The greater political divisions of Austria retained their own *Landtags,* or local legislatures, and to these belonged considerable legislative powers. The Emperor named the chairmen of the *Landtags* and their substitutes; he called, opened, and might close, adjourn, or dissolve the *Landtags;* and his assent was necessary to all their acts. But their consent was necessary to almost all laws which affected the provinces which they represented, and their privileges constituted an important part of the total of legislative power which rested with the representatives of the people.   The provinces had also extensive rights of self-administration.

Local Government. — The *Landtags* were the most conspicuous organs of self-government.   Each *Landtag* consisted of a single chamber and represented the same classes of voters that sent members to the national *Reichsrat* (page 501), — with the addition of another, an official class.   The administrative organ of the province was a provincial committee, as in France.   The central government was represented in the exercise of its many local powers by a *Statthalter* or *Landespräsident*, whose powers were very extensive.   Within the province there were, in some parts of the country, districts or circles, which were areas of financial administration; and throughout the country the smallest areas of local government were the Communes, local bodies which, acting within the commission of general statutes, exercised considerable powers of self-direction through a communal committee and a communal president chosen, together with a certain number of assistants, by the committee.   The Communes were organs of the provinces, and their presidents to a certain extent served the general state administration.

The Government of Hungary : the Executive. — The king bore substantially the same relations to the other powers of the state in Hungary that he bore in Austria.   The directing head of the state, he yet must act in all administrative matters through the ministers, and in all legislative matters through the national chamber.   Even his treaty-making power was limited as regards Hungary in the same way that it was limited as regards Austria (page 502).

The Hungarian Ministry consisted of a Minister-President and, if he held no portfolio, of nine other ministers : a minister attendant upon the king, a minister of the Interior, a minister of Finance, a minister of Industry and Commerce, a minister of Agriculture, a minister of Justice, a minister of Religion and Education, a minister of National Defence, and a special minister for Croatia-Slavonia.

The ministers attended the sittings of the chambers and played there the same part that the Austrian ministers played in the *Reichsrat* (page 501).   The Hungarian ministers were, however, subject to a real responsibility to the parliament of the kingdom. The Magyars maintained a veritable majority in the Hungarian Houses, and they knew their own minds and the right methods of party discipline, besides. They have been statesmen and rulers time out of mind, and the king's ministers in Hungary obeyed and represented the majority in parliament, resigning as of course when defeated.

The Diet. — The *Diet* (*Országgyülés*), the national representative body, consisted of a Table of Magnates and a Table of Representatives. To the former went all hereditary peers who paid an annual land tax of three thousand florins, the highest officials of the Roman Catholic and Greek churches, certain ecclesiastical and lay representatives of the Protestant churches, eighty-four life peers appointed by the king, certain members *ex officio*, three delegates from Croatia-Slavonia, and those royal archdukes who had reached their majority and who owned landed estates in Hungary. The Table of Representatives consisted of four hundred and fifty-three members elected by direct vote for a term of five years. The membership of the House for ordinary business, however, was only four hundred and thirteen. The forty additional members represented Croatia-Slavonia; and, inasmuch as that great province had an almost independent legislature of its own, its members in the national House voted only upon questions of national action which affected their own province. These subjects were understood to be, the army, trade, and finance. As must always happen where there is real ministerial responsibility, the lower House was the governing House. The Magnates yielded, in the long run, every point upon which the purpose of the Representatives was definitely fixed.

The franchise rested upon the payment of a small amount of taxes on land or on income. Members of certain learned and professional classes, however, possessed the franchise without any property qualification.

The president and vice-president of the upper House were nominated by the king. As in the case of the Austrian representative bodies, so also in the case of the Hungarian, the king convened and opened, and might close, adjourn, or dissolve them.

Local Government. — For purposes of local government Hungary was divided into shires, self-administered cities, and Communes. The organization was throughout substantially the same. In each area, — the Commune excepted, — there was a president who represented the central government ; in each, without exception, there was an administrative committee which was the executive representative of the local body and an assembly, in part representative and in part primary (inasmuch as those who are most highly taxed are entitled to be present), with which rested the general direction of affairs.

Croatia-Slavonia. — There was not in Hungary the provincial organization which existed in Austria. Croatia-Slavonia was the only constituent part of the Hungarian lands which had its own separate *Landtag.* The organization of this territory was in all respects exceptional. It was given legal rights which could not be taken away from it without its own consent ; and it had a distinct administration responsible to the king and to its own *Landtag.* It was, nevertheless, an integral part of the Hungarian monarchy.

Revolution and the Breaking Up of the Austro-Hungarian Empire.[1] — The war has brought the long-anticipated dissolution of the power of the Habsburgs and the proclamation of a number of independent republican states. The Emperor Charles II. has abdicated and the Union of Austria and Hungary has been dissolved. Hungary has been proclaimed a republic and will doubtless be greatly reduced in size through the loss of territories that will become independent or that will join with Rumania and Serbia. The Czecho-Slovaks in Bohemia and Slavonia have proclaimed themselves independent and are establishing a republic, as have the Jugo-Slavs in the South. The fate of the German Austrians is not yet determined. The Austrian Poles have joined in the new Republic of Poland ; Transylvania will probably unite with Rumania, since they are of the same nationality. The Croats and Serbians in Bosnia and Herzegovina have proposed a union with Serbia, and Italia Irredenta will return to Italy.

Whatever the exact territorial arrangements may be, the Austrian and the Hungarian power over the subject races in the

[1] Written December 1, 1918.

Empire has been broken, and out of the disruption of the Empire will come a number of small, national states in which the national aspirations for independence will be realized.

SOME REPRESENTATIVE AUTHORITIES.

On Austria-Hungary:

Andrassy, J., Development of Hungarian Constitutional Liberty, London, 1908.

Arnold-Foster, F., Francis Déak, A Memoir, London, 1880.

Borgeaud, Charles, The Adoption and Amendment of Constitutions in Europe and America. Translated by C. D. *Hazen* and J. M. *Vincent*. N.Y. and London, 1895.

Demombynes, G., Les Constitutions Européennes, II., pp. 167–304, 2 vols., Paris, 1883.

Dickinson, Reginald, Summary of the Constitution and Procedure of Foreign Parliaments, 2d ed., 8vo, London, 1890.

Dodd, W. F., Modern Constitutions, 2 vols., Chicago, 1909.

Gumplowicz, Das Oesterreichische Staatsrecht, 3d ed., Vienna, 1907.

Knatchbull-Hugessen, C. M., The Political Evolution of the Hungarian Nation, London, 1908.

Leger, Louis, A History of Austro-Hungary from the Earliest Time to the Year 1889. Translated by Mrs. Birkbeck *Hill*. London, 1889.

Lévy, D., L'Autriche-Hongrie, ses Institutions, etc., Paris, 1872.

Lowell, A. L., Governments and Parties in Continental Europe, Vol. II., Chaps. VIII.–X., 2 vols., Boston, 1896.

Ogg, F. A., The Governments of Europe, N.Y., 1913.

Patterson, Arthur J., The Magyars: Their Country and Its Institutions, 2 vols., 8vo, London, 1870.

Ulbrich, J., Das Staatsrecht der oesterreichisch-ungarischen Monarchie, in *Marquardsen's* Handbuch des oeffentlichen Rechts der Gegenwart, Freiburg im B., 1884.

Von Ferdinandy, G., Staats und Verwaltungsrecht des Königreichs Ungarn, Hanover, 1909.

Vámbéry, Arminius, and *Heilprin*, Louis, Hungary (Stories of the Nations Series), N.Y. and London, 1886.

Whitman, C. S., The Realms of the Hapsburgs, London and N.Y., 1893.

Worms, Baron H. de, The Austro-Hungarian Empire, 8vo, London, 1877. Historical and descriptive.

Zuylen de Nyevelt, Baroness, Austria: Its Society; Politics, and Religion, *National Review*, October, 1891.

XV.

THE GOVERNMENT OF SERBIA.

———o◦⦂◦⦂◦o———

THE struggle for Serbian independence began in 1804 and continued until by the Treaty of Adrianople in 1829 the pachalik of Belgrade was erected into an autonomous and tributary principality under the suzerainty of Turkey and the protection of Russia. Miloch Obrenovitch was proclaimed hereditary prince by the national *Skupshtina* and was recognized as such by the Porte in 1830. Under him a constitution was prepared and after approval by the Grand *Skupshtina* was promulgated in 1835. It created a Council of State charged with the duty of preparing the laws, but as it met for only two days a year it could not perform its function and became merely a chamber for enrolling the laws. This constitution was of short duration and was succeeded by another, called the *Oustav*, or Statute, which went into effect in 1839. For twenty years the Statute was the fundamental law of the principality. By the Treaty of Paris in 1856, the Russian protectorate of the principality was abolished, and Serbia was recognized as a semi-independent state. In 1861 the functions of the *Skupshtina* were by law determined in some detail and a distinction made between the ordinary *Skupshtina* and the *Grand Skupshtina* which had no stated meetings. The *Skupshtina* was a sort of popular assembly, whose origin lay in very remote time.

In 1878, by the Treaty of Berlin, the complete independence of the principality was recognized, and in 1882 the national *Skupshtina* proclaimed the principality a kingdom and Prince Milan Obrenovitch IV took the title of Milan I, King of Serbia.

In 1869, following the assassination of Prince Michel, the *Grand Skupshtina* had, through a committee, prepared and proclaimed a constitution. This lasted until 1888 when King Milan yielded to the oft-repeated demands for a revision, and appointed a committee of seventy, composed of members of the different parties. The work of the committee was ratified by a Grand *Skupshtina* and the new constitution was promulgated in February, 1889. Its existence was brief, for it was suspended by a royal proclamation in May, 1894, and the constitution of 1869 was again put into effect. Seven years later this constitution was again repealed and a new one was proclaimed in April, 1901.

The constitution of 1901 was elaborated in conjunction with the leaders of the radical and progressive parties and contained an innovation in the form of a senate. Following the assassination of King Alexander and Queen Draga in 1903, the *Skupshtina* revived the constitution of 1888 and proclaimed Peter Karageorgevitch king, with the title of Peter I.

According to the constitution the kingdom is an hereditary and constitutional monarchy combined with representation of the people. The state religion is that of the Orthodox Greek Church.

For purposes of administration the kingdom is divided into departments (*okroug*), the departments into arrondissements (*srez*), and the arrondissements into communes (*opchtina*).

The constitution contains a statement of the rights of citizens : all are equal before the law and no titles of nobility can be granted or recognized ; individual liberty is guaranteed and no one can be tried except by a competent tribunal ; private domicile and private property are inviolable ; freedom of conscience is absolute and instruction is free in so far as it is not contrary to public order and morality ; primary instruction is obligatory and free in the public schools ; liberty of speech and of the press, freedom of assembly and of association, and the right of petition are guaranteed.

The King. — The executive power is vested in the King and is exercised through responsible ministers who are appointed and dismissed by the King. He is the head of the state and his person is inviolable ; he cannot be held responsible ; he sanctions and promulgates the laws ; he appoints the officers of the state and they exercise their authority in his name and under his supervision ; he is commander-in-chief of the army ; he conducts the foreign affairs of the state, declares war, makes treaties of peace, of alliance, and of all other sorts and communicates them to the *Skupshtina* as soon as national interests permit; treaties of commerce and those which require the expenditure of money or a modification of the laws or which affect the rights of citizens must be approved by the *Skupshtina* before they become binding; he convokes the *Skupshtina* in ordinary or extraordinary sessions; he opens and closes its sessions; he may prorogue it, but not for a longer period than two months and not oftener than once in the same session without its consent; he may dissolve it, but new elections must be held within two months and the new assembly must meet within three months. The decree of dissolution must be countersigned by all the ministers.

No act of the King touching state affairs is valid unless countersigned by a competent minister who thereby assumes the responsibility. In case the throne becomes vacant, the *Grand Skupshtina* shall determine the question of a successor.

The Skupshtina. — The national *Skupshtina*, which represents the country, is ordinary (*obitchna*) or grand (*velika*); it is composed of deputies freely chosen by the people in accordance with the provisions of the constitution. The election is direct and voting is secret and by ballot. There are one hundred and sixty-six deputies, chosen by districts; the electors comprise all Serbian citizens twenty-one years of age and over who pay an annual direct tax to the state of five dollars.

No one can be elected who is not qualified to vote, and in addition he must, if a naturalized citizen, have been a resident for five years, and must be at least thirty years of age, enjoy full political and civil rights, be a permanent resident and pay at least six dollars direct tax a year. Deputies who enter the service of the state, except ministers, lose their membership but may stand for reëlection. The term is four years and there is an annual session which cannot end until the Budget is passed; its sessions are public unless a secret session is demanded by the president or ten members, in which case the *Skupshtina* decides. All proposed laws, except those relating to the Budget, must first be considered by the Council of State, and all bills must be referred to a committee and cannot be considered unless favorably reported by the committee. Every deputy has the right to address questions and interpellations to ministers, who must answer before the close of the session.

The *Grand Skupshtina* is composed of twice as many members as the ordinary *Skupshtina* and is summoned when it is necessary to decide the succession to the throne, to appoint a Council of Regency, to decide upon amendments to the Constitution, to determine upon the alienation or exchange of national territory, and when the King deems it necessary to consult it.

Ministers. — The ministers are the heads of the executive departments, except the president of the council of ministers, who may be without portfolio. They are appointed and dismissed by the King. They have the right of free access to the *Skupshtina*, but may not vote unless they are members; the *Skupshtina* may demand their presence at its sittings. They are responsible to the King and to the *Skupshtina* for all official acts ; and may be tried by a special court composed of members of the Council of State and the Court of Cassation.

Council of State. — The Council of State is composed of sixteen members, eight of whom are appointed by the King and eight by the *Skupshtina;* the King sends to the *Skupshtina* a list of sixteen names from which the *Skupshtina* chooses eight and it in turn sends a similar list to the King from which he chooses eight. They are appointed for life. The chief functions of the Council are to draft, at the invitation of the government, proposals for laws, to give its advice upon questions submitted by the government, and to examine all proposals for laws introduced by the government or initiated by the *Skupshtina*, and no discussion of any proposed law may take place until the Council has given its opinion. The Council may appoint one or more of its members to defend its report before the *Skupshtina*.

The Courts. — The courts are declared independent and it is forbidden to the executive or to the legislative departments to interfere in judicial matters. No special tribunals or commissions to exercise judicial functions may be created.

There is a Court of Cassation for the whole country which determines solely questions of law ; it also has jurisdiction in cases of conflict between the judicial and the administrative authorities,

Below the Court of Cassation are courts of appeal and courts of first instance.

Judges are appointed by the King; they are not liable to removal except by a judgment of a regular tribunal or by the Court of Cassation for a disciplinary offence, nor can they be transferred without their consent.

Amendment of the Constitution. — The proposal for an amendment, revision, or interpretation of the Constitution may originate with the King or with the *Skupshtina;* if with the King it shall be communicated to the *Skupshtina* which shall at once be dissolved and the *Grand Skupshtina* summoned within four months; if the proposal originates with the *Skupshtina*, it must be passed by that body by an absolute majority of the deputies twice at an interval of ten days ; thereupon the *Skupshtina* is dissolved and the *Grand Skupshtina* must be summoned within four months.

The decision in each case by the *Grand Skupshtina* shall be by an absolute majority of the members, and its decisions, when sanctioned by the King, become binding.

Some Representative Authorities.

Church, L. F., Story of Serbia, London, 1914.

Crawford, H., The Balkan Cockpit, London, 1915.

Cvijić, J., Questions Balkanesques, Paris, 1916.

Dareste, F. R., Les Constitutions Modernes, 3d ed., Paris, 1910.

Demombynes, G., Constitutions Européennes, 2d ed., Paris, 1883.

Peritch, J., La Nouvelle Constitution au royaume de Serbie, Paris, 1903–1904.

Petrovitch, V. M., Serbia; Her History and Her Customs, London, 1905.

Sentupéry, L., L'Europe Politique, 3d ed., Paris, 1895.

Temperly, H. W. V., A History of Serbia, London, 1907.

Ubicini, Constitution (de 1869) de la principauté de Serbie, Paris, 1871.

XVI.

THE GOVERNMENT OF RUMANIA.

By the treaty of Adrianople of September 14, 1829, Moldavia and Wallachia acquired the title of Principalities and became vassal territories of Turkey. With the cessation of the military occupation in 1834, two organic laws, prepared under the influence of Russia, were put into effect and served for twenty-seven years as the bases of the organization of the Principalities, which during that period were under the protection of Russia. By the Treaty of Paris of 1856, the Russian pretectorate was abolished and the Principalities were recognized as semi-independent states, each with its separate Prince; but in 1859 Colonel Cuza was elected ' Hospodar,' or Lord, by each and took the title of Prince Alexander-Joan I. The union of the Principalities under the name of Rumania was formally proclaimed at Bucharest and at Jassy on December 23, 1861.

In July, 1864, a statute was promulgated by which a Senate and a Council of State was created and in 1866 as a result of a revolution Prince Alexander-Joan abdicated ; a few months afterward Prince Charles of Hohenzollern-Sigmaringen was called to the throne by popular vote and took the name of Charles I. The Sultan confirmed this choice and conferred on him the title of the hereditary prince. Charles summoned a constituent assembly for the purpose of framing a constitution which on June 30, 1866, was proclaimed, and, with modifications, is the constitution in force to-day.

As a result of the Russo-Turkish war of 1877, Rumania was recognized as an independent state by the Treaty of Berlin in 1878, but upon condition of a modification in the constitution which should remove all distinctions and incapacities arising out of religious beliefs. In 1881 Rumania became a kingdom and its Prince took the title of King.

Constitution. — The constitution of 1866, as amended in 1879 and 1884, is divided into eight titles dealing with the territory, the rights of Rumanians, the powers of the state, finances, the army, general provisions, amendment, and temporary and supplemental provisions.

Rights of Rumanians. — The declaration of the rights of Rumanians contains the usual provisions upon liberty of conscience, of speech, of the press, of meeting and upon individual freedom, protection from arbitrary arrest and prosecution except as provided by law, inviolability of residence and property, and the right of peaceable assembly and of association. In a number of respects the exercise of these rights is subject to the provisions of law.

The Powers of the State. — All power emanates from the people and can be exercised only by delegation and in the manner prescribed in the constitution. The legislative power is exercised by the King and the national assembly, which is composed of two houses. The King and each house is a separate part of the legislative power and each can initiate legislation. The interpretation of the law belongs solely to the legislative power. The executive power is in the hands of the King, and the judicial, of the courts.

National Assembly. — The national assembly is composed of two houses, the members of which represent the nation and not merely the district from which they are chosen. Members of either house, except ministers who accept a salaried post from the government, cease to be members but may again become members by a new election. The houses enjoy the ordinary rights and privileges of constitutional assemblies.

Chamber of Deputies. — The chamber is composed of 183 members, chosen for a term of four years. Members must be twenty-five years of age, Rumanian citizens enjoying full civil and political rights and domiciled in the country. The electors are all male citizens of full age who pay taxes. The electors in each district are divided into three colleges; the first comprises all owners of property producing an income of at least two hundred and fifty dollars, the second those domiciled and resident in urban communes and paying direct taxes to the state of at least four dollars a year, and those who exercise the liberal professions, officers, state pensioners and those who have been through the primary course; the third, all others who pay taxes. Within this last college those who can read and write and have an income of at least sixty dollars from rural land, priests, and village schoolmasters vote directly; all the rest vote indirectly. Every fifty indirect electors choose a delegate and the delegates vote with the direct electors of the colleges. The first college elects seventy-five deputies, the second seventy, and the third thirty-eight.

The Senate. — The Senate is composed of one hundred and twenty members, of whom two represent the universities, eight are high ecclesiastical dignitaries, and one hundred and ten are elected. The electors in each district are divided into two colleges; in the first are all electors having property yielding an annual income of at least $400, and in the second those having property yielding from $160 to $400. In each college certain individuals are enrolled irrespective of the property qualification. In general they include the high officials of state, of the army and the courts, members of the professions, professors, and teachers.

The first college elects sixty senators and the second fifty. Senators must be at least forty years of age, Rumanian citizens enjoying full civil and political rights, domiciled in Rumania, and have an assured income of about $1800. The property qualification is dispensed with in the case of a number of high officials. The heir to the throne has a right to membership at eighteen but no right to vote until he is twenty-five. The term of senators is eight years, and one half are elected every four years. In case of dissolution the entire Senate is renewed.

The King and the Ministers. — The constitution declares that "the constitutional powers of the King are hereditary" in the House of Hohenzollern-Sigmaringen according to the Salic law. In the event the throne becomes vacant, choice of a new King devolves upon the two Houses sitting together; they must meet at once and choose a successor within eight days. During the vacancy the Houses united shall choose a commission of three who shall exercise the royal power until a King is chosen. The person of the King is inviolable. The ministers are responsible, and no act of the King is valid unless countersigned by a minister who thereby assumes responsibility for it.

The King appoints and dismisses the ministers; sanctions and promulgates the laws, and may refuse his sanction; he may issue ordinances to aid in carrying out the laws but cannot suspend them; he is chief of the army and he concludes treaties, but to become binding they must be approved by the legislative power. He summons and closes the sessions of the Houses, though the Houses must meet annually on a given date if not previously summoned by the King; he may adjourn the Houses, but not for longer than a month and not oftener than once in a session without the consent of the Houses; he may dissolve either or both of the Houses, but in case of dissolution, the Houses must be convoked within three months.

Ministers have the right to appear in either chamber and take part in the debates but can vote only in the House of which they are members. At least one minister must be present before the Houses can deliberate, and the Houses can demand the presence of ministers. Every member of both Houses has the right to interpellate the ministers.

The judicial power is established by law and no commissions or extraordinary courts can be created on any pretext. There is a Court of Cassation established by the constitution and inferior courts by law. Jury trials are assured for criminal cases and for political and press offences.

Finances. — The Budget is prepared annually by the Chamber of Deputies and must be passed by it and sanctioned by the King. If the Budget is not passed in time, the executive power may expend for the public service in accordance with the Budget of the previous year, but no Budget can be extended more than a year beyond the year for which it was passed.

SOME REPRESENTATIVE AUTHORITIES.

Bellesort, A., La Roumanie contemporaine, Paris, 1905.

Benger, G., Rumania in 1900. Translation, London, 1901.

Blaramberg, N., Essai comparé sur les institutions et les lois de la Roumanie, Bucharest, 1886.

Dareste, F. R., Les Constitutions Modernes, Paris, 3d ed., 1910.

Dissescu, C. G., Cursul de drept public român, Bucharest, 2d ed., 1909.

Miller, W., The Balkans, London, 1896.

Pointe, H. Le, La Roumanie Moderne, Paris, 1910.

XVII

THE GOVERNMENT OF BULGARIA.

—◦◦⦂◉⦂◦◦—

By the Treaty of Berlin of 1878 Bulgaria was severed from the Turkish Empire and established as an autonomous and tributary principality under the suzerainty of the Sultan. During the Russo-Turkish War of 1877 the Russians took possession of Bulgaria and established an imperial commissioner. This commissioner summoned an assembly composed of representatives in part appointed by himself, in part chosen by the people and in part by virtue of their official positions. The assembly was composed of 233 members and met at Tirnovo in February, 1879, and on the 16th of April proclaimed a constitution. In April of the same year the great *Sobranje* assembled for the choice of a ruler. Prince Alexander of Battenberg was chosen and assumed the direction of the new principality. He regarded the constitution with disfavor, and following a number of dissolutions of the assembly he issued a proclamation on the 27th of April, 1881, in which he declared that he would resign his throne unless extraordinary power should be conferred upon him for a period of seven years in order to reform the administration and to create new institutions, particularly a Council of State composed of Bulgarians; he also demanded the cessation of the annual meeting of the *Sobranje* and the extension of the current budget to the following year with provision for the summoning of a great *Sobranje* at the end of the seven years.

These conditions were accepted by the *Sobranje* and until September, 1883, Alexander ruled as an absolute prince; it then became necessary for him to declare the constitution of 1879 again in operation but upon condition that it should be amended by a great *Sobranje*. The revision of the constitution was published in December, 1883. The principal change was in the establishment of a second Chamber which should be composed of members in part appointed by the Prince, in part elected by the people, and in part of members attending by virtue of their offices. This provision for a second Chamber was never accepted by the ordinary *Sobranje* and, therefore, never became effective. For the next ten years it could hardly be said that the government of Bulgaria was conducted in accordance with constitutional provisions.

By the Treaty of Berlin, the province of East Rumelia was constituted a separate principality under the suzerainty of the Sultan, but the separation between Bulgaria and East Rumelia was an artificial one and was brought to a close in 1885 when Rumelia rebelled against Turkish domination, drove out the governor, and proclaimed Alexander as Prince. Rumelia thereby became a part of Bulgaria.

In 1893 the Bulgarian constitution was revised and by the revision it was provided that there should be a representative chosen for every twenty thousand inhabitants. From that time on Bulgaria may be said to have been, in form at least, governed in accordance with the constitution. In October, 1908, Prince Ferdinand proclaimed Bulgaria an independent kingdom and assumed the title of Czar. In October, 1918, he abdicated in favor of his son Boris, who likewise abdicated within a month, and Bulgaria was proclaimed a republic.

The principal features of the constitution of 1879 were the existence of an hereditary prince in a state called a constitutional monarchy with popular representation and a popular assembly. The Prince, later the Czar, was the head of the state; his person was sacred and inviolable; he conducted foreign affairs; was commander-in-chief of the military forces in war and in peace, and he had the right of refusing his sanction to laws passed by the popular assembly.

The *Sobranje.* — Popular representation existed in two bodies : the ordinary *Sobranje* and the great *Sobranje*. Both were elected directly by the people in accordance with the same election laws and procedure. The great *Sobranje* was composed of twice as many members as the ordinary *Sobranje ;* it met only on special occasions, which were determined in the constitution as follows : for the consideration of the question of the cession or exchange of territory, for amendment or revision of the constitution, and for the filling of a vacancy in the succession to the throne and to receive the oath from a new Prince when he ascended the throne. The ordinary *Sobranje* was elected for a period of four years on the basis of universal and direct suffrage and consisted of one deputy for every twenty thousand inhabitants. It was the legislative body of the kingdom and was endowed with the ordinary rights and privileges of legislative bodies. The executive power was exercised by ministers appointed and dismissed by the Czar and they were responsible by counter-signature for all his acts ; also they could be held legally and politically responsible by the *Sobranje* which controlled the executive by means of the necessity for an annual approval of the budget.

Some Representative Authorities.

L'Annuaire, 1880, p. 774 ff., and 1894, p. 682 ff., contain French translation of the Constitution of 1879 and the revision of 1893.

British and Foreign State Papers, vol. 70, 1878–1879, p. 1303 ff., contains French translation of the Constitution of 1879.

De Cauny, L., La Bulgarie, d'hier et de demain, Paris, 1914.

Forbes, N., The Balkans, Oxford, 1915.

Fox, F., Bulgaria, London, 1915.

Murray, W. S., The Making of the Balkan States, London, 1913.

Rankin, R., The Inner History of the Balkan War, London, 1914.

XVIII.

THE GOVERNMENT OF GREECE.

GREECE was a Turkish province from the latter part of the 15th century until its independence was achieved in the revolution of 1821–1829. During the revolutionary period several constitutions were framed but they were never put into effect. At the conference of London in 1830 Greece was declared a kingdom and put under the protection of Great Britain, France, and Russia. Prince Otto of Bavaria was accepted by Greece as king by the treaty of 1832 and ascended the throne January 25, 1833. He ruled for eleven years without a constitution but assisted by a council of state which had, however, only advisory powers. Following a revolution in 1843, a constituent assembly was summoned at Athens which adopted a constitution in February, 1844, modeled on the French constitution of 1830 and the constitution of Belgium.

King Otto was expelled in October, 1862, and in the following year Prince George of Denmark was elected and became King George the First. This election was made under the guidance of the three protecting powers. In the following year a general revision of the constitution was undertaken by the national assembly which had elected the new King, and the constitution thus framed was adopted in October, 1864. This is the constitution which is in force at the present time. It contains provisions regarding the rights of Greek subjects, the powers of the state, the King, the ministers, the legislative branch, and the judicial power.

Rights of Greek Subjects. — The constitutional provisions touching the rights of Greek subjects provide for equality of all

Greeks before the law and a contribution by them without distinction, in accordance with their wealth, to the expenses of the state; titles of nobility may neither be conferred nor recognized; individual liberty, freedom from arrest and imprisonment except in pursuance of the forms of law, the right of peaceable assembly, of association, and of petition are established; private domicile and private property are inviolable and private property may not be taken for public use without payment. Likewise there is freedom of speech and of the press.

Powers of the State. — All power emanates from the nation, and can be exercised only in the manner established by the constitution. The legislative power is exercised jointly by the King and by the chamber (*Boulé*). Laws may be initiated either by the chamber or by the King, who exercises his initiative through ministers. Proposals relating to increase of public expense for the establishment of pensions, or in general for any individual interest, must be originated by the chamber. Authoritative interpretation of the laws belongs to the legislative authority.

Executive power belongs to the King, who exercises it through responsible ministers appointed by him.

The judicial authority is exercised by the courts, whose judgments are executed in the name of the King.

The King. — The King cannot be held responsible and his person is inviolable. Responsibility rests upon his ministers, and no act of his is valid unless countersigned by a competent minister who thereby assumes the responsibility. Ministers are appointed and dismissed by the King.

The King is the supreme head of the state; he commands the military and naval forces; declares war; makes treaties of peace, of alliance and of commerce; he must give information to the chamber, with the necessary explanations concerning these treaties, as soon as the safety of the state permits. Treaties of commerce and other treaties containing provisions which require the sanction of the law, or which affect the Greeks individually, must receive the consent of the chamber before they become binding. The King has the power to issue ordinances necessary to carry out the laws but an ordinance may never suspend the operation of a law.

Laws must be sanctioned and promulgated by the King. A bill passed by the chamber which does not receive the sanction of the King within a period of two months following the close of a session is regarded as rejected by the King.

The King must convoke the chamber at least once a year in ordinary session and he may summon extraordinary sessions as often as he deems it necessary ; he opens and closes each session and has the right to dissolve the chamber, but the ordinance of dissolution, countersigned by the ministers, must contain a provision for an election within two months and for a re-assembling of the chamber within three months ; the King has the right to adjourn or to prorogue a session of the chamber but not for a period longer than forty days nor more than once in the same session without the consent of the chamber. In the event of a vacancy in the succession to the crown an assembly composed of twice as many members as the chamber chooses a King by a vote of a two-thirds majority of all the members.

Ministers. — The ministers, appointed and dismissed by the King, have free access to the chamber and have the right to be heard at any time they choose, but they may not vote unless they are members. The chamber in turn may require the presence of ministers. The ministers may not be relieved of their responsibility by any written or verbal order of the King; they may be accused by the chamber and tried before a special court.

Ministerial political responsibility to the chamber is secured by convention rather than by law, though the numerous constitutional provisions relating to the relations between the chamber and the ministers, combined with the unquestioned supremacy of the popular will, would make any other result out of harmony with the entire constitutional arrangements.

The Chamber. — The chamber meets annually on the first of November for a session which may not be less than three months nor longer than six. It deliberates in public but may, upon the demand of ten members, decide by a majority vote to hold a secret session. No taxes may be levied or collected unless previously voted by the chamber and sanctioned by the King. The naval and military contingents and the budget must be passed annually. Members of the chamber enjoy the ordinary immunity from arrest and freedom from responsibility for what they may say in the chamber. The number of deputies in each province is fixed at the ratio of one to every 16,000 inhabitants. At present there are 332 members in the chamber, who are elected for a maximum period of four years. Qualifications of a deputy are Greek citizenship, enjoyment of full civil and political rights for a period of two years previous to the election, at least twenty-five years of age and the qualifications of an elector. The electorate is based upon universal manhood suffrage.

Council of State. — By an amendment to the constitution in 1911 a council of state was established as a substitute for a second chamber of the legislative body. It has the duty of examining all proposals for laws and of annulling official decisions and acts contrary to the law.

The Judicial Power. — Judges are appointed by the king in accordance with the law. There are a supreme court, courts of appeal, and courts of first instance. Judges hold office for life and may not be removed save by judicial sentence. The constitution forbids the creation of judicial commissions and extraordinary tribunals. The sessions of the court are ordinarily public and the decisions must be accompanied by statement of the reasons therefor, and must be pronounced in public.

The constitution contains a prohibition against a total revision, but revisions that are not fundamental in character may be proposed after a lapse of ten years from the promulgation of the constitution if the necessity arises. Such a revision must be demanded by the chamber in two votes passed by two-thirds majority, providing the second vote is taken at least one month after the first and that the revision shall be carried out by a newly elected chamber.

SOME REPRESENTATIVE AUTHORITIES.

Cassavetti, D. J., Hellas and the Balkan Wars, London, 1914.
Dareste, F. R., Les Constitutions Modernes, 3d ed., Paris, 1910.
Demombynes, G., Les Constitutions Européennes, 2d ed., Paris, 1883.
Deschamps, G., La Grèce d'aujourd'hui, Paris, 1910.
Martin, P. F., Greece of the Twentieth Century.
Saripolis, N. K., Das Staatsrecht des Königreichs Griechenland, Vol. 8 of Das öffentliche Recht der Gegenwart.

XIX

THE GOVERNMENTS OF RUSSIA AND TURKEY.

Russia.

Autocracy reached its highest development in Russia, where the power of the Czar was, until 1906, unlimited by law. Previous to that time certain fundamental laws had been issued but they had been issued by an imperial ukase and could be withdrawn or modified at the pleasure of the Czar. Following the war with Japan a revolution broke out in 1905, and in February, 1906, there appeared two imperial ukases, by one of which a Council of the Empire and by the other, a *Douma*, or popular house, was created. The Czar, however, retained the "supreme autocratic power" of all the Russias, though he exercised the legislative power in conjunction with the Council of the Empire and the Douma.

All executive and administrative functions rested with the Czar; he appointed and dismissed the ministers; he was head of the army and navy; he declared war and concluded peace and made treaties, but all of his acts must be countersigned by a minister.

The Council of the Empire was composed of members, partly appointed by the Czar and partly elected, but the number appointed could not exceed that of the elected members. The latter were chosen by a variety of organizations, including the church, the nobles, chambers of commerce, the universities and the *zemstvos*, for a term of nine years, one third retiring every three years.

The Douma was composed of 442 members elected by the people under a complicated system of indirect election for a term

of five years, but could be dissolved by the Czar. The Council of
the Empire and the Douma had equal rights in the matter of
legislation, and each might propose laws ; but the initiative of
all laws amending the fundamental laws rested with the Czar.
In the matter of the Budget, credits necessary for the payment
of the public debt and the other obligations contracted by the
government could not be refused or lessened and the expenses of
the ministry of the court were not subject to consideration by
the Council and the Douma unless they exceeded the Budget of
1906.

In the event the Budget was not adopted by the beginning of
the budgetary year, the last Budget remained in force with such
additions as were necessary by reason of laws subsequently
adopted.

The Douma never acquired a position of influence and control,
but survived until the revolution in 1917. As a result of the
military disasters and scandals, including the betrayal of the
army to the Germans, the Czar was deposed in March, 1917, and
a republic proclaimed under a provisional government. A constituent assembly was to be chosen to determine a constitution,
but before it assembled the Bolshevik régime was inaugurated.
Soldiers and Workmen's Councils were established in Petrograd
and other places and the radical Socialist element secured control
of the machinery of the central government. Lenine, as president of the Council, and Trotzky, as Foreign Minister, have been
the controlling forces in what government there has been.

A condition bordering on anarchy has existed for more than a
year. The Ukraine proclaimed its independence as a republic ;
other parts of the Empire broke away from the central authorities
and proclaimed republics, notably Murman in the north and
Siberia, and more recently an All-Russian government has been
proclaimed with the object of reuniting the separate parts.

The Lenine-Trotzky government made peace with the Central
Empires by the Brest-Litovsk Treaty, by which several of the
western provinces passed under German control. The United
States and the Allies have from the first taken the position that
this treaty was secured by treachery and bad faith and as victors
they have compelled the Central Powers to abandon it.

It is not possible to tell what the outcome in Russia will be, but it is not probable that autocracy will be reinstated. It is equally unlikely that the Bolsheviki will much longer retain the power.

TURKEY.

The government of Turkey has always been regarded as an absolute monarchy despite the fact that it at times has had the form of constitutional arrangements. In 1856 at the Conference of Paris, following the Crimean War, Turkey was recognized as a member of the Family of Nations and it was anticipated that internal reforms would be carried out, assuring equality before the law, respect for private property, liberty of religious beliefs, equality in taxation, public trials and the abolition of confiscation and torture, but the promised reforms were not realized.

Under pressure from the European powers, Sultan Abdul Hamid II. proclaimed a constitution in 1876 providing for a Senate whose members were appointed for life and a Chamber of Deputies. The first parliament met on the 19th of March, 1877, but the war with Russia of that year led to the indefinite proroguing of that body in 1878. From that time until 1908 the constitution was a dead letter, but under the influence of the Young Turk party, which then came into power, the constitution of 1876 was again proclaimed and in the following year was revised. Though the Parliament met thereafter, the government remained autocratic. No real control was exercised by the Chamber of Deputies.

XX

THE GOVERNMENT OF JAPAN.

THE constitution of Japan was promulgated by the Emperor on February 11, 1889, and in accordance with its preamble came into force with the opening of the first session of the Diet on November 29, 1890. In an imperial rescript of October 12, 1881, the Emperor had declared his intention of promulgating a constitution so soon as the country was ready for it; and when it is recalled that Japan was opened to foreigners only twenty-one years before the constitution was promulgated, some conception may be gained of the rapidity with which the country had progressed and some allowance be made for the inexperience shown in the early attempts at constitutional government. To understand the government of Japan it must be borne in mind that for centuries the country had been under the rule of an Emperor in whom was vested in theory the supreme power. During several centuries, to be sure, the Emperors enjoyed no actual authority, the government being in the hands of the Shoguns. Nevertheless there centered about the Emperors a feeling akin to religious awe and reverence, and when the last of the Shoguns in 1868 voluntarily gave back his power into the hands of the Emperor, the combination of veneration and power made him the most absolute of rulers. But the Emperor pursued an enlightened and liberal policy and sought to adapt the Japanese government along with the rest of the national life to Western models. Accordingly, following the rescript of 1881, a commission was appointed, of whom Prince Ito was the most conspicuous member, to study the constitutions of the European countries and the United States, and to frame a constitution for Japan.

The effects of the centuries of absolutism and feudalism through which Japan had passed could not be thrown off in the brief space of a generation, and the constitution must be viewed in the light of this history. The remarkable fact is not that the constitution of Japan is less liberal than the most advanced constitutions of the Western world, but that a constitution should have been given at all within so brief a space of time.

When one takes into consideration the steady progress toward a greater liberalism in the government and the equally steady development of democracy among the people, no surprise will be felt on finding that custom has greatly modified the spirit of the government if not the letter of the constitution in the twenty-nine years of its existence.

The Emperor. — It was natural in view of the history of Japan that the sovereignty of the Empire should be regarded as in the Emperor; but the constitution provides that it shall be exercised in accordance with its provisions. The Emperor is proclaimed sacred and inviolable; he exercises the legislative power with the consent of the Diet; he sanctions the laws and orders them promulgated and executed; he convokes, opens, closes and prorogues the Diet, and he may dissolve the House of Representatives; when the public safety demands, or to avert public calamities, he may, if the Diet is not sitting, issue imperial ordinances in place of laws, but such ordinances must be submitted to the Diet at its next session and if not approved by the Diet, they are invalid for the future. He has also the right to issue ordinances to carry out the laws, to preserve the public peace and order, and to promote the welfare of the people, but these ordinances shall not in any way alter the existing laws.

The Emperor determines the organization of the different branches of the administration, the salaries of all civil and military officers, and appoints and dismisses the same. He is commander-in-chief of the army and navy and determines their organization and peace standing; he declares war, makes peace and concludes treaties: he confers titles of nobility, rank, orders, and other marks of honor, and has the right to grant pardons, amnesty, and commutation of punishments. This is a formidable list of powers and were they exercised directly by the Emperor would make him the most powerful monarch ruling to-day, but all laws, imperial ordinances, and imperial rescripts that relate to

state affairs must be countersigned by a minister of state. The
constitution provides that the ministers of state shall give advice
to the Emperor and shall be responsible for it. To whom they are
to be responsible the constitution does not state but the custom may
be regarded as established that they are responsible to the Diet.

The Privy Council. — An imperial ordinance of 1888,
amended in 1890, provided that the Privy Council should consist
of a President, a Vice-President, twenty-five Councillors, a Chief
Secretary, and five Secretaries. Among the Councillors are *ex
officio* the ministers of state who form the Cabinet. The Council
may advice the Emperor upon doubtful points relating to articles
of the constitution and to laws and ordinances dependent upon
the constitution, upon proclamations of a state of siege, certain
imperial ordinances, treaties, the organization of the Privy Council and other matters specially called for. It may be consulted
in times of political crises concerning the organization of the
cabinet and all cabinet measures may be referred to it, either
before presentation to the Diet or after acceptance by the Diet.
It is the highest body of constitutional advisers to the Emperor
and in this respect has taken the place, in part, which the Cabinet
would naturally fill. Those who have been seeking to establish
complete parliamentary government and ministerial responsibility
to the Diet regard the power of the Privy Council as a usurpation and wish to see it limited. The so-called Elder-Statesmen,
the Genro, composed of the survivors of the men who brought
about the Restoration of 1868, are an extra-constitutional body
which has occupied a position of influence next to the Emperor
and the Privy Council. These men have rendered great service
to their country, but they and their position are not in harmony
with the development of constitutional government and popular
institutions. They have been the power behind the throne, who,
without official position, have nevertheless been called upon for
advice in political crises. Death has already removed all but
two or three of them and this anomaly will soon vanish entirely.

The Cabinet. — The Cabinet as such is not mentioned in
the constitution, which speaks only of Ministers of State who are
ten in number ; the Minister President of State, the Ministers of
Foreign Affairs, of Home Affairs, of Finance, of War, of the Navy,

of Justice, of Education, of Agriculture and Commerce, of Communications. There is also a Minister of the Imperial Household, but he is not a member of the cabinet.

The ministers may be members of either House of the Diet and, whether members or not, have the right to speak in either House.

The earlier view and practice was that the ministers were responsible to the Emperor alone, who had the right to appoint and to dismiss them at pleasure, but this view has begun to give way before the demand for the control by the Diet; in 1914 Count Okuma dissolved the House of Representatives and appealed to the people in a general election in which he obtained a large majority. Party government may be regarded as an established fact, but the change from ministerial responsibility to the Emperor to responsibility to the Diet has not yet been fully accomplished, although the tendency is in this direction and the present state of affairs may be regarded as transitional. Nowhere outside of Japan is there an upper house, not popular in character, which has maintained it supremacy over the lower popular house; and it is reasonable to suppose that with the further development of popular control of the government, Japan will prove no exception to the rule. For the first time in its history, a real Liberal party is at present in power in Japan and further increase in the power of the House of Representatives may be expected.

The Diet. — The Imperial Diet is composed of the House of Peers and the House of Representatives. Though the constitution vests the legislative power in the Emperor with the consent of the Diet, the development of parliamentary government has deprived the Emperor of the power formerly attributed to him of vetoing laws passed by the Diet.

Bills may be initiated by the government and by each of the Houses and the two Houses have the same rights with respect to all measures except that the Budget must be first laid before the House of Representatives. The House of Peers, however, has won the right to reinsert in the Budget items which have been stricken out in the House of Representatives.

The Diet meets annually and the session lasts three months, but may be prolonged by imperial order. Extraordinary sessions may be summoned by the Emperor. The deliberations of the

Houses are public, but secret sittings may be held upon the demand of the government or upon resolution of the House. No member of either House may be held responsible outside the respective Houses for any opinion expressed or for any vote given in the House, but for his opinions expressed in public speeches or in writing a member is amenable to the general law. Members are free from arrest during the session for all ordinary offences, not of a flagrant character and not connected with internal disorder or foreign trouble, unless with the consent of the House.

The Emperor appoints the President and the Vice-President of the House of Peers from among the members for a period of seven years, and the President and Vice-President of the House of Representatives from among the three candidates respectively elected by the House for each office.

The Presidents of the Houses receive an annual allowance of 5000 *yen*, the Vice-Presidents 3000 *yen*, while the elected and appointed members of the House of Peers and the members of the House of Representatives receive 2000 *yen*.[1] They also receive a certain allowance for travelling expenses — but members who are in the service of the government do not receive such annual allowance.

Sections and Committees. — Each House divides itself into sections by lot and the sections elect, from among the members of the House, an equal number of members to the standing committee, which is divided into branches according to the requirements of business. Special committees are chosen by the House for the examination of particular matters.

House of Peers. — The constitution provides merely that "the House of Peers shall, in accordance with the ordinance concerning the House of Peers, be composed of the members of the Imperial Family, of the orders of nobility, and of those persons who have been nominated thereto by the Emperor."

By the Imperial ordinance of February 11, 1889, the composition of the House of Peers was determined as follows: The members of the Imperial family; princes and marquises; counts, viscounts, and barons who have been elected thereto by the members of their respective orders; persons who have been elected,

---

[1] A *yen* equals about fifty cents.

one member for each city and prefecture, by and from among the tax payers of the highest amount of direct national taxes on land, industry or trade therein, and who have afterwards been nominated thereto by the Emperor.

The members of the Imperial family take their seats upon attaining their majority, the princes and marquises at the age of twenty-five, the members of the orders of counts, viscounts and barons at the age of twenty-five; the latter are elected by the orders for a term of seven years, and their number shall not exceed one-fifth of the entire number of the respective orders.

The Emperor may appoint for life any man thirty years of age on the ground of meritorious services to the state, or for his learning.

One member is elected in each city and prefecture by and from among the fifteen male inhabitants thereof above the age of thirty who pay the highest amount of direct national taxes on land, industry, or trade. Those so chosen must be appointed by the Emperor and serve for a term of seven years. The number of members appointed by the Emperor for meritorious services, for their learning and from among the highest tax payers, shall not exceed the number of members having the title of nobility.

The number of members of the House of Peers is variable and at present is 374. The House of Peers has been a very conservative body. Having an equal voice with the House of Representatives in all legislation it has blocked progressive and radical legislation; being secure of its tenure of office, since it cannot be dissolved, it has proved stronger than the House of Representatives. With the further development of parliamentary government and a firmer establishment of ministerial responsibility, it will be indeed strange if the House of Representatives does not become the stronger.

House of Representatives. — The only constitutional provision respecting the House of Representatives is that it shall be composed of members elected by the people according to the provisions of the Law of Election.

Any male Japanese subject of thirty years of age is eligible for election except the heads of noble families, men in the active service of the army or navy; students; Shinto priests, ministers, priests and teachers of religion of all kinds; certain government officials, government contractors, and persons suffering from legal disabilities.

Qualifications for electors are the age of twenty-five, permanent residence in the district for not less than one year previous to the date of drawing up the electoral list, and payment of direct national taxes to the amount of not less than ten *yen*. Inasmuch as voting is by secret ballot and the elector must write the name of the candidate upon his ballot, the ability to write is really a qualification.

There are at present 381 members who are chosen in electoral districts, but each elector votes for one person only. The term of members is four years unless sooner terminated by dissolution of the House.

Rights and Duties of Subjects. — Fifteen articles of the constitution deal with the rights and duties of Japanese subjects, but in almost every instance the rights are to be enjoyed subject to the limits provided by law — and in many instances these limits have set very great restrictions from the standpoint of American ideas of individual rights. The constitution in fact affords no absolute guarantees of civil rights and liberties. There has been, however, a constant and rapid extension of popular liberties through legislative enactment. The extension of the suffrage, greater liberty of the press and of speech, of public meeting and political association and reform of the criminal law are evidence of the growth of popular rights.

Political Parties. — When the constitution was promulgated there were no political parties for there had been no opportunity or occasion for their development. The intervening period has witnessed at least the beginning of party organization and for the past ten years parties have assumed somewhat of the position and functions of parties in other constitutional states. The development of parties has gone hand in hand with the establishment of a system of cabinet responsibility.

The weakness of Japanese parties lies in the fact that they have centered around individuals rather than principles. The feudal conception of personal allegiance has lingered on into the new era, but with the passing away of the generation that knew the old régime and the coming into power of the younger men the character of parties is becoming less personal ; policies, not men, are forming the cohesive element. All of which is but further evidence of the complete acceptance by the Japanese of the political conceptions and arrangements of the Western world.

The Judiciary. — Justice is administered by the courts according to law in the name of the Emperor. He is the fountain and source of law and of justice. The organization and jurisdiction of the courts is left entirely to the law. The constitution affords protection to judges through the provision that "no judge shall be deprived of his position, unless by way of criminal sentence or disciplinary punishment," and to individuals by requiring that trials and judgments shall be public, but this requirement may be suspended by law or by the court if publicity might be prejudicial to peace and order or to the maintenance of public morality.

Suits relating to rights alleged to have been infringed by illegal measures of the executive authority come before the court of Administrative Litigation and not before the ordinary courts of law. The courts have no power to interpret the constitution ; that function belongs exclusively to the Emperor who was its author.

Amendment of the Constitution. — In consonance with its origin as a gift from the Emperor, the power of initiating amendments rests with him ; he must submit a proposed amendment to the Diet. The amendment cannot be debated in either House unless two-thirds of its members are present nor can an amendment be passed by either House unless approved by two-thirds of the members present.

Some Representative Authorities.

Clement, E. W., Constitutional Imperialism in Japan, Proceedings of the Academy of Political Science, Vol. VI., No. 3, N.Y., 1916.

Ito, Commentaries on the Constitution of Japan, Tokyo, 1889.

Jyenago, The Constitutional Development of Japan, Baltimore, 1891.

Kawakami, K. K., The Political Ideas of Modern Japan, Tokyo, 1903.

McLaren, Japanese Government Documents, Asiatic Society of Japan, Tokyo, 1914.

Masoaka, Japan to America, N.Y., 1914.

Satoh, Evolution of Political Parties in Japan, Tokyo, 1914.

Uyehara, The Political Progress of Japan (1867–1909), N.Y., 1910.

XXI.

SUMMARY: CONSTITUTIONAL AND ADMINIS-
TRATIVE DEVELOPMENTS.

———∽∘⚬∘∾———

Continuity of Development. — From the dim morning hours of history until now, the law of coherence and continuity in political development has suffered no serious breach. Human choice has in all stages of the great world-processes of politics had its part in the shaping of institutions; but it has never been within its power to proceed by leaps and bounds: it has been confined to adaptation, altogether shut out from raw invention. Institutions, like morals, like all other forms of life and conduct, have had to wait upon the slow, the almost imperceptible formations of habit. The most absolute monarchs have had to learn the moods, observe the traditions, and respect the prejudices of their subjects; the most ardent reformers have had to learn that too far to outrun the more sluggish masses was to render themselves powerless. Revolution has always been followed by reaction, by a return to even less than the normal speed of political movement. Political growth refuses to be forced; and institutions have grown with the slow growth of social relationships; have changed in response, not to new theories, but to new circumstances.

The Order discoverable in Institutional Development is not, indeed, the order of perfect uniformity: institutions, like the races which have developed them, have varied infinitely according to their environment. Climate, war, geographical situation, have shaped them: the infinite play of human thought, the infinite many-sidedness of human character have been reflected in them. But the great stages of development have remained throughout clear and almost free from considerable irregularities. Tested by history's long measurements, the lines of advance are seen to be singularly straight.

Course of Development in the Ancient World. — If the bond of kinship was at first clear and unmistakable, it must ere long have become much less defined in the broadened Family. When the Family became merged in the still wider Community, solidarity remained and a strong *sense* of kinship, but the reality of kinship had no doubt largely departed, and law had begun to take on a public character, to bear the sanction of all rather than the sanction of a single supreme person. Kinship was typified still in the hereditary character of the kingship; but the king was now the representative of the community rather than its master. The Community developed into the city-state: and further than this the ancient peoples did not go. In Rome and in the great city-states of Greece the conception of *citizenship* supplanted the idea of kinship. The state became virtually personified in the thought of the time. It was the centre of civic affection and the object of all civic virtue. The public officer ruled not in his own name but in the name of the State. Around Rome at last there grew up a vast Empire; but it was *Rome's* Empire, — the world had fallen into the hands of a city, and the only citizenship that Caracalla could bestow was the citizenship of Rome. This city-statehood was the last word of the ancient world in politics.

The Feudal System and the Modern Monarch. — When the Germans emerge upon the European field we have the State in a new aspect. Nations are moving in arms, and the Host is the State. Commanders of Hosts are the kings of the new order of things. The Host settles on the lands of the old Roman dominions, and that military tenure is developed which we have learned to call the Feudal System. This Feudal System, when it has worked its perfect work, in such countries as France and Germany, brings forth still a third type of kinship: we presently have the king who *owns* his kingdom as supreme feudal lord: the king who, having absorbed fief after fief, at last possesses his kingdom by a perfected legal title; the king whose realm is his estate. This is the king who becomes the sole source of law and of justice, the king who, in our day, has granted out of his abundant grace rights and constitutions to his people.

England's Contribution. — Where the Feudal System fails of its full fruitage, as in England, where freehold estates are not entirely blotted out, where tenure of the king as overlord is a theory but never a reality, and where local self-government obtains a lasting rootage in the national habit, political development takes another course. There political liberty abides continually, in one form or another, with the people, and it is their operative power which gives to liberty expansion, and which finally creates the constitutional state, the limited monarchy, the free self-governing nation. Out of the fief grew the kingdom; out of the freehold and local self-government grew the constitutional state; out of the constitutional state grew that greatest of political developments, the free, organic, self-conscious, self-directing nation, with its great organs of popular representation and its constitutional guarantees of liberty.

The Romans and the English. — In the general history of European development two nations stand forth preëminent for their political capacity: the Roman nation, which welded the whole ancient world together under one great organic system of government, and which has given to the modern world the groundwork of its systems of law; and the English nation, which gave birth to America, which has "dotted over the whole surface of the globe with her possessions and military posts," and from which all the great nations of our time have borrowed much of their political thought and more of their political practice. And what is most noteworthy is this, that these two nations closely resemble each other, not only in the mental peculiarities which constitute the chief element of their political strength, but also in the institutional foundations which they have successively laid for their political achievements.

Likenesses between the Two Imperial Nations. — Both have been much stronger in creating and working institutions than in explaining them: both of them have framed such a philosophy as they chose to entertain 'after the fact': neither has been too curious in examining the causes of its success or in working out logical sequences of practice. Above all, neither has suffered any taint of artificial thoroughness to attach itself to its political methods. Slowly, and without much concern for theories of government, each has made compromise its method, adaptation its standing procedure. Illogical, unimaginative their mode of procedure must be said to have been throughout, a mode for slow, practical men, without speed or boldness. Revolution has never fallen within their calculations; even change they have seldom consciously undertaken. If old institutions must perish, they must perish within the Roman or English system by decay, by disuse, not by deliberate destruction: if new institutions must be constructed, they must be grafted on the old in such wise that they may at least seem to be parts of the same stock, and may partake as largely as may be of that one vitalizing sap, old custom. As the Roman Senate, from being the chief motive power of the state, came at last to exercise only such prerogatives as the people and the people's officers suffered it to retain, so the English House of Lords, from being the single coadjutor of the king in legislation, has been reduced to a subordinate part which it plays only upon a sort of sufferance, and all without any sudden or premeditated step of revolution. As the consular power in Rome was slowly pared down to be dealt out in parts to plebeian officials, so has the royal power in England been piece by piece transferred to the hands of ministers, the people's representatives. The whole political method of the two peoples is the same: the method of change so gradual, so tempered with compromise and discretion, so retarded and moderated by persistent habit that only under the most extraordinary pressure is it ever hastened into actual revolution.

Popular Initiative in Rome and England. — Doubtless much of this likeness of temperament and method is due to the fact that both in Rome and in England it has been the nation, and not merely a small governing class, which has been behind political change. The motive power was popular initiative: the process of change was the labored process of legislation, the piece-meal construction which is to be compounded out of the general thought. Measures have had in both cases to be prepared for the general acceptance; and popular action, wherever it is the wont for the people to act, is always conservative action. A king's law-making is apt to be rapid, thorough, consistent; but a nation's law-making, devised and struggled for piece by piece, cannot be. The plebeians in Rome fighting inch by inch towards the privileges which they coveted, the people in England making their way by long-protracted efforts towards the control they desired to exercise, have had to advance with painful slowness, and to be content with one piece at a time of the power they strove for.

Rome's Change of System under the Empire. — With the full establishment of imperial forms of government Rome lost the conservative habit of her republican period. The methods of the first emperor, indeed, were slow and cautious in the highest degree : Augustus avoided all show or name of imperial power. Carefully regardful of republican sentiment and spirit, which he knew to be not yet extinct, he simply accumulated to himself one by one every republican office, professing the while merely to exercise for somewhat extended periods, — periods which steadily lengthened from terms of years to tenure for life, — but by free gift of the Senate and people, the old offices of self-government. But later emperors were by no means so careful or so considerate of popular prejudices : their power was open, bold, oftentimes even wanton. And with these changes in the nature of the government came radical changes in political method : there came the wilful creation of new offices known to no Roman custom, the constant breach of old practices hallowed by immemorial Roman habit, — the whole familiar process, in brief, of arbitrary power. What Rome gained thus in discipline, in military efficiency, she lost in political capacity. For that capacity so characteristic of the Romans and the English, the capacity namely for political organization, is beyond question inseparably connected with popular initiative, with national self-direction, with self-government.

Fundamental Contrast between English and Roman Political Method. — The most striking contrast between the English and the Romans consists in a vital and far-reaching difference in political organization. What I have said touching the national action of the two peoples, the slow, conservative concert of the people as a whole in the origination and effectuation of policy must be understood in different senses in the two cases. It was true of the Romans only during the period of the Republic and while the Roman people could take a direct part in affairs. The Teuton brought into force, particularly in England, the principle of _representation_, that organization by representative assemblies which enabled the people to act over wide areas through trusted men elected to speak and act in their stead, and which thus enabled the organization of the nation to extend without loss of vitality. Of such methods the Roman knew nothing. Only the people of the city of Rome had any part in Roman legislation, for the Roman had conceived of no way of acting by a delegation of the law-making power on the part of the people. The equal and concerted action of widely diffused populations through the instrumentality of representation was utterly unknown to the ancient world. The county court with its reeve and four selected men from each township, the parliament with its knights from the shire and its burgesses from the towns, instrumentalities so familiar everywhere now that the world has gone to school to the English in politics, were for a long time peculiar to England in their best features. They were the peculiar fruit of Teutonic political organization where that organization had grown most apart from the Roman influence, in England, not on the Continent, penetrated as the continental lands were everywhere by the Roman example. Rome had had no similar means of holding her vast populations together in active political coöperation and living union. Therefore, as her conquests spread, her system became more and more centralized and autocratic. The English could hold populations together, however large they might be, by means of representative assemblies; but the Roman, who knew no method of admitting scattered peoples to a part in the central government, who knew no popular assemblies except those in which all citizens should be actually present and vote, could hold an extended empire together only by military force and the stern discipline of official subordination.

The Development of Legislatures. — Perhaps the most distinguishing feature of modern as compared with ancient politics is the difference between the sphere, the mode, and the instrumentalities of legislation now, and the character and methods of legislation among the classical nations. Representative law-making bodies are among the common-place institutions of the political world as we know it: but no such assembly was ever dreamed of by any ancient politician, Greek or barbarian. Every citizen either took direct part in legislation or took no part in it at all. Aristotle believed, consequently, that no free state could exist with a wide territory or a population so scattered as to be unable to attend the assemblies. But what the Greeks and Romans did not know at all the Teuton seems to have known almost from the first: representation is one of the most matter-of-course devices of his native polity, and from him the modern world has received it.

> Our early colonial history furnishes at least two very curious examples of a transition from primary to representative assemblies. The earliest legislature of Maryland was a primary assembly composed of all the freemen of the colony ; to the next assembly some were allowed to send proxies ; and before representation was finally established there appeared the singular anomaly of a body partly representative, partly primary, at least one freeman insisting upon attending in person (Doyle, I., pp. 287–290). The other example is to be found in the history of Rhode Island, whose citizens for some time insisted upon meeting at Newport in primary assembly for the purpose of electing the persons who were to represent them in the colonial legislature, thus as it were jointly inaugurating the session, to use Mr. Foster's words, and then leaving the legislature "to run for itself for .he remainder of the time " (W. E. Foster, *Town Government in Rhode Island*, p. 26).

The Powers of a Representative. — But only very modern times have settled the theory of a representative's power. The strong tendency among all vigorously political, all self-reliant self-governing peoples has been to reduce their representatives to the position and functions of mere delegates, bound to act, not under the sole direction of their own judgments, but upon instruction from their constituents. The better thought of later times has, however, declared for a far different view of the representative's office, has claimed for the representative the privilege of following his own judgment upon public questions, of acting, not as the mouthpiece but rather as the fully empowered substitute of his constituents.

Scope of Modern Legislation. — The question is of the greater importance because of the extraordinary scope of legislation in the modern state, and of the extreme complexity nowadays attaching to all legislative questions. Time was, in the infancy of national representative bodies, when the representatives of the people were called upon simply to give or refuse their assent to laws prepared by a king or by a privileged class in the state; but that time is far passed. The modern representative has to judge of the gravest affairs of government, and has to judge as an originator of policies. It is his duty to adjust every weighty plan, preside over every important reform, provide for every passing need of the state. All the motive power of government rests with him. His task, therefore, is as complex as the task of governing, and the task of governing is as complex as is the play of economic and social forces over which it has to preside. Law-making now moves with a freedom, now sweeps through a field unknown to any ancient legislator; it no longer provides for the simple needs of small city-states, but for the complex necessities of vast nations, numbering their tens of millions. If the representative be a mere delegate, local interests must clash and contend in legislation to the destruction of all unity and consistency in policy; if, however, the representative be not a mere delegate, but a fully empowered member of the central government, coherence, consistency, and power may be given to all national movements of self-direction.[1]

The Making, Execution, and Interpretation of Law. — The question of the place, character, and functions of legislation is in our days a very different question from any that faced the ancient politician. The separation of legislative, judicial, and executive functions is a quite modern development in politics, and we have questions to settle concerning the integration of these three functions which could not have arisen in any ancient state. In the early days when the family was the state; in the later days when the political organization, although it had lost the father's omnipotent jurisdiction, still rested upon the idea of

---

[1] The introduction of the initiative and the referendum is evidence of the distrust felt by the people for their representatives, — often not *their* representative, but that of special interests.

kinship; and even in still later times when forms of government inherited from these primitive conceptions still persisted, all the functions of government were vested in a single individual or in a single body of individuals, in a father-king or in an assembly of elders. Even in highly developed free states like Athens no adequate or complete recognition of any essential difference in the character of the several duties of the judge, the executive officer, and the law-maker is discoverable. It was a very modern conception that governmental functions ought to be parcelled out according to a careful classification. The ancient assembly made laws, elected officers, passed judgment upon offenders against the laws, and yet was conscious of no incongruity. It was before the day when any one could be shocked by such a confusion of powers.

Modern politicians are, however, greatly shocked by such confusions of function. They insist, as of course, that every constitution shall separate the three 'departments' of government, and that these departments shall be in some real sense independent of each other; so that if one go wrong the others may check it by refusing to coöperate with it. In no enlightened modern system may the legislator force the judge, or the judge interfere with the privileges of the legislator, or judge or legislator wrongly control the executive officer.

Charters and Constitutions. — This division of powers between distinct branches of government has been greatly emphasized and developed by the written constitutions so characteristic of modern political practice. These constitutions have by no means all had the same history, and they differ as widely in character as in origin; but in every case they give sharp definiteness to the organs and methods of government which illustrate the most salient points of modern political development. Our own constitutions, as we have seen (page 283), originated in grants from the English crown, for which were substituted, in the days following the war for Independence, grants by the people. Originally royal, they are now national charters: and they have been kept close to the people, firmly based upon their direct and explicit sanction. The constitutions of Switzerland bear a like character: proceeding from the people, they rest in all points upon the people's continuing free choice.

In France, on the contrary, the people have as yet had no direct part in constitution-making. French constitutions have in all cases been both made and adopted by constituent assemblies: at no stage are the people directly called upon for their opinion, — not even after the constitution has been formulated. Its adoption, like its construction, is a matter for the constituent assembly alone : it is given to the people, not accepted by them. The present constitution of the Republic was even framed and adopted by a convention which could show no indisputable right to act as a constituent assembly (page 148).

Creation vs. Confirmation of Liberties by Constitution. — This process, of the gift of a constitution to the people by an assembly of their own choice, may be said to be intermediate between our own or the Swiss practice, on the one hand, and the practice of the monarchial states of Europe, on the other, whose constitutions are the gift of monarchs to their people. In many cases they have been forced from reluctant monarchs, as Magna Charta was wrung by the barons from John : but whether created by stress of revolution, as in so many states in 1848 (page 445), or framed later and more at leisure, as in Prussia (page 445), they have been in the form of royal gifts of right, have not confirmed but *created* liberties and privileges.

Our own charters and constitutions have, on the contrary, been little more than formal statements of rights and immunities which had come to belong to Englishmen quite independently of royal gift or favor. The Acts of Parliament upon which the governments of such modern English colonies as Canada and Australia rest do scarcely more, aside from their outlining of forms of government, than extend to the colonists the immemorial privileges of Englishmen in England. And so our own colonial charters, besides providing for governors, courts, and legislatures, simply granted the usual rights of English freemen. Our constitutions have formulated our political progress, but the progress came first. European constitutions, on the other hand, have for the most part created the rights and immunities, as well as the popular institutions, which they embody : they institute reform, instead of merely confirming and crystallizing it.

The Modern Federal State : contrasted with Confeder-ations. — In no part of modern political development have written constitutions played a more important, a more indis-pensable rôle than in the definite expression of the nice balance of institutions and functions upon which the carefully adjusted organism of the modern federal state depends. The federal state, as we know it, is a creation of modern politics. Ancient times afford many instances of confederated states, but none of a federal state. The mere confederations of ancient and of modern times, however long preserved, and of however distin-guished history, were still not states in the proper sense of the term. The most prominent example of a confederation in ancient times was the celebrated Achæan League. In modern times we have had the early Swiss confederation, the several German con-federacies, and our own short-lived Confederation.

They were composed of states, and their only constituent law was treaty. They were themselves, as confederacies, without sovereign power : sovereignty remained unimpaired with their component states. Their members did not unite : they simply agreed, as equals, to act in concert touching certain matters of common interest.

The modern federal state, on the contrary, is a single and com-plete political personality among nations : it is not a mere rela-tionship existing between separate states, but is itself a State. Confederation and federal state have this peculiarity in common, that they are both constituted by the association of distinct, inde-pendent communities : but under a confederation these com-munities practically remain distinct and independent, while within a federal state they are practically welded together into a single state, into one nation.

Under both forms, however, it has proved possible to make pro-vision for the association, upon the best terms of mutual help and support, of communities unlike in almost every feature of local life, and even of communities diverse in race, without any sur-render of their individuality or of their freedom to develop each its characteristic life. Nothing could well be conceived more flexible than a system which can hold together German, French, and Italian elements as the Swiss constitution does.

Distinguishing Marks of the Federal State. — The federal state has, as contrasted with a federation, these distinguishing features : (*a*) a permanent surrender on the part of the constituent communities of their right to act independently of each other in matters which touch the common interest, and the consequent fusion of these communities, in respect of these matters, into a single state. As regards other states they have merged their individuality into one national whole : the lines which separate them are none of them on the outside but all on the inside. (*b*) The federal state possesses a special body of federal law and a special federal jurisprudence in which is expressed the national authority of the compound state. This is not a law agreed to by the constituent communities : it is the spoken will of the new community, the Union. (*c*) There results a new conception of sovereignty. The functions of political authority are parcelled out. In certain spheres of action the authorities of the Union are entitled to utter laws which are the supreme law of the land ; in other spheres of action the constituent communities still act with the full autonomy of independent states. The one set of authorities is sovereign ; for it presides, and the range of its powers is, in the last resort, determined by itself ; but the other set of authorities exercises full dominion, though in a narrower sphere. Its powers are independent and self-sufficient, neither given nor subject to be taken away by the government of the Union, originative of rights, and exercised at will.

All modern federal states have written constitutions ; but a written constitution is not an essential characteristic of federalism, it is only a feature of high convenience ; such delicate co-ordinate rights and functions as are characteristic of federalism must be carefully defined ; each set of authorities must have its definite commission.

It is not certain that the federal state, as at present established, is not a merely temporary phenomenon of politics. It is plain from the history of modern federal states, — a history as yet extremely brief, — that the strong tendency of such organization is towards the transmutation of the federal into a unitary state. After union is once firmly established, not in the interest only but also in the affections of the people, the drift would seem to be in all cases towards consolidation.

Existing Parallels and Contrasts in Organization. — The differences which emerge most prominently upon a comparison of modern systems of government are differences of administrative organization chiefly and differences in the relationship borne by Executives to Legislatures.

Administrative Integration : Relation of Ministers to the Head of the Executive. — One of the chief points of interest and importance touching any system of administration is the relation which the ministers of state bear to the head of the Executive. Of course much of the consistency and success of policy depends upon the presence or absence of a single guiding will : if ministers be without real leadership, they are apt to be without energy or success in policy, if not actually at odds with each other.

Under our own system the heads of departments are brought together into at least nominal unity by their common subordination to the President. Although they are, as we have seen (page 374), rather the colleagues than the servants of the President, his authority is yet always in the last resort final and decisive: the secretaries have had very few powers conferred upon them by Congress in the exercise of which they are not more or less subject to presidential oversight and control. The President is in a very real sense head of the Executive. In France and England, on the contrary, the nominal head of the Executive is not its real head. Not the President or the sovereign but the Prime Minister speaks the decisive word in administration and in the initiation of policy, — and the Prime Minister only so far as he can carry his colleagues with him. The headship of the President and the sovereign is in large part formal merely, being real only in proportion to the influence given them by their interior position as regards affairs. The influence of the Prime Minister is the vital integrating force.

Perhaps it is safe to say that only in Germany, among constitutional states, has there been an example of a really sovereign guiding will in administration. The Emperor's own will or that of the vice-regent Chancellor was the real centre and source of policy, and the heads of department were ministers of that will. And there is under such a system an energy and coherence of administrative action such as no other system can secure. The grave objection to it is the absorption of so much vitality by the head of the state that its outlying parts, its great constituent members, the people, are apt to be drained of their political life.

Relations of the Administration as a Whole to the Ministers as a Body. — Scarcely less important from an administrative point of view than the relations of the ministers to the head of the Executive is the relation of the administration as a whole, both central and local, to the ministers as a body. We have seen (pages 330, 335, 336) that in the commonwealths of our own Union there is in this regard practically no administrative integration; that the central officers of administration do not as a rule constitute a controlling but only a superior sort of clerical body. In our federal organization we have the President as supreme chief, but the cabinet as a body does not usually exercise any concerted control over administration taken as a whole. Its conferences as a body are confined for the most part to political questions: administrative questions are decided separately, by each department for itself, the only real central authority in administrative matters being the President's opinion, not the counsel of his ministers. As regards points of administrative policy each department is a law unto itself. In England we find a slightly greater degree of administrative control exercised by the Cabinet as a body. A "Treasury minute," for instance, is required for any redivision of business among the departments, and such redivisions are presumably matters of agreement in Cabinet council. But even in England the administrative control of the Cabinet is rather the result of the political responsibility of the Cabinet than of any conscious effort to integrate administration by the constitution of a body which shall habitually regulate, by semi-judicial processes, the main features and when necessary even the details of executive management. In France and Prussia, on the contrary, such an effort is made, and is made with effect. In France, besides a Cabinet of ministers whose function is wholly political, there is a *Council* of ministers whose single office is systematic administrative oversight, the harmonizing of methods, the proper distribution of business among the departments, etc. (page 158) ; and above this Council of ministers, again, there is a Council of State, a judicial body whose part it is to accommodate all disputes and adjust all conflicts of jurisdiction between the departments, as well as to act as the supreme administrative tribunal (page 173). In Prussia there was a like system : a *Staatsministerium* which to a certain extent combined the duties given in France to the Council of Ministers and to the Council of State, and also a Council of State which was by degrees being elevated to high judicial functions.

The Administration and the Legislature. — The relations borne by the Administration, the branch which executes the laws, to the Legislature, the branch which makes the laws, touch the very essence of a system of government. Legislation and administration ought under every well-devised system to go hand in hand. Laws must receive test of their wisdom and feasibility at the hands of administration : administration must take its energy and its policy from legislation. Without legislation administration must limp, and without administration legislation must fail of effect. The vital connection between the two is well illustrated in the matter of money appropriations for the support of administration. Legislators hold, and properly hold, the purse-strings of the nation : only with their consent can taxes be raised or expended. Without the appropriations for which they ask, administrators cannot efficiently perform the tasks imposed upon them : but without full explanation of the necessity for granting the sums asked and of the modes in which it is proposed to spend them legislators cannot in good conscience vote them. A perfect understanding between Executive and Legislature is, therefore, indispensable, and no such understanding can exist in the absence of relations of full confidence and intimacy between the two branches.

The absence of such a coöperative understanding has

led in France to the gravest financial impotency on the part of the government. The Chambers trust almost nothing concerning appropriations to the authoritative suggestion of the ministers. The great Budget Committee (page 162) not only examines and revises but also at pleasure annuls or utterly reverses the financial proposals of the ministers : the ministers are for the most part left entirely without power, and therefore entirely without responsibility, in the matter, and appropriations follow the whim of the Chambers rather than the necessities of administration. In England the ministers are allowed to insist upon the appropriation of the sums they ask for, because they are held strictly responsible to Parliament for the policy involved in every financial proposal. The means of raising the money desired Parliament is to a certain extent at liberty to suggest without implying distrust of the ministers ; but the amounts the ministers ask for must be voted unless Parliament wishes the ministers to resign. Confidence and responsibility go hand in hand (pages 196, 197). Under our own system there is practically no commerce between the heads of departments and Congress : the administration sends in estimates, but the Appropriations Committees of the houses decide without ministerial interference the amounts to be granted.

The relations existing between the Executive and the Legislature equally affect every other question of policy, from mere administrative questions, such as the erection of new departments, increases of clerical force, or the redistribution of departmental business, to the gravest questions of commerce, diplomacy, and war. The integration or separation of the Executive and the Legislature may be made an interesting and important criterion of the grade and character, in this day of representative institutions, of political organization in the case of existing governments. Thus in England we have complete leadership in legislation intrusted to the ministers, and to complete leadership is added complete responsibility (pages 196, 197). In France we have partial leadership (financial matters being excluded) with entire responsibility (page 160). In Prussia, leadership without responsibility (pages 460, 461) ; and in Switzerland the same (page 403). Under our own system we have isolation *plus* irresponsibility, — isolation and *therefore* irresponsibility. At this point more widely than at any other our government differs from the other governments of the world. Other Executives lead ; our Executive obeys.[1]

[1] In recent years the President has steadily gained in his influence to direct legislation, but it is only through his ability to act as the spokesman of public opinion.   So-called " administration measures " now constitute the leading features of the legislative programme, but the Executive still lacks the true position of leadership.

XXII.

AFTER THE WAR.

———◦◦⚬◦◦———

THE governments of all the powers actively participating in the war have experienced important changes. Germany, Austria-Hungary and Russia are in the midst of revolution; in place of kingdoms and empires, republics have been proclaimed; in place of autocracy, democracy has been enthroned. The governments of the other belligerent countries have not escaped the growing sense of popular supremacy, but have everywhere been brought into closer contact with the people.

An important result of these changes will be a greater unity among the states of the world; competing forms of government, with their different ideals, will, we believe, be replaced by governments organized on the common basis of popular representation and control: dynastic rivalries will no longer vex the world with wars nor will it be possible again for ambitious rulers to plunge the world into warfare for the accomplishment of their personal ends. A surer basis for peace has been laid in the common and universal control of governments by their peoples.

Though it be true that democratic government will make wars less likely, it will not eliminate all causes of conflict between nations, and if the enormous sacrifices of this war are not to be made in vain, not merely must democracy triumph in the individual states, but in the society of states as well.

The development of modern democracy has meant two things: equality of rights and the assurance of those rights through popular control of government. Within the individual states special privilege has steadily been replaced by equality of all men before the law, and the right of a few to administer government as their private possession has made way for the conception that the whole people has the right to direct government for the welfare of all. To put it in another way, democracy may be regarded as the realization of human rights through the agency of government in channels determined by the popular will.

In the field of international relations all states have been regarded theoretically as equal; this has been the basis upon which international law has rested, yet outside the realm of theory this equality has been confronted by a doctrine of state action directly in conflict with it. The modern state is a territorial state and in the realm of international politics the possession or lack of territory has largely determined the influence and importance of states. Consequently the acquisition of territory came to be regarded as a necessity in the expansion of national life. But new territory could be acquired only at the expense of some other power. Here was a frequent source of animosities and wars. In this struggle for territory no small state could successfully compete, but worse still no small state could feel itself safe from the menace of imperialism. Moreover every large state was jealous of the extension of the power of every other and each bit of territory brought within the control of one, excited both the antagonism and the greed of every other whose relative position of power and influence was thereby affected. The logical result was deep-seated distrust and a fear of being overreached, accompanied by standing armies and powerful navies on whose existence the peace of Europe was said to depend. Over against this whole conception of armed imperialism there arose the movement to do away with armies and navies and the oppressive tax burdens which they uselessly imposed. Many different motives animated the people who sympathized with this idea; some adhered to it out of antagonism to war as in itself a brutal and unreasonable thing; some because they desired to see the expenditures hitherto directed to preparation for war diverted to improving the social well-being of humanity.

The stages in the development of this idea are clearly marked by the means which were to replace war in the settlement of international difficulties. Following the adjustment of the Alabama claims by arbitration at Geneva in 1871, this method of settlement was eagerly taken up and pressed upon the attention of the world. The First Hague Conference in 1899, summoned to consider the question of disarmament and heralded as a Peace Conference, was unable to agree upon any measures whatever looking toward disarmament, but in behalf of peace it adopted a plan providing a general scheme of arbitration and a so-called permanent court of arbitration available for any states desiring to make use of it. The establishment of the permanent court of arbitration was received as a great achievement and stimulated to renewed activity those who looked upon arbitration as the means by which peace could be maintained. Numerous arbitration treaties were concluded but as they almost universally excluded questions touching national honor and interests, little was accomplished by them.

Arbitration, moreover, did not seem adequate to many who were seeking a peaceful settlement of international disputes and the judicial settlement of such disputes was advocated by individuals and societies. At the Second Hague Conference in 1907 an international prize court was provided but due to a failure to agree upon the law which this court should enforce, it remained a dead letter. Finally in 1914 the great European conflict, so long anticipated, became a reality through the wanton aggression of Germany and Austria. The doctrine of imperialism became in the hands of Germany a demand for "a place in the sun," a demand for a conquest as the right of the strong over the weak, as the supremacy of might over right, and a determination to extend her boundaries and acquire territory at the expense of her neighbors and in utter disregard of international law, of right, and of humanity. The sentiment aroused in the United States by Germany's violation of the neutrality of Belgium in complete disregard of solemn treaty obligations, the terrible atrocities committed by her armed forces upon the civilian population of Belgium and northern France, her defiance and disregard of neutral rights, and the menace of her conduct to the existence of the society of states led to the establishment of a society for the advocacy of a League to Enforce Peace. The fundamental principle of the society was to secure the establishment among the nations of a League, the members of which would bind themselves to use economic pressure or military force against any state which should go to war without first resorting to peaceful means, including arbitration, for the settlement of the difficulty. It was the application to the society of nations of the principle in force in every individual state. The law-breaker who violates the rights of another finds the combined force of the society arrayed against him.

The success of such a League must depend upon the whole-hearted acceptance by its members of the obligations it imposes. The small states will find in it a source of protection that will free them from the fear of aggression and conquest and their acceptance of it may naturally be anticipated; but the large and powerful states will be equally benefited through the prevention of a repetition of another world-war. It will mean, however, a certain limitation upon their freedom of action; they must renounce any claim to overcome the weaker by their superior strength, and they must forego the right in any dispute to resort straightway to force; they must be prepared to use their power in behalf of the established law though their own rights be not immediately endangered. Secret treaties and alliances must be forbidden, and disarmament be brought about.

President Wilson has declared that the United States can never again be a neutral in a great European war. The world has become too closely knit together for us to pursue in the future the policy of isolation.

The hope of such a League and the possibility of its realization have been immeasurably advanced by the destruction of autocracy and the universal establishment of democracy.